International Business
Theories, Policies and Practices

We work with leading authors to develop the
strongest educational materials in business,
bringing cutting-edge thinking and best learning
practice to a global market.

Under a range of well-known imprints, including
Financial Times Prentice Hall, we craft high quality
print and electronic publications which help
readers to understand and apply their content,
whether studying or at work.

To find out more about the complete range of our
publishing please visit us on the World Wide Web at:
www.pearsoneduc.com

INTERNATIONAL BUSINESS

THEORIES, POLICIES AND PRACTICES

Edited by **Monir H. Tayeb**

FINANCIAL TIMES
Prentice Hall

An imprint of **PEARSON EDUCATION**

Harlow, England · London · New York · Reading, Massachusetts · San Francisco · Toronto · Don Mills, Ontario · Sydney ·
Tokyo · Singapore · Hong Kong · Seoul · Taipei · Cape Town · Madrid · Mexico City · Amsterdam · Munich · Paris · Milan

Pearson Education Limited
Edinburgh Gate
Harlow
Essex CM20 2JE
England

and Associated Companies around the world

Visit us on the World Wide Web at:
www.pearsoneduc.com

First published 2000

Many of the designations used by manufacturers and sellers to distinguish
their products are claimed as trademarks. Pearson Education Limited has made
every attempt to supply trademark information about manufacturers and their
products mentioned in this book.

ISBN 0 273 63712 6

British Library Cataloguing in Publication Data
A catalogue record for this book can be obtained from the British Library.

Library of Congress Cataloguing-in-Publication Data

International business : theories, policies, and practices / edited by Monir H. Tayeb.
    p. cm.
  Includes bibliographical references and index.
  ISBN 0-273-63712-6 (pbk. : alk. paper)
    1. International business enterprises. 2. International trade. 3. Free trade. 4.
  Commercial policy. 5. International business enterprices--Management. I. Tayeb, Monir
H.

HD2755.5 .I5385 1999
338.8'8--dc21

                                        99-051883

10 9 8 7 6 5 4 3 2 1
04 03 02 01 00

Typeset by Pantek Arts, Maidstone, Kent
Printed by Ashford Colour Press Ltd., Gosport

Contents

Chapter 10   Political Risk in International Business Brent Burmester   247

Chapter 11   Government Intervention in International Trade Angelica Cortes   273

Foreword

In writing a foreword to this text on International Business, I shall confine myself to generalities rather than specifics as this will be done by the Editor in the Introduction. It is clear that the subject matter to follow is of vital importance to today's and tomorrow's managers.

International Business is now becoming increasingly important as a subject as we move into the new millennium. As globalisation proceeds apace, managers need to know more and more about the worldwide environment in which their businesses operate. The international and cross-cultural dimensions of managerial activity are now critical even to managers operating in SMEs (small and medium size enterprises), let alone MNCs (multinational corporations). This represents a sea-change from the immediate postwar period when national markets were relatively more protected and trade more restricted. Since the 1970s and 1980s, the scale of internationalisation has expanded and GATT (General Agreement on Tariffs and Trade) has been transformed into the WTO (World Trade Organisation). Managers need to know more these days about such wider arrangements, as well as regional accords such as the EU (European Union) or NAFTA (North American Free Trade Agreement). Latin American economies lately began to seek to set up comparable links, as did Pacific Asian ones.

Giant firms began to span the globe, linked by electronic communications, not only dealing in manufactures but increasingly in services. The 'immaterial economy' was upon us. 'Technology transfer' and 'joint ventures' became catchwords of the early and middle 1990s. Strategic alliances proliferated, as global links were constructed. International managers now had to cope with such wider perspectives and business schools sought to internationalise their courses accordingly. It was often hard not to teach international management, as locally oriented management became less and less relevant. Many leading such schools internationalised their faculty to cope with the increasingly culturally and nationally diverse student populations, especially at MBA levels. The newsmagazine *The Economist* was full of advertisements for such courses, whether in Europe at INSEAD or at the Harvard Business School. While Hong Kong featured similar courses, only a limited number of Japanese universities had business schools along US lines and even fewer promoted international business courses. For these, some of their MNCs sent their young managers overseas to Stanford or Wharton.

So, we were now living in an organisationally interdependent world, as the Asian Crisis of the later 1990s revealed. Some economies were less affected than others, but most have felt the chill winds of the downturn in the Pacific Rim. Firms had to learn how to diversify and adopt defensive strategies when threatened. A new text reflecting the problems of the end of the old century and the new millennium has to cope with such intellectual and practical challenges.

This textbook, ably edited by Monir Tayeb, of Heriot-Watt University, will prove to be of great use not only to students of management but also to practising managers in understanding the changing face of international business. Dr Tayeb has written extensively in the cross-cultural field and has a wide knowledge of doing business in many parts of the world. She herself has been raised in the Near East and educated in the West, as well as doing her doctoral research in South Asia. Her edited text reflects her wide range of managerial concerns. Her own chapters on national institutions and management, multicultural workforces and transferring management policies across borders aptly reflect her interests. She brings more than a passing interest in international management to her text.

It covers the widest possible range of topics in the field and each chapter is written by experts in the respective areas of management and business. The focus is not only by discipline but also by areas of the globe, thus making the resulting publication most comprehensive and in a form not normally found in such texts. It is an up-to-date guide to new ways of managing in the global economy and combines the broad sweep of conjecture with the detailed analysis of the specialist contributors. The old certainties no longer can be relied on as the reader seeks new ways of looking at the global managerial world.

In the 21 chapters, the editor has assembled contributors who cover everything from international trade theories and practices to managing a multicultural workforce, in the wide-ranging chapters, to the more nationally focused accounts of management-defined territories such as in the Arab world, China, Western and Eastern Europe, India, Japan, China and the United States. There are 20 general chapters and a nationally focused one with three sections. The range of countries chosen is wider than found in most comparable works. The contributors come from a range of disciplines and this helps to give the text a useful interdisciplinary character. Some come from an economic background, while others teach OB (Organisational Behaviour) or HRM (Human Resource Management) among other relevant business school subjects. Yet others teach finance or marketing. All these fuse into a deeper understanding of international management than if reliant on just one discipline.

All chapters include exhibits and case studies, so that there is a link with practical examples of the wider issues. There are altogether 42 opening and closing case studies introduced as part of the wider chapters. Case studies can be useful adjuncts to academic analysis. This text very neatly combines the two. A good example of this is the case relating to the internationalisation of SMEs.

The increasing connectivity of international economies and markets has made an appreciation of the global implications of a decision in any specific functional area vital. This text helps to increase the awareness of the reader to such links. The internationalisation process, for instance, is given considerable prominence. The international institutional framework is also well covered, as is the financial and political risk environment. An analysis of strategic management, managing international operations, international logistics and the structuring of international firms also find a place.

Comparisons of management styles and practices are a necessary part of such a wide-ranging text; here, the Editor has included a number of chapters to do this, as well as summing up the main substance of the book.

The future may hold many uncertainties as far as emerging markets are concerned but is not possibly too fully prescient. The main task is to alert managers to the economic environmental and institutional uncertainties which will face their firms and corporations and show them the options for coping with change, as we advance into the *terra incognita* of the next millennium.

While it is not possible to be totally comprehensive in coverage, this text deals with most areas that undergraduates, MBAs and interested managers need to know about the subject from an international perspective. Others taking international economics or international trade courses and the like may also profit from this work. It is likely that those studying international relations, for instance, may be interested in delving into such a text. There is no doubt a wider level of interest among practitioners these days than ever before. Readers of the *Asahi Shimbun*, *Financial Times* or *Wall Street Journal* have keen appetites for enhancing their understanding of international business in greater depth, whether with MBAs or not.

Many existing textbooks reflect a North American point of view and have been criticised for this reason. This text tries to avoid taking any given cultural or national perspective, although admittedly most contributors come from an English-speaking background. There is less bias here than found in many comparable works and this is a great advantage. It is not of course possible to produce a wholly 'value-free' endeavour but Tayeb has done better than most here. It may be read to advantage whether you are in North America, Europe or Pacific Asia, to cite but a few of the possible venues. If it has a bias, it is clearly 'managerial'; critics of MNCs may be less receptive but it is not specifically aimed at this readership.

To sum up, Tayeb as Editor has tried to create a coherent, cohesive and distinct textbook on international management, for students and practitioners at a number of levels. Teachers of management will no doubt also appreciate the usefulness of this product. She has succeeded in tying these strands together in an interdisciplinary way and has integrated them closely. Using an internationally diverse set of contributors, she has deftly interwoven their chapters to form a coherent whole and has provided cross-referenced links across the chosen themes and countries.

This is no mean achievement. The upshot is definitely a truly internationalised teaching-oriented volume of the right length, particularly for the undergraduate market, and I am sure it will stand the test of time in the textbook market. The text is both timely and lucid, thus making it doubly appealing to both students and practitioners.

Malcolm Warner
Professor and Fellow
Wolfson College, Cambridge
and
Judge Institute of Management Studies
University of Cambridge
Cambridge
UK

July 1999

Preface

This book is the culmination of a two-year project which brought together an academic and publishing team in a fruitful and exciting venture.

All the chapters have been specifically written for the book by the contributors. They are all experts in their field and have a wide range of teaching, research and other professional experiences in different parts of the world. The book has a Companion Web Site for interactive use by students and their teachers throughout the world.

I should like to take this opportunity to express my deep gratitude to all the co-authors, without whose unfailing support and encouragement this project would not have materialised.

At the Press I pay tribute to the staff of Financial Times Management and Addison Wesley, both now part of Pearson Education, who supported me throughout the project. I am in particular indebted to Tina Cadle, Michelle Graham, Anna Herbert, Sadie McClelland, Julianne Mulholland, Jane Powell and Penelope Woolf who were always ready to offer assistance through thick and thin. My special thanks go to Caroline Ellerby and Valerie Mendes for their professionalism and excellent proofreading and copy editing.

I am also grateful to Heriot-Watt University for granting me a five-month sabbatical leave at the initial stages of the project which greatly helped me to get it off the ground.

Monir Tayeb
Heriot-Watt University,
Edinburgh

July 1999

A Companion Web Site
accompanies *International Business*
edited by Monir Tayeb

Visit the **International Business** Companion Web Site at *www.booksites.net/tayeb* to find valuable teaching and learning material including:

For students:
- Study material designed to help you improve your results
- Links to valuable resources on the web
- Search for specific information on the site
- A linked glossary

For lecturers:
- A secure, password protected site with teaching material
- Links to articles and resources on the web
- A syllabus manager that will build and host a course web page
- Downloadable supplementary material

List of Contributors

Dr Mike Bowe is a Senior Lecturer in Economics and International Finance at Manchester School of Management. He has extensive international teaching experience and has held visiting academic positions in various countries. His research interest is in the area of international capital markets and he has published widely in relevant academic journals. Dr Bowe's extensive consulting experience lies in the area of international finance and derivatives markets. Contact address: Manchester School of Management, UMIST, P.O.Box 88, Sackville Street, Manchester M60 1QD.

Dr Chris Brewster is Professor of International Human Resource Management at Cranfield School of Management in the UK. He is Director of the School's Centre for European HRM. In addition to his teaching role, Professor Brewster has acted as a consultant to UK and international organisations mainly in the areas of personnel policies and management training. Professor Brewster is the author of some dozen books and is currently directing a major research programme on international strategic human resource management which is assessing developments across Europe. Contact address: Cranfield School of Management, Cranfield, Bedford MK43 0AL.

Dr Susan Bridgewater is a lecturer in marketing and strategy at Warwick Business School which she joined in 1991 after an extensive professional experience. She teaches international marketing and international business on undergraduate and MBA programmes and on executive courses for clients from major UK companies. Her research interests lie in the areas of internationalisation, emerging markets and relationships and networks. Contact address: Warwick Business School, Warwick University, Coventry CV4 7AL. E-mail: S.H.Bridgewater@warwick.ac.uk

Dr Pawan Budhwar is a Lecturer in HRM at Cardiff Business School. He has been conducting research in human resources management and cognition since 1989. His current research interests are in comparative and international HRM, managerial cognition and HRM policies and practices of MNCs in India. His publications include several articles in academic journals, a book and contributions to edited books. Contact address: Cardiff Business School, Colum Drive, Cardiff CF1 3EU. E-mail: Budhwar@Cardiff.ac.Uk

Mr Brent Burmester is a Lecturer in International Business at the University of Auckland, New Zealand. His principal area of interest is the interface between international business and its political environment. He is presently engaged in a four-year study of the non-market implications of international business relocation. Contact address: Department of International Business, Faculty of Business and Economics, The University of Auckland, Private Bag 92019, Auckland, New Zealand. E-mail: b.burmester@auckland.ac.nz

Dr Farok J. Contractor is Professor of International Business at Rutgers University, and a Fellow of the Academy of International Business. He has been known worldwide for over a decade for his research on International Investment, in particular the negotiated, interfirm aspects of international business such as joint ventures, licensing and negotiations between investors and governments. The author of seven books and over 50 articles and a member of the editorial board of a number of academic journals, his research has focused on the technology transfer process, financing, negotiations, setting a price on technology, and the strategic implications of companies sharing their expertise and markets with other firms. Professor Contractor has an extensive professional experience at a high level in the world of international business. Contact address: School of Management, Rutgers University, 81 New Street, Newark, NJ 07102, USA. E-mail: Farok@Andromeda.Rutgers.edu

Dr Angelica Cortes is a member of the Faculty of Marketing, Management and International Business of the Graduate School and the College of Business at University of Texas - Pan American. Her research interests have been in cross-cultural management and marketing from 1989, with an emphasis on the importance of culture and its effects on international business. Contact address: College of Business at University of Texas – Pan American, Edinburg, Texas 78539, USA. E-mail: Cortesa@panam.edu

Mr Adam Cross is a Lecturer at the Centre for International Business (CIBUL), Leeds University Business School. His research interests focus on the foreign market servicing strategies of firms, particularly licensing and franchising. He has recently edited a volume on international business and has contributed chapters on entry mode choice to a number of books.

Dr Tony Fang is a Lecturer at the Department of Management and Economics, Linköping University in Sweden. He recently completed an in-depth study into Chinese business culture and its influence on Chinese negotiating behaviours and tactics in Sino-Western business negotiation settings.

Dr Pervez Ghauri is Professor of Marketing and International Business at the Faculty of Management, University of Groningen in The Netherlands. He has previously taught for many years in Sweden and Norway and is currently Director of International Business Programme at Groningen. Professor Ghauri is the author/co-author of a number of books and articles on international business and international marketing and is the Editor in Chief of the *International Business Review*.

Dr Anne-Wil Harzing is a Lecturer in International Management at the University of Bradford Management Centre. Her research interests are in the areas of cross-cultural management, international human resource management and headquarters-subsidiary relations. She has published two books and contributed chapters to several edited books and articles to academic journals.

Contact address: University of Bradford Management Centre, Emm Lane, Bradford BD9 4JL. E-mail: a.harzing@bradford.ac.uk

Dr Svend Hollensen is an Associate Professor of International Marketing at University of Southern Denmark. After working in industry as an International Marketing Manager he has published several articles and books. Contact address: University of Southern Denmark, Grundtvigs Allé 150, 6400 Sønderborg, Denmark. E-mail: svend@sb.hhs.dk

Dr Katalin Illes is a Senior Lecturer in the Business School of Anglia Polytechnic University in Cambridge. She teaches international business, strategic management, human resource management and creative management. Dr Illes's main research interest is in the transition process of the Central and Eastern European Economies. She has published several articles concerning the responsibilities of multinationals investing into the region, the impact of change on SMEs and also on higher education. Contact address: Anglia Polytechnic University, Business School, East Road, Cambridge CB1 1PT. E-mail: K.Illes@anglia.ac.uk

Dr Peter Lawrence is Professor of International Management at Loughborough University, England, and has previously held posts at other British universities as well as in France, Sweden, Germany, The Netherlands, Israel and in the USA. His main interests are in management in other countries and in current business developments worldwide.

Dr Alan McKinnon is Professor of Logistics at the School of Management, Heriot-Watt University, Scotland. He teaches undergraduate and MSc courses and has conducted several in-depth studies in the past decade or so and has published widely in the field.

Dr V. K. Narayanan is Associate Dean and Professor of Strategic Management at the University of Kansas. He is an active member of the Strategic Management Society and consultant to several global firms. Contact address: The University of Kansas School of Business, 203 Summerfield Hall, Lawrence, KS 66044-2003, USA. E-mail: VNarayanan@bschool.wpo.ukans.edu

Dr Andrew Solocha is an Associate Professor of International Business at the University of Toledo. He has written many articles on international financial linkages, international trade issues, and determinants of foreign direct investment. Professor Solocha has been active in North American business seminars and has consulted for both industry and government. He has conducted executive training programmes for Russian, Yugoslavian, Scottish business leaders, and Japanese educators. He has also developed multimedia study guides for international finance.

Dr Monir Tayeb is a Reader at the School of Management, Heriot-Watt University, Scotland. She has been conducting research in cross-cultural studies of organisation since 1976. Her current interest is in the human resource management policies and practices of foreign multinational companies located in the UK. Her publications include several articles in academic journals, books and contributions to edited books. Contact address: School of Management, Heriot-Watt University, Edinburgh EH14 4AS. E-mail: m.h.tayeb@hw.ac.uk

Dr George Tsogas is a Lecturer in Human Resource Management at Cardiff Business School, Cardiff University. He has researched and written on labour standards in international trade agreements, and on corporate codes of conduct in global sourcing. Contact address: Cardiff Business School, Colum Drive, Cardiff CF1 3EU. E-mail: tsogas@cf.ac.uk

Dr Allan Webster was Professor of International Business at the Centre for International Business and Economic Research (CIBER), Anglia Business School, Anglia Polytechnic University at the time of writing his contribution to the current book, between January 1998 until September 1999. He subsequently took up the position of Professor of Economics at the University of the West Indies in Barbados. Professor Webster has worked at the Universities of Reading and Warwick and as an economic consultant with Maxwell Stamp PLC. He is an economist with a number of research publications in the area of international trade and in the economics of the multinational enterprise.

Professor David Weir is Dean and Director of Newcastle Business School, at the University of Northumbria, Newcastle. He has been conducting and supervising research on management in the Arab Middle East since 1979. He has supervised studies in Jordan, Algeria, Egypt, Iraq, The Yemen, The Sudan, Saudi, Bahrain, Kuwait, Oman and the United Arab Emirates on such topics as management development and training, the impact of privatisation and economic liberalisation, the employment of women, and the replacement of expatriate workers by nationals. His publications include articles in academic journals, books and contributions to edited books.

Dr Hugh Whittaker is a Lecturer in Japanese Studies and Senior Tutor of Clare Hall, University of Cambridge. His current research looks at corporate restructuring among large Japanese firms, and entrepreneurial business from a comparative perspective. His publications include *Managing Innovation: a study of British and Japanese factories*, and *Small Firms in the Japanese Economy* (both published by Cambridge University Press). Contact address: Faculty of Oriental Studies, Cambridge University, Sidgwick Avenue, Cambridge CB3 9DA. E-mail: dhw1000@cam.ac.uk

Dr Heather Wilson was born in Scotland. She emigrated to New Zealand in 1993 to take up a lectureship at the University of Auckland. She teaches entrepreneurship, strategic management and international business. Her research interests include internationalisation, entrepreneurial networks and knowledge development. She has had articles and case studies published on these topics in academic journals and books.

Acknowledgements

We are grateful to the following for permission to reproduce copyright material:

Figure 5.2 from 'International investment and international trade in the product cycle' in *The Quarterly Journal of Economics* 80:2, pp.190–207 © 1966 by the President and Fellows of Harvard College, MIT Press Journals (Vernon, 1966); Figure 5.3 from 'The internationalisation of the firm: four Swedish cases' from *The Journal of Management Studies* October 1975, pp.305–22, Blackwell Science (Johanson and Wiedersham-Paul, 1975); Table 3.2 from *Chinese Business Negotiating Style*, p.166, Sage Publications (Fang); Table 6.1 adapted from *International Business Studies*, Blackwell Science (Buckley and Brookes, 1992); Table 8.2 from 'Relationship of small firms to large firms' © A.Rainnie, (Rainnie, 1991).

The Financial Times Ltd. for extracts from articles that appeared on their CD-Rom 1 January to 31 December 1998, as follows: Opportunities are growing in Greece; $51bn fall in bank lending to Asia is biggest in decade; Agencies to target Europe's burgeoning bond market; Mexican companies and NAFTA; Japan's $100bn Asia aid plan wins; ASEAN agrees to speed up regional tariff cuts; Bangladesh's garment industry sector gets a rude shock; Ethical codes of practice 'not being implemented'; Germany's once-mighty industrial machine starts to misfire; A range of ties for all occasions; Software goes global: a race to internationalise; Building a global energy business to stay on top; Body Shop expands with £7.1m Cosmo buy; Foreign business looks beyond Tuscany and tenors; On a mission to go for the throat of the world fizzy drinks market; An invitation to think big; Japanese traders put under review; Business travel hostage fears: how to avoid the kidnappers' hit list; Arabian fights as state-of-art ports vie for scarce business; Philippines fears lead to poor performance; Canada seeks to protect local magazine publishers; Singapore government's grip on society loosens slightly; NCB auditors fear shareholders may sue; America through the rose-tinted spectacles of a Briton; Why can't the present be just like the past?; Engineers braced against the wind from the East; Tamed in the West by expensive drugs, Aids is exploding among the poor; Doing the knowledge: a new species of corporate official; A new chip from diverse blocks; Siemens and 3Com in joint venture deal; ABB aims to maximise payoffs and at the same time avoid stifling risk-taking; Cultural barriers as Europe dials M for Middleman; Ocean drive to enter global logistics arena; Moving vehicles made easier; Supply chain logistics: In pole position in the race to innovate; Percy Barnevik eliminates hierarchy; France and the United States: two countries divided by more than an ocean; Coping with corruption; A language to unite our multicultural team: Geoff Unwin's secret weapon; In Egypt red tape has been turned into high art; Changes on the shop floors in South Africa; East meets West: Western classical music in China; MBA goes to Poland; Microsoft, IBM and Intel. Faris Badawi for an extract from 'A Christian secular Moslem' that appeared on the Financial Times CD-Rom 1 January to 31 December 1998; Vinod Mehta for an extract from 'Striking fear in political hearts' that appeared on the Financial Times Website on 1 August 1997.

Extracts as follows: 'Builders of a new Russia', Time, 15 June 1998 © Time Inc.; 'Transfer of HRM Policies and practices across cultures: an American company in Scotland', *International Journal of Human Resource Management*, Vol 9, No 2, pp. 332–58 (Tayeb, 1998); 'Japanese managers and British culture: a comparative case study', *International Journal of Human Resource Management*, Vol 5, No 1, pp. 145–66 (Tayeb, 1994); and 'Foreign remedies for local difficulties: the case of Scottish manufacturing firms', *International Journal of Human Resource Management* Vol 10, No 5, pp. 842–57 (Tayeb, 1999) all with permission from Cardiff Business School, University of Wales College of Cardiff. In case study 8.1 'Convex plastics looks to new overseas markets', *Export News*, 7 July 1987 (Storey, 1987). In case study 8.2 'Child's play at Galloway International' *Export News* 10 November 1997 (author unknown). In case study 8.3 'Potato crisp venture underway' *Export News* 28 October 1996 (author unknown).

Whilst every effort has been made to trace the owners of copyright material, in a few cases this has proved impossible and we take this opportunity to offer our apologies to any copyright holders whose rights we may have unwittingly infringed.

Introduction

Monir Tayeb

We are living in a complex world, where peoples and countries are more than ever interdependent. When Japan's stock market sneezes US and Europe catch cold and the rest of the world might even develop pneumonia. Indonesia gets its economic policies wrong; as a result a South-Korean-owned chip factory in Scotland is abandoned half-built.

Mass communication media and fast and far-reaching means of transport are also bringing closer together people from various parts of the world. The electronic revolution which started in the first half of the twentieth century and achieved an incredible speed in the late 1980s and the 1990s, has contributed greatly to the shrinking of our world. It would now take us only a few minutes to search the entire world through the Internet to find the best producer for the goods and services we want, place orders and pay for them. We are literally just a few seconds away from any information on any subject in any part of the world we may wish.

Other technical and scientific discoveries and innovations, such as biotechnology and 'green' energy, have also left their imprints on our lifestyles. International companies play a significant part in this complex, fast-moving and multifaceted world. They sponsor innovations and apply scientific breakthroughs; they produce and move goods and services around the world; they transfer ways of doing things from one country to another; and they also transform societies along the way.

Moreover, these firms operate, like the rest of us, in a world that has recently witnessed rapid political and social changes. The collapse of the Soviet bloc, the forging ahead of European countries' integration, the Balkan region's conflict, the emergence of China as a major economic player, the economic crisis in South East Asia, the end of apartheid in South Africa and the nuclear race in the Indian sub-continent are but a few of these changes. These not only have implications for us as individuals, but also for the international companies that are moving within and between various countries around the world.

For these reasons and many more it is important to understand international companies and their business world. This is where the present book comes in, with its many-fold objectives: to explain the rationale for international business, to explore the reasons why certain firms engage in international business, to take a look at the internal and external environments within which such firms operate, to appreciate the major challenges that they face, to examine the ways in which these challenges could be and are met, and to look into the future and see where these companies might go from here.

The book also has a companion Website for interactive use by students and their teachers throughout the world. The address of this site is http://www/booksites.net/tayeb.

Plan of the book

The book consists of six parts divided into 21 chapters, each of which deals with a major aspect of international business. Each chapter starts with a learning objective section and an opening case study, and ends with a summary, followed by a closing case study and an annotated recommended further reading list, as well as references. Each chapter also includes vignettes and exhibits related to the topics discussed as well as real-life examples.

Part I consists of two chapters. Chapter 1 sets the scene and focuses on international trade theories and practices. It examines these issues at both national and firm levels and discusses both theoretically and practically the launching pads of international firms. Chapter 2 concentrates on global capital markets and emphasises the importance of foreign exchange markets and major stock exchanges for international firms.

The two chapters in Part II discuss two major aspects of the global environment in which international firms operate. Chapter 3 gives a description of the objectives and structures of major global and regional institutions and trade blocs, the World Bank, the International Monetary Fund (IMF), the World Trade Organisation, the European Union and its single market, NAFTA and ASEAN. This description is then followed by a critical assessment of the way in which these institutions function. The implications of these for the firms whose home and/or host countries are member states and those whose countries are not part of these institutions is examined.

Chapter 4 focuses on the concept of international labour standards and their relationship with trade and corporate practices. It also discusses the ethical issues involved in the management of supply chains and examines some of the remedial options available to corporations.

Part III, comprising Chapters 5 to 8, brings the focus of the book down to the firm level – the factors that influence their decisions to go international, and how they might choose to do so.

Chapter 5 discusses the organisational and environmental determinants of decisions to internationalise, while Chapter 6 focuses on modes of internationalisation, ranging from those which do not involve managerial control to those which do. The factors that influence the choice of any one mode, or a combination of some of them, is also explored.

Chapter 7 discusses the issue of internationalisation from a different angle: the type of firms in terms of sector and scope of the market served, that is, manufacturing, service firms, large multinational firms and large global firms. The chapter also points out the limits to internationalisation.

Chapter 8 examines the question of internationalisation from the perspective of small- and medium-sized enterprises, and analyses the emerging modes of internationalisation for these categories of firms.

The five chapters in Part IV point out the potential external challenges, threats and opportunities that international firms face and the ways in which they might handle them. In each chapter the issues concerned are discussed with respect to the type of international firms and the scope of their markets.

Chapters 9 and 10 concentrate respectively on financial and political risks, at both national and firm levels. Chapter 11 makes a distinction between open-door and closed-door trade policies. It then discusses the issues arising from government intervention in domestic and foreign trade and its implications specifically for foreign firms.

Chapters 12 and 13 explore the varied range of national institutions and cultural characteristics around the world with which international companies have to deal. The former will concentrate on such institutions as education, political economic systems and the role of state, infrastructure, legal system, accounting practices, taxation policies, and industrial relations. The latter will discuss the origins of culture and critically examines major models proposed by various scholars writing within management and related disciplines.

The chapters in Part V concentrate on the potential problems and opportunities within the international firm itself. The strength and relevance of the issues discussed depend on the activities of the firm and on its internationalisation mode. One of the major issues confronted by international firms is the cultural diversity of their markets, business partners and employees. Arguably, the ways in which this diversity is handled could make or break the firm.

The activities of the firms are grouped under strategic, operational, organisational and employee management categories. Each will be discussed within the culturally diverse world in which international firms operate.

Chapter 14 deals with strategic management and focuses on issues such as strategies for market expansion, exploiting emerging opportunities (e.g. regional trading blocs, central and Eastern European countries, the Middle East, ex-Soviet union republics, South-East Asian nations, especially China, emerging third world economies, such as India), and strategies related to internal matters.

Chapters 15 to 17 concentrate, respectively, on managing technology globally, international marketing and international logistics.

Chapter 18 examines various models of international organisational structure, the implications of modern technology for organisational structure and the issue of control in international firms.

Chapter 19 is aimed at enhancing our understanding of and managing a multicultural workforce. It goes deep inside the organisation and examines its management–employee relationships. The chapter discusses major work-related values and attitudes and examines their implications for the management of international firms.

The two chapters in Part VI deal with national models of management styles and their transferability. Chapter 20 describes major management styles practised in various western and eastern countries, which, according to research evidence, have contributed to the success of their international firms. Here, management practices of the UK, Germany, France, the US, Central and Eastern Europe, Japan and other Asian nations, especially China, India, and Muslim/Arab countries, will be discussed and compared. They are selected on the basis of their actual and potential economic success in international markets, and their attraction as trade partners and investment locations for multinational firms.

Chapter 21 discusses the problems and challenges involved in the cross-border transfers of management policies and practices. It explores issues such as the prerequisites for the successful transfer of other nations' practices, and makes a distinction between management policies and practices. The chapter also examines the modifications and adaptations required for the successful cross-border transfers of both management practices and management-education practices.

Part I International Business and Trade

CHAPTER 1

International Trade Theories and Practices

Allan Webster

Learning objectives

By the end of this chapter you will have:

- an understanding of why international trade occurs and how the nature of trade varies according to the type of firm and industry concerned

- an appreciation of the different economic forces that generate international trade

- a general introduction to the different instruments of trade policy used by governments

- an overview of the free trade versus protectionism debate

- an overall perspective of the evidence on international trade in practice.

Opening Case Study:
Opportunities are growing in Greece

Renewed links help to counter diminishing business with EU nations. The re-opening of Greece's historic markets in the Balkans could not have come at a better time for the country's struggling exporters. By gaining access to a region with a population of more than 50m, Greek companies have been able to counter the effects of their declining competitiveness in the European Union.

Because of Greece's isolated position at the edge of Europe, and a small domestic market of only 10m people, trade has focused on sectors with little international potential, such as tourism and services.

Now that links are restored with the Balkan countries, which are rich in natural resources by comparison with Greece and have a much bigger industrial base, trade prospects are brightening. The region's roads, railways and ports are in urgent need of improvement, but the basic infrastructure is already in place.

Despite the sharp decline in output across the region which followed the demise of communism and the violent break-up of the Yugoslav federation,

Greece's trade with its northern neighbours has grown steadily. Exports to Balkan countries accounted for 20 per cent of total exports last year, compared with just 7 per cent in 1989.

The value of Greek exports to the Balkans – including Turkey – reached $1.6bn in 1996, compared with $326m in 1989. Over the same period imports grew from $505m to $933m, according to figures from the Panhellenic Exporters' Association.

These figures are higher than the central bank's statistics because they are based on customs documents rather than repatriated earnings which fail to take account of income retained outside Greece or of the large numbers of transactions carried out in drachmas in the Balkan countries.

Economic transition has created steadily growing demand for fresh and processed food, white and brown goods and building materials from the region's new consumers. Despite a fall in per capita incomes in the southern Balkans, amounting to more than 30 per cent since 1989 according to official figures, the sustained expansion of the grey economy provides a wealth of opportunity for Greek traders.

By contrast, Greece's trade with the EU has started to decline, partly as result of the 'hard' drachma policy pursued until earlier this year which reduced the competitiveness of exports. Between 1995 and 1997, the share of exports going to EU partners fell from 61 per cent to 46 per cent as Greek companies concentrated their efforts on penetrating the Balkans, central Europe and the former Soviet Union.

'These are fragile and unpredictable markets with a high degree of risk,' says Christina Sakellarides, president of the exporters' association. 'Last year, exports to Bulgaria, Romania and Albania fell because of economic and political crises – although by a smaller margin than you'd expect.'

A rise in exports to Serbia and Macedonia, however, compensated for the decline elsewhere in the Balkans, while exports to Ukraine and Russia also increased. Across the region, small trading concerns, often consisting of one or two entrepreneurs, have revived the tradition of the travelling Greek merchants who bought and sold goods between the Black Sea and the Adriatic under the Ottoman empire. In Romania and Bulgaria, these companies have prospered by channelling products of state enterprises which had lost their markets in the former Soviet Union to Greece, Cyprus and the Middle East.

Spyros Argyropoulos, who imports chemicals and timber and sells Greek thread and textiles in Bulgaria, says: 'State-owned companies were desperate to unload products, often at very low prices, just to be able to pay salaries.

'These opportunities are shrinking as companies are privatised, but trading relationships have become more stable, even if margins are lower.' The Greek government has provided more than $150m in revolving credits to boost trade in the Balkans. Over the past year, the fastest-growing market has been Macedonia, which has become a target for small Greek exporters based in Thessaloniki, less than three hours' drive from Skopje, the Macedonian capital.

The unresolved dispute over Macedonia's name has not deterred Greek exporters, although Macedonian businessmen complain about restrictions on the issue of visas for visiting Greece.

However, more must be done to encourage cross-border links and develop 'intra-industry' trade, which involves goods in the same product category that are differentiated by price and quality. At present Greece lags behind the rest of the EU in focusing on less favourable 'inter-industry' trade, which deals in widely varying types of goods.

Closer links with towns across the border would bring opportunities for Greek companies to co-operate with low-cost Balkan producers to develop specialised products that could compete internationally. The services sector would also develop rapidly as contacts increased.

Greece has made a start by agreeing with Albania and Bulgaria to open three new border crossings with each country. The additional crossings would also relieve worsening traffic jams at the handful of existing crossing points. The unrest still prevailing in Albania has caused a postponement, but local residents on both sides of the Bulgarian border are impatiently awaiting the opening of new crossing points in the Rodope mountains.

Source: *Financial Times* CD-ROM, 1 January–31 December 1998.

Introduction

This chapter is intended to provide an overview of current thinking about international trade. Explanations of international trade tend not to directly address issues of why firms engage in international trade. Quite simply firms are presumed to supply foreign markets because it is profitable for them to do so. Instead theories of international trade tend to focus much more on its underlying determinants. That is, they are much more focused on the elements of the business and economic environment that, for example, mean that firms in one industry are successful exporters while firms in another industry export very little and face high levels of import penetration.

A key feature of this chapter is that explanations of international trade are divided into two main types. These are:

- inter-industry trade
- intra-industry trade.

Inter-industry trade occurs when a country tends to export one good and import a wholly different type of good. For example, the UK on balance exports whisky but imports brandy. Intra-industry trade occurs when two countries exchange different varieties of essentially the same type of good. For example, Italy exports wine to Germany at the same time that it also imports German wines. As the chapter will show, the two types of trade are generated by fundamentally different sets of forces. For this reason they are presented separately.

The chapter starts with theoretical explanations of inter-industry trade and, in particular, the theory of comparative advantage. Comparative advantage, which is distinct from competitive advantage, is the oldest theory of trade and remains the dominant explanation of inter-industry trade. On page 25 we move on to explanations of intra-industry trade and on page 31 review issues concerning government policy towards international trade. Particular emphasis is given to the issue of free trade versus protectionism. On page 33 the methodologies and findings of those who have sought to provide evidence on the various different forces affecting international trade are briefly reviewed. Finally, two case studies of international trade are presented.

The theory of inter-industry trade: comparative advantage

This section is concerned with the theoretical explanation of why countries specialise in producing and exporting certain kinds of good and largely import other types of good. The main concept involved is that of comparative advantage, which is the subject of most of the section. The differences and similarities between the concepts of comparative and competitive advantage are also discussed.

Basic concepts

Absolute advantage

The theory of international trade is as old as the subject of Economics. Adam Smith, writing in 1766, set out the theory of **absolute advantage**. He argued that countries would tend to specialise in international trade and, in particular, that they would export goods they produced more cheaply than their trading partners and import goods they produced more expensively. Table 1.1 provides a simple hypothetical example of absolute advantage.

Table 1.1 Absolute advantage

Country	Cost per unit: Whisky	Brandy
United Kingdom	£7.00	£8.50
France	£8.50	£7.00

In the example the UK produces whisky more cheaply than France, causing French consumers to buy from British sources, while France produces brandy more cheaply than the UK causing British consumers to buy from French suppliers. Note the two key features of international trade: specialisation and exchange. Both countries specialise in the production of the good they produce more cheaply than the other and exchange this for the good they produce more expensively. By so doing British consumers, for example, are able to buy brandy for £7.00 rather than £8.50. This enables British residents to consume more brandy, more whisky or more of both and, hence, makes them better off.

Comparative advantage

Absolute advantage is easy for us to understand because we are all used to prices expressed in terms of money. To understand comparative advantage it is necessary to first understand the key economic concept of **opportunity cost**. We are all familiar with prices in terms of money and with exchange rates as the rate at which one currency can be exchanged for another. Any two prices expressed in terms of money do, in fact, give us a rate of exchange between two goods.

For example, suppose a pair of jeans costs £30 and a compact disc £15. This implies that two CDs are worth one pair of jeans. That is, the opportunity cost (the price of one good expressed in terms of the amount of the other good needed to forego in order to purchase it) of a pair of jeans is two CDs.

Ricardo, writing in 1817, had the insight that international trade depends more on these opportunity costs. Consider the hypothetical example given in Table 1.2 below.

Table 1. 2 Comparative advantage

Country	Whisky Cost (£)	Opportunity cost	Schnapps Cost (£)	Opportunity cost
UK	£7.00	0.5	£14.00	2
Germany	£30.00	2	£15.00	0.5

Under the theory of absolute advantage no two-way trade can occur because Germany produces both goods more expensively than the UK. However, Ricardo's insight was to show that the potential gains from international trade and, hence, the incentives to undertake it depend on relative prices (opportunity costs) more than on absolute prices. In the example for consumers in the UK, one bottle of schnapps is worth two bottles of whisky in the absence of trade, while in Germany one bottle of whisky is worth two bottles of schnapps. Suppose now that both British and German residents can exchange British whisky for German schnapps at the rate of one bottle for one bottle. British consumers would now be able to obtain schnapps at one-half of its previous cost and German consumers whisky at one-half of its previous cost. Consumers in both countries would, therefore, be able to consume more and are made better off.

An important feature of this is not just the international trade itself (the act of exchanging British whisky for German schnapps) but the consequences for production in both economies. Trade provides an incentive for Britain to specialise in whisky production and Germany to specialise in the production of schnapps.

This process of specialisation and exchange is by no means limited to international trade but is a fundamental feature of human life. Very few of us as individuals would even contemplate becoming self-sufficient in all our individual needs. This is precisely because it is far more efficient to specialise in an activity in which we are relatively effective and to exchange our labour services, through the medium of money, for a package of other goods and services. Exhibit 1.1. shows the importance of exchange and specialisation to human activity.

The principle of comparative advantage suggests that international trade is determined by differences between countries in pre-trade relative prices such that countries export goods they produce relatively cheaply (in which they have a comparative advantage) and import goods they produce relatively

Exhibit 1.1 Exchange and specialisation

Suppose that two women, Emily and Sharon, are marooned on a desert island in separate locations. Emily is effective at gathering coconuts and fruits but is poor at fishing. Sharon, in contrast, is excellent at fishing but poor at finding fruits and coconuts. Before the two women meet we would, therefore, expect Emily's hut to contain an ample supply of fruit and coconuts but a limited quantity of fish. Sharon's hut would contain an abundance of fish but little in the way of coconuts or fruit.

Once the two women meet it should be obvious that both women can gain from exchanging fish and fruit without either changing their behaviour in terms of fishing and fruit-gathering. This the gain from exchange.

However, further gains are available. Because Sharon is relatively efficient at fishing she could specialise in catching fish, allowing Emily to specialise in gathering fruit and coconuts. Both women could be made better off by specialising in their production of foods. This is the gain from specialisation in production.

expensively (in which they have a comparative disadvantage) compared to trading partners. This trade occurs because the difference in relative prices prior to trade provides potential gains to both countries from international exchange and from specialisation in production. An important implication of this is that the mix of goods and services produced in each country will be determined by comparative advantage.

While the principle of comparative advantage tells us how international differences in relative prices leads to trade, it is only a part of the story. We also need to know how these differences in costs and prices arise. This issue is the focal point of the following theories.

The role of costs and technology

Comparative advantage arises from differences between countries in pre-trade relative prices which, given competitive markets, arise in turn from differences in relative costs. Theories of comparative advantage, therefore, focus on how these cost differences between countries might arise. To understand these we must first understand two key economic concepts: production and cost functions.

The process of production involves the firm using a set of inputs such as land, labour, capital and raw materials to produce an output in the form of a good or service. In principle, the relationship between these inputs and outputs could be represented mathematically. Economists refer to this mathematical relationship between inputs and outputs as a ***production function***. The production function, if known, gives the range of different production techniques open to the firm. In effect, it can be thought of as representing the available technology.

The production function summarises the relationship between physical quantities of inputs and of outputs. In its own right it provides no information about costs. However, for any given set of production techniques it does tell us how much land, labour, capital and other inputs are needed to produce a given output. This can readily be converted to total or average production costs when the cost of each of these inputs is known. A *cost function* gives the mathematical relationship between output and costs for any given set of production techniques and any given output.

Note carefully that the cost function contains two sets of influences: technology (as represented by the production function) and the cost of inputs. Differences in relative costs and ultimately comparative advantage must therefore depend on either or both of two sets of influences:

- technological differences between countries
- differences in key input costs between countries.

This chain of reasoning is summarised by Figure 1.1 below. We then outline the theory of comparative advantage which emphasises the role of technological differences and the theory that emphasises differences in input costs. Recent efforts to synthesise the two are also discussed.

Productivity and technology: Ricardian comparative advantage

David Ricardo, the originator of the concept of comparative advantage in 1817, saw comparative advantage as arising from differences between countries in labour productivities. For a pure Ricardian model of trade it is necessary to simplify greatly and to assume that goods are produced in all countries using labour alone. With the benefit of further assumptions (most notably constant returns to scale and perfect competition) it can be readily demonstrated that there are mutual gains from trade for any two countries and, hence, trade will occur if there are international differences in *relative* labour productivities. That is, if labour is relatively more efficient at producing, say, whisky in the UK and relatively more efficient in Germany at producing schnapps, comparative advantage and a basis for trade will exist. Since the argument involved is very close in spirit to the discussion on previous pages, no more detail is provided here.

However, several important issues of interpretation arise here. Labour productivity is normally defined to be the quantity of output per worker or per unit of labour (hours worked, for example). There are a number of reasons why

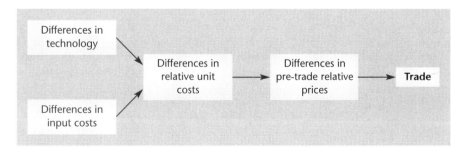

Fig. 1.1 Comparative advantage summarised

labour productivities across industries may vary across countries. The most important of these are:

- labour is not, in reality, the only relevant input and, for example, one country may use more capital per worker than another;
- labour may not be a single homogeneous input;
- technological differences between countries may result in productivity differences;
- cultural, political, legal and sociological differences can result in significant differences between countries in terms of labour productivity.

The Ricardian model can be seen as a mental experiment in which key inputs such as land, capital and natural resources are assumed away in order to clearly identify the role of differences in relative labour productivities in determining trade. This does not mean that economists believe these other inputs to be irrelevant: it is necessary to engage in a degree of simplification to make clear the role of these differences in determining trade. Naïve interpretation of the theoretical model by, for example, asserting that trade is solely determined by technological differences would also be equally misleading.

Productivity differences, when the role of land, capital and raw materials are taken into account, are often treated by economists as being the same as technological differences. While technology must be a key source of these differences it stretches imagination somewhat to conclude that they are the only source.

First, labour is unlikely to be homogeneous: that is, one hour of one person's labour is often not the same as one hour of another person's. In particular, productivity is usually higher with workers who have a high degree of education or are highly skilled than with workers who are not. Productivity differences may, therefore, arise from differences in the level of skill or education (what economists refer to as **human capital**) between countries as well as technology.

Second, there are other important influences on labour productivity. It is well documented, for example, that for many years American workers have exhibited a higher level of productivity than their European counterparts. Early evidence of this was produced by Leontief in 1953. While the evidence is not conclusive it is at least questionable whether these differences can be accounted for solely by greater use of capital or better technology in the US. It is at least plausible to suggest that sociocultural factors such as the American work ethic and the high degree of flexibility in US labour markets have had an important impact on labour productivity.

To conclude, the Ricardian model clearly demonstrates that international differences in (relative) labour productivities are a potentially important source of comparative advantage and trade. It is too simple to suggest that they are the only potential source and it is too simple to conclude that they arise from technology alone. Technological differences are an important source of productivity differences but cultural and institutional factors may also be relevant.

Supplies of capital and labour: Heckscher–Ohlin

In this section we turn to the other key element of costs: the costs of key inputs such as labour, capital or land.

The Core Theory

Probably the most influential model of comparative advantage was first developed by Heckscher (1919) and Ohlin (1933) and, consequently, is referred to as the Heckscher-Ohlin (H-O) theorem. The model predicts that countries with relatively high levels of capital per worker would export goods whose production is capital intensive (and to import goods whose production is labour intensive) and that countries with low levels of capital per worker would export goods whose production is labour intensive (and to import capital intensive goods).

To understand the model we must again introduce another element of economic terminology: **factors of production**. Factors of production are inputs needed to produce a good or service but are generally treated as those that are not produced in the current period. Labour, land and crude natural resources are factors of production because they are not produced by the economy. Capital is a factor of production because production typically relies on machinery and equipment produced in earlier time periods. Components, packaging and electricity are not factors of production because they are produced by the economy for current use. The critical difference is that the stock of factors of production is not determined by current production decisions whereas other inputs are.

The insight of the model involves several stages of reasoning. These are:

- *Stage 1* differences in the prices of factors of production between countries arise from differences in the endowments (supplies) of factors of production between countries. For example, a country with a relative abundance of capital and a relative scarcity of labour will have relatively cheap capital and relatively expensive labour. Conversely, a country with relatively abundant labour but relatively scarce capital will have relatively cheap labour but relatively expensive capital.
- *Stage 2* these differences in the relative costs of factors of production will feed through to differences in relative production costs and pre-trade relative prices under certain key assumptions. This would imply that a good whose production is intensive in the use of capital would be relatively cheap in the capital-abundant country and a good whose production is intensive in the use of labour relatively cheap in the labour-abundant country.
- *Stage 3* the international differences in relative production costs feed through to differences in pre-trade prices and generate trade (the standard comparative advantage argument).

In the same way that we adopted unrealistic assumptions to construct a mental experiment that isolated the effects of technology on trade it is necessary to make a series of assumptions to hypothetically isolate the effects of factor abundance or scarcity on comparative advantage. There is no suggestion that these assumptions necessarily hold.

The assumption of two countries, two goods and two factors has the effect of keeping the mental experiment simple. The basic model can in large measure be extended to many countries, many goods and many factors but at the expense of considerable additional complication. We know, from the preceding discussion of Ricardian comparative advantage, that technology can be a source of trade. By assuming away technological differences we focus the attention of our mental experiment on other sources of comparative advantage and, by further assuming

Table 1.3 Assumptions of the basic H–O model

- there are two countries, two goods and two factors of production (capital and labour);
- technology is the same in both countries and exhibits constant returns to scale;
- capital and labour are freely mobile between industries in the same country but are immobile between countries;
- there are no factor-intensity reversals (explained below);
- both countries have identical consumer preferences of a form that means that the share of each good in total expenditure remains the same when income increases;
- all markets are competitive.

constant returns to scale (doubling input quantities doubles the output quantity), we hypothetically eliminate the possibility that one country may have an initial cost advantage from a larger scale of production.

Consider now the behaviour of labour and capital markets. Comparative advantage, as we discovered on the preceding pages, implies that countries will specialise in production. They are only able to specialise if capital and labour are able to move from one industry to another. However, if both capital and labour are themselves freely traded across international boundaries then the process of this international trade would remove any international differences in the costs of factors of production. In this case, trade in the inputs would eliminate any possibility of comparative advantage and, hence, trade in the outputs.

The logic of the H-O model is that differences in factor costs lead to differences in the costs of goods such that, for example, a labour abundant country will have an advantage in labour intensive goods. However, this can only work if goods are unambiguously capital or labour intensive, whatever the costs of capital or labour. In reality it is possible that they might not be. Japanese firms make substantial use of robots to assemble motor vehicles whereas Spanish firms, who have access to the same technology, do not. A key reason is that labour is relatively expensive compared to capital in Japan but less so in Spain. This provides incentives for manufacturers in Japan to use more capital intensive techniques. Suppose now that a second good, refrigerators for example, uses the same techniques of production in both Japan and Spain. The differences in production techniques in the motor industry could mean that motor vehicles are the more capital intensive industry at Japanese prices of capital and labour but refrigerators the more capital intensive industry at Spanish prices of capital and labour. This would be called a **factor intensity reversal**. The existence of factor intensity reversals would invalidate the H-O model because no uniquely labour intensive or capital intensive good would exist.

Finally the assumption of competitive markets is needed for all comparative advantage models. It ensures that differences in costs are reflected in differences in pre-trade prices rather than in pre-trade profit margins.

Having covered the assumptions of the H-O model we can now move to a simple hypothetical example. Let the two countries be the UK and Turkey with labour and capital costs as follows:

UK   Daily rate for labour = £75
Daily rental for capital = £50
Implied cost of labour in terms of capital = 1.5 (£75 divided by £50)

Turkey Daily rate for labour = 750 Turkish Lira (TL)
Daily rental of capital = 1000 TL
Implied cost of labour in terms of capital = 0.75

Note that this example implies that the UK is capital abundant (capital relatively cheap – one day's labour has the same cost as one and a half day's use of capital) and that Turkey is labour abundant (labour relatively cheap – one day's labour has the same cost as 75 per cent of a day's use of capital).

Suppose now that the two goods are fabric of man-made fibres and cotton fabric which have the following production requirements in common to both countries (to produce one unit of each):

- fabric of man-made fibre: two person/days of labour and three units of capital for one day
- cotton fabric: three person/days of labour and two units of capital for one day.

Note that man-made fibres are relatively capital intensive (using three units of capital for every two workers) and cotton fabric relatively labour intensive (using two units of capital for every three workers). Taking the cost of producing one unit of cotton fabric in Turkey as a specimen calculation:

Labour cost: three days at 750 TL = 2250 TL
Capital cost: two units at 1000 TL = 2000 TL
Total cost = 4250 TL.

If we repeat these calculations for both goods in both countries we derive the costs set out in Table 1.4 below.

Table 1.4 Example of Heckscher–Ohlin comparative advantage

	Man-made fabric Actual cost	Opportunity cost	Cotton fabric Actual cost	Opportunity cost
UK	£300	0.92	£325	1.08
Turkey	4500 TL	1.06	4250 TL	0.94

Note that, because of the costs of labour and capital in the UK, producing one unit of man-made fabric requires the economy to forego less than one unit (92 per cent) of a unit of cotton fabric. If the UK could produce man-made fabric and exchange each unit for a unit of cotton fabric it would be able to obtain cotton fabric at about 92 per cent of its previous cost and would be made better off. Similarly, if Turkey could produce cotton fabric and exchange each unit for one unit of man-made fabric it would obtain man-made fabric at about 96 per cent of its previous cost and would also be better off. That is, in a very similar way to our earlier exposition of comparative advantage, differences in capital and labour costs create an incentive to trade. Specifically, the example illustrates the basic H-O proposition that a capital abundant country (the UK) will export the capital intensive good (man-made fabric) and the labour abundant country (Turkey) the labour intensive good (cotton fabric).

Finally, the basic model needs to be interpreted with care. There are clearly more than two countries, more than two goods and more than two factors of production. Technology is generally not the same in all countries. However, the basic model can be generalised to provide a much more realistic representation of the world (discussed later in the chapter) and these generalisations retain much of the insight of the simpler, less realistic version. The H-O model, therefore, remains arguably the most important theoretical explanation of international trade. Moreover, there are a number of implications of the model which, as we shall see, have important implications for our understanding of the way that international trade links different countries together.

Key implications

One of the reasons for the enduring popularity and importance of the H-O trade model is its richness in understanding the wider implications of trade. There are three main theorems of relevance, each of which can be expressed as a corollary of at least one other. These are:

- the equalisation of wage rates and capital charges between different countries (*the factor price equalisation theorem*);
- the effects of changes in the endowments of capital, labour and other factors of production on trade and specialisation (*the Rybczynski theorem*);
- the impact of trade on the returns to labour and capital (*the Stolper-Samuelson theorem*).

Trade, in the H-O model, results in the capital abundant country, in which capital is initially relatively cheap and labour relatively expensive, exporting the capital intensive good and importing the labour intensive good. This results in a degree of specialisation as the capital abundant country will now produce more of the capital intensive (export) good and less of the labour intensive (import) good. As a consequence of the increased production of the capital intensive good and the reduced production of the labour intensive good this would, under most circumstances, result in an increase in the demand for capital and a reduction in the demand for labour.

However, because the supply of both labour and capital is fixed in the short run at least, the economy cannot supply more capital or labour. Trade creates an additional demand for capital and a reduced demand for labour but supply is unable to respond. From basic supply and demand analysis there can be only one outcome: the price of capital (initially relatively cheap but subject to increased demand) must rise relative to that of labour (initially relatively expensive but subject to reduced demand).

This is not the only effect. The country must produce more of the capital intensive good and less of the labour intensive good without being able to immediately increase the stock of capital and, hopefully, without leaving labour unemployed. This is only possible if both the capital intensive and labour intensive industries use more labour and less capital in their different production techniques than they did before. The change in the prices of labour and capital make this possible. Because labour is now relatively cheaper and capital relatively more expensive, firms in both industries are encouraged to substitute labour for capital in their production processes.

Trade in the H-O model, as we have seen, would tend to increase the price of capital relative to labour for the capital abundant country. For the labour abundant country the effect, by an identical process of reasoning, would be to increase the price of labour (its abundant factor) relative to capital (its scarce factor). To state this more concisely, trade will tend to increase the price of the abundant factor of production relative to the scarce factor for any participating country. This is the core of the theorem set out by Stolper and Samuelson (1941).

Stolper and Samuelson also demonstrate that, under certain conditions, the change in the price of the abundant factor relative to the scarce factor will make the scarce factor worse off in absolute terms. That is, in a capital abundant country, labour would be made worse off not just in relation to capital but also worse off than it was before trade.

This link between trade and wages or the returns to capital may seem at first to be a somewhat obscure implication of the H-O model but it is a potentially powerful tool for explaining key aspects of debates about trade. First, it suggests that while trade may lead to overall gains for a country, some groups may lose out while others receive disproportionately large gains. Second, it predicts the groups likely to gain and those to lose. For example, the theorem predicts that, in countries such as the UK or the US, which can generally be regarded as capital abundant, workers may be adversely affected by trade. In practice, groups representing workers in both countries have been at the forefront of calls for protection against imports at various stages of recent history. The theorem provides a basis for understanding why these pressures to resist freer trade arise. It shows that policy-makers need not only to consider the overall gains from trade but also the potentially adverse effects on a specific group.

The line of reasoning provided by the Stolper-Samuelson theorem has taken a prominent role in recent concerns about trade and labour markets. Concerns about the effects of trade on labour markets first arose with the debates about the formation of the North American Free Trade Area (NAFTA): see, for example, Garber (1993). More recently there has been concern about the widening gap in wages between highly skilled and educated workers and less skilled and educated workers in the UK and the US. In both countries there has been a marked and persistent trend for white-collar wages to rise while blue-collar wages stagnate or fall. Although this trend is not apparent in a number of other countries there has been an active and occasionally heated debate about its causes. On the one hand some economists such as Leamer (1995) and Wood (1994) have highlighted the role of Stolper-Samuelson effects, arguing in effect that Britain and the US are abundant in **human capital** (skills and education) rather than physical capital and scarce in unskilled labour. In this view the greater globalisation of the world economy has, by creating further specialisation in the UK and US in goods intensive in skilled and educated labour, resulted in gains for highly skilled workers and losses for unskilled ones. Economists with a contrary view, such as Lawrence and Slaughter (1993) or Sachs and Shatz (1994), have argued that these changes can be explained by technological progress rather than by trade.

Closely related to the Stolper-Samuelson theorem is the **factor price equalisation (fpe)** theorem. As we have seen in the preceding discussion, trade in the H-O model means that wages will tend to fall relative to the returns to capital in the capital abundant country, where they are initially high. Similarly, wages will tend to rise relative to the returns to capital in the labour abundant country, where they are initially low. The result, as demonstrated by Samuelson (1948), is a clear tendency for the relative prices of capital and labour in both countries to converge. The theory does not predict that this convergence will normally result in the full equalisation of factor prices between the two countries. This is only likely to happen where countries are initially similar in the amounts of capital per worker.

The factor price equalisation theorem again has practical relevance. Consider, for example, trade between a capital abundant (developed) country and a labour abundant (developing) country. If trade leads to a convergence in factor prices as predicted by the fpe theorem this would mean that workers in the poorer country would receive higher wages as a consequence of trade. For this and other reasons, many concerned with the problems of economic development have seen international trade as an important route for improving conditions in developing countries.

Finally, the H-O model deals with given supplies of labour and capital. At any point in time a country has a fixed supply of labour and capital and these supplies of labour and capital ultimately determine how it specialises in the process of international trade. However, we know that the supply of both labour and capital change over time. The effects of these changes are dealt with in the H-O model by the **Rybczynski theorem**. Rybczynski (1955) showed how these changes would affect trade and specialisation.

Suppose that the capital abundant country which is already engaging in trade and, hence, already specialised in the capital intensive good increases its capital through investment at the same time that its labour force remains constant. It would now have more capital per worker than before and, from the logic of the H-O model, we should expect it to become yet more specialised in the production of its export good (capital intensive). Rybczynski demonstrates that, if the prices of goods and factors of production do not change, an increase in the amount of capital per worker would indeed lead the capital intensive country to produce and export more of the capital intensive good and to produce less and import more of the labour intensive good.

This is not restricted to the capital abundant country. By an identical process, growth in the labour force in a labour intensive country with no increase in its capital stock would lead it to become yet more specialised in producing the labour intensive good. It could be argued, for example, that this line of reasoning is particularly pertinent for the experience of Sub-Saharan Africa in the 1980s and 1990s. Sub-Saharan Africa has traditionally depended on the exports of raw materials and agricultural produce which tend to be intensive in low skilled labour. In the 1980s and 1990s they have tended to experience low rates of investment (low or minimal increases in the capital stock) at the same time as rapid population growth (large increases in the labour force). The Rybczysnki theorem predicts that this would make the countries concerned yet more dependent on their traditional exports and less able to develop new exports such as manufactures. In practice, Sub-Saharan Africa, with some important exceptions, has persistently shown the lowest growth, and often reductions, in manufactured exports of any region in the world.

To conclude, the attraction of the H-O model to many trade economists is not just its ability to explain certain types of international trade but also its ability to show how trade links with key aspects of the domestic economy. In the H-O world, trade has important implications not just for goods which are internationally traded but also factors of production such as labour which are not. Trade can also be expected to play an important role in economic development by allowing workers in poor countries to earn higher wages than they would in isolation. Finally, trade provides a key mechanism by which high or low rates of investment in relation to the growth of the labour force feed through into changes in the types of good produced by any country.

The specific factors theory

The specific factors model, associated with Jones (1971), can be seen as another variant of the comparative advantage tradition. The Ricardian model considers only one factor of production (labour) which can freely move between industries but cannot move between countries. The H-O model extends this to two factors (labour and capital) which again are freely mobile between industries but not between countries. The specific factors model, like the other two, assumes two goods for simplicity (call these agriculture and manufactures) but assumes three factors of production – say, land, labour and capital – each of which cannot be traded internationally.

In the specific factors model two of these factors can only be used in one industry and cannot be switched from one to another. Thus, land is only used by the agricultural sector and capital only used by the manufacturing sector. Labour, however, is assumed to be mobile between both sectors.

The model produces predictions of trade that are similar to those of the H-O model. That is, a country relatively abundant in capital will tend to export the capital intensive good (manufactures) and the country relatively abundant in land the land intensive good (agriculture).

Extensions and adaptations of the core theories

By the 1980s it was becoming increasingly clear that the simple two country, two good, two factor of production version of the Heckscher-Ohlin theory had for long been an inadequate representation of the realities of international trade despite its prominence among economists. The main criticisms were:

- there are clearly more than two countries engaged in world trade, more than two factors of production and more than two goods;
- factors of production and labour, in particular, are not homogeneous (i.e. are not a single input of uniform quality equally capable of being employed in any activity);
- technology and other influences on productivity are important determinants of comparative advantage together with the relative abundance or scarcity of supplies of factors of production;
- the existence of economies of scale in important industries means that comparative advantage explanations, which rely on constant returns to scale, are not relevant;

- volumes of international trade are highest between one developed country and another, which are similar in their capital stock per worker, rather than between the more dissimilar developed and developing countries as might be expected from the H-O theory;
- intra-industry trade, which is not readily explained by any theory of comparative advantage, accounts for a substantial part of world trade.

This section outlines as briefly and simply as possible how these criticisms have led to modifications, extensions and different interpretations of the core theories of comparative advantage in a way which makes them much more plausible explanations of international trade.

Let us start with extensions of the H-O model to more than two countries. In principle, this is relatively straightforward as long as there are only two factors and two goods. Countries can be ranked according to the amount of capital per worker. Countries with higher amounts of capital per worker will tend to export the capital intensive good and countries with lower amounts of capital per worker the labour intensive good.

Likewise the H-O model is readily extended to many goods provided there remains two factors and two countries. This time, goods rather than countries can be ranked according to their capital intensity (the amount of capital per worker used in their production). The capital abundant country would then tend to export goods with high capital intensities and the labour abundant country goods with low capital intensities.

Extending the H-O model to more than two factors of production poses much more substantial problems. With two factors of production countries can be ranked according to the capital stock per worker and industries according to the capital employed per worker. With many factors of production, no unique ranking is possible. Should countries, for example, be ranked by capital per worker, land per worker or land per unit of capital?

Work by Ethier (1984) has successfully extended the H-O model to (simultaneously) many factors of production, many countries and many goods. Reference to the original author will quickly reveal that this requires a lengthy, complex and advanced mathematical exposition which is not summarised here. However, the key result is that the H-O model can be successfully extended to a more realistic number of goods, factors and countries with one subtle but important modification. The fuller model, unlike the simple version, does not predict that a capital abundant country, for example, *will* export capital intensive goods. It predicts that the capital, labour or other factor intensity of a country's exports and imports will be correlated with its relative factor supplies: that is, countries will *tend* to export goods whose production is intensive in their abundant factors of production.

Evidence on the performance of the H-O model as an explanation of comparative advantage in practice has persistently highlighted the importance of technology and productivity differences between countries as well as differences in supplies of capital, labour or other factors of production. This evidence is discussed in more detail later in this chapter. In effect, this evidence suggests that a synthesis between the H-O model (based on differences in factor supplies) and the Ricardian model (based on differences in labour productivities) is a more appropriate representation of inter-industry trade than either theory in its own right.

A synthesis of the two can be simply derived by treating factors in terms of their **efficiency units** rather than in physical units. Suppose, for example, German workers are capable of producing twice as much as comparable workers in, say, Tunisia. To measure the German labour force in the same efficiency units as Tunisian workers it would be necessary to multiply the number of German workers by two. In this adapted version, countries would, therefore, tend to export goods which are intensive in factors in which they are abundant in terms of efficiency rather than physical units. Trade would depend both on productivity and physical supplies. A more sophisticated synthesis of the Ricardian and H-O models has recently been provided by Davies (1995), allowing both differences in labour productivities and in factor supplies to determine comparative advantage.

Another key reinterpretation rather than modification of the H-O model concerns the treatment of labour. It is increasingly clear that labour is not a single homogeneous factor of production: that is, not all workers are equally well employed in all possible uses. For example, it is clear that it is not possible to readily use a car mechanic to programme computers or a computer programmer to repair cars. The reason why these workers are not interchangeable between different occupations is because they are not just selling their labour time but are also selling their **human capital** (their skills, experience and education). One type of worker can, therefore, possess both different levels of human capital (for example, a higher level of education) or different types of human capital (for example, pharmacists and accountants have comparable levels of education but entirely different sets of capabilities). These differences can readily be incorporated into a many-factor version of the H-O model with each distinct type of worker constituting a different factor of production. Many economists such as Wood (1994), concerned with identifying the way international trade operates in practice, are now moving towards a view in which physical capital, which is increasingly traded internationally, is a less important source of specialisation and human capital much more important. In this view, then, the comparative advantage of countries is critically determined by the level and nature of skills and education in their labour forces.

Two sets of criticisms, however, cannot be addressed by modifications or reinterpretations of the comparative advantage theories. These are the existence of intra-industry trade and economies of scale. These require further theoretical explanations which are discussed in a later section of this chapter. However, it is worth noting that key theories of intra-industry trade have now been synthesised with the H-O model to provide a coherent explanation of both sets of influences on international trade.

Finally, there is the criticism that trade is greatest between (similar) developed countries and not between (dissimilar) developed and developing countries as we would expect from the H-O model. There are two possible explanations for this which are not necessarily contradictory. First, volumes of intra-industry trade are greatest between one developed country and another. For these, trade flows, as discussed later, are simply more appropriate explanations. Second, even when intra-industry trade is taken into account there remains significant volumes of inter-industry trade between developed countries. There is some evidence that trade between developed and developing countries depends on differences in the levels of human capital in the workforce. Thus, for example, the UK and US tend to export goods intensive in the use of highly educated workers to developing countries and to import goods intensive in the use of manual workers. In trade between developed countries the type rather than the level of human capital becomes more important. For example, the UK tends to export financial services and pharmaceuticals, both of which make intensive use of specialised, highly educated workers which are relatively abundant in the UK. Germany, in contrast, tends to be specialised in engineering and vehicles, in which they have an abundant supply of workers with the requisite skills.

Competitive advantage

This chapter's focus on international trade means that Porter's (1990) theory of competitive advantage cannot be given the detailed treatment it deserves. The objective of this section is to outline its linkages with and its relevance for the theory of international trade. Readers requiring a detailed discussion of competitive advantage are referred to Porter's book.

Porter (1990) produces a critique of comparative advantage and proposes the alternative concept of competitive advantage. Competitive advantage differs from comparative advantage in that it quite explicitly refers to the advantages of geographical regions of countries rather than countries themselves. For example, competitive advantage is more an explanation of how silicon valley in California came to have a marked advantage in computers and information technology rather than a theory of US exports specifically. In this respect, Porter provides a useful reminder rather than a new outlook. Trade economists have long known that comparative advantage can apply within countries as well between them. For example, studies have looked at the comparative advantage of the southern US states within the US and of Scotland within the UK.

Competitive advantage is determined by a wide range of factors, including:

- the availability of skilled labour
- locally available technology and know-how
- access to suppliers of key inputs
- market proximity
- the local cost of inputs.

Although at first glance the list of influences appears quite distinct from comparative advantage, many of them would also be included in the more modern, sophisticated versions of comparative advantage. For example, the preceding discussion of comparative advantage has emphasised the importance of technology and the availability of highly skilled labour in determining comparative advantage. In these cases the key differences between competitive and comparative advantage are more in terminology than content. In the language of comparative advantage, technology and the availability of skilled labour are translated into cost differences between locations.

An important difference is that competitive advantage emphasises the cost and availability of all inputs in a particular location. Comparative advantage, in contrast, focuses only on the availability and cost of those inputs referred to as factors of production (land, labour, capital, natural resources). Trade economists would disagree with Porter concerning those other inputs that are nationally or internationally traded. If a good is freely traded internationally then, by definition, it is available throughout the global economy at prevailing world prices and cannot be the source of advantage for any location. For those inputs which are not traded – infrastructure, electricity, water supply, certain financial and technical services to name a few – Porter has a much stronger case. The absence of trade in these inputs means that their cost and availability can vary from one location to another or between one country and another. They are clearly a potential source of advantage and, hence, a significant omission from the theory of comparative advantage.

Comparative advantage and the multinational

The theory of international trade is, in large measure, a theory of the location of production. It seeks to explain why certain countries produce certain goods and not others. The theory of the multinational must necessarily cover a wider range of issues. Since the multinational is a firm owned by residents of one country but producing in others, its theory involves issues of the ownership of the firm as well as the location of its production activities. In some key areas there are important overlaps between the theory of trade and the theory of the multinational.

The most important of these is Vernon's (1966) product cycle theory. Vernon argued that each product has its own life cycle in the following stages. Starting with a new product the most important factors determining success are proximity to consumers (to ensure effective feedback and modification of the product) and to suppliers (to ensure reliable supply and quality of the yet unstandardised inputs). Over time, once the new product has become accepted by local consumers and has started to become standardised, the product starts to be exported but production remains located in the home country as communication with suppliers and the availability of skilled labour remain important. As the product matures it becomes a fully standardised, established good accepted by consumers and with standardised components. Once this stage has been reached production costs become the most important element in the choice of location and production will be switched to foreign locations if they offer lower production costs (see also Chapter 5).

It is this locational choice of the multinational where there is the greatest potential for overlap between explanations of comparative advantage and the multinational. If multinationals locate their production in countries where production costs are most favourable this would normally be in whichever location has a competitive or comparative advantage in the good concerned. Studies, such as that by Maskus and Webster (1995), have produced evidence of a relationship between the comparative advantages of a location and the degree of inward foreign direct investment in the location concerned.

The theory of intra-industry trade

We now consider explanations of intra-industry trade: the simultaneous export and import of essentially the same good. The explanations of this type of trade tend to rely heavily on the similarities between countries, unlike comparative advantage which relies heavily on the differences between them.

Basic concepts

Central to understanding the theories of intra-industry trade is what economists call **imperfect competition**. Comparative advantage depends on **perfect competition** in which markets have many buyers and sellers and trade in homogeneous (identical) goods. Imperfect competition arises either when there are few buyers or sellers or where goods are not identical.

The extreme version of imperfect competition, where there is only one seller, is known as **monopoly** and a market where there are few rather than many sellers is referred to as an **oligopoly**. Oligopolies are behaviourally distinct from other types of industry because firms need to take into account the interdependence between their own decisions and those of their rivals. If there are many small suppliers, no individual seller can affect market prices. If, however, there are a few large suppliers, then both the firm's decisions and those of its rivals can affect market conditions. Under these circumstances firms are forced to consider the likely responses of their rivals.

Whether or not there are large numbers of suppliers, markets often differ from perfect competition in that the goods traded are essentially the same good but are differentiated from each other. Economists refer to this as **product differentiation**. Goods can be differentiated from each other either by quality or by simply being different in some respect from other goods of similar qualities (different flavours of ice cream would be a simple example). Lancaster (1979) probably provides the most coherent clarification of this. He points out that consumers do not buy goods because they have intrinsic value but because they embody important characteristics. Thus, consumers buy stereo sound equipment because it reproduces music in a way they find pleasurable. Stereo sound equipment is different from, say, a washing machine because it has very few characteristics in common and certainly cannot be used to wash clothes.

Even when we have accepted the distinction between one good and another there remains distinctions within what would normally be described as the same good. There is a large range of different types of stereo equipment available to consumers. In some cases, they are of different quality because higher quality inputs (better components or more highly skilled design or manufacture) have been used. A higher quality version, therefore, embodies more in total than does a lower quality version. However, it is also possible to buy a large number of different products of essentially the same quality but which are different from each other. These are said to be different **varieties** of the same good because, unlike different qualities, they use approximately the same value of inputs but exhibit the different characteristics which define an object to be a stereo in different proportions. For example, one variety may offer the facility to change compact discs by remote control but not allow tape to tape recording. Another may offer tape to tape recording but not permit the remote switching of CDs.

Comparative advantage in different qualities of the same good

In an article that has probably received far less attention than it deserved Falvey (1981) set out a theory of how trade in different qualities of the same good may arise. The model is essentially an adaptation of the H-O model in which there are two countries, two factors of production but only one good. The good is differentiated by quality, with the quality of the good being determined by the amount of capital per worker used in its production. Thus, high quality versions use large amounts of capital per worker and low quality versions small amounts. As with the H-O model it follows that a capital abundant country would export higher quality (capital intensive) versions and import lower quality versions (labour intensive) from a labour abundant country.

The model is an attractive explanation of trade flows, particularly if we were to swap human capital for physical capital. For example, Italy has tended to export high quality men's suits which are intensive in the skilled labour of designers and tailors, and tends to import lower quality suits from Eastern Europe which require less highly developed labour skills to produce.

Trade arising from consumers' taste for variety

The most widely known and commonly used theories of intra-industry trade are based on a taste for variety among consumers. As with comparative advantage these theories start with very basic and fundamental observations of human behaviour. At the level of the individual a taste for variety in certain goods is so intrinsic to our behaviour that we are accustomed to it. How many people would be willing to buy several sets of identical clothing so that they can dress in the same way each day or how many would be prepared to eat the same food every day?

The starting point for our analysis is that consumers each have a taste for variety. It follows that the more different varieties of the same good they are able to consume the better off they are made. If, then, consumers desire variety and are made better off by more varieties, why do we not simply provide the maximum number of possible varieties by making each individual item to a different specification? In practice this would be extremely costly because economies of scale would be wholly unexploited. Consumers, therefore, face a trade-off between an increased number of varieties and the increased cost of each. Achieving a balance between the two is likely to mean that consumers' taste for variety is not fully satisfied because economies of scale make this too expensive. On the other hand economies of scale are not fully exploited because the willingness of consumers to pay more for increased variety leads to shorter production runs for each variety than would be justified if consumers were concerned only with minimum cost.

Examples of goods where individuals have a taste for variety would include goods such as clothing or foods. However, it is clear that goods exist that are differentiated but for which individual consumers do not have a taste for variety. For example, how many individuals have a taste for variety in refrigerators or washing machines? Similarly, many consumers have a preferred variety of, say, beer and normally purchase the same variety. Although, in these cases, there is no individual taste for variety there remains a taste for variety in aggregate.

This aggregate taste for variety arises because different individuals have a different specification of their ideal variety. That is, each consumer has a different concept of, say, their ideal beer and buy whichever variety is closest in its specification to this ideal. Note that economies of scale again mean it is not viable to produce a variety that corresponds to each consumer's ideal specification and, in consequence, consumers are restricted to buying whichever available variety is closest to this ideal. Consumers are also made better off in general if the number of varieties is increased without an increase in costs because at least some will be able to buy varieties that are nearer to the specification of their ideal. The properties of markets for these goods are in aggregate very similar to those where there is an individual taste for variety. Economies of scale are not fully exploited because consumers are willing to pay extra for a variety nearer to their ideal but the aggregate taste for variety is not fully satisfied because economies of scale make this prohibitively expensive.

To see how this leads to international trade and to show that trade is simply one manifestation of fundamental human behaviour, Exhibit 1.2 provides a simple hypothetical experiment.

Exhibit 1.2 A taste for variety and exchange

Experiment 1
Take two children aged between, say, 6 and 11 years old under the supervision of an adult to prevent the use of force or threats. Give the first child two chocolate bars of the same brand (brand A) and give the second child two chocolate bars of the same brand (brand B) but of a different brand from the first child. If the experiment is repeated with a number of pairs of children it is likely we would observe in many cases that the two children will exchange a bar of brand A for a bar of brand B.

In this case the children engage in trade because (a) they have a taste for variety and (b) they are restricted in the number of varieties they initially have available.

Experiment 2
Take a number of the children who did not exchange chocolate bars in the first experiment. Give each two identical bars but each child a different brand. With a sufficiently large number of children it is likely that at least two children will exchange both of their bars for two bars of a different variety.

In this case the children do not have an individual taste for variety but each has a different ideal variety and is prepared to engage in trade to obtain a variety nearer this ideal.

What these hypothetical experiments show is that a taste for variety at the level of the individual or in aggregate, when combined with restrictions on the number of available varieties, provides an incentive to trade. Theoretical models of intra-industry trade are based on this insight. Some models, such as those by Dixit and Stiglitz (1977), are based on a taste for variety at the level of the individual. Others, such as that by Lancaster (1980), are based on a taste for variety in aggregate.

Both sets of models consider two identical countries which, in a mental experiment, do not initially engage in trade. As we have already seen, the existence of economies of scale means that a taste for variety (either individually or in aggregate) will not be fully satisfied in each country. At the same time economies of scale will not be fully exploited in either country because of the willingness of consumers to pay for some additional variety. Opening two identical countries to trade – that is, making them in effect a single market of twice the size – offers two extreme possibilities:

- consumers in each country can have access to twice the number of varieties, each of which is produced at the same cost as before;
- consumers can have access to the same number of varieties as before but face lower prices because of improved exploitation of economies of scale.

In practice it is much more likely that trade would lead to a combination of the two sources of potential gain. That is, international trade makes each economy better off because they are able simultaneously to consume more varieties at lower cost than before. Trade, therefore, is generated by these potential gains. Note that, unlike trade based on comparative advantage, this trade occurs between similar rather than dissimilar countries.

Finally, work by Helpman and Krugman (1985) has integrated intra-industry trade models of this type with the Heckscher-Ohlin trade model. Suppose there is an undifferentiated labour intensive good ('agriculture') and a differentiated capital intensive good ('manufacture') for which there is a taste for variety in both countries. Let one country initially be capital intensive and the other initially labour intensive. While the two countries have significantly different capital stocks per worker the capital abundant country would tend to export the differentiated capital intensive good and the labour abundant country the undifferentiated labour intensive good. Next change the capital stocks per worker to become much more similar between the two countries. As they become more similar, comparative advantage disappears so trade in the undifferentiated good disappears but intra-industry trade in the differentiated good starts to arise.

Trade arising from the rivalry of large firms

To show that product differentiation is not the only potential source of trade, now assume for the purposes of mental experimentation that goods are homogeneous (i.e. not capable of differentiation). As before, take two countries, say the UK and France, not currently engaging in international trade and which we artificially assume to be identical in all respects. Take a single good which is initially produced by only one firm (a monopoly) in each country.

Before proceeding further it is necessary to introduce some basic results of economic analysis. These are:

- a monopoly earns higher profits than the combined profits of all firms in a perfectly competitive market but will sell less of the good at a higher price than a perfectly competitive market;
- an oligopoly (few firms) also earns higher profits, charges higher prices and sells a smaller volume than a perfectly competitive market but earns lower combined profits, charges lower prices and sells higher volumes than would a monopoly.

Note that these properties imply that moving from a monopoly to an oligopoly would provide overall gains. The greater degree of competition means that consumers are charged lower prices and buy more than under a monopoly. Although the profits of producers are reduced, the gains to consumers would normally more than offset this.

The implication for international trade in our example is that, by opening the two countries with national monopolies to international trade, both countries could gain by the creation of duopolies (industries with two suppliers rather than one) in each of their markets. Consumers in both countries would gain by lower prices. However, it is clear that the firms concerned do not gain from trade because they receive lower profits, so why do they engage in trade? Exhibit 1.3 provides a hypothetical case.

Exhibit 1.3 Firm rivalry and trade

The UK and French firm are both free to supply each other's markets. Both firms would earn $100 million profit if they remained a monopolist in their own market. Both firms would earn $40 million if they share either their own market or their rival's market (i.e. combined profits are less than monopoly at $80 million which is shared equally between the firms). The potential returns to both firms are set out in the following table, with the returns to the French firm given first in each cell in normal type and the returns to the British firm second and in italics.

| | UK FIRM | | | |
	Supply France		Do not supply France	
FRENCH FIRM				
Supply UK	80	*80*	140	*40*
Do not supply UK	40	*140*	100	*100*

Thus, there are four possible outcomes:

- both firms remain national monopolists and do not supply each other's markets (giving the highest combined profit of $200 million);
- both firms supply each other's markets (giving the lowest combined profit of $160 million);
- the French firm supplies the British market but the British firm does not supply France (giving the best possible outcome of $140 million for the French firm but the worst possible outcome of $40 million for the British firm);
- the British firm supplies the French market but the French firm does not supply the UK (giving the best possible outcome of $140 million to the British firm but the worst possible outcome of $40 million for the French firm).

Consider now the decision-making of the French firm. It can decide to supply or not supply the British market but cannot possibly know what the British firm would do. If the British firm does decide to supply the French market (first column) it receives $80 million if it has also decided to supply the UK but only receives $40 million if it has decided not to supply the UK. If, however, the British firm decides not to supply (second column) the French market it receives $140 million if it has decided to supply the UK but only $100 million if it has decided not to supply the UK. Thus, the French firm is better off by deciding to supply the UK market whichever decision the British firm makes. The French firm will, therefore, choose to supply the British market.

Consider now the decision of the British firm. It, too, cannot know what decision its French rival will take but is better off (first row) by $80 million compared to $40 million if the French firm chooses to supply the British market and it has chosen to supply France. Likewise (second row) it is better off by $140 million to $100 million if it decides to supply the French market if its rival chooses not to supply the UK. Thus, whatever decision the French firm takes the British firm is better off if it has decided to supply the French market. The British firm will, therefore, also choose to supply its rival's market.

Since both the French and British firms can only adopt decisions to supply each other's markets there is only one possible outcome: the top left-hand cell in which the firms of both countries supply each other's markets.

Note that the example suggests that international trade in the same good can result simply from the rivalry of a small number of firms. Both firms supply each other's markets although the combined profits are less than maintaining national monopolies. They do so because international trade introduces actual or potential competition from foreign rivals which forces them to respond. Consumers in both markets face lower prices because of the increased competition. Theoretical models based on this type of reasoning include that by Brander and Krugman (1983).

Government policy and international trade

When governments intervene in international trade the results, if favourable to domestic producers, are called **protection**. Protection means that government engineers a situation in which domestic producers receive higher prices or returns than they would under free trade. Later in the book Chapter 11 discusses in detail protectionist policies, the mechanisms employed by governments to implement them and their pros and cons. The current section focuses on the strategic aspects of trade policy.

Strategic trade policy

As we shall see in Chapter 11, there are very few circumstances where *economic* arguments provide a strong case for government intervention in international trade. With the arrival of theories of intra-industry trade and, in particular, those based on international oligopoly (industries with a few large firms) Brander and Spencer (1985) were able to introduce a new dimension to the theory of trade policy: a strategic trade policy.

Strategic in this sense has nothing to do with military or political considerations. It means that the government may be able to pursue an *economic* strategy of earning abnormally high profits on foreign markets. As we saw earlier both monopolies and oligopolies earn higher profits than would firms in more competitive markets. The argument of a strategic trade policy is that the government could take measures to ensure that domestic firms win a larger market share of foreign markets in which these higher profits are available. Because domestic firms would be extracting a greater share of high profit markets, the country would be made better off.

Strategic trade policy quickly becomes highly complicated and readers interested in more detailed discussion are referred to Krugman (1986). These complications arise because, as we saw earlier, oligopoly requires firms to recognise the interdependence between their decisions and those of their rivals. In particular, it requires firms to construct hypotheses as to how rivals will react to any course of action taken by themselves. The hypotheses that firms construct are critical to how the industry will behave.

For strategic trade policy this provides serious problems. For example, suppose that firms set outputs rather than prices and use the hypothesis that their rivals will not change their outputs in response to a change in the firm's own output. If firms behave in this way a government subsidy would cause domestic firms to secure a larger share of foreign markets and the objective of the strategic trade policy (an increased share of abnormally high profits) would be achieved. If, however, firms set prices rather than outputs and use the hypothesis that their rivals will not change prices in response to their own price changes, an export subsidy would be entirely the wrong policy to obtain an increased share of abnormally high profits. In this case an export tax not an export subsidy would be needed.

For a strategic trade policy to be workable it would impose substantial informational requirements on the government concerned. It would need to know which industries earn these abnormally high profits. This is not simple because some industries earn higher profits as a reward for higher risk and not as a result of the additional profit earned by oligopolists. If these industries can be identified successfully the government must then know how firms construct their hypotheses about the way in which rivals respond. If the government gets this wrong it could use the wrong policy (say, a subsidy rather than a tax). This would make the domestic country worse off rather than better off. Finally, a strategic trade policy presumes that other governments do not retaliate. If they do retaliate by adopting a similar policy it is not clear that the initiating country will be better or worse off.

Strategic trade policy is of interest because it does raise the possibility that the view that 'free trade is always best' is questionable in certain, specific cases. However, as a practical policy prescription it is highly limited. Governments that attempt to pursue a strategic trade policy are at least as likely to make their own country worse off than better off.

International trade in practice: evidence

This section provides a broad outline of the techniques and findings of empirical studies of international trade.

Simple measures of trade

In this section it is necessary to use some basic mathematical notation. Readers are encouraged to persist but, if it is really too much, you can skip the section without affecting your understanding of subsequent sections.

Comparative advantage indices

Comparative advantage indices are based on the principle of **revealed comparative advantage**. This asserts that, since trade is determined by comparative advantage, we can identify the underlying pattern of advantages and disadvantages by both country and industry by observing actual trade flows. The first of these indices was developed by Balassa (1965). The index is defined as:

$$B_{jk} = x_{jk}/x_{jw}$$

where: B_{jk} is the Balassa index for industry j in country k,
   x_{jk} is the share of industry j in country k's total exports, and
   x_{jw} is the share of industry j in the world's total exports.

The logic of the index is that if country k has a greater propensity to export good j (as shown by a greater export share) than does the world at large, it can be argued to be revealing a comparative advantage. Values greater than one show that country k has a greater propensity to export good j than the world and are interpreted as revealing an advantage. Values less than one show that country k has a lesser propensity to export good j than the world and are interpreted as revealing a disadvantage.

Some economists would see the Balassa index as limited because it presumes all exports are generated by comparative advantage. The existence of intra-industry trade could, for example, lead to misleading conclusions. An alternative measure, put forward by Ballance (1988), is the **net export ratio**. This ratio is defined as:

$$NER_{jk} = (X_{jk} - M_{jk}) / (X_{jk} + M_{jk})$$

where: NER_{jk} is the net export ratio for industry j in country k,
   X_{jk} are the exports of good j by country k, and
   M_{jk} are the imports of good j by country k.

Note that the basis of the index is the calculation of net exports (exports less imports). Suppose a country has a 'pure' comparative advantage and exports good j and has no imports. With M_{jk} set at zero the index becomes X_{jk} divided by itself and takes the value of +1. Alternatively, if the country has a 'pure' disadvantage and exports none of the good while importing some quantity the index becomes M_{jk} divided by itself and takes on the value of –1. The net export ratio, therefore, has the following interpretation:

- values between 0 and +1 – a revealed advantage
- values between –1 and 0 – a revealed disadvantage
- values of approximately zero – only intra-industry trade is relevant.

The last measure, initially proposed by Finger and Kreinin (1979), is not so much a measure of comparative advantage as a means of identifying countries with a similar pattern of comparative advantage. It is known as the **export similarity index** and is defined as:

$$XSIM_{k,l} = \text{sum } [\min(x_{jk}, x_{jl})]$$

where: $XSIM_{k,l}$ is the index of export similarity between countries k and l,
x_{jk} is the share of good j in country k's total exports, and
x_{jl} is the share of good j in country l's total exports.

The index is calculated in the following way:

- step 1:   calculate the share of each and every good in the total exports of each country
- step 2:   for each good take the minimum of the two values for each country
- step 3:   sum these minimum values across all goods.

The maximum value of the index is 1 (both countries have an identical composition of their exports) and its minimum value zero (both countries have entirely dissimilar export compositions).

To see how the index works consider a hypothetical comparison between Japan and Saudi Arabia. In calculating the shares of each good in total exports for Japan there would be a zero share for crude petroleum since Japan has no deposits but a positive share for a wide variety of other goods. Repeating the calculations for Saudi Arabia would produce the reverse: a large share for crude petroleum and a zero share for most other goods. Taking minimum values the minimum for crude petroleum is zero (its share in Japan's total exports) and for most other goods also zero (their shares in Saudi Arabia's total exports). Summing across all goods would produce a total of approximately zero, suggesting that the pattern of Japan's and Saudi Arabia's exports are almost completely dissimilar.

Intra-industry trade

The most common measure of intra-industry trade is the index first proposed by Grubel and Lloyd (see Greenaway and Milner 1984 for a detailed exposition). The measure is defined as:

$$IIT_{jk} = 1 - |NER_{jk}|$$

where: IIT_{jk} is the index of intra-industry trade for good j in country k and
$|NER_{jk}|$ is the absolute value (i.e. ignoring the positive or negative sign) of the net export ratio for good j in country k.

Note that, if the net export ratio is zero (exports and imports of the same good are balanced) the intra-industry trade index takes on its maximum value of 1. If the net export ratio takes on its maximum value of +1 ('pure' comparative advantage) or its minimum value of –1 ('pure' comparative disadvantage) the intra-industry trade index takes on its minimum value of zero.

Comparative advantage and specialisation

There are a very large number of empirical studies of comparative advantage which generally fall into one of three groups. These are:

- factor content analysis
- econometric studies
- computable general equilibrium models.

The following sections provide a brief outline of each.

Factor content analysis.

The seminal study was conducted by Wassily Leontief in 1953. In essence, his study looked at the capital and labour intensities of US exports and imports for 1947. His findings were that US imports were less labour intensive and more capital intensive than US exports. This was a particularly surprising result since in 1947 the US was unquestionably the country with the highest amount of capital per worker and the H-O trade theory would consequently have predicted the reverse conclusion.

Subsequently there have been a large number of studies which make use of an extended and modified version of Leontief's approach: see Webster (1993) as a more recent example for the UK. The technique relies on two sets of information. First, it requires information on production techniques which, for example, tell us how much capital or how much skilled labour is used to produce, say, £1000 worth of each good. Second, it requires information on the exports and imports of each good. Using both sets of information it is possible to derive an estimate of how much capital or skilled labour was embodied in the exports and imports of each good. Adding this up across all goods provides an estimate of the total value of the services of capital and skilled labour that were embodied in the total value of national exports and imports.

Factor content analysis provides estimates of, for example, the implied trade of the UK stated in terms of the services of different factors of production. Factors whose services are on balance exported (exports exceed imports) are regarded as those which constitute a source of advantage (those in which the country is relatively abundant) and those which are on balance imported are regarded as a source of disadvantage in which the country is relatively scarce.

Although a number of the early factor content studies, not least Leontief's work, produced evidence which tended to contradict the H-O trade model, many more recent studies have tended to provide at least partial support. Many studies point towards the importance of different types of labour and, in particular, different skill levels as an important determinant of comparative advantage and trade.

Econometric studies

Econometric studies of comparative advantage are somewhat less common than would be normal for many other areas of economics. There are particular difficulties in conducting econometric studies which remain consistent with the underlying theory. Nonetheless some good work has been produced. Readers who are interested in following this subject further are referred to Leamer (1984). Studies of this type generally offer evidence in support of comparative advantage and the H-O trade model.

Computable General Equilibrium models

Computable General Equilibrium (CGE) models do not, strictly speaking, provide estimates. They are highly complex and sophisticated simulation models which cover not only comparative advantage but many other aspects of the behaviour of an economy. A common use of CGE models is to provide simulations of the effects on the domestic economy of changes in international trade policy.

Because of the high degree of technicality and complexity of these models, no detailed exposition of them can be offered here. Readers interested in pursuing this topic further are referred to Kendrick (1990).

Intra-industry trade

Although there continues to be an extensive new literature concerning the evidence for intra-industry trade and its determinants, probably the best overview of the different methodologies involved is given by Greenaway and Milner (1984). Studies have tended to fall into one of three main categories. These are:

- documentary studies
- econometric analysis
- calibration models.

Documentary studies tend to make intensive use of indices of intra-industry trade such as the Grubel-Lloyd index (see page 34). These typically focus on measuring the extent of intra-industry trade and almost all of these studies have found that intra-industry trade accounts for a substantial and growing share of world trade.

Econometric analysis has tended to focus on the evidence for the different theoretical determinants of intra-industry trade. Although there have been many good studies it is probably fair to say that results have been mixed. At the time of writing there remains no real consensus of evidence on which determinants of intra-industry trade are the most important or on the precise way in which they determine trade.

Calibration models provide simulations of behaviour within an oligopolistic trade model rather than estimates. They are most commonly used to provide an analysis of the likely consequences of a strategic trade policy. A useful example of such a model is given by Dixit (1988).

Chapter summary

As this chapter has shown international trade is not just important in its own right but is a key element in understanding the business environment for any country or industry. Explanations of inter-industry trade do not just provide a basis for understanding trade itself. They also explain why any particular country produces more of certain goods and less of others. That is, an understanding of international trade provides an explanation of why certain countries are success-ful locations for the production of some goods but not others.

It is clear that many different elements are important in this process. For exam-ple, technology, productivity and the costs of factors of production (land, labour and capital) are important in understanding inter-industry trade, whereas market structure and demand conditions are of particular importance for intra-industry trade. Trade, therefore, not only helps to shape the business and economic envi-ronment but is also itself shaped by the same environment.

The controversy between free trade and protectionism remains an active debate for many governments as it has done periodically for at least the last 200 years. Given that free trade, leaving aside the rather special circumstances of a strategic trade policy, is one of the few areas where there is a long-standing con-sensus among economists this is perhaps surprising. One possibility is that economists have done a poor job of explaining to others their reasons for this conclusion. It is to be hoped that this chapter has provided a modest contribu-tion to creating greater understanding.

Finally, the chapter has sought to equip the reader with some basic and rela-tively simple techniques for the analysis of international trade. Hopefully these will prove of use to those who would like to undertake their own assessment of international trade in practice.

Discussion questions

1 What are the key differences between countries that give rise to comparative advantage?
2 What types of good would you expect a country, say the UK, with a large number of highly educated and skilled workers per unskilled worker to export to a country, say Nigeria, with relatively few highly educated workers per unskilled worker?
3 How would persistently high rates of investment and low rates of population growth tend to change the UK's pattern of comparative advantage?
4 What elements of consumer behaviour are likely to generate intra-industry trade?
5 What would be the likely economic costs of increasing tariff protection against imports?

Closing Case Studies:
Case Study 1: Labour skills and the UK's trade

In this study, Webster (1993) looked at the way in which the UK's exports depend on highly detailed categories of labour. The starting point of the study was that labour can be differentiated in two main ways. First, labour can have different levels of skill or education, what economists refer to as 'human capital'. Thus, for example, skilled manual workers have more human capital than unskilled workers and professional workers more human capital than skilled manual workers.

Second, different types of labour may have approximately the same level of human capital but a set of skills that are distinct from each other. For example, pharmacists and accountants have broadly similar levels of education and training but the skills of each group are distinct from each other.

There has been a tendency, since the discovery of intra-industry trade, for economists to argue that comparative advantage is not particularly relevant in explaining trade between countries at a similar level of development. For example, the UK and Germany have broadly similar numbers of professional workers per unskilled worker. As predicted by the Heckscher-Ohlin theory this would suggest that the countries have no real differences in their relative endowments of different types of labour and would be unlikely to be engaged in much inter-industry trade.

This argument, however, is only valid if all types of labour at a certain skill level are the same. If, as was argued earlier, pharmacists and accountants have essentially the same amount of human capital but in distinct and differentiated forms, there remains a possibility that countries with similar relative endowments would engage in inter-industry trade. That is, countries with similar endowments of workers by the overall level of skill may still differ substantially in the types of skill at each level. This would create a basis for specialisation and trade.

The study, using information on some 162 occupational categories, found that the UK did indeed specialise in international trade according to both the level of human capital and the type of skill. Specifically, it found that variations in different levels of skill and in different types of skill at the same level were of roughly equal importance in explaining inter-industry trade.

Source: Webster (1993).

Case Study 2: Comparative advantage and foreign direct investment

This study, by Maskus and Webster (1995), looked at the locational decision of the multinational enterprise. Generally multinationals are considered to have some firm specific or 'ownership' advantages which gives them the potential to make profits in domestic or foreign markets. Under certain conditions firms with such advantages will choose to exploit them through multinational production rather than by franchising or exporting. Given that firms have made this decision to become multinational they must also decide where to locate their production.

This choice of location is likely to be determined by costs. That is, provided there are no significant barriers to trade, multinationals are likely to produce in whichever location has the most favourable costs and to export from these locations to consumers in other markets. This suggests that multinationals in economic activities which have few barriers to trade will choose to locate production wherever there is an absolute advantage and, to the extent that absolute and comparative advantages coincide, wherever there is a comparative advantage.

The study looked at both trade and inward foreign investment for the UK and for South Korea. For the UK inward foreign investment tended to be focused on the same types of economic activity in which the UK had a comparative advantage in trade. This evidence tends to support the proposition that multinationals locate their activities according to comparative advantage.

For South Korea there was a much weaker relationship between inward foreign investment and comparative advantage. This is most likely explained by the fact that investment is necessarily forward looking. That is, firms are likely to invest in those activities in which there is likely to be a cost advantage in the future. For a rapidly changing country like Korea, which was still on the path of economic development, the activities that were likely to have a comparative advantage in the near future are unlikely to be the same as those that had an advantage in the recent past.

Source: Maskus and Webster (1995).

Questions

1 In what ways can labour be differentiated and what are the implications for the arguments put forward by the Heckscher-Ohlin theory and its proponents?
2 Why are the UK and South Korea different from one another in terms of the relationship between inward foreign investment and their respective comparative advantage?

Further reading

Greenaway, D. (1983) *International Trade Policy: From Tariffs to the New Protectinism*, Basingstoke: Macmillan.

Greenaway, D. and **Milner, C.** (1986) *The Economics of Intra-Industry Trade*, Oxford: Basil Blackwell.

Krugman, P. (1991) *Geography and Trade*, Cambridge MA: MIT Press.

Krugman, P. (1997) *Pop Internationalism*, Cambridge MA: MIT Press.

Sodersten, B. and **Reed, G.** (1994) *International Economics*, Basingstoke: Macmillan.

References

Balassa, B. (1965) Trade liberalization and revealed comparative advantage, *The Manchester School* 23: 99–123.

Ballance, R.H. (1988) Trade performance as an indicator of comparative advantage, in D. Greenaway (ed.) *Economic Development and International Trade*, London: Macmillan.

Brander, J.A. and Krugman, P. R. (1983) A reciprocal dumping model of international trade, *Journal of International Economics* 13: 313–21.

Brander, J.A. and Spencer, B.J. (1985) Export subsidies and market share rivalry, *Journal of International Economics* 18: 83–100.

Davies, D.R. (1995) Intra-industry trade: a Heckscher-Ohlin-Ricardo approach, *Journal of International Economics* 39: 201–26.

Dixit, A.K. (1988) Optimal trade and industrial policies for the US automobile industry, in R. C. Feenstra (ed.) *Empirical Methods for International Trade*, Cambridge MA: MIT Press.

Dixit, A.K. and Stiglitz, J. (1977) Monopolistic competition and optimum product diversity, *American Economic Review* 67: 297–308.

Ethier, W.J. (1984) Higher dimensional issues in trade theory, in R. W. Jones and P. B. Kenen (eds) *Handbook of International Economics*, Amsterdam: North Holland.

Falvey, R.E. (1981) Commercial policy and intra-industry trade, *Journal of International Economics* 11: 495–511.

Finger, J. and Kreinin, M. (1979) A measure of 'export similarity' and its possible uses, *Economic Journal* 89: 905–13.

Garber, P. M. (ed.) (1993) *The Mexico–U.S. Free Trade Agreement*, Cambridge MA: MIT Press.

Greenaway, D. and Milner, C. (1984) *The Economics of Intra Industry Trade*, London: Macmillan.

Heckscher, E.F. (1919) Utrikeshandelns verkan pa inkomstfodelningen, *Eknonomisk Tidskrift* 21: 1–32.

Helpman, E. and Krugman, P.R. (1985) *Market Structure and Foreign Trade*, Cambridge MA: MIT Press.

Jones, R.W. (1971) A three factor model in theory, trade and history, in J.N. Bhagwati *et al* (eds) *Trade, Balance of Payments and Growth: Essays in Honour of C P Kindleberger*, Amsterdam: North Holland.

Kendrick, D.A. (1990) *Models for Analyzing Comparative Advantage*, Dordecht: Kluwer.

Krugman, P.R. (ed.) (1986) *Strategic Trade Policy and the New International Economics*, Cambridge MA: MIT Press.

Lancaster, K. (1979) *Variety, Equity and Efficiency*, Oxford: Basil Blackwell.

Lancaster, K. (1980) Intra-industry trade under perfect monopolistic competition, *Journal of International Economics* 10: 151–76.

Lawrence, R.Z. and **Slaughter, M.J.** (1993) International trade and American wages in the 1980s: giant sucking sound or small hiccup, *Brookings Papers on Economic Activity: Microeconomics* 2: 161–226.

Leamer, E.E. (1984) *Sources of International Comparative Advantage: Theory and Evidence*, Cambridge MA: MIT Press.

Leamer, E.E. (1995) The Heckscher-Ohlin model in theory and practice, *Princeton Studies in International Finance* 77.

Leontief, W.W. (1953) Domestic production and foreign trade: the American capital position re-examined, *Economica Internazionale* 7: 3–32.

Maskus, K.E. and **Webster, A.** (1995) Comparative advantage and the location of inward foreign direct investment, *The World Economy* 18: 315–28, Oxford: Blackwell.

Ohlin, B. (1933) *Inter-regional and International Trade*, Cambridge MA: Harvard University Press.

Porter, M.E. (1990) *The Competitive Advantage of Nations*, London: Macmillan.

Ricardo, D. (1817) *Principles of Political Economy and Taxation*, reprinted as Vol. 1 of P. Sraffa (ed.) (1951) *The Works of David Ricardo*, London: Cambridge University Press.

Rybczynski, T.M. (1955) Factor endowment and relative commodity prices, *Economica* 22: 336–41.

Sachs, J.D. and **Shatz, H.J.** (1994) Trade and jobs in US manufacturing, *Brookings Papers on Economic Activity* 1: 1–84.

Samuelson, P.A. (1948) International trade and the equalization of factor prices, *Economic Journal* 58: 163–84.

Smith, A. (1766) *The Wealth of Nations*, reprinted as E. Cannan (ed.) (1961) London: Methuen.

Stolper, W.F. and **Samuelson, P.A.** (1941) Protection and real wages, *Review of Economic Studies* 9: 58–73.

Vernon, R. (1966) International investment and international trade in the product cycle, *Quarterly Journal of Economics* 80: 190–207.

Webster, A. (1993) The skill and higher educational content of UK net exports, *Oxford Bulletin of Economics and Statistics* 55: 141–60, Oxford: Blackwell.

Wood, A. (1994) *North–South Trade, Employment and Inequality: Changing Fortunes in a Skill-Driven World*, Oxford: Clarendon Press.

CHAPTER 2

International Financial Markets

Andrew Solocha

Learning objectives

By the end of this chapter you will be able to:

- describe the structure of the foreign exchange market and present basic exchange rate terminology

- explain rudimentary factors that can affect exchange rates

- describe the currency futures market and how future contracts are used in international finance

- outline the structure of the options market

- explain factors that influence option values and basic option hedging strategies

- examine the factors that can affect the cost of capital

- understand the sources for international capital

- describe international equity markets and probe future trends.

Opening Case Study:
$51bn fall in bank lending to Asia is biggest in decade

International bank lending to Asia fell by $51.7bn (£31.3bn), or 14 per cent, in the first half of the year, the biggest decline in a decade. Figures published today by the Bank for International Settlements (BIS) provide more evidence of the extent of the shift of funds out of the region as a result of the economic downturn.

The Basle-based central bankers' organisation said cross-border lending by banks in leading industrial countries to Asia fell to $324.8bn at the end of June.

The $51.7bn decline on the previous six months was equivalent to Thailand's or Indonesia's estimated annual export income for the current year.

The organisation paints an even starker global picture for the three months to September, with figures for the quarter indicating liquidity in international debt markets virtually dried up. 'Financial turbulence in the first half of 1998 was associated with a massive withdrawing of international banking funds from Asia,' says the BIS.

It shows that the retreat covered all countries in the region, but affected South Korea and Thailand particularly strongly. For a while, the shift of capital was partly offset by an increase of $14.9bn in lending to Latin America, with the bulk going to Brazil. But that stopped in the summer and the turmoil assumed global proportions in August when the Asian crisis was compounded by Russia's decision to float the rouble and renege on debt. Russia's move triggered a huge flight to safety, 'a rush to liquidity . . . the unwinding of large and highly leveraged exposures (and) fears of a systemic disruption,' says the BIS.

Global retrenchment was accentuated by the near collapse of Long-Term Capital Management, the US hedge fund, and has led to a marked downturn in international banking and securities activity.

In the third quarter, syndicated loan volume dropped by 23 per cent to $204bn. This was partly because of the bleak economic outlook, but also because Japanese banks had clamped down on lending and consolidation had cut the pool of European lenders.

Overall, net issuance of international debt almost halved to $126.3bn as volatility reached record levels. 'Demand dried up for all but the most highly rated names while primary activity contracted for the second consecutive quarter,' says the BIS.

Fixed rate bond issuance fell by 17 per cent during the quarter and floating rate issues shrank by 6 per cent.

Royal Bank of Scotland is expected to announce a charge of at least £100m for its exposure to Asia when it gives its annual figures on Thursday.

Source: *Financial Times* CD-ROM, 1 January–31 December 1998.

Introduction

International financial markets consist of the foreign exchange, derivative, debt and equity markets. They are important to governments, multinational firms and investors in achieving their individual goals. International financial markets assist governments and central banks in financing their fiscal and current account deficits (when nations buy more than they sell), and to maintain their exchange rates. Firms engaged in international transactions require international financial markets for their currency requirements, assistance in management of currency risk, and the ability to raise capital at a lower cost. Investors use international financial markets to diversify their portfolios and to achieve higher rates of return.

The interrelationship of governments, multinational firms and international investors is illustrated in the case study at the end of the chapter. Thailand was running a current account deficit and borrowed from international investors to finance the deficit. The central bank used their international reserves (foreign currency) to maintain their exchange rate in the foreign exchange market. It became evident to international investors that Thailand could no longer maintain their exchange rate and they withdrew their funds. This led to the collapse of the Thai Baht and applied pressure to all the other currencies in Asia.

Foreign exchange markets

The volume of international trade and investment increased dramatically after the Second World War and created the need for foreign currency. The **foreign exchange market** is where the financial instruments are traded and the price is the **exchange rate**.

The foreign exchange market is an informal market with no physical location. All transactions are conducted over telephone lines and by computer screens. The market is open continuously and as shown in Figure 2.1, the largest trading volume is done in the UK, US, and Japan. The Bank for International Settlements (BIS) found that the other important markets include Singapore, Hong Kong, Switzerland, Germany and France. Furthermore, the BIS estimated the average daily volume of trade on foreign exchange markets at $1.49 trillion dollars in 1998 with approximately 20 banks accounting for 50 per cent of the total volume.

Participants

There are four main participants in the foreign exchange market:

- **Banks** and other financial institutions in the major money markets are the largest participants;
- **Brokers** act as intermediaries between banks and the trades are confidential;
- **Multinational firms** require foreign currency for operations;
- **Central banks** participate in foreign exchange to either change the value of the exchange rate or to bring order to the market in a crisis.

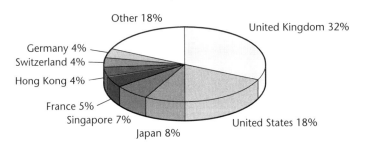

Figure 2.1 Percentage of daily turnover in foreign exchange markets: 1998
Source: Bank of International Settlements survey.

The participants in foreign exchange markets typically involve arbitrage, trading, hedging, or speculating. **Arbitrageurs** take advantage of market imperfections to gain risk-free profits. **Traders** use foreign currency for their accounts receivables and accounts payable. **Hedgers**, usually multinational firms, use off-setting contracts, such as forward, futures, options, and swaps, to eliminate their exchange rate risk. **Speculators** expose themselves (gamble) to foreign exchange rate risk so they can profit from favourable movements in foreign exchange rates.

There are two principal types of foreign exchange markets: the interbank and the retail markets. Transactions in the interbank market are generally for very large sums (millions of dollars) and are sometimes called the wholesale market. This is a highly competitive market where quotations are valid for only one minute. The retail markets are generally for transactions of a specific amount and involve a bank and its client. Typically, travellers obtain their foreign exchange in retail markets.

Basic terminology

- There are two ways of quoting exchange rates. **American terms** are the number of US dollars to buy foreign currency. **European terms** are the number of foreign currency to buy the US dollar;
- **Cross rates** are exchange rates that do not involve the US dollar;
- Transaction costs are represented by the **bid-ask spread**. The bid price at which the currency is bought and the asking price at which the currency is sold;
- There are three major types of markets: the spot, forward, and swap foreign exchange markets. The **spot market** is the foreign exchange market where transactions are settled within two business days. The **forward market** is the foreign exchange market where transactions are settled at a future date. A **swap** transaction is the simultaneous purchase and sale of foreign currency for different maturity dates. The spot for forward is the most common type of swap; however, forward for forward swaps are also conducted.

The spot market accounts for approximately half of all foreign exchange transactions. Most dollar transactions are cleared through the Clearing House Interbank Payments System in New York. In addition, many large international banks act as market markers in the foreign exchange market. They specialise in particular currencies by maintaining an inventory, and are willing to buy or sell these currencies within established trading limits.

The forward market

The forward rate is determined at the time of the agreement but payment is not required until maturity of the contract. Interbank forward rates are generally quoted for one, two, three, six, and twelve months. Retail forward rates can be quoted for a particular date. Occasionally, forward rates may be quoted for periods of more than one year.

Forward exchange rates can be offered at a premium or a discount. A **premium** is when the forward rate is greater than the spot rate, while a **discount** is when the forward rate is less than the spot rate. The discount or premium depends on the interest rate differential between instruments in the two countries (difference in yield curves). Although forward markets are derivative markets, a natural hedge could be established. For instance, if IBM had an accounts payable in Swiss francs due in 90 days, it would ask CITIBANK for a forward quote to buy Swiss francs with US dollars in 90 days. CITIBANK would immediately exchange dollars for Swiss francs and buy Swiss T-bills that mature in 90 days. At maturity, the Swiss T-bills mature and IBM receives its US dollars. If Swiss interest rates are lower than US interest rates, then CITIBANK will incur an opportunity cost and pass it on to IBM as an exchange rate premium. If Swiss interest rates are higher than US interest rates, then CITIBANK would pass on a portion of the extra interest in the form of a discount on foreign currency.

Exchange rate regimes

There are three main types of foreign exchange rate regimes. **Floating exchange rates** are determined by supply and demand for the currency. For a currency to truly float, the market for their currency must have sufficient liquidity. **Fixed exchange rates** are pegged to the value of another currency, such as the dollar, a basket of currencies or pegged to the value of gold. The Gold Standard (1792–1913), the Gold Exchange Standard (1944–1973), the EURO (1999) are examples of international fixed exchange rate systems. Similarly, Argentina pegs its currency to the US dollar. **Managed floats** or **dirty floats** are exchange rates that are allowed to float within a range. Once the exchange rate reaches the upper or lower limit of the range, the central bank intervenes to bring the exchange rate back into the range.

There are a number of arguments for and against fixed exchange rates that relate to the independence of monetary and fiscal policy and international trade flows. First, central banks need large amounts of international reserves to defend their currencies. Second, fixed exchange rates reduce the currency risks inherent in international trade. This may induce greater levels of international trade. Third, fixed exchange rates require the convergence of national monetary and fiscal policies. This generally results in price stability and provides a basis for sound monetary and fiscal policy. Nevertheless, since fixed exchange rates link national economies, shocks from one country are quickly transmitted to other countries. The interrelationship between national economies was shown in 1982 when East and West Germany unified and Germany borrowed large amounts of international capital at high real interest rates (adjusted for inflation). This caused a recession in Germany that spread to the rest of Europe. The interrelationship between national economies was also demonstrated in the Asia crisis where the collapse of the Thai Baht spread to the other currencies of Asia.

Foreign exchange rate determinations

There are many theories of exchange rate determination. These include traditional approaches that focus on international flows such as the Keynesian and absorption theories, asset-based theories such as the monetary and portfolio balance approaches, or expectations, approaches that focus on 'news'. These theories examine factors relating to the balance of payments statistics, monetary and fiscal policy, news from financial markets, political developments and business cycles. Each of these factors influences the supply and demand for foreign currency through the components of the balance of payments: the capital account (debt instruments, stocks, and foreign direct investment), and the current account (goods and services).

Income

A change in income has an impact on both the current and capital account. Nevertheless, the result on exchange rates is complicated and controversial. From the current account, an increase in a country's income with a positive marginal propensity to import would increase the demand for foreign products and foreign currency. This is the same thing as an increase in the supply of domestic currency in the foreign exchange market, thus causing the currency to depreciate.

From the capital account, an increase in income signals that the country's economy is strong. This would attract more investors and increase the supply of foreign currency in the foreign exchange markets. This is equivalent to an increase in the demand for the domestic currency and would result in currency appreciation. The ultimate affect on exchange rates would be determined by whether the impact on the capital or current account is strongest.

Inflation rates

An increase in inflation rates relative to other countries causes the country's products to become less competitive and the other country's products to become more competitive. Therefore, the demand for foreign currency increases (supply of domestic currency) and the supply of foreign currency decreases (demand for domestic currency) and the country's exchange rate would depreciate.

Real interest rates

An increase in a country's real interest rate (adjusted for inflation) represents an increase in purchasing power. Therefore, if a country's real interest rate were to increase, investment flows to the country would increase, while investment flows out of the country would decrease. The demand for foreign currency (supply of domestic currency) would decrease and the supply of foreign currency would rise (demand for domestic currency) thereby causing the exchange rate to increase. There is some evidence that high levels of fiscal deficits can increase real interest rates through their efforts to bid for capital away from the private sector. Therefore, high levels of fiscal deficits and debt can have an influence on exchange rates.

Balance of payments

Countries with persistent current account deficits are buying more than they are selling and are living beyond their means. If international reserves levels are also declining, then the country's ability to maintain its exchange rates are reduced. This is a clear sign of a weak currency and leads to expectations of a fall in exchange rate values. Countries have several ways to maintain their exchange rates. These include methods aimed at reducing imports, increases in domestic saving, reducing government deficits and attracting foreign capital.

Safe havens

Increases in political risk would cause capital to flow to safe havens. Higher interest rates are no longer the prime concern as investors seek to protect their principal. The US, Switzerland and Costa Rica tend to be safe havens and the demand for their currencies increases during periods of political instability. Costa Rica has been politically stable for over 100 years and has not had an army in that time period.

News

Foreign exchange rate markets respond to a vast array of fundamental and psychological events. Under the efficient markets' hypothesis, asset prices embody all available information. News is additional information that arrives randomly and therefore asset prices move randomly.

Futures markets

The breakdown of the gold exchange standard became evident by late 1971 and a need for foreign exchange risk management arose. Futures markets developed in 1972 as an instrument to reduce risk. The primary US market for foreign currency futures is the International Monetary Market (IMM) on the Chicago Mercantile Exchange. Contracts traded on the IMM became interchangeable with those on the Singapore International Monetary Exchange (SIMEX) in 1985.

Eurex is the German options and futures exchange and is gaining importance in international financial markets. Eurex is currently negotiating with the Chicago Board of Trade to create standardised instruments that can be traded simultaneously on both exchanges. The Eurex has also negotiated with the French Bourses, and Amsterdam and Swiss Exchanges.

A foreign currency futures contract is a financial derivative that calls for delivery of a fixed amount of foreign currency at a set time and price. The futures exchange acts as a clearing-house and is party to all transactions. Therefore, the risk of default on a contract is the risk that the futures exchange will default.

Some important features of futures contracts include:

- Standard contract size: foreign futures can only be traded in whole contracts specified by the exchange. Contract specifications are available on their web sites given at the end of the chapter.
- Standard maturity date: contracts mature on the third Wednesday of January, March, April, June, July, September, October, or December. Spot month contracts are also traded and these mature on the next following third Wednesday.
- Margin requirement: futures contracts are highly leveraged with margin requirements of 5 per cent or less. The initial margin is similar to a perfor-

mance bond and can be met by a letter of credit, treasury bills, or cash. The maintenance requirement is approximately 75 per cent of the initial requirement. When the value of the contract falls so that the initial margin falls below the maintenance margin, the initial margin must be restored. The margin requirement is monitored on a daily basis
- Settlement: 5 per cent or less of foreign futures contracts are settled by physical delivery. In other words, people are buying something they do not want and are selling something they do not have.
- Commissions: customers pay a commission based on a round turn, buying and selling of the futures contract since most contracts are not delivered.

Example

An investor takes a long position (buy) in a British-pound futures contract on 1 May (Monday) that matures in June. The price for the contract is $1.6136/£ and the value of the contract is $100,850 ($1.6136/£ * £62,500). The initial margin is $2000 and the maintenance margin is $1500.

Table 2.1 Example of Futures Margin Account

Date	Settle price	Contract value	Mark-to-market (change in value)	Margin account balance
5/1	1.6136	$100,850	0	$2,000
5/2	1.6120	$100,750	$100	$1,900
5/3	1.6100	$100,625	$225	$1,775
5/4	1.6000	$100,000	$850	$1,150

When the margin balance falls below the maintenance margin of $1500, the investor receives a margin call and additional funds must be deposited in cash to bring the balance back to $2000.

Options markets

Foreign currency options are another financial derivative that is gaining importance as a hedging tool, particularly with the liberalisation of trade in services and intellectual property rights. The popularity in foreign currency options stems from their flexibility. Unlike forward and future contracts, options allow the purchaser the right, but not the obligation, to buy or sell a fixed amount of foreign currency for a set time period (expiration date). Options should be viewed as insurance against future currency losses. There are several important basic terms to understanding options.

Basic terminology

- There are two basic types of options. A **call option** gives the purchaser the right to buy foreign currency (sell domestic currency). A **put option** gives the purchaser the right to sell foreign currency (buy domestic for foreign currency);
- The purchaser of the option is called the **holder**. The seller is called the **writer** or **grantee**;
- Options can be exercised in two styles. **European options** can only be exercised on the expiration date. **American options** can be exercised at any time during the life of the option;
- The **exercise** or **strike price** is the exchange rate that foreign currency can be purchased (call) or sold (put). The **premium** is the cost of the option, which is determined by open outcry between buyers and sellers on the trading floor. The total financial gain from an option is: (1) the difference between the strike price and spot price; and (2) the value of the premium;
- An option that is profitable if exercised immediately is called *in-the-money* (ITM). Similarly, an option that cannot be profitably exercised is *out-of-the-money* (OTM). Finally, an option whose value is zero is *at-the-money* (ATM).

Structure of the options market

Options are traded on formal organised exchanges and on informal over-the-counter (OTC) markets. Multinational firms using currency options for risk management or financial institutions with international portfolios generally engage in the OTC market, while financial institutions trade in the organised exchanges. The BIS estimates the OTC derivative average daily turnover at $362 bn in 1998, an increase of 85 per cent from 1995. The UK increased its market share in OTC derivatives from 27 per cent in 1996 to 36 per cent in 1998. The increase in UK market share stems from the growth in Eurocurrency trading. Similarly, as shown in Figure 2.2, France and Germany increased their OTC derivative market share while Japan and Singapore lost their prominent positions.

OTC options market

OTC options are similar to forward contracts because the amount, exercise price and rights, underlying instrument, and expiration of the contract can be negotiated and

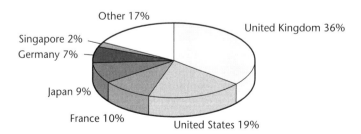

Figure 2.2 Market share of OTC derivatives turnover on selected exchanges
Source: Bank of International Settlements survey.

tailored to the firm's needs. OTC currency options are traded by financial institutions in most major money centres with the two most important OTC markets located in London and New York. The contracts involve the major currencies and are generally traded in round lots of $5–$10m in New York and $2–3m in London. Although most contracts involve US dollars against the major currencies, branches of foreign banks can write options against their home currency. Although this market was not liquid at its inception, it is currently considered to be reasonably liquid. Nevertheless, there have been failures in international markets, most notably the Bank of New England and Drexel-Burnham Lambert, and legal risks associated with financial institutions in the UK.

Organised exchanges

The Philadelphia Stock Exchange (PHLX) introduced standardised foreign currency option contracts in 1982. The PHLX offers customised, standardised, and 'virtual' or '3-D' currency options, and is currently the most diverse and comprehensive market for currency options trading. The PHLX offers Virtual Currencies of 3-D (Dollar-Denominated-Delivery) options on the Deutschemark and Japanese yen. These are settled at expiration in US dollars for the difference between the spot and the strike price; thus the underlying currency does not have to be delivered. Other organised options exchanges are located in London (LIFFE), Amsterdam (European Options Exchange), Chicago (Chicago Mercantile Exchange), and Montreal (Montreal Stock Exchange). Organised exchanges are important to investors who do not have access to the OTC market and to banks because they can offset the risk of options incurred on the OTC market.

Options strategies

There are several strategies in hedging foreign exchange rate risk uses options. These include synthetic forwards and other second generations option products. With a synthetic forward, two options contracts can be used to create an instrument that resembles a forward contract. One contract provides insurance against foreign exchange rate losses and the other locks in or 'collars' the exchange rate. This reduces the cost of the option but eliminates potential gains from exchange rate changes. The creation of a synthetic forward stems from the definition of a call and put option.

A range forward is an extension of the synthetic forward that allows the firm to engage in limited profits from favourable exchange rate movements while still providing an insurance against unfavourable exchange rate losses. A participating forward is also called a zero-cost option and allows the firm to participate in favourable exchange rate movements.

Option pricing and valuation

Black and Scholes developed the original option pricing model and it has been extended by Cox-Rubinstein, and Garmen-Kohlhagen. The total value (premium) of an option consists of two components: the intrinsic value and the time value. The intrinsic value is the difference between the spot value and the strike price and is the financial gain if the option is exercised immediately. A put option has intrinsic value when the spot price is below the strike price. Similarly, a call option has intrinsic value when the spot price is above the strike price.

The time value of an option is based on the probability that the spot rate can move further ITM during its time to maturity (expiration date). The time value component is complex and is sensitive to the following: (1) changes in forward rates; (2) changes in spot rates; (3) time to maturity; (4) changes in volatility; and (5) changes in interest differentials.

An American option will always have a positive time value because there is a positive probability that the spot rate can move the option ITM. This is why an American option is not exercised prior to expiration. Since American options have time value before expiration, they can be sold to capture this value. This is not necessarily the case for European options since they can only be exercised on the maturity date. While a European currency option may be ITM before expiration, it may be OTM on the expiration date.

International sources of capital

Cost of capital

Multinational firms require capital for their operation, including working capital and expansion into new markets. Capital can be obtained through debt and equity financing. The cost of capital is a weighted average of the two. The degree to which capital markets are segmented have an important impact on the cost of capital. Market segmentation reduces market liquidity and is influenced by factors such as asymmetry in information, transaction costs, exchange rate risk, and regulatory barriers.

Asymmetry in information

Market imperfections can be caused by language barriers, differing accounting standards, and level of disclosure. These give local investors an informational advantage because of familiarity. For instance, many financial markets do not require that a prospectus be prepared in English, thereby restricting access to their markets from foreign borrowers and investors. Accounting standards and the level of disclosure vary among financial markets and create uncertainty for foreign investors.

Transaction costs

Brokerage commissions and taxes on capital gains that differ according to the investor's nationality are transaction costs that create market imperfections.

Exchange rate risks

Volatility in exchange rates creates a risk premium for investors and financial institutions that can impede capital flows. If instruments for hedging are not readily available, the financial markets become less liquid.

Regulatory barriers

Governments impose many regulatory barriers on foreign investors. These include restrictions on cross-border borrowing and lending, constraints on ownership of securities, enforcement of insider trading rules, and exchange controls.

The introduction of the Euro may potentially have an important impact on the cost of capital in European financial markets. The Euro is forcing accounting standards in Europe to converge, regulatory barriers in trading securities are minimised, and exchange rates risk is eliminated with the single currency. This has stimulated negotiations for European financial markets mergers and spurred the euro-equity market.

Exhibit 2.1 Agencies to target Europe's burgeoning bond market

Monetary union, as economists and bankers never tire of pointing out, is expected to awaken Europe's corporate bond market from its hitherto sleepy existence. One set of players who are undoubtedly wide awake and at each others' throats (at least proverbially) are the world's leading credit-rating agencies.

Fitch IBCA, the world's third largest agency but still very much in the second division, believes Emu could provide it with the opportunity to join Standard & Poor's and Moody's Investors Service in the premier league. 'It is much easier to grow into an undeveloped market than into one which is not (the US),' said Christopher Huhne, head of sovereign ratings at Fitch IBCA in London. 'We have found this previously in Eastern and Southern Europe and in international banking and structured finance – all areas where we are now market leaders.'

But Fitch IBCA, the product of a merger last year between IBCA, the European agency, and Fitch Investors Service, the domestic US agency, will be competing with the 'big two' at their most aggressive. Both Moody's and S&P have increased their European staff levels by around 30 per cent over the last 12 months and expect their European payrolls to continue to grow at double-digit rates for the next few years.

Both agencies, which have several thousand ratings in the US market, have set targets to derive at least 30 per cent of revenues from non-US ratings in the next year or two. At present the proportion of international ratings is about 20 per cent of overall levels. The majority of this growth is expected to be stimulated by Emu.

Duff & Phelps, the US agency which has tended to concentrate on specialist and corporate ratings but has recently moved more openly into sovereign ratings, has also stepped up its presence in London. 'The rating agencies know they are on to a good thing,' said John Langton, chief executive of the International Securities Market Association, the leading trade body for the Eurobond market. 'Emu and its effects on the corporate bond market is a one-off opportunity for a very rapid growth in ratings.'

Chester Murray, head of Moody's European operations in London, says that the fastest ratings growth will be concentrated on three areas: corpo-

▶

rate bonds, Europe's nascent municipal bond market and structured finance, including asset-backed securities. The agencies already have Europe's sovereign bond market well covered. 'We are bullish on the prospects for the growth of a corporate bond market in Europe,' said Mr Murray, who added that Moody's had rated about 100 European companies for the first time this year. This brings Moody's total number of corporate rating relationships (companies have more than one rating for different types of debt) up to 300 in Europe.

However, Moody's and its competitors still face a steep climb to bring Europe up to the levels of credit awareness common in the US. First, many European companies, especially household names such as Porsche and Carrefour (who can rely on name-recognition alone to attract retail investors) are unrated despite coming to the markets with bond offerings recently.

Rating agencies derive the vast bulk of their revenues from those they rate. Unsolicited ratings are therefore uneconomic and often viewed as hostile by the borrower. It may take some time for European companies to view ratings more positively, say the agencies. 'The change will have to come from investors,' said one rating official. 'Pension funds happily buy unrated bonds when the company is a local one within their domestic currency zone, but when that zone suddenly expands to become the Euro-zone the investor will want to buy less familiar names and will require them to be rated.'

Second, Europe's municipal bond market is unlikely to grow at the ambitious rates which many have anticipated. Last year there were $214bn (£128.90bn) worth of municipal bonds issued in the US – a major source of revenue for the rating agencies. In Europe it totalled less than $10bn. Nevertheless, there were some encouraging signs: Catalonia, Naples and Lazio have all issued debut bonds in the last 12 months. And many others – given the increased trend towards devolution of central government finance to the regional and provincial level – will be compelled to follow suit in the next few months.

Third, Europe's asset-backed market is also dwarfed by its counterpart in the US, although this means the scope for dramatic growth in Europe is correspondingly greater. Last year there were $50bn worth of securitised offerings in Europe and roughly the same again so far in 1998, even though the market has been closed for the final third of the year. In the US total issuance was $149bn for the first three-quarters of 1998, according to Moody's.

Again, there are persuasive signs that this market will take off. For example, Italy, Spain and Germany have all recently amended domestic regulations to allow for mortgages and loans to be securitised. Leading players, such as Deutsche Bank, have already taken advantage of this and issued large-scale asset-backed bonds. Given their poor return on equity, most of Europe's leading banks will inevitably use this sort of balance-sheet management more frequently in the next year or two.

Last, there are factors independent of Emu which are also helping to stimulate the development of a corporate bond market in Europe. Most important is the reduction in long-term interest rates with yields on ten-year government bonds falling to below 4 per cent in recent weeks. This has encouraged companies that were hitherto reliant on bank debt to tap longer-term capital from the financial markets. The fact that banks are reluctant to provide longer-term funding and increasingly disenchanted with the low returns in the loan market, can only compound this trend. 'All the signs are pointing our way,' said one rating official. 'Volumes in the European bond market can only go one way.'

Source: *Financial Times* CD-ROM, 1 January–31 December 1998.

International debt financing

Multinational firms can reduce their cost of capital by obtaining debt on international financial markets. Multinational firms use international financial markets to match maturities of their assets with debt instruments to reduce exposure to interest rate movements. Multinational firms with foreign assets may want to match currencies to reduce their economic or operating exposure. By matching assets with liabilities in the same currency, exchange rate exposure is reduced. Euro-financial markets play a dominant role in international debt markets.

Eurocurrency markets

Eurodollars are US denominated bank deposits held in banks outside the US. Eurocurrencies extend this concept by including other currencies such as the mark and the yen. This is sometimes referred to as off-shore banking.

The Eurodollar market was established in the early 1950s when the Soviet Union sold gold to purchase grain and other goods. The dollars the Soviet Union received for the gold did not earn interest; however, Soviet banks would not leave them on deposit in New York because of the cold war. A strong reminder of the political risk occurred when the US froze all Chinese accounts after the Chinese revolution. Another early impetus for the Eurodollar market was the inflow of dollars into Europe from continued US BOP deficits and the dollars generated by the Marshall Plan.

The Eurodollar market grew during the 1960s and 1970s because of restrictive US banking rules and US tax laws. The Eurocurrency market developed when European currencies attained convertability in the 1950s. The US restrictions were Regulation Q, Regulation M, and the US interest equalisation tax (1963–74). The Eurodollar market provided an avenue for US banks to avoid US banking rules and the equalisation tax. Further impetus for the Eurodollar market occurred when US banks began to channel loans to less developed countries (LDCs) through their off-shore banks.

A small Asiacurrency market has developed in similar fashion to the Eurocurrency market. It is dominated by dollar transactions and provides Asian countries with funds for investment and a facility to deposit dollar receipts.

Euronote

Euronotes are short- to medium-term debt instruments that originate from the Eurocurrency markets. Euronotes are both underwritten by commercial and investment banks and sold directly in financial markets. Eurobanks, acting as financial intermediaries, have created facilities for multinational firms to issue their own Euronotes. Note issuance facilities, standby note issuance facilities, and revolving underwriting facilities provide a market for unsecured short- to medium-term debt issued by firms with excellent credit ratings.

Euro-commercial papers (ECPs) are short-term debt instruments that are usually sold at a discount. Although ECPs were originally underwritten, currently ECPs are generally not underwritten. Most ECPs are denominated in dollars and compete directly with local credit markets. Deregulation in financial markets globally has lowered the cost of borrowing in domestic markets and reduced the importance of ECPs as a source of international capital.

Euro-medium-term notes (Euro-MTNs) are not underwritten and are one of the most important and fastest growing Euromarkets. Euro-MTNs are less costly, can be offered quickly, and are flexible in their specifications. Euro-MTNs are offered continuously instead of a large issue on bond markets. Euro-MTNs can also change with respect to the amount of offering, maturity, currency, and whether the interest rate is fixed or floating. This gives the firm the flexibility to lower its interest payments by exploiting the yield curve.

Eurobond

A Eurobond is underwritten by investment banks and sold only in countries other than the currency written in. Eurobonds are generally issued by large multinational firms, governments and international institutions. Moody's and Standard & Poor's rate international bonds on the ability to repay the issue at the original terms.

There are several types of Eurobonds. Fixed-rate issues are similar to domestic bearer bonds and have a fixed coupon paid annually. Floating-rate notes have a coupon that is paid semi-annually and the amount is determined by an interest rate such as the London Interbank Offer Rate (LIBOR). Convertible bonds combine the characteristics of a fixed-rate bond with the option for the bearer to convert the bond to stock issues before the maturity date at a set price (warrants). This reduces the cost of borrowing for multinational firms. In particular, Japanese multinational firms issued large amounts of dollar-denominated bonds with detachable warrants at low interest rates. This created a separate market for warrants since, in essence, warrants are similar to stock options.

There are several advantages to the Eurobond market. These include the lack of regulatory supervision, fewer disclosure requirements, and tax advantages. Interest on Eurobonds is generally not subject to income-withholding tax.

Currency swaps

Multinational firms can reduce their economic and transaction exposure to foreign exchange rate movements through swap markets. In these markets, multinational firms agree to exchange a specified amount of currency for a set time. Swaps are usually arranged by a swap bank or dealer located in a money centre. Each firm borrows funds in their own financial markets where they have established lines of credit and the interest rates would be lowest; they then swap loans. The swap market is closely linked to the Eurocurrency markets where the loans are arranged. Swap markets are an extension of parallel loans except that the transaction is arranged by an agent and the two parties do not know the other firm on the other side of the transaction.

For instance, a Swiss affiliate operating in Japan would require yen and a Japanese affiliate operating in Switzerland would require Swiss francs. The Swiss parent firm would borrow Swiss francs in its local financial market and the Japanese parent would borrow yen. The Swiss parent would swap its obligation to the Japanese affiliate and the Japanese parent would swap its obligation to the Swiss affiliate through the agent. Therefore, each affiliate has access to the local financial market at the lowest cost with no exchange rate risk. Another important advantage to swaps is that the transaction does not appear on the firm's balance sheet. Nevertheless, there are problems arising from interest rate differentials and preference for floating or fixed interest rates increase the complexity of the market. Swap transactions have been combined with options to form swaptions.

International equity markets

Multinational firms have raised capital through foreign equity issues. There are several benefits of cross-listing on foreign equity markets. The most important benefit is to reduce the cost of capital. Large multinationals in small segmented financial markets with limited liquidity may find that the cost of raising equity is difficult and expensive.

Multinationals cross-list their equity issues to increase their visibility in the host country and international community. By issuing equity in the host financial markets, local investors increase their knowledge of the firm and, more importantly, now have a stake in the multinational firm. Cross-listing may also increase the international financial community's awareness of the multinational firm. Furthermore, local ownership may improve relations with the host government, suppliers and customers. Local investors may be more inclined to buy the multinational's products because they have ownership in the firm.

Another potential benefit to cross-listing is to increase share prices. There is evidence that share price increases in value for multinationals with small segmented domestic equity markets after cross-listing on large integrated foreign equity markets. Nevertheless, the evidence is mixed for multinationals with large integrated equity markets that cross-list on other large integrated foreign equity markets. By cross-listing, the firm reduces its cost of capital and required rate of return. This may instead reduce share prices. Finally, cross-listing provides secondary markets to facilitate acquisitions in the host country. Multinationals can acquire rival firms in the host market by using shares as payment; thus they do not have to use cash.

The New York Stock Exchange

The New York Stock Exchange (NYSE) consists of members who are allowed to trade on the floor. An important characteristic of the NYSE is the specialist system. Specialists are members that deal with assigned shares and are responsible for creating an orderly market even in a crisis situation. There are several important characteristics of the NYSE including transaction costs, a notion of fairness that includes insider-trading rules, and limit orders. The NYSE has low transactions costs because of the deregulation of the securities industry by the Securities Exchange Commission (SEC). This has resulted in low commissions on the NYSE. Changes in share prices on sequential transactions are also limited depending on trade volume, thereby further reducing costs.

To ensure that the public has open access to the trading floor, orders are executed in the order they arrive. The SEC has imposed strict regulations to prevent insider trading. The SEC aggressively enforces insider trading through a variety of methods including the constant monitoring of share prices by a computer-surveillance system. An important aspect of the NYSE is limit orders. These allow an investor to place an order to be executed at a specific price as soon this limit is reached. Specialists are required to fill limit orders as soon as the spot price reaches the specified price in chronological order.

The London Stock Exchange

The London Stock Exchange (LSE) is known as the centre for international business. The LSE is a prominent player in the foreign exchange, equity, banking, international bond, and derivative markets. The LSE is the world's third largest stock market, and has the highest number of foreign companies listed. The LSE accounts for almost 60 per cent of global turnover in foreign stocks. Furthermore, nearly 90 per cent of foreign equity turnover in Europe is managed by LSE member firms. The number of foreign firms listed on the LSE at the end of 1998 was 522, compared to 392 listed on the New York Stock Exchange, 441 on the NASDAQ, 224 on the Luxembourg stock market, and 178 on the Paris Stock Exchange.

Unlike the NYSE, the LSE is a computer-based system patterned after the NASDAQ in New York. There are no specialists, orders are not chronologically executed, and transaction costs are higher. Limit orders do not have to be executed chronologically or executed at the specified price. The LSE does not have the same ability to manage a financial crisis on its system.

Nevertheless, there are important advantages for foreign firms to list shares on the LSE. The LSE requires lower levels of disclosure, lower costs of listing, and

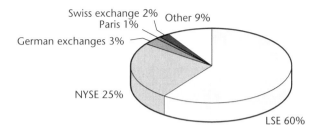

Figure 2.3 Market share of foreign equity turnover on selected exchanges (end–1997)
Source: London Stock Exchange web page.

fewer restrictions on financial reporting. This has resulted in more foreign firms listing on the LSE than on the NYSE.

The Tokyo Stock Exchange

The Japanese stock market is dominated by the Tokyo and Osaka Stock Exchanges. The Japanese stock market was the world's largest until the burst of the speculative real estate and stock market bubbles in the late 1980s. The impact of the collapse is still felt in the consumer-spending sector and by financial institutions.

The Tokyo Stock Exchange (TSE) has some characteristics of the NYSE but there are several important differences. First, although trading in the most active stocks are conducted on the TSE floor, the majority of the shares are traded on an automated computer system. Second, the TSE maintains a 'Saitori' system that supports limit orders, but they are not responsible for creating an orderly market. Third, commissions on the TSE are considerably higher than other equity markets. Finally, although insider-trading laws on the TSE are patterned on the NYSE, their enforcement is not nearly as energetic.

The TSE allows foreign firms to become members; however, the market is not liquid for foreign firms. Disclosure and other requirements are similar to those on the NYSE which increase the cost of raising equity on the TSE. Therefore, the TSE has not been an important source of equity for foreign firms.

Frankfurt

The Frankfurt Bourse is the largest German stock market and a member of the Deutsche Bourse. The Deutsche Bourse regulates the securities and derivatives markets. It guarantees the settlement of transactions, and is controlled by banking institutions. The Frankfurt Bourse is the fourth largest in the world and has many foreign firms listed. Trading is done either through its Xetra® (Exchange Electronic Trading) computerised trading system or through its electronically linked trading floor. The Xetra system was instituted to increase liquidity and efficiency in its financial markets and reduce the cost of trading.

The Frankfurt Bourse supports three types of limit orders. Unrestricted limit orders are valid until cancelled or until a set date. Restricted limit orders can either be executed in full or partially executed and the rest cancelled. Finally, there is a limit order valid for one day.

Euro-equity markets

The formation of the single currency, the Euro, has increased the pace of integration of European equity markets. Firms can issue equity in several countries through investment banks and do not necessarily have to be listed on the country's exchange. These Euro-equities are generally listed on the computer trading system on the International Stock Exchange in London. The Frankfurt Stock Exchange is another important equity market for foreign firms. Currently negotiations are underway to unify the London and Frankfurt stock markets for Europe's 300 largest firms.

Chapter summary

This chapter has shown the importance of foreign exchange markets for firms engaged in international transactions and central banks seeking to stabilise their exchange rates. Market participants must understand the determinants of foreign exchange rates and their volatility. Derivatives such as forwards, futures, and options are important to multinational firms for risk reduction resulting from international transactions. Each instrument has its own advantage in forming an optimal hedging strategy for multinational firms.

International capital markets have had an increasingly important role in reducing a firm's cost of capital. International markets, such as the Eurocurrency and Eurobond markets, provide firms with a low cost source of debt. At the same time, the international debt markets compete with domestic capital markets and increase the complexity of conducting national monetary policy. The London Stock Exchange and the New York Stock Exchange are the most important sources for equity for foreign firms. The LSE has an advantage because of ease in listing on its exchange, while the NYSE is the largest source of capital.

The closing case study, as you will see, illustrates the relationship between an overvalued currency, current account deficit, investor confidence, and excessive dependence on international borrowing to finance its spending. To restore investor confidence and to obtain IMF funding, Thailand had to resort to drastic measures in restructuring its financial institutional framework. The case study also demonstrates the importance of properly regulating national financial institutions.

Discussion questions

1 Using web sites, find the current British pound/yen exchange rate. Find other cross-rates.
2 Explain the impact of volatility on option premiums.

3 Using the Federal Reserve Bank of New York web site, examine the volatility of the Japanese yen.

4 Using web sites, what kinds of products are listed on the Frankfurt exchange?

5 Using web sites, what are the Euro-products introduced on the Philadelphia Stock Exchange?

6 Are there advantages to using futures over forward contracts? Option contracts?

7 Do Eurocurrency markets create problems for central banks in controlling their nation's money supply?

8 Are domestic credit markets obsolete? How could they compete against Euromarkets?

Closing Case Study:
Crisis in international capital markets: focus on Thailand

The Asian capital markets were thrown into turmoil in 1997 with the Thai financial markets in the centre. Thailand had several serious financial and political problems. These included problems with its current account, property bubbles, falling exports, pressures on its exchange rate, poor management of its financial institutions, and corrupt politics. Investor confidence was badly shaken and a crisis in the financial markets ensued. Capital quickly left Asia for safe havens in other capital markets. There were several factors that led up to the collapse of the Thai Baht which are discussed below.

First, Thailand consistently ran a current account deficit since 1975, with the current account deficit to GNP ratio reaching 8 per cent of GDP in 1996. This was the same as Mexico's before its collapse in 1994. The current account deficit can be attributed to a rapidly growing GDP, increasing inflation rates, and an overvalued exchange rate. The current account deficit was financed to a large extent by foreign capital inflows. Part of the problem with Thailand's exchange rate value was the rigidity of its exchange rate regime that tied the Baht to the US dollar. During times when the yen was strong against the dollar, Thailand received large inflows of foreign direct investment. Nevertheless, when the dollar appreciated against the yen, Thailand began to experience serious financial problems because the Baht also became stronger. As exports fell, the Thai government attempted to defend its currency with foreign exchange intervention, higher interest rates, and selective capital controls.

Second, in the 1980s and 1990s, Thailand experienced rapid economic growth and began a building spree. The loans were provided by Thai financial institutions, and as the economy slowed and interest rates increased the number of bad loans increased. A substantial number of Thai loans were denominated in dollars, and the strength of the dollar put additional pressure on borrowers. The number of loans defaulting threatened the safety of the financial institutions and the Thai government intervened to keep the companies afloat. Although Thailand lent more than $19bn (more than 10 per cent of GDP) to keep the 91 Thai finance companies partially solvent, the government still needed at least $15bn in foreign loans to prevent a financial meltdown. Its only source of funding was from the International Monetary Fund (IMF).

Third, the massive spending on Thai financial institutions led to its first budget deficit since 1987. This created an additional need for funds which could potentially increase real interest rates. Austerity measures were needed to bal-

▶

ance the budget; however, political corruption undermined the traditional independence of the central bank and the Ministry of Finance. The political instability made it difficult for the government to reduce government spending. Foreign investors perceived greater levels of political risk that put further pressure on the Baht.

Finally, the Japanese economy had slowed down after the speculative bubbles burst in its real estate and stock markets. This reduced demand for products throughout Asia. The Japanese yen was falling dramatically in value and was approaching 150 yen per dollar. The impact on Chinese and Korean exports was devastating, and they signalled that they might conduct competitive devaluations. These actions could throw the entire Asian economy into chaos. To stabilise the situations, the Japanese and US central banks engaged in a massive coordinated exchange rate invention. After the Japanese government eventually promised to reform its financial markets, the yen began to stabilise.

Thailand was able to borrow funds from the IMF after agreeing to its terms. The immediate result was that 58 of 91 Thai finance firms failed, the new financial regulations were instituted, and the Baht depreciated to 20 per cent of its former value. The Thai Baht is slowly regaining some of its value, investor confidence has been stabilised, and the current account is improving.

Sources: Adapted from Mydans (1997), Cohen (1997), Sapsford and Sherer (1997), Sugawara (1997).

Questions

1 Explain the relationship between the current account, international reserves, and the Thai Baht.
2 Briefly outline the factors that influenced the Thai Baht's value.
3 How did the Thailand real estate bubble contribute to the crisis?
4 Are high levels of personal savings and government surpluses important in reducing the impact of a financial crisis?
5 Should the Thai government have allowed 58 Thai financial firms to fail? Will this improve Thailand's prospect for the future?
6 Was the IMF's role appropriate in reducing the crisis in Thailand? Could its role be improved?

References

Cohen, Y. (1997) Asia's market woes ricachet into politics, *Christian Scientist Monitor*, 23 October, p. 1.

Mydans, S. (1997) An 'Asian Miracle' now seems like a mirage, *New York Times*, 23 October, p. 1.

Sapsford, J. and **Sherer, R.** (1997) Rescue Package for Thailand takes shape, *Wall Street Journal*, 8 August, p. 10.

Sugawara, S. (1997) Global meltdown in Thailand; Economists say many ignored warning signals of looming crisis, *The Washington Post*, 24 October, p. 34.

Sources of information

Web sites:

Chatroom

You are invited to participate in an on-line chatroom organised by the author of this chapter, Professor Andrew Solocha. Please e-mail him at: *Soloch@UTNet. UToledo.Edu* for further information and joining instructions.

Foreign exchange markets

- Currency Converter from Olsen Associates. You can view an exchange rate for any day from 1 January 1990 to yesterday. The O&A currency converter is updated daily at 06:00 MET (Middle European Time) with information from the previous day.
  http://www.oanda.com/cgi-bin/ncc
- Bloomberg. Contains financial news and a currency converter.
  http://www.bloomberg.com/welcome.html
- Federal Reserve Bank of New York. The FRB of NY has information on asset volatility, exchange rates, and interest rates.
  http://www.ny.frb.org/pihome/mktrates/

Futures and options

Futures markets
- Exchange Rate Futures: IMM
  http://www.cme.com/market/institutional/currency/currncs.html
- Chicago Mercantile Exchange Home Page http://www.cme.com/

Currency options
- Chicago Board of Options Exchange Home Page http://www.cboe.com/
- The London International Financial Futures and Options Exchange
  http://www.liffe.com/
- Philadelphia Stock Exchange http://www.phlx.com/
- INO Global Markets. INO Global Markets has information on futures, options, and foreign currency quotes on an intraday, daily and weekly basis.
  http://www.ino.com/

World capital markets

- New York Stock Exchange http://www.nyse.com/

- London Stock Exchange http://www.stockex.co.uk/aim/
- Tokyo Stock Exchange http://www.tse.or.jp/eindex.html
- SBF- Paris Bourse http://www.bourse-de-paris.fr/bourse/sbf/homesbf.fcgi?GB
- Singapore International Monetary Exchange http://www.simex.com.sg/
- Links to World Stock Markets http://www.finix.at/fin/selinks.html
- Emerging Markets. Asset prices and exchange rates for emerging markets with limited liquidity and highly regulated. http://www.emgmkts.com/
- Morgan Stanley Capital International http://www.ms.com/msci/perform/
- Standard & Poor's: http://www.standardandpoors.com/ratings/
- Moody's http://www.moodys.com/repldata/ratings/ratsov.htm

Central banks

- Bank for International Settlements Home Page. BIS has monetary policies of major central banks and economic performance measures. http://www.bis.org/
- All central banks on the web. http://www.bis.org/cbanks.htm

North America
- Bank of Canada http://www.bank-banque-canada.ca/english/intro-e.htm
- US Federal Reserve http://www.bog.frb.fed.us/
- Banco de Mexico http://www.banxico.org.mx/public_html/indices/indexe.html

Asia
- Bank of Thailand http://www.bot.or.th
- Hong Kong Monetary Authority http://www.info.gov.hk/hkma
- Central Bank of Japan http://www.boj.or.jp/en/index.htm

Europe
- Banque Central du Luxembourg http://www.bcl.lu/
- Banco de España http://www.bde.es/welcomee.htm
- Banque de France http://www.banque-france.fr/us/home.htm
- Central Bank of Austria http://www.oenb.co.at/english/index_e.htm
- Central Bank of Denmark http://www.nationalbanken.dk/uk
- Central Bank of Finland http://www.bof.fi/env/startpge.htm
- Central Bank of Italy http://www.bancaditalia.it/
- Central Bank of Norway http://www.norges-bank.no/english/
- Central Bank of Sweden http://www.riksbank.se/eng/
- Deutsche Bundesbank http://www.bundesbank.de/index_e.html
- Bank of Greece http://www.greekgov.ariadne-t.gr/gov/uk-bank24.html
- Bank of England http://www.bankofengland.co.uk/
- Banco de Portugal http://www.bportugal.pt/
- Swiss National Bank http://www.snb.ch/
- European Central Bank (ECB) http://www.ecb.int/

Further reading

Foreign exchange markets

The following booklet is available free from the Federal Reserve Bank of New York at its web site and provides a basic background of international trade and finance. The Federal Reserve System provides a wealth of free information on numerous topics in finance and is a valuable resource.

Gonnelli, Adam, (1993) *The Basics of Foreign Trade and Exchange*, New York: Federal Reserve Bank of New York.

Option pricing

These are some of the classic articles in foreign currency option pricing. Although option pricing theory is highly mathematical, the conclusions in the articles should be understandable by most international business students with a solid foundation in finance.

Amin, K. and Jarrow, R.A. (1991) Pricing foreign currency options under stochastic interest rates,' *Journal of International Money and Finance*, September: 310–29.

Black, F. and Scholes, M. (1973) The pricing of options and corporate liabilities, *Journal of Political Economy*, May/June: 637–59.

Cox, J., Ross, S.A. and Rubinstein, M. (1979) Option pricing: a simplified approach, *Journal of Financial Economics* 7: 229–63.

Garman, M.B. and Kohlhagen, S.W. (1983) Foreign currency option values, *Journal of International Money and Finance*, December: 231–37.

International debt and equity markets

These articles provide empirical evidence background material on international financial market integration, the impact of cross-listing, and debt-financing alternatives. By entering international finance markets, the firm is able to access a wide variety of financing. Nevertheless, the choice of financing has an impact on the firm's value and this is discussed in the following articles.

Marr, M.W., Trimble, J.L. and Varma, R. (1991) On the integration of international capital markets: evidence from Euro-equity offerings, *Financial Management*, Winter: 11–21.

Meek, G.K. and Gray, S.J. (1989) Globalization of stock markets and foreign listing requirements: voluntary disclosures by continental European companies listed on the London Stock Exchange, *Journal of International Business Studies*, Summer: 315–36.

Rhee, S.G., Chang, R.P. and Koveos, P.E. (1985) The currency-of-denomination decision for debt financing, *Journal of International Business Studies*, Fall: 143–50.

Saudagaran, S.M. and Biddle, G.C. (1992) Financial disclosure levels and foreign stock exchange listing decisions, *Journal of International Financial Management and Accounting*, Summer: 106–48.

Stulz, R.M. (1995) The cost of capital in internationally integrated markets: the case of Nestlé, *European Financial Management*, March: 11–22.

Sundaram, A.K. and Logue, D.E. (1996) Valuation effects of foreign company listings on US Exchanges, *Journal of International Business Studies*, Spring: 67–88.

Part II International Trade Institutions

Global and Regional Institutions: The International Governance of International Business

Brent Burmester

Learning objectives

By the end of this chapter you will be able to understand:

- the case for and against the regulation of international business

- the identities, objectives and capacities of the governing institutions

- the problems specific to governing international business activities

- the history of international governance of international business

- the emergent forms of governance in global civil society.

Opening Case Study:
Mexican companies and NAFTA

Antonio Madero Bracho, chairman and chief executive of Mexico's Sanluis Corporacion, is a walking advertisement for the North American Free Trade Area.

Before Mexico joined NAFTA in 1994, Sanluis was a medium-sized gold and silver producer that had diversified into manufacturing vehicle components. Today, it can hardly keep up with the orders pouring in from the big three car makers in Detroit. Exports now account for almost 90 per cent of the company's revenues.

Over the past four years, Sanluis has doubled its parts sales, captured a 40 per cent share of the US market for leaf-springs used in pick-up trucks and sport utility vehicles, and secured enough long-term contracts to ensure that sales will double again, to $500m, by 2001.

'NAFTA opened the door for us,' says Mr Madero. 'We realised Mexico, Canada and the US would become a single production market, with converging engineering and manufacturing practices that would allow car makers to switch production across plants. We saw the opportunity to supply not only the Mexican-based vehicle assembly plants, but to jump into the larger US market – competitively, without protection and without subsidies.'

Mr Madero began by establishing a bigger presence in Detroit, sending Mexican engineers to work with Ford, Chrysler and General Motors in the design and development of Sanluis' suspension and brake components. 'It was a major step,' he recalls, 'because it convinced our customers of our commitment to the North American market.'

At home, Sanluis worked on improving quality control systems for the more demanding US market. It hired Japanese and American consultants, and sent its technicians on training courses abroad.

Sanluis' manufacturing plants are equipped with classrooms, where employees attend 'virtual university' courses beamed by satellite from the Tec of Monterrey, one of Mexico's most prestigious universities. 'Our goal is to have our entire management and technical team proficient in English and computing by the turn of the century,' Mr Madero says.

For the production chain to work smoothly, Sanluis has also provided capital and technology to its Mexican suppliers, in order to secure the right quality of inputs, delivered on time.

The company established joint ventures with Hendrickson International, and with Brembo, the Italian manufacturer of brake systems for Formula 1 racing cars. Brembo took a 35 per cent stake in Rassini Frenos, Sanluis' brake components subsidiary. 'We gained access to their technology, and Brembo established a beachhead into the North American market,' Mr Madero explains.

Last year, Rassini Frenos won its first long-term contract in the US – a $360m order to supply rear wheel discs for General Motors' new line of pick-up trucks and utility vehicles for the next eight to ten years. This year, it will also begin exporting brake components to BMW's plants in North Carolina and Germany. As a result of these and other big contracts, Sanluis last year embarked on a $140m expansion, its biggest capital investment programme to date.

At Piedras Negras, a border town in the northern state of Coahuila, Hendrickson-Rassini built a state-of-the-art plant to manufacture leaf-springs for export to Navistar in the US. Production began in August 1997, and it is already being expanded to accommodate new orders from Nissan.

Suspensiones Rassini, a fully-owned Sanluis subsidiary, built a separate plant in Piedras Negras to manufacture rear suspensions for GM and Ford.

A new plant in the state of Puebla, in central Mexico, equipped with computer-controlled robots, will supply the $360m contract with GM. But Sanluis' ambitions have not stopped with NAFTA. In 1996, it saw the promise of the Mercosur market, the customs union which encompasses Brazil, Argentina, Paraguay and Uruguay, and launched itself as a multinational, acquiring Molas Fabrini, a Brazilian manufacturer of coil and leaf-springs for Mercedes-Benz, Volkswagen, Ford and Chrysler. 'In the space of four years, Sanluis has gone

from being a Mexican company, to a NAFTA company, to a continental operation,' Mr Madero says. 'Our strategy is to supply our customers wherever they
are located, and to consolidate our presence in the global autoparts industry.'

Source: *Financial Times* CD-ROM, 1 January–31 December 1998.

Introduction

Competition plays a dominant role at all levels of modern society. In the developed world and much of the developing, competition is clearly the favoured
strategy in relationships beyond the realm of friends and family, and in business
success and survival hinge on being competitive. However, competition in any
social context is beneficial only if it is conducted according to commonly understood and applicable rules. This chapter deals with the international institutions
that share responsibility alongside national governments for setting and enforcing the rules of international business. It shows why their intervention is
necessary in the current international order, not only to those communities and
interest groups disinterested in or opposed to international business, but to international businesses themselves.

Governments and governance

Sovereignty

International business activities are subject, first and foremost, to rules laid down
by particular nation-states. For example, should a South Korean company establish a foreign subsidiary in Hungary, that subsidiary must comply with
Hungarian law, not the laws of South Korea that bind the parent firm. This
arrangement stems from the way in which political and legal authority is distributed on an international basis, consistent with the **doctrine of sovereignty**.

Sovereignty describes the power to rule without constraint and, for the last
three centuries, this power has been identified with the nation state. That is, the
world is conceived as a patchwork of territories, within which different peoples
live, each of these peoples determining for themselves (in theory, at least!) a
system of government that has complete authority over affairs within their territory. This divisionalisation of the world into mutually exclusive sovereignties
implies that there can be only one supreme governing institution, the **state**,
within each territory, and no state may intervene within the rightful jurisdiction
of another. Thus, Brazil's state apparatus, its **government**, may freely create and
enforce law in Brazil, but it is powerless in Argentina, and vice versa. This is by
no means the only way in which political power can be distributed and exercised

on a worldwide basis; indeed, since its inception in the sixteenth century, the international power-sharing system has frequently been put to the test. The present era of economic globalisation may prove to be the system's most trying time yet, but for the foreseeable future the political world remains comprised of sovereign nation states. The significance of this for **inter-national** business should not be underestimated.

The legal equality of all nation states means that there exists no overarching global authority with an exclusive power to exercise comprehensive governance. In other words, international relations remain in an **anarchic** (ruler-less) state, uncontrolled by the decisive force of a sovereign world government. Anarchy does not necessarily imply chaos, however, for nation states are obviously capable of conducting their relationships with one another in a peaceful and constructive manner. Nonetheless, the equilibrium of peace may be upset at any time, and with devastating consequences. The fragility of the anarchic international system was highlighted by the nuclear weapon tests carried out by India and Pakistan in May 1998. Although they created general uneasiness worldwide, and attracted international condemnation, no supervisory body was capable of commanding the end to further shows of aggression on the Asian sub-continent, or elsewhere for that matter.

The impact of globalisation

The last quarter of the twentieth century has been a time of considerable change in the international political economy, not least because of the activities of international businesses. Observers have expressed concern over the capacity of the system of sovereign states to withstand the integrative pressures of globalisation (Ohmae 1995). Governments exist to govern, but when technology and growing social, economic and political integration between states renders their borders so porous that money, goods, information and people can move across them virtually at will, how are they to exercise any control? Although national borders are not yet so completely permeable, the direction of change is clear and has been for some time (Dichter 1962; Levitt 1983). Consider the helplessness of the Indonesian government during the 1997/8 Asian financial crisis, when vast quantities of capital flowed out of the local economy at the instigation of offshore investors, leaving the nation all but bankrupt. Meanwhile, Italian, Greek and Turkish authorities were struggling to prevent thousands of North African economic refugees entering the European Union (*The Economist* 1997), and the US fought a losing battle against the flow of narcotics across its southern border from Central America (*The Economist* 1998c).

Institutions capable of providing governance where a single national government cannot seem poised to play a much stronger role in future international affairs. Many exist, and some of the most important to international business are discussed below. All remain constrained by their ambiguous status within the community of sovereign states, however, which constitutes both an advantage and disadvantage. An advantage, for none is competent, individually or collectively, to assert dominance over global affairs. A disadvantage, because their capacity to solve international problems can be compromised by the unwillingness of nation states to co-operate to the full.

Governance and markets

Governance, the control of behaviour, is not the exclusive province of governments or government-like institutions. International business behaviour is controlled not only by legislation, but national, business and corporate cultures (Terpstra and David 1991), and the natural laws of supply and demand. Could these forces alone ensure that international business is executed in the interests of international society at large?

Every economics' student learns that perfect competition generates socially optimal outcomes with respect to the efficient allocation of scarce resources. The global market context most nearly approximates the theoretically infinite buyers and sellers of the neo-classical model of perfect competition, given the great many potential and existing competitors and buyers in a globally defined industry. We might conclude that on this scale free markets will deliver benefits like nowhere else, and the need for deliberate external intervention is therefore slight. However, when it comes to an equal distribution among current and potential participants of know-how, access to information, and ability to influence demand and supply, it is clear that international markets are far from perfect.

Market fundamentalists, adherents to the policy of deregulation, argue that only through liberalising international trade and investment can prosperity be assured to the greatest number of the world's inhabitants. In doing so, they assume that, with full deregulation, the present failure of real international markets to conform to the necessary conditions underlying the structural model of perfectly competitive markets would be self-correcting, so far as correction is possible. Their opponents observe that the structural characteristics of most international markets are utterly unlike that of the theoretical ideal, and conclude that the conduct of enterprises in international industries will never automatically safeguard the interests of international society at large. A typical outcome of greater market autonomy was recently reported by the International Labour Organisation, to the effect that recent trade liberalisation in Bangladesh has raised average per capita income, but also widened the gap between rich and poor in that country (Reuters 1999). Is this all-too common observation the result of imperfect liberalisation, or will the benefits of unconstrained markets always elude a significant proportion of society?

We cannot do justice here to the arguments for and against intervention in international markets by governing institutions, let alone to those for and against capitalism itself. However, acknowledging the existence of these debates serves to remind us that business may serve society by the pursuit of private profit, but that private business profits are not in isolation a social benefit. It is reasonable to require that international business should create opportunities for societal development on sub-national, national and international levels. Furthermore, it should not harm those living in non-conformity with the rules of the market, peoples to whom the principles of capitalism are unknown or inimical for reasons of tradition or belief. Yet when powerful companies have operated across borders without adequate national and international regulation, history reveals a pattern of antisocial, self-serving behaviour quite at odds with outcomes desired by the nations implicated. Market forces can ensure only a limited form of business conformance to the diverse needs of societies, such as security, growth, freedom and justice. Karl Polanyi, one of the most influential political economists of the twentieth century, maintained that in the long term a self-regulating market system would 'annihilate the human and natural substance of society' (Polanyi 1944: 3). Though this may seem an extreme view, few would deny the case for the retention and augmentation of external sources of governance over international business in the international community.

The present level of international debate regarding economic governance and the role of markets therein has not been matched in intensity since the time of the severe monetary crises of the early 1970s. Almost daily, influential figures, such as British Prime Minister Tony Blair and wealthy financier George Soros, are calling for reform to key institutions, while many others are beginning to publicly question long-held beliefs regarding the societal advantages of uncontrolled markets, particularly markets for monetary assets. These contemporary issues are met again in the following sections, which outline in passing the historical and structural framework out of which the current controversies surfaced.

The United Nations system

Background

There is one international organisation to which all others refer in their decision making, either because they are formally affiliated to it, or because of its operating scope and six decades of accumulated experience. This institution is the United Nations, or UN. It was in formation even as the Second World War was raging, and the impetus for its creation came from the severe international conflicts that dominated the first half of the twentieth century, conflicts that the UN's predecessor, the League of Nations, had been unable to prevent. Accordingly, the UN's mission is to establish a world order based on peace, prosperity and freedom (Kennedy and Russett 1995).

The UN can be thought of as an incorporated society whose members are nation states rather than individuals. As of 31 May 1998, there were 185 members (*United Nations Handbook* 1998), two notable exceptions being Taiwan, which remains ineligible for membership while China disputes its independence, and Switzerland, whose constitutional neutrality limits the country to observer status. The UN is a forum where nations can share their views on issues of international concern, with a view to generating solutions acceptable to as many member states as possible. This implies that the will of the UN is a reflection of the majority view or consensus of its members, and that it is not appropriate to regard the UN as an entity capable of defying the international community of states.

Established by Charter in 1945, the UN's principal organ is the General Assembly, in which all members participate. The Assembly creates subsidiary organs, such as agencies, councils and committees, each composed of representatives from subsets of the Assembly membership, to deal with specific issue-areas, such as health, development and human rights. These bodies report to the Assembly, which in turn acts according to resolutions carried by majority vote. The UN 'acts' by communicating its position to individual members, by instructing its Security Council, and through directing the actions of its subsidiary organs within the territories of its members. Overseeing both the General Assembly and the Security Council is the Secretary General, an elected individual with considerable moral influence in world affairs.

Governance of international business

All the key intergovernmental institutions influencing the environment of international business are components in the UN system. Bodies subsidiary or related to the UN include the International Centre for the Settlement of Investment Disputes, the International Civil Aviation Organisation, the International Labor Organisation, the International Monetary Fund, the International Telecommunications Union, the World Bank Group, the World Intellectual Property Organisation, the World Tourism Organisation, and the World Trade Organisation (*United Nations Handbook* 1998). A review of these bodies' titles indicates the heavy involvement of the UN family in the governance of international business. However, these represent only a small sample of the different bodies in the UN system, and it should be borne in mind that those listed here are by no means the only ones worth monitoring by business decision-makers. Others, despite their apparent disinterest in commercial affairs, may be even more immediately implicated in the operations of particular international business enterprises.

Comprehensive documentation of the UN's various opinion-making, monitoring, financing and advisory activities impacting on the conduct of international business goes well beyond the scope of this chapter. As one legal scholar remarks: 'Few areas of private business decision-making escape the attention of one or another agency' (Weidenbaum 1985: 350). Three notable initiatives deserve mention before moving on, however.

The UNCTC

Socioeconomic advancement lies at the core of the UN's mission. Particularly instrumental in this regard is the UN's Economic and Social Council, or ECOSOC, for short. In 1974, ECOSOC established an intergovernmental Commission on Transnational Corporations, together with a subsidiary Centre on Transnational Corporations (UNCTC) to undertake research into the practices of the more prominent international business enterprises. One of the Commission's more ambitious contributions to the regulation of international business is the Code of Conduct on Transnational Corporations. Impetus for this document came largely from the less developed countries, which sought to limit the scope and scale for exploitation of their resources by large international businesses and, by extension, their home nations. On the other hand, developed nations were concerned to gain a measure of protection for their corporate citizens against volatile host governments in the developing world.

Negotiations began in 1975, and the draft was finally submitted for consideration to ECOSOC in 1989. The draft Code is comprehensive and unambiguous on issues concerning national sovereignty, compensation for expropriation, the protection of socio-cultural values, anti-corruption measures and political non-interference (Bassiry 1990). Its main weakness lies in implementation and enforcement, for the Commission on Transnational Corporations, responsible for the Code's administration, had no means of guaranteeing compliance by transnational corporations. Although widely regarded as an influential and necessary statement of international consensus on the matter of international business ethics, the Code remains unadopted by the General Assembly. Delay in the UN forum has prompted not entirely welcome moves elsewhere, of which more can be read below.

In addition to generating the Code of Conduct, the UNCTC published an extensive library on the practices of international business enterprises and, in doing so, gained a reputation for vigilance over MNE affairs. With the Code of Conduct in limbo, and attitudes toward MNEs changing, the Centre was dismantled and its duties transferred elsewhere in the UN system. It is interesting to note that the body assuming responsibility for foreign investment issues, the Transnationals and Management Division of the Commission on Trade and Development (UNCTAD), is quite differently disposed toward FDI. While the UNCTC tended to view FDI with caution, regarding it very much a mixed blessing for host nations, UNCTAD takes the view that FDI is instrumental in the development of the non-industrialised nations, and seems less concerned by the potential for corporate malpractice.

Exhibit 3.1 Japan's $100bn Asia aid plan wins

Japanese aid to the crisis-hit Asian economies, as proposed earlier this month by Kiichi Miyazawa, Japan's finance minister, would give a far bigger boost to world activity than the equivalent spent on boosting the domestic economy, according to the United Nations Conference on Trade and Development (UNCTAD).

UNCTAD's economists said yesterday that a Japanese aid package to Asia of $100bn could add up to $380bn to global output over the three years 1998–2000, with significant benefits to the US and Europe as well as the affected Asian economies. 'These figures are considerably higher than would result from a domestic fiscal expansion in Japan of similar magnitude,' UNCTAD said, arguing that structural problems in the Japanese economy will continue to handicap growth.

Based on model simulations, its economists believe the cumulative effect on the global economy of an aid package could be a third higher than that of a fiscal stimulus. Yilmaz Akyuz, UNCTAD's chief economist, said yesterday that Washington and Brussels would do better to press for implementation of the Miyazawa plan than to belabour Tokyo for not doing more to stimulate the domestic economy. Mr Miyazawa recently announced some $30bn in bilateral help for the five worst-hit Asian economies: Indonesia, South Korea, Malaysia, the Philippines and Thailand.

Japan has already pledged $43bn in financing for the region, much of which has been channelled through the IMF as part of bail-out operations. While the countries in crisis would gain considerably from an assistance package compared with a fiscal stimulus in Japan, so too would other countries including the US and European Union, UNCTAD estimates.

The impact on their GDP growth would be more than twice as large as that of a domestic fiscal stimulus. 'If you give $100 to a Japanese consumer, he will save part of it and spend most of the rest on Japanese goods,' Mr Akyuz said. 'If you give the same amount to an Indonesian, he will spend most of it on imported goods from the US, Europe and Japan.'

The US in particular would not have to bear such a large burden of adjustment through a rapidly growing balance of payments deficit, which would in turn help to reduce protectionist pressures. Even Japan would benefit in the long run because, while a fiscal stimulus is needed to trigger recovery, it would not be sustainable in the absence of structural reforms, UNCTAD's economists believe.

Their study suggests Japan is now broadly on the right track in combining a fiscal stimulus with an aid package to the Asian region and efforts to tackle structural problems in the financial sector.

Source: *Financial Times* CD-ROM, 1 January–31 December 1998.

UN Convention on Contracts for the International Sale of Goods

Unlike contracts for the sale of goods between parties in the same jurisdiction, international sales transactions are complicated by the lack of an international contract law. This means that export/import contracts must be specific about what nation's law will decide disputes arising over the contract's execution. If contracts are silent or ambiguous on this issue then costly litigation may arise over the issue of where the dispute should ultimately be heard; in other words the parties may be forced to go to court over where to go to court.

To help reduce the uncertainty and complexity inherent in contracting internationally for the sale of goods, the UN set out to create a uniform law to which all traders and courts could resort. In 1966 the UN Commission on International Trade Law (UNICITRAL) was established by the General Assembly to promote the harmonisation and unification of international trade law. UNICITRAL went on to help establish important conventions on international arbitration, but its most far-reaching project is the UN Convention on Contracts for the International Sale of Goods. This Convention establishes internationally applicable rules governing the formation of contracts, sets out the obligations of parties, and stipulates remedies for parties when problems arise. It not only reduces legal uncertainty in trade between states accepting the Convention, but increases the range of options available to traders with regard to the form and process of legal protection.

International Code of Marketing of Breastmilk Substitutes

The International Code of Marketing of Breastmilk Substitutes is a joint initiative of the World Health Organisation (WHO) and UNICEF, the UN's Childrens' Fund.

The Code was a response to the avoidable deaths and illness of many thousands of infants in developing countries during the 1960s and 1970s, due to improper feeding with breastmilk substitutes aggressively marketed by MNEs, including Swiss conglomerate, Nestlé. Finalised in 1981, it called for a stop to consumer marketing of such products anywhere, and remains remarkably effective, although nothing approaching full compliance was ever secured (Beauchamp 1993).

The future of the UN

Despite its scope and mission, there is no legal or geographic territory within which the UN possesses an undisputed authority. As a result it is unable to guarantee its own financial means of survival through taxation or carry out its resolutions with the backing of a powerful coercive force, such as an army. The UN's Security Council has often deployed military resources in an international peace-keeping capacity, but no mechanism exists for the UN to physically exert itself in defiance of a competent nation state. Like all large 'public' organisations, the UN has had many failures and partial successes, and become bureaucratic and guilty of inefficiencies. It remains, however, a vitally important institution, and one worth working to save in a globalising political economy, where international problems grow in number and complexity. Its contribution to creating the world within which international business has flourished is significant, and in future international businesses may be called on to return the favour by providing a measure of financial support to the UN (Kennedy and Russett 1995).

The Bretton Woods–GATT troika

At the time the UN concept was in development, plans were devised for two more specialised international organisations. These were to deal with the general collapse in economic relations between nations that presaged the Second World War. The following peace could only be sustained if the international economic system was in good health and as inclusive of as many countries as possible. In 1944, a 44-nation meeting of the UN Monetary and Financial Conference was convened in the New Hampshire mountain resort of Bretton Woods, to consider the rebuilding and regulation of the international economy. Plans were agreed for the creation of two institutions representing a major development in international economic governance. They consisted of a bank for lending in cases of special need, and a fund to maintain international monetary stability. A third organisation to oversee the conduct of international trade regulation took rather longer to establish, but became irrevocably linked with the other two in the history of international economic governance.

Thanks to remarkable adaptability, all three intergovernmental organisations (IGOs) continue to play key roles in the regulation of the world economy. In the following sections the history and prospects of each are considered in turn.

The World Bank

Origins

The World Bank Group consists of three international non-profit financial institutions. The purpose of the senior is evident in its full title, i.e. the International Bank for Reconstruction and Development (IBRD). At the time of its creation, many important nations were in ruins as a result of the Second World War. In order that they should be politically and economically restored as quickly as possible, the IBRD was established with the primary aim of providing funds for their reconstruction. These reconstruction and development funds were generated in financial markets on the strength of guarantees made by the Bank's member states. Despite the clarity, immediacy and obvious importance of its mission, the Bank got off to an unpromising start, to the extent that it was very difficult to recruit senior management in the first years of its life (Kamarck 1996). These problems are well behind the World Bank now, but throughout its history it has never been far from controversy.

Postwar reconstruction played a minor role in the Bank's history. A very large part of the resources that helped Western Europe and Japan back on their feet were provided directly by the United States as aid and private investment (Urquidi 1996). With these nations quickly restored to economic health, the second critical function of the Bank became salient. This was, and is, providing credit facilities for the financing of well-defined, developmental (productive capacity-enhancing) projects in nations that are unable to fund these projects by other means. Over time the Bank has increasingly made macroeconomic reform by the borrower a condition of lending. This broadens the scope for financing institutional development centred around a project or projects, for the required changes to policies and their administration oblige the Bank to provide the wherewithal to bring these changes about (Kamarck 1996).

In 1958 the member nations of the IMF and IBRD created a second lending institution to operate in conjunction with the IBRD. This was the International Development Association (IDA), an institution intended to provide development finance to nations too poor to service the IBRD's loans. Credit from the World Bank might have been more accessible to developing nations than from private sources, but interest remained aligned with market rates, because private financial markets were the ultimate source of the Bank's capital. The IDA dispersed funds made up in part of donations from member states, and could therefore offer lower interest rates (Owen 1994). The third member of the World Bank Group, known as the International Finance Corporation (IFC), joined in 1959, and differs from the other two in that it focuses on lending to private borrowers involved in development related ventures. The creation of the IFC allowed the Bank to extend its lending operations beyond the public sphere, and was a consequence of the growing participation of private businesses in international economic relations. As the 1960s began, development clearly had top priority on the Bank's agenda.

During the 1980s, the Bank shifted its focus away from financing projects such as building dams, roads, power plants and telecommunication infrastructure. There was little evidence that this form of lending was having any positive effect on development, and the Bank could not ignore the fact that some project lending had siphoned capital into the black hole of corrupt and incompetent governments from which it would never return. In addition, many developing countries were struggling to such a degree during this period, thanks to the economic shocks of the 1970s, high indebtedness, and inept political and economic management, that they became unable to meet even the favourable terms of the Bank's lending. Hard times led to a deprioritisation of development projects by governments, since money was more urgently needed to pay for imports, to honour debt repayments to other lenders, or to contain domestic variables such as interest rates and inflation. Until these more pressing financial problems were solved and positive growth was returned to these nations, the development programme was effectively on hold. The Bank therefore created a new form of debt facility, known as the Structural Adjustment Loan (SAL). These 12–18 month loans, later increased to 3–5 years, were to help in the reformation of macro-economic policy and government administration in developing nations.

It did not take long for this new lending practice to attract unflattering criticism. In particular, critics argued that SALs displaced private investment, both local and foreign, and without any appreciable impact on growth. Furthermore, the type of adjustment forced on borrowing countries was not demonstrably appropriate to their needs, smacked to many of short-termism, and was not feasible in many cases. This growing disquiet with Bank operations was partly a response to the Bank's emphasis on maximising lending volumes, as opposed to achieving the best developmental outcomes (Kamarck 1996).

The Bank's present role

It is perhaps unclear how the World Bank acts as a regulator of international economic competition. To appreciate the role played by the Bank in its capacity as a lender, consider the impact of its removal from the international economy. Developing countries would then be forced to finance self-improving projects alone, through private credit arrangements, or with aid donated by the industrialised countries. Competition for private funds between the developing countries would increase, raising the cost and availability of private credit, which would be scarce in any case, as the return on development investment is slow in coming. This economic competition would almost certainly spill over into political rivalry, and the developing world might now resemble the least developed of the west and central African states, locked in a downward spiral of warfare, poverty, vulnerability to disease and natural disaster, and lack of meaningful participation in international society. Private capital financing would ensure that the benefits of development investment were skewed toward foreign investors, rather than indigenous populations, and this would further exacerbate political instability and civil conflict within and between less developed nations.

It is also important to appreciate that, like the IMF, the World Bank is as much a consultant as a financier. It has long been concerned not only to lend funds, but to help maximise the value of project loans through involvement in resource-allocation decisions. Furthermore, many countries have sought out the Bank's advice on economic policy, or accepted it in return for loan capital, for that advice constitutes a valuable resource to poorer nations in this role. The financial and technical assistance of the Bank helped save India from a devastating famine-induced collapse in the years directly after that immense country gained independence. Had there been no such institution the world political economy might still be recovering from the shock of that narrowly averted disaster. On a related front, the World Bank's Economic Development Institute has been responsible for training administrators from many developing member countries, and the long-term benefits of this enhanced human capital should not be underestimated (Kamarck 1996).

On the lending side, however, and by its own admission, extensive revision to the Bank's policies is long overdue, since for over 20 years private capital has accounted for the majority of development financing, and the soundness of the economic models underlying past Bank activities is now in doubt. However, the international disposition of private capital takes place in the shadow of institutions like the Bank and IMF. Were there not such institutions to pick up the pieces in times of emergency, private capital would behave far more cautiously, and less generously. In emergencies, such as the global recession of 1998/9, the sense in retaining a World Bank in a globalised political economy is clearer than during times of growth and general prosperity, when private capital is more bold.

The International Monetary Fund

Origins

To understand the evolution of the International Monetary Fund (IMF), we must bear in mind that, for a quarter-century following the Bretton Woods conference, convertible currencies were maintained at fixed exchange values, anchored by the $35/ounce gold-convertibility of the US dollar. This system of international monetary management could be costly in terms of the strain put on national reserves of gold and foreign exchange. Countries with non-convertible currencies were forced to barter or buy imports with export earnings, running reserves down in times of balance of payments deficit, while those with convertible currencies often needed to sell foreign exchange to buy their own currency, thus preserving its official exchange value.

As a result, countries needed help to support the exchange value of their currency, or to pay for much needed imports. This help could take the form of temporary assistance from other governments, or access to an independent, impartial and informed source of emergency funds, such as the IMF. Capitalised by its member countries, the Fund, as the IMF is also known, lent reserves to its members to prevent devaluation, thus maintaining monetary stability. In support of its exchange-rate and payments functions, the IMF's Articles of Agreement stipulated that it was also to promote international monetary co-operation, and facilitate the growth of international trade, employment and income. As a regulator of international economic rivalry, the IMF served to reduce the incidence of competitive currency devaluation by nations seeking to capture greater international market shares at one another's expense.

Crises and changes

The IMF was reasonably comfortable in this role from its inception in 1946 until the collapse of the gold exchange standard in 1971, which caused first Germany then other major trading nations to allow their currency exchange values to float. In the latter half of 1973 inflation rates in the industrialised countries ballooned into double digits. Then came the oil crises, where the price of this vital commodity skyrocketed because of collusive supply restrictions by producer nations. The IMF was compelled to create new lending facilities to prevent oil-induced deficits from wreaking havoc. Once the system of floating rates was formalised in 1976, the IMF was left in an awkward position. Many exchange rates remained pegged to key monies like the dollar, deutchmark or pound sterling, or floated with continued government intervention. However, the governments responsible for the principal convertible currencies, those most important to the conduct of international business, were no longer in need of the IMF, as the exchange values of their currencies were free to find natural market-clearing levels. When the Russian and South Korean emergencies of the late 1990s occurred, it had been 20 years since a major industrialised nation had used the Fund's credit facilities.

Responding to the threat of obsolescence, and to the new challenges of gold's abandonment as a reserve asset and floating exchange rates, the IMF amended its Articles of Agreement. It placed greater emphasis on the general health of the international monetary system, and moved away from the less flexible, rule-based practices of the past. Although it continued to assist its members in its capacity as a monetary stabilisation fund, the IMF focused less on short-term loans to correct balance of payments deficits, providing instead longer-term finance in line with its more generously specified supervisory role. Consequently, the Fund was able to come to the assistance of Mexico, Brazil and Poland in the 1980s, as these countries struggled under the weight of foreign debts. Similarly, thanks to its mid-1970s reinvention, the IMF has played and continues to play an important role in the ex-communist territories' transition to market-based economic management.

Surveillance and sovereignty

International monetary supervision by the IMF implies **surveillance**: monitoring national economic management, in order to forecast crises, and propose alterations to policy. Surveillance arms the IMF with the information it needs to advise governments for the good of their national economies and that of the world (Harold 1995). It has become the principal activity of the IMF since the late 1970s, and the issues it raises are evident in the Fund's recent well-publicised activities in Indonesia, for which it endured considerable criticism. In this case the IMF was called on as a lender of last resort when the national economy had reached the verge of collapse. Indonesia's woes were due in large part to the complex interaction of political corruption, over-reliance on foreign debt, knock-on effects from other economic failures in the region, and unrestricted capital flight.

The IMF came to the aid of Indonesia with a multi-billion dollar loan package, granted on the condition that significant changes would be made to the borrower's economic management. Through its preceding and ongoing surveillance activities, the IMF knew the full extent to which Indonesia had pursued macroeconomic policies of which the Fund did not approve. Critics argue that the IMF supervenes national sovereignty in demanding changes to national policies as a condition of financial assistance. There is also concern over the severity of the austerity measures advocated by the IMF, particularly with regard to the way the costs of adjustment are distributed in the borrowing country.

To be fair, national governments are understandably reluctant to heed the IMF's policy suggestions when they do not have to, and they do not have to when they do not need, or qualify for, the money the IMF can make available. We may therefore sympathise with the Fund's decision to leverage one of the few bargaining advantages it possesses when negotiating with sovereign states. Although it often finds itself the target of condemnation for the harsh policies it imposes on national governments in crisis, it must be said that governments sometimes place themselves in harm's way by ignoring the IMF's urgings in less trying times. Thailand, the nation triggering the Asian financial crisis, was guilty in this regard. What is more, in some instances large proportions of IMF loans are siphoned away to supplement the private wealth of the borrowing country's elite, as evidenced recently in Russia. Such facts hardly support the image of an all-powerful IMF loftily presiding over the economic affairs of nations.

However, it is also true that the type of policy changes demanded by the Fund are not a proven winning formula in every case, even when they are faithfully instituted. Also, like the World Bank, the Fund is accused of obstructing international market solutions to economic problems. The IMF is also criticised for being too like the Bank – lending long term and thereby intruding on the territory of the World Bank Group and other international development banks. The Fund's First Deputy Managing Director has made much of the collaboration between the two institutions (Fischer 1998), but the fact remains that the IMF was not conceived as an instrument of development, and if its resources are needed in this regard it seems redundant to administer them independently (Urquidi 1996).

Whatever the IMF's future as a financier, its accumulated expertise in monetary affairs will certainly not be allowed to go to waste. International debate currently centres on whether and how private flows of international capital should be regulated. It is increasingly obvious that the key decision makers in the international monetary economy are no longer reserve banks and treasuries carrying out government policies, but private sector banks and investors effectively unregulated at the international level. In early 1999, with Asia still struggling to revive after its economic collapse, Brazil finds itself facing a similar fate, also with global market implications, and the IMF is again responding with multi-billion dollar conditional loans. As these crises multiply and deepen, the imposition of inhibitory controls on the world's capital markets is increasingly likely and, if a regulatory scheme is eventually installed, the Fund will have a key role in its design and administration.

The World Trade Organisation

Origins

The third member of the Bretton Woods troika is much younger than the other two: in fact it came into being on 1 January, 1995. Yet it too has amassed 50 years of experience in international economic governance! This puzzle is easily solved. The Bretton Woods conference did not establish an IGO to administer trade as it had for monetary stabilisation and development lending, but both the IMF and World Bank were intended to contribute to the expansion of world trade, and there was acknowledgement of the further need for a specialised body (Urquidi 1996; Jackson 1998). In 1946, the UN's Economic and Social

Council, ECOSOC, began moves to introduce an International Trade Organisation (ITO) to administer a treaty laying down rules governing the national regulation of trade. The ITO was to help create and sustain a competitive multilateral trading system, minimally encumbered by obstacles to free trade.

To show this was a viable idea, 23 countries entered into a model agreement called the General Agreement on Trade and Tariffs, or the GATT for short. Inspired by bilateral trade agreements to which the US was party, it set down a framework for multilateral negotiation of trade concessions, and contained schedules listing the tariffs established among the signatories. On 1 January 1948, the GATT entered into force. This was prior to the creation of the ITO, because officials from several founding members, the US in particular, were unsure that the political will to join such a venture would last until the ITO was a reality (Jackson 1998). With the ITO imminent, the GATT was silent on matters such as employment, investment, restrictive business practices, and an administering institutional framework (Reisman 1996).

The GATT would probably have been replaced by a more comprehensive and sophisticated agreement under the auspices of the ITO, had ECOSOC's original plans gone ahead. Instead the ITO design, finalised in Havana in 1948, was never given life. The US Congress refused to consider the ITO charter, primarily because it was not comfortable with the notion of an external organisation authorised to demand changes to US trade policy (Reisman 1996). With the world's most influential nation not prepared to join, the ITO scheme simply fizzled out. The GATT remained, however, modified to account for the final form of the ITO Charter, and in need of an independent administrating structure. With the Interim Commission established to prepare the way for the ITO now suddenly surplus to requirements, its staff were netted by the GATT members, and set up as an unofficial GATT secretariat. Thus emerged the Geneva-based institution that would eventually become the WTO.

Over the years the GATT attracted over 100 members, and, periodically, negotiating 'Rounds' were staged in which the Contracting Parties, as the members were formally termed, would agree new tariff levels and make amendments to the Agreement. In the eight Rounds called to date, trade representatives negotiated among each other bilaterally, or in small groups, agreeing to lower tariffs on different product categories in exchange for the same from another country on some other category. Australia might therefore agree to lower its tariffs on consumer electronics imports, in return for a Japanese offer to reduce import tariffs on aluminium. This reciprocity is a fundamental principle of the GATT process, and is considered vital to its success.

Once new tariff levels are established among Contracting Parties on a bilateral basis, the lowest tariff level set by a nation in any particular product category becomes the maximum tariff imposed by that country, in that category, on imports from *any other* Contracting Party. This is known as the **most favoured nation** principle, or MFN, and it has proved to be a vital component in non-discriminatory multilateral trade liberalisation. Assume that during a negotiating Round, Australia's promised reduction of consumer electronics tariffs for Japan were not surpassed in its negotiations with any other Contracting Party. The MFN principle requires that Australia's tariff on consumer electronics imports from all GATT participants holds at the level bargained for by Japan. Conversely, say Japan reduced its tariff on French aluminium to a level unmatched in any other bilateral negotiation involving Japan. Australian aluminium exports to Japan would then attract the same tariff as French aluminium, as would aluminium exports from all other members. In any given product category, the tariff negotiated by the most favoured nation is that enjoyed by all Contracting Parties.

The GATT was almost entirely devoted to tariffs and their reduction. Under its regime, tariffs steadily fell to under a tenth of their average levels in 1948 (*The Economist* 1998b). The circumstances of the GATT's conception left it impotent with regard to other international business issues. So long as trade accounted for most international economic transactions, and tariffs remained the favoured instrument of protective regulation, this was not a serious drawback. However, that situation did not last long. As tariff levels diminished over time, and international business intensified, national regulators began deploying other, less obvious, forms of protective instrument. To understand why, we must appreciate that as well as cushioning national industries from competition in the form of imported goods, protectionism is often a weapon in mercantilist competition between nation states. Non-tariff barriers (NTBs), a useful weapon in these contests, come in many forms, including quotas, product safety standards, and local content requirements, to name but a few. In response to the threat of NTBs, at the 1973–9 Tokyo Round the GATT stipulated that deliberate protection should always take the form of tariffs, as these are visible, well understood, clearly set and amenable to supervised reduction.

The latest GATT Round was launched in 1986 in Punta del Este, Uruguay. Known thereafter as the Uruguay Round, this protracted series of meetings between the Contracting Parties resulted in a virtual revamp of the GATT system, but it took eight years and several near-collapses of the talks to achieve. Not only was the GATT treaty rewritten, but new agreements were formed, and the ITO concept was revived in the modified form of the WTO. The WTO Charter creates an IGO with full legal status, and requires that nations do not interfere with its staff (Jackson 1994). Already established as a central participant in international economic relations, the WTO, continuing in the mode of the GATT secretariat it replaced, oversees the operation of the treaties annexed to its Establishing Agreement, particularly GATT '94, the extended and revised version of the original 1948 agreement. Unlike its predecessor, GATT '94 covers agricultural products, and, thanks to the Uruguay Round, has a set of new siblings, including the General Agreement on Trade in Services (GATS), and treaties covering trade-related intellectual property rights (TRIPS), and trade-related investment measures (TRIMS: more on this later). GATS extends the principles of GATT to the realm of services and the NTBs impeding service trade. TRIPS requires that member countries comply with minimum standards of intellectual property protection. Most non-industrialised countries have until 1 January 2000, while the poorest have an extension to 2006.

Dispute settlement

Of the WTO functions not already discussed, its dispute settlement responsibilities are of particular interest. The GATT secretariat played an important role as arbitrator and adjudicator in trade disputes between Contracting Parties, but the

WTO is better equipped in this regard. A dispute settlement procedure involving a panel of impartial individuals may be initiated by any nation with a complaint that another WTO member is in violation of its obligations under any of the agreements annexed to the WTO Charter, and appeal hearings are also obtainable. Panel and Appellate Body decisions become binding on the disputants once they are adopted by the General Council, meeting in its guise as the Dispute Settlement Body. A serious failing of the old GATT system was that any nation might block adoption of panel decisions when under consideration by the Council, but in the WTO, according to its Dispute Settlement Understanding, adoption is agreed by a majority vote. The success of the new dispute settlement system is evidenced by the use to which it is being put: in only four years the WTO has heard over half the number of complaints ever entertained by the GATT secretariat (*The Economist* 1998b).

Consider the following demonstration of the WTO's new powers, and problems, in the dispute settlement arena. In 1997 a dispute settlement panel ruled that the European Union's banana import regime violated global trade rules by discriminating against banana producers such as Mexico, Honduras, Guatemala and Ecuador, and indirectly the US, thanks to foreign direct investments in these Latin American countries by US multinationals like Chiquita. Bananas from these countries were largely excluded from European markets by imports from Costa Rica, Colombia, Venezuela and Nicaragua, and from nations in Africa, the Caribbean and the Pacific. After the EU revised its banana import regime, the still-dissatisfied complainants asked another dispute settlement panel to rule on whether or not the EU properly fulfilled its obligations under the 1997 WTO ruling. Perhaps the most striking feature of the banana feud up to this point was the submission of the economic superpowers to the trade dispute settlement process as dutiful WTO members, albeit with little grace. Unfortunately, the second panel was slow to make a finding, spurring the US to unilaterally impose trade penalties, threatening hundreds of jobs and jeopardising millions of dollars worth of export sales. The penalties took the form of bond payments equivalent to 100 per cent duties on a disparate range of European products ranging from Italian cheese to German coffee-makers, deferring collection of the money until completion of the WTO inquiry into the effects of the EU regime (*The Economist* 1999a). The subsequent panel finding against the EU authorised the complainants to impose retaliatory measures, but the unilateral action of the US considerably complicated the achievement of a resolution via WTO channels. Still to be clarified is the WTO's role in prescribing solutions to disputes such as these: one potential course is for it to stipulate the actions a country should take in order to comply with WTO rules, but both America and the EU oppose this innovation (*The Economist* 1999b).

Without underestimating the importance of the historical context of the banana dispute, the EU's inertia, the aggressiveness of the US, and the hesitancy of the WTO may be understood as institutional responses to the turbulence created in international governance structures as a new international actor asserts itself. Remote though these affairs may seem from the day-to-day of business activities, it is salutary to note the very tangible effects such high-level conflicts have on the operations of exporters and importers.

The future

The future of the WTO appears to be one of increased influence over international economic relations. Now boasting 134 members – notably excluding China, Taiwan and Russia – the WTO is heavily involved with the further development of international trade governance. Tariffs are still a main area of concern, particularly in agriculture, while trade liberalisation in services remains in its infancy. Agreements and the trade policies of member states are scheduled for periodic review, and working parties are examining whether and how trade rules could be modified to achieve objectives relating to workers' rights and environmental protection. A year-2000 review of the WTO, and the agreements it administers, have been planned since Uruguay. Agriculture and services will be the principal areas of attention, but some WTO members, notably the US, Japan, and the EU, are pressing for a more comprehensive set of negotiations in the form of a 'Millennium Round'. With talk of labour standards and environmental protection as areas for rule development in the Millennium Round, some governments are disturbed that the WTO is moving too quickly and will intrude on domestic policy-making. The technical competence and authorisation of the WTO has also been called into question in this regard – despite a general consensus that environmental and social issues deserve better governance at the international level, the specialised nature of the WTO makes it unlikely that it can function optimally in this capacity (Jones 1998).

The risk of future WTO incursions on national sovereignty is limited by the requirement that most decisions be made by consensus among its members, or, failing that, a 75 per cent majority. Amendment to the WTO Agreements requires unanimity, or a two-thirds majority in favour, and should a members' rights and obligations be altered as a consequence, they may refuse to be bound by it (Jackson 1998). It is apparent that in this regard the WTO is unlike the World Bank and IMF which have historically enjoyed a higher degree of independence from their national 'shareholders'.

Present indicators suggest the WTO, IMF, World Bank and other UN organs will work more closely together in future. In doing so they will not join forces to preside over the international society of sovereign states, but in an effort to more effectively perform their functions within the inter-state system. All four institutions are responsible to the nations that give them life, and only through increased co-ordination can these IGOs fully address their members' complex and often conflicting concerns.

Supranational governance

The bodies discussed above are characterised by their purpose to influence relationships between and within nation states, irrespective of national identity or geographic location. Operating on a more confined geopolitical scale are a number of institutions and associations exercising governance on a supranational scale. This entails exercising authority over certain events in a territory comprised of a well-defined set of countries, often with shared boundaries, as in the European Union, or in a more or less definable conceptual space, such as the developed world in the case of the OECD.

This section looks at examples of supranational governance arrangements. Note at the outset that all have far to go before assuming the sort of comprehensive powers their individual members wield within their own nationally defined territories.

The European Union

The EU may be regarded as a quasi-supranational state evolving out of a postwar economic integrative agreement. It possesses a governing apparatus exhibiting the model separation of powers between a judiciary, legislature and executive, very like a national government, and has arguably wrested aspects of sovereign authority away from the states that comprise the union. At the time of writing, the EU is composed of 15 national members, although some accept a higher degree of integration than others. Membership is comprised of: Austria, Belgium, Britain, Denmark, Finland, France, Germany, Greece, Ireland, Italy, The Netherlands, Portugal, Spain, Sweden and Switzerland. Several central and eastern European nations are eager to join, as are Cyprus and Turkey.

The EU did not begin so grandly. Its inception is typically dated to 1957, when two international agreements were signed in Rome by Belgium, France, Germany, Italy, Luxembourg and The Netherlands. These established two new European Communities to join the European Coal and Steel Community (ECSC), formed in 1951. One of the two new creations was the European Atomic Energy Community (Euratom), but it was the direct ancestor of the EU, the European Economic Community (EEC), that captured the public's attention. Like the UN, these communities were created in a climate of determination that international economic competition should not be allowed to lead to war. It was also hoped that prosperity and competitiveness would be enhanced if European industries had access to larger markets than any individual nation could provide (Nicoll and Salmon 1990).

In its founding document, the Treaty of Rome, the EEC was established as a customs union, but the Treaty made clear that this was only the start of greater things to come. Accordingly the trade bloc gradually expanded in membership and became more fully economically integrated in the following three decades. It took on the new name of the European Communities (EC) to signify the widening and deepening economic and political integration between its members. Although the EC still formally exist, they are now subsumed within the larger idea of the European Union, which came into existence in January 1993.

The EU represents a substantial realisation of the objectives set down in the Treaty of Rome to create a federal Europe. In the first place it is characterised by the unimpeded movement of goods, services, people and capital, creating a single market of about 370 million people. Legislative impetus for this aspect of the EU came in 1985 in the form of the Single European Act. The close of 1992 was set therein as the deadline for completion of the Single Market, and the unanimity previously required in many areas of community decision making was abandoned in favour of qualified majority voting. The formation of the Single Market aroused much concern elsewhere in the world that a 'Fortress Europe' was in the making, a region where international business was unencumbered by frontier barriers within, but entry from outside would be next to impossible. In the 1980s and early 1990s, FDI poured into the region from companies determined to establish a market presence before 'lock-out'. However, the EU remains bound to multilateral trade liberalisation through its WTO membership so, with the exception of agriculture, where subsidies under the Common Agricultural Policy (CAP) continue to seriously distort output, fears of discriminatory exclusion from this region have proved generally unfounded.

Further advancement came in the form of the Maastricht Treaty, finalised in December 1991 and ratified, not without difficulty, by the various member states in the following two years. This agreement is as important to the history of European regional integration as the Treaty of Rome itself. It sets the 1999 target and qualifying criteria for monetary union, but it also contains a social policy agreement (the 'social chapter' or 'social protocol') stating the procedure for creating European policy in areas such as workers' rights, and a resolution to create regional security and foreign policy. Despite initial setbacks, particularly the formal British opt-out of the monetary union provisions, accompanied by Danish and Swedish reservations over the same, and the practical failure to establish anything resembling a coherent EU foreign policy, the Maastricht Treaty has so far proved a substantial advance toward greater political union.

The objectives of the EU may be summarised as: the promotion of economic and social progress; assertion of the Union's identity as a unified actor in international relations; the introduction of Union citizenship to protect and strengthen individual rights; the development of intra-Union cooperation on justice and home affairs; and the development of the cooperative spirit of the European Communities. Of these, the emergence of the EU as an entity capable of forming relationships in international society alongside its members is particularly interesting in the context of this chapter. One of the first fruits of the EU's international status is its membership of the WTO, continuing the EC's membership of the GATT. Increasingly, the EU represents its members in international affairs beyond the economic domain, as exemplified recently by the February 1999 call from EU foreign ministers to the warring parties in the Yugoslavian Federation urging the negotiation of a peace settlement. This type of unity would not be possible were it not for the wider and deeper non-economic integration between the member states.

The principal governing institutions of the EU were created during its earlier Community incarnations, and continue as fundamental and evolving parts of the EU system. They are headed by its Council, a body comprised of Heads of State, which provides the Union's political direction. There is also an elected body, the European Parliament, made up of representatives from the different national members. In the past the Parliament was clearly the weakest member in the EU's institutional family, but it is increasingly asserting itself, and this is to be commended if the Union is to possess the democratic credentials it requires to deepen the integration of its members. The EU's executive body is the Commission, and it is this organ that has held the reigns of power within the Union. The Commission drafts directives and regulations that are placed before the Council for passage into law. These laws then apply automatically within the 15 member states and are upheld by national courts. The Union also has its own court, sited in Luxembourg, which began life under the original Coal and Steel Community. The European Court of Justice (ECJ) hears disputes arising between members and between the Commission and members in breach of EU law. The ECJ also sits as the final court of appeal from national courts in cases involving EU law.

With the evolution of European integration from a customs union to a political union, the EU's influence over all business between its member states begins to rival, even overtake, that of the members within their territories. As noted above, EU law applies directly within the member states, and is enforced by the national courts of those states. In future, business enterprises expanding into or within the Union will give as much consideration to the EU institutions as to particular host states when engaged in political risk assessment. The establishment of a Single European Currency exemplifies the depth of involvement of the Union's institutions in economic affairs within the member states. Since 1 January 1999, citizens of 11 EU members have had to contend with prices denominated in the **Euro**, a regional currency destined to become a permanent fixture of the European monetary scene, and a likely challenger to the international financial dominance of the dollar (Bergsten 1999). By 2002, the national currencies of the current EMU members will be phased out of circulation. This move represents an apparent abandonment of monetary sovereignty by members of the EMU to the new European Central Bank. Britain, Denmark and Sweden notably abstain from EMU participation, all remaining to be convinced that the economic gains outweigh the political losses.

The OECD

The Organisation for Economic Co-operation and Development (OECD) is a Paris-based association of the industrialised nations, perhaps 'the most powerful grouping of nations the world has ever known' (Dischamps 1993: 104–5). Established in late 1948 as the 18-member Organisation for European Economic Co-operation (OEEC), its original purpose was to manage funds donated by the US to speed Europe's reconstruction. Under the Marshall Plan, devised by the US Secretary of State, General George C. Marshall, US aid rebuilt European markets for US exports and created a secure environment for US FDI (it was this capital that rendered the IBRD redundant in its reconstruction role).

After the Marshall Plan, the OEEC studied and advised on pan-European economic problems and promoted liberalised trade between its members (Dischamps 1993). In 1961 it became the OECD when Canada and the US, previously only associate members, assumed full membership. Many countries have since become members, with the roll now including Australia, Austria, Belgium, the Czech Republic, Denmark, Finland, France, Germany, Greece, Hungary, Iceland, Ireland, Italy, Japan, Luxembourg, Mexico, The Netherlands, New Zealand, Norway, Poland, Portugal, Spain, South Korea, Sweden, Switzerland, Turkey and the UK.

The OECD Convention states that this IGO should promote policies designed to:

- achieve the highest sustainable economic growth and employment and a rising standard of living in member countries, while maintaining financial stability, and thus contribute to the development of the world economy;
- contribute to sound economic expansion in member as well as non-member countries in the process of economic development;
- contribute to the expansion of world trade on a multilateral, non-discriminatory basis in accordance with international obligations.

How have these objectives translated into tangible outcomes? Some examples give the flavour of the OECD's efforts. Like the UN, the OECD devised a code of conduct for international businesses, known as the Guidelines for Multinational Enterprises. Finalised in 1976, the OECD's version predates the UN's by 13 years, but incorporates ideas brought to the Code of Conduct negotiations by the industrialised countries, and the two are therefore alike in many respects. In November 1997 the OECD countries and Argentina, Brazil, Bulgaria, Chile, and the Slovak Republic adopted a formal Convention on Combating Bribery in International Business Transactions, the first of its kind (Hotchkiss 1998). This convention, in effect since February 1999, criminalises and abolishes tax deductibility for bribery of foreign public officials.

The latest high-profile activity of the OECD with regard to international business governance is the design of the Multilateral Agreement on Investment (MAI). This initiative was intended to create a framework establishing rules for the national regulation of FDI and MNEs. In general terms, the MAI would be to FDI what the GATT is to trade.

This comparison has interesting historical resonances: the ITO was to have dealt with investment alongside trade, but the GATT was not extended to cover aspects of international investment until comprehensively revised in the Uruguay Round.

Despite, or because of the fact that OECD members are the source of 80 per cent and the recipients of 60 per cent of FDI, the WTO may be a more appropriate forum for its development and implementation (*The Economist* 1998b). The WTO supervises several multilateral agreements establishing rules for the treatment of FDI by national governments. Chiefs among these are GATS and TRIMS. GATS deals with FDI regulation only in so far as it impinges on trade in services, while the more general TRIMS attempts to alleviate trade distortions introduced by FDI policy (Daniels *et al.* 1995). The WTO agreements do not constitute a comprehensive international investment regime, so the OECD's MAI initiative may be seen as an effort to close the gaps.

The MAI talks, begun in September 1995, ground to an inauspicious halt in mid-1998, two months after the April completion deadline. International public opposition to the MAI was extraordinary, because of the secrecy with which negotiations were first conducted, the perception that the agreement is staunchly pro-MNE, and its lack of provision for environmental and labour protection. Further difficulties emerged as the negotiating parties failed to reach consensus on whether and which strategic industries should enjoy special exemptions (*The Economist* 1998a). There was also complaint from developing countries over their exclusion from drafting an agreement that might potentially effect many more changes in their investment regimes than in those of the industrialised nations. Furthermore, WTO rules, binding most of the world's nations, make negotiated trade-facilitating investment measures subject to WTO-wide application, based on the MFN principle. Signatories to the MAI would have to maintain the same investment regime standards for all WTO members, regardless of their commitment to the MAI (*The Economist* 1998a). For these reasons any future multilateral FDI negotiations will probably take place under WTO supervision.

Regional integration in the Americas and Asia

Regional economic integration is a distinctive feature of the late twentieth century. Seen at its most advanced in the evolution of the EU, it involves nation states entering into binding agreements to reduce regulatory barriers to resource flow between them, and reduces regulatory discrimination against business involving citizens of the other integrating parties. In its simplest form, the free trade area (FTA), two or more countries contract with one another to lower tariff and non-tariff barriers to goods traded between one another. The members of **customs unions** take this idea one step further, by adopting a common external tariff as well. **Common markets** go further still, and introduce liberalisation of the international provision of services and investment capital within the integrated region. During its 41-year history the EU acquired almost all these forms, at times mixing and matching elements of several at once, and it continues to advance the political and economic integration of its members into historically uncharted territory.

Within a bloc of nations, regional economic integration shifts the locus of governance of international business away from individual states and into markets of multinational geographic dimensions and concomitantly greater competitiveness. For this to be possible, the integrating nations must be geographically, economically or culturally proximate, otherwise a mutually advantageous compromise cannot be reached. The need for proximity along these dimensions leads to exclusivity in regional economic integration, in that these agreements are made among relatively few nations, and therefore run counter to the principle of multilateralism expounded by the WTO.

There is a danger that the absence of respect for the WTO's MFN ideal in regional integration may serve only to lift adversarial trade relations from the international level to the inter-trade bloc level. It may, on the other hand, advance the cause of globalisation by promoting the ideal of economic integration and providing larger building blocks to piece together into an integrated global economy. Whatever the eventual outcome, regional integration is an increasingly popular device to widen and deepen economic relations between states, and with the number of integrative agreements almost quadrupling to over 90 since 1990, it shows no sign of waning in the twenty-first century (*The Economist* 1998b).

The following sub-sections briefly introduce three of the main agreements representing significant developments in international business governance at the supranational level.

The Americas

NAFTA

The North American Free Trade Area is sold short in its title. NAFTA, composed of Mexico, the US and Canada, is a good deal more than a simple free trade area. Formed in 1994, it is the largest integrated region after the EU. Apart from the free trade area in goods and services established between the three members, NAFTA also eliminates barriers to investment, contains specific provisions on intellectual property right protection, and creates a Trade Commission and Commission for Environmental Cooperation with powers to impose fines and settle disputes.

Illustrating the extent to which NAFTA shifts the balance of economic governance in favour of international business is the provision entitling private companies to sue member states for violation of the Agreement. The first challenge brought to court was from chemical manufacturer Ethyl Corporation, of the US. Ethyl complained that Canada had banned the import of a fuel additive without sufficient cause, such as evidence that the additive constituted a health hazard. In July 1988, Canada settled out of court for US$13m and lifted the import ban (Sissell 1998). Similarly, NAFTA's Chapter 11 allows an investor to seek compensation through the courts if a government acts directly or indirectly to expropriate an investment in that country.

As to NAFTA's benefits, the jury is very much still out. Debate continues over which, if any, of the NAFTA members is gaining meaningfully from their membership. It was widely believed at the outset of the agreement that the member with the most to gain would be the US, thanks to its considerable power advantage. However, the Clinton administration announced in September 1998 that NAFTA merely had a 'modest positive effect' on the US economy in the four years since its commencement (*International Business* 1997). The long-term success of NAFTA will hinge not only on the further integration of its existing members, but also on its expansion southwards, which brings us to our second American integrative agreement.

Mercosur

Mercosur is the Southern Cone Common Market, the cone in question being that of the South American continent, where the member countries Argentina, Brazil, Paraguay, Uruguay and Chile, latterly an associate member, are located. Mercosur, formed in 1991, is the world's third largest integrative agreement in economic terms, behind the EU and NAFTA. Total GDP for the four member countries, excluding Chile, accounts for around 70 per cent of South America's GDP and more than 50 per cent of Latin America's (Kotabe and de Arruda 1998). Like NAFTA, Mercosur is dominated by a large national economy, in this case Brazil, the giant of Latin America. Uruguay and Paraguay are economically tiny by comparison, while Argentina and Chile combined are still only one-third as big. Brazil's disproportionate influence is a serious problem in the integrated regional economy, as its economy is highly unstable.

The largest members, Argentina and Brazil, and associate member, Chile, are all committed to global economic integration. Argentina and Brazil, who entered a bilateral agreement to ease trade restrictions in 1985, see Mercosur as an opportunity to develop their competitiveness on global markets, and as a buffer to international economic volatility. The two smaller members are more immediately concerned with gaining access to the large markets of their fellow participants.

Mercosur has demolished tariff barriers between its members and erected common tariff levels to extra-regional trade on a large, but not exhaustive, cross-section of products. However, intra-regional trade amounts to only 3 per cent of combined GDP of the member nations, despite a tenfold growth between 1991 and 1996. This represents poor performance compared to NAFTA's 5 per cent and 15 per cent for the EU (Kotabe and de Arruda 1998). Undaunted, the bloc is now concentrating on liberalising intra-regional factor mobility. Its success should not, therefore, be measured exclusively by the extent of intra-regional trade: interest shown by foreign investors is also a telling factor. MNEs are now able to access five national markets from a single production site, leading to a significant upturn in FDI flowing into the region. The development of the common market has been cited as a major determinant in the decision of automobile manufacturers like Fiat, GM and Toyota to directly invest in Argentina, despite previously experienced misfortunes in that market (Hinchberger 1995).

Links between Mercosur and other major trading blocs are beginning to strengthen. The European Commission is prepared to negotiate a trade agreement between the EU and Mercosur to remove tariffs over ten years, although resistance from the agricultural lobby within the EU is sure to be high. Closer to home, Mercosur and the Andean Pact (Bolivia, Colombia, Ecuador and Venezuela) are concluding an agreement that would merge the two groupings into a South American Free Trade Area. The combined Mercosur–Andean group would establish

Exhibit 3.2 ASEAN agrees to speed up regional tariff cuts

South-East Asian countries yesterday agreed to accelerate the development of a regional free trade area in advance of a 2003 deadline for its establishment. The commitment, made at a meeting in Manila of economic and trade ministers from the Association of South East Asian Nations (ASEAN), aims to counter concern that economic turmoil would slow the pace of trade liberalisation. 'We are sending a signal to the global community,' said Jose Pardo, chairman of the Asean Free Trade Area (AFTA) council and the Philippines trade and industry secretary.

The AFTA council said member countries intended to reduce tariffs on inter-ASEAN trade to zero on 'as many products as possible' by 2003, rather than the earlier target of between zero and 5 per cent. The council also said member states had made 'substantial' individual plans to step up the pace of tariff reductions and bring more products under AFTA. 'ASEAN means business. Despite current difficulties, ASEAN countries have individually and collectively agreed to step up their commitments to tariff reductions,' said Lee Yock Suan, the Singaporean minister for trade and industry.

Under planned tariff reductions for 1998, 82.8 per cent of all products will be subject to tariffs of between zero and 5 per cent for inter-ASEAN trade. This is expected to rise to 84.8 per cent in 1999 and 85.2 per cent in 2000. Average tariffs for trades under AFTA would be reduced from 5.37 per cent in 1998 to 2.68 per cent in 2003. For the new ASEAN countries, the deadline for reducing tariffs on a wide range of products is later than for other member countries.

The AFTA council said increasing trade in the region would help overcome the negative impact of currency devaluations in ASEAN countries. It added that AFTA would provide the impetus for economies to restructure, improve competitiveness and engineer an export-led recovery. The council also said there had been substantial progress in strengthening the transparency and predictability of its members' trade regimes. It said conditions under which member states could carry out unilateral trade restrictions in times of crisis to protect an industry or prevent a run on foreign exchange reserves had been made more stringent. A protocol had also been finalised under which member states would have to give 60 days' notice of any measures that may impair the AFTA agreement.

Source: *Financial Times* CD-ROM, 1 January–31 December 1998.

a common market with 300m consumers. Indeed, Mercosur's ultimate goal is to incorporate all South American countries before linking up with NAFTA to form a transcontinental free trade zone (Kotabe and de Arruda 1998). Chile, already in a FTA with Canada, is set to become the next national member of NAFTA, and Mercosur may join as a regional member early next century. At the first Americas Summit in 1994, a Free Trade Agreement of the Americas (FTAA) was signed. This established a plan for a Western hemispheric free trade area involving 34 countries to come into force by 2005 (Hill and D'Souza 1998). The expansive future of regional economic integration (REI) in the Americas may confirm the hypothesis that REI augments, rather than supplants, the multilateral integration striven for by the GATT and WTO.

Asia

Asia is the site of considerable international integrative activity: in West Asia is the Gulf Cooperation Council consisting of Bahrain, Kuwait, Oman, Qatar, Saudi Arabia, and the United Arab Emirates; and in South Asia, the South Asian Agreement for Regional Cooperation incorporating Bangladesh, Bhutan, India, Maldives, Nepal, Pakistan and Sri Lanka. Here we focus on the most advanced of the Asian integrative agreements, the Association of South East Asian Nations (ASEAN). Formed in 1976, ASEAN's nine members are Brunei, Burma (Myanmar), Indonesia, Laos, Malaysia, the Philippines, Singapore, Thailand and Vietnam. Although several ASEAN members remain very poor by OECD standards, almost all have enjoyed very high rates of growth in the last few years, particularly in trade and investment. This condition changed very quickly in 1997 with the general collapse into recession brought about by the Asian financial crisis.

There has always existed disagreement in ASEAN over the function and evolution of the association. Singapore, and to a lesser extent the Philippines, are for economic liberalisation and regional integration. Indonesia and Malaysia are less keen, and prefer ASEAN to remain primarily a political grouping in which forces are joined to influence international decision making. Despite the reservations of some members, ASEAN is due to create a free trade area (AFTA) by 2002, phasing in Myanmar, Laos and Vietnam over the following four to six years. Strong measures are also being adopted to restore investor confidence in the region, including allowing 100 per cent ownership to foreign direct investors. Plans to avert future shocks, and to minimise their impact, include increased levels of economic monitoring of member countries, and greater monetary integration within the region. ASEAN members are also beginning to co-ordinate environmental policy making.

ASEAN and the other examples of regional economic integration discussed above represent only the highest profile agreements of their kind. A great many others exist around the world, including Africa and the Pacific. Integration of this kind shows no signs of diminishing in the twenty-first century, as the steady flow of media coverage of new negotiations attests. Even in Japan, a nation historically aloof from formal integrative agreements, officials have begun to acknowledge a potential role for FTAs in the near future (*Business Korea* 1998). Current bilateral trade talks between the EU and Mexico (*World Trade* 1999) draw attention to the fact that economic integration is increasingly taking place beyond the confines of geopolitical clusters, and is becoming a truly global phenomenon.

International non-governmental organisations (NGOs)

The international institutions discussed so far rely, for whatever influence they possess, on the formal co-operation of nation states. Defiance by any country is always a possibility, and one for which none of these bodies is effectively prepared. Consider the UN's inability to disarm Iraq, or Britain's regular refusals to participate fully in EU initiatives. It is apparent that the legitimacy of these institutions, their right to exercise governance, can always be traced back to a delegation of power from nation states. State sovereignty, then, is the glue holding the official international system of governance together.

Partly in reaction to the continued primacy of the nation state in the regulation of global affairs, and partly because of the inadequacies of IGOs in responding to changes in global society, another species of transnational organisation has come to the fore. These bodies do not combine national governments in co-operative governing ventures, but draw their membership from the grassroots of international society. The generic term for these associations is 'non-governmental organisation', or simply, 'NGO'. Some international NGOs, like the Roman Catholic Church, Greenpeace, and Amnesty International, are household names. A far greater number have lower public profiles, smaller memberships, and more modest aims but, as constituents of an emergent class of major international actor, all are important.

The influence of NGOs is not their ability to issue commands to governments or international business corporations. NGOs cannot enforce their will by threat or application of military might, as can governments. They are composed of ordinary civilians, individuals and corporations voluntarily joining forces as members of civil society rather than as state officials. People form and join these organisations, often at significant personal expense, because they share certain beliefs, interests and concerns, ranging from the rights of the unborn child, to the protection of the environment, to the ethics of international business. NGOs exert influence over market and non-market actors primarily through public awareness campaigns. They make use of television, newspapers, internet sites, schools, community meetings, display posters, and other information disseminating media to arm societies with knowledge and to sway opinion. Unlike national governments and IGOs, they are not constrained by the niceties of diplomacy, and will call attention to malfeasance wherever they perceive it.

Although many NGOs are purely local in action and may exist for only a short while, others have gained sufficient status, thanks to their longevity, experience and membership size and distribution, to act in a consultative role with international organisations. Article 71 of the original UN Charter gives NGOs a non-voting role in ECOSOC decision making, and by 1993 almost 1000 NGOs possessed consultative status (Otto 1996). IGOs, such as the Bretton Woods Institutions and the WTO, are beginning to appreciate the potential advantages of forming closer relationships with NGOs, and civil society at large. These advantages include information exchange, policy debate, access to public opinion, increased legitimacy, better public understanding of the IGOs, and an example-setting democratic inclusiveness in decision making. The work by NGOs in concentrating IMF attention on the multilateral debt burdens of the least developed countries in the mid-1990s demonstrates the practical benefits of forming closer relationships between civil society groups and the IGOs (Scholte 1998).

Multinational enterprises are learning to pay closer attention to the NGOs. This is unavoidable in some cases, as in Shell's confrontation with German Greenpeace activists over the disposal of the Brent Spar oil storage buoy (Guyon 1997). However, NGOs can make also themselves and their causes noticed by less dramatic means. For example, since 1993, Transparency International (TI) has done a great deal to raise awareness of corruption in international business, which it believes to be a large and growing problem. Its activities include international coalition building, lobbying IGOs, and research-based assistance for its affiliates and governments seeking to combat corruption. It has founded 72 national chapters, published a best practice Source Book, helped establish corruption-free zones in the developing world, pressured the OECD and EU for corruption-deterring law changes, created a comprehensive web site, and established a much-discussed international Corruption Perception Index (Hotchkiss 1998). Thanks to the efforts of TI and NGOs like it, international businesses can no longer assume that their deviations from socially responsible practice will be hidden from public view.

More recently, NGOs and corporations have engaged in cooperative projects, to one another's mutual benefit. In Britain, for example, the Ethical Trading Initiative is a government-supported scheme that brings food retailers and producers together with development NGOs and labour unions to draw up standard codes on trading practices and independently audit them (Wilkinson 1999). Similarly, in 1995 the UK division of the World Wide Fund for Nature assembled more than 80 companies to promote sustainable forestry practices. There remains considerable mutual suspicion, however, in the wake of the MAI blockage and scandals involving prominent NGO involvement in fraudulent 'green' investments. NGOs have played a key role in catalysing opposition to economic initiatives, and participants in international business have been put on guard.

The impact of NGOs on decision making in business and government seems destined to grow. The obstruction of the MAI represents a major win for civil society, and is indicative of the future importance of these organisations in international governance. Pressure is increasing for them to have greater participation in bodies such as APEC, the club of Pacific Rim nations negotiating Asia Pacific Economic Cooperation, and in the development of new trade relationships, such as the emergent pan-American Free Trade Agreement of the Americas (FTAA), the potential trade partnership between the EU and US. Having begun to overcome their earlier lack of credibility, NGOs are eventually constrained by their relative lack of resources (Scholte 1998). This is not entirely unfortunate: valid questions revolve around the legitimacy of the NGOs' self-appointed representation in decision-making processes at the highest levels. Organisations such as the UN possess a clear legal mandate to act, but the status of NGOs is far less clear – they often lack the democratic qualities they demand so fiercely of governments and IGOs.

Chapter summary

The internationalising world economy represents a 'new frontier' for business where, to paraphrase noted international business scholar Mark Casson (1986), effective governance lags behind the pioneering enterprises that are now consolidating their international competitive positions. The regulation of international competition between and among consumers, firms and nations is the responsibility of a fragmented, multitiered, divisionalised but increasingly interdependent governing system. That system remains far from complete, and events such as the Russian and Asian economic crises, hostilities in Rwanda and ex-Yugoslavia, and Iraq's intransigence over disarmament are proof to some that time has rendered old stalwarts like the UN and Bretton Woods institutions redundant. There are increasing demands for radical change to the present system of international governance, such as greater reliance on deregulated markets, new and more powerful IGOs, or reform of the existing institutional system (Kennedy and Russett 1995; Hogland 1998).

It is likely that the system of international governance will undergo historic revisions in the near future, but the organisations discussed above will continue to play key roles in that system. Nation states will remain the political engines powering it, but will increasingly understand their interests to be aligned with that of the international political economy as a whole, and issues surrounding state sovereignty will gradually seem less critical. Non-governmental organisations are destined to play a greater role than before, but they require internal checks on their power if they are to be a force for positive change. In all this, international business enterprises can also look forward to fuller participation. Their combined voice should continue to advocate liberty, non-discrimination, and co-operation as guiding principles in the governance of their affairs. They cannot always expect to be heard over the demands of rival interests, but so long as there exists an international culture of fair competition in the governance of international competitive relationships, global society will continue to evolve constructively.

Discussion questions

1 What is the relationship between governments and governance?
2 Why have some called for the merger of the World Bank and IMF?
3 Why did the OECD fail to institute the MAI?
4 How do international NGOs influence the behaviour of international businesses?

Closing Case Study:
An International Business Court

Introduction

In international business, as in business generally, there is always the chance that a law may be broken, a contract dishonoured, or an injury suffered. The resolution of disputes arising from these instances often demands the services of courts. Since sovereignty is retained at the national level, legal procedures involving international business enterprises and their agents are carried out within national legal systems. For all the multilateral regulatory instruments in existence, it is national law that decides legal liability in a given case. This situation has prevailed for centuries, but it reflects a less mobile, less interdependent and more disparate era than that of today. In the future the compartmentalisation of the legal world will be increasingly problematic for individuals and organisations, and for the institutions that govern their conduct.

A quick primer on international law

There are two varieties of international law. Public international law concerns relations between nation states and, although it may not entirely qualify as law to some legal scholars, it is truly international. In the international environment there exists no entity with the overarching power of a national government in its territory. If laws are only those rules enforceable by a superior over its subordinates, then in the society of states, where all nations are considered equal, there are rules, but no law. Private international law is used to resolve conflicts between domestic or municipal laws of different nations, such as those arising in international business disputes. Although private international law definitely qualifies as law, because it is composed of rules determined and enforced on a national basis, it occupies the same plane as land law or criminal law, and it is therefore not really international.

Putting the legal theory to one side, what you need to understand is that nothing akin to law prevailing within a nation exists at the international level. As discussed in the preceding chapter, this is a direct consequence of the sovereignty of the nation state, and is therefore not likely to change in the foreseeable future.

Implications for actors in the international domain

To cope with the absence of substantively and procedurally complete international law, international business contracts often contain a term stipulating what nation's law and courts will be decisive in any dispute arising from transactions between the parties. This might result in one party being at the mercy of the other's national legal system, where impartiality is not guaranteed, especially in times of diplomatic tension between the nations concerned. However, without such implied or explicit terms, considerable legal uncertainty is inherent in international business dealings.

Nation states also face difficulties. Many international business activities have unwanted repercussions across national boundaries. A negligent or malicious act performed by an MNE or one of its employees may cause injury on an international scale. Affected nations enforcing their laws independently of one another in such cases may create avoidable effort, conflict and confusion. In order to prosecute Nicholas Leeson, the prime culprit in the Barings Bank collapse, attorneys in three different countries vied for his extradition from Germany.

Similarly, when a Union Carbide pesticide subsidiary leaked a toxic chemical over a wide area of the Indian city of Bhopal, legal relief was delayed by a dispute between India and the US over which nation should try the case. Furthermore, some countries possess no legal remedies, because the malfeasance takes place in a foreign jurisdiction, does not involve their citizens, or causes only indirect damage to their interests. Finally, many developing nations are unable to secure reparations because their domestic legal institutions – their courts, laws, lawyers and legislature – are not properly equipped. India's courts found Union Carbide liable to pay millions in compensation, but the victims of the disaster have yet to be properly apportioned their shares because of inadequacies in the execution of the court's orders.

Self-regulation

Voluntary codes of conduct for international businesses are posited by industry associations, free-market proponents, even some regulatory bodies, as the best means to guarantee good corporate behaviour. However, the effectiveness of voluntary codes is compromised by the lack of a credible external threat of punishment for their breach. Nike offers a useful case in point: its subcontractors in Indonesia, China and Vietnam were ostensibly operating under an internal code of conduct for all Nike affiliates when the sportswear MNE came under fire for workers' rights abuses. Self-regulation is not necessarily doomed to fail – there are many examples of MNEs acting responsibly according to self-imposed codes of conduct – but there is always the temptation to bend the rules when imperfectly competitive conditions allow.

A cosmopolitan court for international business

An alternative to reliance on voluntary codes is the creation of an international business court, to try both criminal and civil cases, and in which private individuals, bodies corporate and nation states have legal standing. Such a court might apply rules laid down by the UN and its affiliated organisations, such as the UN Convention of Contracts for the International Sale of Goods, thereby complementing, rather than replacing, individual national efforts to regulate international business conduct. Although the establishment of such a court is not currently on the agenda of the UN, it is an intriguing possibility and the issues it raises are instructive.

An international tribunal of the type envisaged here need not deal exclusively with international business issues. The recently established International Criminal Court, intended to preside over trials for the like of war crimes and genocide, might develop a corporate crime division, or recognise certain corporate misdemeanours as sufficiently heinous to try as crimes against humanity. Although this is unlikely, it remains a great deal more feasible than the creation of an international court with general jurisdiction over criminal and civil matters.

The proposal to create a specialised international business court also encounters a variety of technical, ideological and political obstacles, yet the idea has considerable merit. It would serve as a neutral forum, reduce legal uncertainty and avoid political fallout between nations. MNEs would be less able to avoid prosecution through the tactic of situating questionable activities in countries with lax regulation or law enforcement. Governments could bring one another to account for extraterritorial applications of national law or policy. For their part, MNEs would possess an international forum where they might oppose host-government actions against them. As a deterrent, the reputational damage to a global company if tried and found liable by the court would be enough to ensure that firms change their operating procedures.

However, for such a court to be fully effective, particularly with respect to decisions against national governments, states must multilaterally undertake to enforce its orders with respect to persons or property within their jurisdictions. Once again, as the current international political system stands, only consent from the world's sovereign states to give effect to the court's decisions would ensure its workability.

Sources: This case draws mainly from Jackson, K.T. (1998) Information on the Nike case was sourced from Saporito (1998).

Questions

1 What is the difference between public and private international law?
2 What happens under the current system of different national laws when a contract dispute arises between two companies in different countries?
3 Is there any virtue in self-regulation by MNEs, or should the idea be dropped entirely?
4 What are some technical, ideological and political obstacles to the formation of an international business court?

Further reading

Kirshner, O. (ed.) (1996) *The Bretton Woods–GATT System*, Armonk, NY: M.E. Sharpe: 128–42. Interesting and often entertaining insights into the formation and evolution of the IMF, World Bank, and GATT/WTO.

Mander, J. and **Goldsmith, E.** (1996) *The Case Against the Global Economy: and for a Turn Toward the Local*. San Francisco: Sierra Club Books. A compilation of views from many authors sceptical about the increased role of deregulated markets in national and international economic governance.

Preston, L.E. and **Windsor, D.** (1997) *The Rules of the Game in the Global Economy: Policy Regimes for International Business*, 2nd edn, Boston: Kluwer Academic Press. A comprehensive analysis of international business governance, recommended for students taking study of these issues beyond the level of this chapter.

United Nations Library on Transnational Corporations (1993/94) London: Routledge on behalf of the UN Transnational Corporations and Management Division. An inestimably valuable compilation of research related to the governance of international business, especially volumes 7, 9, 19, and 20, published in 1993 and 1994.

References

Bassiry, G.R. (1990) Business ethics and the United Nations: a code of conduct, *SAM Advanced Management Journal*, Autumn: 38–41.

Beauchamp, T. (1993) Marketing infant formula, in T. Moran (ed.) *Governments and Transnational Corporations*, New York: UNCTAD Division on Transnational Corporations and Management.

Bergsten, F. (1999) America and Europe: clash of the titans?, *Foreign Affairs* 78, March/April: 20–34.

Business Korea (1998) Common interests, economic needs pull nations closer, November: 16–9.

Casson, M. (1986) General theories of the multinational enterprise: their relevance to business history, in P. Hertner and G. Jones (eds) *Multinationals: Theory and History*, Aldershot: Gower: 42–63.

Daniels, M., King, R. and Bernstein, P. (1995) TRIMming protectionism, *China Business Review*, March/April: 20–21.

Dichter, E. (1962) The world customer, *Harvard Business Review*, July–August: 113–22.

Dischamps, J.C. (1993) The European Community, international trade, and world unity, *California Management Review*, Winter: 104–17.

Fischer, S. (1998) The Asian crisis and the changing role of the IMF, *Finance and Development* 35: 2–5.

Guyon, J. (1997) Why is the world's most profitable company turning itself inside out?, *Fortune*, 4 August: 120–25.

Harold, J. (1995) The historical development of the principal of surveillance, *IMF Staff Papers* 42: 762–91.

Hill, J.S, and D'Souza, G. (1998) Tapping the emerging Americas market, *Journal of Business Strategy* 19: 8–12.

Hinchberger, B. (1995) Mercosur's pain and presence, *International Business*, June: 46–9.

Hogland, J. (1998) Weakness at top underlines need for reforms, *New Zealand Herald*, 16 October: C1.

Hotchkiss, C. (1998) The sleeping dog stirs: new signs of life in efforts to end corruption in international business, *Journal of Public Policy and Marketing* 17: 108–15

International Business (1997) In other developments, September/October: 26.

Jackson, J. (1994) The World Trade Organisation, dispute settlement, and codes of conduct, in S.M. Collins and B.P. Bosworth (eds) *The New GATT: Implications for the United States*, Washington D.C.: The Brookings Institution.

Jackson, J. (1998) *The World Trade Organisation*, London: Pinter.

Jackson, K.T. (1998) A cosmopolitan court for transnational wrongdoing? Why its time has come, *Journal of Business Ethics* 17: 757–83.

Jones, K. (1998) Who's afraid of the WTO?, *Challenge* 41: 105–19.

Kamarck, A. (1996) The World Bank: challenges and creative responses, in O. Kirshner (ed.) *The Bretton Woods–GATT System*, Armonk, NY: M.E. Sharpe.

Kennedy. P. and **Russett, B.** (1995) Reforming the United Nations, *Foreign Affairs* 74: 56–71.

Kotabe, M. and **de Arruda, M.** (1998) South America's free trade gambit, *Marketing Management* 7: 38–46.

Levitt, T. (1983) The globalization of markets, *Harvard Business Review*, May–June: 92–102.

Nicoll, W. and **Salmon, T.C.** (1990) *Understanding the European Communities*, Hemel Hempstead: Phillip Allan.

Ohmae, K. (1995) *The End of the Nation State*, London: HarperCollins.

Otto, D. (1996) Nongovernmental organisations in the United Nations system: the emerging role of civil society, *Human Rights Quarterly* 18: 107–41.

Owen, H. (1994) The World Bank: is fifty years enough?, *Foreign Affairs* 73: 97–108.

Polanyi, K. (1944) *The Great Transformation*, Boston, MA: Beacon.

Reisman, S. (1996) The birth of a world trading system: the ITO and GATT, in O. Kirshner (ed.) *The Bretton Woods–GATT System*, Armonk, NY: M.E. Sharpe.

Reuters (1999) Free trade widens rich–poor gap in Bangladesh, 15 February.

Saporito, B. (1998) Taking a look inside Nike's factories, *Time*, 30 March: 52–3.

Scholte, J. (1998) The IMF meets civil society, *Finance and Development* 35: 42–5.

Sissell, K. (1998) Canada rescinds MMT restrictions, *Chemical Week*, 29 July: 11.

Terpstra, V. and **David. K.** (1991) *The Cultural Environment of International Business*, 3rd edn, Cincinnati, OH: South Western Publishing.

The Economist (1997) Magnetic south, 4 January: 49.

The Economist (1998a) The sinking of the MAI, 14 March: 81–2.

The Economist (1998b) World trade: fifty years on, 16 May: 21–3.

The Economist (1998c) So legalise them?, 8 August: 32.

The Economist (1999a) The beef over bananas, 6 March: 65.

The Economist (1999b) Going bananas, 6 March: 20.

United Nations Handbook (1998). Wellington: New Zealand Ministry of Foreign Affairs and Trade.

Urquidi, V.L. (1996) Reconstruction vs development: the IMF and the World Bank, in O. Kirshner (ed.) *The Bretton Woods–GATT System*, Armonk, NY: M.E. Sharpe.

Weidenbaum, M.L. (1985) The UN as a regulator of private enterprise, *Notre Dame Journal of Law, Ethics, and Public Policy* 1: 341–65.

Wilkinson, A. (1999) Cause for concern, *Marketing Week*, 11 February: 28–31.

World Trade (1999) European Union moves ahead with Mexico trade pact, 12 January: 16.

Labour Standards, Corporate Codes of Conduct and Labour Regulation in International Trade

George Tsogas

Learning objectives

By the end of this chapter you will:

■ be familiar with the concept of international labour standards and their relationship with trade and corporate practices

■ have an understanding of the experiences in linking trade with the observance of labour rights

■ be aware of the ethical issues involved in the management of supply chains

■ appreciate some of the remedial options available to corporations.

Opening Case Study:
In defence of international reputations

Nike and Shell, two companies with strong global reputations, have recently been targets of international protest campaigns.

On 18 October pressure groups in the US organised a series of demonstrations worldwide against Nike's use of cheap labour in developing economies. Allegations of subsistence-level pay rates, worker intimidation and the use of child labour which have dogged Nike for several years culminated in this month's protest in 50 US cities and 11 countries. Shell faced public outrage in Europe in the summer of 1995 when its subsidiary tried to sink the obsolete

Brent Spar oil storage platform in the Atlantic Ocean . . . The Brent Spar fiasco was followed by international revulsion over the execution of Ken Saro-Wiwa, the Nigerian minority rights activist who had led a local protest movement against Shell in Ogoniland, in the heart of Nigeria's oil production region.

Both companies, used to thinking of themselves as model citizens, were taken aback – and are now rethinking how they deal with such issues.

While denying claims of exploitation and hostile working conditions at its factories in China, Vietnam and elsewhere, Nike is aware that the issues raised cannot be treated lightly . . . 'Our corporate image is our greater strength,' said a Nike spokesman.

Nike has reacted to the criticisms with a range of defensive measures designed to refute the claims while also protecting the company's public image. It joined the Apparel Industry partnership, a new group of clothing manufacturers that hopes to eradicate the use of sweatshops by enforcing an industry-wide code of conduct in their factories overseas . . . Shell is also having to respond on a wide-front. . . . In its revised statement of business principles published earlier this year, Shell for the first time said it supports 'fundamental human rights in line with the legitimate role of business.'

Source: Harverson and Carzine (1997).

Introduction

In this chapter we provide an introduction to and overview of labour standards and their relationship with international trade and corporate codes of conduct. We look at recent experience in the US and the UK. Key issues analysed include:

- the regulatory framework set by international trade regimes
- International Labour Organisation (ILO) conventions
- national legislation, including the North American Free Trade Agreement (NAFTA), and the Generalised System of Preferences (GSP) both in the European Union and US
- individual company codes of conduct.

Labour standards in a global economy

During the 1980s, advocacy for the inclusion of standards regarding conditions of employment in the regulatory framework of international trade relations gained momentum first in the US and then throughout the world in the 1990s. Even though the proposition for a 'social clause' in trade agreements is quite old (Hansson 1983: 11–29; Charnovitz 1986, 1987) it has acquired special significance nowadays, within the context of a global economy. Supporters of labour standards in international trade agreements claim that in a global economy, the rights of workers in developed countries can be safeguarded only when labour rights in less-developed countries are also protected (Faux 1990). Ensuring that social standards are 'harmonised' up, not down, is seen as a fundamental social challenge faced by advanced and developing countries as they become more economically integrated.

Advocates of labour standards emphasise that the international trade system is not without its rules. Just as these already include codes on intellectual property rights, market access and subsidies, they could also include rules on labour standards and environmental protection (Charnovitz 1992). Otherwise, they claim, there is a risk of a global race to the absolute minimum that could undercut employment standards and leave everyone worse off. For that purpose, labour standards legislation intends to ensure that the benefits of expanded international trade are fairly distributed.

The practical opportunity to achieve this goal arose with the establishment in 1995 of a global regulatory body for trade, the World Trade Organisation (WTO). A social charter that defines minimum labour standards and a procedure for enforcement could potentially be included. The International Labour Organisation (ILO) has also been considered as another possible forum. ILO Conventions and Recommendations (the 'International Labour Code') are a steadfast point of reference for international standardisation of conditions of employment. All discussions on labour standards in trade refer to ILO Conventions and Recommendations and all definitions of labour standards are based on this Code.

On the other hand, others argue that national development policy has priority over international requirements. The importance of foreign investment for national development results in demands for 'competitive' labour market structures, where wage levels, labour conditions and labour institutions have to adapt to the level of economic 'realities'. Industrialising countries' governments, and several others, are not convinced of the necessity for a social clause in trade. Disguised protectionism is the most common argument used against such a proposal. Currently, the debate is far from conclusive. The issues involved are many and complex (for a detailed discussion of the arguments, see Tsogas 1999).

Labour standards clauses in international trade agreements

The gained experiences from attempts or cases of successful implementation of a social clause in trade agreements fall into four categories: unilateral, bilateral, multilateral and regional (Tsogas 1999).

The unilateral approach includes national trade legislation, containing a social clause that covers all trade relations. Examples include legislation on imports produced by child or prison labour. Codes of conduct introduced by corporations to regulate employment standards in their suppliers could also be included, as policy measures taken unilaterally by a corporation and involving its intra-firm trade.

Examples of the bilateral track include the European Communities' labour standards clauses in its Generalised System of Preferences (GSP); and the inclusion of labour standards in US trade legislation, the most prominent of which are in the US GSP. The multilateral track includes attempts to incorporate a labour standards clause in the recently established WTO as well as GATT (General Agreement on Tariffs and Trade) that preceded it.

Finally, the regional track includes social clauses in regional trade agreements such as in the North American Free Trade Area (NAFTA) and the Social Chapter of the EU.

What are labour standards?

The most generally accepted labour standards in existing or proposed trade-related schemes include the following:

- freedom of association
- right to organise and collective bargaining
- minimum age for employment of children
- right to occupational health and safety
- prohibition of forced labour
- prohibition of discrimination in employment.

All these standards have as a common reference point relevant ILO Conventions: Convention No. 87 (freedom of association); No. 98 (right to organise and collective bargaining); No. 5 and 138 (minimum age for employment of children); 29 and 105 (forced labour); 111 (prohibition of discrimination in employment and occupation on the grounds of race, sex, religion, political opinion, etc.); and finally, various Conventions covering occupational safety and health.

These labour standards form a core of fundamental rights (see also Netherlands Advisory Council 1984; Teunissen 1986; van Liemt 1989). Core worker rights are based on human rights. These rights are provided for in the ILO Constitution and Conventions, as the ones identified above. They are fundamental principles that every human being is entitled to in their employment relationship. These are rights that men and women of all races and nationalities are equally entitled to and should be equally guaranteed of, regardless of their level of economic development.

Other labour standards, such as wages, hours of employment, length of holiday entitlement and other benefits reflect a country's level of development. These labour standards – unlike the basic labour/human rights – are and could remain different from country to country. It makes perfect sense, for example, to expect higher wages and longer annual holidays in the UK, than in India and Mexico and, in turn, in India and Mexico than in Haiti (Swinnerton and Schoepfle 1994: 53).

Labour standards in US trade legislation

In this section we review the extensive US experience in linking labour standards to international trade (see also Charnovitz 1986, 1987, 1992; Ballon 1987; Herzenberg 1988; Perez-Lopez 1988, 1990; Amato 1990; Compa 1993; Compa and Diamond 1996). Since 1983, the US Congress has introduced labour standards clauses in several trade legislative items. Of these, the most significant is the Generalised System of Preferences (GSP).

GSP permits duty-free entry in the US of selected products from designated developing countries on the premise that easier access to the US market would promote the economic development of these nations. Eligibility for GSP benefits depends on whether a country is respecting 'internationally recognised workers' rights'. The term includes:

- the right of association
- the right to organise and bargain collectively
- prohibition on the use of any form of forced or compulsory labour
- minimum age for the employment of children
- acceptable conditions of work with respect to minimum wages, hours of work, and occupational health and safety.

The law does not aim at bringing developing countries' standards up to the prevailing labour standards in the US, but rather to encourage developing countries to demonstrate respect for the internationally recognised worker rights of its workers (Perez-Lopez 1990: 224).

A petition and review process of workers' rights violations in beneficiary countries is in place. The first step in the process is the submission of petitions, by 1 June of each year, to the United States Trade Representative (USTR) requesting examination of workers' rights violations and the subsequent suspension of GSP privileges. It may be filed by 'any person', including an organisation or any interested party, who has 'a significant economic interest' in the subject of the petition for review (Amato 1990: 98). By 15 July the USTR announces the acceptance or denial of the petition. If the petition is accepted, public hearings, testimonies, and various investigations and consultations take place. Finally, by 1 April the following year, an official announcement has to be made to take effect from 1 July. These annual cycles have taken place since 1987.

Labour standards in the European Union's generalised system of preferences

The EU has operated its GSP since 1971. It offers preferential duty to a list of products from developing countries. Beneficiary countries include Asian NICs, Latin American, and East European countries and former Soviet Republics. Like the US, the European GSP is unilateral and requires no concessions from beneficiary countries (*Business Europe* 1994). A major reform of the GSP was carried out in 1994–5. The final text adopted included provisions for granting preferential treatment to countries that observe a core of labour standards (Council Regulation No 3281/94, Article 6). These standards are:

- International Labour Organisation Conventions No. 87 concerning freedom of association and protection of the right to organise

- No. 98 concerning the application of the principles of the right to organise and to bargain collectively
- No. 138 concerning the minimum age for admission to employment.

Total or partial temporary withdrawal of GSP tariff benefits (Council Regulation No 3281/94, Article 9{1}) may occur in cases of:

- practice of any form of *forced labour*
- export of goods made by *prison labour*.

From 1 January 1998 additional tariff concessions were granted to countries that have introduced and applied labour legislation regarding ILO Conventions Nos. 87 and 98 concerning freedom of association and protection of the right to organise and bargain collectively, and Convention No. 138 concerning minimum age for admission to employment. In order for GSP countries to take advantage of these lower tariffs, they must have taken measures to implement and monitor that legislation effectively.

Similarly to the US GSP, a review and consultation process is described. EU member states, individuals or associations may bring violations of the aforementioned standards to the attention of the Commission of the EU. A process of consultations, investigations and hearings takes place. At the end, the Commission may propose to the Council of Ministers – which has the final say – withdrawal of preferences.

Comparison of workers' rights provisions in the EU and US trade legislation

Inclusion of a social clause in the EU trade legislation has been very recent. Therefore, the effects and experiences that such incorporation would have brought are very limited, in comparison with those from the US. Nonetheless, both schemes favour unilateralism, either in the provisions of the law, or in actions resulting from its enforcement. They deal with labour standards provisions covering only developing countries, while leaving aside the issue of workers' rights in the US and the EU. They provide for sanctions before co-operation among all parties involved can be achieved. Indeed, there is no co-operation between European countries, the US and the beneficiary developing countries, and between the social partners themselves. There is no aim or any provisions to further both the economic and social progress of the developing countries.

In the US GSP the social partners do not appear at all. Trade unions are marginalised, at the roles of either the victim or the party who tries to ameliorate suffering (the 'petitioner' in the GSP review process). Employers appear only as the accused. The whole system is run and tightly controlled by the state apparatus. Politicians and unaccountable federal bureaucrats investigate the petitions, judge the merits of each case and execute unilaterally the decision, under a complete lack of transparent rules (other than US foreign policy considerations). The process is only influenced by lobbying from various interest groups. At the end, the US simply exercises its economic and political power over whomever government dislikes and whenever it deems appropriate to do so. Cooperation among *all* parties involved to correct abusive labour practices and promote growth and long-term development does not take place in the US practice.

In the newly introduced EU legislation, there is a clear, positive element of encouragement. The scheme is not just punitive in character but also rewards good labour standards practice. Moreover, it embraces internationally recognised ILO Conventions and international treaties and does not put forward its own selective interpretation of labour standards. On the other hand, the set of labour standards chosen is very narrow and a dual approach is followed. For a developing country to qualify for additional tariff concessions, freedom of association, the right to organise and bargain collectively and minimum age for employment are taken into account, whereas in cases of withdrawal of GSP privileges, only the use of forced or prison labour is considered. To that end, in a hypothetical scenario, a country that outlaws trade unions and collective bargaining may qualify for the same GSP status as one that respects all democratic freedoms, and as long as it does not use forced or prison labour it would continue to enjoy, uninterrupted, GSP privileges!

Furthermore, as in the US GSP, withdrawal of preferences is a political decision taken, in the case of the EU, by 'qualifying majority' in the Council of Ministers, where a small group of countries can block any action. The whole process is run by unelected EU bureaucrats. The involvement of the European Parliament is notably absent. However, all of the above remain to be seen how they will work in practice. It might possibly suffer from the same shortcomings of the American GSPs, plus some unique European ones. The social partners – unlike many other EU institutions – are absent from the GSP consultation process. As in the US, the system is open to excessive lobbying from various interest groups and bound to conduct its business away from public accountability. Its dual character sets a worrisome precedence. One of the basic ILO principles is the universality of its standards. The labour standards are the same for all countries regardless of the stage of development or the economic and political situation. A two-tier system has specifically and repeatedly been discouraged. The EU GSP – with all good purposes and intentions – seems to do exactly that.

 ### Exhibit 4.1 Bangladesh's garment industry sector gets a rude shock

There is concern that the industry will struggle to meet competitive challenges. The garment industry, which has almost single-handedly driven Bangladesh's export drive, recently received a rude shock – and a discomforting portent of things to come.

Canada last year removed cotton shirts from its list of items subject to quota restrictions under the Multi-Fibre Arrangement (MFA), which governs global garment trading. Seen from Dhaka, the effects were alarming. 'Almost 95 per cent of the orders straight away were switched to Chinese producers,' says Mostafa Golam Quddus, president of the Bangladesh Garment Manufacturers & Exporters Association (BGMEA). 'We lost out – and we're obviously concerned about this.'

Garment exports last year earned $3.5bn and, recovering from a dip caused by a row over point of origin certification with the European Union, are rising again at about 15 per cent annually. Mr Quddus sees growth reaching 20 per cent in coming years. Such growth has arisen partly because of a generous MFA quota and European Generalised System of Preferences (GSP) market access granted by virtue of Bangladesh's low-income status. It was aided, too, in the 1980s by a shift of trade from strife-torn Sri Lanka. But it was fuelled by industrious low-wage labour and smart, energetic entrepreneurs.

Today, the BGMEA embraces 2600 units ranging from workshops where rows of women at sewing machines cut and seam T-shirts beneath strip lights and ceiling fans, to companies turning over as much as $40m a year directly supplying US and European high street retailers. 'The garment sector is a leader in Bangladesh because it showed people how quickly things can happen here,' says Runa Alam, managing director of Union Capital, a Dhaka investment bank.

The sector has also effected significant social change, chiefly by drawing so many women into work – many from rural areas, most of whom had never previously been employed. Mr Quddus estimates that 90 per cent of the sector's 1.4m employees are women. The consequence for female 'empowerment' in an otherwise male-oriented Islamic society has been exhaustively documented by aid agencies and foreign donors, which see it as transforming their social and economic status, and with it Bangladesh's fertility rate. 'Before the garments industry, the husband used to beat his wife around the house,' is how Mr Quddus describes the social transformation. 'These days he's waiting for her after work in a rickshaw to take her home.'

There were uglier social effects, too, notably the high incidence of child labour in the industry. But the industry has concertedly addressed the problem under pressure from the US and Europe, coming some way towards solving what many garment manufacturers see as a foreign attempt to impose a non-tariff barrier to their surging exports.

The industry is also rebounding from a row with the EU over abuse of rules of origin certification. Duty-free access to the European market under its GSP rules require several degrees of local processing, and certified proof of yarn and fabric originating within Bangladesh for those gaining duty-free access under the scheme. In 1996, however, the EU opened an investigation into thousands of certificates of origin, having discovered exporters claiming GSP rights exceeding by five times the amount of yarn and fabric known to be produced in the country.

Bangladesh investigated the matter and blushingly conceded there had been widespread abuse. In a compromise, the EU has offered limited derogations from its GSP rules while Bangladesh has redoubled policing of the sector's paperwork. 'We hope and believe the problems are over,' says Michael Drury, European Commission ambassador in Dhaka.

Source: Financial Times CD-ROM, 1 January–31 December 1998.

Objectivity of the review process

Questions regarding the objectivity of the review and petition process arise in relation to the criteria employed by the petitioners, when selecting countries, on the one hand, and the US government, when judging the merits of each case, on the other.

Petitions have been filed by a plethora of trade union, solidarity and human rights organisations, but most come from a few sources. The detailed work, documentation and substantiated evidence required, in order for a petition to stand a good chance to be accepted, demand dedicated research staff and resources that only bigger organisations can afford. The criteria by which interested parties chose a country for petition have not always been transparent. Foreign policy considerations and economic nationalism have considerably affected the selection (or non-selection) of countries.

Further, the openness of a particular country to outside scrutiny, its political relationship with the US, and the links that any local trade unions or human rights organisations may have with international bodies can also be decisive. In 1986, Taiwan protested its selection for review as what it saw as a gross double standard with respect to the Chinese mainland (Amato 1990: 110). To that end, the more open or politically closer to the US developing countries are, the more likely they are to have their labour practices placed under scrutiny.

On the other hand, the unwillingness of various US administrations to accept for review even petitions against countries that have been well-known for human and worker rights violations, questions the objectivity and commitment to human and worker rights of the review process. The very few countries that were suspended from the GSP were done so either because their governments were not liked by the US (Nicaragua, Syria) or because their trade with the US was totally minimal (Romania, Paraguay, Burma, Central African Republic, Liberia, Sudan, Mauritania). From 1987 to 1990, petitions against El Salvador (at the highest point of civil strife and death squads' actions) were denied for review, while Nicaragua, under the Santinistas' government, was among the first country to be removed from the GSP programme, by the Reagan Administration, even though a US trade embargo was in full force.

But even if a petition is accepted for review, a simple promise on behalf of the foreign country's government, often coupled with intensive lobbying, or the introduction of some new legislation, with no guarantee for enforcement, can be enough for the USTR to declare that the country in question is 'taking steps' to comply with 'internationally recognised worker rights'. Major violators of worker rights who, for political and economic reasons, cannot be suspended or removed from the GSP programme, usually end up in this category

Under these circumstances, serious questions arise regarding the fairness and objectivity of the worker rights review procedure. The experience since 1985 has shown that worker rights considerations are usually at the bottom of the list of the US government agencies. 'National security' and economic interests overwhelmingly take precedence over concerns for human and worker rights. Inevitably, when such interests conflict, worker rights are yielded. No close ally of the US has ever been removed from the GSP programme regardless of their state of human and worker rights. Labour conditions in many countries were not placed under US government review, in spite of well-documented evidence of prosecutions against trade unionists and gross violations of human rights.

Labour standards in the North American Free Trade Agreement

This section examines a case where labour standards have been introduced in a regional trade agreement.

The North American Free Trade Agreement (NAFTA), signed in August 1992 between Canada, Mexico and the US, came into force on 1 January 1993. NAFTA – as its name suggests – is a regional trade agreement, where labour issues (as well as environmental) were included after substantial political debate and intensive campaigning. The Bush Administration, that negotiated the agreement, fiercely opposed any consideration of labour or environmental issues. Under pressure from organised labour and aware of the need to fulfil its electoral promise, the Clinton Administration negotiated the North American Agreement on Labor Cooperation (NAALC), commonly known as the NAFTA 'labour side agreement'. It came into effect on 1 January 1994.

The North American Agreement on Labor Cooperation

NAALC does not put forward any labour standards, nor does it provide for harmonisation of existing labour legislation. Signatory countries (Canada, the US and Mexico) undertake the responsibility simply to comply with and enforce their own labour laws fairly (NAALC, Articles 3–7). Each Party maintains its right 'to establish its own domestic labour standards, and to adopt or modify accordingly its labour laws and regulations' (NAALC, Article 2). But NAALC is the first trade agreement to establish contractual rights and obligations, with trade sanctions provisions, regarding violations of labour standards (see www.naalc.org).

Labour Standards in the NAALC

The NAALC provides for a National Administrative Office (NAO) in each country. The NAO is a forum for public input and the dissemination point for information on North American employment matters. Any interested organisation or person may request the NAO to examine any issues under the provisions of the NAALC in *another* NAFTA country.

Labour rights violations may result in different responses, depending on their nature. In terms of its treatment of violations of labour standards, the NAALC contains a dichotomy. On the one hand, it specifically defines a set of 'technical labour standards' (NAALC, Article 49{1}) which are related to:

- prohibition of forced labour
- labour protections for children and young persons
- minimum employment standards, such as minimum wages and overtime pay covering wage earners, including those not covered by collective bargaining agreements
- elimination of employment discrimination on the basis of grounds such as race, religion, age, sex, or other grounds as determined by each Party's domestic laws

- equal pay for men and women
- prevention of occupational injuries and illnesses
- compensation in cases of occupational injuries and illnesses
- protection of migrant workers.

That leaves aside a set of basic worker rights, described as:

- freedom of association and protection of the right to organise
- the right to bargain collectively
- the right to strike.

In cases where a NAFTA member state is involved in a 'persistent pattern of failure . . . to effectively enforce its occupational safety and health, child labour or minimum wage technical labour standards' then the NAALC provides for the implementation of an 'action plan' to remedy such violations (NAALC, Article 38). Failure by the country complained against to fully implement the 'action plan' will result in a monetary fine set at no greater than 0.007 per cent of the total trade in goods between the countries involved (NAALC, Annex). Such trade sanctions are, however, only applicable in cases of violations of the aforementioned 'technical labour standards'. *Violations of the basic worker rights do not carry any punitive sanction.* The 'penalty' in such serious matters is reduced to a series of consultations among the labour minister of the NAFTA countries.

The significance of labour regulation under NAFTA

The NAALC has introduced a new way to confront labour abuses by large corporations. It is indeed the very first time that the practical opportunity arises for an interested party to pursue a corporation for its activities, not only in the country where these took place, but also in a third country that maintains a trade relationship with the former. In the Sony case, for example, a Japanese corporation, with its regional headquarters in New Jersey, US is questioned for its labour practices in Mexico by a governmental body in the US.

However, the practical experience so far from the complaints procedure has demonstrated the extremely narrow scope and ineffectiveness of this legislation. The NAALC calls for what is essentially an obligation of any government: adherence to, and enforcement of, its own labour legislation. The procedural system for resolving disputes under the NAALC has demonstrated its inability to remedy violations of even the most fundamental labour rights such as freedom of association. The process itself is effort and time consuming and its outcome has been deemed to be morale-crippling for workers and trade unions.

Nevertheless, it has been acknowledged that NAFTA's labour side agreement can have some practical usefulness. The threat that a corporation can be dragged into a public hearing and its labour practices be exposed and receive media attention, can act as a deterrent.

The NAALC would have been a success story if workers, employers and governments in North America could feel that such an agreement has helped their economic and political advancement. In turn, that would have been achieved if, first, workers felt protected from the excessiveness of the market forces, through increased job security; second, employers felt content with a regulatory framework which would prohibit undercutting each other and would not jeopardise those who seek to promote sound human resource policies in their enterprises; and third, governments and political parties felt that the provisions of the agreement have actually helped economic progress and social stability.

The question, therefore, that arises is whether the first few years of operation of the NAALC have provided any encouraging signals. The answer is negative. Some corporations have managed to get away with violations of every fundamental worker right. Those employers who treat their workers as assets, not as mere human capital, would certainly have to lose if this downward spiral continues. Workers, their organisations and various grassroots movements have been left disappointed. Workers who were dismissed because of their activism, in most cases, have not been reinstated. Trade union democracy in Mexico is still in its infancy and government interference (on the employer side, of course) is still the norm. US workers have to fight for their legal right to join a union and bargain collectively while in practice their right to strike is severely curtailed. And to make matters worse, no political development from political parties and governments in North America that could alter this situation is expected.

Corporate codes of conduct

The emergence of global sourcing has drawn many manufacturers and retailers from developed countries into contact with suppliers operating at standards and in regulatory environments very different to those of their home markets. The developing world is now a producer not just of raw materials for European or US industry but of finished products which are manufactured at world standards but at wages which are a fraction of those payable in the industrialised countries and under conditions of employment which are often markedly worse. In a number of countries the freedom to join trade unions and bargain collectively is highly restricted, and union organisers and activists are subjected to serious harassment and violence. In Export Processing Zones (EPZs), some 845 of which are now operating worldwide, national labour law is often relaxed or weakly enforced as an additional inducement to inward investment (International Confederation of Free Trade Unions 1998).

The intensity of competition in some industries is such that once a company makes use of this vast reserve of workers, others must follow, leading to a proliferation of supplier countries and individual suppliers and a constant search for ever cheaper locations. Supply chains have become so complex that retailers and corporate buyers may often not even know precisely where goods are sourced and in many cases are ignorant of the employment standards prevailing in plants that supply them.

Price pressure and fashion cycles

In some industries, notably clothing, the price pressures that have led to global sourcing have combined with ever more rapidly changing fashion cycles to revive 'sweatshop' conditions in industrialised countries as well as drawing in new suppliers with low employment standards in developing countries. Both developments, combined with the huge financial investment in brand names, have made manufacturers and fashion retailers vulnerable to campaigners on child labour and related issues.

In the US in particular, garment companies and sportswear brands have been in the forefront of addressing these issues, but with varying degrees of success. Many major brands in the US and now in the UK accept that they have a corporate responsibility for the working conditions not only of their own employees but also of those engaged in the factories and workshops of their suppliers.

Social responsibility and business ethics

Up until the early-1990s, ethical issues have primarily been concerned with internal conduct (honesty, non-discrimination) and customer relations, with a growing role for the environment; few dealt with the ethical issues raised by the behaviour of the company and its subcontractors and suppliers. Employment issues – such as whether firms used child labour, complied with basic health and safety standards, or allowed employees to join trade unions – were not seen as corporate issues at all, but were kept at arm's length behind the veil of subcontracting. This began to change dramatically in the US in the early- and mid-1990s with the exposure of extensive labour abuses in the supply chains of some of the leading brand names in sportswear and fashion, both within the US and abroad.

Exhibit 4.2 **Ethical codes of practice 'not being implemented'**

Companies are failing to put into effect their well-meaning codes of ethical practice, for example, with widespread lack of protection for corporate whistleblowers, according to a survey published today.

The Institute of Business Ethics found more than half of the companies surveyed had a code of conduct or ethics, but in practice its content was often unknown to staff, customers and other stakeholders. Roderick Chamberlain, the institute's chairman, said: 'A code is a dead letter if it is not communicated. People must know about the code if it is to function properly – it must become part of the corporate culture. 'It is also worrying that external stakeholders – particularly suppliers and contractors – are not aware of the obligations imposed by these codes. Until they are, companies may have no real defence to offer if malpractice occurs,' he warned.

The IBE report says 'worryingly, almost half of the companies have either no procedures or inadequate ones in place to protect corporate whistleblowers, despite new legislation to encourage insiders to inform about illegal practices.' Some 30 per cent of companies have no formal whistleblowing procedures. Of those that do, 20 per cent have no arrangements to protect the informant's identity. Under new legislation, staff in companies without proper whistleblowing arrangements can obtain protection from reprisals if they raise issues of concern with the media directly.

Ian McCartney, British trade minister, is eager for companies to try harder to enforce codes of conduct. The survey of 178 of Britain's top 500 companies also found that although staff are usually required to comply with the terms of the code – and in 42 per cent of cases it is part of their conditions of employment – few companies involve employees in developing them. Some 30 per cent of companies fail to give a copy of their code to every employee, and only 11 per cent use staff surveys to help revise their code.

The survey says that external communication is also poor. Only one-third of companies make any public reference to their code, normally in the annual report. Three-quarters say they have codes because they wish to safeguard their reputations and two-thirds say they have introduced codes at the initiative of the chairman or chief executive. Social and ethical auditing are not widely seen as part of the solution, as only 5 per cent have had their behaviour audited in this way.

Source: Financial Times CD-ROM, 1 January–31 December 1998.

Several incidents achieved high media attention. Thai garment workers were discovered to be kept as virtual slaves in California; child labour was found to be used in making footballs in Pakistan or famous label brands in El Salvador; and a persistent campaigning has been sustained around Nike and its involvement in Indonesia and Vietnam.

Companies found themselves vulnerable to such exposure because of:

- their commitment to global sourcing to lower costs of production in a ferociously competitive market
- concerns on the part of trade unions, labour activists and development NGOs that global sourcing would lower standards and cut jobs in developed countries while doing little to remedy – or even encouraging – employment abuses in developing countries
- the emergence of the 'ethical consumer': sensitised to human rights and environmental issues, and seeing shopping on an ethical basis as a complement to (or substitute for) other forms of direct social activity
- access by NGOs to the broadcasting media: eager for popular, human-interest-focused stories and with hours of broadcasting time to fill
- rise of the internet and electronic communications which make direct access to large audiences possible at fairly low costs and allow rapid and effective campaigning with quick feedback.

Similarly, in Europe the widespread use of child labour for the production of footballs in Pakistan also caused a high public concern and promoted a number of initiatives to tackle child labour. Benetton was obliged to review its operations in Turkey following exposures of child labour in that country. In Germany, concern over child labour in rugmaking in India and Pakistan played a key role in launching the RUGMARK Initiative, which offers manufacturers an opportunity to label their products if they meet the scheme's criteria.

Impact on companies

The impact of campaigning on companies has not been easy to quantify in terms of revenue or sales lost. Claims that share prices are affected by campaigns have been difficult to sustain against the general turmoil of equity markets. This does not mean that there is *no* impact on company performance. Mismanagement of ethical issues can spiral out of control (as Shell and BP found out in their management of environmental issues), and can lead to consumer boycotts or brand avoidance.

Responding to risks posed to companies by the exposure of poor labour standards in their own plants and those of their suppliers has been viewed as prudent risk and reputation management by many companies in the US and the UK, often following an episode of 'crisis management'. The evidence so far is that many leading companies in the US, a number of large and influential corporations in the UK and some pioneers in mainland Europe are attempting to manage this turbulence by:

- understanding and managing their supply chains
- producing codes of conduct on employment standards for their operations and those of their suppliers
- appointing specialist staff to set up and monitor codes of conduct, or deploying existing specialists – primarily with sourcing or environmental management experience
- engaging with NGOs to address the issues and establish the means of verifying the implementation of their codes
- initiating remedial action.

On the other hand, some corporations simply do not care about ethical considerations at all. A minority would even regard the corporation as an inappropriate place for social accountability to rear its head. However, some businesses which have reluctantly gone down this path or sought to fend off NGO criticisms with aggressive counter-attacks have often ultimately been obliged to make a more constructive response.

Not just garments?

As yet, the focus of campaigning organisations has been on sectors with a proven record of human rights difficulties: garments, shoes, woven textiles and carpets, toys, sports goods, and some agricultural products. Some furniture-makers, such as the Swedish-based IKEA and the the UK retailer B&Q, have also initiated action.

However, a glance at the composition of exports from developing countries with a record of human rights violations shows that the 'Third World garment sweatshop' by no means exhausts the potential for difficulties in the international supply chain. Possible examples include:

- cut flowers and other horticultural products
- child labour in deep-sea and coastal factory-fishing
- electrical goods and automotive components
- products of the extractive industries, for example where children work in small-scale mines.

Points of caution

Companies will need to be very careful before embarking on what might be a substantial review of their operations and principles, and a commitment of resources to put in place a monitoring system. At present, the number of companies in the UK which have made a commitment to this remains small – both compared to those with global supply-chains and with activity and interest in the US. Some companies which have looked at their operations have found it is almost impossible for them to match all the calls placed on them – despite a willingness to bring about improvements.

Others are adamant in their refusal to discuss these issues, regarding it an open door to external interference and an intrusion into their commercial autonomy; they are more worried about maintaining margins and about retaining good suppliers. Anticipation of a disruptive ethical issue is sensible risk management – an ethical issue in the supply chain represents an unaccounted for 'contingent liability'. Planning is always better than crisis management.

Evidence from companies which have devoted resources to ethical sourcing has shown that there may be gains in efficiency and quality through the close attention to the supply chain implied by a 'social accountability' or 'ethical risk' review. Moreover, many managers and employees want to work in companies which are not rooted on abuses of labour standards. As employment relationships take on a larger role in the shaping of social life and attitudes, attending to ethical issues may just be 'doing the right thing' both morally and for the long-term coherence and survival of the business.

Proliferating campaigns and standards

The issue that therefore emerges is: what are the options available to the 'concerned' and proactive manager?

The response by NGOs, governments, sectoral associations and individual companies to this evolving environment has given rise to a proliferation of initiatives. There are currently numerous schemes in existence or proposed (see Tsogas and Incomes Data Services 1998).

Corporate codes of conduct, intended to regulate the behaviour, practices and standards of the participants in supply chains, have assumed a new prominence because of the problems in developing and enforcing effective trade-related regulation of labour standards (i.e. GSP, NAFTA). For the most part, codes have so far been embraced by retailers and owners of high-profile brands with their own manufacturing facilities in developing countries. Industrial manufacturers from the developed countries have generally not figured in the debate as yet, although, as we noted above, they have been found vulnerable under the NAFTA labour side agreement.

Codes represent one of the first steps companies can take when tackling the issue of how to respond to criticism of standards in their supply chains. Codes also allow companies to respond to the challenges of NGOs by initiating improvements immediately.

Codes may also be the *only* form of regulation that can be realistically developed in the medium-term, given the low probability that an effective, global trade-related regulatory framework (such as the one proposed at the WTO) will appear in the near future. However, scepticism about codes on the part of NGOs and trade unions means that in the late-1990s companies need to do more than simply issue a text without specifying effective means for *implementation* and *monitoring*, and some procedure for verifying that implementation is taking place.

It could be argued that corporate codes reflect:

- 'consumer choice', in that companies are responding to the demands of their customers for 'ethically-sourced' products
- 'purchaser choice', in that companies can source from where they like and on the conditions they can negotiate: for the supplier, they are the customer – and the customer is king.

Background

Although the modern phase of codes of conduct dates back to the late-1960s and 1970s, with various attempts to regulate the actions of transnational corporations, codes expressly aimed at regulating labour standards began to appear in the early-1990s in the US. The first such company code in the US apparel industry is thought to be that of Levi Strauss & Co, introduced in 1991 (US DoL 1996).

Since then there has been a proliferation of codes. Their style and format varies considerably. They tend to be general in character and are intended to convey a company's values externally, but may also be supported by more detailed documentation on particular issues which is used in the field by the group's employees when visiting suppliers.

The main components of codes of conduct are:

- prohibitions on child labour, either in terms of national law, their own definition or sometimes no precise definition
- prohibitions on forced or indentured labour
- prohibitions on discrimination based on race, religion or ethnic origin
- prohibitions on certain types of disciplinary practice (physical or psychological punishment or unreasonable fines)
- provisions on health and safety, both at the workplace and in some cases in employee accommodation
- provisions on pay, hours of work, rest breaks and time-off, and the regulation of overtime
- in some cases, provisions on the rights to organise and engage in collective bargaining.

The precise standards vary considerably. Some codes refer to the 'core' ILO Conventions (see above), some simply to compliance with local laws and regulations, while others make less specific provisions. Many codes contain a blanket provision requiring compliance with all applicable national laws and regulations. The bulk of existing codes in the US and UK seek to base themselves on the core ILO Conventions, either expressly or at least by using the same broad language. However, a number have been criticised for vagueness or the deliberate selection of criteria which minimise the impact on their operations.

The business response: is there 'one best way'?

Experience so far suggests that different sectors and different types of business need different approaches. As we note in the case study below, whereas a large company – such as Levis or C&A – can commit the resources to take an independent path, smaller enterprises have been looking for an acceptable external standard and external forms of support. Whether such standards and support can be delivered remains to be seen.

Chapter summary

This chapter has introduced a framework for the study of labour standards in international trade agreements. It reviewed the experience in Europe and the US and focused on corporate codes of conduct. It presents the case of C&A and the way it has chosen to respond to the issues and the internal capacities and competences it has developed.

Discussion questions

1 Which are the labour standards internationally recognised as fundamental?
2 What is the significance of the labour 'side agreement' of NAFTA for an international business operating in North America?
3 Define a corporate code of conduct. What does it include as far as labour standards are concerned?

Closing Case Study:
The C&A Approach

C&A began to develop an explicit policy on social standards in its relations with suppliers during 1996, after a period in which it had begun to become aware of the potential problems for its reputation and practices of increased global sourcing. During 1996/97 it also engaged in discussions with a number of NGOs, including Oxfam in the UK. The company had had a code of practice for dealing with its suppliers since the 1970s, and also had a code of conduct for executives. C&A has not traditionally been a company with an open culture of information towards the outside world, and the decision to respond to external criticism with more public statements of policy and practice was not an easy one to take. The policy has been championed by the Head of Corporate Communications, who is the public face of C&A on ethical trading issues.

C&A moved to a formal Code of Conduct for the Supply of Merchandise in 1996, at the same time developing a database of all its suppliers and issuing compliance forms to them. The code sets out C&A's policy on supplier relationships, emphasising its desire to 'develop long-term business relationships'.

▶

Specifically, the Code:

- bans the exploitation of child labour or other vulnerable groups, such as illegal immigrants
- bans forced labour or labour which involves physical or mental abuse
- requires pay and benefits to be 'fully comparable with local norms' and to comply with local laws and 'conform with the general principle of fair and honest dealing'
- requires suppliers to ensure that all manufacturing processes are carried out under conditions which have 'proper and adequate' regard for the health and safety of those involved.

The Code was amended in May 1998 to include a provision on freedom of association. There is also a general clause stating the company's commitment to 'comply fully with the legal requirements of the countries' in which C&A operates, an injunction which also applies to the company's suppliers.

Monitoring

The outstanding innovation which C&A introduced was the development of a sophisticated internal mechanism for monitoring and ensuring compliance. Monitoring suppliers' standards was easier in the past when many of the suppliers delivering to C&A produced in Western Europe. This is no longer the case. Almost all suppliers based in the European countries now produce offshore, in the Far East, India, Africa or East European countries. It is also common for a European-based supplier or importer to use more than one production facility. Because buyers could not be expected to visit every factory and because of the need to separate the tasks of social audit from other business relationships with suppliers, C&A established a specialised unit – SOCAM – in March 1996 to audit production facilities on an arms-length but internal basis. This separated the social audit function from the broader management of the company's sourcing arrangements, which are carried out through its sourcing operation, called Mondial.

SOCAM has its co-ordinating office in Brussels and has set up offices in Singapore, Hong Kong and Madras. SOCAM stands for 'Service Organisation for Compliance Audit Management'. SOCAM has full and independent authority to monitor the standards which are defined by C&A's Code of Conduct and the legally binding requirements contained in every merchandise order. SOCAM is structured so as to be fully independent of the buying function.

SOCAM auditors use a standard questionnaire containing detailed requirements transposing the principles embodied in the code of conduct. All information on production facilities provided by C&A to SOCAM is used by SOCAM only, and only SOCAM staff have access to SOCAM's database. C&A requires all its worldwide suppliers to disclose the factories they produce in – or intend to produce in – for C&A. Since June 1997, C&A has refused to trade with any supplier who has not disclosed all their production units producing for C&A. The company also endeavours to establish whether its suppliers are using subcontractors, and trains its auditors to be aware of this possibility. The Sourcing Department has confirmation letters from every C&A supplier throughout the world that they will permit SOCAM to make unannounced visits at any time to factories that are being used to make merchandise for C&A. Managements of these factories are required to inform their employees that they must allow SOCAM immediate access, irrespective of whether the manager of the factory is present or not. If auditors are subject to deliberate delay, C&A will take the appropriate actions against the relevant supplier.

SOCAM's co-ordinating office advises the auditors based in Europe and Asia which production units should be visited. All visits are surprise visits made without any prior announcement. SOCAM auditors assess the factory in regard to working conditions, exploitation of child labour and any other form of unacceptable practices. When a production unit gives cause for concern SOCAM will audit in more detail and will issue a detailed report covering all aspects in regard to: data on the factory and its employees; the appearance of the factory (working conditions, safety, toilet, washing and canteen facilities); and whether C&A merchandise was being produced during the time of visit. If the auditors find under-aged workers, those findings will be supported by photographs, age certificates (birth/school certificates, identity cards, medical proof, etc.). All observations are sent in a comprehensive report to the SOCAM co-ordinating office in Brussels. On the basis of these reports SOCAM will inform the C&A Sourcing Department and make recommendations.

The SOCAM auditing team makes annually over 1000 unannounced visits to production units. In addition the SOCAM management team, based in Brussels, annually visits 150 of the largest and most important suppliers to explain SOCAM's strategy and C&A's company philosophy in detail. SOCAM also sees its task as one of educating suppliers and making them aware of their responsibilities in ensuring that merchandise is produced within C&A's code of conduct as well as in accordance with local labour legislation.

SOCAM is managed by a single director who co-ordinates all its activities from the office in Brussels. Apart from the secretarial support, all members of the company – including the director – are actively involved in making unannounced audits of production units which make merchandise for C&A. All the auditors previously worked for C&A or the Mondial organisation which co-ordinates C&A's buying. They have extensive and detailed experience of the garment industry throughout Europe, the Far East and the Indian subcontinent. The auditors spend 95 per cent of their time visiting production units. Those who have the best knowledge of local conditions tend to make the audits for those countries. Visits involving mostly female workforce will be carried out using a female member of staff where possible.

C&A expects and requires that every executive should take a direct and personal responsibility for the quality of the resources they use. The primary responsibility therefore rests with a very large number of executives throughout the company. SOCAM then has the responsibility of providing support and back-up in the form of audits and other activities such as additional briefings for suppliers.

Infringements of the code of conduct

Should suppliers be found to have infringed the Code of Conduct SOCAM informs C&A's Sourcing Department and then decides on the actions to be taken. These can be: permanent termination of business; termination of business for a certain period of time; cancellation of orders produced under infringing conditions; cancellation of all outstanding orders; and suspension of business. Any decision to restart business relations at a later stage depends on the supplier presenting a convincing corrective plan which would avoid future infringements of the code.

▶

In the company's view, experience has shown that for every unannounced visit made by SOCAM, there are many other suppliers in the area who become aware that visits can happen without warning. Equally, every supplier with whom business is stopped has served as a warning to all other suppliers, creating a powerful 'multiplier effect' which is likely to have a cumulative impact.

Source: Tsogas and IDS (1998: 109–12).

Questions

1 What does the C&A Code of Conduct for the Supply of Merchandise contain?
2 Why are issues of quality control and assurance separated institutionally from those of social auditing?
3 How are the monitoring and auditing functions performed?
4 To what extent could the monitoring and auditing process satisfy demands from NGOs and activists for an independent third-party verification? How could you, in the position of a C&A executive, defend your company's approach?
5 Do you think the C&A example can readily be followed by other corporations? If so which ones?

Further reading

Tsogas, G. and **Incomes Data Services** (1998) *Corporate Codes of Conduct and Labour Standards in Global Sourcing*, London: IDS and Cardiff Business School. This gives an overview of the main issues involved, explores the remedial options on offer and looks at the capacities and competences companies need to develop.

References

Amato, T.A. (1990) Labor rights conditionality: United States Trade Legislation and the International Trade Order, *New York University Law Review* 65: 79–125.

Ballon, I.C. (1987) The implications of making the denial of internationally recognized worker rights actionable under section 301 of the Trade Act of 1974, *Virginia Journal of International Law* 28(1): 73–127.

Business Europe (1994) World labour rights and the EU, 34(16): 1–2.

Charnovitz, S. (1986) Fair labor standards and international trade, *Journal of World Trade Law*, January–February: 61–78.

Charnovitz, S. (1987) The influence of international labour standards on the world trading regime. A historical overview, *International Labour Review* 126(5): 565–84.

Charnovitz, S. (1992) Environmental and labour standards in trade, *The World Economy* 15(3): 335–56.

Compa, L. (1993) Labor rights and labor standards in international trade, *Law and Policy in International Business* 25(1): 165–91.

Compa, L. and Diamond, S. (1996) *Human Rights, Labor Rights and International Trade.* University of Pennsylvania Press.

Council Regulation (EC) No 3281/94 of 19 December 1994, Applying a four-year scheme of generalised tariff preferences (1995 to 1998) in respect of certain industrial products originating in developing countries, *Official Journal* No. L 348, 31/12/94.

Council Regulation (EC) No 11541/98 of 25 May 1998, Applying the special incentive arrangements concerning labour rights and environmental protection in Articles 7 and 8 of regulations (EC) No 3281/94 and (EC) No 1256/96 applying multiannual schemes of generalised tariff preferences in respect of certain industrial and agricultural products originating in developing countries, *Official Journal* No. L 160, 4/6/98.

Faux, J. (1990) Labor in a Global Economy, *Dissent,* Summer: 376–82.

Hansson, G. (1983) *Social Clauses and International Trade,* London: Croom Helm.

Harverson, P. and Carzine, R. (1997) In defence of international reputations, *Financial Times,* 31 October.

Herzenberg, S.A. (1988) Institutionalizing constructive competition: international labor standards and trade, Washington, DC: US Department of Labor, Bureau of International Affairs. Economic Discussion Paper 32.

International Confederation of Free Trade Unions (1998) *Annual Survey of Violations of Trade Union Rights 1998,* Brussels: ICFTU.

International Labour Review (1988) Labour and Social Issues Relating to Export Processing Zones, Geneva: ILO.

NAALC (1993) North American agreement on labor cooperation between the government of the United States of America, the government of Canada and the government of the United Mexican States, 13 September.

Netherlands Advisory Council for Development Cooperation (1984) *Recommendation on Minimum International Labour Standards,* The Hague, Netherlands: Ministry of Foreign Affairs.

Perez-Lopez, J.F. (1988) Conditioning trade on foreign labor law: the US approach, *Comparative Labor Law Journal* 9(2): 253–92.

Perez-Lopez, J.F. (1990) Worker rights in the US Omnibus Trade and Competitiveness Act, *Labor Law Journal,* April: 222–34.

Swinnerton K.A. and Schoepfle, G.K. (1994) Labor standards in the context of a global economy, *Monthly Labor Review* 117(9): 52–8.

Teunissen, Hans J.J. (1986) Recommendation on minimum international labour standards, *The American Journal of International Law* 80: 385–6.

Tsogas, G. (1999) Labour standards in international trade agreements: a critical assessment of the arguments, *International Journal of Human Resource Management* 10 (2): 351–75.

US Department of Labor [Bureau of International Labor Affairs] (1996) The *Apparel Industry and Codes of Conduct: A Solution to the International Child Labor Problem?*, Washington DC: US Department of Labor.

van Liemt, G. (1989) Minimum labour standards and international trade: would a social clause work? *International Labour Review* 128(4): 433–48.

Part III Internationalisation of Firms

CHAPTER 5
Internationalisation of the Firm

Pervez Ghauri

Learning objectives

By the end of this chapter you will:

■ be able to understand why companies go abroad

■ comprehend how the decisions are made with regard to market selection

■ understand whether internationalisation decisions are fully made by the companies or dictated by changes in the environment

■ understand different theories and approaches to the internationalisation process.

Opening Case Study:
Germany's once-mighty industrial machine starts to misfire

The cogs of Germany's famous industrial machine, long the engine of its economic prosperity, are whirring a little less briskly, and Josef Gerstner, an industrialist from Germany's south-western Palatinate region, knows why. 'Markets are moving away from Germany, away from Europe. And Germany has problems, high salaries, long vacation times, which means companies like mine that want to grow go to other countries.'

When even a traditionally German company like Mr Gerstner's is talking about shifting production abroad, then Germany really does have problems. Over the past three years, his company, KSB, which makes industrial pumps, has laid off 1200 workers at its German plants while hiring 200 in Brazil, India and the US. 'We now want to grow, but this will be in Asia-Pacific and America, the most important markets for us,' he said.

Mr Gerstner's KSB exemplifies an important and dangerous phenomenon for Germany. German companies still boast the discipline, precision and engineering skills which powered the nation's postwar industrial renaissance.

But increasingly they are finding that Germany is no longer an attractive place to do business, because of its slow economic growth and high labour costs. In

▶

response, they are moving their jobs abroad. The result is a painful national paradox: while German industry is arguably stronger than ever before, assuming leading positions globally, Germany itself and the nation's army of unemployed are not reaping the benefits. 'Many German companies have been strong in internationalising their production. German companies are doing very well, the major players are making big profits, but this is not so good for Germany as a manufacturing centre,' said Hans-Gunther Vieweg, industrial economist at the Ifo research institute in Munich.

The giants of German industry, such as car groups Daimler-Benz and Volkswagen and chemicals group Hoechst, are also shifting their focus abroad. VW has factories in South America and has moved swathes of Western European car production to cheaper Eastern European and Spanish plants. Daimler-Benz opened its first US car factory, in Alabama, last year. Siemens, the big engineering group, now earns two-thirds of revenues from foreign markets and has more than half of its employment abroad.

There are two main explanations for this corporate exodus. The first has to do with the explosive expansion of foreign markets, especially compared with Germany's own sluggish economy. 'The most important market for us is the Asia-Pacific region, even with the crisis. This is growing by 7 per cent each year. In Germany it is less than 1.5 per cent,' said Mr Gerstner.

As a result, industrialists such as Mr Gerstner find it profitable to move their factories abroad to be closer to rapidly growing foreign markets. By contrast, economic growth in Germany has been slow. Even now, with a gradual upturn, the engine of growth is outside Germany's borders: the slightly improved economic performance has been driven by a surge in exports. Meanwhile at home, unemployment is stuck above 4m.

The second reason for the shift is the high cost of doing business in Germany. Workers are sheltered by powerful trade unions and an extensive and expensive welfare state. Wages are high and rigid, set according to a creaking national pay-bargaining system, and working hours are strictly regulated.

Source: *Financial Times* CD-ROM, 1 January–31 December 1998.

Introduction

In international business research, the area of decision making for going abroad has attracted considerable attention. As a result, a number of controversial views have been put forward. Do firms make well-calculated decisions to go abroad or are they forced by environmental factors to go international? The relationship between a firm's decision to go international and how a particular market is served is an interesting issue. The conditions under which a firm will choose to go to a particular market or in a particular way – export, licensing or manufacturing – influence the decision-making process (Buckley and Ghauri 1999a).

In earlier studies on international business, a foreign investment decision was considered a complex social process influenced by social relationships both within and outside the firm. In his classical work, Aharoni (1966) provided a rich description of individual and organisational behaviour over time and showed the crucial effect of perception and uncertainty in the course of this process.

The first elements to analyse for a decision process for internationalisation are the organisation and the environment in which the decision is to be made. An organisation has an established strategy, procedures and operating policies, which involve individuals with different aspirations and goals. The goals and policies of an organisation influence the behaviour of its individuals, which in turn influences the reactions of these individuals towards the environment. The relationships of these individuals within and outside the organisation also influence these decisions.

Decision to go international

Here we first discuss how the decisions to go abroad are made and discuss the factors that influence these decisions. Then we present and discuss some theoretical developments on the internationalisation of the firm. Finally, we present the different methods through which a particular foreign market is served.

Time, uncertainty, the goals of the decision-makers and environmental constraints are important elements in the decision-making process. For a decision to go international, it first has to be realised that it is worthwhile to go abroad, only the expected high profit is not enough. Moreover, decisions are often made out of existing alternatives or those that emerge out of previous experience or research and development. In the case of the first international experience or entry, there are some factors that push the organisation toward internationalisation. These factors can be divided into two categories: one coming out of the organisation and the individuals working in the organisation and the second coming from the environment. In the first category the factors include the ambitions and goals of individuals and the organisation as regard to resources, capabilities and strategies. The second category relates to environments at home and in the foreign market such as tax, regulations, legal requirements, financial considerations, the type of industry, investigation costs and potential profit possibilities.

Generally, the first decision to go abroad is a specific one. It is a decision to look at the possibility of a specific investment in a specific country, not a general decision to look around the globe for investment opportunities. At this stage the organisation has no experience with the complexities of foreign investment, although it has often had some export experience. There are no standard operating guidelines which can be given to deal with these complexities. What is needed most is a strong push and/or commitment to go abroad. A company benefits from these earlier experiences in its subsequent investment decisions. The organisational factors include:

- the role of management
- the motives of the organisation
- success at home.

Other than these internal forces, a number of factors in the environment, outside the organisation, may also force a company to go abroad. These drivers of internationalisation may include:

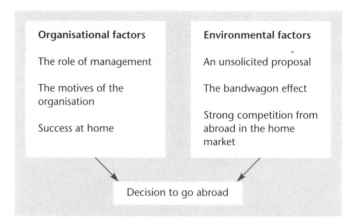

Figure 5.1 Factors influencing the decision to go abroad

- unsolicited proposal that cannot be ignored. These may include proposals from a foreign government, distributor or customer;
- competitive drive or *bandwagon* effect following other competitors or a general belief that presence in a certain market is a **must**;
- strong competition from abroad in the home market.

Normally, a combination of internal and external factors is the reason behind a decision to go abroad. Although it is sometimes possible to explain investment in a certain market with one of the above factors, e.g. a number of investments in China can be directly related to the bandwagon effect, it is generally not possible to pinpoint one particular force behind a particular investment decision.

When a decision is to be made for a subsequent investment abroad, the experience gained from the earlier ones helps, and gradually someone is given the task to head the so-called international division. The creation of such a division drives the organisation towards increasing commitment and expansion in international operations.

Organisational factors

The role of management

The ambitions and dynamism of management are considered the most important factors in a decision to go abroad. Internationalisation demands an active and committed management. This is particularly true in the initial stages of internationalisation. A fundamental strategic decision has to be made for going international. This is often done at the higher levels of management, quite often at President or Vice-President level. Top management has first to become aware of the opportunities in the international market place, but an international business orientation develops over time. A change in Chief Executive Officer, President or Vice-President can often bring in individuals who already have an international orientation.

One major factor that influences individual commitment towards internationalisation is special knowledge about a particular market or foreign customers in a market. Such motivation can result from a particular insight of a manager gained through earlier experience or background. This can lead to an enthusiastic drive toward international business activities. It can also be a reflection of a genuine entrepreneurial motivation, a desire for continuous growth and expansion of the business. Although management, in many firms, is much too occupied with short-term immediate problems than in long-term planning for expansion and internationalisation, more and more managers are discovering the value of going international. Managers who have lived abroad and are bilingual, are interested in foreign cultures and particularly interested in exploring business opportunities abroad.

Top management can also influence this through employing new staff with such backgrounds and interests. Managers want to be part of a firm that is internationally recognised. In other words, the more international a firm is, the more chances it has to attract managers who are internationally oriented.

Motives of the organisation

There can be several reasons why a firm chooses to go abroad. A number of factors, in fact, work both ways, as a motive as well as a constraint. For example, as there are increasing returns to scale in many activities, companies tend to operate only in one market to achieve these economies of scale. However, if the economies of scale are related to production or transportation and the size of the market, it creates incentives for firms to operate in more than one market to offset production. This also leads to the fact that production or some parts of the production are moved to the least cost location. For example, the location of R&D will depend on the regional differences in the price of the most important non-traded input skilled labour. Another important factor is that MNCs normally function in imperfectly competitive markets. That means the companies tend to move to the areas or markets where they can force down or control prices. In short, the motives of companies going abroad can be categorised in three main motives; market seeking, efficiency seeking and resource seeking.

Market seeking
Many companies go international rather proactively seeking new markets for their products and services. This is done for many reasons such as profit advantage, unique product, patents, exclusive market information and tax benefits. A firm normally perceives the international market as a potential source of higher profits quite often because of the size of the market. A number of companies go to emerging markets with a big population for this reason. Markets such as China, India and Brazil have thus been popular countries for many companies. The size factor for these three markets, as compared to the US – the largest homogenous market in the Western world – is presented in Table 5.1.

Despite the uncertainty and Asian crisis, MNEs have no choice than to enter these markets as the consumer base of hundreds of millions is emerging in these markets. A huge middle class, with an appetite for most Western-styled products, has attracted many companies to these markets. Companies like McDonald's, Nestlé, Unilever and Procter & Gamble are some of the companies that derive a major part of their revenues from these markets. However, companies need to calculate their customer base more carefully. The total population of a country

Table 5.1 Market size of the three biggest emerging markets as compared to the US

Product	China	India	Brazil	United States
Televisions (million units)	13.6	5.2	7.8	23.0
Automobiles (million units)	1.6	0.7	2.1	15.5
Pharmaceuticals (billion $)	5.0	2.8	8.0	60.6
Detergent (million tons)	3.5	2.3	1.1	3.9
Shampoo (billion $)	1.0	0.8	1.0	1.5
Power (megawatt capacity)	236,542	81,736	59,950	810,964

Source: Based on Prahalad and Liberthal (1998).

can be misleading. For example, China with a population of 1.2bn or India with a population of 925m might have only 20–30 per cent of the population that can afford Western products such as shampoos, cosmetics or cars such as Ford Escort or VW Golf. In India, the most popular middle-class car is Maruti (Suzuki), selling for less than $10,000. Fiat, for example, has developed a special low price and simpler car, Palio, for the emerging markets of Brazil and India. This small car is more robust and will sell at around $9000.

Efficiency seeking

Experience has shown that a number of companies move to certain markets seeking for efficiencies in their production or distribution. Philips' move of consumer electronics and semi-conductors to Singapore and Malaysia is one such example. These two countries have over the years specialised in the efficient production and development of these products. Any company working in this product category can take part in the development of these fast-moving products. In the same way, a number of Scandinavian and American companies have opened their distribution and logistic centres in The Netherlands. The availability of an efficient port, the skilled and English-speaking labour force and closeness to the EU market are some of the reasons behind these moves.

Resource seeking

The third type of market entry is often dependent on the availability of a certain resource or input in a certain market. Most oil companies have invested in oil refineries in the Middle East for this reason. In the same way, several textile producers and fashion houses from Hennes & Maurits to Marco Polo and Mexx have opened production units in India and Pakistan as these are two major cotton-producing countries.

Success at home

When a firm has been successful in the domestic market, growth is its natural course. This success at home also drives the firm to grow beyond its domestic market, because it has been encouraged by success itself. This is particularly true in the present time of globalisation where most products are demanded in most countries almost simultaneously. Companies like Ericsson and Nokia might have started as domestic companies in Sweden and Finland but their success at home has led these companies to foreign markets. This factor can also influence the behaviour of managers in gaining more confidence in their product and firm and in pursuing higher growth. The success of a product at home can also create additional resources in the company thus enabling it to spend more efforts on foreign markets. It will attract new people with fresh ideas and ambitions.

Exhibit 5.1 A range of ties for all occasions

Ermenegildo Zegna is a classic example of one of those highly successful family companies that are sometimes called the 'hidden champions' of the Italian economy. But in recent weeks, the four-generation-old north Italian textile and exclusive men's clothing manufacturer has been forced out of its hiding in the Piedmontese Alps and thrown into the international limelight, all because of one of its ties.

For the now world famous blue and gold diamond-shaped tie that Monica Lewinsky gave US President Bill Clinton was made by Zegna. Overnight, Zegna became a household name in the US and around the world. At first, the company was tempted to cash in on this free advertising bonanza. However, discretion prevailed. 'It all took us completely by surprise,' says Paolo Zegna, joint Chief Executive with his cousin, Gildo. 'We decided not to reproduce the tie or launch into a publicity campaign. It's simply not our style,' he explains.

Zegna's style is to manufacture top quality textiles and an expanding line of men's clothing from its traditional made-to-measure suits to a growing range of sports and casual wear. Started in 1910, it has been a remarkable family story of steady expansion into world markets. About 75 per cent of its annual revenues of £875bn last year came from overseas sales. 'North America accounts for 40 per cent of our sales, Europe another 40 per cent and Asia 20 per cent,' says Gildo Zegna. The company not only has shops all round the world but a strong manufacturing presence in Switzerland and Spain and plants in Turkey and Mexico.

The advent of the new single European market does not worry Gildo Zegna. 'We are well prepared,' he says. 'For a long time we have internationalised ourselves as well as diversifying ourselves to create a global collection without undermining our traditional quality.'

Zegna's internationalisation was pushed by the third generation: Angelo and Aldo, the fathers of Gildo and Paolo. 'They realised we were based in a small country and that the only way to grow was to go overseas,' Gildo says.

Already in the 1960s, Zegna established a trading company. In the 1970s, it embarked on a multinationalisation of its operations to ensure 'that not all our eggs were in the same basket,' says Gildo. At the time, Italy was rocked by labour strife and Zegna decided to invest in production facilities in Spain and Switzerland. In addition, four plants in Spain employ about 1,000 people. 'Spain was an excellent market for tailors and we felt it could become a little

Italy for our business,' says Gildo. Spain also opened up prospects for the Latin American market now strengthened by the Mexico plant.

Another important turning point for the company and its internationalisation came in the 1980s. Zegna decided to develop its own strong retailing presence by opening shops to move even closer the traditional textile operations to the final customer. 'The first shop was opened in Paris, not Milan, as a showcase,' says Paolo Zegna. 'Milan followed in 1985 but we soon realised it was not just a showcase but had potential to become a good business.'

Zegna now has nearly 250 shops worldwide – from Beijing to Beverly Hills, from Tokyo to Beirut. These shops, coupled with the company's expanding men's wear collection, have been behind a doubling in annual revenues over the past four years. Clothes now make up the bulk of the company's sales with the traditional textile operations accounting for less than 15 per cent of annual revenues. Yet the two Zegna joint chief executives insist that this sharp growth would in no manner compromise the company's traditional emphasis on quality. 'We will continue to control everything in-house, avoid licensing and maintain our focus on top quality men's wear. We want to develop even closer relations with our customers worldwide to provide them with quality of product and service,' says Gildo.

An example of this approach is Zegna's recent decision to offer customers next year not only made-to-measure suits but also made-to-measure ties. 'They will be able to choose their material and design, the length and width they want,' he explains. Presumably this means that, if they really want, customers will be able also choose their own variation of the famous – perhaps infamous – Clinton tie.

Source: *Financial Times* CD-ROM, 1 January–31 December 1998.

Environmental factors

As explained in Figure 5.1, other than the organisational factors, a number of factors in the external environment play a role in a company's internationalisation decisions. These factors include an unsolicited proposal, the bandwagon effect and strong competition from abroad in the home market (Aharoni 1966).

Unsolicited proposal

Generally it is very difficult to point out one factor as the reason for a decision to go abroad. The decision depends on a number of factors or events, such as knowledge of a market, unique product or a company's commitment. A number of studies have pointed out that an unsolicited order plays an important role in the initial internationalisation activities of a firm.

Once an outside proposal by a foreign firm, distributor, customer or government arrives in a company the first decision to be made is whether to take this proposal seriously or not. Sometimes a company rejects such a proposal only because it comes from abroad. But if it decides to take it seriously, it shows that the firm is at least not against going abroad and then a decision is made to do some research or investigation. In such an investigation a particular market is considered on its own merits rather than as a choice among many markets. Here the initial force or proposal also plays a role in the investigation and provides information convincing the company to go ahead with the proposal. In such a case not only the market but also the provider (initiator) is investigated. Two factors are particularly investigated: the risk involved and the market potential.

Because of the lack of knowledge about the market and the lack of experience of international activities, it is generally believed that in some countries the risk is higher. The countries situated far away through physical or psychic distance are often considered more risky. In such a case, depending on the organisational factors, discussed earlier, a decision is made not to enter into this venture as it would take a lot of management time, or because the individual or the organisation is not motivated enough. The nature of risk may vary in different markets ranging from unstable government to a lack of infrastructure or foreign exchange risk.

As for market potential, estimates are made as to the existence and size of the market segment for the firm's products, cost and income levels and the availability of basic requirements such as distribution channels, etc. The more a company gets involved in these investigations, the more it feels committed to the market. It is thus important that a quick decision is made at an early stage about the attractiveness of the market. In reality it has been shown that sometimes the decision to go to a particular market has already been made before the investigation is started. In such cases, the investigation can still reveal additional information, which forces the company to reverse the initial decision. The fact, however, remains that starting and doing an investigation creates commitments as some investment is made to do these investigations. The people involved feel more and more committed to the idea of going international. The commitments or investments are not only financial but also psychological and emotional.

The bandwagon effect

As most industries today are of oligopolistic nature, the prices and outputs of firms are interdependent and independent actions result in uncertainty concerning competitive position of an individual firm. No matter what a firm does, in such a competitive situation, the other firms are cognisant of that firm's actions on their own competitive position. Any decision by one company on a new product or on internationalisation, entering a specific market, induces a chain reaction in other firms towards similar actions. An internationalisation decision by one firm is thus followed by similar moves by other leading firms in that industry. When one firm establishes its office or manufacturing in a lucrative market, other firms realise they have to do the same, as they fear that otherwise they might lose their overall competitive position (Schnitzer *et al.* 1985).

Companies competing with each other keep an eye on each others' activities. The successful activities of one firm in a particular market induce other firms in the same line or in a related business to enter that market. Some markets are also considered a must for a company to demonstrate its competitive strength or positioning. A number of Western firms' entrance into China, when it opened its doors, is a very good example. In the early years, late 1980s, before the Tiananmen Square incident, companies and executives used to brag about their entrance into the Chinese market. The same type of rush was experienced in bigger Eastern European and ex-Soviet markets. A number of firms later had to get out of these markets because of risks, heavy losses and no profits in sight. Philips' move out of Russia in 1998 is one example.

A number of studies have revealed that companies often go abroad following not only their competitors but also their customers and alliance partners. A number of Dutch and Swedish banks followed their customers to Asian markets to be able to serve or not lose their customers (Engwall 1992). As a result, a number of markets have become central for a certain industry or product: for example, Taiwan, Singapore and Malaysia for consumer electronics and semi-conductors and India and Pakistan for textiles and garments.

Strong competition from abroad

The third environmental factor that influences the decision to go abroad is the presence of foreign companies, especially competitors, in the home market of a firm. It is a kind of defensive or retaliation strategy against competing foreign firms. It is not only to defend but also because companies gain confidence by handling the competition often from multinational firms in its home market. It is also quite common that a firm realises that its product/service, as compared to its competitors, is not that bad after all.

In some cases the competition from abroad reveals additional applications or customer segments to the firm for its products. While in some cases a firm, being successful in competing with foreign firms, wants to give back by entering into the domestic market of a particular competitor. If that foreign firm had not entered this firm's domestic market, it would perhaps not have realised the market potential and strength of its product. It has also been proven that foreign competition enhances the competitiveness of local firms as they then have to compete with more resourceful international players and to improve the quality of their products and technologies in order to compete.

The internationalisation process: theoretical perspectives

Early theories on international trade and investments were written by classical economists, whose main concern was not international trade but the political economy of a nation. After the industrial revolution, trade, mainly exports and imports, between nations expanded. When technology became more advanced and products more complex, researchers started talking about firms and companies and producers and consumers. Companies started producing in foreign markets and more complex products required well-controlled sales and distribution as well as repairs and service centres. This meant that the firm took control over its costs, prices and distribution channels. This development gave birth to so-called multinational corporations. We therefore avoid the discussion on whether internationalisation or foreign investment belongs to economics, industrial organisation or to more international trade or business studies and concentrate on theories related to the behaviour of the firm, in regard to internationalisation.

The product life cycle model

Raymond Vernon's seminal article, *International investment and international trade in the product cycle* (1966) argues that firms are highly stimulated by their local environment and are more likely to innovate when their immediate surroundings are more conducive to the creation of (particular) new techniques or products. For internationalisation to occur, these innovations must be transferable to other economies. In adapting to its market, the firm moves through stages from innovation to standardisation and maturity according to the developing forces of supply and demand for its product. This model of sequential decision making has had a great influence on internationalisation theory. The model was originally developed to explain US investments in Europe and also in cheap labour countries. Its usefulness goes beyond Vernon's reappraisal of its efficacy under changed world conditions. Its relevance arises from the fact that the dynamic of the model lies in the interaction of the evolving forces of demand (taste) patterns and production possibilities. The twin rationales of cost imperatives and market pull are simply explained in Vernon's model. Although its validity for the explanation of the behaviour of modern multinationals may be questioned, this article spawned much of the empirical literature on international business.

According to this theory a product goes through several stages of development. The first stage is the innovation stage of the product, the second stage is the introduction in the domestic market (US, the innovating country in this example). The third stage is the export of the product. The next stage is the maturity of the product. As it becomes standardised at this stage, it is being imitated and even produced overseas by foreign firms. The product when newly invented, attracts high-income groups as customers. Its demands grow rapidly in more advanced countries. At this stage the production also starts in other advanced countries, sometimes in a subsidiary of the inventing company. If the cost benefits of producing in the second or third country are large enough to offset transportation cost, then the subsidiary or a foreign producer may even export back to the US. Having seen the benefits of these operations, a number of firms will then start producing and exporting the product. The companies just imitate the original innovating company and often, even produce in the same geographic locations. In the final stage new competitors even from far away markets rise and start producing the same products. And, if they can achieve better production costs, due to cheaper labour, other input, or standardisation of production system, they start exporting back to the US and other early producer countries such as Western Europe. A number of products have followed this pattern. Television invention in the US, typically followed this pattern. When production and marketing was standardised, costs reduced and prices dropped, so it moved to Europe and later to Japan and Korea. Vernon's product life cycle model is depicted in Figure 5.2.

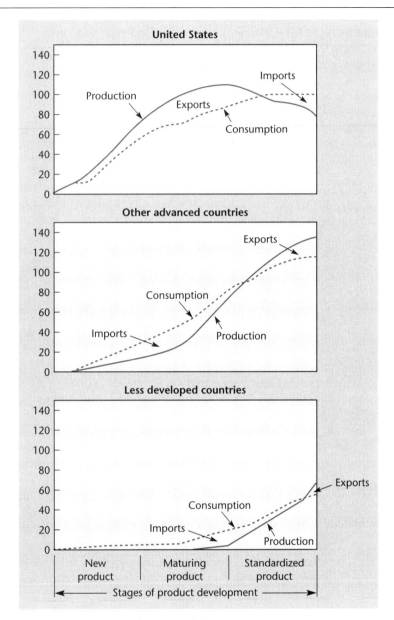

Figure 5.2 The product life cycle model
Source: Vernon (1996).

The establishment chain

In a milestone study, Johanson and Wiedersheim-Paul (1975) examined the internationalisation of four Swedish firms. They found a regular process of gradual incremental change. The firm progresses from no regular exports to export through independent representatives and the establishment of sales subsidiaries to the establishment of production facilities. Flows of information between the firm and the market are (as in Vernon's model) crucial in this process and the cultural distance between spatially separated units of the firm is termed psychic distance. The establishment profiles of the four firms are mapped across a number of countries in time and the gradualist pattern is confirmed. According to this approach internationalisation refers either to an attitude of the firm towards foreign activities or to the actual carrying out of activities abroad. There is a close relationship between attitudes and actual behaviour. The attitudes are the bases for the decision for internationalisation and international activities influence these attitudes. The internationalisation process is thus an interaction between attitudes and actual behaviour.

The assumption of this study is that the firm first develops in the home market (success at home) and that internationalisation is a consequence of a series of incremental decisions. Also, lack of knowledge and resources are the most important obstacles. These obstacles are reduced through incremental decision making and learning about foreign markets and operations. As the perceived risk decreases and a continued internationalisation is stimulated by the increased need to gain control over its activities abroad, the firm starts exporting to neighbouring or similar countries that are relatively better known with regard to business practices. In the first step the firm starts selling through independent representatives, as it demands less of a resource commitment. These activities are extended stepwise. These steps or stages are classified as:

1 No regular export
2 Exports via agents
3 Sales subsidiary
4 Production in a foreign market.

These four stages involve successively larger resource commitment and they also lead to progressive experience and information for the firm. In the first stage, the firm has made no commitment of resources to the market as it does not possess enough information about the market. In the second stage, the firm creates a channel of information (an agent), through which it can influence its activities. It also means more commitment to the market. In the third stage, the firm establishes a controlled information channel (own sales subsidiary) to the market enabling the firm to control its activities even better. In this stage the firm also gets direct experience of influencing factors in the market. In the final (fourth) stage, the firm makes a still larger resource commitment and fully controls supply and sales in that market. An example of one such internationalisation process is given in Figure 5.3.

This sequence of stages is called the **establishment chain**. Although it is quite difficult to have a clear demarcation between these four stages, and firms might jump one or more stages, they explain a firm's attitude and activities (behaviour) towards the internationalisation process. The concept of **psychic distance**, is also introduced to explain this sequence of activities.

This concept is defined as factors preventing or disturbing the flows of information between firms and markets. These factors may include language, culture, political systems, level of education, the level of industrial development, etc. The psychic distance is often related to geographical (physical) distance. But exceptions can be easily found – Britain and Australia, although physically far located from each other, are near to each other in psychic distance. There are

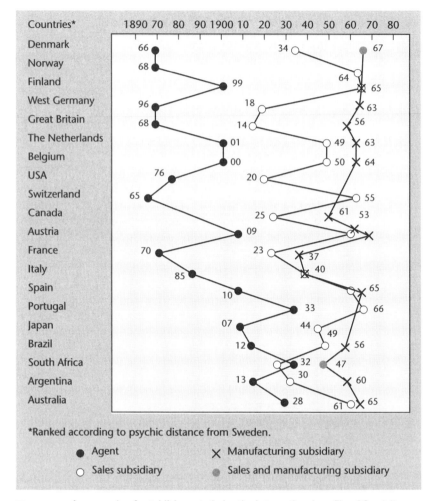

Figure 5.3 An example of establishment chain: the International profile of Sandvik
Source: Johanson and Wiedersheim-Paul (1975).

other factors that influence a firm's activities and choice of market such as the size of the market and market opportunity. There are also different factors that influence a firm's decision about internationalisation at different stages.

Johanson and Vahlne (1977) examined the internationalisation process by investigating the development of knowledge and the building of a commitment within the firm to foreign markets. The twin notions of increasing knowledge about foreign markets as a means of reducing uncertainty and the creation of a commitment to foreign ventures had been examined and the authors here tie these notions to the framework of the behavioural theory of the firm. Internationalisation is again envisaged as the product of a series of incremental decisions. Decisions taken at a point in time affect subsequent steps in the process. Psychic distance is invoked and is defined as **the sum of the factors preventing the flow of information from and to the market**. The decision-making process is dependent on the firm's previous experience. Again, the empirical evidence is based on a very small number of companies. After this study, the two notions of market commitment and market knowledge entered the literature as key elements of internationalisation.

The model presented is considered dynamic as the outcome of one decision or stage constitutes the input for the next. It suggests that the present state of internationalisation is an important factor explaining the course of following internationalisation. It is assumed that the firm strives to grow and to keep risk taking at a low level. These two purposes influence decision making at all levels. The state of internationalisation thus affects perceived opportunities and risks, which in turn influence commitment decisions and current activities.

Two aspects, resource commitment to foreign markets (market commitment) and knowledge about foreign markets possessed by the firm at a particular point of time, are the most important factors. The commitment to the market affects and is effected by the firm's perceived opportunities and risks. This is illustrated in Figure 5.4.

Market commitment

This concept is composed of two factors: the amount of resources committed and the degree of commitment that there is no better alternative use for these resources. Resources located in a particular market or allocated at home to that market are considered committed to that market.

Market knowledge

Commitment decisions are based on several kinds of knowledge. Knowledge on opportunities, market environment, performance of activities, competition and channels of distribution, etc. can vary from market to market and time to time. In this context, experiential knowledge is most critical as it cannot be otherwise acquired. This knowledge then provides the base for perceiving and formulating opportunities. It is different from the general knowledge of characteristics in a specific market. There is thus a direct relationship between market knowledge and market commitment. Knowledge is considered as a resource and consequently the better the knowledge about a market, the more valuable are the resources and the stronger the commitment to the market.

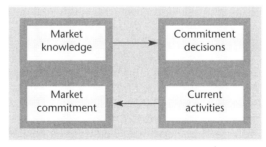

Figure 5.4 The basic mechanism of
internationalisation – state and change aspects
Source: Johanson and Vahlne (1977).

Current business activities

Towards the other end are the change aspects. Current activities are prime sources of experience. These are two kinds of experience: market experience and firm experience. For the performance of marketing activities, both kinds of experience are required. To some extent it is possible to hire persons with market experience and to use them efficiently and profitably, for example by hiring a local sales manager.

Commitment decisions

The second change aspect is the decision to commit resources to foreign operations. This decision depends on what alternatives are available and is based on perceived problems or opportunities on the market. These problems and opportunities in their turn depend on experience: firm as well as market experience. Problems are primarily discovered by those who are responsible for operations on the market and most probably by those who are working in the market. Opportunities are mainly perceived by those who are working on the market and will lead to the extension of operations on the market. So whether problems or opportunities, they will initiate decisions related to the activities currently performed in the market.

Exhibit 5.2 Software goes global: A race to internationalise

The arrival of the Euro is likely to accelerate the trend towards international software. Accounting software is rapidly becoming internationalised as business becomes more global and developers seek broader markets.

The trend first became apparent in the late 1980s and in the 1990s it has gathered pace. Through the 1990s, the top end of the market was pushed towards internationalisation by leading vendors such as SAP, System Software Associates (SSA) and JD Edwards. They have convinced most of the largest multinationals that it makes sense to standardise on software products which can handle their business requirements all round the world. At the same time, the middle of the market, comprising a much larger number of medium-sized companies and their systems suppliers, has been moving in the same direction. Most companies which trade internationally still run different accounting systems in each country – but many want to change that.

The trend has also created a fast expanding market for mid-range accounting software developers such as Scala, Navision, Agresso and Systems Union. Even at the lower end of the market, where software has usually been designed for small businesses with no international involvement, a few products aimed at users across borders such as Intuit's Quicken and Microsoft's Money have become popular. 'Without a shadow of a doubt, the market is now headed towards internationalisation,' concludes John Tate, a director of the software consultancy, Tate Bramald. The two main reasons for this, he says, are that many more businesses are operating in more than one country and developers can see the financial advantages of being able to sell their products more widely.

International businesses are deciding that they want to use the same systems in every country where they have a presence, not least so that staff can move from one place to another and be able to carry on working normally. Yash Nagpal, UK managing director of Navision, says that large companies feel more secure in buying from a global supplier than from a national one.

Suppliers such as Navision now sell in more than 70 countries. For developers, the extra cost of incorporating features to meet the different requirements of other countries on top of a development budget of tens of millions of dollars is relatively slight, while there are good prospects of greatly increasing revenue.

For European developers, the single country market has become too small to justify the high cost of being in the business. The arrival of the Euro is likely to accelerate the process of product internationalisation, as it should help to consolidate a single European market.

Another reason for the shift to international products is that they are now capable of being scaled down by multinationals to suit the requirements of their smaller subsidiaries abroad, notes Dennis Keeling, director of the UK's Business And Accounting Software Developers' Association.

The standard model is now a single package for the world, sharing the same data and easily adaptable to the requirements of each country. Vendors who have stuck with different versions of their product in different countries have generally fared less well than those which have moved to international products. Some of those which used to hold strong positions in national markets are now losing ground to other software suppliers who have entered their markets from abroad with international products.

An apparent exception to the trend is the very successful UK developer, Sage. It owns market-leading but different personal computer-accounting software products in the UK, France and Germany, with a strong contender in the US. Its growth strategy has been not to internationalise its existing products but to build on its dominant position among small businesses in Britain by acquiring similar products in other countries. Its theory is that brand name is more important than standard features and that to internationalise necessarily means to make products which are more complex and less user-friendly. Whether Sage continues to prosper could be a test of whether the lower end of the market will remain at least partly national or whether it will follow the rest towards internationalisation.

Mr Tate argues that most low-end developers who do not internationalise their products, either because they think there is no need or because they cannot afford to, are likely to get squeezed out. 'They cannot gain the benefits of economies of scale from the international market and customers may move up to international packages to get the benefits of being supported by a larger supplier,' he says.

Neil Robertson, UK managing director of US PC product developer Great Plains Software, says that users are more astute as they come to buy their second-generation or third-generation system. 'They see the disadvantages of buying from a single country supplier and know that there will be a limited amount of new functionality which it can afford to develop,' he says.

Most of the development budget for smaller suppliers will be taken up just in achieving year 2000 and Economic and Monetary Union (EMU) compliance, he says. Doubts about the ability of suppliers to meet these two crucial objectives are causing a huge amount of migration in the market.

There is also the risk that a leading vendor could launch a new internationalised low-end accounting package market and push out existing suppliers. SAP and its competitors are evidently keen to expand down-market.

The rush to upgrade could soon be past its peak. Mr Keeling thinks that by 2000 all the activity caused by the date change problem will be over and the software industry could suffer a recession similar to that which followed sterling decimalisation in 1971.

Source: *Financial Times* CD-ROM, 1 January–31 December 1998.

The internalisation approach

Buckley and Casson, whose book the *Future of the Multinational Enterprise* (1976) was a basic contribution, attempted to explain the division of national markets (and therefore of the world market) between domestic firms and foreign multinationals. They did so by reference to two effects: the location effect and the ownership effect. The location effect determines where value-adding activities take place and the ownership effect explains who owns and controls those activities. The concepts of least cost location and growth by internalisation of markets are thus introduced to the internationalisation theory.

Firms grow by replacing the (imperfect) external market and earn a return by doing this, until the point at which the benefits of further internalisation are outweighed by the costs. The types of benefit and cost of growth by internalisation are listed and it is suggested that certain types of market are more likely to be internalised than others, given the configuration of the world economy. Thus, the direction of internationalisation can be predicted by predicting changes in cost and market conditions. These factors are classified as industry specific, region specific, firm specific and nation specific. A national market for a final product can be served in four main ways:

1 By indigenous firms
2 By subsidiaries of MNEs located in the market
3 By exports to the market from foreign locally owned firms
4 By exports from foreign plants owned by MNEs.

In the first two methods, the market is served by local production, **location effect**, while in the last two the market is served by foreign production. In the second and fourth the production is owned and controlled by foreign-owned companies, **ownership effect**. Combining location and ownership effects, allows us to give the reasons for the division of particular markets between domestic producers and foreign firms. The division between exports and local servicing is largely the result of the economics of the location. But as MNEs can internalise a market through ownership, the question of servicing a final market is tied up with the nature and ownership of internal markets. Location and ownership effects are thus interdependent for the least cost location of an activity, which is at least partly determined by the ownership of the activities integrated with it (Buckley and Casson 1979).

The eclectic theory

John Dunning has produced a massive corpus of work in international business. From them, Dunning's **eclectic paradigm** is the most relevant for our purpose. This approach uses three sets of explanatory factors to analyse international business issues: locational factors, internalisation factors and ownership factors. Essentially, firms transfer their ownership-specific assets to combine with the most favourable sets of traditionally fixed elements in the global economy. They do this, where appropriate, internally, in order to retain control of the revenue generation. Later versions of the eclectic approach refined this position and extended its taxonomy and it has become familiar to many generations of researchers and students as a set of key organising principles in international business. Dunning's work helps us to understand in which ways production financed by MNEs has affected our thinking about the international allocation of resources and exchange of goods and services between countries. The eclectic theory suggests that, given the distribution of location-specific endowments, the companies, which have the greatest opportunities for and derive the most from, internalising activities will be most competitive in foreign markets. These advantages will however differ according to industry, country and company characteristics (Dunning 1977/1995).

Dunning took the starting point in the Heckscher-Ohlin model which asserted that, provided certain conditions were met, countries would specialise in the production of goods which required relatively large inputs of resources with which they were comparatively well endowed, and would export these in exchange for others which required relatively large inputs of factors with which they were comparatively poorly endowed. The conditions included that countries had two homogeneous inputs, labour and capital, both of which were: locationally immobile (i.e. they were to be used where they were located); converted into outputs by the most efficient (and internationally identical) production functions; all enterprises were price-takers, operating under conditions of atomistic competition; there were no barriers to trade and no transaction costs; and international tastes were similar (Ohlin 1939/1967).

This model had three assumptions: factory immobility, the identity of production functions and atomistic competition. These implied first, that all markets operate efficiently; second, that there are no external economies of production or marketing; and third, that information is costless and there are no barriers to trade or competition. In such a situation international trade is the only possible form of international involvement; production by one country's enterprises for a foreign market must be undertaken within the exporting country; and all enterprises have equal access to location-specific endowments.

Although the Heckscher-Ohlin theory dominated the scene for a long time, later studies concentrating on ownership advantages of foreign firms really provide the base to understand internationalisation (Hymer 1970). It was also made clear that it is sufficient for the exporting country to have a location-endowment advantage over the importing country; that is, it is not necessary for the exporting firms to have ownership advantage over indigenous firms in the importing country. The third type of advantage was more specific for multinational enterprises, whose input arises out of multivariability of a company. The larger the number and the greater the differences between economic environments in which an enterprise operates, the better placed it is to take advantage of different factor endowments and market situations.

Dunning's studies re-evaluated the benefits of going abroad and pointed out that both country and company factors have changed considerably. For firms, a systematic approach of combining production and marketing was becoming strategically important. For countries, a positive attitude towards foreign companies is considered an important means of enhancing the competitiveness of their local firms. These changing attitudes from both sides are creating a new balance of costs and benefits for both parties. Some of the reasons behind these changing attitudes are considered to be renewed faith in market economy system, increasing globalisation, the emergence of emerging markets, the changing scope of competition, changes in criteria to judge foreign firms, and the experience of countries about what foreign firms can do for them. Firms have shown increased interest in going abroad because of the increasing need to go international, pressure to procure cheapest inputs, efficiency seeking, the opening up of new markets, considerable changes in location costs and benefits and a strive to strike a balance between globalisation and localisation.

The network approach

The above-mentioned approaches and theories are the most established ones. The stage theory has initiated a lot of research in favour and against. Studies have suggested that jumps in the stage pattern in *any one foreign market* may result from learning across the firm, i.e. from other foreign markets. Thus, overall foreign knowledge may diffuse through the firm and allow more rapid penetration of foreign markets tackled at a later date. More recently, the internationalisation of industrial firms has been explained through networks and relationships between firms. According to this approach, firms internationalise because other firms in their national network internationalise. The industrial system is composed of firms engaged in production, distribution and the use of goods and services. The relationships between firms are described as a network. The firms within the network are dependent on each other, and their activities therefore need to be co-ordinated. These networks are stable or/are changing, but the transactions take place within the framework of these established relationships. In the process however, some new relationships are developed and some old ones are disrupted because of the competitive activities of different actors (Johanson and Mattson 1988; Thorelli 1990; Ghauri 1992).

Thus, although there are competitive relationships, interdependencies are stressed in the network approach. Firms have to develop and maintain relationships with other firms in the network. This process of developing and maintaining relationships is of a cumulative nature and firms are striving to establish a prominent position in their networks. At each point the firm has a position in the network which explains its relationship to other firms. Here one basic assumption is that the firm is dependent on external resources controlled by other firms. Therefore, it is dependent on its network in foreign markets while internationalising. The firm thus has to work for international integration. A higher degree of internationalisation means that there are strong relationships between different national networks. These relationships developed by the firm are thus considered as market investments. Moreover, the firms, which are highly internationalised, would prefer to have a number of activities performed externally by subcontractors and can still have the desired control arising from these relationships. See also Chapter 8 of this volume for further discussion of the network model and some of the other models mentioned above within the context of small- and medium-sized enterprises (SMEs).

Chapter summary

The field of international business has received much attention from scholars. The focus of earlier studies was on business–government relationship. This was inevitable as it was the feature of a multinational enterprise that it must deal with at least two governments: the host and the home. This led to a period of conflict between companies and governments. Over the last two decades, however, international business has taken a quantum leap and is now considered strategically important both by firms and governments. The growing interdependence is manifested by an ever-increasing amount of international trade (UNCTAD 1998). From a period of conflict followed by the Second World War to a period of suspicion towards company activities in foreign countries in the 1970s, there has been considerable change. The 1980s thus saw the building of co-operative relationships between companies and governments to such an extent that there has been a danger of oversubsidising inward investment through excessive locational competition (Buckley and Ghauri 1999b).

Other than these theoretical developments, there have been, in recent years, enormous changes in the environment of international trade and business. Among these developments four can be characterised as the drivers of globalisation:

1 The increasing interdependence between the economies of the world at national as well as corporate level
2 The increasing amount of wealth and growth in all parts of the world
3 Liberalisation of most economies towards free trade and open economies
4 Regionalisation, a strive towards block building and creating free trade areas in most parts of the world from NAFTA to EU and ASEAN.

All these factors are forcing countries and companies to do business with each other. This is one of the reasons why today there is hardly any company that can claim that it is a domestic company. If they do not sell abroad they buy their products/ingredients from abroad. And most companies today are competing with foreign companies at home as well as in foreign markets.

Discussion questions

1 What are the factors that influence a company's decision to go abroad? Explain how these are related to each other.
2 In the discussion on the internationalisation process of a firm, the product life cycle model played a major role. Explain this model and discuss its usefulness.
3 The establishment chain model is considered to be a milestone study in the theory development on the internationalisation process of the firm. Explain what is meant by the *establishment chain*, and what is the main assumption of this model. Explain what is meant by *psychic distance*.
4 Buckley and Casson attempted to explain the division of a national market between domestic and foreign firms. Explain the main argument in their approach (internalisation approach). What are the main ways in which a national market for a final product can be served?

Closing Case Study:
Builders of a new Russia: Turkish firms are quietly winning scores of big contracts in the former Soviet Union
Monir Tayeb

Since the fall of communism, investors have swooped on the former Soviet Union, eyeing it as a treasure trove of natural resources and a bargain basement of business opportunities. But many of these adventure capitalists, breezing into town for a quick profit, encounter unforeseen obstacles, and return home empty-handed. Sometimes quieter virtues – like vision, flexibility and a canny patience – win the day.

That's how Turkish firms have scooped up 85 per cent of the foreign construction business in the former Soviet empire. With a steadiness and a cultural rapport few Westerners possess, 46 contractors have won business worth $14bn in nine years. Thanks to a reputation for doing good work cheaply, Turks are busily building steel mills, refineries, hospitals, shopping centres and ceramics plants.

Turkey has been laying the groundwork for this success for more than a decade. A 1984 agreement to import 120bn cubic metres of natural gas from the Soviet Union over 25 years proved a good wedge when Turkey secured the right to pay for 30 per cent of the gas in contracting services. In 1988, it was one of the first countries to organise a private business council with the Soviet Union; within two weeks of the USSR's collapse, there were similar links with the newly independent republics. It was a useful foothold. When Moscow signed the 1990 treaty reuniting Germany, Bonn agreed to finance housing for 100,000 soldiers returning to Russia. At the insistence of the Russians – and even though German firms had priority – Turks were allowed to bid. To German consternation, Turks won nearly half of the $5bn project.

Historically well-placed between East and West, Turkey bridges both geographical and cultural gaps. 'We Turks understand the Russians,' says Ishak Alaton, co-director of Alarko, a construction firm that does 75 per cent of its business – earning $650 million annually – in Russia and Central Asia. 'Russians are often reluctant to deal with Americans and Europeans due to an inferiority complex, but they're at ease with us.' Alaton says he first looked for Russian business during the Brezhnev era because 'we smelled change coming'. Since then, the jolly 72-year-old multimillionaire has learned to accommodate his clients in Russia and Central Asia. For example, deals can take several years to consummate. 'Most European and US companies won't wait that long,' he says. 'You need patience, guile and a sweet nature to do business in this region.' Until recently, he did business in Russia without lawyers. 'We still do handshake deals, with lawyers doing only the fine-tuning. But Central Asia is still handshake country. In that part of the world, lawyers don't solve problems; they create them.'

A willingness to adapt to local culture certainly helps, but Alaton has also gently prodded his business partners in new directions. At first, he says, businessmen in the former Soviet Union didn't know how to finance construction deals, 'so we taught them.' Now the former communists are savvier, and Alaton is hatching joint ventures with budding Russian construction firms instead of competing with them. Alarko's partner in sprucing up Moscow's skyline is Mayor Yuri Luzhkov. Alarko staffers in Russia were once 99 per cent Turks; now more than half are Russian.

Rich in natural resources and with a decaying infrastructure, the former Soviet states that span ten time zones are a builder's dream. ENKA – which claims to be Turkey's largest construction company and the biggest foreign owner of property in Russia – is diversifying into specialised projects such as the construction of a $1bn petro-chemical plant and refinery in Kazakstan, a $10m exploration camp for underwater oil surveys of the Caspian Sea for Shell and a $22m gold mine 4200 metres high in the remote Tian Shan Mountains on the Chinese and Kyrgyzstan border. In the past nine years, ENKA earned $1.2bn from projects in Russia, $122m in Belarus, $55m in Kyrgyzstan and $30m in Ukraine.

But perhaps ENKA's most important project – one that indicates its standing in Russia – had nothing to do with exploiting natural resources. After the storming of the Russian Duma in 1991, ENKA and another Turkish firm, GAMA, rather than a Russian builder, won the contract to rebuild the damaged White House, finishing the job on time in only three months. Operating in Turkey provides good practice. Says managing director Mehmet Draz, 'We are the grandmasters of circumventing bureaucracy. In Turkey, it takes 276 signatures to build a house.'

Turkish construction companies also have an edge when it comes to workers. They are close – within bussing distance of most of Central Asia – and adaptable, says Ugur Yurdakul, who is in charge of operations in the former Soviet Union for GAMA. On the White House job, says Yurdakul, 'We had 2500 workers toiling 24 hours a day for three months. It was like a giant battle.' Along with patience, Turks have demonstrated a willingness to gamble. European and American firms usually want credit guarantees, says Yurdakul. 'We don't insist. To enter the Russian market, we took risks unacceptable to Western companies. This is a volatile region in full transformation,' Yurdakul admits. But he also says Turkish firms are there to stay: 'We've paid the entrance fee. We are building the future of these countries: their infrastructure.'

While their motives are plainly commercial, there is a personal quality to the deals Turks are striking in Russia and Central Asia. 'Do you know why we like you?' Moscow Mayor Luzhkov reportedly asked Nihat Gokyigit, the chairman of TEFEN, a construction conglomerate. 'You don't bring lawyers. We look into each other's eyes. Then we put the contract on the shelf and never look at it again.' The hottest toys in the business world may be palm-top computers and video conferencing, but the oldest tools – handshakes and eye contact – are as essential as ever.

Source: *Time*, (1998) 15 June: 96–7. © 1998 Time Inc. Printed by permission.

Questions

1 What major internal characteristics of Turkish firms have helped them win contracts in Russia?
2 What opportunities does Russia offer to foreign firms and how have the Turks exploited these?
3 In what forms do Turkish companies seeking business in Russia have an edge over their European and American counterparts?
4 What specific skill have the Turkish construction companies acquired in their own country which has helped them succeed in Russia?

References

Aharoni, Y. (1966) *The Foreign Investment Decision Process*, Boston, Mass: Harvard University.

Buckley, P. and **Casson, M.** (1976) *The Future of Multinational Enterprise*, London: Macmillan.

Buckley, P. and **Casson, M.** (1979) A theory of international operations, *European Research in International Business*, Amsterdam: North Holland, pp. 1–8.

Buckley, P. and **Ghauri, P.** (eds) (1999a) *The Internationalisation of the Firm: A Reader*, 2nd edn, London: International Thompson Press.

Buckley, P. and **Ghauri, P.** (eds) (1999b) *The Global Challenge for Multinational Enterprises: Managing Increasing Interdependence*, Oxford, Pergamon.

Dunning, J. (1977) Trade, location of economic activity and multinational enterprise: a search for an eclectic approach, in B. Ohlin, P.O. Hesselbosu and P. M. Wijkman (eds) *The International Allocation of Economic Activity*, London: Macmillan.

Dunning, J. (1995) Trade, location of economic activity and the multinational enterprise: a search for an eclectic approach, in J. Drew (ed.) *Readings in International Enterprise*, London: Routledge, pp. 250–74.

Engwall, L. (1992) Barriers in International Banking Networks, in M. Forsgren and J. Johanson (eds) *Managing Networks in International Business*, Philadelphia: Gordon & Breach, pp. 167–77.

Ghauri, P. (1992) New structures in MNCs based in small countries: a network approach, *European Management Journal* 10(3): 357–64.

Hymer, S. (1970) The multinational corporation and the law of uneven development, in J. Bahgwati (ed.) *Economics and World Order*, New York: World Law Fund.

Johanson, J. and **Mattson, L.-G.** (1988) Internationalisation in industrial systems: a network approach, in N. Hood and J.E. Vahlne (eds) *Strategies in Global Competition*, New York: Croom Helm.

Johanson, J. and Vahlne, J.-E. (1977) The internationalisation process of the firm: a model of knowledge development and increasing foreign market commitments, *Journal of International Business Studies* 8(1): 23–32.

Johanson, J. and Wiedersheim-Paul F. (1975) The internationalisation of the firm: four Swedish cases, *Journal of Management Studies*, October: 305–22.

Ohlin, B. (1939/1967) *Interregional and International Trade*, Cambridge, Mass: Harvard University Press.

Prahalad, C.K. and Liberthal, K. (1998) The end of corporate imperialism, *Harvard Business Review*, July–August 76:4, 69–78.

Schnitzer, M.C., Liebrenz, M.L. and Kublin, K.W. (1985) *International Business*, Cincinnati: South Western Publishing Company.

Thorelli, H. (1990) Networks: the gay nineties in international marketing, in H. Thorelli and T. Cavusgil (eds) *International Marketing Strategy*, 3rd edn, Oxford: Pergamon, pp. 73–85.

UNCTAD (1998) *World Development Report*.

Vernon, R. (1966) International investment and international trade in the product cycle, *Quarterly Journal of Economics* 80: 190–307.

CHAPTER 6

Modes of Internationalisation

Adam Cross

Learning objectives

By the end of this chapter you will:

- be familiar with the various methods that firms use to enter foreign markets, and to appreciate their principal characteristics

- understand the main advantages and disadvantages associated with using each foreign market entry mode

- be aware of the circumstances in which a particular entry mode might best be employed by a foreign market entrant.

Opening Case Study: Building a global energy business to stay on top

State-owned Gaz de France may not be everyone's idea of an international energy predator. But the French gas company is set to make waves outside its home market as Pierre Gadonneix, its president, seeks to keep it among the world's top five gas companies. The group has budgeted FFr5bn ($817.5m) for foreign investment in 1997 to 1999, as it strives to double to 20 per cent the proportion of its FFr55bn turnover generated outside France.

It is poised to take a significant step towards that goal by winning a contest to buy 51.2 per cent of Gasag, Berlin's gas distributor, in what would be its biggest foreign investment to date. Gaz de France won the contract in partnership with Bewag, the Berlin electricity utility. Under the DM1.41bn ($790m) deal, which has to be ratified by parliament, Gaz de France would take 38.2 per cent of Gasag's capital.

Mr Gadonneix says the internationalisation strategy is needed to keep pace with other operators, which are getting bigger and bigger, and because of the opening of European gas markets to greater competition.

EU energy ministers decided in December to open a third of Europe's natural gas market to competition. Each state will have to open at least 20 per cent of its gas market to competition within two years of the new law being adopted. 'As soon as the market is opened, we will lose clients,' Mr Gadonneix says, 'as few as possible, but we will lose them. So we have to find new activities. There will no longer be single-product, single-country companies. If we want to remain a world leader, we must internationalise ourselves – and quickly.' He wants alliances with other companies, 'since we cannot do everything alone at once'.

On the gas production side, the company has signed agreements with Elf Aquitaine and Total, the French oil companies, covering 15bn cubic metres of North Sea gas supplies. He believes such deals are vital to 'reinforce the credibility of our commercial offers. Clients prefer to deal with sellers which have, at least in part, their own resources. In 1997, according to a Salomon Brothers study, the 15 main US companies increased their upstream gas investments by 12 per cent, while their sales only rose by 0.5 per cent. Gaz de France, at risk of being marginalised, cannot stay outside this general practice.'

He emphasises, nevertheless, the need for such resources to be accessible to the French market and to have an acceptable price/quality relationship. It is also important for France to emerge as a 'hub' of Europe's gas network. He suggests contracts signed last year with the Italian groups Snam and Enel would help realise this goal, since they would 'practically triple' the volume of gas passing through France to other countries. The contracts would result in nearly FFr4bn of investment in the country.

In distribution, in addition to the Berlin agreement, the company recently acquired 25 per cent of Estag, an Austrian electricity and gas producer and distributor, in partnership with Electricite de France. Gaz de France says it is aiming to win control of four or five of the 30 private distribution companies being created in Mexico. It has also tendered, with mixed success, for contracts in Argentina, Colombia and Brazil.

Source: *Financial Times* CD-ROM, 1 January–31 December 1998.

Introduction

Chapter 5 demonstrated that there are many reasons why a firm might choose to internationalise part or all of its business activity. Once managers have decided to 'go international' they are confronted by two questions: which foreign market should the firm enter, and what business method should it use to achieve entry? The response of managers to the first of these questions, the 'where' of internationalisation, is shaped by their strategic motives for internationalising. Managers looking to sell products and services to new customers (a market-seeking strategy), for instance, might choose a foreign country with a growing market, or a large or affluent target population or perhaps one that is geographically or culturally close to the home country. Meanwhile, a firm looking to reduce production costs (an efficiency-seeking strategy) might prefer to relocate production to a country with low factor input costs, such as labour, land or raw materials costs (Dunning 1993). The approaches used by firms to identify a suitable host country, and how factors within the firm and in its external business environment influence the decision-making process, are considered elsewhere in this volume, especially Chapters 5 and 7. This chapter focuses on the second question faced by the internationalising firm – the 'how' of the internationalisation process.

Developing a new international market is a formidable challenge for any firm. This is especially true for those that are inexperienced or under-resourced. As we shall see, there are many business options that firms can use to enter and service a host market (see also Table 6.1 on page 158). An important, if not crucial, element of the internationalisation process is to identify which of these is the most appropriate for a particular circumstance and then implement it effectively. Selection must be done with care, because the entry method will determine to a considerable degree whether or not entry is successful and corporate objectives are achieved. It is therefore essential for managers of international business to understand the principal characteristics of the various foreign market servicing strategies available, and to have insight into some of the benefits and problems that each can confer on a firm's foreign market entry strategy. This chapter seeks to introduce readers to these issues.

Foreign market entry modes: towards a typology

In broad terms, there are three generic forms of international competition, depending on whether production occurs in the home market or abroad, and whether the internationalising firm or another party carries out production.

The first and most straightforward form of international competition is for the internationalising firm to continue producing goods and services in its **domestic** market and to **export** this output to foreign markets. The physical movement of goods across borders normally happens by air-freight, sea-freight, road haulage or rail. However, rapid advances in telecommunication and information technology have introduced to this list another medium – electronic-based exchange – and the cross-border trade of computer software and other digitised media (such as music, graphic images and the written word) 'on-line' via the Internet and the World Wide Web has proliferated in recent years. Some services, notably certain marketing, banking and insurance products, are also now sold internationally in this way. Although clearly not on the same scale (in volume and value terms) as more traditional means, the continued growth in electronic-based methods of exporting seems assured in certain service industries.

In the second form of international competition the production of goods and services is relocated to the foreign market under a **contract-based** agreement with an **independent** local company. There are many types of contract, depending on the major provisions, terms and conditions contained therein, but usually they fall into one of the following categories: technology licenses (the most common), franchises, technical service agreements, management contracts, turnkey operations, international subcontracts and contractual joint ventures. These contracts are generally of fixed duration, involve a relatively limited degree of technology transfer to the contracted party and often restrict geographically the markets that contracted parties can supply.

In the third form of international competition, production also takes place in the foreign market, but it is carried out by an entity in which the internationalising firm has taken a significant **equity** position; that is, one that the international firm owns, either in whole or in part (above a 10 per cent threshold). When this ownership secures **control** of the assets, output and decision-making processes of the foreign operation, the flow of capital is called foreign direct investment (FDI) and the firm making this investment can be regarded as a multinational enterprise (MNE). The issue of control is central to distinguishing between direct and portfolio capital flows. Both are capital transactions, but in portfolio investments the investing firm has no control over productive activity in foreign markets – it is merely a means of wealth holding. Nevertheless, many firms do make portfolio investments abroad for this reason, albeit often with a view to increasing their stake and obtaining control at some point in the future.

When the MNE has secured 10 per cent or more – the precise percentage varies depending on the national jurisdiction concerned – of the voting stock of the foreign operation, this operation is referred to as an affiliate. Three types of affiliate are possible: an associate firm, in which the MNE has a minority holding (that is, up to, but not over, 50 per cent of its voting stock); a subsidiary firm, in which the MNE has a majority holding (over 50 per cent), and in which the MNE can be presumed to have outright control; and, third, as a special case of an associate or affiliate firm, an equity joint venture (in which two or more parent firms have a shared holding). With any FDI, unlike contract-based agreements, the MNE often transfers a comprehensive 'bundle' of factors of production to its affiliates, rather than a selected few elements. This package can include capital equipment, finance, technology (often embodied in intellectual property rights such as brand-names, patents, trademarks, formulae, copyright and so forth), business know-how, marketing knowledge and managerial resources, among other things.

The total foreign business sales (TFS) of an internationally active firm can therefore be derived from three possible sources (Buckley *et al.* 1992):

TFS = sales from exports + sales from contractual agreements + sales from foreign direct production.

The relative importance of each element will differ as a result of industry-specific and firm-specific factors. However, most large internationally active firms engage extensively in each area of international business, globally co-ordinating a portfolio of foreign direct investments, various contractual agreements and exporting channels in an integrated and complementary manner. So, these firms may sell products and services using different entry modes in different markets. Smaller internationally active firms, on the other hand, generally use a narrower range of modes, which are typically substitutable for each other. Some firms may exhibit a distinct leaning towards a particular mode, perhaps because of the industry they are in, their corporate culture, or the particular expertise of their decision-makers and managers.

In the text that follows, we highlight the distinctive characteristics of each mode of supply (summarised in Table 6.1) possible under the three broad forms of international competition and discuss in more detail the circumstances in which a particular entry method might best be employed. This account is somewhat idealised, however, because distinctions between entry modes are often less clear in real-world situations. Also, while each method is described in the context of international business, domestic equivalents exist as well.

Table 6.1 A typology of international technology transfer

Form of co-operation	Equity or non-equity	Time limited or unlimited	Geographically limited	Transfer of resources or rights	Mode of transfer
Wholly-owned foreign subsidiaries	Equity	Unlimited	At discretion of multinational enterprise	Typically, whole range	Internal
Equity joint ventures	Equity	Unlimited	Agreed	Wide range	Internal
Foreign minority holdings	Equity	Unlimited	Limited	Wide range	Internal
Fade-out agreements	Equity	Limited	Nature of agreement	Wide range, but for limited period	Internal, changing to market
Licensing	Non-equity	Limited by terms of contract	May include limitation in contract	Limited range	Market
Franchising	Non-equity	Limited by terms of contract	Yes	Wide range, including support	Market
Management contracts	Non-equity	Limited by contract	May be specified	Limited	Market
Turnkey projects	Non-equity	Limited	Not usually	Limited in time	Market
Contractual joint ventures	Non-equity	Limited by contract	May be agreed contract	Specified by	Mixed
International sub-contracting	Non-equity	Limited	Yes	Small	Market

Source: Adapted from Buckley and Brooke (1992).

Exporting as a mode of market entry

As already indicated, exporting involves the transfer of goods and services between firms in different countries. As such, it is perhaps the oldest and most straightforward method for conducting international business. As data on international trade flows illustrate (see also Chapter 1), exporting is an increasingly common activity, although often confined to a small – but growing – proportion of firms in the industrialised economies. A number of developments explain this increase. Probably most significant is the rapid liberalisation of trade that has taken place globally and within regional trade blocs during the 1990s. In particular, as we saw in Chapter 3, the Uruguay Round of trade negotiations under the auspices of the GATT (General Agreement on Tariffs and Trade) completed in 1993, and its successor the World Trade Organisation (WTO), has significantly reduced, on a multilateral basis, tariff rates and quotas for most imports. Other protectionist measures relating to technical standards and import licenses are also being phased out by the WTO and certain trade-enhancing measures introduced. Tariff and non-tariff barriers to trade are being lowered at the regional level also, in free trade areas such as NAFTA (North American Free Trade Agreement), ASEAN (Association of South East Asian Nations) and APEC (Asia-Pacific Economic Cooperation); in customs unions such as the Andean Pact and Mercosur, and in economic unions, most notably the European Union (EU). At the same time, international transportation and communication costs continue to fall and many cultural barriers to international business are diminishing through the process coined 'globalisation' (Radice 1999). The response of firms to these trends is to export a greater share of their output. Proactive exporters are taking advantage of lower costs and improved access to foreign markets, while reactive firms are being compelled to seek international sales to compensate for increased competitive pressures and an eroding share of their domestic market as foreign imports rise. Many governments assist indigenous exporters in this activity with export credit guarantees and other export-promoting initiatives, in recognition of the benefits of exporting for a country's balance of payments.

Several channels of distribution are available to an exporting firm. For descriptive purposes, it is usual to divide these into indirect exporting and direct exporting, depending on whether or not the producer is responsible for the export function (Brooke and Buckley 1988; Young *et al*. 1989).

Indirect exporting

A firm becomes an **indirect exporter** when its products are sold in foreign markets without any special international activity on its part. Instead, other firms carry out the export function. This might involve, for example, the preparation of export documentation, responsibility for the physical movement of goods and setting up sales and distribution channels in the foreign market. Indeed, an indirect exporter may not even be aware that its products are being sold overseas. A variety of firms adopt the role of intermediary. These include export houses, confirming houses and buying houses (see Table 6.2 for a description of each and their main advantages and disadvantages for the exporting firm). The principal disadvantage to indirect exporting is that, because indirect exporters are isolated from the export process, they have little or no control over local marketing issues. This may be in respect of, for example, price setting, packaging and promotion of their products. Interaction with the end-user is also minimal. Consequently, indirect exporters receive little or no feedback from the market place. This is a major shortcoming if products and marketing approaches need to be adapted, as is often the case, to suit local market conditions. Much of the goodwill associated with the exporter's products, accumulated during pre-sales contact and after-sales care with the end-user, is also dependent on the performance of another firm. For these reasons, indirect exporting usually generates only modest non-domestic sales. It is most appropriate for the smaller or inexperienced exporter, and for low value or occasional orders.

Direct exporting

Firms with more a proactive view to international expansion will probably prefer the greater 'hands on' control associated with direct exporting (Welford and Prescott 1992). A firm becomes a **direct exporter** when it undertakes to export

Table 6.2 Indirect versus direct exporting

Export Mode	Advantages for the domestic exporter	Disadvantages for the domestic exporter
Indirect Exporting *Export houses* An organisation that buys goods from a domestic firm which it sells abroad on its own account	✓ the export process is handled by another firm ✓ the sale is domestic and local laws apply (allowing legal recourse to recover bad debts, for example) ✓ needs no experience of operating internationally	• allows little or no control over the export process • little or no information flowing back about local market conditions • sales opportunities will be limited • local goodwill is dependent on another firm • allows no contact with end-user • export house may not even divulge name of end-user
Confirming houses Act for foreign buyers and are paid on a commission basis	as above, plus: ✓ payment is guaranteed by confirming house on behalf of the foreign end-user ✓ seller and buyer are in direct contact via the confirming house	• as above, except that greater contact is allowed with the end-user
Buying houses Act on behalf of foreign clients (such as department stores and foreign government agencies)	as for export house, plus: ✓ buying house often makes the first contact	• as for export house
Piggybacking The exporter sells its goods abroad through the foreign sales distribution of another, usually larger intermediary firm	✓ access to the resources of an experienced exporter	• difficulty in finding a suitable business partner • low priority placed by intermediary on domestic firm's products • contracts may limit future sales growth
Direct Exporting *Direct selling* Sales representatives from home country may be used in foreign sales territories	✓ domestic sales reps have detailed knowledge of the company and its products/services ✓ high level of market control ✓ promotes good flow of information back to exporter best used when host market is limited or spasmodic	• reliant on the drive and character of local reps • domestic reps may lack local knowledge • considerable travelling time and contact may be involved • domestic reps may experience language problems • may be continuity problems if rep leaves market

Export Mode	Advantages for the domestic exporter	Disadvantages for the domestic exporter
Agents Act as direct representation for the exporter in the foreign country. An agent is usually a local party, paid on commission on the value of sales made. Agents do not take title of goods. Agreements can be exclusive (the agent acts as the exporter abroad); semi-exclusive (the agent also handles non-competing goods of other firms) or non-exclusive (the agent may handle competing goods).	✓ allows greater market control than the indirect methods above ✓ agent will often have good local knowledge of the host market ✓ agent will have permanent presence in the market	• contracts with agents need to be comprehensive and binding • identifying a suitable agent may prove difficult • agents must be viable firms with a strong local reputation • agent may sell the products of other companies, producing conflicts of loyalties • agreements can be difficult and costly to terminate • the agent may act as a barrier rather than link to host markets • important to develop good, long-term working relationship with agent • agreements can be difficult and costly to terminate
Distributors Take title to goods (distinguishing them from agents) and earn revenue from mark-up rather than commission	As for agents above, plus: ✓ distributor can provide better after sales service	• as for agents
Local sales office/affiliate Run by staff from home country or host country	✓ identifiable commitment to market ✓ easier for local customers to deal with exporter ✓ flexible and can accommodate growth ✓ affiliate will be treated as local firm which may provide access to markets otherwise closed (because, for example, of 'buy local' policies of government)	• selecting sales personnel and other staff • domestic staff may be reluctant to go abroad • local employees have less company knowledge but more host country/market knowledge • requires knowledge of local employment laws re hiring/firing, social security, pensions, insurance, etc.

Source: Adapted from Young *et al.* (1989); and Buckley and Brooke (1992).

its own products. Certain in-house expertise will need to be developed. This might involve, for example, nurturing local contacts, conducting market research, processing the necessary documentation and transportation (often via a freight-forwarding company) and establishing local pricing policies (Young *et al.* 1989). These functions may later be centralised in a separate export department or division. The direct exporter typically sells its products in the foreign market through an independent local agent or distributor,[1] or by using specialist company representatives and sales affiliates. Having this local presence generally reflects a greater and longer-term commitment to servicing a foreign market than indirect exporting. It allows the exporter to monitor closely developments and/or the competition in the host market, so the firm can respond rapidly to opportunities or threats as they emerge. It also promotes the flow of information to and from the foreign end-user, facilitating the adaptation of products to meet local needs. As Brooke and Buckley (1988) observe, a visible commitment to the host market gives customers greater confidence in after-sales service and care (promoting a positive purchasing decision) and helps to concentrate the exporter on its key markets.

Exporting is generally recognised as being the least risky method of internationalisation (Young et al. 1989). For this reason, firms frequently export their products when they first sell to non-domestic customers. For many firms, exporting represents a 'toe in the water' strategy, allowing them to gain experience of doing business in unfamiliar environments (from which they can withdraw with relative ease if necessary), as a precursor to more substantial foreign involvement. Of course, exporting is not risk-free. Exchange rate movements, for example, can influence dramatically the profitability of individual orders in the short term, as well as a firm's international competitiveness in the longer term (see Chapter 9).[2] It would also be wrong to presume that exporting is the preserve of inexperienced or under-resourced firms. Today less than half of world trade (some estimates suggest around one-third) is between independent companies (UNCTAD 1996). The majority of trade, and therefore exporting activity, is actually intra-firm and takes place between firms which form part of an MNE. Of this, approximately half consists of exports by the MNE, or its affiliates, to sales and distribution affiliates for sale in the host country or neighbouring markets (a type of direct exporting between affiliates), and about half involves the export of intermediate goods for processing or final assembly before being returned to the MNE (which is international subcontracting between affiliates) (UNCTAD 1996).

Non-equity modes of foreign market entry

In non-equity modes of foreign market entry, firms sell proprietary technology or know-how to foreign companies under some form of contract. More often than not, this technology and know-how is embodied in legal instruments such as patents, trademarks and copyright. Collectively referred to as intellectual property rights (IPR), these legally sanctioned monopolies seek to protect in law the technology created or acquired by the firm and so prevent other companies from appropriating it, for example, by pirating or counterfeiting. Intellectual property, and the knowledge underpinning it, is an important commercial asset and in many respects represents a significant, if not a key, source of competitive advantage (Sullivan 1998). Whether the firm chooses to exploit its IPR 'in-house' or sell it on to independent foreign companies under contract is central to much theorising on the *raison d'être* of the MNE (see, for example, Buckley and Casson 1976; Dunning 1993).

Cross-border payments for IPR and specialised services sold under contract have increased in value considerably since the mid-1980s. Although certain methodological inadequacies in the way authorities collect this type of data make precise quantification difficult, it is generally estimated that global payments for technology alone (that is, excluding service-related agreements) quadrupled to around $48bn between 1983 and 1995 (UNCTAD 1997). The majority of this licensing is between firms from just a few developed countries, typically US firms on the one hand (as both donor and recipient) and Japanese, German, British, French or Dutch firms on the other. The bulk of transactions concerned payments for patents, and these cover a wide range of products and manufacturing processes, in sectors as diverse as biotechnology and information technologies to industrial automation, software, telecommunications, chemicals and food and beverages (UNCTAD 1997).

The scale and scope of licensing activity is certainly indicative of its importance in international business strategy. This observation must be qualified, however. It has been estimated, using US data as a guide, that the majority, probably around 80 per cent, of global fees and payments for technology and know-how occur *within* rather than between firms (UNCTAD 1997). This is 'affiliate licensing', and it involves agreements (of all types, but especially technology licensing and management contracts) made to bolster and regulate the transfer of technology and capital between parent firms of MNEs and their overseas affiliates. Nevertheless, 'non-affiliate licensing' (that is, agreements between independent firms of different nationalities, whereby the licensor owns less than 10 per cent of the equity in the licensee) remains a potent, and probably underutilised mode of foreign market entry, which we elaborate upon below.[3]

Technology licensing

At its narrowest, international technology licensing is merely permission, granted by the owner of a proprietary product or process (the licensor) to a foreign concern (the licensee) in the form of a contract, which allows the latter to engage in an activity otherwise legally forbidden to it (Young *et al.* 1989). Under this contract the licensee purchases the right to commercially exploit a fairly limited set of technologies and know-how from the licensor. The licensor is compensated financially in a number of ways. Most agreements allow for an 'upfront' lump-sum payment and also royalties, normally calculated as a percentage (typically around 5 per cent and seldom exceeding 15 per cent) of the net sale price or on annual turnover and which are paid periodically during the lifetime of the contract (Brooke and Skilbeck 1994). The licensor may also earn revenue on the goods and services it provides the licensee, although tied purchases are now illegal in many jurisdictions.

In the past, only rights relating to patents and trademarks were normally exchanged but, increasingly, agreements now also allow for the provision to the licensee of managerial and technical assistance and training, as well as product up-grades and improvements. The amount of additional support provided by the licensor is largely dependent on the competence and absorptive capacity of the licensee. Generally, it is usual for the licensee to make most, if not all, the capital investment necessary to run the business locally, for example in machinery, land, inventory and labour. It is not uncommon, however, for licensors to take a minority equity stake in their licensees. Most licenses will constrain the business activities of the contracted parties in some way, most commonly with respect to exclusivity and territory (Brooke and Skilbeck 1994). For example, a non-exclusive license may be granted to a licensee. Here the licensor may continue to use the licensed property and may grant other non-exclusive licenses. This contrasts with an exclusive license, in which the licensor agrees with the licensee not to exploit the technology itself nor grant further licenses. Between these extremes is the sole license, under which the licensor can continue to exploit its own technology, but has agreed with the sole licensee not to grant additional licenses. Similarly, licenses may limit to a specific geographical region the markets that the parties can supply. Clearly, a licensee will tend to prefer a high degree of exclusivity in activity and territory, as this will reduce the level of competition to which it is exposed.

Franchising

Franchising is another contractual method of internationalising. It shares many of the characteristics of technology licensing. Although literally meaning 'freedom from servitude', as a business activity the term 'franchising' is actually difficult to define in practice. Nevertheless, two types of franchising are generally recognised – first generation and second generation franchising (Felstead 1993). First generation franchising is often seen in the soft drink-bottling industry and in automobile and petrol retailing. It is very similar to technology licensing except that the franchisee purchases the right to undertake a business activity using the franchisor's trademark or brand name rather than patented technology, and the provision of additional support and guidance is limited. In second generation franchising (or business format franchising as it is more commonly known), by contrast, the franchisor transfers a much more comprehensive business package (the format) to buyers of the franchise. This contains most of the elements needed by the buyer to establish and replicate the business in the foreign market, in what are often 'start-up' situations. In addition to the franchisor's brand-name and marks, therefore, the buyer also receives detailed instructions and guidance on how to operate the franchise, together with managerial expertise, training and perhaps even financial support. The buyer also often benefits from the goodwill that the franchisor has established in its brand names through centralised advertising. In general, in business format franchising the franchisor exerts considerable influence on the day-to-day running of the local operations, unlike first generation franchising, where the business relationship is somewhat distant. Business format franchising is common in the fast food restaurant, hotel and vehicle rental industries, and companies with 'household' names such as McDonald's, Holiday Inn, Hertz and Avis regularly franchise their business into foreign markets. Although franchises are sold directly to individual operators, or franchisees, in the host market, it is more common for master franchising to be used. Here, the franchise is sold to an intermediary company, the sub-franchisor, who is allowed to operate its own outlets or sell the franchise on to independent operators, called sub-franchisees. It is also not unusual for franchising firms to invest equity in host markets, in the form of company-owned outlets and affiliates (Burton and Cross 1997). To this extent, international franchising can lead to the creation of a multi-national enterprise.

Exhibit 6.1 Body Shop expands with £7.1m Cosmo buy

Body Shop International is paying DM20m (£7.1m) for Cosmo Trading, a private company which operates its head franchise in Germany, in the first significant move by Patrick Gournay, the new chief executive. The shares rose 6p to 88p.

Since Mr Gournay took over in July, he has been 'looking at the whole structure of the business', Jeremy Kett, Finance Director, said yesterday. Other changes, to be announced early next year, could include a move out of manufacturing.

Mr Kett said no decisions had yet been taken on the manufacturing side. Body Shop still makes half of the products it sells, although the proportion of in-house manufacturing has dropped over the years. However, other vertically integrated retailers have found it difficult to balance the interests of manufacturing and retailing.

It is thought that Mr Gournay is keen to concentrate on the retailing side of the group. Mr Gournay said: 'The acquisition of the Body Shop in Germany will significantly increase our direct retail presence within central Europe.' The deal is intended to complete on 31 December in order to avoid a rise in the tax rate on corporate disposals in Germany, which takes effect next year.

Cosmo, which took on the Body Shop franchise in 1992, operates 20 Body Shop stores in Germany and sub-franchises another 53. By taking control of Cosmo, Body Shop will remove one link in the chain, but the 53 sub-franchisees will remain.

Mr Kett said the deal could add about £2m to Body Shop's pre-tax profits. Under the franchise deal, it earns a margin on the goods it sells to Cosmo, which had a total sales value of DM21.9m in 1997.

In 1997 Cosmo made a pre-tax profit of DM2.67m after owners' salaries and fees of DM1.96m. Cosmo's profits should have benefited in 1998 by the move in the exchange rate during the year.

Mr Kett said Body Shop had been happy with the operation of the German business, but felt it could be expanded faster under its own control. He predicted it would double in size over the next three to five years. He said there were no plans to buy out the head franchisees in other countries.

Source: *Financial Times* CD-ROM, 1 January–31 December 1998.

Other contract–based entry modes

There are numerous other ways to provide business services to firms in a foreign market under contract besides technology licensing and franchising. In **management contracting**, for example, a supplier in one country undertakes to provide to a client in another country certain on-going management functions which would otherwise be the responsibility of that client. Management contracts are used to provide a wide range of skills and services to customers (including general management, financial administration, personnel administration, production management services). A large element will often concern the training of the local workforce with a view to management responsibility reverting to the client firm at some point in the future. Such agreements are common in the hotel industry, public utilities, health care (notably hospital management), transportation, agriculture and mining industries. **Technical service agreements** have a similar but more precise function, to provide for the supply of technical services across borders, for example, to run or maintain machinery and equipment. An increasingly common instance of a technical service agreement occurs when a company out-sources to a foreign firm the maintenance and management of its computer and telecommunications networks. Finally, firms also enter into contractual international joint ventures. These are contract-based partnerships formed between firms of different nationalities, as well as government agencies, to share, typically, the cost (and therefore the risk) of an investment. In contrast to equity joint ventures, no legally separate firm is created. Examples of contractual joint ventures include the co-production, co-research and co-development activities frequently observed in the automotive, pharmaceutical and electrical goods industries; the co-publishing arrangements between publishing companies and consortium ventures undertaken by many multinational banks.

Disadvantages of contractual modes of entry

Contracting out production to independent local companies has a number of disadvantages (Contractor 1985; Welch 1999). This discussion looks at technology licensing, although much also pertains to franchising and other contract-based modes of market entry. The greatest disadvantage is that, because production is effectively delegated to the licensee, licensing is generally a low-control strategy that does not allow the firm to maximise returns on its technology. The licensor is dependent on the licensee to generate revenues, of which the former only receives a minor portion in the form of fees and royalties. Government restrictions and withdrawal taxes on the repatriation of licensing royalties may further dilute this share. The volume and quality of production, local distribution channels and many of the marketing issues are usually also under the licensee's control. The licensor and licensee will probably have established a common business strategy prior to signing the agreement and will normally be able to hammer out any disagreements during regular meetings. Nevertheless, the potential for conflict remains strong. Common areas for dispute include the setting and achievement of production targets and business growth rates, the amount of support provided and the level of fees to be paid. Reconciling a business relationship that has broken down can prove an expensive and time-consuming exercise for the licensor.

The second disadvantage to licensing is that it is very difficult, if not impossible, for the licensor to recover its technology and know-how once it has been transferred and assimilated by the licensee. The constant threat in licensing, therefore, is that the licensee will be able to use the product or process technology 'in ways which have not been paid for' (Buckley and Ghauri 1999: xiv). The licensee may then become a competitor, either during the lifetime of the contract or, more likely, after it has expired.

The third disadvantage relates to the costs associated with contracting with independent companies in the market place. We can refer to these as transactions costs, and there are several types (Contractor 1990). First, there are search and negotiation costs. Unless the licensor receives an adequate number of unsolicited enquiries, it will have to locate a suitable foreign partner in the target market and, once identified, its suitability and productive capacity assessed. If acceptable, agreements need to be negotiated, contracts drawn up and legal fees paid. If not already done so, the licensor will also need to codify its technology and know-how in a tangible way (as blueprints, designs, operating manuals, computer software) so that it can be readily transferred and assimilated by the licensee. The licensor will also need to protect its IPR in each market entered. Indeed, licensees are often reluctant to buy unpatented technology. Levels of protection vary between jurisdictions (despite attempts by the WTO to harmonise national legislation), but legal systems that protect the rights of owners of technology enable those owners to feel more secure in licensing to independent firms and reduce associated costs.[4] Collectively, these are known as technology-transfer costs.

When the business is up and running, the licensor will also incur the cost of providing managerial and technical assistance and training. These are servicing costs. At the same time, the licensor will need to monitor and, if necessary, police the licensee, to obviate any likelihood that the licensee will behave opportunistically. For instance, the licensor may have to install counting equipment, make regular inspection visits and periodically audit the business of the licensee. This is to ensure that correct sales are declared and appropriate fees paid. More importantly, monitoring ensures that a certain level of quality in the delivery of product and service is met. While important in technology licensing, this is particularly important in franchising, in which the franchisee has the incentive to reduce its costs, and perhaps deliver a substandard quality product or service as a result, in order to inflate its margins on sales. If unchecked, such action could have a disastrous impact on the goodwill associated with the brand-name and therefore the value of future sales of the franchise.

The transaction costs associated with contracting with an independent company in a foreign market can therefore be appreciable. This is especially true between firms that are spatially distant from each other or are from widely contrasting cultures, for example. When the transaction costs of dealing with independent companies in host markets are greater than the costs of corporate governance, firms will have a strong incentive to internalise their technological advantage, and develop foreign markets using equity-based means of internationalising (that is, using foreign affiliates). The high transaction costs of conducting international business at 'arm's length' between independent firms (that is, non-affiliate licensing) serves to explain the preponderance of FDI: internalised transacting negates many of the costs associated with negotiating and policing inter-firm agreements.

The advantages of contractual modes of entry

Nevertheless, in a seminal study, Contractor (1985) found many advantages to licensing. The two most important reasons given by firms was that licensing enabled them to service foreign markets in which investment restrictions (by sector and/or level of foreign ownership) militated against FDI and when trade barriers or high transport costs (relative to value) rendered exporting impractical.

This finding suggests that licensing is a suboptimal strategy compared with the alternative modes of market entry. However, despite the fact that, since the time of Contractor's study, both investment restrictions and barriers to trade have diminished, the popularity of international licensing is unabated. The additional advantages of licensing identified by Contractor go some way to explaining this. In particular, because the foreign entrant makes little or no resource commitment in host-market operations, it is generally viewed as a low-risk strategy. This makes it an ideal method to use when political risk in the host-market, whether perceived or actual, is high. It also makes licensing appropriate when servicing markets that are uncertain or volatile, or those that are too small to warrant an equity investment. It follows that, despite the transaction costs already discussed, licensing tends to be a low-cost strategy, certainly in comparison to equity modes of international competition. This makes it particularly attractive to smaller firms that are financially constrained or lack the necessary international management skills to invest directly in and run a foreign plant. Its low-cost characteristic also enables firms, irrespective of size, to enter one or more markets rapidly and simultaneously by licensing out, accelerating the internationalisation process. In each of these cases, the foreign entrant also benefits from the licensee's local market knowledge and distribution channels, which it might find costly and time-consuming to develop on its own.

In addition to its low-cost, low-risk characteristics, licensing is also a feasible option in circumstances where the foreign market entrant is unconcerned about the danger of creating a competitor in the licensee. Contractor (1985) found, for example, that licensing was favoured among firms that were able to remain technologically superior to the licensee, either because of their own fast rate of product development, or because of imminent technology or model changes typical in dynamic, rapidly evolving industries. In such situations, the licensee is likely to gain greater benefit from product up-grades and other technical improvements it receives from the licensor than if it reneged on the agreement by exploiting the technology in competition with the licensor. This explains, in part, the preponderance of licensing in 'high-tech' industries. On the other hand, many licensors also license out technology that is becoming obsolete in their home or major markets, in order to extend its life cycle in less technologically advanced foreign markets (for example, in developing countries). Many large and diversified firms are also increasingly prepared to license out their technology and brand-names, as a means of earning revenue on products that are not 'core' to them. Finally, contracts are also used widely as a means of formalising the reciprocal exchange of technology between independent firms, for example, in joint ventures.

It is important, therefore, that firms do not view licensing as second best. It is often the optimal foreign market entry and servicing strategy, even when FDI and exporting are viable options. Firms should constantly appraise their IPR portfolio, and be prepared to license-out their technology and brand-names if opportunities to generate revenue in this way are presented.

Equity modes of foreign market entry

Foreign direct investment is the principal way that firms compete internationally in the modern global economy. In general, by internalising international produc-

Exhibit 6.2 **Foreign business looks beyond Tuscany and tenors**

If lifestyle were the measure on which companies base their location strategies, Italy would probably come out on top. Artistic and architectural treasures abound in historic towns and cities. Excellent food, fine wines, world leadership in fashion and furnishing, a Mediterranean climate in much of the country, marvellous beaches, Alpine slopes: Italy seems to have everything. Add in Italian hospitality and how can the country be beaten on lifestyle? And, even when using the more stolid criteria that corporate bosses employ when making their decisions on where to site factories and offices, Italy scores well.

It was one of the European Economic Community's six founding members in 1957 and is now a qualifier for Europe's single currency. Although the Italian boot pushes south-eastwards into the Mediterranean, a substantial part of the country can fairly claim to be at or near the heart of Europe. Yet Italy has been a huge underperformer in attracting direct inward investment. Figures from UNCTAD show that direct inward investment into the *bel paese* was just $3.5bn last year, compared with $36.9bn for Britain and $18.2bn for France. The Benelux countries and Spain did significantly better than Italy and even tiny Ireland had greater appeal.

Last year was not an exception in a run of good years. Italy has never done well in the global competition for direct investment. A study by the Bank of Italy shows that Italy's annual average share of total world direct investment has been around 3 per cent since 1970, a percentage consistently much lower than its European partners. In 1980, for example, Italy took 2 per cent of the global total while Britain had 12.7 per cent, Germany 5.1 per cent and France 4.6 per cent.

One reason advanced for the low level of direct inward investment is that, however hospitable they may be, where business is concerned Italians simply do not like having outsiders on their patch. Hands are thrown up in horror at the idea of foreign companies taking control of Italian businesses, particularly those being privatised. The Bank of Italy is thought to be unenthusiastic about foreign banks controlling Italian institutions.

Despite the talk about an open economy, nostalgia for Fascist-type autarchy lingers. 'Other countries compete to attract foreign investment, while in the south we still ask whether this (foreign investment) is appropriate. Foreign capital is viewed with suspicion,' observes Pietro Busetta, an economist and president of the Fondazione Curella in Palermo.

Sergio de Nardis, an economist with Confindustria, the industrialists' federation, says that there are several reasons why Italy fails to attract more foreigners. 'It is a question of convenience. Excessive labour costs, inadequate infrastructure, high taxation and a Byzantine bureaucracy are enormous deterrents. Italy is just not competitive,' says Mr de Nardis.

Conditions were favourable for outsiders to invest in Italy during the early and mid-1990s, thanks to the lira's devaluation and to opportunities arising from privatisation and corporate restructuring. But they did not arrive then any more than they did before or have since. 'Foreigners are just not interested,' concludes Mr de Nardis. For just more than a year, however, an agency based in Turin has been trying to drum up interest among reluctant or indifferent foreigners. ITP Agenzia pergli Investimenti a Torino e in Piemonte, Italy's first regional investment agency, has achieved some results. By mid-November it had helped 15 companies establish themselves in Turin and the surrounding Piedmont region.

So far ITP's efforts have created 340 jobs. ITP seems well placed to meet its modest target of 1000 jobs by April 2000. Some of the jobs already created are with Italian firms, though most have been generated by foreign businesses which account for two-thirds of the set-ups. 'Foreign companies provide work directly for 70,000 people in Piedmont.

'Until now they have been almost completely ignored by the authorities. These are an obvious starting point for us,' says Paolo Corradini, ITP's director. ITP is still the only regional investment agency in Italy, where many industrialists point enviously towards the examples offered by Britain's Welsh Development Agency. 'In order to be a model for other Italian regions, we must adopt best practice. This means copying Britain and France,' says Mr Corradini. He adds, however, that a small budget limits what ITP can do abroad.

Outsiders may find it strange that a region in the north-west, where Italy's industrialisation started and where unemployment is around the national average, should be the first to organise for attracting inward direct investment. Surely the unindustrialised south where some regions have unemployment that is more than twice the national average is the logical place for such efforts?

GDP growth of 3 per cent is needed just to keep employment at present levels; double that is required to start reducing the queues of jobless in the mezzogiorno. 'We need to offer advantages in order to make the south a location as appetising as Ireland, Wales or Eastern Europe,' says Mr Busetta. He admits that the south will never have the same labour flexibility and costs as Taiwan but it could do much better than now.

Italy's southern regions, and Sicily particularly, suffer from being at the periphery. There is little that Palermo can do about being 1400 km. from Milan but this raw fact of geography makes first-class infrastructure a precondition for direct investment, whether the investment be Italian or foreign.

Beating the organised crime which exists across the south, and not just in Sicily, is another precondition. 'It is unrealistic to imagine outsiders investing unless they have absolute guarantees of locating in areas that are secure,' remarks Mr Busetta.

Italians themselves have shown scarce enthusiasm for investing in the mezzogiorno. Little wonder, therefore, that foreigners have steered clear.

Source: *Financial Times* CD-ROM, 1 January–31 December 1998.

tion (that is, bringing it under direct control within an MNE) the firm secures the greatest level of control over its proprietary information, IPR, product quality and, therefore, its technological advantage compared to other entry methods. The firm also maximises potential returns on this technology because profits are not shared with an independent local party, such as an agent, distributor or licensee (Buckley and Casson 1976; Dunning 1993). The co-ordination and integration of production and marketing in different countries allows the firm to spread its risk, so that economic downturns or setbacks in one market can be compensated for by diverting production to other locations, without the complications of renegotiations of contracts with third parties. Firms may also benefit from the financial incentives of host-country governments to attract inward investment.

Further benefits and costs of FDI compared to the alternative methods of international supply are determined in part by the motive for the investment, the scale of investment (that is, an equity joint venture or wholly owned subsidiary) and the vehicle used (that is, by acquisition or greenfield entry). We consider first the motive for investment. Four generic motives are recognised: market-oriented, cost-oriented, raw-materials oriented and strategic asset-seeking motives (Dunning 1993).

In a market-oriented investment, the decision is taken to supply a foreign market by producing goods locally in an affiliate rather than by shipping goods directly from the home market. This is import-substituting FDI. It is usually a response by MNEs, most often those from the manufacturing industries, to the costs associated with serving a foreign market from a distance, particularly tariff and transport costs. When production involves large volumes of goods or goods that are heavy or bulky relative to their value, it may be cheaper to produce in the host market and circumvent these costs, even when the manufacturing cost per unit is higher abroad than at home. Direct investment is preferable because, at high sales volume, the high fixed costs of setting up an affiliate are apportioned over such a large sales volume that the total costs of FDI are lower than the transaction costs of negotiating and policing a license. Closer contact with markets and customers also promotes information flow to the firm, increasing its local responsiveness in terms of product adaptation, delivery and aftersales care. Many US and Japanese firms invested in the EU in the 1980s and 1990s for import-substitution reasons (Cross 1999). In addition to economising on transport costs, they were able to negate the threat, albeit unrealised, that punitive tariffs would be levied on imports from non-member states. The market-oriented motive may result in the whole of a value-adding chain of production processes being transferred to the foreign market, or just some stages of production. Typically, an MNE might establish a sales affiliate, which transfers only the selling function, as an early stage of market-oriented FDI, or an assembly plant, at a later stage (or perhaps to circumvent tariffs). The main function of the sales affiliate is to sell imported goods and provide additional marketing and aftersales services, thus benefiting the MNE in terms of closer proximity to its final customers and markets.

Cost-oriented investments take place to reduce input costs, such as labour, energy and transport costs. Many firms from the industrialised economies, particularly those in mature industries, have responded to high domestic labour costs by combining existing production technology with host country labour to lower production costs and increase their competitiveness. Cost-oriented investment is distinct from market-oriented FDI in that the final market to be supplied is usually outside the host country. For example, firms often export semi-finished goods from the parent to a foreign affiliate, where the goods undergo further processing and finishing before being re-exported to the home or third countries. This is 'off-shore production' and it occurs in export-platform countries that have a comparative advantage in the production of low-skilled labour intensive goods (for example, Mexico for many US firms and Spain and Portugal for European firms). The same principle applies to MNEs that invest in countries with a large pool of scientists, engineers and highly skilled labour in order to develop and undertake technology and skills-intensive production. This is evidenced by Japanese FDI in the EU, where skills-intensive production tends to be located in Germany in preference to, for example, the UK (Cross 1999).

The third type, raw-materials oriented investment, occurs to obtain security in the supply of inputs. It occurs because high transaction costs of using contracts to supply raw materials over the long term renders this inferior to owning and controlling a foreign affiliate to supply the MNE indefinitely. This type of investment is still very important in certain industries – notably the extractive industries such as oil and minerals – and in certain parts of the world. Much of Japan's investment in the 1950s and 1960s, for example, was made to secure the supply of natural resources lacking at home. As a proportion of global FDI flows today, however, this type of investment is in decline (UNCTAD 1997).

Finally, firms make strategic asset-seeking investments. These are undertaken to promote long-term strategic objectives. It typically takes the form of an acquisition of an existing firm, although establishing a joint venture yields similar benefits (see below). The aim is to add to the acquiring firm's existing portfolio of assets in a manner intended to sustain or advance their international competitiveness *vis-à-vis* that of their competitors. Expected benefits might include gaining access to new markets via the foreign party involved (for example, distribution networks, government contacts); creating synergies and economies in R&D, production and marketing; or acquiring a range of tangible and intangible assets through the acquisition of a foreign firm that compliments the MNE's current offerings.

Owning and controlling a foreign operation represents the greatest level of commitment of capital and managerial effort that a firm can make to a foreign market. The investing firm needs to have in place effective decision-making procedures in all the major functional areas of business, including production, marketing, organisation, human resources management and financial management. This will involve, for example, procurement policies, staffing policies, reporting relationships between parent and affiliate, financial planning and control systems. Tensions between the parent and its affiliates will also need to be managed regarding the centralisation or decentralisation of decision making in these areas.

The cost of investing in and co-ordinating the functions of a foreign operation, and the inevitable increase in exposure to economic and political risk experienced by the foreign market entrant means that FDI tends to be undertaken by larger firms, especially those from the industrialised economies. However, smaller firms, in terms of both financial and managerial resources, as well as those firms from the developing countries, have demonstrated an increasing willingness to invest in overseas subsidiaries, assisted by a greater awareness of the importance of foreign markets and falling trade barriers.

The 'vehicle' of FDI

In practice, a firm can make a foreign direct investment in one of several ways: by establishing a foreign operation 'from scratch', by acquiring an existing foreign firm, or by creating an equity joint venture which is located in a non-domestic market. We consider now the role of equity joint ventures in international strategy.

Equity joint ventures

An equity joint venture (EJV) is a foreign affiliate in which ownership is incomplete and more than one party has an effective voice in the control of its day-to-day operations. In addition to private firms, these parties can be government agencies and public sector organisations. The parent firms in the EJV (the 'child') join forces to undertake a long-term (typically five years or more) business objective regarding, for example, production, purchasing, sales, maintenance, repair, research co-operation, consultation and/or financing. The EJV is a separate legal entity, and quasi-autonomous in that it is distinct from the management of each parent. Each partner contributes assets to the venture in the form of capital, technology, IPR, managerial know-how, marketing experience, personnel, physical assets and access to distribution networks. The combined monetary value of these assets constitutes the EJV's capitalisation, which is shared according to the interests of each parent. Typically, one partner will have a majority shareholding and therefore some dominance in decision making. Profits and risks are usually shared in proportion to the respective capital contribution of the partners, of which there may be several.

MNEs often prefer complete control in the form of wholly-owned affiliates over inter-firm EJVs. In the past, EJVs were the only practical means of investing in countries such as the USSR, China, Mexico and India that imposed limitations on the proportion of FDI permitted in a given operation. Nevertheless, despite the fact that many host countries have relaxed these restrictions – especially in non-sensitive sectors – the use of EJVs as an international strategy has not waned (Beamish and Banks 1987; Glaister and Buckley 1994). Why is this so?

First, because capital contributions are shared, an EJV reduces the entrant's start-up costs relative to the initial costs of greenfield entry or the capital costs of outright foreign acquisition. Many smaller firms are often attracted to EJVs for this reason, particularly when they can capitalise their know-how and IPR as part, if not all, of their contribution, while the host-country partner supplies the land, buildings and labour, for example. Using the partner's local production facilities often means that the entrant does not have to start a local business from scratch and potential initial losses are minimised. Where time is crucial, an EJV may shorten the period for market entry and development compared to greenfield entry, and immediate access may be gained to the local partner's competencies, foreign market knowledge and distribution facilities. Indeed, synergistic benefits may be created from the amalgam of two business activities in one 'child' firm. The EJV may be able to use the partners' technological inputs to provide goods and services that each partner would not be able to develop alone cheaply, if at all. The EJV may generate economies of scale and scope not otherwise readily available to participating firms, by allowing the partners to complement each other.

Local involvement in an EJV may benefit the entrant in other ways. For example, it may be easier for foreign firms to win tender contracts in a host country when a local partner is involved, and local consumers may be more willing to purchase from a firm viewed as domestic rather than foreign. Similarly, an EJV between a foreign firm and a local partner may be treated by governments as an entirely domestic firm, and so benefit from tax holidays, tax concessions, preferential loans and fewer profit-repatriation limitations than would be the case if the operation were fully foreign-owned. Equity joint ventures also allow the spreading of financial and political risk between the parties. Consequently, they are common in high-risk, capital-intensive industries, especially in the extractive industries. In these instances, the partners are most likely to both be MNEs, operating outside their home countries or normal territory, for example, in oil exploration.

Despite these benefits, failure rates among EJVs are high. EJVs between developed and developing country firms are particularly afflicted, as are those in high technology industries where the control of technology is especially difficult. Numerous sources of difficulty account for the instability of EJVs, and these mainly derive from the conflict that can arise between the two parent firms.

In addition to disagreements in the day-to-day running of the EJV and its business functions, the partners may well seek differing objectives for the EJV. Misunderstandings and conflicts of interest can easily arise between the partners regarding, for example, whether to pursue a global or a local strategy, to supply domestic or export markets, or to repatriate or reinvest profits. In many cases, the EJV has a justifiable right to question the authority of the foreign parent firm, which in itself can lead to tension. Differences in management culture and language between the parents (between say European and Japanese managers) may exaggerate and exacerbate these difficulties.

Partners to an EJV may demonstrate an unwillingness to share earnings. This problem is most pronounced in technologically based industries where the foreign parent is commonly from an industrialised economy and enjoys a monopoly or near monopoly position in its market. One or more of the partners may also be reluctant to share control over its IPR and technology. For many local firms, access to foreign technology is the prime motivator for undertaking an EJV, and the partner with the greater technological input will be concerned that the other firm does not dissipate the technology (that is, damage its value) or become a competitor. For these reasons, EJVs are inherently unstable, particularly as their relative bargaining strengths change over the duration of the EJV. They tend to be most scarce and least successful in research-intensive industries, where the diffusion of intangible assets and technology to a local partner disturbs the internal balance of power between the parent firms.

Acquisition and wholly owned greenfield operations

Wholly owned affiliates avoid many of the problems inherent in EJVs, especially those due to shared decision making. Wholly owned affiliates can be created from scratch (a greenfield investment), or by merging with or acquiring an existing firm in the foreign market. Mergers and acquisitions have become the most important international supply method, at least in terms of the value of assets employed (UNCTAD 1997).

A greenfield investment has many advantages over acquisition (Brooke and Buckley 1988). The scale of entry and the development rate of greenfield entry can be matched to the firm's resources and the size and potential of the market. It may overall be cheaper than acquisition and there is certainly little danger of overpayment, which is not always the case when buying an existing business. Building a tailor-made facility also allows the entrant to select its preferred location and install the most modern technology and management techniques if it wishes. The entrant will also not inherit any problems from an acquired firm (regarding, for example, ageing technology, inappropriate production methods or a demoralised work-force). Host-country governments often welcome (with financial incentives) greenfield investments in preference to acquisition, as the former is likely to generate greater employment and increased competition rather than be anti-competitive, which acquisitions may well be. Greenfield entry is often preferred by smaller investors without the financial ability to purchase outright an existing firm. Furthermore, it will be the only viable form of investment if the host country lacks a suitable company to purchase, which is often the case, for example, in less-developed countries.

However, acquisitions do have their advantages. An acquisition permits rapid market entry and allows a quicker return on capital and ready access to knowledge of the local market (via the acquired firm) than does greenfield entry. Acquisitions may also be essential to pre-empt a rival's entry to the same market. By assimilating a local company, many of the cultural, legal and management problems associated with foreign market entry, especially those pertaining to 'start-up' situations, are avoided, at least in part. In addition to acquiring local management and local market knowledge (often the most important motives for the takeover in the first instance), established brand-names, distribution networks and R&D facilities may also be purchased. To this extent, a strategic asset-seeking acquisition is most likely to succeed. Finally, because an acquisition involves a change in ownership and does not disturb the local competitive environment as much as a new greenfield entry might, it often attracts a lesser competitive reaction from local firms.

There are several disadvantages to acquisition. First, there is the problem of accurately identifying the worth of the assets (especially intangible assets such as IPR, know-how and goodwill) to be acquired, and a danger of overpayment exists. As Brooke and Buckley (1988) point out, the purchase price should represent the value of the assets when combined with the acquiring firm, not the value of the independent entity prior to purchase. Also, there are the problems of integrating a previously independent unit into a larger whole, with different goals, procedures, management styles and – of heightened importance today – computer and telecommunications infrastructure. Finally, the search for the ideal takeover candidate can involve heavy costs, especially in management time, and this should also be taken into account by the acquisitive firm.

Chapter summary

There are many different routes that firms can employ to enter foreign markets. Each method places its own unique demands on the firm and has its particular implications for management. Consequently, when selecting the appropriate entry method, decision-makers must evaluate a complex yet interdependent set of factors, many of which cannot be readily quantified. Managers need to balance the degree of *control* they seek over local operations with the *cost* of entry – the level of resources they are willing to commit to that market. They also need to assess the actual *risk* associated with an entry mode (as opposed to that perceived), and the potential *returns* which can be appropriated (as a proportion of the total maximum income that could be generated in the host market) using that mode. Indirect exporting is a low-control, low-risk mode of market entry, but likely returns are commensurately lower. Progressing along a continuum from licensing to joint ventures to wholly owned subsidiaries heightens the cost of entry and exposes the firm to greater risk, but yields greater control and increases the firm's ability to appropriate the profits generated by the foreign operation.

Although choosing the optimal entry method for a particular market is probably more of an art than a science, care must be taken to correctly match the entry mode to the circumstances of the firm and of the foreign market. It is likely that a suboptimal choice, or inadequate commitment to this choice, will lead to the unsatisfactory performance of a foreign sales drive or operation. Should this occur, managers will probably need to expend a considerable amount of time and effort, as well as financial resources, to extricate themselves from the business arrangement or switch to an alternative market-servicing mode. Any consequent diversion of resources from areas (both geographical and functional) where they are more productively employed may be detrimental to the firm's ability to service other international markets or, at worst, its home market, where sales and profits are often the greatest, especially for smaller firms. Although this caution applies to MNEs with extensive international operations, the effect on smaller and novice international firms is often more pronounced, and perhaps may cause them to postpone or indefinitely delay further international expansion plans. It is therefore important that firms monitor changing circumstances to ensure they are supplying foreign markets in the most appropriate manner.

Discussion questions

1 'The theoretical generalisation that multinational firms will prefer "internalisation" via direct investment over the sale of technology via licensing is a proposition that needs to be examined with greater circumspection in the emerging climate for international business' (Contractor 1985). Discuss the validity of this statement in the context of today's international business environment.
2 In a global economy characterised by increasing liberalisation of trade and a relaxation in investment restrictions, why do equity joint ventures continue to be a popular means of servicing foreign markets?
3 What key factors should a medium-sized British consumer goods manufacturer take into account when deciding between a 'greenfield' entry and acquisition as a route into a developing country market?

Closing Case Study:
Marks & Spencer – retailing to the world

In 1884, a Pole, Michael Marks, established a chain of shops in the north of England that sold everything at one price – a penny. After joining forces with Thomas Spencer in 1894 a business empire – Marks & Spencer Ltd – was created which was to become the largest retailer in the UK. Growth was achieved through a philosophy of commitment to both customers and employees. M&S

has traditionally sold durable merchandise at a moderate price, with high turnover compensating for low margins, and its St Michael brand-name has become synonymous with quality and value. Offering good salaries, as well as other benefits such as advantageous pension schemes, sponsored social and recreational facilities, and assistance with the costs of chiropodist services (needed by shop-workers who stand a lot), the company benefited greatly from its loyal and committed workforce.

By the mid-1970s, however, growth opportunities for M&S in the UK were diminishing. Attempts to add new products and appeal to new market segments had failed. The Harrods-type customer refused to switch to M&S following the introduction of higher-priced and finer-quality clothes, while the company was unable to respond to the fast changes demanded by the more fashion-conscious market when it targeted the younger consumer. It was soon recognised that the company faced near saturation in the UK and the best prospects for expansion lay overseas.

Taking advantage of reduced tariff barriers brought about by the creation of the European Community, M&S opened its first stores on the European continent in 1975. Since then, M&S has used a variety of methods to develop overseas markets. However, success in international markets has been mixed and, as like many firms, M&S has discovered that replicating abroad a competitive advantage created at home is a challenge often difficult to overcome.

In France, Belgium and The Netherlands, M&S chose to open its own stores. However, M&S was not well received initially. Although the company was highly reputed in the UK, this encouraged a degree of complacency among its managers who presumed that the names M&S and St Michael would be equally well known in Paris and Brussels. It was belatedly discovered that less than 3 per cent of the French had even heard of the company. Store location was also a problem. Because store space was at a premium in the most popular shopping streets of Paris and Brussels, the company was forced to accept stores with limited walk-by pedestrian traffic and with small frontage which failed to give an impression of copious merchandise within. Once its continental stores were up and running, M&S was forced to respond to a number of operational difficulties. In the UK, M&S enjoyed considerable purchasing power over its UK suppliers, and could negotiate very advantageous prices and terms. However, on entering continental markets, M&S decided to contract the bulk of its sourcing to local suppliers, who were unwilling to treat M&S more favourably than other European retailers. The company also found that French customers had different tastes. French women, for example, tended to prefer tighter fitting clothes and longer skirts than their British counterparts, while French men preferred jackets and trousers rather than formal suits, and a wider range of colours in their sweaters. Many French customers found the M&S stores austere and complained about the lack of changing-rooms (which was *de rigeur* in the company's UK stores). As a result, M&S had to adapt their procurement of supplies and their marketing mix to target a particular market niche. M&S now buys very little from continental suppliers, and instead capitalises on the 'Britishness' of the St Michael brand to sell UK-made goods to Britons living in Paris, as well as Parisians, rather than competing head-on with French styles and couture. In deference to French tastes, the stores are now carpeted and have dressing-rooms. Despite the problems M&S experienced in gaining local market knowledge, by responding to the specific needs of the market the company has become one of the leading retailers in France. Following the lessons learnt, M&S now owns 37 stores in the major capital cities and important conurbations of continental Europe, in France, Belgium, Holland, Spain, the Republic of Ireland and, latterly, Germany.

The importance of operating company-owned outlets to gain market knowledge is evidenced by the company's Far East strategy. The only directly-owned outlets M&S has in the Far East can be found in Hong Kong, now a Special Administrative Region of China. In operating these stores, M&S is developing valuable first-hand expertise and knowledge of the Chinese consumer. This should prove vital to the company's representative office in Shanghai, from where the grassroots of what may prove to be a huge retail business in mainland China is being established.

In North America M&S decided to adopt an acquisitive approach. It entered the Canadian market in 1976 first using company-owned outlets that operated the UK business formula, and then by the acquisition of D'Alliard's and Peoples. It was hoped that the Canadian operation would be a springboard into the lucrative markets of the United States, and in 1987, D'Alliard's expanded into three shopping malls in New York. In 1988, following extensive market research, M&S purchased the US retailer Brooks Brothers. This move surprised analysts, not only because of the high price paid, but because Brooks Brothers had an up-market image, a high level of personal service, and expensive clothing which did not fit well with the goods typically offered by M&S. However, a significant element of the purchase was the operations that Brooks Brothers owned in Japan, which provided M&S with an important toehold in an otherwise difficult market to access. Despite promises to the contrary, M&S imposed many of its UK practices on the Brooks Brothers organisation in the US. It reduced the size of the workforce, replaced glass cabinet displays with open displays, changed promotional policies and reduced the range of clothing on offer. Within two years, the sales and profits of Brooks Brothers dropped sharply. This was only turned around when M&S increased the rate of sales commission and introduced improved cost controls and inventory systems. With 119 outlets in the US today, Brooks Brothers is consistently among the best performing US retailers in like-for-like sales of men's clothing.

Since the mid-1980s, M&S has also successfully franchised its brand-name and business format around the globe. Multiple unit franchises have been sold to markets in Europe (for example, Austria, Cyprus, Czech Republic, Gibraltar, Greece, Guernsey, Hungary, Jersey, Malta, Poland, Portugal and Turkey), the Middle East (Abu-Dhabi, Bahrain and Dubai), North Africa (Gran Canaria and Tenerife) and South-East Asia (Indonesia, Malaysia, Philippines, Singapore, South Korea and Thailand). In most of these cases, the franchise was sold to businesses that had previously enjoyed a long-term relationship (in some cases over 30 years) with M&S as importers of St Michael merchandise and where levels of mutual trust were high. By franchising, the company has been able to quickly tap local entrepreneurial capabilities with regard to recruitment, local sourcing, distribution channels and understanding customer needs, while at the same time limiting its exposure to capital expenditure and risk. For M&S, franchising has proved to be an effective and profitable method for extending its brand name into geographically dispersed foreign markets, especially those with relatively limited sales prospects and where a degree of uncertainty over future market developments exists.

Source: Adapted from Welford and Prescott (1996), Daniels and Radebaugh (1995), and various company annual reports.

Questions

1 What were the main difficulties that Marks & Spencer experienced when it set up stores from scratch in Continental Europe?
2 What advantages did M&S derive from purchasing Brooks Brothers in the US rather than setting up stores from scratch?
3 Do the countries that M&S has entered using franchising have any common characteristics and, if so, what are they? Why has franchising been used to enter these markets?

Notes

1 The term 'agent' and 'distributor' should not be used interchangeably; a distributor takes title to the goods it imports whereas an agent does not.
2 The elimination of exchange rate risk to promote greater trade was one of the principal reasons why European monetary union was conceived and introduced in 1999 among 12 member states of the European Union.
3 In other words, non-affiliate contractual relationships necessarily imply an absence of contracts.
4 Countries with a strong patent protection (such as the industrialised countries) tend to attract greater inward licensing activity because companies are reassured that contracted parties will not appropriate the technology and so become a competitor, either before or after the contract expires.

References

Beamish, P.W. and Banks, J.C. (1987) Equity joint ventures and the theory of the multinational enterprise, *Journal of International Business Studies* 18 (3): 1–16.

Brooke, M.Z. and Buckley, P.J. (eds) (1988) *Handbook of International Trade*, London: Macmillan.

Brooke, M.Z. and Skilbeck, J.M. (1994) *Licensing: The International Sale of Patents and Technical Know-How*, Aldershot: Gower.

Buckley, P.J. and Brooke, M.Z. (1992) *International Business Studies: An overview*, Oxford: Blackwell Publishers.

Buckley, P.J. and Casson, M. (1976) *The Future of the Multinational Enterprise*, London: Macmillan.

Buckley, P.J. and Ghauri, P.N. (1999) *The Internationalization of the Firm: A Reader*, London: International Thomson Business Press.

Buckley, P.J., Pass, C.L. and Prescott, K. (1992) The internationalization of service firms: a comparison with the manufacturing sector, *Scandinavian International Business Review* 1 (1): 39–56.

Burton, F.N. and Cross, A.R. (1997) International franchising: market vs hierarchy, Chapter 7 in G. Chryssochoidis, C. Millar and J. Clegg (eds), *Internationalization Strategies*, London: Macmillan.

Contractor, F.J. (1985) *Licensing in International Strategy: A Guide for Planning and Negotiations,* Westport, Connecticut: Quorum Books.

Contractor, F.J. (1990) Contractual and cooperative forms of international business: towards a unified theory of modal choice, *Management International Review* 30 (1): 31–54.

Cross, A.R. (1999) Foreign direct investment and the European Union, Chapter 16 in F. McDonald and S. Dearden (eds) *European Economic Integration*, 3rd edn, Harlow: Longman.

Daniels, J.D. and Radebough, L.H. (1995) *International Business: Environments and Operations*, 7th edn, New York: Addison Wesley.

Dunning, J.H. (1993) *Multinational Enterprises and the Global Economy*, Wokingham: Addison-Wesley.

Felstead, A. (1993) *The Corporate Paradox: Power and Control in the Business Franchise*, London: Routledge.

Glaister, K.W. and Buckley, P.J. (1994) UK international joint ventures: an analysis of patterns of activity and distribution, *British Journal of Management*, 5 (1): 33–51.

Radice, H. (1999) 'Globalization' and the convergence of national business systems, Chapter 13 in F.N. Burton, M.K. Chapman and A.R. Cross (eds), *International Business Organisation: Subsidiary Management, Entry Strategies and Emerging Markets*, Basingstoke: Macmillan.

Sullivan, P.H. (1998) *Profiting from Intellectual Capital: Extracting Value from Innovation*, New York: John Wiley.

UNCTAD (1996) *World Investment Report: Investment, Trade and International Policy Arrangements*, United Nations Conference on Trade and Development, UNCTAD: New York and Geneva.

UNCTAD (1997) *World Investment Report: Transnational Corporations, Market Structure and Competition Policy*, United Nations Conference on Trade and Development, UNCTAD: New York and Geneva.

Welch, L. (1999) Outward foreign licensing by Australian companies, Chapter 15 in P.J. Buckley and P.N. Ghauri (eds) *The Internationalization of the Firm: A Reader*, London: International Thomson Business Press.

Welford, R. and Prescott, K. (1992) *European Business: An Issue-Based Approach*, 3rd edn, London: Pitman Publishing.

Welford, R. and Prescott, K. (1996) *European Business: An Issue-based Approach*, 3rd edn, London: Pitman Publishing.

Young, S., Hamill, J., Wheeler, C. and Davies, J.R. (1989) *International Market Entry and Development: Strategies and Management*, Hemel Hempstead: Harvester Wheatsheaf.

CHAPTER 7

The Internationalisation Process and Types of Firms

Susan Bridgewater

Learning objectives

By the end of this chapter you will:

■ understand the concepts of simultaneous and sequential internationalisation

■ be familiar with the arguments for each of these processes

■ be aware of different processes of internationalisation, which may be found in services and manufacturing firms and between large, multinational or global, and small firms

■ understand the network view of internationalisation.

Opening Case Study:
On a mission to go for the throat of the world fizzy drinks market

Though 'Coca-Cola – Always' is the current advertising slogan for the world's favourite fizzy drink, 'Coca-Cola – Everywhere' is the mantra for the The Coca-Cola Company of Atlanta, which sells almost 1bn servings a day of its cola and other soft drinks such as Fanta and Sprite.

Coke's mission is to ensure its products are within 'an arm's length of desire', and it is building a worldwide network of anchor bottlers to achieve that. This week the latest piece in its global jigsaw fell into place with the announcement of the flotation in London of Coca-Cola Beverages, covering 13 countries of Central and Eastern Europe.

The new company will be the latest addition to the family of listed Coke bottlers, which includes Coca-Cola Enterprises of the US and Coca-Cola Amatil in the Asia-Pacific region. Coca-Cola Beverages is likely to prove particularly interesting to investors, however, because of its position in the emerging economies of Europe's former communist bloc.

▶

'The company will offer focused exposure to the significant potential of these territories,' says Neville Isdell, Chairman and Chief Executive, who was formerly Senior Vice-President of the parent company.

Until the fall of communism, Pepsi-Cola was dominant in Eastern and Central Europe. By slotting into state distribution systems, it outsold Coke in the countries of the region by multiples of between two and four.

When the old economies crumbled, Coke allotted 10 of the eastern bloc countries to Coca-Cola Amatil, the Australia-based bottler that had been so successful in emerging Asian countries. Within a few years, it had overhauled its old rival and now outsells Pepsi two-to-one in the region.

That has been done by heavy investment in state-of-the-art manufacturing and distribution capacity – almost £500m ($835m) in Amatil's European area over the past three years.

The challenge now, according to Mr Isdell, is to shift the emphasis into building 'marketplace assets' such as cooler cabinets and vending machines to raise consumption to the sort of levels seen in Western European countries. Coke believes this marketing job will be done better by a regionally based operation – hence the creation of Coca-Cola Beverages. It will take in Amatil's European operation, which includes Austria and Switzerland as well as the 10 former communist countries.

It will also acquire Coca-Cola Bevande Italia, which covers Italy from Rome northwards and is currently owned by the parent company in Atlanta. Like much of Central Europe, this part of Italy is classed by Coke as a 'developing territory' because average consumption per head was 93 eight-ounce servings last year – against 195 in Spain and 193 in Greece.

Austria and Switzerland have made Coke's top tier as 'established territories', with more than 150 servings a head. But most of the CCB countries are well below the European Union average of 139 servings, providing plenty of room for growth. And three countries fall into Coke's least-developed category of 'emerging territories': they include Ukraine, where 50m people managed to down only 18 servings each on average last year, and neighbouring Belarus where the average was 19 servings.

Neither of these two former Soviet countries has made the strides towards a market economy achieved by Poland or the Czech Republic. But Mr Isdell – a veteran in the region who helped build up Amatil's operation there – believes they are moving towards the same destination, heavily influenced by the success of their neighbours. 'There will be dips,' he says, 'but I am confident in the future of these countries.'

His task will be to increase market share for the Coke stable in the CCB countries, already more than 25 per cent in carbonated soft drinks and as high as 70 per cent in some countries. But as in the rest of the world, Coca-Cola sees the competition as much more than just the other fizzy-drink makers: this is the group that sees the water tap as its main competitor. So it will also aim to lift Coke's 'share of throat' – currently 11 per cent of the non-alcoholic beverages market. The targets will include producers of fruit juices, tea, coffee and milk.

For potential investors, then, CCB offers an intriguing punt. The attractions are obvious: it sells a consumer product with a proven track record in one of the world's faster-growing regions.

On the downside, it is exposed to the risks of operating in countries where the commitment to a market economy is often tenuous. On the assumption that it achieves the forecast market capitalisation of about £1.5bn, however, success is probably assured. Apart from its merits as a Coke bottler, it will be a constituent of the FTSE 250 and thus in demand from the growing number of index-tracking funds.

'Everything we've heard and seen shows a great deal of interest out there,' says Mr Isdell.

Source: Financial Times CD-ROM, 1 January–31 December 1998.

Introduction

This chapter first explains why internationalisation should be viewed as a process. Second, it studies two models of this process. While some firms, like AuditCo (see Exhibit 7.2), expand rapidly into new international markets and use high-investment modes of operation on entry, others, such as ComputerCo (see Exhibit 7.1) enter more gradually using low levels of investment to establish the potential of the market before expanding their operations. The arguments underlying the former, simultaneous and latter, sequential model are explored. The internationalisation process of service and product firms, and of large international and small organisations are contrasted to see which model more accurately explains their behaviour. The alternative network view of internationalisation is explored to see what it adds to understanding of firms' decisions. The chapter concludes by studying Bohomin Steel Works' internationalisation choices so that managers understand the complex influences on the internationalisation process.

Simultaneous and sequential models of internationalisation

Aharoni (1966) argues that international investment decisions should not be viewed in isolation as each decision influences later decisions. If a firm enters a country using a distributor, but then disagrees over the terms of the contract, it may not make any further investment in the country. Were this decision to be viewed in isolation, the full explanation for it might not be apparent. Study of internationalisation as a process offers a fuller understanding of international investment decisions. A number of models of the internationalisation process have been proposed. These models can broadly be divided into sequential and simultaneous models.

Sequential models of the internationalisation process identify different stages of internationalisation between first international activity and a high degree of internationalisation. However, the number and nature of the stages varies. Perlmutter (1969) bases the stages on the 'cultural orientation' of the firm. Three distinct orientations are identified. In the 'ethnocentric orientation', the domestic culture dominates the firm. A polycentric orientation is achieved when the distinction between the domestic and 'foreign' culture becomes blurred. Geocentric orientation refers to the stage at which the firm operates as a multinational or global player.

As we saw in Chapter 5, probably the best-known model of the internationalisation process is that of the Uppsala school (Johanson and Wiedersheim-Paul 1975; Johanson and Vahlne 1977). This model describes a sequential progression from export through knowledge agreements, such as licensing or franchising, to foreign direct investment.

High levels of uncertainty, which the firm faces on first entering an international market, favour entry via low 'commitment' modes of operation, such as export or the use of an agent. As the firm increases its knowledge and understanding of the market, it may increase its commitment by entering knowledge agreements and finally by foreign direct investment. Furthermore, firms will tend to invest first in countries culturally similar to their own, which they find easier to understand (Kogut and Singh 1988) and move towards those which are culturally dissimilar as their international experience grows.

Although the model was originally a description of the internationalisation process of Scandinavian firms (Johanson and Wiedersheim-Paul 1975; Johanson and Vahlne 1977), the Uppsala incremental model has been validated for firms in some industries in Japan (Yoshihara 1978), Germany (Dichtl *et al.* 1984) and the US (Davidson 1980).

The Johanson and Vahlne model demonstrates the underlying belief of sequential models that international markets are uncertain and that firms will internationalise gradually to minimise the risks resulting from this uncertainty. The Exhibit 7.1 example of ComputerCo's entry into East and Central Europe shows a sequential process of internationalisation. ComputerCo has had long-term involvement in Hungary and Poland using a distributor and export respectively and only invested in these countries many years later when market potential was improved by liberalisation.

Exhibit 7.1 ComputerCo

ComputerCo is a British-based multinational producer and distributor of computers. It has over 60 years of international experience. In Eastern Europe, ComputerCo has a broad portfolio of investments. It has a direct trading subsidiary in Russia, which distributes the company's products. It also has a joint venture to assemble computers. There are wholly owned subsidiaries in Poland, the Czech and Slovak Republics, Hungary, Bulgaria and Romania.

ComputerCo had links with three of these markets before liberalisation. It has 20 years of experience in the USSR. It has had a distributor in Hungary since 1964 and has exported to Poland for more than 20 years. The Manager of ComputerCo says that 'while the rules of operation in the Soviet Union were complex, once you had learned them, they were easy to play. It has become a lot more difficult since liberalisation. It is hard to determine what the new rules are.'

The years since liberalisation have brought an increase in the level of investment activity of the firm in Eastern Europe. In 1990, it invested in a joint venture in Hungary, additional offices were established in Debrecen in 1991 and in Pecs in 1992. Sales and marketing subsidiaries were established in Poland and the Czech Republic in 1990. Investments in Bulgaria and Romania followed in 1991. In Kazakhstan, ComputerCo has a licence agreement for the production of PCs and mid-range systems. In Ukraine, ComputerCo established links with an independent distributor in 1992.

The use of a distributor in Ukraine provides the benefits of local knowledge and buys time, while the firm assesses the market potential. It is foreseen that a joint venture agreement might be entered into in Ukraine, dependent on market potential. Clearly, there is an opportunity in Ukraine. The local partner is an American–Ukrainian national who has the advantage of speaking the language and having a good network of contacts. He had returned to work in Ukraine with one of the international aid agencies prior to liberalisation.

In contrast, simultaneous models are based on arguments of global convergence. The current level of international trade has reduced national differences:

> On a political map, the boundaries between countries are as clear as ever. But on a competitive map, a map showing the real flows of financial and industrial activity, those boundaries have largely disappeared. (Ohmae 1989: 54)

The increasingly global nature of trade has led theorists such as Levitt (1983) to argue that customers' tastes around the world are becoming more similar. In justification he points to technological advances which improve communication and the ease of international travel, to growing similarities in the fashion and music preferences of youths around the world, and to the prevalence of global products such as Coca Cola, Levi Jeans or Sony Walkman. This increasing similarity or 'homogenisation' of tastes leads Levitt to believe that there are global markets for some products and services. Serving these global markets with standardised products or services offers valuable economies of scale and scope. While critics believe that Levitt's views exaggerate the extent of homogenisation and the savings it may offer, nonetheless, a number of authors (Quelch and Hoff 1986; Douglas and Wind 1987; Ohmae 1989; Riesenbeck and Freeling 1991) suggest some degree of standardisation can offer savings.

If tastes are becoming more similar, and communication and travel easier, then the uncertainty, which Johanson and Vahlne (1977) associated with entry into new international markets, must have reduced. Casson (1994) suggests that this may favour simultaneous, rather than sequential models of internationalisation. Riesenbeck and Freeling (1991) show that the speed of international expansion of new brands has reduced from around 20 years for the traditional, sequential or 'waterfall' process to one to two years for simultaneous or 'sprinkler' launches.

These findings seem to support a simultaneous model of international expansion. AuditCo is an example of a firm that has internationalised rapidly within the East and Central European region.

Exhibit 7.2 AuditCo

AuditCo was created by the merger of two of the big eight accounting firms in 1987 and in 1995 ranked as the second largest of the Big Six globally. It has been involved in international operations since the late 1940s. As it provides business-to-business services, it has links with other firms around the world. The size of such customers is such that AuditCo is very concerned to protect its business by offering consistent levels of international service: 'Business is centred mainly on international clients. AuditCo must offer worldwide service in order to develop relationships with these clients across markets.' Any reduction in customer service might result in the loss of accounts to its international rivals. When entering Ukraine, AuditCo opted to take a majority stake in a joint venture with a local partner. The local partner provided necessary knowledge of the turbulent Ukrainian market.

AuditCo set up an office in Hungary in 1987. The success of this venture, and the subsequent liberalisation of the market, resulted in rapid expansion, during 1990, into the Czech and Slovak Republics, into Poland and into Moscow. As the Moscow office was established 18 months before the Ukrainian subsidiary, experienced individuals from this subsidiary identified a likely joint venture partner. The decision to enter Ukraine was prompted by the US Headquarters, which has the strongest links with the international client. Subsidiaries in Germany and Britain, which were near to the target market, were also involved in the investment decision.

While AuditCo has had international experience spanning a considerable time, its entry into the East and Central European region shows virtually simultaneous entry and the use of high commitment modes of operation on entry.

Limitations of sequential and simultaneous models

Critics point to a number of limitations of both sequential and simultaneous models of internationalisation. For Johanson and Vahlne's sequential model, critics question where the boundaries lie between the different stages and whether export or use of a distributor involve less commitment (Turnbull 1987). Indeed, the concept of 'commitment' is not fully explained in earlier papers, although it can be assumed that this is some measure of the firm's total investment in the market.

Second, data shows that firms may not follow a one-directional process. Jatar (1992) examines the way in which multinational corporations opened up the brewing industry in Venezuela by investing in distribution outlets, which were franchised once the path to market was established. To achieve economies of scale in its manufacturing, Ford has moved towards production of its different models in European hubs. This has led to the closing down of manufacturing plants in some European countries. In both cases, Johanson and Vahlne's model (1977) might suggest that the firms are reverting from high to lower levels of commitment. However, these actions are motivated by broader international strategies.

Research also questions the applicability of the model to different types of product or service. Erramilli (1990) points out that inseparable services, such as restaurants or hotels, require a minimum level of investment in premises which makes franchising the lowest level of commitment possible. Furthermore, critics suggest that multinational corporations, which have both high levels of resources and significant international experience (Forsgren 1989) are likely to skip the lower commitment stages of the process and face less uncertainty in new international markets. Johanson and Vahlne (1990) later accept that the model may have limited value in understanding large, highly internationalised firms.

Critics of the simultaneous model question the assumptions on which it is based. Both standardisation literature and simultaneous models are based on the idea that the similarity between people in different countries has increased and that uncertainty, in consequence, has decreased. However, critics suggest that while there may be some convergence in tastes, there is little evidence of homogenisation (Douglas and Wind 1987). Views range from convergence allowing global success for some 'high-technology' and 'high-touch' luxury items (Ohmae 1990) to the counter-arguments of Toffler (1970) that sophisticated consumers are demanding greater customisation. Moreover, simultaneous market entry may be possible for large firms with high levels of resources but is not feasible for smaller or less experienced firms.

While both sequential and simultaneous models offer some interesting insights into the internationalisation process, neither can be universally applied to all industry sectors and sizes of firms. The following section reviews some of the principal influences on manufacturing and service firms and on large multinational and global firms and on small firms.

Manufacturing

The models presented in the preceding discussion are largely based on manufacturing firms. Whether firms follow a sequential or simultaneous process of internationalisation depends in part on demographic factors such as size and level of international experience. As suggested above, large, more highly internationalised firms may internationalise more rapidly and use high commitment modes on entry. However, the pattern varies between sectors. High-commitment foreign investment in the chemical industry requires much higher levels of capital expenditure in exploration, pipelines and refineries than high-commitment investment in a manufacturing plant in an industry, such as tobacco or household goods. Firms in industry sectors where foreign direct investment involves higher levels of capital outlay are more likely to use a low-commitment organisation before taking this step.

Some variation in the internationalisation process can be seen between firms in the same sector who are broadly comparable in terms of size and international experience. These differences may relate to the nature of the firm's competitive advantage and strategy for delivering this to the market. For example, a tobacco firm entering Eastern Europe suggested that while rivals may be entering the market directly with manufacturing joint ventures, it was 'more risk averse' in nature and so opted to begin by exporting. Given the firm's policy of requiring a payback on any international investment within three years, the firm wished to be sure that foreign direct investment could deliver a short-term return. Johnson Wax (see case study at the end of Chapter 14) said that it traditionally takes a pioneering approach and enters markets more rapidly and with higher levels of investment than sector rivals.

Services

The term 'services' is used to encompass a spectrum from highly intangible services, such as holidays, to services that have a tangible element, such as software, creating architectural plans or producing accounts. Erramilli (1990) calls the first of these 'soft' services and the latter 'hard' services. Soft services cannot be separated from the service provider, while the tangible output of hard services can be delivered across borders.

The distinction between hard and soft services provides a useful insight into the issues that service firms face in the internationalisation process. Hard services can use export, knowledge agreements or foreign direct investment. An accountant or architect can receive a commission from an international customer, work on this in their home market and later deliver the final accounts or plans to the customer. The Internet, video-conferencing and other technological advances have improved the ability to provide such services across international borders. In this way, hard services can be exported, although for soft services, the minimum level of international operation required is a knowledge agreement such as a franchise. Well-known examples of soft services franchised internationally are McDonald's restaurants and Best Western hotels.

Erramilli (1991) finds a 'U-shaped' rather than linear sequential progression for service firms as the level of international experience increases. Both firms with little and high levels of international experience opt for high-commitment investment modes. Erramilli puts this down to the level of control the firms wish to have over their international operations. Firms with little international experience may wish to retain control, while those with high levels of experience may wish to protect brands or service quality. It is noticeable that while McDonald's use franchises in most countries, it initially enters new international markets by investment in a joint venture.

Valikängas and Lehtinen (1991) suggest that firms in different types of service industry will pursue different internationalisation strategies. Firms such as

McDonald's, with a mass-market focus, aim for consistent service quality, which can be successfully delivered through a franchise, provided the procedures are clearly established and policed. However, specialist services require the greater levels of control provided by foreign direct investment.

Studies of the internationalisation process of services show that service firms are more likely to encounter non-tariff barriers (Dahringer and Mühlbacher 1991). Suggestions to overcome non-tariff barriers include:

- encapsulate the service in a product. Examples include designer clothes or software
- use technological advances to deliver the service remotely
- use customer 'pull' by creating distinctively better services or by superior management or marketing ability, which customers demand to have.

Multinational and global firms

The distinction between multinational and global firms in this chapter is that the latter are geocentric (Perlmutter 1969) and may have a greater level of global standardisation of activities. Firms which are highly internationalised may have made significant investments in brands, in creating technological advantages or in developing international customer relationships. For these firms, damage to brand value or the loss of a customer does not only have an impact in one market, but potentially across a large number. So great may be the potential impact of any damage to reputation, that the firm is likely to opt for high-commitment modes to retain control of the operation to prevent this happening. The international experience of these firms may reduce the level of uncertainty they face, as they can draw lessons from other similar markets (Forsgren 1989). Moreover, such firms have sufficient resources that they might view the expenditure required for foreign direct investment as relatively low.

Small firms

If external finance is not available, expansion of small firms can only be financed by profits, which may be limited. However, management constraints may be the most significant difference between small and large firms. Shortage of management time may lead to 'short cuts in decision making and information gathering which can be disastrous' (Buckley 1989: 93).

In small firms, decisions are more likely to be championed by individuals and opportunities may be pursued without evaluation of alternatives, in order to minimise the costs of information gathering. One consequence may be that small firms opt to enter first those markets where there are lower levels of uncertainty. As we shall see in Chapter 8, both financial and managerial constraints may make it more likely that small firms will follow a sequential process of internationalisation (Johanson and Vahlne 1977; Buckley 1989).

On the other hand, global convergence would have an impact on small firms, as well as on large. Oviatt and McDougall (1994) suggest that many new, small firms are international from inception. Such new international ventures, they argue, arise because in the current environment:

> An internationally experienced person who can attract a moderate amount of capital can conduct business anywhere in the time it takes to press the buttons of a telephone and, when required, he or she can travel virtually anywhere on the globe in less than a day. Such facile use of low-cost communication technology and transportation means that the ability to discover and take advantage of business opportunities in multiple countries is not the preserve of large, mature corporations. (Oviatt and McDougall 1994: 46)

Network views of internationalisation

We saw in Chapter 5 that both sequential and simultaneous models of internationalisation make the same assumptions about the nature of the firm. Firms exist in a 'faceless' competitive environment. Game theorists have referred to this as a 'zero-sum' game as a firm can only gain (+1) at the expense of a competitor (–1) making zero. Network theory, which has its roots in sociology rather than economics, takes a contrasting view of the firm's links with its environment (Johanson and Mattsson 1988; Axelsson and Johanson 1992; Blankenburg-Holm 1995). Network studies of the firm show firms embedded in a web of interdependent relationships with other firms and in the broader environment. This is referred to as a 'full-faced' interface with the environment. Firms operate in an environment where 'win-win' situations are possible, that is two or more firms can gain (+1) from a relationship with each other.

From a network perspective, the process of internationalisation is that of building on existing relationships or creating new relationships in international markets. Definitions include: 'the way in which existing relationships in the domestic and in third markets as well as those in the entry market are utilised in the entry process' (Axelsson and Johanson 1992: 219) and: 'the process whereby the strength of the relationships in different parts of the global network increases' (Johanson and Mattsson 1988).

A number of different levels of relationship play a role. The first level is that of the macro-environment. Firms embedded in a 'full-faced' environment encounter different sets of challenges from those suggested for a faceless environment:

> Rather than viewing the environment as a set of separate anonymous forces – political, competitive, legal, cultural, economic, etc. – all the actors are considered bearers of diverse interests, power and characteristics. It is in the meetings in the international business arena that such factors impinge on the development of business. (Johanson and Mattsson 1988: 302)

One of the principal challenges of entering a new international market is that developing network connections may involve restructuring the firm's network:

To become established in a new market, that is, a network which is new to the firm, it has to build relationships which are new both to itself and its counterparts. This is sometimes done by breaking old, existing relationships, and sometimes by adding a relationship to already existing ones. (Johanson and Mattsson 1988: 306)

From a network perspective, internationalisation involves entry into markets which each have a different web of actors and relationships. Kinch (1992) highlights the difficulties of breaking into advanced economies where the actors tend to have long-established and stable relationships. A new entrant might find it difficult to form links with a distributor who is not supplying products for one of his competitors. At the opposite end of the scale, if the network of relationships in the host market is rapidly changing, as in emerging markets, there may appear to be greater opportunities, but it may be difficult to identify appropriate partners and attractive investments (see also Chapters 5 and 8).

TelecomCo below is an example of a firm finding it difficult to understand the networks in a new market.

Exhibit 7.3 TelecomCo

TelecomCo expanded into Europe and the US in the late 1960s. By 1991, 44 per cent of its sales were outside the UK. TelecomCo takes a risk-averse approach to international expansion, but the decline of its cash cow in the UK dictates rapid entry into markets which are less technologically developed. The firm has a successful joint venture in Moscow and had been studying the potential of Ukraine for two years before winning a contract to supply the Ukrainian government with equipment to modernise the telecommunications infrastructure. An export representative went out to Ukraine in 1993. Since then, he has been assessing market potential with a view to setting up a joint venture.

A number of business opportunities seemed open to the representative from TelecomCo. Yet he found it difficult to find out to whom he should speak or what procedure he should follow: 'There is so much political instability that you can sign an agreement with someone one week, who will not be there next week. Then they say that the previous agreement was invalid and ask for a bribe. Success is possible if you are prepared to pay the right people.'

Twice, he was asked to make payments in order to ensure the smooth running of the authorisation process. On each occasion, Head Office refused to sanction any such payment as they felt it might damage their international reputation.

Finally, the local representative produced a business idea which he believed would work in Ukraine. However, Head Office had decided that the risks for the firm were too great. In March 1994, the representative was about to leave Ukraine, en route to a new posting in Azerbaijan. TelecomCo were withdrawing in the face of worsening market conditions, but might reconsider investment at a future stage. The representative of TelecomCo felt that he had gained personal knowledge of the conditions in Ukraine, but it was difficult to convey to Head Office the fact that business was possible there. From a distance the level of uncertainty seemed unacceptable.

The second type of relationships which influence the process of internationalisation are between organisations. A complex web of relationships may have a bearing on the decisions a firm makes. Firms may stand in different relation to each other in different international markets:

> Competitors in one market co-operate in another and are suppliers and customers to each other in a third.

> A Swedish firm might increase its penetration in a South American market because of its relationship in Japan with an internationalising Japanese firm. Other examples of such international interdependence are 'big projects' in which design, equipment, supply, construction, ownership and operation can all be allocated to firms of different national origin. (Johanson and Mattsson 1988: 315)

Finally, relationships within the organisation may influence the process. Multinational corporations and global firms may have relatively large subsidiaries in a number of countries. Decision making in this type of organisation may take place at the subsidiary level rather than always at the centre. Forsgren (1989) argues that when this happens, there may be cultural distance between different parts of the firm as well as with the host market. Individuals and subsidiaries that are further away from the target investment may perceive it as higher risk than those who are closer and have a better understanding may.

An instance of this can be seen in the case of TelecomCo. When the firm made decisions about further investment in Ukraine, the local representative considered there to be less risk than did Head Office who were further away. In the earlier example, AuditCo's subsidiaries in Germany and the UK played a role in the entry into Eastern Europe. Once the Moscow office was established, it helped with later investments in the region.

From a network perspective, relationships at the macro-, inter-organisational and firm level all play a role in investment decisions and each decision is influenced by others which have gone before.

Chapter summary

A range of firm, industry and country factors influence each international investment decision. International business theory proposes sequential and simultaneous models of the process of internationalisation. These take different views of the level of uncertainty involved in internationalisation. Sequential models see new international markets as uncertain and suggest entry into more culturally similar markets first. Simultaneous models build on the convergence of customer tastes, which they believe reduce the uncertainty of international markets. Provided the firm has sufficient resources, the barriers to more rapid internationalisation and entry via foreign direct investment are lower. Network theory provides an alternative view of internationalisation. Greater attention is paid to the web of relationships, which influence investment decisions. From a network perspective, internationalisation is the process of forming relationships in new international markets. This may involve building on existing relationships in the home, host or a third country.

Discussion questions

1 According to incremental or sequential models of internationalisation, what role does psychic distance play in determining the mode of initial international market entry and subsequent international expansion?
2 In which respects does globalisation literature raise different expectations of internationalisation?
3 What contribution does network theory make to an understanding of the internationalisation process?
4 Identify the issues which may influence the internationalisation of small firms; service firms; and multinational corporations? To what extent are these similar and in which ways do they differ?

Closing Case Study:
Bohomin Steel Works[*]

Until the dramatic events of November 1989, when the Czech people, led by students and dissident writers, crowded into Wenceslas Square, Prague, to protest against Soviet oppression, Czechoslovakia had been under communist totalitarian rule for 41 years. The tremendous spirit of the Czech people in rallying to support the revolutionary cause drew worldwide attention.

For the Czech Republic, the years since liberalisation have been no less momentous. The transition from centrally planned to free market economy has brought many changes. In 1991 the newly formed Czech and Slovak Federal Republic split into separate Czech and Slovak states. In October 1993, the Czech Republic was accepted as an associate member of the EC and is now seeking full membership. Among the former COMECON countries, the Czech Republic vies with Hungary as the nation which has progressed furthest in its reforms. A key part of the reform process in the Czech Republic has been the mass-privatisation of the previously state-owned monopolies. This has been achieved by issue of vouchers to Czech citizens, with which they can purchase shares in their chosen company. While this has proved a rapid way of decentralising control, it has not been without critics. In some instances, people have taken loans to purchase shares in companies, which have no experience of competition and flounder in the free market within a short period.

One firm, which has successfully completed the first phase of privatisation and now operates as an independent company, is Bohomin; a major producer of pressed steel goods and wires. Berlin entrepreneurs A. Hahn and H. Eisner set up the Bohomin factory in 1885, to manufacture nails and screws. The location of the plant, 12 km from Ostrava on the Czech-Polish border, was seen to be advantageous, both because of the local availability of raw materials and because of the excellent road and rail links with Northern, Eastern and Southern Europe.

In 1896 the firm merged with wire producer, Moravian-Silesian Co., to become a limited company. In the following years, the plant expanded to become the largest producer of wires in the country. After the Second World War, Bohomin set up plants to manufacture pressed steel castings for a variety of purposes. Currently, Bohomin has six manufacturing plants: wires, cables and ropes, radiators and generators, pressed steel goods, railway wheels and undercarriages and wire meshes. Since liberalisation, Bohomin has experienced radical changes. It has lost its guaranteed Soviet markets, and now has to compete in the international market. In practice, Bohomin has much to recommend it. The low wage costs in the Czech Republic allow it to price its products at below world prices, for comparable quality. Bohomin has already achieved ISO 9001 quality certification. It has a go-ahead management team, who are currently in the process of a second rights issue to raise funds to modernise the plant. Indeed, the entire management team is in the process of improving its own managerial ability by studying for an In-Company MBA through Prague International Business School.

At the same time, there are some significant issues which Bohomin will have to resolve in order to ensure its future profitability. A significant proportion of the, formerly guaranteed, markets in Russia and Slovakia have been lost, for which replacements must be found. Bohomin gains a significant proportion of its sales through export. The industry sectors in which Bohomin operates are characterised by high levels of competition. Within the EU, protectionist measures in the steel and predominantly state-owned railway industries limit the access which they can gain to customers. The steel cast panels which Bohomin sells to automotive manufacturers are subject to ever increasing quality and delivery requirements. Bohomin's ability to compete on cost may be eroded as the Czech economy moves forward and wage levels become comparable with the rest of Europe. Moreover, it is heavily reliant on supplies of oil and coal, which are still bought from Russia at less than world market price.

However, as a result of the privatisation process new potential markets have opened up for Bohomin within the Czech Republic and former COMECON countries. COMECON may no longer exist, but opportunities arise from the new economic groupings of the Visegrad countries (Czech and Slovak Republics, Hungary, Poland), the revived Hapsburg grouping (Austria, Italy, Czech and Slovak Republics, Poland) and the EU.

Indeed, in some of its market sectors Bohomin has little choice but to compete internationally. Czech Railways is replacing less rolling stock as shifting priorities have resulted in less governmental expenditure on infrastructure. The board of directors of Bohomin considers it unlikely that the situation will change in the foreseeable future. However, possible privatisation of the railway systems in a number of other countries may open up new international markets. Bohomin also makes wheels and undercarriages for trams and light railways. Increasing concern about traffic density has made this a growth area in recent years.

The market for automotive panels is almost exclusively international. Even Skoda, the leading Czech car manufacturer, is now in partnership with Germany's VW. The leading firms in the automotive industry are primarily multinationals, who make tough demands on their component suppliers. Bohomin supplies some international automotive firms, in Russia and Italy, but would like to expand its business in this area.

One major problem facing Bohomin is that the majority of its plant is very old. Accordingly it is expensive in terms of maintenance and also oriented towards previous production patterns. Hence, Bohomin has a massive capacity for the production of semi-finished and finished wires. Its finished wires are made to an extremely high specification and are capable of competing internationally on quality.

As its market is changing, Bohomin will have to rethink the way in which it operates. Orders were previously organised centrally through the state-controlled system. Order quantities were large and quality relatively unimportant. Bohomin had little knowledge about its final customers. The firm deals with the EU via one distributor, but currently has no direct links with potential customers. New private distribution channels such as builder's merchants are springing up in the Czech Republic. However, meeting the requirements of these channels would require Bohomin to supply much smaller order quantities. Order lead times may have to be reduced and consistent quality standards assured. In some geographic areas, Bohomin would have to decide on the most appropriate mode of international operation.

As part of their MBA marketing course, the Board of Directors of Bohomin arrived at the following SWOT analysis of their firm:

Strengths	Weaknesses
Broad customer base Skilled workforce International quality Certification Management dynamism	○ No experience of marketing ○ Low profitability ○ Not marketing-led
Opportunities	Threats
Pursue differentiation on quality Restructure to cut costs Find new Western markets New private customers (domestic) Form a joint venture Find new suppliers	○ World recession ○ Protectionism ○ Disruption of raw material supplies ○ Competition

The management team recognises that they have, as yet, little experience in analysing their business. They also have relatively little internal data on which products have been responsible for their profitability to date.

At this stage in their development, the management team at Bohomin is anxious to make the best strategic choices. It is currently deciding on the priorities for allocating resources between the different areas of its product portfolio. This requires an analysis of the product areas with the best potential for the future. Several Czech firms have entered joint ventures with foreign partners. A number of the Board members favour this option, as it seems to them that this will provide Western managerial skills. If an EU partner is chosen, it may also offer access to markets currently blocked by protectionist measures. However, this suggestion raises considerable concern among other Board members, who fear the loss of autonomy which may be associated with this course of action.

* This case is intended as a basis for discussion rather than to illustrate the effective or ineffective handling of a business situation. © Sue Bridgewater 1994.

Questions

1 Assess the potential of Bohomin Steel Works to compete internationally?
2 What would be the advantages and disadvantages of a joint venture for Bohomin?
3 What other strategic options do Bohomin have?
4 What would be your preferred internationalisation strategy and why?

Further reading

Buckley, P.J. and **Ghauri**, P. (eds) (1999) *The Internationalisation of the Firm: A Reader*, 2nd edn, London: Academic Press. This recently updated collection of readings provides a comprehensive range of views of the internationalisation process.

Easton, G. and **Axelsson**, B. (eds) (1992) *Industrial Networks: A New View of Reality*, London: Routledge. This book contains contributions from some of the main researchers in network theory. The final section applies network theory to strategic topics, such as internationalisation.

Forsgren, M. and **Johanson**, J. (eds) (1992) *Managing Networks in International Business*, London: Gordon & Breach. One of the major applications of network theory to international business.

References

Aharoni, Y. (1966) *The Foreign Direct Investment Decision Process*, Boston, Mass: Harvard University.

Axelsson, B. and **Johanson**, J. (1992) Foreign market entry – the textbook versus the network view, in G. Easton and B. Axelsson (eds) *Industrial Networks: A New View of Reality*, London: Routledge.

Blankenburg-Holm, D. (1995) A network approach to foreign market entry, in K. Möller and D. Wilson (eds) *Business Marketing: An Interaction and Network Perspective*, The Netherlands: Kluwer, pp. 375–410.

Buckley, P. J. (1989) Foreign direct investment by small and medium-sized enterprises: the theoretical background, *Small Business Economics* 1: 89–100.

Casson, M. (1994) Internationalisation as a learning process: a model of corporate growth and geographic diversification, in J. Sapsford and N. Balasubramanyam (eds) *The Economics of International Investment*, London: Edward Elgar.

Dahringer, L. and **Mühlbacher**, H. (1991) Marketing Services Internationally: Barriers and Mangement Strategies, *Journal of Services Marketing* 5(3): 5–17.

Davidson, W.H. (1980) The location of foreign direct investment activity, *Journal of International Business Studies* 11(1): 9–22.

Dichtl, L.E.M., Liebold, M., Köglmayr, H.G. and Müller, S. (1984) The foreign orientation of management as a central construct in export centred decision-making processes, *Research for Marketing* 10, 7 4.

Douglas, S. and Wind, Y. (1987) The myth of globalization, *Columbia Journal of World Business*, Winter: 19–29.

Erramilli, M.K (1990) Entry mode choice in service industries, *International Marketing Review* 7(5): 50–61.

Forsgren, M. (1989) *Managing the Internationalisation Process: The Swedish Case*, London: Routledge.

Jatar, A. (1992) Unpublished PhD Dissertation, Warwick University.

Johanson, J. and Mattsson, L.-G. (1988) Internationalisation in industrial systems – a network approach, in N. Hood and J.-E. Vahlne (eds) *Strategies in Global Competition*, reproduced in P.J. Buckley and P. Ghauri (eds) *The Internationalisation of the Firm: A Reader*, London: Academic Press.

Johanson, J. and Vahlne, J.-E. (1990) The Mechanism of Internationalisation, *International Marketing Review* 7 (4) 11–24.

Johanson, J. and Wiedersheim-Paul, F. (1975 The internationalisation of the firm – four Swedish cases, *Journal of Management Studies*, October: 305–22.

Kinch, N. (1992) Entering a tightly structured network – strategic visions or network realities, in M. Forsgren and J. Johanson (eds) *Managing Networks in International Business*, London: Gordon & Breach.

Kogut, B. and Singh, H. (1988) The effect of national culture on the choice of entry mode, *Journal of International Business Studies* 19 (3): 411–32.

Levitt, T. (1983) The globalization of markets, *Harvard Business Review*, May–June: 92–102.

Ohmae, K. (1989) Managing in a borderless world, *Harvard Business Review*, May–June. Reprinted in R.B. Buzzell, J.A. Quelch and C.A. Bartlett (eds) *Global Marketing Management: Cases and Readings*, Boston: Harvard Business School Press.

Ohmae, K. (1990) The borderless world, *The McKinsey Quarterly* 3: 3–19.

Oviatt, B.M. and McDougall, P.P. (1994) Toward a theory of international new ventures, *Journal of International Business Studies*, Spring: 45–64.

Perlmutter, H. (1969) The tortuous evolution of the multinational corporation, *Columbia Journal of World Business*, January–February: 9–18.

Quelch, J.A. and Hoff, E.J. (1986) Customising global marketing, *Harvard Business Review*, May–June: 59–68.

Riesenbeck, H. and Freeling, A. (1991) How global are global brands?, *McKinsey Quarterly* 4: 3–18.

Toffler, A. (1970) *Future Shock*, New York: Bantam Books.

Turnbull, P.W. (1987) A challenge to the stages theory of the internationalisation process, in R.J. Rosson and S.D. Reed (eds) *Managing Export Entry and Expansion*, Praeger: New York.

Valikängas, L. and Lehtinen, U. (1991) Strategic types of services and international marketing, *International Journal of Service Industry*, 5 (2): 72–84.

Yoshihara, K. (1978) Determinants of Japanese investments in South-East Asia, *International Social Sciences Journal* 30: 2.

CHAPTER 8

Internationalisation of Small- and Medium-sized Enterprises (SMEs)

Heather Wilson

Learning objectives

By the end of this chapter you will be able to:

■ understand the relationship between small and large firms

■ understand the specific advantages and disadvantages of the SME

■ understand the three principal models of internationalisation relevant to the SME, namely the stages, network and international new ventures models

■ evaluate how the different internationalisation models contribute to our understanding of SME international operations.

Opening Case Study:
An invitation to think big

Export Explorer will encourage SMEs to become exporters. Ian Hamilton Fazey spoke to Barbara Roche, the minister spearheading the initiative. The UK government is to promote a new export drive among small- and medium-sized enterprises. Barbara Roche, the UK's small firms minister, says that many small businesses do not export simply because they do not know how to. Special help will be offered through the national business links network and will include guided package tours for first-timers to export markets and trade fairs.

'Exporting is a good issue for small firms. We are operating in global markets and that applies to all sizes of business. SMEs have to think globally,' says Mrs Roche. 'But for many there is a barrier to exporting for the first time. It sometimes seems too daunting a task. What many small firms want to know is how to do it. They need knowledge about markets, languages, legal systems and how to minimise credit and financial risk.'

Guided package tours will be one of the more visible features of the SME export drive. They will be run under a programme called Export Explorer, which will be launched in the next few weeks. Only 'export virgins' will qualify, although the Department of Trade and Industry says there will be some discretionary flexibility over businesses which have already done a little passive exporting through taking unsolicited orders from abroad.

The tours will be subsidised with £1m of public funds and will cost participants only £99, plus travel and accommodation. Mrs Roche says initial trips would concentrate on markets nearest home and would provide 'basic hand-holding' and on-the-job training in how to export.

Tour guides are likely to be export experts drawn from the DTI and the private sector. The DTI currently has about 100 managers on loan from the private sector as export promoters. Other specialists may be drawn from business links, where there is now a national network of export development counsellors, and chambers of commerce.

Mrs Roche says the main task of the new initiative is to convince small businesses that they can export. 'We want to persuade them to take it in stages, exporting to Europe first, but the next thing will be to convince them that there are other markets with potential, such as Latin America, where they can also do good business,' she says. 'British companies in the components industry are prime targets for this export drive.'

One of the most important features of Export Explorer will be a readiness to cater for the smallest of small businesses, down to traders who employ only one, two or a handful of people. It will be a matter of official judgement whether such businesses have an export potential but an example might be a computer software business which is developing a globally marketable product.

Crocodile Clips, the winner of last year's NatWest-FT Export Excellence Award for new exporters, employs more than ten people now but was exactly in the position envisaged by Mrs Roche three years ago.

The point about size of business is also a crucial indicator of government attitudes to helping small enterprises. Under the Conservatives, business links were discouraged from helping businesses with fewer than ten employees. Where possible, these were pointed at enterprise agencies.

However, the enterprise agency network has neither the influence nor the resources of 12 years ago, when it peaked at more than 300 strong under Sir David Trippier, one of Mrs Roche's predecessors. Training and enterprise councils (TECs), then business links, took over many of their functions and sources of funds.

Funding difficulties have since sown confusion in the business links network, with some having to be rescued by TECs and others by chambers of commerce. Meanwhile, some chambers have merged with TECs.

Mrs Roche is determined to clarify the situation by making business links the principal point of contact for business support from the government. They were already the official channel for accessing export services but Mrs Roche intends to strengthen their role and promote it vigorously.

Each business link will be expected to reflect the business profile in its area, so that the right sorts of experts are available to offer local help, but none will be expected to be all things to all businesses. Specialised services will be concentrated where they can do the most good but national networking will ensure national access to any particular expertise.

Business links are also expected to play a part in developing contacts between European business associations to match SMEs capable of doing business with each other across frontiers. Worldwide, the United Nations Industrial Development Organisation in Vienna last year started a similar scheme to promote joint ventures between compatible tenants in business innovation centres but Mrs Roche wants something wider and more inclusive.

She also stresses that exporting should never be a mere add-on function to a domestically oriented business but part of general marketing strategy – a consistent line of the Institute of Export and a central theme of the annual NatWest-FT Export Forums.

Of about 1.13m businesses in England alone, nearly 960,000 employ fewer than ten people. By ensuring that the full range of government help is available to all of them, Mrs Roche is trying to tap a rich seam of potential international trade.

Source: *Financial Times* CD-ROM, 1 January–31 December 1998.

Introduction

Chapter 5 discussed the main approaches to internationalisation; this chapter examines some of these within the context of small- and medium-sized enterprises.

International business teaching and research attention has tended to focus on multinational enterprises (MNEs) leading to implicit assumptions of 'older' age and 'larger' size. However, it is generally recognised that traditional MNE theories do not explain the international activities of 'younger' and 'smaller' firms. Younger and smaller firms do not own the resource pool of their larger counterparts, and MNE theory is primarily concerned with the effective international management of this resource pool. SMEs, because they are small, do not have the purchasing power of their larger counterparts and this means they pay a premium for resources or even have difficulty attracting resources.

There are three major approaches to overcoming such resource constraints to enter international markets, of which three are relevant to this chapter. The first, termed the stages model of internationalisation, also known as the establishment chain model (see Chapter 5), assumes a growing international presence building on an established domestic base of operations. Thus, domestic sales provide the resource fuel to enter the first international market, and the progressive accumulation of resources allows the firm to exploit successive international opportunities. The second approach focuses on the impact of the use of networks, or relationships with other organisations, on the internationalisation process. This method recognises that most firms, including SMEs, interact with firms that are international themselves and that this international exposure is influential in terms of the firm's own international decisions and operations. The final approach outlined in this chapter assumes early entry into international markets following the start-up of the enterprise. Under this scenario, the domestic activities of the firm are secondary to its international operations, and the international connections and previous international experience of the founder(s) becomes critical to determining the structure and resource position of the enterprise. All three approaches will be discussed in the context of strategies built on the inherent advantages of the SME, namely flexibility and innovation.

Characteristics of SMEs

Definition of the SME

There is no single international definition of SMEs. For example, the OECD has used the figure of 100 employees or fewer to define the small enterprise (Loveman and Sengenberger 1990). In the UK, employment and turnover figures have been used to define small firms in different industrial sectors, with 200 employees being the maximum threshold for manufacturing firms and a maximum turnover of £450,000 (1990 prices) for retailing firms (Stanworth and Gray 1991). Finally, 500 employees or fewer has been the limit applied by the Small Business Administration in the US when considering SMEs (Stanworth and Gray 1991). Recognising that these employment definitions fail to capture that section of the SME population where new firm births and deaths are likely to be highest, the European Commission disaggregates the SME sector into micro-, small- and medium-sized firms with fewer than 10, 100 and 500 employees respectively (Storey, 1994).

Regardless of definition, SMEs constitute the bulk of all enterprises around the world. They also, because of their sheer numbers, contribute significantly to economic output and employment, whereas large firms contribute significantly because of their sheer scale. However, there is debate about whether SMEs contribute disproportionately to economic development when compared to their larger counterparts. For example, research has established that small firms employ research and development (R&D) resources more efficiently than large firms do and contribute disproportionately to innovative outputs (Bannock and Peacock 1989). This is often interpreted as meaning that small firms are more innovative than large firms. Stated more precisely, 'small firms have a higher share of major innovations than their share of employment. However it is *not* the case that there is a higher probability that an individual small firm will introduce a new product than that an individual large firm will introduce a new product' (Storey 1994: 324). Likewise, with employment, statistics have been used to contend that small firms contribute disproportionately to new job growth (Birch 1979).[1] However, the relative contribution of small and large firms to employment share has been shown to vary according to prevailing economic conditions, with large firms being more important during times of prosperity and small firms being more consistent job creators over time (Storey 1994). Thus, it is possible to conclude that small and large firms play a complementary role, and the following pages consider their relationship in the context of the inherent advantages and disadvantages of the SME (see Table 8.1).

Table 8.1 Advantages and disadvantages of SMEs

Advantages of the SME	Disadvantages of the SME
Flexibility	Liabilities of smallness
Innovation	Liabilities of newness

Advantages of the SME

Interestingly, when we consider the size structure of enterprises over time, an inverse relationship exists between large and small firms (Bannock and Peacock 1989). In the early part of the twentieth century small firms were prevalent but were soon overtaken by large firms. One explanation was that, during the Fordist era, emphasis was placed on mass production for mass consumption (Curran and Blackburn 1991). This approach was suited to large firms that could achieve cost advantages via economies of scale, with small firms consigned to the role of suppliers of customised machinery for mass production or filling market niches too unprofitable for their larger counterparts. The small firm could be considered to be operating in a dependent or isolated relationship (Rainnie 1991) with larger firms under this model (see Table 8.2). The Post-Fordist era resulted in an increasing focus on the customisation of products and services to meet more individualised needs where, it was argued, SMEs had an advantage because of their ability to pursue more flexible strategies compared to their larger counterparts. Flexible specialisation is the term used by Piore and Sabel (1984) to describe the situation where SMEs employ skilled workers to exploit sophisticated, general-purpose machinery to produce a wide and constantly changing, craft-based assortment of goods for large and constantly shifting markets or, in other words, the SME focuses on permanent innovation (see Table 8.2).

Table 8.2 Relationships of small firms to large firms

- Dependent – complementing and serving the interests of large firms, e.g. through sub-contracting
- Isolated – operating in specialised and/or geographically discrete markets or niches of demand that are not attractive to larger firms (either because they are unproductive for, or they have been overlooked by, larger firms)
- Innovative – operating in (often founding and developing) specialised/new products or markets (where larger firms eventually seek to exploit, or counter, the more productive innovative developments)

Source: Adapted from Rainnie (1991: 188).

The role of innovation, in the context of cycle theory, is the basis of the second explanation for alternating small and large firm emphases. Cycle theory explains how economies cycle through periods of prosperity, recession, depression and recovery and, according to Schumpeter (1939), these waves are caused by innovation, the effects of innovation and the response to innovation by the system. The initiation of the wave, characterised by prosperity, is associated with smaller enterprises developing and diffusing new technologies. This is because small firms are often less committed to existing products and practices (Pavitt *et al.* 1987), whereas large firms have greater investments, or sunk costs, associated with their pursuit of advantages based on efficiencies and scale. Later stages of the cycle are characterised by larger firms exploiting these precise advantages once the technologies have been proven in the marketplace. Waves associated with fundamental innovative advances have been termed Kondratieffs, after their founder, and have been observed to last for around 50 years (Pavitt *et al.* 1987). Subscribers to this view contend that advanced economies are currently entering the fifth Kondratieff wave where, again, SMEs are in the ascendance based on their innovative exploitation of knowledge and information technologies (Storey 1994).

Disadvantages of the SME

Again, in order to highlight the disadvantages of the SME, comparisons will be drawn with larger firms. Liabilities of smallness and, in the case of new ventures, liabilities of newness are two main areas of disadvantage associated with the SME according to Aldrich and Auster (1986). Difficulty in raising capital is one liability of smallness. Compared to their larger counterparts, SMEs often have fewer options when raising capital, face higher interest rates and are subject to greater intervention by their financiers. In addition, complying with government rules and regulations is often a higher administrative burden for SMEs, as they are unlikely to have the number of administrative staff or specialists, or the lobbying power, of larger firms. Liabilities of newness centre on the ability of SMEs to attract resources. The new enterprise does not have an operating track record and, as such, finds it hard to attract financiers, suppliers, customers and employees who are concerned that the venture might fail. This is the case even where the business founder has been previously associated with a successful enterprise. It is the history of the company, or lack thereof, rather than the history of the entrepreneur, on which suppliers of resources focus when entering into contracts with the new firm. Also, the financially constrained SME is often unable to compete with larger firms for resources, especially if these resources are scarce and competition is increasing their value on the market.

Resource leveraging

If SMEs lack resources, this does not necessarily have to inhibit the firm's operations because entrepreneurship is ' . . . the pursuit of opportunity without regard to resources currently controlled' (Stevenson *et al.* 1994: 5). The entrepreneurial SME can overcome inherent disadvantages by leveraging its resource base; that is, the firm seeks to do more with less (Timmons 1994). Essentially, the entrepreneur and the SME assume a co-ordination role: obtaining and using resources which are not well marketed; visualising alternative, more productive, uses for existing resources; and co-opting other people and/or organisations to exploit opportunities (Leibenstein 1978; Timmons 1994). The following advantages have been identified by Timmons (1994). Resource leveraging contributes to the firm's flexibility where it can decide quickly to commit or decommit to particular activities because of the lower overall sunk costs in the venture. Ownership results in greater inflexibility because organisations cannot afford to incur the costs associated with resources lying idle. SMEs employing fewer resources carry lower fixed costs, and this favourably affects the break-even position of the enterprise. The SME will also have lower capital requirements, reducing financial exposure or limiting potential losses, as well as avoiding the dilution of the founder's equity, or ownership of the company. The above measures limit total exposure, while further risk reduction can result from avoiding the costs of resource obsolescence.

Thus, we have two perspectives on the role of SMEs: as initiators of change, from a cycle theory perspective; and as responders to change, under the flexible specialisation model. Both perspectives are based on the inherent advantages of the SME: namely innovation and flexibility. The disadvantages associated with the liabilities of newness and smallness often result in resource constraints which, if applied to maintaining flexibility, can be turned to the advantage of the SME through a strategy of resource leveraging. The characteristics highlighted above should be borne in mind when considering the following pages on models of internationalisation since they are presented in order of increasing flexibility for the SME.

Exhibit 8.1 Cookie Time

Christchurch-based company Mayell Foods, founded by entrepreneur Mike Mayell and later supported by his brother Guy, produces cookies under the Cookie Time brand for the New Zealand market. At start up, Mike realised that he would need three times the capital he had available to start the business, nor could he find a baker to produce the cookies. To overcome these constraints he called a friend in the United States to get hold of a household cookie recipe; baked the cookies himself; went out on the streets to test market the product; rented existing bakery facilities, during their down time, and used them overnight; used his parents' help to produce the first batch; delivered the cookies by courier to existing shops; ignored supermarket outlets, conventional retailers of biscuits, and focused on point-of-sale positioning in service stations, cafés and corner shops. Twelve years after establishment the company was turning over sales of NZ$7.5m.

Source: Adapted from Goulter (1995: 14–21).

The stages model of internationalisation and the SME

The stages model of internationalisation assumes that internationalisation is the consequence of a series of incremental decisions where the firm starts from a domestic base and makes increasing commitments to international markets (Johanson and Wiedersheim-Paul 1975). It is also assumed that the firm employs more diverse international methods as internationalisation progresses (Welch and Luostarinen 1994). These increasing commitments, or international methods, can be identified as distinct incremental stages of internationalisation.

The stages model has been criticised by many researchers (see, for example, Turnbull 1987). However, a study of small software manufacturers in Ireland, Norway and Finland (Bell 1995) found limited resources were an important factor in determining the firm's choice of market entry mode and its capability to expand international operations. Thus, servicing the international market from a domestic base via exporting, or Stage 2 of the establishment chain (see Chapter 5), was prevalent for the studied SMEs.

The originators of the model, in addressing some of the criticisms levelled at the theory, did not alter their position regarding the inevitability of the internationalisation process once started, although they recognised that the combination of strategic and deterministic perspectives might prove useful (Johanson and Vahlne 1990). For the moment, though, the basic mechanism concept is useful for directing attention to the *process* of internationalisation: that is, why and how firms embark on their international endeavours and how their international efforts develop over time. As such, it provides one possible reference point when looking at SMEs that have focused on serving the domestic market prior to developing international sales. Convex Plastics provides a good example here.

Case Study 8.1 **Convex Plastics**

Hamilton-based Convex Plastics, a supplier of fill and seal plastics for machine packaging, had no sales outside the North Island of New Zealand in 1991. The company made its first international sales to Australia in 1993 and now has a sales office of two staff located in Sydney to support sales of 20 per cent of overall turnover. Currently, it is considering whether to develop a manufacturing base or take over an existing operation in the Australian market. The company has also set its sights on the Asian market, and is investigating a manufacturing joint venture opportunity in the Philippines. According to management, 'While we've managed to crack the Australian market on our own, we recognise that we cannot duplicate this approach in Asia. As a result, we're being versed in Asian protocol.'

Source: Adapted from Story (1997: 6).

The network model of internationalisation and the SME

There has been growing interest in the use of networks or collaborative strategies in international business and how these relationships impact on the international activities of the firm. The following pages first define what is meant by the term network and, second, explore the implications of network-based approaches for SME internationalisation.

Definition of a network

A firm, in its normal course of operations, will be involved in transactions with other organisations. Where these transactions are relatively uncomplicated, unlikely to be repeated and do not involve the purchaser making any substantial transaction-specific investments in terms of resources, they are expected to take place via the market mechanism (Powell 1991). That is, buyers and sellers will use price as the co-ordination mechanism for the transaction (Johanson and Mattsson 1991). Under the reverse conditions, the transaction is deemed to represent high costs to an organisation and it is expected that it will attempt to reduce these costs by internalising the transaction: that is, using horizontal and/or vertical integration to co-ordinate activities more efficiently (Powell 1991). The co-ordinating mechanism for these transactions is the hierarchy or ownership and control structure (Johanson and Mattsson 1991). These two perspectives form the foundation of transaction-cost economics (Williamson 1981). However, networks do not involve pure market-based exchanges, nor do they involve the ownership element of integration.

Understanding the network approach requires switching explanatory emphasis from the economic exchange to the social exchange between firms (Holm *et al.* 1996). The economic exchange perspective encourages a focus on costs and allocative decisions are made to reduce both production and transaction costs; whereas the social exchange perspective focuses on the added value accruing from learning and innovation as a result of the relationship (Lundvall 1993). 'The development and utilization of foreign networks is . . . closely related to the learning process that underlies overall internationalisation. Indeed, an important part of a company's knowledge is often created and maintained through actors in its relevant networks,' (Welch and Welch 1996: 12). Relationships with other organisations tend to evolve from more traditional forms of economic exchange, and a process of continued interaction leads to the organisations synchronising activities and resources (Håkansson and Snehota 1995). In contrast to price and hierarchy controls, the co-ordinating mechanism under the network approach is the interaction between firms engaged in the network structure (Johanson and Mattsson 1991). Network structures can be vertical, between the firm and its suppliers and/or customers, horizontal, among firms that offer competing products/services, or conglomerate in nature, where the firm is engaged in regular interactions with organisations outside the industry.

The network model

Because the learning, innovation and resource co-ordination elements are relevant issues for the SME seeking to enter international markets, the network model of internationalisation represents a useful framework. This model of internationalisation involves considering how relationships in the domestic, target and third markets are utilised for market entry (Axelsson and Johanson 1992; Johanson and Mattsson 1995). Figure 8.1 illustrates the four different approaches to internationalisation proposed by Johanson and Mattsson (1995) according to the degree of the internationalisation of the market and the degree of internationalisation of the firm.

The early starter is characterised as having few and/or unimportant relationships with overseas organisations and this situation is typical of the market as a whole (Johanson and Mattsson 1995). Entry into international markets would not be dissimilar to the stages model of internationalisation described earlier. In

		Degree of internationalisation of the market	
		Low	High
Degree of internationalisation of the firm	Low	The early starter	The late starter
	High	The lonely international	The international among others

Figure 8.1. Network model of internationalisation
Source: Johanson and Mattsson (1995: 63).

order to offset the uncertainty and lack of experience in international operations, as well as the lack of resources, the early starter targets psychically close markets via the medium of agents.

The lonely international is ahead of the rest of the market in having established overseas relationships and experience, and in having the resource complement to allow it to act independently (Johanson and Mattsson 1995). The network focus of this type of firm is on how it enables other market players, like suppliers, customers and competitors, to initiate international operations. This lonely international category may not be a good descriptor of the internationalising SME from the traditional stages model perspective, but may encapsulate the situation described later in this chapter where the firm is 'born international'.

By contrast, the late starter is less internationally oriented than the rest of the market. However, it has indirect international relationships through the international operations of its customers, suppliers and competitors (Johanson and Mattsson 1995). It is conjectured that this firm can be pulled into international markets by virtue of its domestic relationships with international suppliers and/or customers. Such firms will also take larger international steps, in terms of investments and markets, than would be expected given the stages model of internationalisation. Thus, this situation might help to describe some of the exceptions noted to the stages model of internationalisation (see earlier). For smaller firms to be able to establish an international presence in an already well-established international market, it is hypothesised that they will be highly specialised and/or operating in a market that is loosely structured, enabling additional relationship establishments to support the firm's internationalisation efforts (Johanson and Mattsson 1995).

The firm that is international among others is less focused on market extension and penetration than it is on market co-ordination and, as such, this category is less fitting for the SME. It is, perhaps, best described by traditional MNE theories of international operations (see, for example, Dunning 1977), and their extensions involving alliance or network relationships (see, for example, Dunning 1995).

There have been limited tests of the network-based internationalisation approach. However, one study indicated that, 'While most research on foreign market entry has focused on entry mode selection, our findings indicate that the development of cooperative relationships with customers, suppliers or other business partners may be critical' (Holm *et al*. 1996: 1049). It is also generally acknowledged that, even under the stages model of internationalisation, relationships with other parties need to be taken into account in helping to explain the current activities of the firm and its commitment decisions (Johanson and Vahlne 1990). Therefore, the network model of internationalisation is useful in drawing our attention to **external influences** and **interactions** in relation to the internationalisation process, and especially the effect of networks on the rate of internationalisation. As such, it provides one possible reference point for determining how other organisations impact, or are impacted by, the internationalisation efforts of the SME.

Case Study 8.2 **Galloway International**

'Connecting colourful pods and tubes into a revolutionary playground structure is building an expanding niche export market for Galloway International. The patented plastic playground concept was designed and developed by rotational moulding company, Galloway International, with McDonald's Systems New Zealand and Canadian joint venture partner, Superior Plastics Industries (SPI). Galloway and SPI target the international market, with Galloway concentrating on Australia and the Asia Pacific region. The first playgrounds were installed in 1993 at McDonald's restaurants around New Zealand. Since then sales have risen by more than 500 per cent. In just four years of exporting Auckland-based Galloway International has installed playgrounds in Australia, China, Korea, Indonesia, Thailand and Taiwan and with SPI in more than 17 countries. Total export foreign exchange earnings . . . [represent] more than 65 per cent of total sales.'

Source: *Export News* (1997: 4).

The international new venture model and the SME

Definition of an 'international new venture'

The international new venture model of internationalisation has also been termed the born international or born global approach. The term 'international new venture' will be employed in this chapter because it is, technically, the correct description as the phenomenon being observed is early, rather than instantaneous, internationalisation. Early internationalisation has been variously defined as firms which within two years (Roberts and Senturia 1996) to eight years (McDougall 1989) were achieving international sales comprising 5 per cent (McDougall 1989) to more than 40 per cent (Roberts and Senturia 1996) of their overall output. The question arises as to how this is different to the stages model, which predicts that a domestic base will precede international efforts. The following pages, on empirical counter evidence and theory development, will highlight the crucial differences between the international new ventures model and the stages and network frameworks.

Empirical evidence of international new ventures

The study of software companies, highlighted in the stages model of the internationalisation section, identified a number of companies which serviced international markets before developing a domestic presence, and even some where domestic sales resulted from international endeavours (Bell 1995). An earlier study of firms in the computer and communications equipment manufacturing industries identified that the industry structure and strategic content of international new ventures was significantly different to domestic new ventures, and that strategy was the principal distinguishing factor (McDougall 1989). The international new ventures entered multiple markets, competed on a large scale and employed external resources. The emphasis on the strategic differences contrasts with the stages model of internationalisation which assumes that internationalisation proceeds regardless of the strategic actions of the firm. The follow-up study of these organisations two years later focused on the differential performance of the more highly internationalised firms (McDougall and Oviatt 1996), and found that the firm's level of international sales at the time of the first study was a good indicator of relative market share at the follow-up stage.

Another study focused on the analysis of four cases from different countries and the difficulties encountered in establishing market access, especially when compared to the incumbents in the industry; the problems of establishing a global presence because of the lack of foreign market investment or international contacts; and the imperfect nature of the global market, where even highly globalised companies are compelled to adopt country-based strategies to service some markets (Jolly et al. 1992). Given these impediments, firms would be expected to pursue a more staged-approach to internationalisation, keeping fixed costs low and, perhaps, concentrating on geographically protected niche markets. On the contrary, the four technology-based, start-up companies had been positioned to compete effectively in their respective global industries, and the strategies employed exhibited the common elements elaborated on below.

The global vision created by the founder for the organisation stemmed from an attitudinal predisposition to being involved in international markets (Jolly et al. 1992). Even with the establishment chain model it is acknowledged that internationalisation is a function of both attitude and activity (Johanson and Wiedersheim-Paul 1975), but subsequent studies tended to focus on the more observable activity element of internationalisation. The study of international new ventures has re-established the importance of the attitude element to the firm's international orientation and, in the case of international new ventures, the focus centres on the role of the founding entrepreneur.

The international entry strategy coincided with industry shifts from old to new technologies, and the start-ups possessed incrementally innovative products and processes which were well placed to exploit this shift (Jolly et al. 1992). Because of the shakeout in the industry, and the lag associated with larger companies transferring to the new technology, the small start-ups were able to obtain a rapid and strong market presence. They remained on top of the technological wave by establishing an early orientation to introducing successor products, either based on next generation developments or entirely new technologies.

The four companies exploited products which required minimal adjustments to the marketing mix in homogeneous market segments (Jolly et al. 1992), perhaps reflecting the early stage of the product life cycle as highlighted in the previous paragraph. Broad market access and penetration in these markets was facilitated by the use of partners with established distributive mechanisms. Both the stages and network models cover this approach to international development. However, the network model is more relevant because the companies proceeded to focus their efforts on what they did best, namely product development and manufacturing. They did not exhibit any interest in exerting more control over distributive structures as predicted by the stages model and, therefore, established partnerships for this purpose in the target markets. The firms engaged rapidly in limited foreign direct investment for supply purposes, thus separating the decision regarding market access from decisions relating to other functional investments (Jolly *et al.* 1992). This is the strongest point of departure for the international new venture when compared with firms employing a staged or network approach to internationalisation. In all cases, research and development and manufacturing were also situated on separate continents and, in two cases, the finance and administrative functions of the organisations were geographically separate.

This investment strategy allowed the firms to serve the global market from different locations, although limited in number, and this was further facilitated by the formation of a tightly networked global organisation (Jolly *et al.* 1992). That is, the principal officers of the company were geographically distant with oversight of regional markets as well as functional specialities. However, the principal site of each of the functional areas had prime responsibility for the worldwide operation of that function. Again, neither the stages nor network models help to explain such international organisational structures.

The insights provided by case and empirical studies, such as the above, and the recognition that traditional business theories (see Chapters 1 and 5) also fail to explain the *process* of internationalisation, led to the development of the international new venture framework.

The international new venture framework

It is on the age issue that the international new venture framework is distinguished from: traditional international business theories, since they start from the assumption of existing operations; and the stages model of internationalisation, which assumes an established domestic base of operations. For the international new venture, the origins of the firm are international and the pertinent age of the firm is what is termed 'inception,' in a legal sense, or 'observable resource commitments' (Oviatt and McDougall 1994: 49), recognising that some new ventures become progressively more established over time (Vesper 1990). The international new venture framework, developed by Oviatt and McDougall (1994) and presented in Figure 8.2 draws on theories from economics, entrepreneurship, international business and strategic management to explain the phenomenon and each of these contributory theoretical perspectives will be explored in turn.

First, as highlighted in the networks section of this chapter, transaction cost economics explain the circumstances under which firms internalise transactions versus contracting for resources on the open market (Oviatt and McDougall 1994). The internalisation of some transactions under Element 1 of the model, or the

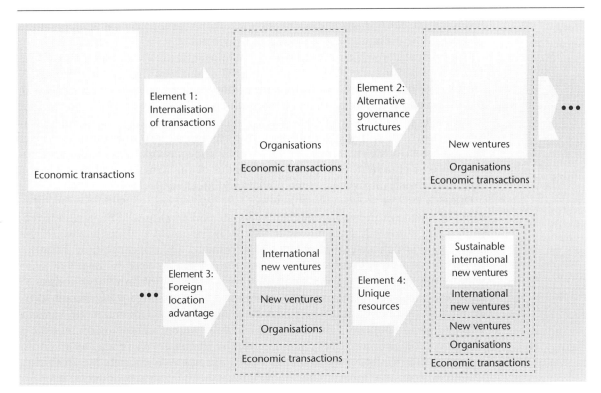

Figure 8.2 International new ventures framework
Source: Oviatt and McDougall (1994: 54).

accumulation of resources, corresponds with the definition of the inception stage of the firm. However, rapidly internationalising, resource-constrained SMEs are expected to utilise alternative governance structures to complement their internal resource base, as per Element 2 (Oviatt and McDougall 1994). Drawing on the insights from both the entrepreneurial and network literature highlighted earlier, entrepreneurial companies are expected to leverage and complement resources by engaging in network relationships with other organisations, or by licensing or franchising their new venture concept. However, the network approach is considered to be a more powerful co-ordinating mechanism than licensing or franchising because it minimises the risk of asset appropriation by partners.

The concept of foreign location advantage from the MNE-based international business literature explains how foreign companies effectively compete with domestic firms. Although MNEs have competed traditionally on the basis of economies of scale, knowledge is becoming an increasingly important basis of international competition (see, for example, Archibugi and Michie 1998). International new ventures are less able to compete on scale economies. However, they are able to combine knowledge advantages with less mobile resources in order to compete with domestic companies in multiple locations (Oviatt and McDougall 1994). An interesting question arises from Element 3 of the model: since the empirical evidence on international new ventures has been centred on high-technology firms, and since knowledge is expected to be a defining element, is the framework a theory of technology-based international new ventures? The model has not been limited specifically to such industries, and empirical work on more diverse industries is required to answer this question.

The last element of the framework – unique resources – is derived from the resource-based view of the firm in the field of strategic management (Barney 1991). The international new venture model focuses on two elements of the resource-based framework: the means by which SMEs maintain the value of their knowledge, preventing appropriation via such means as patents, internalisation and network relationships; and the emphasis on the promotion of imperfect imitability, through the SME's unique history and network organisational structure, so that competitors only see the product of the firm's endeavours not the means by which this was achieved (Oviatt and McDougall 1994).

Drawing on the international new venture framework, a predictive model of types of new venture was developed by Oviatt and McDougall (1994) and is presented in Figure 8.3. This model is based on the number of activities on the value chain which are co-ordinated across countries and the number of countries in which the firm is involved. New international market-makers consist of firms with a small number of value chain activities, namely inbound and outbound logistics, co-ordinated across countries: export/import start-up businesses focus on a small number of countries; multinational start-up traders operate across a larger range of countries. The historical literature on entrepreneurship reinforces these typologies since it emphasises the role of the entrepreneur as an inter-market operator, obtaining resources which are not well marketed, transferring resources from one location to the other and seeing more productive uses for resources (Leibenstein 1978; Casson 1982; Jennings 1994). It is also important to note that the international trading company has, for the first time, been incorporated explicitly into a theory of international business.

The geographically focused start-up engages in the international co-ordination of many value chain activities to service the specialised needs of a geographical region, such that the input activities are geographically unlimited while the output activities are geographically concentrated (Oviatt and McDougall 1994). On the other hand, the final international new venture category, the global start-up, exhibits no geographical constraints in terms of its input and output

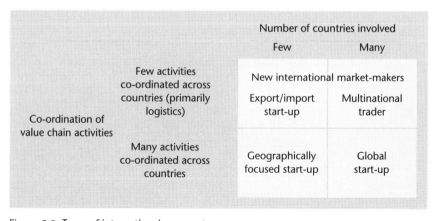

Figure 8.3 Types of international new ventures
Source: Oviatt and McDougall (1994: 59).

activities (Oviatt and McDougall 1994). These categorisations may help to explain the case study examples, mentioned under the empirical evidence heading of this section, where supply activities were internalised, eventually, while distribution activities were handled via network relations.

Notwithstanding, more research needs to be conducted on the international new venture type in order to increase our understanding of this important phenomenon. For the moment, the framework is useful for highlighting the role of the *individual* in the internationalisation process of the SME, elaborating on the use of *networks*, and allowing for *strategic action* in relation to the international success of the SME.

Case Study 8.3 Horticultural Developments New Zealand

Laurie Rennie . . . and David Eder . . . formed Horticultural Developments NZ Ltd two years ago to invest in a potato crisp manufacturing plant in China. Neither had set up an offshore manufacturing plant before but they had identified the opportunity to manufacture and sell snack foods in China during seven years of travel there sourcing rare dehydrated herbs for a business in New Zealand. . . . It went into a 50:50 joint venture with a Hong Kong partner and . . . set up a factory in Heiliongjiang in north-east China. The factory was built there because it is among the most agriculturally productive regions in China and the Hong Kong company already had a snack food factory there. . . . The plant was designed by Food Systems Ltd in Melbourne and manufactured by Palmerston North-based company Weld Fabricators Ltd. The packers came from Australia and the weighers were bought in Japan. . . . Negotiations are . . . under way with two Beijing companies to distribute the product in east China .... One snack good company wants to sell the product under its own house brand while another is interested in exporting it to Europe where its organic nature appeals.

Source: Adapted from *Export News* (1996: 9).

Chapter summary

An SME is not a little big firm and, therefore, it is important to recognise that traditional international business models do not explain SME internationalisation. This chapter presented three models of internationalisation which, when combined with an understanding of the inherent advantages and disadvantages of the SME, are more suited to understanding the facilitating and impeding factors of internationalisation. The review of the stages model of internationalisation explained how firms, from a domestic base, make incremental commitments to international markets in the context of resource and international knowledge constraints. The explanation of the network model of internationalisation highlighted the effect of other organisations on the SME's internationalisation process, focusing primarily on how interactions can speed up the pace of development by helping to overcome resource and international knowledge constraints. The discussion of the international new venture model centred on the phenomenon of rapid illustration that, in some instances, may even involve establishing an international sales presence ahead, or even instead, of domestic sales. The review focused on how individuals with international experience and networks can overcome internationalisation constraints while exploiting the specific innovation and flexibility advantages of the SME.

Discussion questions

1 Discuss the advantages and disadvantages of building a strong domestic base of operations before developing an international presence.

2 In the networks model, discuss how the situation of 'the lonely international' compares and contrasts with the situation of 'the late starter'.

3 Discuss how the advantages of flexibility and innovation, and the process of resource leveraging, are fundamental to understanding the international new venture (INV) model of internationalisation.

4 Knowledge is a fundamental concept for the stages, network and international new ventures models. Discuss the similarities and differences in the definition and extent of knowledge across the three models.

Closing Case Study
Trends Publishing International

The present situation

1998 New Zealand Entrepreneur of the Year, David Johnson, and the company he formed in 1983, Trends Publishing, reached a critical stage in terms of future international growth at the point where the company employed 52 people in four countries.

Background

In partnership with Gordon Dryden, David formed the Dryden Johnson Group, a media-buying business (Gordon was subsequently bought out of the business by David). One client, the New Zealand Kitchen and Bathroom Association, asked the company to conduct an advertising campaign to publicise colour kitchen units and bathroom suites. It was soon decided that the black and white medium of the national newspaper was inappropriate and the company began to design a colour insert. Meanwhile, David talked to some of his other clients and they wanted to be associated with the campaign. The colour insert grew quickly to become a 30- or 40-page booklet just on this one advertising campaign. The company knew it could no longer distribute this with the national newspaper. So they called it a book, the company charged NZ$4.95 for the resulting 148 pages and David became a publisher. The book consisted of 75 per cent advertorial and advertising, all paid for before the book was placed on the advertisers' shelves. The company used the radio to advertise the newspaper and the newspaper to advertise the book, which was positioned as the authority on contemporary kitchen and bathroom designs. The book was sold from the advertisers' showrooms. The cash flow from this first book was used to fund two followup books, one solely on kitchen design and another focusing on bathroom design. Eventually, with five books in the New Zealand market, David developed the Trends name to establish a consistent brand identity and began to think about overseas markets.

Trends Publishing International

The United States No. 1

In 1987, Trends Publishing approached the national kitchen and bathroom association in the United States and the organisation was extremely enthusiastic about the product concept. David admits he did no research on the United States market and acted on intuition; however, in his haste he made a serious mistake. He forgot about distribution which, in those days, was controlled by organised crime. The failed entry cost the company NZ$150,000, but the lesson was that it was vulnerable distribution-wise and future market entries required research.

Singapore No. 1

The United States experience had confirmed that the basic product concept was good and David was determined to break into the international market in order to become a global communications company. The problem was how to finance this while keeping costs in control. In the late 1980s, David moved the printing and lithographic operation to Singapore and saved NZ$350,000. He found out, subsequently, that he had managed to negotiate a price comparable to Australian entrepreneur Kerry Packer who, at the time, managed a multi-million dollar business, and this was despite the lower volumes involved in the Trends print runs.

Australia

In 1989, Trends tackled the Australian market. David took a no-frills approach to researching and developing the market, a practice he maintains today. He flew economy class, he stayed at his sister's house and borrowed her car, and he avoided hiring any new people at this initial stage. He knew, in production terms, that he could get a book to the market at an internationally competitive price. He also focused, initially, on the same clients in Australia as in New Zealand; for example, DuPont and Formica. They were familiar with the Trends approach and David did not have to reinvent the wheel.

Trends came under great pressure to adapt the concept to the Australian market. For example, David was encouraged to drop the price (then set at the equivalent of NZ$9.95) and to copy the approach taken by competitors in the market. He insisted on sticking to the unique formula that had served the company well in the New Zealand market and focused on creating a sales and distribution operation in Australia. The lesson on distribution had been learned, with David having already established his own distribution company in New Zealand. Both of the New Zealand and Australian distribution companies catered for 55 per cent of Trends' overall distribution, with the remaining distribution controlled by MNEs. According to David, the establishment of his own distributive mechanisms gave Trends some strategic power. Subsequently, the company established a sales team in Australia and published 14 titles there, with successive product launches financed by the income of earlier books.

Singapore No. 2

In 1991, Trends grabbed the Asian tiger by the tail and focused its development efforts on Singapore. Singapore was chosen for a number of reasons: David was familiar with the market because the printing business was located there; he could also insulate the company's exchange-rate risk. Again, the same successful formula was employed with the introduction of a Kitchen Trends book, which financed two more books and led to nine titles overall in the market. By this stage, the company employed 25 people in three countries.

Malaysia

David changed the formula for the Malaysian entry and started out with six titles. 'I got cocky and expanded too quickly. We still haven't recovered in Malaysia despite the economic problems,' David observed. The larger-scale entry drew staff away from the Singaporean operation, and required financial support from the New Zealand and Australian activities. The company remained in Malaysia despite these difficulties.

Hong Kong

Hong Kong was a strategic choice for positioning the company to address the Chinese market. According to David, Hong Kong had 80 per cent of the design and construction influence for the whole of the Chinese market. As with the Malaysian market, Hong Kong was serviced from the Singaporean hub.

United States No. 2

The United States re-entry in 1996 was focused on organising distribution first, and it took David eight months to organise. After the Malaysian experience, David was even more determined to stick to the successful formula. This proved particularly troublesome. For example: the company established exclusive distributorships with major chains, a first in the United States; the insistence on a 12-month shelf life for the product was also a first; and David refused to place the word 'advertisement' at the top of each page of the book, again a unique approach.

By this time, David had managed to leverage his operations across all his international markets. For example, the company could put 12 pages of a client's advertorial in the United States edition, put four of these pages into a New Zealand version, and put eight into an Australian publication. In this way, the one source of information was multiplied many times under the Trends brand.

However, although Trends could produce a book for under US$2, it cost the company US$1.2 million to launch the Kitchen Trends book in the United States, and this was followed by two more and then five. All were financed from reinvested earnings that, with a 12- to 15-month lead time, stretched the company to its limits. At this point, David concluded that the company had reached a critical juncture in its growth aspirations. He began to investigate potential partnerships with major corporations around the world, among them Time Warner, Inc. and CNN International.

Questions

1 How would you explain the internationalisation of Trends Publishing International?
2 What options are available for the future international development of Trends Publishing International and what advice would you offer?

Note

1 This study was cited widely and, later, doubts were cast on the credibility of the results because of methodological problems.

Further reading

Haahti, A., **Hall**, G. and **Donckels**, R. (1998) *The Internationalization of SMEs: The Interstratos Project*, London: Routledge. Reports the results of a pan-European study of SME internationalisation.

Hisrich, R.D., **McDougall**, P.P. and **Oviatt**, B.M. (1997) *Cases in International Entrepreneurship*, London: Irwin. Provides case examples to illustrate the models introduced in this chapter.

Jenster, P.V. and **Jarillo**, J.C. (1994) *Internationalizing the Medium-Sized Enterprise*. Copenhagen: Munksgaard International Publishers. Provides case examples on medium-sized firms that can be used to explore the models introduced in this chapter.

Nielsen, K., **Pedersen**, K. and **Vestergaard**, J. (1999) *Internationalization of SMEs*, London: Macmillan. Introduces a conceptual framework designed specifically to understand the internationalisation process of SMEs.

Root, F.R. (1994) *Entry Strategies for International Markets*, Oxford: Maxwell Macmillan International. Includes useful 'how to' lists for alternative market entry strategies.

References

Aldrich, H. and **Auster**, E.R. (1986) Even dwarfs started small: liabilities of age and size and their strategic implications, *Research in Organizational Behavior* 8: 165–98.

Archibugi, D. and **Michie**, J. (1998) *Trade, Growth and Technical Change*, Cambridge: Cambridge University Press.

Axelsson, B. and **Johanson, J.** (1992) Foreign market entry – the textbook vs the network view, in B. Axelsson and G. Easton (eds) *Industrial Networks: A New View of Reality*, London: Routledge, pp. 218–34.

Bannock, G. and **Peacock, A.** (1989) *Governments and Small Business*, London: Paul Chapman Publishing.

Barney, J. (1991) Firm resources and sustained competitive advantage, *Journal of Management* 17 (1): 99–120.

Bell, J. (1995) The internationalization of small computer software firms: a further challenge to 'stage' theories, *European Journal of Marketing* 29 (8): 60–75.

Birch, D. (1979) *The Job Generation Process*, Cambridge, Mass.: MIT Program on Neighborhood and Regional Change.

Casson, M. (1982) *Alternative Theories of the Entrepreneur*, Oxford: Martin Robertson.

Curran, J. and **Blackburn, R.A.** (1991) Changes in the context of enterprise: some socio-economic and environmental factors facing small firms in the 1990s, in J. Curran and R.A. Blackburn (eds) *Paths of Enterprise: The Future of the Small Business*, London: Routledge, pp. 163–92.

Dunning, J.H. (1977) Trade, location of economic activity and the multinational enterprise: a search for an eclectic approach, in B. Ohlin, P.O. Hesselborn and P.M. Wikman (eds) *The International Allocation of Economic Activity*, London: Macmillan, pp. 395–418.

Dunning, J.H. (1995) Reappraising the eclectic paradigm in an age of alliance capitalism, *Journal of International Business Studies* 26 (3): 461–91.

Export News (1996) Potato crisp venture under way, 28 October: 9.

Export News (1997) Child's play at Galloway International, 10 November: 4.

Goulter, J. (1995) Just do it: and learn along the way, *NZ Business*, March: 14–21.

Håkansson, H. and **Snehota, I.** (1995) Analysing business relationships, in H. Håkansson and I. Snehota (eds) *Developing Relationships in Business Networks*, London: Routledge, pp. 24–49.

Holm, D.B., Eriksson, K. and **Johanson, J.** (1996) Business networks and co-operation in international business relationships, *Journal of International Business Studies, Special Issue* 27 (5): 1033–53.

Jennings, D.F. (1994) *Multiple Perspectives on Entrepreneurship*, Cincinnati, OH: South Western Publishing.

Johanson, J. and **Mattsson, L.-G.** (1991) Interorganizational relations in industrial systems: a network approach compared with the transactions-cost approach, in G. Thompson, J. Frances, R. Levacic and J. Mitchell (eds) *Markets, Hierarchies and Networks: The Coordination of Social Life*, London: Sage Publications, pp. 256–64.

Johanson, J. and **Mattsson, L.-G.** (1995) International marketing and internationalization processes, in S.J. Paliwoda and J.K. Ryan (eds) *International Marketing Reader*, London: Routledge, pp. 51–71.

Johanson, J. and **Vahlne, J.-E.** (1990) The mechanism of internationalisation, *International Marketing Review* 7 (4): 11–24.

Johanson, J. and **Wiedersheim-Paul, F.** (1975) The internationalization of the firm – four Swedish cases, *Journal of Management Studies*, October: 305–22.

Jolly, V.K., Alahuhta, M. and Jeannet, J.-P. (1992) Challenging the incumbents: how high technology start-ups compete globally, *Journal of Strategic Change* 1: 71–82.

Leibenstein, H. (1978) *General X-Efficiency Theory and Economic Development*, London: Oxford University Press.

Loveman, G. and Sengenberger, W. (1990) Introduction: economic and social reorganisation in the small and medium-sized enterprise sector, in W. Sengenberger, G.W. Loveman and M.J. Piore (eds) *The Re-emergence of Small Enterprises: Industrial Restructuring in Industrialised Countries*, Geneva: International Institute for Labour Studies, pp. 1–61.

Lundvall, B.-A. (1993) Explaining interfirm cooperation and innovation: limits of the transaction-cost approach, in G. Grabher (ed.) *The Embedded Firm: On the Socioeconomics of Industrial Networks*, London: Routledge, pp. 52–64.

McDougall, P.P. (1989) International versus domestic entrepreneurship: new venture strategic behavior and industry structure, *Journal of Business Venturing* 4: 387–400.

McDougall, P.P. and Oviatt, B.M. (1996) New venture internationalization, strategic change, and performance: a follow-up study, *Journal of Business Venturing* 11: 23–40.

Oviatt, B.M. and McDougall, P.P. (1994) Toward a theory of international new ventures, *Journal of International Business Studies* 25 (1): 45–64.

Pavitt, K., Robson, M. and Townsend, J. (1987) The size distribution of innovating firms in the UK: 1945–1983. *Journal of Industrial Economics* 45: 297–306.

Piore, M.J. and Sabel, C.F. (1984) *The Second Industrial Divide: Possibilities for Prosperity*, New York: Basic Books, Inc.

Powell, W.W. (1991) Neither market nor hierarchy: network forms of organization, in G. Thompson, J. Frances, R. Levacic and J. Mitchell (eds) *Markets, Hierarchies and Networks: The Coordination of Social Life*, London: Sage Publications, pp. 265–76.

Rainnie, A. (1991) Small firms: between the enterprise culture and 'New Times', in R. Burrows (ed.) *Deciphering the Enterprise Culture: Entrepreneurship, Petty Capitalism and the Restructuring of Britain*, London: Routledge, pp. 176–99.

Roberts, E.B. and Senturia, T.A. (1996) Globalizing the emerging high-technology company, *Industrial Marketing Management* 25: 491–506.

Schumpeter, J.A. (1939) *Business Cycles: A Theoretical, Historical, and Statistical Analysis of the Capitalist Process*, Vol. I, London: McGraw-Hill.

Stanworth, J. and Gray, C. (1991) *Bolton 20 Years On: The Small Firm in the 1990s*, London: Paul Chapman Publishing.

Stevenson, H.H., Roberts, M.J. and Grousbeck, H.I. (1994) *New Business Ventures and the Entrepreneur*, 4th edn, Boston: Irwin.

Storey, D. (1994) *Understanding the Small Business Sector*, London: Routledge.

Story, M. (1997) Convex Plastics looks to new overseas markets, *Export News*, 7 July: 6.

Timmons, J.A. (1994) *New Venture Creation: Entrepreneurship for the 21st Century*, 4th edn, Boston: Irwin.

Turnbull, P.W. (1987) A challenge to the stages theory of the internationalization process, in P.J. Rosson and S.D. Reid (eds) *Managing Export Entry and Expansion*, New York: Praeger.

Vesper, K.H. (1990) *New Venture Strategies*, Englewood Cliffs, NJ: Prentice Hall.

Welch, L.S. and **Luostarinen, R.** (1994) Internationalization: evolution of a concept, in P.J. Buckley and P.N. Ghauri (eds) *The Internationalization of the Firm: A Reader*, London: Dryden, pp. 155–71.

Welch, D.E. and **Welch, L.S.** (1996) The internationalization process and networks: a strategic management perspective, *Journal of International Marketing* 4 (3): 11–28.

Williamson, E.E. (1981) The economics of organizations: the transaction cost approach, *American Journal of Sociology* 87: 548–77.

Part IV The External Challenges of International Firms

CHAPTER 9
Financial Risk
Mike Bowe

Learning objectives

By the end of this chapter, you will:

- be familiar with the sources of financial risk and the impact of financial risk on multinational corporations

- understand why managing financial risk can increase the value of a multinational firm by reducing taxes, lowering transaction costs and decreasing the likelihood of making incorrect investment decisions

- be aware of the basic techniques for implementing a risk-management programme and evaluating its performance

- understand the state of the art techniques such as value at risk and cash flow at risk for measuring exposure to financial risk both internally and externally.

Opening Case Study:
Japanese traders put under review

Moody's, the US credit rating agency, placed the debt ratings of three of Japan's largest trading houses under review for downgrade yesterday, adding to concern about their financial stability.

The review of Mitsubishi, Mitsui and Sumitomo brings to five the number of Japanese trading houses on watch for credit problems, and highlights the impact of the Asian financial crisis on Japanese companies.

In May, Moody's put Marubeni and Nissho Iwai, both of which have heavy exposure to south-east Asia, under review for a downgrade. Moody's said the reviews came in response to a weakening in the trading houses' profitability and financial position because of the effects of the Asian financial turmoil and Japan's domestic economic downturn.

The trading houses' unusually heavy reliance on commercial paper for funding created additional financial risk, the agency said. 'I think it reflects the very

▶

weak financial fundamentals of the Japanese trading companies, especially in terms of capitalisation, earnings and profitability,' said Mutsuo Suzuki, senior analyst at Moody's.

The companies' core businesses – known as keiretsu – were hit last year by the sharp decline in the Asian and Japanese economies. Profits plunged in the oil, construction, machinery, and car industries, which in turn increased the financial burden on the trading houses, Mr Suzuki said. The riskiness of these core businesses prompted the review, he added. All the Japanese trading houses are heavily exposed to Asian markets and therefore at risk of suffering losses because of currency fluctuations and falling domestic demand through their keiretsu businesses. Mitsubishi's exposure to Asian markets was Y273.3bn last year, mainly in trade insurance. Sumitomo reported Y203.66bn in exposure to five countries in the region.

Exposure to Indonesia had been particularly damaging, Mr Suzuki said. Even worse for the trading companies, stock prices have plunged to new lows this year. Mitsubishi hit a year-to-date low in June, dropping to Y715. Yesterday, Mitsubishi gained Y70 to close at Y930, while Mitsui closed up Y29 at Y779. Sumitomo improved Y83 to Y750.

Source: *Financial Times* CD-ROM, 1 January–31 December 1998.

Introduction

This chapter begins by identifying the nature of these financial risks and goes on to demonstrate the way in which tactical and strategic risk-management activity can increase the present value of the corporation's expected cash flow, thereby augmenting shareholder returns. The chapter then examines the strengths and weaknesses of internal and external mechanisms for quantifying financial risk in conjunction with approaches to identifying basic strategies for implementing a risk-management system and evaluating its performance.

Definition of financial and other international business risks

Managing financial risk, through the identification, measurement and control of relevant risk exposures, is the major corporate responsibility of the treasury department and the senior financial officers in a multinational corporation. While some firms are passive in accepting financial risk, others use such exposure to risk as a business opportunity, attempting to create a competitive advantage through the strategies they adopt to manage these risks.

To begin, it is necessary to provide a formal definition of financial risk. In practical terms, in order to define risk, we must first select the financial variable(s) of interest. The value of the corporation's portfolio of assets and liabilities, corporate earnings, equity capital or a specific cash flow arising from an operating or contractual exposure, are all natural potential candidates. Focusing on the former variable for illustrative purposes, financial risk can now be defined as *unexpected* changes in the valuation of a multinational corporation's portfolio of assets and/or liabilities arising either from changes in the value of financial instruments, or consequent on the corporation's activities in financial markets. Movements in the prices of financial instruments, such as exchange rates, interest rates, commodity and equity prices, in a manner which was not predicted by the firm's managers, are the major sources of financial risk for most multinational corporations.

Financial risk is just one of the three main categories of risk to which multinational firms are exposed, and before proceeding further it is worthwhile to briefly discuss the two others. They are customarily termed business risk and country risk. Business or operating risk incorporates those risks which a multinational corporation chooses to confront in order to enhance its shareholder's wealth. These risks arise in the product market within which the corporation operates, and include innovations in technology, personnel practices, product and manufacturing design, and marketing. Unexpected changes in a corporation's cost structure relating to the balance between fixed and variable costs are also a source of business risk to the extent that operating leverage is also a choice variable. Developing a strategic framework to appropriately select and manage business risk is a 'core competency' of multinational business activity.

Country risk, which incorporates the subsets of political and macroeconomic risk, arises when fundamental changes in the political, social or macroeconomic environment of a host country result in unforeseen changes in the valuation of the corporation. Events creating country risk cover a wide range of possibilities and circumstances, as the following non-exhaustive list of examples demonstrates:

- the imposition of tax regulations or foreign exchange controls, especially those which discriminate against foreign-owned corporations
- capital controls restricting access to host-country sources of finance
- new host-country stipulations regarding local sourcing, production or hiring practices
- expropriation or nationalisation of the corporation's assets without adequate compensation
- destruction of plant and equipment or harm to personnel arising from catastrophic effects such as rioting, civil war or revolution
- social upheaval involving discrimination against foreign-owned products or businesses.

The variety of techniques multinational firms have adopted to manage country risk, whether for the purposes of foreign direct investment or establishing international operations, involve the implementation of a framework for strategic planning and are discussed in the following chapter. The remainder of this chapter is devoted to financial risk and the recent techniques that have evolved in order to manage it.

The nature of financial risk

The emphasis on financial risk and the evolution of risk-management practices have been motivated by a number of factors, the most important being the increased volatility in the financial environment within which multinational firms operate. These financial risks emanate from several sources. We start by chronicling selective recent developments in the global financial environment, in order to provide a classification of the risk categories impacting on multinationals' operations, namely: market risk, credit risk (including sovereign and settlement risk), liquidity risk, operational risk and legal risk. We begin with the former.

Market risk

Market risk relates to the impact on the value of the multinational corporation of changes in exchange rates, interest rates, and the price of equity or commodities. It can be quantified using some measure of the dispersion (or volatility) of changes in the value of the variable of interest, for example, earnings or a particular cash flow, caused by unexpected price movements in these financial instruments. The increasing impact of market risk in global financial markets, and consequently on multinationals' risk-management behaviour can be illustrated with reference to the following developments.

Exchange rate variability

Following the collapse of the Bretton Woods system of fixed exchange rates in the early 1970s, exchange rate fluctuations have become increasingly volatile, punctuated by occasional episodes of exchange rate crises. In the past 30 years, the Yen/US dollar exchange rate has moved from 361 to 118.5 and the Deutschemark/US dollar rate has fallen from 4.2 to 1.67 (at the time of writing). The dollar has, however, appreciated by about two-thirds against sterling over the same period. The crisis in the European Monetary Systems exchange-rate mechanism, in September 1992, led to significant falls in the value of sterling and the Italian Lira, while the currencies of Thailand, Indonesia, Malaysia, the Philippines and South Korea lost between one-third and three-quarters of their value in the second half of 1997. There have also been major movements in exchange rates following shifts in the monetary policy stance of certain governments, such as the tighter monetary policy followed in the early days of the Thatcher administration in the UK. Indeed, the average volatility of exchange rates, which is in the region of 10–15 per cent per year, is sufficient to eliminate the average profit margin for multinational corporations, which is typically of a similar magnitude.

Interest rate variability

Corporate funding costs, cash flows and net asset values have been greatly impacted by the interest rate volatility which has arisen periodically since the early 1970s. Inflationary pressures caused interest rates to increase in the first half of the 1970s in the US, and although they subsequently declined, a change in policy by the Federal Reserve caused a sharp increase in both the level and volatility of rates in 1979. Interest rates peaked in 1981, and then fell slowly. There have been four more interest rate cycles in the US since 1983. According to Jorion (1996), the increase in 1994 is estimated to have wiped-out over $1.5 trillion from the value of fixed income portfolios (see Exhibit 9.5). Interest rates have also become more volatile since many central banks began to abandon targeting interest rates as a policy objective in favour of targeting money supply growth or inflation. In the UK, interest rates shot up in the late 1980s and early 1990s because of inflationary pressures caused by a relaxation in monetary policy, but then fell substantially with sterling's withdrawal from the ERM in September 1992.

Equity market variability

Equity markets have also become extremely volatile. During the inflationary periods of the early 1970s, prices increased significantly only to fall sharply during the bear market of 1974–5 following the 300 per cent oil price rise. A global recovery then ensued, with minor price reversals in 1982–3, and the market peaked in 1987. On Black Monday, 19 October, 1987, prices plunged throughout the world's stock markets. US equities lost 23 per cent of their value, equivalent to over US $1 trillion in equity capital. This was followed by another sustained recovery worldwide for the next ten years with the exception of Japan, where the Nikkei index fell from 39,000 in 1989 to 17,000 in 1992, representing a capital loss of US $2.7 trillion. Finally from mid- to end 1997, the stock markets of Bangkok, Jakarta, Kuala Lumpur and Manila lost US $370 billion, or 63 per cent of the four countries' combined GDP, while the Seoul stock market declined 60 per cent over the same period.

Commodity price variability and other sources of increased risk

Commodity prices, particularly for those in primary product markets, have also been subject to large fluctuations since the 1970s, a trend established subsequent to the oil price rises of 1973–4. This variability also had spillover effects in other financial markets, particularly equity markets, thereby corroborating the view that it is fundamentally incorrect to treat financial markets in isolation from one another. Significant changes in regulatory and legal emphasis, the globalisation of the financial services industry, and the emergence of offshore financial activity have also increased financial risks. Finally, the risk associated with the enhanced global nature of competition has become apparent following increasing levels of world trade and major changes in trade policy, all exacerbated by the economic and political transition of the former Soviet bloc, the growth of the EU, and the emergence of the Asian 'tiger' economies as economic powers.

Credit risk

Credit risk captures the impact of counterparty default on the value of the financial variable of interest to the corporation. Default is simply the failure of a contractually obligated party to undertake a financial payment which has been stipulated under the terms of a contract. Credit risk essentially encompasses two elements. The quantitative component is market risk as considered in the previous section. The additional qualitative feature is default risk, which is an objective assessment of the probability that a counterparty will default. Credit risk for a given counterparty is measured over the life of a contractual obligation by summing current and potential exposure. Current exposure is an estimate of the current least-cost method of replicating any existing contractual obligations, while potential exposure is a measure of future replacement cost. Both are measured net of the value of any assets that are expected to be recovered from the counterparty.

A major component of credit risk is presettlement risk, which occurs when counterparties are either unwilling or unable to carry out their on-going contractual obligations. Credit risk can also result in losses when a counterparty is downgraded by a credit-rating agency. Such an occurrence usually results in a fall in the market value of the counterparty's outstanding financial obligations, which are assets of the corporation. Credit risk also includes sovereign risk. This type of risk is often associated with the imposition of exchange or capital controls by governments which make it impossible for counterparties to satisfy their contractual obligations. The distinction between sovereign risk and credit risk is that the former generally relates to country-specific events, while the latter is firm-specific.

Exhibit 9.1 Sovereign Risk and Eurodeposits

In October 1983, the Philippine government imposed controls limiting the transfer of foreign currency denominated funds from Philippines' banks. Citibank of New York responded by freezing hundreds of millions of dollars worth of Eurodollar deposits in its Manila branch, saying 'it had no choice but to freeze the deposits when the cash-strapped Philippine government imposed controls banning foreign-exchange outflows' (*Wall Street Journal*, 23 February 1984). A Singapore-based subsidiary of Wells Fargo Bank of San Francisco, Wells Fargo Asia Limited, had placed two £1 million deposits with Citibank Manila in June 1983, both due to mature in December 1983, and which were expected to be paid on maturity. When repayment did not occur, Wells Fargo Asia sued Citibank New York in a New York federal court.

Source: Adapted from *Wall Street Journal*, 23 February 1984.

A second component of credit risk is settlement risk, which is of particular relevance for multinational financial institutions. Settlement is the actual physical or electronic event when a contracted exchange occurs following which both parties to the contract are deemed to have satisfied their obligations. Settlement risk exists when there are simultaneous exchanges required in the transaction and stems from three sources. One is the failure of one of the contracting parties to deliver the promised commodity, securities or cash when required at contract termination. Another is the risk that a middleman, or a settlement agent such as a financial intermediary utilised for the purposes of executing the transfer of securities or commodities, will fail to perform. Finally, it is possible that markets will confront difficulties leading to systemic contagion.

Exhibit 9. 2 Settlement Risk and Financial Crisis

Settlement risk is also known as Herstatt risk, after Bankhaus Herstatt which declared bankruptcy and was closed by German regulators in 1974 after receiving daily settlement payments from a number of counterparties, but before it had made payments on the other leg of the transaction. This event potentially destabilised the global banking system, and was a major impetus in the formation of the Basle Committee for Banking Supervision. Central Bankers are becoming increasingly concerned over settlement risk, given that daily currency settlement payments have escalated to over $3 trillion. This has led to the introduction of bilateral and multilateral netting systems. The former allow offsetting cash flows between two counterparties on any given day to be netted prior to payment, while the latter allow each member bank to settle daily balances in each currency with a group of banks. Multinet, established in 1994 as a clearinghouse for multilateral currency netting, is an example of a multilateral system.

Source: Various, adapted by author.

Legal risk

Legal risk encompasses situations where there is uncertainty concerning the enforceability of a contract. It arises in situations where a counterparty may not have the statutory authority to undertake a contractual obligation (resulting in a situation where the contract may be declared invalid) and where there are disputes over insufficient documentation.

Exhibit 9.3 Legal Risk and Derivatives

In January 1991 the British High Court ruled that the large interest rate swap positions entered into by city councils were illegal, as the municipalities did not have the power to enter these transactions. The existing swap contracts were declared null and void which meant that the city councils were no longer responsible for paying the large losses that the contracts had accumulated. As a result of this decision, the swap counterparties had to swallow losses of about £500 million.

Source: Various, adapted by author.

As such circumstances effectively result in a contractual default, legal risk bears a direct relationship to default risk. Legal risk also incorporates compliance and regulatory risk relating to activities which may contravene government regulations such as market manipulation, insider trading and suitability regulations.

Clearly this regulatory framework will vary across jurisdictions, and even within a country possibly subject to amendments and differences of interpretation.

Operational risk

Operational risk encompasses potential unexpected losses arising from:

- management failure to implement the requisite controls or engage in the appropriate monitoring of employee behaviour, for example through internal audits
- technology risk, including the requirement to insulate systems from unauthorised access and tampering
- fraudulent behaviour relating to unauthorised trading, the intentional falsification of information, and/or the deliberate incorrect recording of contractual details or financial transactions
- execution risk arising from human error, which includes situations where contracts fail to be completed appropriately, leading to costly delays or penalties, or general difficulties in back-office operations including the inability to reconcile individual contractual obligations with the firm's aggregate position.

The recommended mechanism for managing operational risk consists of making obsolete systems redundant, clearly separating front-office and back-office responsibilities, coupled with strong internal monitoring and control, and contingency planning on a regular basis.

Operational difficulties are also connected to valuation issues through the potential for model risk. This is the danger that the model outcomes, which

Exhibit 9.4 Operational Risk and the Barings Fiasco

A notable example of ineffective and ultimately disastrous management of operational risk is provided by the example of the February 1995 failure of Barings Bank. The trading activities of its manager in Singapore, Nick Leeson, resulted in a £700 million loss from derivatives trading, which wiped out the Bank's entire capital. Prior to its failure, Barings violated the majority of the rules of sound operational risk management which were outlined above.

The bank committed the cardinal error of allowing Leeson to control both the front and back office functions.

Management in London failed to monitor Leeson's activities, or verify the recording of contractual details or trading records.

Auditors' warnings that Leeson had too much operational control, that he should be relieved of back-office control, and recommendations to tighten up management-control functions were consistently ignored.

Simple checks, which would have uncovered the fraud, consistently failed to be undertaken.

Source: Various, adapted by author from (Dowd, K. 1998).

form a key input into corporate strategy and management decision making, are incorrect. This can arise either as a result of model misspecification or faulty parameterisation, and leads to incorrect estimation. To insulate the corporation from the effects of model risk, the model outcomes must be constantly subjected to independent verification, or objective out-of-sample verification.

Liquidity risk

Liquidity risk may be defined as the risk of unexpected losses occurring when attempting to alter the portfolio composition of the corporation's assets and/or liabilities. It arises when markets do not operate without 'friction', in the sense that they manifest significant search or transaction costs, low turnover of transactions, and significant buy–sell spreads. Clearly, this situation characterises most financial and commodity markets most of the time, with the arguable exception of the large capital, money and foreign exchange markets. However, while these markets usually attain a high degree of liquidity, they occasionally experience crises when liquidity dries up. Notable examples are the ERM and Asian currency crises of 1992 and 1997, respectively, and the stock market debacles of 1987. The conclusion to be reached is that no market can be assumed to be fully liquid at all times so it is always important to consider the effect of liquidity risk.

In the context of a multinational firm's risk-management strategy, it is worthwhile distinguishing two classes of liquidity risk. The first is generic liquidity risk arising from operating in markets which, owing to the factors enumerated above, are less than fully liquid in their daily operations. As the corporations primary concern is unexpected change in the valuation of its asset/liability portfolio, the institution must incorporate estimates of liquidation costs into measures of market and credit risk. A plausible method of doing this would be to measure illiquidity by the expected buy–sell (bid-ask) spread suitably normalised by the average of the expected buy and sell prices. The importance of liquidity costs will vary across positions, but reasonable estimates (Lawrence and Robinson 1995) of liquidation costs

Exhibit 9.5 Liquidity Risk and Hedge Fund Activity

David Askin was manager of a $600 million hedge fund invested in collateralised mortgage obligations at the time of the 1994 US bond-market crisis. Although marketed as market neutral, this fund had leveraged itself into a total of $2 billion and was actually exposed to increases in interest rates. From February to April 1994, when the Federal Reserve was increasing interest rates, the fund had to satisfy increasingly large collateral call payments, which eventually Askin could not meet. After brokers liquidated their positions, all that remained of the $600 million hedge fund was $30 million and some very angry investors. Askin was sanctioned by the Securities and Exchange Commission for misrepresenting the value of his funds, and barred from the investment industry for two years.

Source: Adapted from Jorion (1997).

suggest that they can easily dominate market risk. The second type of liquidity risk is inherently more dangerous. As events during 1997 in emerging financial markets indicate, markets can be liquid most of the time but such liquidity can evaporate during periods of large price volatility, especially drastic collapses in the level of market prices. In these situations, the market bid-ask spread can increase dramatically, and the time taken to unwind positions rises drastically. Any risk-management strategy that relies on timely and orderly liquidation of market positions then encounters serious difficulties in its effective implementation. The only real resolution of this problem is for institutions to make worst-case assumptions about liquidation costs and see if the resulting risks encountered are acceptable.

Implementing risk–management systems

The augmented volatility of prices in financial markets discussed earlier has led corporations to discover that their value has become more subject to the risks occasioned by changes in the financial environment within which they operate, as well as the risks inherent in their core business activities. Faced with this increased volatility, the treasury divisions of international firms initially undertook the obvious step of attempting to utilise models to forecast future price changes. Such forecasts were to be used as inputs into a business strategy which would enable the firm to circumvent the effects of unexpected financial price changes. This strategy generally proved to be unsuccessful, which in one sense is reassuring. If financial markets operate efficiently, in the sense that asset prices reflect relevant information, then attempts to predict future asset price changes and the attendant risks are unlikely to be successful as this would require the forecaster to have access to information which was not available to other market participants.

As financial forecasting has proved to be inadequate for eliminating the impact of financial risk, the alternative is to manage the risk. Treasury departments can attempt to undertake this by two strategies, on- or off-balance sheets. The former strategies should only be adopted in response to extreme structural changes in the firm's competitive environment, as they are inflexible, costly and difficult to reverse. For example, in principle a firm can manage a foreign exchange exposure resulting from foreign competitive activity by borrowing in the competitor's currency, or by relocating production to the foreign country. However, the impact of such action needs to be carefully assessed.

The alternative is to manage financial risk by utilising off-balance sheet financial instruments, generally known as derivative instruments: forwards, futures, swaps and options. These instruments provide the building blocks which have enabled corporations to utilise both standardised exchange-traded instruments and customised financial products obtained in over-the-counter markets, to manage the risks associated with currency, interest rate and commodity price fluctuations far more flexibly, cheaply and efficiently than is possible with on-balance sheet strategies. Risk management using such derivatives is the focus of the remainder of this chapter. Before proceeding we note that the mere fact that the value of the international firm is sensitive to changes in financial asset prices does not itself imply that corporate value will increase if this exposure is managed with derivatives. While such sensitivity is a necessary condition for implementation of an effective risk-management strategy, the strategy should be utilised if and only if it increases the present value of the firm's net cash flows. This impact can originate from considerations relating to both corporate funding and corporate strategy. Smithson (1998) terms these tactical and strategic motives for managing risk, respectively. Tactical motives increase the present value of a firm's expected cash flows, while strategic motives for risk management additionally reduce the volatility of the value of the firm.

Tactical risk management and corporate funding

Reducing funding costs by reducing transaction costs

Transaction costs such as the bid-ask spread in a financial market, the costs of acquiring information and those associated with liquidity are the natural consequences of raising funds in any financial market. Multinational firms can to some extent mitigate these costs by the appropriate use of certain derivative instruments which allow them to separate the cash flow obligations on their original borrowing from the ultimate cash flow characteristics they face. For example, a multinational corporation may be able to exploit its comparative advantage by utilising excess borrowing capacity in one particular segment of the international capital markets, where they can obtain relatively cheap funds, and by means of a currency swap convert this into synthetic funding in a capital market segment where they have no particular comparative advantage, but where for business reasons they would like to obtain the funds.

Reducing funding costs by arbitraging markets

The appropriate use of derivative instruments can also exploit artificial market segmentation caused by an asymmetric incidence of governmental regulation or tax treatment. Barriers to entry are often found in certain capital markets. For example, prior to 1992, the Subcommittee for Foreign Issues of the Central Capital Markets Committee regulated the timing and amount of issues in the German external bond markets by establishing monthly quotas for bond issuance. As the supply of securities was thereby restricted, the price was higher than the market-determined price, and accordingly the instruments carried below-market interest rates. The corporations or other end-users with privileged access to the market could exploit this anomaly through judicious borrowing combined with appropriate derivatives positions.

Differences in national taxation practices often also present arbitrage opportunities, which can be exploited through derivative positions. A commonly cited example concerns the existence of withholding taxes on offshore borrowings in some countries. In the 1980s the Australian government levied a withholding tax on interest payments made by Australian companies on all offshore borrowings denominated in Australian dollars. This tax, combined with high interest rates in Australia and a relatively stable currency, prompted a substantial volume of swap-driven Australian dollar Eurobond issues in early 1986. A similar situation arose in New Zealand in 1990. Other examples arise when differences in taxation laws provide incentives to raise capital in one country to finance investment in another. Historically, generous capital consumption allowances in some European countries, such as France, implied that interest expenses provided only a minimal tax shield in those countries. Multinational corporations then had an incentive to raise finance in countries where interest expenses provide a considerable tax shield, and to invest the funds in countries with high depreciation allowances. This procedure, while reducing funding costs, provides a foreign exchange exposure in at least one currency, the risk of which can be managed with the appropriate derivatives portfolio.

Reducing funding costs through embedded options

Multinational corporations may also be able to reduce their funding costs by issuing hybrid debt, essentially debt which contains an implicit or embedded option, for example a bond with an equity warrant attached, a convertible bond, or a callable bond. There is some evidence that in the past this option feature of the debt has been underpriced by investors in the terms of the debt contract. Astute financial management by the corporation is able to sell an asset (perhaps another option) with the same or similar features which trades on an exchange or over-the-counter after issuing the bond. Amortising the price received for this asset effectively implies the corporation has issued debt at below market rates.

Risk management and strategic motives for hedging financial risk

Theories of optimal hedging are designed to demonstrate how financial risk management can increase firm value in the presence of capital market imperfections. The relation between the present value of a corporation's cash flow and its financial policies was demonstrated in a classic paper by Modigliani and Miller (1958), in developing the seminal M&M propositions. These propositions demonstrate that in the absence of capital market imperfections, investors can just as cost effectively undertake their own risk management policies as the firm's managers, by holding diversified investment portfolios. The relevance of the M&M proposition for strategic risk-management becomes evident by considering its corollary: a necessary condition for strategic risk-management to effect firm value is that it impacts on the firm's taxes, transaction costs or investment decision. While necessary, this is not sufficient. Given the incentives created by capital market imperfections, a corporation's choice to use derivative instruments also depends on its level of financial risk exposure and the costs of managing financial risk. In the following pages we adopt a framework developed by Geczy *et al.* (1997), in order to organise the various theories explaining a firm's derivative use for risk-management purposes.

Managers

Managers of international firms invest much of their human capital or intangible wealth in the corporation. They may also hold significant amounts of common shares. If management are averse to bearing uncompensated risk, the value of these two components of their wealth will be significantly adversely effected by volatility in the corporation's earnings. As risk management reduces the volatility of the value of the firm, the management will direct the firm to hedge if it can do so at a lower cost than compensating the managers for bearing the additional risk through, for example, a management compensation scheme containing share options (Smith and Stultz (1985). DeMarzo and Duffie (1995) suggest an alternative but complementary argument focusing on managerial reputation. A corporation's value is determined both by the quality of managerial decisions relating to its core business competencies, and also by financial risk, which impacts on the firm's earnings but which lies outside the domain of managerial control. Managers may choose to manage the effect of financial risk through hedging, as the information content of corporate earnings as a signal of managerial ability is thereby enhanced. Managerial labour markets and the market for corporate control are then more able to isolate the effects of good luck from good judgement when assessing managerial performance.

Bondholders

Bondholders of the corporation have an incentive to support strategic risk-management activity in order to reduce the probability and, therefore, the expected costs of financial distress (or bankruptcy). Financial distress arises when the firm's income stream is insufficient to cover its liabilities, or its probability of default rises because of increased volatility in its income stream. The associated costs include not only the direct costs associated with bankruptcy or liquidation, but also the indirect costs of a deterioration or loss of long-term relationships with suppliers and customers, or a reduction in the firm's borrowing capacity through a downgrading of its credit rating. We note that a risk-management strategy will only reduce expected financial distress costs if the firm can credibly commit to following a hedging strategy, through, for example, bond covenants or credit agreements.

As first demonstrated by Myers (1977) financial distress costs also induce suboptimal investment decisions. As the perception that the firm may encounter financial distress increases, it becomes more difficult and costly to raise external finance. This leads to capital rationing constraints and the consequent rejection of profitable investment opportunities. Froot *et al.* (1993) develop this argument, noting that hedging mitigates this underinvestment problem by reducing not only the costs of raising finance externally, but also the firm's reliance on external funds.

Equityholders

Smith and Stultz (1985) were the first to demonstrate that risk management can increase shareholders' expected wealth when the firm operates in a fiscal environment where corporate tax rates increase more than in proportion to corporate income. This is known as a convex tax liability schedule. The existence of tax-preference items, such as various forms of tax credits, which are subtracted from pretax income, indirectly create convexity in the tax-liability schedule, as the present value of unused tax shields decreases as they are postponed to future periods. Mian (1996) among others has pointed out that by reducing the variance of corporate earnings, risk management increases the expected value of tax shields because the probability of using preference items increases with the level of a firm's taxable income. DeMarzo and Duffie (1991) have also shown that equityholders in the corporation will support risk management when the firm's managers have better information about the risks which affect the corporation's earnings. As hedging reduces the volatility of the firm's earnings, it enables equityholders to better distinguish the effects of luck and managerial ability, and consequently make better-informed portfolio optimisation decisions.

Empirical evidence

The previous pages identified the reasons why various parties have a vested interest in ensuring that a corporation engages in the appropriate level of risk management activity. We now pose the following question: to what extent is the available empirical evidence consistent with the motives which have been identified? Concerning managerial motives, Geczy *et al.* (1997) argue that empirical proxies for managerial risk aversion are positively correlated with derivatives usage, while Francis and Stephan (1990) found strong evidence for the managerial signalling arguments using multivariate and time series empirical techniques. Both sets of results are in accordance with *a priori* theoretical expectations. The available evidence is also broadly consistent with the use of risk-management tools to avoid the costs of financial distress as advocated by Froot *et al.* (1993) and Smith and Stultz (1985). A significant relationship has been found between a corporation's derivative usage and the following variables: its level of debt service coverage (negative); its leverage (positive); its level of foreign operations (positive); and changes in its credit-rating (negative). The sign in parentheses refers to the direction of the relationship, which are in accordance with the theory. Finally, the available evidence is also weakly consistent with the view that risk management is used to increase shareholder wealth through reducing taxes. Positive relationships have been uncovered between both tax loss carryforwards and tax credits and the use of derivatives. These results are encouraging in the sense that not only do theoretical arguments demonstrate how corporations should be managing risk in order to maximise their shareholders' wealth, but empirical evidence demonstrates they are behaving in the appropriate manner.

Quantifying a multinational firm's exposure to market risk

The key question that any financial officer of a multinational corporation must address is: to what extent is the value of the firm exposed to changes in financial asset prices? There are several means available to treasury departments for quantifying expose to these risks, and the purpose of the following pages is to convey a flavour of these measurement alternatives. Broadly speaking, they can be divided into two types: internal and market-based measures. We begin with the former.

Internal measures of market risk: value at risk (VaR)

The majority of the recently developed internal techniques for measuring financial risk recognise that market risk should not be considered as exposure to individual financial asset-price changes, but rather as constituting an integrated set of interrelated asset-price risks. Moreover, any proposed definition must be both easily understood, and easily communicated by those responsible for risk-management activities to the senior management and the executive Board of the corporation. This has led to the development of probability-based summary measures of exposure, the most notable being value-at-risk (VaR). VaR is a valuation technique based on the current net asset value of the portfolio. It is specified in terms of a confidence level (Jorion 1996), and enables the risk manager to calculate the maximum that the corporation can lose over a specified time horizon at a specified probability level. This calculation is undertaken utilising either historical simulation of past data, using Monte Carlo simulation, or analytic variance-covariance methods. The method chosen should depend on the composition of the portfolio and the desired time horizon. The calculated VaR is then translated into a probability statement about the likely changes in portfolio valuation resulting from financial asset-price changes over a given time period. For example, the risk manager should be able to define the maximum loss for a one-day, one-week, one-month period that the firm will incur with 95 per cent probability (implying that this loss should be exceeded on only five occasions in 100).

The relevance of VaR

The VaR concept has been embraced by many multinational corporations, particularly those where the firm's value is closely linked to their current portfolio net asset value. These firms would be market-value driven, with business assets marked to market daily, securities and derivatives trading being a primary business focus, and the companies' investment horizon measured over short time periods. They would, therefore, have a keen interest in managing the volatility of their current asset value. As such VaR is particularly suitable for financial institutions, institutional investors and the treasury divisions located in manufacturing corporations where such trading divisions function as a profit centre. An example of the later is British Petroleum, where BP Finance not only manages the companies' natural financial risk exposures, but is also expected to trade foreign exchange and interest rate products with the intention of contributing to BP's profits.

Alternatives to VaR: cash flow at risk

For other multinational corporations, however, the VaR approach is potentially less relevant. These corporations can be characterised as cash-flow driven, and their value is linked closely to the judicial exercise of the real growth options arising from their investment and research and development activities. In these corporations, business assets are marked to market infrequently, derivatives are used only as tools to manage financial risks, and investment horizons are measured in months or even years. Their primary focus, therefore, is to manage cash-flow volatility so they can judicially exercise their growth options at the appropriate time.

Corroboration of such an approach is provided by the results of a survey undertaken in 1994 by the Wharton Business School at the University of Pennsylvania, which concluded that 62 per cent of non-financial firms stated that their primary risk-management objective was to reduce their cash-flow volatility. The issue then becomes how best to translate this information into a summary, operational measure of financial exposure which focuses on the impact of price changes on the firm's cash flows: in other words, a cash-flow ana-logue to VaR. This would relate the magnitude and timing of cash inflows to a corporation's contractually committed liabilities and investment opportunities, as suggested by Froot *et al.* (1993). Smithson (1998) refers to this as cash-flow sensitivity analysis, while Dowd (1998) terms it cash-flow at risk. The former author proposes the following cash-flow-based measure of exposure. A corpora-tion's consolidated exposure to financial risk is the probability that the company will fail to satisfy its performance targets over a given time period as the result of unexpected changes in financial asset prices.

The natural question to ask is how do we go about implementing such an expo-sure measure? Smithson (1998), on which this section is based, suggests the following approach. The desired model must be sufficiently rich to capture the interactions between commodity inputs, product prices, foreign and domestic operations and contractual payment obligations. As such, the corporation's plan-ning model provides a useful place to begin this exercise, but it must be supplemented to address two critical shortcomings. First, simulation exercises must be undertaken with variable prices in order to realistically model the various pric-ing scenarios that the firm is likely to face in the future. Second, an acceptable method must be found for modelling the relationship between market risk and changes in the companies' operating or non-contractual future cash flows. The factor that complicates the analysis here is that the impact of market risk depends on the operating cash flows of the corporation. These depend on both the eco-nomic environment the firm faces, and how, given this competitive environment, the corporation's strategy is impacted by changes in the exchange rate.

The nature of cash–flow exposure

The nature of the companies' operations is a critical determinant of the ability to successfully model the dependency of cash flows on market risk. Multinational corporations with global production operations are obviously at the complex end of the modelling spectrum relative to single-product or commodity-driven firms. The class of exposure faced by an international firm is generally divided into two broad types. Contractual exposure, which is also known as transaction exposure, and operating (or competitive) exposure. The most powerful, simple way to measure these exposures is through the use of the concept of elasticity, which measures the percentage change in the firm's cash flow with respect to the percentage change in the variable which is the source of the exposure, for exam-ple the exchange rate.

Most multinational treasury departments customarily focus on contractual exposure. Contractual exposure arises from a corporation's fixed contractual obligations: accounts payable/receivable, long-term purchase/sales contracts and financial positions expressed in foreign currency. If the source of information on contractual exposure is accounting data, then it becomes relatively transparent and easy to quantify for most types of market risk. Moreover, contractual cash flows are fixed either in domestic (reference) currency units or in units of the firm's output. Their nominal value in domestic currency then changes in the same proportion as the change in the exchange rate, foreign currency price, or amount sold, all things being equal. Alternatively stated, contractual exposures have an elasticity of one.

Another class of exposure, operating exposure, is much more complex to quantify, as it requires a detailed understanding of the firm's competitive position and the macroeconomic environment in which it operates. Moreover, operating cash flows will fluctuate because the amount of product the corporation sells, or the quantity of resources committed will vary as the product's price varies, implying operating cash flows are subject to both price and quantity uncertainty. Consider a UK multinational with a subsidiary in Thailand. The subsidiary's local currency (baht) cash flow, and ultimately its competitive position, might depend on the value of the baht relative to other currencies. As fluctuations in exchange rates impact on both the baht cash flow and the (domestic) sterling value of that cash flow, the total effect an exchange rate change in terms of sterling could imply an elasticity greater or less than one.

Capturing operating exposures through accurate elasticity estimates is critical to cash-flow sensitivity analysis. How corporations obtain elasticity estimates, for example, using economic models or simulations will vary. However, while the translation of financial price risk into changes in the corporations' operating performance is perhaps the most challenging aspect of ascertaining cash flow exposure, it compels multinational treasurers to be explicit about their operating parameters. These parameters can then be re-evaluated in the context of the model utilised.

Market–based measures of market risk

As their name suggests, market-based measures of financial risk utilise market-determined values of financial data to measure the market's perception of how changes in the corporation's value (or other preselected measures of financial performance) are related to changes in the prices of financial assets. Market-based approaches to risk measurement vary in the details of their implementation, but can broadly be said to utilise economic and/or statistical models to estimate the sensitivity of a corporation's earnings, cash flow or share price to movements in the value of selected financial prices. These would include changes in selected exchange rates, interest rates and commodity prices. The models can also be used to estimate the exposures of the corporation's main competitors, providing an input into the firm's strategic decision making, and contributing insights into the competitive environment. Whether the firm chooses to utilise internal or market-based systems, the following pages considers the appropriate organising framework within which a multinational can co-ordinate its risk-management policies.

Effective risk-management strategy for multinational corporations

Implementing an effective risk-management strategy involves establishing processes which deliver the requisite knowledge and ensure appropriate accountability. It is the responsibility of the corporation's Board of Directors to:

- understand how risk management impacts on the corporation's overall business plan
- ensure that the team of managers entrusted with implementing the corporation's risk-management policies have the required expertise
- evaluate the performance of the risk-management activity, and ensure it is reviewed periodically.

In order to operationalise the implementation of this procedure, the corporation must carefully consider the following issues:

Define the objective of financial risk-management activity

For most multinational corporations, the objective of risk-management activity is the reduction in some form of volatility. The 1995 Wharton/CIBC World Market's Survey of US Derivatives Users indicated that for 49 per cent of respondents, reducing cash-flow volatility was their primary objective, while 42 per cent cited reducing earnings volatility. Such activity only makes sense if it simultaneously serves to increase the value of the corporation. While some corporations may use exposure to risk and its management as a business opportunity, and attempt to enhance corporate value through this activity, as this objective is totally separate from volatility reduction it must be managed differently.

Isolate and measure financial risk exposures

To effectively manage risk, the corporation must know exactly what financial risks it faces and how to quantify them. This requires the design and implementation of a risk-management system. Possible alternatives here include VaR, stress-testing, simulation/sensitivity analysis, and the customary gap and duration analysis. This chapter has emphasised the VaR approach, but emphasised its limitations in the context of non-financial corporations. Moreover, the above listed measures all indicate the impact of financial risk on the present value of the variable of interest; as such they are all stock measures. Perhaps of more relevance for the non-financial corporation is how financial risk impacts on its cash flows or earnings, which would call for an approach emphasising cash flows at risk.

Establish a risk-management strategy

It is important that financial risks are not considered in isolation, but form part of some integrated strategy of dealing with risk. Smithson (1998) identifies the following manner in which this can be achieved, presented in increasing order of strategic complexity in terms of management requirements.

Integrate market risks: Many non-financial firms such as Intel, Hewlett-Packard and Hyundai attempt to implement a portfolio measure of risk through combining all the sources of risk arising from changes in financial prices, and considering their net impact. However, according to the 1995 Wharton/CIBC Survey, two out of three derivatives-users still manage risk on a transaction by transaction basis. Corroboration of this finding is provided in another survey, which concluded that of over 500 multinational firms, only one-quarter had centralised treasury operations.

Integrate market risk and insurance: Effectively this requires the combination of these two risk-management functions, and involves a realisation that the distinction between financial risk and insurance is becoming blurred. Indeed, certain insurance corporations such as Swiss Re and Cigna Property & Casualty now offer insurance policies which resemble options on financial price variables. Corporates such as Honeywell and Union Carbide are proponents of such a risk-management strategy, and have integrated financial price-risk management with the corporation's insurance activities.

Integrate financial with manufacturing and marketing risks: This is the most complex approach to risk management, and involves integrating the treasury department's activities, decisions on how best to handle liquidity, operational and legal risk, and the firm's core businesses. Smithson (1998) notes that the most prominent example of this practice is Merck & Company, which requires that the treasury function becomes an integral part of managing the corporation rather than simply providing the financing, once business decisions have been made. Such a system of 'enterprise-wide risk management' potentially involves major structural changes, and commitments of managerial time. Oldfield and Santomero (1995) suggest that this requires a comprehensive review of all the major business activities along the following lines:

- the specific risks of each business activity must be identified and measured, where possible;
- risk management must 'begin at the point nearest to the assumption of risk' in order to ensure that management control is maintained, data is generated in a consistent fashion, and needless exposure to risk is eliminated;
- senior management (the Board of Directors) must have a clearly formulated and effective overall risk-management strategy, closely integrated into the corporation's business planning and management control processes.

Monitoring and evaluation of the corporate risk-management strategy

Finally, the data derived from the selected risk-management strategy must be used as an informational input into a centralised system of evaluation and performance monitoring. It is crucial that this system of monitoring and evaluation should be independent of the activity itself, and that whatever the strategy selected, corporate management be constantly appraised of the value of the portfolio of risk-management instruments. The analytics of such a system have been concisely summarised by Dowd (1998), and include: data-verification procedures; systems to monitor compliance with constraints imposed on those taking decisions, for example position limits on traders; systems to acquire and analyse data for performance evaluation and adjustments in the riskiness of the corporation's position; and ensuring that the models used in the firm's risk-management system are valid and appropriate for the task at hand.

Chapter summary

The increasing financial risk engendered by the changing financial environment of the past 25 years has stimulated demand for an evolution in corporate risk-management strategy. We began this chapter by identifying the nature of these financial risks. We then proceeded to demonstrate how tactical and strategic risk-management activity can increase the present value of the corporation's expected cash flow, thereby augmenting shareholder returns. Finally, the strengths and weaknesses of internal and external mechanisms for quantifying financial risk, in particular value at risk and cash flow at risk were then examined, in conjunction with approaches to identifying the basic strategies for implementing a risk-management system and evaluating its performance.

Discussion questions

1
  a Explain clearly the central features of fundamental, technical and market-based techniques for forecasting exchange rates.
  b Discuss how the accuracy of such techniques may be evaluated.
  c Identify the major limitations associated with the former two forecasting approaches, and provide a rationale for use of the latter, market-based method.
2 The approach to risk management suggested in this chapter advocates implementing a system of management of overall institutional risk across all risk categories and business units. A necessary input into such a system is a full-scale review of the risk-management implications of all major lines of the corporation's business activity. What guidelines would you suggest such a review process should follow?
3 Corporations have recently begun to provide more public information to actual and potential stakeholders regarding the nature of the risks they are encountering. Identify the reasons why a corporation may wish to increase its risk disclosure, thereby making the risks it is facing more transparent.

Closing Case Study:
Hedge Funds and the Bailout of Long-Term Capital Management

The name 'hedge funds' describes a wide variety of investment and fund-management institutions, some 3000 with over $200 billion in investors' money, according to recent estimates by TASS Management. These funds utilise widely different investment strategies for generating returns for their investors. Moreover, the 1990s have witnessed the emergence of some highly sophisticated hedge-fund operations, including those undertaken by Long Term Capital Management (LTCM) which recently encountered some well-publicised financial difficulties, and was rescued in a bailout operation organised by the Federal Reserve. LTCM is an example of a certain class of hedge fund known as a relative value (or market-neutral) fund. Such funds attempt to detect and profit from arbitrage opportunities arising from temporary discrepancies in the relative prices of financial assets. In order to identify such discrepancies these funds use sophisticated, model-based, mathematically driven trading strategies. The basic input to these models is a detailed financial database that represents many years of asset-price behaviour. On the basis of historical pricing relationships, computer models calculate the exact point at which to enter a buy–sell order together with the appropriate size of transaction, calculated to maximise the fund's returns while exposing the fund's investors to an acceptable level of risk.

In this fashion, hedge-fund strategists (who include Nobel Laureates in economics) hope to be able to outsmart larger institutions and make millions of dollars by buying undervalued securities and selling those that are relatively overvalued. They generate returns from the eighths and quarters of a point relative price discrepancies that small investors, and often even professional proprietary traders, never see. These relative value funds are by no means the only class of hedge funds. Other important types of fund include the Macro funds such as Quantum, run by George Soros, or Julian Robertson's 'Tiger Fund'. These attempt to generate returns by placing large, well-publicised bets on the financial impact of macroeconomic shocks or economic policy decisions impacting on certain economies. There are the short-seller funds which specialise in profiting from their analysts predictions regarding events such as corporate bankruptcies, divestitures or acquisitions; other funds simply play the equity markets. A classification of the various types of hedging funds, together with their return performance in 1998 is provided in Table 9.1.

If the risks undertaken by hedge funds are deemed to be acceptable, the natural question to ask is why did LTCM fail during the recent financial crisis? The answer is straightforward. LTCM's high leverage, the ratio of its debts relative to its capital base, left it vulnerable to the impact of extreme outlying market conditions, events that market practitioners refer to as 'the perfect storm'. Perfect storms in financial markets occur very infrequently. This one was triggered by the Russian default on their domestic debt obligations, which significantly changed the market's perception of the probability of sovereign default relative to that which was incorporated into historical asset-pricing relationships: in this case, relative bond yields on government debt. The difficulty model-based trading strategies such as those employed by LTCM face when encountering a 'perfect storm' is that the assumptions on which the models are constructed often mean they fail to assign appropriate probabilities to the occurrence of such events. Their impact can thereby be underestimated. In particular, it has been revealed that LTCM's postulated worst-case scenario for losses was only 60 per cent as bad as those that

Table 9.1 Banks' LTCM-related losses since 1 July 1998

Investment Bank	Reported losses	LTCM bail-out contribution	Decline in share price
Lehman Brothers	$60m income reduction	$100m	65%
Citicorp	$200m income reduction	n/a	43%
Chase Manhattan	$200m commercial charge-offs	$300m	43%
JP Morgan	Not disclosed	$300m	29%
Morgan Stanley Dean Witter	$110m income reduction	$300m	52%
Salomon Smith Barney	$300m trading loss	$300m	40%
Goldman Sachs	Not disclosed	$300m	n/a
Merrill Lynch	$135m trading loss	$300m	54%
Bankers Trust	$350m trading loss	$300m	55%
Deutsche Bank	Not disclosed	$300m	40%
CS Group	$55m LTCM write-down	$300m	55%
UBS	$600m LTCM write-down	$300m	54%

actually occurred. Its high leverage – it had borrowed over 50 times its capital – meant that such losses eroded its capital base very quickly.

For the first two years following 1994 when it was launched, LTCM had annual returns in excess of 40 per cent yet by the end of 1997 returns had declined to 27 per cent. Some argue that this decline in returns was in part caused by LTCM's own success, and the success of a number of other marginal investors, that made markets more efficient and relative price anomalies rarer. In addition, the strong bull market over the period could possibly raise questions among LTCM's investors about the value of their illiquid investment in the fund. This consideration led LTCM to hand back $2.7 billion to investors, while increasing its leverage through banking borrowing. Since the beginning of 1998, the value of leveraged positions under LTCM's control totalled far more than $100 billion, while the fund's net asset value was never more than $4 billion.

Highly leveraged hedge funds, such as LTCM, bore the main impact of the latest crisis. When losses started to emerge, lenders started demanding more collateral for extending credit lines, forcing hedge funds to shed marginal deals at 'fire-sale' prices, while keeping in place their core arbitrage bets. By extending credit lines to hedge funds, investment banks have increased their risks and, as a result, the correlation of their fortunes with those of funds themselves. The banks declared losses to date in their dealings with LTCM are presented in Table 9.2.

More importantly, the complex relationship between some banks and hedge funds, which was only revealed after the LTCM bailout, may have exacerbated systemic risks. Banks not only extend credit to hedge funds, they invest in them directly, and earn revenues executing trades on their behalf. LTCM had $18 million invested in Bear Stearns, and two senior executives at the bank, Warren Spector and James Cayne, had each invested $10 million in the fund. LTCM also disclosed a $14 million investment in Berkshire Hathaway, Warren Buffet's investment group, which considered taking over the fund. JP Morgan executives had close personal ties with the Chief Executive at LTCM, while Merrill Lynch executives had personal investments in the fund totalling $22 million. Even Banca d'Italia had an investment in LTCM, which is even more questionable

Table 9.2 Various types of hedge funds

Category	Investment strategy	Performance YTD98 (US, Offshore, Global)
Aggressive growth	Investing in small-cap or micro-cap stocks which are expected to experience very rapid growth.	6.1%, 6.0%, 6.2%
Distressed securities	Buying securities of companies that face bankruptcy, hoping that the company will come out of troubles.	−1.9%, −2.1%, −1.8%
Emerging markets	Investing in the equity or debt of emerging markets.	-45.6%, -30.6%, -33.6%
Fund of funds	Investing in other money managers utilising a variety of investment strategies.	-0.5%, -1.6%, -0.5%
Income	Focusing on current income rather than on long term capital gains.	3.2%, -8.8%, -3.0%
Macro	Employing an opportunistic approach, following major changes in countries' economic policies.	8.1%, 6.9%, 7.4%
Market neutral-arbitrage	Focusing on obtaining returns with low or no correlation to the market. They usually trade the spread between different securities of the same issuer.	5.3%, -1.0%, 2.4%
Market timing	Focusing on a limited number of asset classes by predicting the timing of being in or out of the market.	21.4%, 7.0%, 14.4%
Opportunistic	Utilising one or more investment styles and not a consistent investment approach.	7.4%, -1.8%, 3.0%

given one of LTCM's bets was on a narrowing of the spread between Italian and German government bonds!

Source: Adapted from Pagratis and Bowe (1999) and 'Hedge Funds', *Financial World*, January 1999.

Questions

1 Some influential commentators have warned that the regulation of hedge fund activities is not the best response to the LTCM bailout. The Deputy Governor of the Bank of England is quoted as saying that LTCM was an 'isolated' incident and hedge funds would learn from their mistakes. Critically assess this view.

2 Analyse the contention that it is the banks' lending practices that should shoulder primary responsibility for the hedge fund 'crisis'.

3 In terms of the classification of financial risks provided in the chapter, what do you believe was the major lesson to be learned from the LTCM débâcle?

Further reading

Jorion, P. and **Khoury, S.J.** (1996) *Financial Risk Management: Domestic and International Dimensions*, Oxford: Blackwell Publishers. This book incorporates an extensive treatment of all the latest risk management products.

Van Deventen, D.R. and **Imai, K.** (1997) *Financial Risk Analysis*, Homewood, Illinois: Irwin. This explains in a comprehensive yet understandable terminology the analysis of financial risk mangement.

Wilmott, P. (1998) *Derivatives*, Chichester: Wiley. This provides a comprehensive overview of the nature of derivative products and their valuation, as well as a readable introduction to the theory and practice of financial engineering.

References

DeMarzo, P. and **Duffie, D.** (1991) Corporate Financial Hedging with Proprietary Information, *Journal of Economic Theory* 53: 261–86.

DeMarzo, P. and **Duffie, D.** (1995) Corporate incentives for hedging and hedge accounting, *The Review of Financial Studies* 8: 143–71.

Dowd, K. (1998) *Beyond Value at Risk*, Chichester: Wiley.

Francis, K. and **Stephan, J.** (1990) Characteristics of hedging firms, in R. Schwartz and C. Smith Jr. (eds) *Advanced Strategies in Financial Risk Management*, New York: New York Institute of Finance.

Froot, K., Scharfstein, D. and **Stein, J.** (1993) Risk management: co-ordinating corporate investment and financing policies, *Journal of Finance* 48: 1629–59.

Geczy, C., Minton, B. and **Schrand, C.** (1997) Why firms use currency derivatives *Journal of Finance* 52: 1323–54. Pagratis, S. and Bowe, M (1999), Hedge Funds in *Financial World*, Jan, 1999 pp. 40–1.

Jorion, P. (1997) *Value at Risk*, New York: McGraw Hill.

Lawrence, C. and **Robinson G.** (1995) Liquid measures, *Risk* 8: 52–55.

Mian, S. (1996) Evidence on corporate hedging policy, *Journal of Financial and Quantitative Analysis* 31: 419–39.

Modigliani, F. and **Miller, M.** (1958) The cost of capital, corporation finance, and the theory of investment, *American Economic Review* 48: 261–97.

Myers, S. (1977) The Determinants of Corporate Borrowing, *Journal of Financial Economics*, 5: 147–75.

Oldfield, G. and **Santomero, A.** (1995) The Place of Risk Management in Financial Institutions, Wharton School, University of Pennsylvania, working paper.

Pagratis, S. and **Bowe, M.** mimeo, 1999 Manchester School of Management.

Pagratis, S. and **Bowe, M.** (1999): 'Hedge Funds', *Financial World*, Jan. 1999 pp. 40–1

Smith, C. Jr. and **Stultz, R.** (1985) 'The Determinants of Firm's Hedging Policies', *Journal of Financial and Quantitative Analysis*, 20: 391–403.

Smithson, C. (1998) *Managing Financial Risk*, New York: McGraw Hill.

CHAPTER 10

Political Risk in International Business

Brent Burmester

Learning objectives

By the end of this chapter you will understand:

- the origins and implications of political risk

- different forms of political risk

- how political risk is assessed

- the management of political risk.

Opening Case Study:
Business travel hostage fears: how to avoid the kidnappers' hit list

Ask business people what their worst fears are about travelling abroad and most will worry about aircraft crashes, delayed flights or lost luggage. Some will moan about jet lag; others about upset stomachs. Few would think to say 'being taken hostage'.

Yet the threat of being kidnapped while working overseas is very real. According to Rob Davies, a special risks underwriter at Lloyd's syndicate Hiscox, incidents of kidnap have doubled in the past five years. In 1997, there were 881 kidnappings in Colombia, 197 in Mexico and 60 in Brazil. The problem is not unique to South America. Kidnapping has become a global malaise, spreading to many parts of Europe and Asia.

You no longer need to be a multimillionaire or heir to a fortune to be a potential target. In some countries you just need to be perceived as wealthy. 'If you walk through some parts of Latin America in a business suit, you stand out a mile. You may not be very rich but to the locals you are fabulously wealthy and therefore you are a potential target,' says Mr Davies.

Those believed to be most in danger of being kidnapped are expatriates stationed in places such as Guatemala, Mexico and Colombia, where employees from a variety of different multinational corporations have been kidnapped in the past few years.

After pouring millions of pounds in infrastructure and resources into unstable areas, large corporations have become sitting ducks. In worst-case scenarios, as witnessed recently with British Petroleum, they are forced to withdraw totally from trouble hot spots.

Others on the kidnappers' hit list are business travellers in Cambodia, Kashmir, Indonesia, Taiwan, Chechnya and Tajikistan. One reason these countries have become so dangerous is because civil disorder breeds crime and one of the most lucrative crimes is kidnap. According to Hiscox, ransom demands have escalated from an average of just more than $500,000 (£313,000) in 1989 to about $1m in Colombia and $3m in Mexico.

In the UK there are only a couple of kidnappings a year. This is because potential kidnappers know there is a high chance they will be caught. In somewhere such as Colombia, there is not a high enough standard of law and order to act as a deterrent.

Kidnappers have a good chance of getting away with their crime, particularly in countries where the terrain is favourable. There are vast expanses of jungle and vast no-go areas in Latin America where the army and police cannot afford to mount rescues, allowing kidnappers to take hostages into hiding and negotiate for as long as they want.

What can corporations and businessmen do to reduce their vulnerability to extortion? According to Simon Adamsdale at Control Risks, an international consultancy which provides political risk assessment and crisis management, there are five practical principles which can be put into effect to reduce the risk of abduction.

These are: be informed, keep a low profile, surround yourself with protection, maintain lines of communications and do not establish a routine. The message is simple: if you need to travel to high-risk areas, be prepared.

Source: Financial Times CD-ROM, 1 January–31 December 1998.

Introduction

All firms are to some degree exposed to political risk, but to international business managers it is a topic of particular concern. In an international context the risk of events such as the imposition of cost-increasing industry regulations, or unintentionally offending a sector of society by a marketing error, are substantially greater. This is true because risk is a function of ignorance and, in a political context, individual and organisational ignorance is generally much greater abroad than at home. To help future decision-makers in international business alleviate a little of that ignorance, this chapter looks at the nature of political risk, how firms are exposed to it, what they do about it, and why the existence of political risk is not entirely a cause for despair.

The non-market environment

Business enterprises may be conceived as simultaneously occupying two overlapping, but distinct social spaces. One is a business world in which the common goal is economic profit. In this economic or *market* environment, individuals and organisations engage in trade: they buy and sell, and all relationships formed in the market environment are ultimately concerned with this simple, impersonal mode of exchange. Individuals acting in this universe organise into groups called firms, to pursue profit opportunities more effectively and efficiently, and the same individuals take on roles such as employer, shareholder, debtor, entrepreneur, exporter, investor, and consumer. It is this environment that students of business wish to learn about when they pick up a book like the present volume, and it is clearly a complex place that deserves the particular attention of management practitioners and scholars. It does not, however, contain the most powerful, and therefore most dangerous, actors and events that most impact on the fortunes of business corporations.

In the alternative space surrounding and permeating firms, relationships formed between and among individuals and organisations are not about buying and selling for economic profit. They are created in pursuit of other forms of gain, such as security, belonging, respect, love, honour and power. In the political or *non-market* environment, individuals take on roles such as friend, student, helper, guardian and leader. Organisations in the non-market environment include families, clubs, churches, community groups, and governments. These roles and organisations may appear at first glance to be only peripherally relevant to international business. This is never more than temporarily true.

The non-market environment exhibits enormous diversity on an international basis. Although super- and sub-national frontiers may be more appropriate in specific circumstances, it is practical for general international business purposes to let national borders define separate non-market environments. To illustrate the variation and complexity of this realm, consider one form of actor: national governments. These are possessed of different branches, departments and levels, all of which engage in a complex web of interorganisational relations (Boddewyn and Brewer 1994). Governments are extremely influential actors in international business, and the ability to respond to their interventions ahead of business rivals, perhaps even before the government itself acts, constitutes a significant competitive advantage to any company. In the firm's home nation the system of government is difficult enough to comprehend, but on an international basis the task of predicting the behaviour of these political organisations is beyond any company that cannot devote all its energies to non-market analysis. The risks posed by the existence of host national governments – forced divestment, regulatory discrimination against MNEs, imprisonment of employees – exemplify political risk at its most extreme. But political risk implicates many other actors in the immediate and global non-market environments of the international business enterprise.

The nature of political risk

Corporations function in a world where much of the information needed for decision making is unavailable, because it pertains to future events. The unavailability of that information is a function of its futurity – after all, no one knows with certainty what awaits them around the next corner – and the fact that individuals and organisations alike lack the resources and inclination to acquire and assimilate all there is to know about a given event. 'Risk' is a word denoting future events to which decision-makers can attach a probability of occurrence, and almost always refers to events decision makers prefer to not occur (Root 1968). In the context of decision making in international business, 'risk' describes future events that prevent or impede the realisation of strategic objectives, objectives pertaining to the market environment, in the international domain. It is important to appreciate that risks are subjectively defined by the firm, because a disaster to one can be a windfall to another, so the 'riskiness' of an event is not an absolute quality, but depends on the intentions and abilities of the 'victim'. As the above discussion makes clear, political risks occur in the non-market environments of an international business, or are brought about by the external pursuit of non-market objectives, and undermine the firm's market strategies.

Consider the possibility of civil war breaking out in Turkey between Islamists and secular forces in the next ten years. Any business organisation with interests in Europe would be pleased to hear in advance what crisis will lead to the fighting, when the first shot will be fired, the duration of the hostilities, the areas worst affected, and the extent of damage done to private enterprise. Excluding the invention of time-travel or access to supernatural sources, this information cannot be available in advance. Some firms will pay handsomely for it, motivated by the probability they attach to the war occurring, and the extent to which it could damage their interests. Others will pay little, because they imagine a Turkish civil war to be quite unlikely, and/or because they do not see how it could adversely affect their interests, even should it break out tomorrow and continue for years. The different values put on perfect information in this scenario are explained by what the evaluator knows, or thinks it knows, about the probability of occurrence in the time frame, and what it knows, or thinks it knows, about the harmful consequences of those events. The higher the value placed on unobtainable perfect information concerning an event or events in the non-market environment, the higher the political risk to the evaluator.

Political risk was originally synonymous with a particular type of undesirable event, known as forced divestment (discussed below). This risk is embodied in a particular species of non-market actor, namely the host national government, and concerns a particular form of international market entry mode, i.e. foreign direct investment. The definition used in this chapter subsumes this usage, and admits a great deal more. Over time, political risks have been recognised in many different types of occurrence, from civil war to ecological activism, and the concept gradually widened to admit analysis of these contingencies. As the range of events covered by political risk analysis expanded, so did the range of international business modes deemed vulnerable to political risk. Where once FDI alone was treated as attracting political risk, we may now appreciate the more limited, but distinct exposures of exporting and various forms of strategic alliance.

Furthermore, conceptualising the non-market environment draws attention to events and actors in the home nation of the international business enterprise, reminding us that political risk is not confined to foreign places.

In this chapter we prefer 'political risk' to 'non-market risk' simply for reasons of continuity. The literature on political risk is extensive and dates back over 30 years, and the concept has been often revised and augmented in that time, proving to be quite robust (Fitzpatrick 1983). Conversely, the market/non-market distinction took root comparatively recently in international business theory (Kobrin *et al.* 1980), so it is reasonable to apply the older term here, rather than replace it with a label not in common usage.

The discussion to this point gives the impression that future non-market events or states are either for the international business enterprise to guard against, or are not worthy of further consideration. Yet a moment's reflection suggests, if non-market conditions may be the undoing of a firm, they can also create new opportunities to fulfill its strategic objectives. Regrettably, although this was clear enough 20 years ago (Kobrin 1979), research into the transformation of non-market behaviours and relationships into market advantages remains in its infancy, having long been overlooked, or deliberately disregarded.

Sovereign risks

As discussed in Chapter 3, the nation state remains the most potent political force in the international domain. It is hardly surprising that the earliest forms of political risk analysis concentrated exclusively on the acts of national governments. The most discussed form of what may be referred to as sovereign risk, indeed more has been written of it than all other forms put together, is **forced divestment.** Here a host state orders foreign direct investors to give up ownership in assets situated in the territory of the host. The host may offer investors partial or complete compensation, but there exist many examples of expropriation of MNE-operating assets without recompense. Between 1956 and 1972, for example, 20 per cent of all forced divestments went uncompensated (Williams 1975). Forced divestment was at its most popular among the developing countries from the mid-1950s to the mid-1970s. Historically, the industrialised nations resorted far less to this tactic, and it is instructive to examine the reasons behind this difference in the treatment of foreign MNEs.

Between 1960 and 1976 something in the order of 1535 firms were forced to divest from 76 less-developed host nations (Kobrin 1980). Closer examination of the firms in question reveals interesting similarities. Few were manufacturers of consumer products. Fewer, if any, were in service industries. The great majority was involved in the exploitation of natural resources, such as oil drilling and copper mining. Until the period in question, the less-developed world had little to offer direct investors but the wealth embodied in their landscapes, which was, and is, considerable. Without the financial, technological and marketing resources of the industrialised world, commercial exploitation of those assets was not feasible, so governments in Africa, the Middle East, South America, and Asia negotiated resource-development bargains with predominantly North American and European companies, wherein the private investor was granted resource exploitation rights. In return, the host governments received benefits such as know-how, jobs, taxes, export earnings, and shareholdings.

However, once the technology transfer had taken place, with the establishment of plant, local training, infrastructural development, and the formation of critical supply and distribution networks, host governments began to regard foreign control of their strategic industries as unnecessary, or worse, offensive. In many cases renegotiations took place in which the MNEs were compelled to settle for less profitable stakes in these ventures, but frequently the host-government, charged with nationalist and/or anti-capitalist fervour, demanded the immediate withdrawal of the MNE and confiscated their abandoned operations. Investors were left with few remedies, as local laws and courts were generally biased against them, diplomatic intervention was largely ineffectual, and defiance in the face of sovereign force out of the question. This cycle of negotiation – investment – renegotiation/expropriation is known as the obsolescing bargain (Vernon 1971). Although it remains a problem today, the larger proportion of FDI in non-primary sectors, and the more careful disposition of assets in host countries by investors has led to a marked reduction in FDI ending in forced divestment. Even more important in this regard has been the softening of host-government attitudes in the developing world toward FDI. In 1991, according to the Transnational Corporations and Management Division of UNCTAD, 80 of 82 FDI policy changes, adopted by 35 developing countries, reduced restrictions on foreign investors (UNTCMD 1992).

Sovereign risks are inherent in many other government policy changes besides expropriation. Consider the blow dealt to British Nuclear Fuels and its French counterpart COGEMA when the German governing coalition, featuring the Green party, banned the reprocessing of German nuclear fuel beyond 1 January 2000. This deprived the reprocessing contractors of a client worth billions of dollars in future business (*Financial Review*, 28 January 1999). Worse might be yet to come in the form of sympathetic policy changes in other nuclear power-generating nations. Another serious change in the regulatory environment for MNEs comes in the form of restriction on profit expatriation. Unless investors plan to emigrate with their capital, foreign direct investment is little use to a firm if the profits earned by the investment cannot be removed from the host jurisdiction. Governments may limit the ability of international businesses to export cash in a number of ways and for a variety of reasons. For example, the local currency may be declared inconvertible in order to restore the balances of payments to a more acceptable condition; raised capital gains taxes may dissuade the local subsidiary from declaring dividends; or the expatriation of MNE profits may be expressly forbidden as a punitive measure. There are ways to evade restrictions on profit repatriation, but the tax, customs, and serious fraud offices of the host are increasingly quick to catch on to every trick an international business learns.

Sovereign risks can result from discontinuities in politics, such as the displacement of a liberal government by one more socialist, nationalist, religious, environmentalist or otherwise MNE-hostile; or the deterioration of diplomatic relations between home and host states. They may come in response to serious malfeasance by an international business, such as jeopardising national security through the export of sensitive technologies, or to the emergence of new social movements and ideologies. Whatever triggers them, the result is change in the behaviour of a principal non-market actor: change that may be avoided but, in the face of sovereign power, resisted only at far greater risk.

Security risks

In the market environment, the common pursuit of economic profit and the generally accepted norms of market participation condition behaviour. In the non-market environment there are many different means to a far greater number of ends. One such means, and it is very common, is the injurious use of physical force. Although national governments have wielded or threatened the use of military force in cases of expropriation, we are concerned here with violence resorted to by other actors, or where the state deploys force in response to violence used or threatened from elsewhere. Political realists regard sovereign power as ultimately founded on the power to coerce; indeed the sovereign state may be conceived as a monopolist of the use of force in a territory (Weber 1969). We may therefore go so far as to classify all sovereign risk as a special case of violence-derived risk. For the purposes of clearer exposition, here we draw a distinction between sovereign risk, where the use of violence is technically legitimate, and security risks, where it most definitely is not.

On certain scales and levels, violence may represent a serious discontinuity in the non-market environment. Examples of this include the assassination of a head of state, or revolt against the government. At other times, even large-scale violence can be predicted with reasonable assurance. No one professed surprise during the 1998 World Cup when hundreds of supporters from rival footballing nations staged running battles in the streets of French cities. Similarly, politically motivated violence need not constitute a threat to international business. The sudden ejection from office of a presidential incumbent, in a *coup d'etat* for example, can be followed by a remarkably smooth transition of power (Kobrin 1976).

It is important to understand that security risk to the firm does not stem exclusively from violence directed toward the firm's personnel or property. That is not to say that international businesses never directly experience violence, but that the repercussions of violence tend to spread widely through society, and the firm's market capabilities offer it no special insulation.

Civil war

Outright war presents few commercial opportunities to any but the eventual victor and business firms in the weapons industry. Carrying on any other kind of business in a warzone is deemed to be courting disaster by most international enterprises, but withdrawal from the line of fire does not automatically remove the firm from the effects of war. The friends or family of employees may be in harm's way, leading to increased stress in business units that may be far removed from the fighting. Tensions may break out in the workforce between sympathisers of different causes, and international travel through the region may become too dangerous to allow (Brown 1991).

There are a few hardy enterprises that will persevere in a war-torn country because the risks of abandonment are greater still. Consumer-oriented companies appreciate no reason to stay when their customers are preoccupied with seeking refuge in remote areas or neighbouring countries, or arming themselves in a climate of disregard for the finer points of private property. Once the local economy disintegrates, there is little point in industrial suppliers holding on either, unless they dare to seek buyers in the warring forces. In these cases, however, businesses are likely to have already recouped their initial investment costs, perhaps even earned a steady and profitable income for some years. The trade-off between security and profitability is not so clear-cut for enterprises that have sunk large amounts of time, effort and capital into a project that has yet to show any return. In the oil-exploration industry, for example, contractors to an MNE consortium may be distanced from hostilities and self-sufficient within a compound or company village, and thus willing to continue surveying in the expectation that the billion-dollar strike is only another day, week or month away. Since pulling out would mean the expenditure of millions with nothing to show for it, management may be disposed to work on until the heavy artillery drive into view.

Violent crime

All nations suffer from consistent criminal behaviour by a subset of their populations. Crime becomes a serious concern to international business participants, especially foreign direct investors, when it reaches a level at which it seems an inevitable part of daily life. Where this occurs, security becomes a major cost, and no one can count themselves safe from victimisation. Such is currently the case in South Africa, where crime, frequently accompanied by violence, spiralled out of control after the ruling African National Congress assumed power at the end of the disciplinarian apartheid regime. In early 1999, Yong Koo Kwon, the President of the South African subsidiary of Daewoo, a South Korean car manufacturer, was shot and killed, apparently by thieves intent on hijacking his car. Employee safety is now a matter of genuine concern to foreign investors in South Africa (BBC World Service 1999).

Kidnap and ransom

To a small minority in a handful of countries, MNE personnel are valued for reasons unconnected with their technical expertise or spending power. The groups in question are committed to radical political change, but often run into a problem familiar to all: insufficient funds. Terrorists are capable of violence on many levels, and kidnapping may seem rather mild in comparison with blowing up public buildings but when it happens, kidnap impacts directly on the affected firm, and is a form of imprisonment made possible only by the illicit exercise of force.

On top of the risk of physical and psychological harm to personnel, kidnapping can be extremely expensive to resolve. Ransoms commonly range from US$800,000 to $3 million (Frederick 1992). There are also considerable costs involved with setting up crisis-management teams to liaise with local law-enforcement agencies. This calamity may befall any nationality, but British, American and Japanese corporations have suffered most in the past (Barton 1993). The nation in which it is most likely to cluster is Latin America, but parts of Africa, central Asia, and Russia are also problematic, although in Russia the threat is more likely to come from organised criminals than terrorist groups.

Recent events in Yemen, a small oil-dependent nation in the Arabian Peninsula, illustrate the phenomenon. The kidnap and ransom of tourists, aid workers, and employees on foreign assignment, typically in the oil industry, has become standard practice among some northern tribes of the country. These once-nomadic people have learned that this activity is extremely effective for attracting the attention of the government and extracting promises of funding for local development. In 1997 an estimated 45 foreigners were kidnapped, with Americans, Russians, and especially Britains all enduring confinement, albeit hospitable, at the hands of Yemeni tribespeople (BBC World Service 1997). The seriousness of the practice became heightened in late 1998 when four tourists died in a bungled rescue attempt by the Yemeni army. This incident was unusual for its southerly location and the radical Islamic stance of the kidnappers (BBC Online 1999). In August 1998 the Yemeni President had extended capital punishment to the crime of kidnapping (BBC Online 1999), significantly upping the stakes for any would-be kidnappers – and their hostages.

Corruption

For many companies, the prospect of dealing with corrupt officials is both morally abhorrent and unacceptably expensive. Corruption comes in many forms, including nepotism, cronyism and extortion. At one end of the scale is the passport-control official who announces a foreigner's papers aren't in order, with the unspoken suggestion that the 'irregularity' might be overlooked for an immediate cash payment. At the other is the Head of State who indulges in conspicuous consumption using millions of dollars in aid and loans intended to support his nation's development. As officials and their not-so-official associates misappropriate resources for their private profit they raise the costs of business in their jurisdiction. In some countries, corruption ranks well ahead of concerns like political stability and labour costs when it comes to evaluating political risk. A Hong Kong-based political economic consulting group has said of China that corruption is the 'single biggest business risk' (Busse *et al.* 1997).

The thousands of dollars paid by international investors for estimated corruption levels is testimony to the perception of corrupt practice as a risk to international business. Anti-corruption measures taken at the intergovernmental level, such as those of the OECD, and the non-governmental, as exemplified by Transparency International (see Chapter 3), provide further evidence of the seriousness of corruption. International investors and governments are concerned about more than the economic transaction costs inherent in corrupt practices; they perceive a link between corruption and the entrenchment of more sinister and more extreme forms of non-market risk, such as a general collapse of the rule of law. The consequences might include widespread organised and disorganised crime, and frustrating, potentially dangerous bureaucratic capriciousness. One survey suggests that larger MNEs perceive less risk in corruption, perhaps because they can 'buy away' the problem (Busse *et al.* 1997). The tendency for corruption to beget further corruption does not recommend deep pockets as a long-term solution, however.

International risks

The discussion to this point has concentrated mainly on risks identified within the context of national analysis. However, all firms function within a globally defined non-market environment, and an exclusive focus on events at the national level may fail to identify risks resulting from events in the international political economy (Stopford 1994). The international society of states is as liable to experience conflict and change as any other society, and the effects on international business may be profound.

Economic sanctions

National foreign policy has always had a strong commercial content, nowhere better illustrated than in agreements fostering regional economic integration, but there comes a point at which commercial and political interests no longer coincide (Garten 1997). When this occurs and international relations sour, over territorial disputes, human rights abuses, protectionism or ideological differences, a popular instrument of international coercion is the economic sanction. A recurrent problem for some international businesses is their imposition against countries in which they are doing business. In economic sanctions, target states are denied access to export markets, imports, foreign investment, financial transactions, and other forms of international contact, such as landing rights for commercial aircraft (Waelde 1998). These prohibitions may be used in various combinations, unilaterally or multilaterally, depending on the particular nations concerned and the perceived infringement.

It is clear that sanctions may impact on international businesses very seriously. Traders and international licensors and franchisers may be completely denied access to the sanctioned foreign market by virtue of the prohibition on commercial contact. Hard though this may be, once the sanctions are declared the implications for companies using these business modes are clear. This may not be the case for foreign direct investors. Companies incorporated and operating relatively autonomously in the sanctioned country, but controlled by citizens of the sanctioning country, are not legally bound to comply with the sanction. The effect of the sanction on the business unit in the sanctioned country is then largely up to the parent firm. It may prefer to be loyal to the sanctioning home country, or decide that it is free to pursue its business interests abroad, unencumbered by home-nation efforts to exercise extraterritorial jurisdiction. Either choice is fraught with political risk. In cases of multilateral sanctions where no specific legal restrictions are imposed by states in which an international business is operating, the issue of compliance is an ethical question for the company concerned.

Civil protest

Economic sanctions represent an attempt by one or more states to reform the behaviour of another of their number. They are, in isolation, an instrument of economic statecraft that may involve issues stirring relatively little public feeling.

However, there are events attracting international concern at the level of state and in civil society that pose risk to the international business. For example, in the industrialised world, the denial of political freedom is generally regarded as unconscionable. Western nations, intergovernmental organisations and international non-governmental organisations often censure nations that do not observe basic civil and human rights. International businesses engaged in economic relationships involving nations condemned for rights' abuses may experience difficulties with recruitment, employee morale and customer loyalty, not to mention enhanced sovereign and sanction risk at home and abroad. Discouraging though these deleterious effects may be, companies are often able to persevere until their transactions are complete or the offending government alters its practices. This may not be the case, however, when these effects are powerfully amplified by a government's application of capital punishment to political opponents.

One international company acutely aware of this fact is the British and Dutch petro-chemicals giant, Royal Dutch/Shell, or Shell for short. Shell operates in the delta region of Nigeria, a country dogged by dictatorial military rule. Its operations there had been criticised from the start on grounds of ecological and cultural damage, but international public outrage soared when it was revealed that the Nigerian government had used deadly force to quell protests by people living near the Shell plant. Shell Nigeria has a close business relationship with the government through its compulsory joint venture partner the National Nigerian Petroleum Company. Matters were made worse by allegations that security forces seconded from the military by Shell were involved in the violence. As international retail sales dropped appreciably and media attention on Shell reached new heights, the MNE's reputation hit a new low. Acclaimed writer and outspoken critic of the Nigerian military regime, Ken Saro Wiwa, was placed under arrest on scarcely credible murder charges. Saro Wiwa was a leading tribesman of the Ogoni people, who were suffering from pollution and intimidation in the area in which Shell was active. After a summary trial, Saro Wiwa was condemned to death and executed along with eight other activists in November 1995 (International Trade Finance 1995). Shell claimed it was denied an audience with the government head, Sani Abacha, when it attempted to urge restraint (Cragg 1998). The echoes of the global uproar during these events still haunt the Anglo-Dutch MNE, which continues to experience managerial difficulties and shareholder disapproval related to the Nigerian affair (Guyon 1997).

Political risk analysis

No academic discussion of political risk is complete without a complaint about the generally low standard of political risk analysis undertaken by international business firms. This is more than a remark on a literary cliché; it indicates either resistance by business corporations to the notion that non-market environment is amenable to analysis, or a lack of awareness of political risk in business participants. In some cases it may also be attributed to a conceit on the part of international business decision-makers that the non-market environment holds few surprises for the likes of them. Eventually, this always proves not to be the case. The perceived inadequacy of political risk analysis is exhibited in the tendency of firms to initiate the process too late, as in cases where a non-market shock has already occurred, or once international projects and strategies are under way. Judging by the lower incidence of criticism from academics in the last decade, the sophistication and proactivity of international business enterprises is showing improvement in this regard, although there is still far to go before companies develop equal competencies in market and non-market risk analysis.

The techniques of political risk analysis range from the endearingly simple to the strenuously sophisticated. Relatively few firms are reported to formally organise political risk analysis by way of dedicated human, physical and financial resources administered in a specialised department (Fitzpatrick 1983). Even the practice of undertaking a systematic evaluation during FDI decision making is not universal, but evidence suggests that awareness of the importance of political risk is growing. In this section, managerial issues pertaining to political risk analysis are summarised. There is not scope in this chapter to properly acquaint the reader with the methods of political risk analysis, as it is not normally a managerial competence, but rather a specialised research function. Interested readers should supplement what follows with reference to business decision research texts for coverage of research methodology and practice.

Any enterprise interested in undertaking or commissioning a political risk analysis should first take stock of its needs: not all companies operate under the constant threat of demolition by a stray missile or murderous worker revolt. Oil companies such as Mobil, mining firms like US-based MNE Anaconda, and others operating in strategic industries on a large scale, have learned from long and bitter experience that the non-market environment merits continuous expert attention. Yet for most existing or would-be international businesses, the most important element in political risk analysis is taking the non-market environment seriously enough to devote management time and effort to regular systematic appraisal.

The following pages describe some common approaches to political risk analysis in different international business-decision contexts.

Country risk analysis

A typical case of political risk consideration occurs when an internationalising firm conducts an exploratory assessment to identify potential investment locations. This entails an inquiry into nation-level variables such as the system of government, foreign capital controls, industrial regulation, the history of civil unrest, diplomatic tensions, etc. Most firms possess sufficient information about non-market environments to begin the task of analysis without commencing an external search. This information is embodied in general management knowledge and internal databases and libraries. Staff working in or with experience of the environment in question can be surveyed or asked to file a situation report.

External repositories of information include university and public libraries, the internet, news media, industry associations, government agencies, even banks and insurers. Managers may even visit the countries of interest to gain a first-hand, ground-level impression of the relevant threats and opportunities. The information collected from these various sources can be assimilated by decision-makers to form a subjective assessment of the risk the national environment presents to the firm. When economic and market data are simultaneously acquired and combined to form an overall estimate, the resultant rating signifies country risk.

Published country-risk reports are very easily obtained from good libraries, risk-assessment companies and specialist magazines such as *Euromoney*. These usually consist of a country profile and macro-level market/non-market risk assessment. As a starting point for country-risk evaluation these reports are extremely useful, but they are always incomplete in the context of a particular corporation's plans, not to mention potentially out of date. Published country risk analyses, like those of *Euromoney* and *Institutional Investor,* are often geared to the needs of banks lending to national governments and state-owned enterprises, and to large-scale portfolio investors such as pension funds. Much weight may be put on factors such as government debt as a ratio of GNP, or the opinions of international bankers, which may amount to much the same thing (Lee 1993). The variables of interest to direct investors are often very different, so ratings indexes focusing on creditworthiness should be applied in light of the method used to generate the numbers. Even where political factors are accounted for, the concepts and measurements may be quite crude. Political stability, for example, may be proxied by very simple measures such as the number of changes of government in a given period.

Country-risk measures overlook a great deal of fine detail that may prove to be vital to a particular venture, and provide only an indication of sociopolitical conditions. They are best used in a comparative context, for example where an exporter is forced to choose between two national markets, one of which is a large market, but where several competitors are established, and another where the market is small, but competition is weak. The decisive factor, *ceteris paribus,* might then be relative levels of country risk. Another interesting context of application is suggested by the finding that home-country risk is positively correlated with outward FDI (Tallman 1988). This suggests firms may use country risk comparisons as an aid in choosing between domestic and foreign investment.

Exhibit 10.1 Arabian fights as state-of-art ports vie for scarce business

Over the past few years many millions of US dollars have been committed to building two state-of-the-art ports on the southern coast of the Arabian peninsula.

When the projects were drawn up, trade between the east coast of the US, Europe and Asia was growing fast. For this year a growth figure of 9 per cent was predicted. Both the Omani project at Port Raysut which received its first ships this week, and the Yemeni container port at Aden, expected to open in March 1999, were confident of commercial success.

The previous conventional wisdom in the shipping industry was that there could well be room for both. But that is now being reassessed. At a recent shipping conference in Dubai the management companies behind these two projects were closely questioned about who was going to use all this new capacity.

Salalah Port Services, the management company running the Port Raysut project, was able to come up with convincing answers in terms of traffic flow, while the Port of Singapore Authority, which is to run the Aden operation, was unable to be so specific. Aden at first sight would appear to have the edge – a superb geographical position for a hub-container port, where large vessels can off-load their cargoes for the ports of East Africa and the Inner Gulf. The Port of Singapore Authority it has a first-class management highly thought of in the shipping industry.

The opposite is the case, however, and the whole equation hangs on one phrase: 'political stability'. At Oman's Port Raysut, Sea Land of the US, which manages 28 terminals around the world, has committed itself to a very large up-front investment. So has a leading European carrier, the Danish line, Maersk, also in the top five.

The government has contributed about $130m for the infrastructure and Salalah Port Services, in which the two shippers have an interest, has spent approximately the same amount again on superstructure. Although their spokesmen keep well clear of commenting on regional politics, neither company would have committed itself to Yemen, which has become notorious for its unstable political record.

Since the British withdrew from Aden in 1967, leaving two rival groups fighting for power, there has been tribal conflict and civil war. There have also been not infrequent kidnappings of business executives and aid workers in the interior.

Oman, however, since the accession of Sultan Qaboos in 1970, has built itself up as a conciliator with good relations both with the West and other regional powers. That is why the big Western investment has gone to Oman, whereas the Aden project has relied on Yeminvest, a Saudi company, which has looked to Yemeni and Saudi investors. Commercial banks are supplying loans for Aden's $250m first phase but these are subject to political risk guarantees by the World Bank and its private sector affiliate, the International Finance Corporation.

In the Oman project both Sea Land and Maersk have a 15 per cent interest in the management company, Salalah Port Services. Between them they operate about one-third of the total container fleet in the region, and when Port Raysut opened on Tuesday it received container vessels from the two groups. Both have committed themselves to a 30-year partnership with the government of Oman and have pledged to use the port as a link in their US east coast, Europe and Asia container-shipping route. High on the list when presentations are given to potential customers is the stability of Oman.

Salalah Port Services' Chief Executive, Jack Helton, has been seconded from Sea Land to run the project along with several other senior executives from the Middle East and Europe. Mr Helton and his colleagues have become closely involved with plans for developing a larger conventional port, which will also take cruise ships. As part of the deal he is also content to accept conditions laid by government – that more than 50 per cent of the workforce should be Omani, rising to 60 per cent as the project gets under way. Already Omanis have been sent to Sea Land's Hong Kong operation and have come back ready to operate cranes worth more than $5m each.

Source: Financial Times CD-ROM, 1 January–31 December 1998.

Political event risk

It is often the case that firms fear a particular form of non-market event, by virtue of the industries they are in, and/or the propensities of particular actors in their environments. Expropriation risk, for example, remains a special source of agitation for the oil multinationals, despite the warmer ideological climate currently enjoyed by foreign direct investors. Other companies have variously grown wary of, for example, ecological activism, condemnation by religious groups, employee abduction by guerrilla or terrorist organisations, high-profile scrutiny by UN agencies, or protectionist lobbying by foreign competitors. In the cause of accurate risk assessment in such cases, a variety of methods have been tried. These methods are designed to minimise the assessment biases that may undermine casual subjective approaches.

Brainstorming

In brainstorming, a group of people concerned with the events in question assembles for an in-depth, and often protracted session of debate and analysis of the facts currently known. Ideas are shared and expanded on, and different perspectives and knowledge-bases brought to bear on the problem of prediction. The downside of this approach is the tendency for dominant personalities to sway opinion, for less extroverted individuals to participate incompletely, and for unrelated issues to cause factionalisation. These problems can be alleviated to an extent by using skilled facilitators to oversee the brainstorming process.

The Delphi technique

Delphi was the ancient Greek residence of a famous oracle, to which kings and heroes would go in search of prophecy. The risk-assessment technique bearing its name does not rely on a cave-dwelling mystic, but draws on the foresight of multiple expert analysts. A panel of men and women is selected whose opinions on the probability of an event is particularly respectable, by virtue of their experience, formal education or other personal attributes. Isolated from one another, and without knowledge of one another's identity, each member is asked to complete a questionnaire dealing with the future occurrence of the event or events of interest. The data yielded by all the questionnaires is then processed and presented to each panel member. They see how their views compared with the panel as a whole and may then revise their opinions if they so choose. The second-round survey results are then aggregated to establish a final prediction.

   Delphi studies avoid the group dynamics of brainstorming, but are far from perfect. Much depends on the quality of the experts chosen for the survey panel, and their motivation to participate satisfactorily. The survey instrument needs to be well designed, properly administered and accurately analysed if the technique is to be worthwhile. These problems make it wise to secure the services of a professional business researcher to administer a Delphi study (Shubik 1983).

Mathematical multivariate analysis

Both country risk and political event risk may be evaluated using quantitative techniques based on mathematical modelling. This is an approach appealing to the numerate and to companies to whom the last decimal point of accuracy represents millions of dollars saved or lost. Many models exist to be tried in country-risk analysis, while a few address more specific events such as expropriation (Fitzpatrick 1983; Ciarrapico 1992; Thomas and Worrall 1994; Miller 1998). In cases of special need, such as calculating the likelihood that a particular government agency will impose a specific form of regulation, a firm may be forced to devise and refine its own model before undertaking evaluation. As a result, these are methods favoured by analysts with a proclivity for formal rigour, such as academics and professional risk-assessors. In any case, computers running specialised simulation software or advanced statistical packages most effectively perform the data-processing.

Project vulnerability analysis

More recently, as international businesses have come to appreciate the importance and complexity of the non-market environment, a different means of structuring risk analysis has developed. Instead of examining whole nations, or focusing on non-market events that have proved especially troublesome in the past, project vulnerability analysis is based on the assumption that every international business project possesses a unique exposure profile. This profile is contingent on variables such as industry identity and structure, resource commitment, firm strategy and configuration, and project duration. Non-market environmental threat may be treated as a constant, thereby reducing the determination of vulnerability to the market attributes of the project.

In the case of FDI in a developing country, important general factors to consider are the size of the investment, the degree of international competition for the right to invest, the technology implicated in the investment, and the strength of the investor's proprietary brands. The values taken by these variables give an indicator of the investor's bargaining position *vis à vis* the host government. In natural resource industries, for example, these projects exhibit clear patterns in these dimensions, i.e. large low-to-medium-technologically fixed investment in competitive industries with low product differentiation (Moran 1985). The prognosis is not good. Despite generous terms from the host when the initial investment is made, vulnerability to renegotiation will grow with every passing month unless a countervailing strategy is in place.

Before leaving this section, it is worth noting that international businesses are not without support in political risk analysis. A large number of consultant organisations are able to provide expert input into this task, for an appropriate fee. The point is emphasised, however, that over-reliance on outside help limits the business enterprise's opportunities to learn by doing, and in this area of analysis an applied effort can repay itself in many unexpected ways.

Political risk management

Stay informed

Once an appropriate political risk analysis has made management aware of their firm's potential or current exposure, thought must be given to appropriate offset strategies. Strategy number one: stay informed. Even in possession of the best available political risk evaluation on the current facts, decision-makers appreciate risks only as defined in the context of a particular set of firm-specific, spatial and temporal variables, all of which are subject to change.

Although apparently irrational in an economic sense, non-market behaviour is conducted for objectively discernible reasons of self-interest. This means that a good deal of potential harm can be averted if managers stay abreast of events in the environments of interest, and are equipped with a modicum of political, psychological, anthropological, historical, sociological and economic insight. Although this catalogue of social sciences sounds daunting, the thoughtful reader of this volume has already acquired a useful part of what they will need. The point, in any case, is not to develop expert proficiency; rather to appreciate that patterns are discernible in the non-market environment just as they are in the market, and that some knowledge beyond the obvious will render it more legible and therefore more predictable.

Staying informed can also mean investing in expertise pertinent to particular event risks to which the firm is exposed. For example, firms exposed to security risks because of the incidence of terrorism in host countries may go so far as to establish a specialised security department, or have their employees trained in trouble-zone recognition and abduction-survival tactics.

Risk management strategies

Beyond the advice to stay informed, further all-purpose prescription is either very obvious or well-nigh impossible. The obvious strategy in cases of high risk is complete avoidance. This may imply divestiture or the severance of contractual relationships in environments posing worsening risk. Alternatively, the risk might be borne if higher returns can be extracted in some way. For example, a company threatened with anti-trust action by the state-competition authorities should it acquire a dominant market position, might go ahead and acquire it if the resultant monopoly power yields sufficiently high profits before the host enforces its law.

Sovereign risk management

Some sovereign risks and common political event risks are catered for in the literature of political risk management, but these represent only a fraction of what may befall an international business enterprise in the non-market environment. To minimise the risk of renegotiation in obsolescing bargain scenarios, for example, analysts recommend techniques such as investment sequencing. In this manoeuvre an MNE incrementally increases its investment in the threatened venture in order to reassure the host authorities that its commitment remains strong, and to dissuade the government from action that could interrupt the flow of future supplemental investment (Moran 1985). Another useful tactic is to locally source as many inputs as possible. Not only does this reduce the need to import, but the government is less likely to punitively renegotiate if the profitability of domestic interests – local suppliers – are affected. In any case, the initial contract must be carefully negotiated with a view to maximising fairness to both parties.

Where forced divestment is a threat, MNEs may avert danger by globally configuring their value-adding activities so that the worth of sensitive assets becomes greatly diminished if cut off from other parts of the multinational network of production, marketing and support-service units. They may also ensure that no single unit is indispensable by building in redundant capacities in different national locations, so that if the worst occurs internal business units in other jurisdictions can fill the gap (Kogut 1985). Governments can also be constrained if the target investment is financed by an international consortium involving interests in a variety of influential countries – potential diplomatic backlash and jeopardisation of future financing acts as a deterrent (Moran 1985). If international institutions such as the World Bank, IMF, or regional development banks are involved, so much the better. MNEs can also consider lobbying their home government to enter into a bilateral investment treaty with suspect hosts, containing investment guarantees and dispute-resolution mechanisms.

International businesses can immunise themselves against the sovereign risk of profit-expatriation restrictions through the creative use of transfer pricing. Should a government prohibit the payout of dividends to major overseas shareholders, for example, affected companies may effect the transfer in the form of payments to their parent companies, or other affiliates, for goods and services. The restricted company is not compelled to buy great quantities of unwanted stuff: instead the prices set for intra-firm transactions are manipulated so that a given cross-border flow of, say, machine parts or technical advice, is exchanged for an inflated consideration. If the company is not too blatant, this device may work, for the internal accounts that keep track of intra-firm exchanges are not matters of public record nor easy to decipher if scrutinised.

 ### Exhibit 10.2 Philippines fears lead to poor performance

The Philippine stock market suffered a precipitous fall from favour in 1998, eroding its status as one of the 'best of the worst' regional markets amid the Asian economic turmoil of the last 15 months. After avoiding the steepest of the traumatic plunges experienced by some Asian neighbours in 1997, the Philippine market has been one of the poorest-performing bourses in the region this year, contrary to widely held perceptions.

The market initially gained in the first quarter but has since slid sharply to hit a new seven-year low on 11 September of 1082. At Friday's marginally higher closing level of 1195, the PSE (Philippine Stock Exchange) composite index was down 36 per cent on the year and nearly 65 per cent below an 18-month high of 3447 on 3 February 1997.

In US dollar terms, the PSE index tumbled by nearly 42 per cent in 1998 – one of the most dismal returns for investors in the region this year. At the same time, trading volumes have dwindled to paltry levels as foreign interest has dried up.

Driving the market down have been concerns over a sharply slowing economy, increased political risk since the election of the new Estrada administration, expectations of flat corporate earnings growth, and illiquid trading conditions.

Many analysts predict the market may still have some way to fall, with some of the bearish pundits arguing that a drop in the PSE index to below 1000 is inevitable. 'It has not been written off the investment map like some countries such as Malaysia and Indonesia, but there are concerns,' said Alexandra Connor, director of research at Indosuez WI Carr Securities, who forecasts a year-end level for the PSE Index of 1100. 'Given the current volatility of the market, there are likely to be some short-term rallies, but the overall direction is still likely to be lower.'

Few dispute the Philippines is in fundamentally better economic shape than many of the countries around it. The country has not proved immune, however, to the Asian turmoil and its internal problems. The Philippines' government estimates GNP growth will slow from 5.8 per cent in 1997 to 1.5 per cent in 1998, but many analysts forecast the economy will shrink, rather than grow, by as much as 2 per cent.

At the same time, economic concerns have been exacerbated by apprehension over the rough start to the presidency of Joseph Estrada. Since arriving in office, the Estrada administration has faced fierce criticism over a series of controversies, an alleged revival of cronyism, a lack of coherence in its economic policy and the unconventional style of President Estrada himself.

Analysts said the rough start had raised the risk profile of the country at a time when the world was becoming increasingly risk-averse. 'The concern is that there will be a loss of momentum in reforms,' one analyst said. Analysts also said the current lack of liquidity in the market was itself acting as a deterrent to fresh investment.

Trading volumes have slumped to about $10m to $15m a day (excluding a few recent one-off special block deals) – a fraction of the market capitalisation of the PSE Index of about $12.4bn. This has helped to narrow the investable universe for most foreign investors to about six pivotal stocks – Philippine Long Distance Telephone Co (PLDT), SM Prime, Ayala Land, Ayala Corp, San Miguel and Meralco – where trading volumes remain liquid enough to trade without causing significant market distortions. 'A view on the market now essentially boils down to your view on six to seven stocks that account for about 70 to 75 per cent of the market capitalisation,' said Scott Gibson, research director at ABN Amro Securities.

Even within the limited liquid investment universe, analysts said there were concerns outside usual valuation criteria about two of them. Many investors have objected to a recent move by PLDT to introduce a 'poison pill' clause into its articles of association to ward off takeovers.

San Miguel has also been a source of concern for foreign investors since Eduardo 'Danding' Cojuangco, a leading business figure and former friend of Marcos, recently regained control of the food and beverages conglomerate and carried out large asset sales.

Given that the Philippines already represents only a small fraction in the portfolios of most international fund managers, analysts said the country was now likely to face a struggle to stay on the radar screens of foreign investors.

Source: Financial Times CD-ROM, 1 January–31 December 1998.

Insurance

As with most forms of risk, underwriters can be found from whom insurance against political risk can be bought. Premiums depend on the industry and geographic diversification of the international business enterprise, and can be tailored to the firm's particular needs. Kidnap insurance, for example, is available for individuals or groups (Frederick 1992). In this context, however, insurance can be a double-edged sword. Insurance may help pay the ransom, but the apparent liquidity of victimised firms may encourage kidnappers to attack again.

Insurance against forced divestment is available from both public as well as private sources. In the US, for example, the Overseas Private Investment Commission (OPIC) provides insurance to American companies venturing offshore. The advantage of public insurers is their association with the home-nation government. The direct involvement of another state may be sufficient to dissuade host governments from interference with a foreign investor's business operations. In the case of OPIC, for example, investors may be said to 'wrap the American flag around their project' (National Underwriter 1998).

Integration

Many international business enterprises have learned that blending into host-country society, becoming an 'insider', is a valuable hedge against political risk (Stevens 1997). When successfully carried out, generations may grow up perceiving the company and its products as a local concern. Integration is done in many ways, including joint venture partnerships with local enterprises, locally adapted products, promotion and corporate image, the use of local inputs and sponsorship of local non-market causes, such as sport, child health and conservation. In the case of investment in the highly nationalistic Mercosur nations (see Chapter 3), Kotabe and de Arruda (1998) recommend developing a local corporate image by working with local distributors and other partners, retailing in many places in a variety of outlets, rather than through a few large retail outlets, and using country-specific or even location-specific advertising themes. US brewers marketing their products in Mercosur, such as Miller and Anheuser-Busch, possess a strong American image that works against them, thanks to the region's strong European orientation, its nationalism, and entrenched anti-American sentiment. The Coca-Cola company, despite its all-American association, has enjoyed far more success with its Kaiser beer brand. Coca-Cola formulated Kaiser to suit Brazilian tastes, and marketed it as a local brew so convincingly that in 20 years Kaiser grew to be Brazil's third largest brewer (Kotabe and de Arruda 1998).

When foreigners or particular nationalities become *persona non grata* to the general public, the integrated foreign affiliate is unrecognised and therefore may avoid reduced sales, damage to property, or verbal and physical abuse of its personnel. Two contra examples of political discontinuity show how this works. The first involves the July 1985 bombing of the Greenpeace vessel *Rainbow Warrior* in the harbour of Auckland, New Zealand, by French military agents. The attack was meant only to keep Greenpeace away from French nuclear-testing sites in the Pacific, but a Greenpeace volunteer was killed in the blast. The New Zealand public was outraged by the incident, and the *cachet* of French imports and brand-association vanished overnight. The second example comes from Indonesia. In the wake of the financial crisis that struck South-East Asia in late 1997, segments of that country's indigenous population sought a scapegoat for the privations forced on them by the economic collapse. Their target was the relatively affluent resident ethnic Chinese community. The Chinese Indonesians were in no way responsible for the country's economic woes, but their wealth, and incomplete integration with the indigenous people, made them a convenient outlet for frustration and aggression among a viscous minority of indigenous Indonesians.

Integration, or at least downplaying the company's foreignness or HQ nationality, can also serve to protect against terrorism in the form of kidnap and violent attack, and against discrimination in the execution of their official duties by police, judges and other local officials.

Chapter summary

Political risk is intrinsic to international business. In order for it to be properly assessed and managed, business decision-makers must first acknowledge that their non-market environments merit careful monitoring, and that they can be understood as well as the market if a serious effort is made. There are many different forms and intensities of political risk, but not all are relevant to every enterprise. Political risk assessment ideally involves research expertise, and its value to the firm is maximised if management possesses a working understanding of the non-market environments relevant to their decision contexts. Understanding and remaining informed about non-market environments enables firms to manage the political risks to which they are exposed, and facilitates the design of non-market strategies through which the international business can acquire competitive advantages.

Discussion questions

1 What sort of political risk might you represent to an international business that marketed a product of which you did not approve?

2 Why are the general standards of political risk analysis in international businesses criticised by researchers?

3 A major pharmaceutical MNE develops a drug that can guarantee a male child to women about to become pregnant. The company wants to market the drug only in those less-developed countries where regulations allow and where the preference for baby boys is a cultural norm. What are the main political risks of pursuing this strategy?

4 Why do you think so little attention has been paid to the formal development of strategic theory based on advantages acquirable in the non-market domain of the firm?

Closing Case Study:
Pepsi in Burma

Pepsi Cola is one of the world's best-known soft drink brands, alongside its great rival, Coca-Cola. Pepsi was first marketed in 1894 by Caleb Bradham as a dyspepsia medicine under the name 'Brad's Drink', but became a serious contender in the soft-drink market in the 1930s. The US-based PepsiCo Inc., which also owns Taco Bell, Pizza Hut, and KFC, internationalised throughout the 1940s and 50s on Coke's coat-tails, and by the 1960s the two companies were battling head to head for control of the global market. Pepsi scored significantly by being the first of the two into the Soviet Union, and the struggle for the hearts, minds and cash of teenagers rages on to this day.

The pioneering spirit that took PepsiCo to Moscow in the 1970s was evidently still with the company 20 years later, when it established itself in Burma through FDI and a franchising agreement. Until 1988, Burma had been in a state of self-imposed exile for over 25 years. Situated between India and Bangladesh to the north and Thailand to the south, Burma gained independence from Britain after the Second World War. After 14 years of democracy under the leadership of Aung San, a group of military leaders seized power and established a socialist republic in 1962.

In response to demonstrations for political reform, a new executive body in the military government was established in 1988, entitled The State Law and Order Restoration Council, or SLORC. This body set about brutally quelling the government's pro-democracy opposition. In order to foster capitalism, SLORC also began to open the economy to private enterprise, including foreign investment. The name of the country was changed to Myanmar, but this name is not in popular usage. In parallel with the new economic openness, some political change was tentatively begun. In May 1990 a general election was held, which the opposition party, the National League for Democracy (NLD), won by a landslide. SLORC responded by placing the leader of the NLD, Aung San Suu Kyi, daughter of Aung San, under house-arrest. She remained incarcerated for six years, winning the Nobel Peace Prize in absentia in 1991.

SLORC's catalogue of misgovernment was extensive. It was accused of using heroine trafficking to supplement its income, and its dismal human rights abuse record included cases of torture and forced labour. Aung San Suu Kyi remained unable to travel freely within Burma, and other senior NLD members were forced to flee the country. In the meantime PepsiCo had established a successful Pepsi bottling business with local businessman U Thein Tun. The joint venture involved PepsiCo in a 40 per cent stake of the bottling company to which the MNE licensed bottling and distribution rights. PepsiCo also supplied the Burmese plant with soft drink-syrup concentrate by an export arrangement linked to the franchise.

PepsiCo began to feel the ill-effects of consorting with a censured host state in 1990, when boycotts of its products began in the US. With these boycotts came letters and calls of complaint, and demonstrations outside PepsiCo retail outlets. Human rights organisations such as the Free Burma Coalition urged the boycott further, within and outside Burma. Whole communities took up the cause. Eleven US cities, one county, and the State of Massachusetts, passed 'selective contracting' laws to penalise firms trading with Burma. In the Californian town of Berkeley, for example, the City Hall's soft drink dispensers were switched from Pepsi to Coca-Cola. Berkeley residents didn't stop with Pepsi, either. Their boycott extended to other firms active in Burma, including seven oil companies, plus Motorola, IBM, Compaq, Federal Express, and United Parcel. Companies in business in Nigeria, where another government of ill-repute was in power, were also boycotted by the council.

Meanwhile, Aung San Suu Kyi rallied international support from the covers of magazines, and encouraged bans on businesses involved with SLORC. Burma incurred the loss of some tariff privileges from the European Union because of its use of forced labour, and in September 1996 US President Bill Clinton signed a bill authorising him to ban new investment in Burma if conditions worsened. On campuses in the US and UK, students called for the sale of Pepsi products to be stopped until the company pulled out of Burma. This agitation resulted in some universities cancelling supply contracts with PepsiCo, such as one worth US$1 million at Harvard. In a similar move, students at Stanford University prevented the opening of a Taco Bell restaurant. Although few went so far as to accuse PepsiCo of endorsing the SLORC regime, the same could not be said of Thein Tun, the local partner. He went on public record calling for the democracy movement in Burma to be 'ostracised and crushed', and he clearly enjoyed a close relationship with the generals holding political office.

PepsiCo realised it needed to distance itself from the dictatorship in Burma. It announced it would cancel its franchise arrangement with the Burmese bottling plant and no longer supply syrup. The protest action showed no signs of reduction while the company continued to hold 40 per cent in the bottling plant, however. Eventually PepsiCo could no longer endure the loss of goodwill in its home nation and other key markets. In early 1997, Edward V. Lahey, Jr, a Senior Vice-President of PepsiCo, Inc., made the following statement:

> Based on our assessment of the spirit of current US government foreign policy, we are completing our total disengagement from the Burmese market. Accordingly, we have severed all relationships with our former franchise bottler, effective 15 January 1997. The bottler in Burma is taking appropriate steps to ensure that all production and distribution of our products are ceased by 31 May 1997.

With PepsiCo went Carlsberg, Heineken, London Fog, Motorola, Apple Computer, Hewlett-Packard, Walt Disney, J. Crew, and Wente Vineyards, all succumbing to similar pressures, all exiting within the space of six months. The Free Burma Coalition and other pressure groups then turned their attention to a small group of oil companies remaining in the country. This group, enjoying lower public profiles and higher strategic value at home and abroad, will not be as easy to shift as the consumer products companies. Nevertheless, the success of the campaign organised by NGOs like the Free Burma Coalition and Third World First, a UK student organisation, in persuading Pepsi to leave Burma, showed it is possible for ordinary citizens to affect major corporate actors when acting in concert, and without breaking the law.

In April 1997, President Clinton announced a ban on new investment in Burma.

Sources: The Economist (1997); Emond (1997); Francia (1995); Free Burma Coalition (1997); Hobson and Leung (1997); Industry Week (1997); Parrish (1996); Pendergrast (1993); White (1997).

Questions

1 What do you think the initial attraction of the Burmese market was for PepsiCo?
2 Do you think PepsiCo took a calculated risk by entering Burma in the way it did, or was it completely taken by surprise by international condemnation?
3 If you had been asked to undertake a project-vulnerability analysis for PepsiCo's venture in Burma, what attributes of the project would you have isolated as particularly worrisome?
4 If you managed a foreign oil company in Burma, what moves would you make to defend yourself in the light of Pepsi's experience?

Further reading

Brewer, T.L. (ed) (1985) *Political Risk in International Business,* New York, NY: Praeger Publishers. A collection of research monographs on aspects of political risk including illuminating case studies.

Davis, D. (1997) *Business Research for Decision Making,* 4th edn, Belmont, NY: Wadsworth. A sound introduction to the field of business research, and a useful reference to have in an exhaustive political risk analysis.

Kobrin, S.J. (1982) *Managing Political Risk Assessment: Strategic Response to Environmental Change,* Berkeley, CA: University of California Press. Kobrin is a leading academic contributor to the political risk field, and this book remains an excellent resource on the subject.

References

Barton, L. (1993) Terrorism as an international business crisis, *Management Decision* 31: 22–6.

BBC Online (1999) Yemen: playing the hostage card, 9 January.

BBC World Service (1999) Daewoo president killed in South Africa, 4 February.

BBC World Service (1997) Yemen: new kidnap, 30 October.

Boddewyn, J.J. and Brewer. T. (1994) International business political behavior: new theoretical directions, *Journal of International Business Studies* 19: 119–43.

Brown, D. (1991) Under fire: helping the employees back home, *Management Review* 80: 10–14.

Busse, L., Ishikawa, N., Mitra, M., Primmer, D., Doe, K., and Yaveroglu, T. (1997) The perception of corruption: a market discipline approach. Unpublished working paper at the Goizueta Business School, Emory University, Atlanta, GA, USA.

Ciarrapico, A.M. (1992) Country Risk: a Theoretical Framework of Analysis, Aldershot: Dartmouth.

Cragg. C. (1998) Hope and violence in Nigeria, *Energy Economist,* July: 2–4.

Emond, M. (1997) Berkeley's boycotts hit all seven major oil companies in area, *National Petroleum News*, September.

Fitzpatrick, M. (1983) The definition and assessment of political risk in international business: a review of the literature, *Academy of Management Review* 8: 249–54.

Francia, L.-H. (1995) The general's consensus, Worldbusiness 1: 47–51.

Frederick, M.H. (1992) Keeping safe: communism's fall has led to security risks for execs, *International Business* 5: (October) 68–9.

Free Burma Coalition (1997) press release, 27 January.

Garten, J.E. (1997) Business and foreign policy, *Foreign Affairs* 76: 67–79

Guyon, J. (1997) Why is the world's most profitable company turning itself inside out? *Fortune* 136: (4 August) 120–25.

Hobson, J.S.P. and Leung, R. (1997) Hotel development in Myanmar, *Cornell Hotel and Restaurant Adminstration.*

Industry Week (1997) Governing Ingredients, 17 March. *Quarterly* 38: 60–71.

International Trade Finance. (1995) Nigerian crisis prompts IFC withdrawal, 17 November: 9.

Kobrin, S.J. (1976) The environmental determinants of foreign direct investment: an ex-post empirical analysis, *Journal of International Business Studies* 10: 29–42.

Kobrin, S.J. (1979) Political risk: a review and reconsideration, *Journal of International Business Studies* 10: 67–80.

Kobrin, S.J. (1980) Foreign enterprise and forced divestment in less-developed countries, *International Organization* 34: 65–88.

Kobrin, S.J., Basek, J., Blank, S. and La Palombara, J. (1980) The assessment and evaluation of non-economic environments by American firms: a preliminary report, *Journal of International Business Studies* 11: 32–47.

Kogut, B. (1985) 'Designing global strategies: profiting from operational flexibility', *Sloan Management Review:* (Fall) 27–38.

Kotabe, M. and **de Arruda, M.** (1998) South America's free trade gambit, *Marketing Management* 7: 38–46.

Lee, S.H. (1993) Relative importance of political instability and economic variables on perceived country creditworthiness, *Journal of International Business Studies,* 25: 801–12.

Miller, K.D. (1998) 'Economic exposure and integrated risk management' *Strategic Management Journal* 19: 497–514.

Moran, T. (1985) International political risk assessment, corporate planning, and strategies to offset risk, in T. Moran (ed.) *Multinational Corporations,* Lexington, MA: Lexington Books.

National Underwriter (1998) Political risk cover demand surges, 27 April.

Parish P. (1996) Bloc vote for South America, *Corporate Location,* Sep/Oct, 20.

Pendergrast, M. (1993) *For God, Country and Coca-Cola,* London: Phoenix.

Root, F.R. (1968) The expropriation experience of american companies: what happened to 38 companies, *Business Horizons* 11: 69–74.

Shubik, M. (1983) Political risk: analysis, process, and purpose, in R.J. Herring *Managing International Risk,* Cambridge: Cambridge University Press.

Stevens, F.Y. (1997) Quantitative perspective on political risk analysis for direct foreign investment – a closer look, *Multinational Business Review:* (Spring) 77–84.

Stopford, J.M. 1994. The growing interdependence between transnational corporations and governments, *Transnational Corporations* 3: 53–76.

Tallman, S.B. (1988) Home country political risk and foreign direct investment in the United States, *Journal of International Business Studies* 19: 219–34.

The Economist (1997) Sanctioned, but not chastened, 26 April: 34.

Thomas, J. and **Worrall, T.** (1994) Foreign direct investment and the risk of expropriation, *Review of Economic Studies,* 61: 81–108.

UNTCMD (1992) *World Investment Report 1992: Transnational Corporations as Engines of Growth,* New York: United Nations.

Vernon, R. (1971) *Sovereignty at Bay: the Multinational Spread of United States Enterprises,* New York: Basic Books.

Waelde, T.W. (1998) Managing the risk of sanctions in the global oil and gas industry: corporate response under political, legal, and commercial pressures, *CEPMLP On-Line Journal on Natural Resources, Energy and International Business Transactions* 2(1).

White, M. (1997) More and more on Myanmar, *World Trade* 10: 74.

Williams, M. (1975) The extent and significance of the nationalization of foreign owned assets in developing countries 1956–72, *Oxford Economic Papers* 27: 260–73.

Weber, M. (1969) *Economy and Society,* Vol.1, New York, NY: Bedminster Press.

CHAPTER 11

Government Intervention in International Trade

Angelica Cortes

Learning objectives

By the end of this chapter you will:

- be familiar with the reasons and motivations for government intervention in trade

- appreciate the important effects of government intervention in trade as well as its effects on consumers

- become aware of the different mechanisms available to governments that want to restrict international trade in their territories

- be able to understand the interrelation that exists today among and between countries and the World Trade Organisation (WTO) in terms of policies and trade.

Opening Case Study:
Canada seeks to protect local magazine publishers

Canada yesterday unveiled a bold new tactic in its 30-year effort to protect magazine publishers from US competition by banning foreign-owned publications from accepting advertising aimed specifically at a Canadian audience.

The announcement was in response to a World Trade Organisation ruling last year that slapped down Canada's 80 per cent excise tax on advertising in so-called split-run editions, which are separate editions of foreign publications aimed at Canadian readers and designed to attract Canadian advertising revenue.

The issue has become the focus of a long-running battle between Canada and the US over Canada's policies to protect its cultural industries such as film, television, magazines and books from being overwhelmed by US competitors. About 80 per cent of the magazines sold on Canadian shelves are foreign-owned publications, mostly American in origin.

Canada has taken extraordinary measures to keep such publications as *Sports Illustrated*, the US sporting magazine, from setting up separate Canadian editions that might draw scarce advertising dollars away from Canadian-owned

▶

magazines. *Sports Illustrated* folded its Canadian version in 1995 after the excise tax was imposed.

Sheila Copps, Canadian heritage minister, said yesterday that Canada would continue to promote its cultural policy objectives so that Canadians did not lose their 'unique voice'. The US is likely to challenge the new approach as a continued violation of Canada's WTO obligations.

Canada is hoping the measure will withstand WTO scrutiny because it is aimed at the provision of advertising services, which are covered in the weaker WTO agreement on services. The WTO panel decision last July found that Canada had violated the national treatment provisions of the stronger WTO agreement covering trade in goods.

In the services agreement, countries are bound only by the specific commitments made in the Uruguay Round negotiations. Canada made no commitments with respect to advertising services and therefore believes it remains free to discriminate against advertising in foreign-owned publications.

But Clifford Sosnow, an international trade lawyer representing the association of Canadian advertisers, said the WTO had made it clear that advertising was an integral part of magazines, which were considered to be a good. 'As far as I'm concerned the Canadian government is walking back into the wall,' he said.

Canadian advertisers are also considering challenging the measure in the courts as a violation of the free expression guarantee under Canada's charter of rights. Ron Lund, Association President, said US publications were clearly finding an audience in Canada and Canadian advertisers had the right to promote their products to those readers.

Canada will also comply with the WTO panel ruling by ending its importation ban on split-run editions, which dates back to the 1960s, eliminating the 80 per cent excise tax on advertising and lowering the higher postal rates charged to foreign publications.

Source: *Financial Times* CD-ROM, 1 January–31 December 1998.

Introduction

This chapter presents the reasons and motivations why governments limit trade and investments in their territories. Some of these motivations seem to be reasonable and justifiable, such as national defence, the protection of infant industry, and the development of the economic strategic plan. Other motivations appear to be based on the desire to have a competitive position abroad and, at the same time, on not allowing imports to compete in their home markets.

Government policies concerning trade and investments tend to be border bound. However, often these policies, which aim to be domestic, affect the international decisions, trade and relationships with other countries, including policies enacted by the World Trade Organisation, the agency that has jurisdiction over international trade around the world. This chapter shows the interdependency that exists today among countries, regardless of their size and trade volume, and with the World Trade Organisation.

Government intervention: reasons and motivations

It can be argued that governments' principal responsibility is the welfare and protection of their nations. To this end, governments enact policies concerning trade and investments that will be consistent with their plans for developing their industry bases, stimulating economic growth, and attracting direct investments into their country. These policies are also used to encourage direct investments in foreign countries. All these measures are adopted to produce a positive effect on their balance of payments and levels of employment at home.

Government policies are border bound (Ohmae 1990). That is, the emphasis is on how these measures will affect the nation's domestic environment. However, in today's world, all countries are highly interconnected and a domestic policy may have unintended effects on other countries' policies, as well as on business and people abroad. Above all, the regulations and procedures intended for the internal affairs of the nation may violate the policies of the international organisations such as the World Trade Organisation, the International Monetary Fund, and specific functions of the United Nations. For example, one country's policy for economic growth may effectively limit competition from imports. In other cases, policies aimed at protecting the nation's citizens may be viewed as enacting trade barriers. An example of this is the conflict between the European Union (EU) and the United States (US) over the issue involving US cattle being treated with growth hormones. The EU argues that this meat is unsafe for human consumption. Another example is the six-year-long battle between the EU and the US over the importation of bananas.

Governmental policies, in their pursuit to protect their nation's citizens, tiptoe along a fine line between protecting national interests such as economic growth, security and protectionism. Some of the most common arguments for government intervention in the world are:

- protection of an infant industry
- protection of home markets
- protection of the reserve account
- protection of capital accumulation
- maintenance of the standard of living
- conservation of natural resources
- industrialisation of less-developed countries
- maintenance of employment
- creation of employment
- national defence
- transfer of technology and know-how
- retaliation and bargaining
- and the list continues . . .

In general, government intervention in international trade, as we saw from the previous list, can be divided into two major categories of arguments: economic considerations for intervention, and political considerations for intervention. From the nearly endless list of arguments for government intervention, we analyse three of the most common arguments under economic considerations and the three most common under political considerations.

Economic considerations for intervention

Under the economic arguments for policy intervention in trade we find these three issues:

- protection of infant industry
- strategic trade policies
- restructuring the economy.

Protection of infant industry

Historically, it seems to be the oldest argument within the area of economic concerns that prompts government intervention in trade. The first proponent of this argument was Alexander Hamilton in 1791 (Griffin and Pustay 1999). Hamilton based his argument on the belief that many developing countries have a comparative advantage in manufacturing, but new manufacturing industries are not in the position to compete with the mature industries of Europe.

Placing this argument in the historical perspective of the closing of the eighteenth century, Europe had a well-established industry that grew even stronger against the background of the English industrial revolution. The new countries that were starting to gain their independence from the colonial powers had to start creating their industrial base without the infrastructure of capital, organisation and protection provided by the crown in Europe. Protecting these industries in the New World against the competition from the developed economies was a valid argument and an understandable priority of the newly formed governments. Today, it is still a valid argument for the underdeveloped and less-developed countries of the world (Cateora and Graham 1999).

For governments to allow their infant industries to flourish, they must provide temporary protection. GATT recognised this argument as a legitimate reason for protectionism and the World Trade Organisation allows developing countries the use of quantitative import quotas, tariffs and import subsidies until the industry is mature enough to withstand foreign competition.

The argument for infant industry, however, is not without its critics. Basically, criticism comes from two fronts. First, economists argue that protected industries do not develop a need for efficiency, cost containment and product quality. In the long run, without these characteristics, the protected industry is unable to compete in world markets.

The second criticism that economists argue about is based on the assumption that infant industries cannot borrow from domestic and international capital markets and that their government must subsidise the investments. With the development experienced by the global capital markets, this criticism has a strong foundation. Those industries that have a comparative advantage should be able to borrow from the capital markets. Some economies such as those of Taiwan, South Korea, Chile (*Crossborders Monitor* 1996) and others, have allowed their infant industries to borrow from capital markets without strong subsidies from their governments. Most developing economies, however, feel that these subsidies are necessary.

Strategic trade policies

As we saw in Chapter 1, international trade theories have important implications concerning government policies. Michael Porter's (1990) national competitive advantage theory which stresses the importance of a firm to invest in sophisticated advanced factors in production is a trend that is seen today in the US (see Exhibit 11.1). Companies are investing in state-of-the-art technologies, increasing investments in training and research and development to maintain their competitive edge.

Exhibit 11.1 Mystery of global spending: where the money went?

Where the capital spending boom is heading is the biggest mystery. Cash flow is no longer what it used to be. Corporate profits have been roughly flat in the past year. All the spending on new plant and equipment means that many companies now have plenty of spare capacity and little reason to build more.

Still, corporate America has not quenched its thirst for high-technology gear, and continued investment to overcome the year 2000 computer bug may keep capital spending moving up this year. And with productivity jumping at an annual rate of 3.7 per cent in the fourth quarter, the payoff seems obvious. 'Companies keep spending money on technology because that's where they're getting the competitive edge.' Said Bruce Steinberg, chief economist at Merrill Lynch.

Source: *The New York Times*, 27 February 1999.

Porter (1990) recommends that in order for companies to gain or maintain their competitive advantages they should lobby their governments to enact policies that will make the national diamond most favourable to those industries. To illustrate this point, government policies, for example, that have a strong effect in the domestic diamond, are those regarding the development of infrastructure, education, and the promotion of domestic competition. This last point clearly refers to government intervention in the form of subsidies (grants, for example) or other government programmes to facilitate, develop or encourage domestic production and its export to foreign markets.

Another trade theory that has important government implications in terms of policies is the strategic trade theory (Krugman and Smith 1994). This theory proposes the argument that firms which are the first in producing a product may later dominate the market for those products. These first-movers will have a competitive advantage in terms of production and market access over the competitors that may come later.

The propositions of this theory are especially relevant to those industries that can sustain only a few firms. This is because of the high cost of product development or the relatively long period of time it takes to develop experience and expertise in those industries. However, it has also worked in other industries that have a large number of firms competing for the same market, such as cellular phones. For those firms, the commitment of investments and, in some cases, government grants and subsidies, have been critical to the success of those firms.

Governments have the potential to increase their balance of trade if the first-mover firm is domestic, rather than a foreign firm gaining the competitive edge in that particular industry (Lieberman and Montgomery 1988).

The sheer size of the investments required in R&D for the new technologies needed for the future makes it very difficult to raise them exclusively from global capital markets. Therefore, governments support these industries by grants and/or appropriations. Such is the case for industries such as telecommunications, aerospace and those involved in developing components for the space station. Governments must be involved in developing the trade policies for those technologies that will provide their country with a competitive advantage.

Restructuring the economy

During the last two decades we have witnessed a move from planned economies to market economies in several countries (Tayeb 1997). This is the case for the new republics from the ex-Soviet Union, East European countries, emerging economies in Asia and Latin America, and several other developing countries. To make this shift, some countries had enacted temporary protectionist policies with the intention that in a few years they will be changed – and in many countries changed to liberalise trade to allow an open market economy.

The protectionist measures are taken for the period of time that the government and the industrial sector need to adjust to the change in economic policy and philosophy. In some cases, these infant industries need temporary protection given by high tariffs, government subsidies, and/or import quotas. As the country becomes more committed to a market economy and its infant industry is pressed to mature and compete in world markets, the subsidies are decreased with time. Furthermore, tariffs are later lowered to bring them within the range of the rest of the country's tariff schedules.

Political considerations for intervention

The political reasons that governments give for intervention in trade range from specific objectives such as protecting jobs to general objectives such as political objectives, as follows:

- protection of jobs and industry
- national security
- political objectives.

Protection of jobs and industries

One of the most common and emotional arguments is the protection of jobs and industries against foreign competition. Traditionally, the agricultural sector is found within this argument. Almost every country in the world protects the agricultural sector, not only because the country is restructuring its economy, but also because in most countries the farming sector is a powerful and large political constituency.

This type of protection is found in the US, the European Union, and Japan, where governments are careful not to antagonise these powerful groups (Tayeb 1997). Unfortunately, the effects of these types of policies is high prices for the consumers and limited choices in the variety and quality of available products.

National security

National security is a large umbrella for a number of legitimate and sometimes unrelated issues that are placed under this convenient label. The national security argument refers to the need for a government to protect the industries of defence, telecommunications, transportation, and other critical industries that are mainly income-generating and responsible for having a large effect on the balance of payments.

Today, the defence industry also includes industries such as aerospace, semiconductors, and advanced computer and electronic technologies. Nowadays, the telecommunications industry, because of its sophistication and extraordinary investments in technology and equipment, can only be partially controlled by any government. The days when countries had their domestic, independent, government-controlled telephone companies are becoming something of the past. We can appreciate this trend through the privatisation programmes that many countries have with respect to their telecommunications sector.

Political objectives

Within the political objectives of governments we find foreign policies concerning trade as well as foreign aid. Foreign policies can be aimed at enhancing national security through strategic alliances among neighbouring countries such as the European Union, Mercosur, and NAFTA. These agreements, though economic in principle, are also aimed to protect their borders by mutual co-operation in protecting the common interest of the country's members.

Foreign aid is another type of political objective. Several countries, for example, had criticised Japan for its development aid packages to Asian countries. These financial aids carry a number of restrictions, such as that Japanese engineers and designers can judge the project's feasibility. They can also contribute to the project's development. The criticisms are based on the fact that the end result of Japan's aid packages is to increase the Japanese sphere of influence and to be able to control the trade flow in the region.

The US has been criticised for very similar reasons. American foreign aid packages also have a number of restrictions. There is no doubt that besides the altruist nature of the foreign aid packages, they might hide the real political intention of developing or maintaining the sphere of influence in a region by helping or creating economic and trade dependency.

Global trade regulations

At the close of the Second World War, GATT was created as a set of rules to ensure non-discrimination and transparent procedures in international trade. This was intended to liberalise trade and avoid countries adopting protectionist policies that could negatively affect international trade.

GATT has been called the 'remarkable success story of a postwar international organisation that was never intended to become one' (Graham 1983). GATT brought with its policies and rounds, a very significant reduction in tariffs, and the elimination of many of the non-tariff barriers used by countries.

The extraordinary success of GATT is that this institution was never recognised by law as an international organisation. Its provisional constitution was never ratified by any of the original 23 members. Another factor that makes GATT so amazing is that this institution had only advisory authority. It did not have the power to sanction countries' members that violated the fair trading rules.

Because of the complexity and intensity of international trade, it was necessary to create the organisation that was the World Trade Organisation. WTO was created during the Uruguay Round and came to life on 1 January, (wto.org/about/org/ 1999). The GATT's agreements had been amended and incorporated into this new organisation that had the power to sanction. The WTO also increased its jurisdiction to cover areas such as service, intellectual property, agri-culture, textiles, anti-dumping, subsidies, safeguards and other non-tariff barriers.

It is important to realise that countries may enact internal policies that will affect international trade directly or indirectly. The WTO has the jurisdiction to contact the particular government and notify it that the policies are in violation of the WTO's ruling and that they must be changed, even if it is an internal policy. One of the priorities of WTO is to maintain transparency in trade. To this end, WTO conducts periodical reviews focused on member's own trade policies and practices. The frequency of these reviews depends on the country's size (wto.org/about/org/ 1999). A country's size is classified into three major groups:

- *Every two years review*: US, Canada, European Union and Japan
- *Every four years review*: the next 16 countries (in terms of their share of world trade)
- *Every six years review*: the remaining countries.

It is clear by now that the interdependency is not only among the trading part-ners, but also between nations and international organisations. These international organisations, such as the WTO, have been increasing their juris-diction in matters that affect trade and investments, conflict resolutions, and the overall functioning of the world. There are some arguments against this involve-ment of the international organisations in the policy-making of countries. One side of the argument is that it can be seen as an infringement on the democratic processes of individual nations. The counter-argument, however, is that in making their policies, these organisations have a much broader perspective of the whole world than of any particular country. Countries are concerned with their limited partnerships with other nations and their policies tend to be border bound. The international organisations such as the WTO, IMF, UN, and World Bank are concerned with the welfare of the whole world.

Measures for controlling trade

Tariff barriers

Tariffs are taxes (or duties) levied on imports or exports. Most governments impose a tax on the products they import into their territory. The main purposes of these tariffs is to generate revenue and/or to limit the amount of imports into the national territory.

Tariffs have direct consequences on individual businesses. For example, special interest groups lobby their government to raise import tariffs to limit the importation of competitive products. Tariffs also restrict the number of foreign suppliers for manufacturers. In this manner, manufacturers are limited to domestic suppliers, or to those from countries that are given preferential treatment, such as members of multilateral agreements.

Tariffs also affect consumers' choices because high tariffs in imports restrict the competition of available products in the market. Figure 11.1 shows the effect of tariffs on price and product availability. When P1 is the original price, without tariff the quantity of the product available is Q1. Once the tariff is imposed, the price increases to P2. As the price increases, the quantity of the product decreases from Q1 to Q2, effectively reducing the demand for the product.

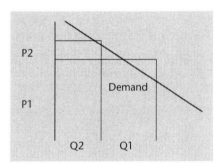

Figure 11.1 Effect of tariff on product availability
Source: Adapted from Hill (1998).

Import tariffs are divided into three main groups:

- *ad valorem* tariff
- specific tariff
- compound tariff.

Ad valorem tariff (Latin expression which means according to value) is levied on a fixed percentage on the imported product, such as 2 per cent for five lbs of sugar.

Specific tariff is levied on a fixed unit amount based on weight, quantity, or other physical characteristics of the imported products, such as 60 cents per kilogram of apples.

Compound tariff is levied on products that have both *ad valorem* and *specific tariffs*, such as the case of textiles. An *ad valorem* tariff is levied on the wool to protect the raw material industry, and a specific tariff is levied on the finished product (sweater) to protect the garment industry of the importing country.

Non–tariff barriers

This is a very extensive collection of measures designed to restrict imports. Any government regulation other than a tariff that has the aim of limiting imports will come under the category of non-tariff. The following chart shows some of the most common non-tariff barriers used by government. From this extensive list (see Exhibit 11.2), only five will be examined: quotas, voluntary export restrictions, standards, monetary restrictions, and subsidies.

Exhibit 11.2 Partial list of non-tariff barriers

Specific limitations on trade:

Global quotas	Embargoes
Country quotas	Boycotts
Import licenses	Voluntary export restraints
Preferential licensing application	Temporary prohibition
Discretionary licensing	Health and sanitary prohibition
Local content requirements	

Customs and administrative procedures:

Valuation systems	Stamp taxes
Anti-dumping procedures	Consular invoice fees
Tariff classification	Statistical taxes
Documentation	Sales taxes
Fees	Consumption taxes
Monetary restrictions	Taxes on transport
Special import authorisation	Value-added taxes
Advance import deposits	Turnover taxes
Foreign exchange licensing	Service charges
Custom surcharges	

Standards:

Standards disparities
Testing and standards
Packaging and labelling

Other:

Multilateral marketing agreements	Export subsidies
Government procurements	Domestic assistant programmes

Sources: Adapted from Cateora and Graham (1999) and Magnier (1989).

Quotas

Quotas are absolute restrictions placed on the number of units or the monetary value to be imported. Like tariffs, the direct effect of quotas on imports is that they tend to increase the prices of these imported products. Quotas are established for imports and also for exports.

Global quotas on imports

These quotas are an absolute restriction on the amount of units or the monetary value world-wide. For example, a government may set a global quota of 65,000 television sets. Once the quota is filled, importers must wait for the next fiscal year to be able to allow new television sets to be brought in. These television sets come from any country of the world and they enter the importing nation on a first-come, first-served basis.

Selected import quotas

A government may impose specific import quotas by country. For example, suppose that a country buys all its oil supply from abroad. In order to avoid dependency from one or two countries, the importing nation divides its purchases among several countries in which no country has a dominant position as a supplier.

Export quotas

In this case, the exporting nation establishes export quotas on the surplus of the product after the needs of the domestic market have been covered. The idea is to serve the domestic needs first. Once these needs are covered, any surplus left can be exported abroad.

Voluntary export restrictions

These are similar to quotas. Voluntary export restrictions (VERs) are designed to help the domestic industries to restructure or recapture their markets (Tayeb 1997). In most cases, *voluntary* is a misnomer. They are called voluntary because the exporting country sets the limits of units to be exported to the importing nation. These limits are agreed to in the face of severe threats from the importing country: threats such as boycotts, high tariffs, absolute quotas, or any other type of trade retaliation.

During the past decade, VERs were common among the textile, steel, automobile and agriculture industries. Because of its voluntary nature, and because it does not violate bilateral or multilateral agreements, the WTO has no jurisdiction on this matter. However, this is one of the non-tariff barriers that the WTO has been targeting for close examination in the future (wto.org/about/org/ 1999).

Standards

Most countries have standards aimed at protecting the health, product quality and safety of their citizens. To this end, countries establish a set of product or testing standards before these imports can be allowed to reach the market in the importing country. Standards is one of the grey areas of trade restrictions. The importing nation's intentions in imposing standards are clearly to protect its people. However, the veiled and sometimes not-so-veiled intentions are to restrict or prohibit the import of certain products into the country in order to protect domestic producers or manufacturers from foreign competition.

Standards as a non-tariff barrier is an area that is open to abuse. For example, Japan requires that all horticultural products imported into Japan should be inspected in the exporting country before being shipped. The US sets standards for a number of agricultural products but inspections are delayed because of the lack of available inspectors (see Exhibit 11.3). In other cases, standards are not clearly spelled out and the interpretation of those standards rest on the judgement of the customs inspectors.

Exhibit 11.3 US raises tariffs for luxury goods

The United States escalated two politically contentious trade disputes with Europe on Wednesday (3 March 1999), imposing 100 per cent tariffs on $520 million in European products and threatening to ban Europe's supersonic pride, the Concorde, from landing in the United States. The tariffs imposed by the Clinton administration essentially double the price of such goods as Louis Vuitton handbags, Parma hams, Pecorino cheese and Scottish cashmere sweaters. They are part of a six-year battle over trade in bananas.

Source: *The New York Times*, 4 March 1999.

Monetary restrictions

These restrictions refer to exchange restrictions aimed at protecting balance of payments, or at encouraging the development of particular industries. This type of trade barrier is most likely to be used by developing countries which find themselves with limited amounts of hard currencies. There are three main types of monetary controls: blocked currencies, differential exchange rates, and government's approval to secure foreign exchange.

Blocked currencies
These refer to the situation in which the conversion of one currency into another foreign currency is prohibited by law. This situation is normally associated with non-convertible currencies in which residents or foreigners cannot convert the domestic currency into another. This case effectively limits imports or imports above an established quota by not allowing the importers to exchange national currency for the exporter's currency.

Differential exchange rates
These are also relatively common among underdeveloped countries. This situation refers to the need to protect a nation's balance of payments and its reserve account by restricting the amount of hard currency that is needed to pay for the imports. The government sets different levels of exchange rates for its currency.

The importers must apply for the exchange of local currencies for the seller's currency. If those imports fall within the government's priority list, then the importers will pay the official exchange rate for that currency. However, those importers that fall within the government's second priority list, will pay a slightly higher exchange rate, and so on. In this manner, the government controls the hard currency that is spent on the imports that meet the country's strategic planning for development, and discourages those imports that can be substituted for domestic products.

Government approval to secure foreign exchange.
This policy may be the accompanying measure for the differential exchange rates. Governments enact this measure when they are experiencing a severe shortage of hard currencies, or when encountering a financial crisis. All importers are required to submit a foreign exchange application with the necessary documentation to be approved by the central bank or some governmental official agency. In some extreme cases, such as the economic crisis of Brazil during the 1980s, the government required that importers deposit months in advance the value of the invoice in local currency before the government could grant the authorisation and disbursement of the foreign exchange. This was an extreme measure caused by the shortage of foreign currencies that Brazil experienced during those years.

Subsidies

This is another type of direct government intervention in trade. Subsidies are some kind of monetary assistance to domestic industries. This assistance may be in the form of tax-breaks, grants, low-interest loans, etc. The aim is to stimulate industrial development in selected sectors, create employment, or to increase the relative advantage of the chosen industry in the global markets.

Subsidies may also be directed to foreign companies to encourage direct foreign investments in the country, as is the case of telecommunications in Asia (*Economist Intelligence Unit* 1999). The effect of these subsidies is to reduce production costs by exempting foreign components from tariffs, domestic components from taxes, or eliminating taxes from export earnings.

The policy of subsidising business firms is consistent with the strategic trade theory that focuses on helping those industries that are in a position to gain a competitive advantage through enough economy of scales in a market that is capable of sustaining only a few firms. The point to keep in mind with subsidies is that they are paid for by taxes and it is difficult to assess when the cost of subsidies exceeds their benefits.

The World Trade Organisation, and its predecessor GATT, have strongly encouraged countries to levy tariffs on their imports rather than other types of non-tariff barriers. Most countries publish tariff schedules which are available to exporters. Today, most countries use the Harmonised Tariff Schedule (HTS) that is a detailed classification of products. The HTS allows for the use of the same number regardless of whether the products are imported or exported, and goes into great detail in classifying products. For the exporter, the key is to classify the product with the appropriate tariff classification.

Consequences of protectionism

Government intervention in trade and investments in the form of protectionist policies has its price both monetarily and socially. First, in terms of monetary consequences, protectionism has to be paid for by somebody. Normally, taxpayers pay the price of subsidies and other similar measures. Consumers also pay higher prices for products that bear high tariff classifications, additional fees, or have a number of taxes through the importation process.

The social costs of protectionism are numerous. We examine only a few of them. First, when foreign competition is discouraged or just eliminated from the scene, consumers are left with few choices. Second, when nations combine the absence of foreign competition and government protection, business firms then do not have the pressing need to turn out products that are efficient, high quality, or to continue improving them.

Third, local manufacturers also suffer because of the limited number of suppliers they can choose from, rather than having access to a wide range of suppliers from around the world. Fourth, there is the danger of other governments retaliating against the nation that resorts to protectionist trade policies in manners that will affect not only the balance of payments, but also create politically hard feelings. Finally, the aftermath of any trade retaliation is that the societies from the disputing countries are the true victims of protectionism. As a consequence, the consumers pay higher prices, have less choices among products, have limited amounts of products, and have limited quality or products' improvement.

Chapter summary

The principal responsibility of governments is the welfare and protection of their nations. To this end, governments enact policies related to international trade that will be consistent to their economic strategic plans for development and growth. By nature, these policies are border bound. That is, the emphasis is on the nation. Often, these domestic policies, such as those concerning the development of certain industries or protection of jobs, are in conflict with other trading partners' policies. Sometimes these conflicts are resolved through the necessary adjustments on the measures taken. Other times, the disputes are resolved through the World Trade Organisation. The WTO is the natural outgrowth of GATT. Today, the WTO is the agency that regulates, monitors and legislates over international trade in order to help trade flow as freely as possible by removing the obstacles to free trade. These obstacles are the policies taken by individual governments to protect their domestic markets from foreign imports by enacting a series of measures that will effectively limit the free flow of goods and services into their territory.

Discussion questions

1 Discuss the political motivations for government intervention in international trade.
2 Discuss why the maintenance of employment is not an accepted reason for government intervention in trade.
3 Discuss why a nation's trade policies can sometimes be in conflict with global trade regulations, especially the role of the World Trade Organisation.
4 Explain the differences between tariff and non-tariff barriers of trade.
5 Discuss the role of voluntary export restrictions in international trade.

Closing Case Study:
Global strategies: are they possible?

Defining global strategies

Global strategies is a term that was coined about 20 years ago and it is still not quite clear what is meant by it. Sometimes companies that have a presence in several countries speak of their global strategies. However, there is a difference between global strategy and multidomestic strategy that is easy to confuse. Business firms apply multidomestic strategy when they treat each country as a separate market. What they do in one country does not carry over to the others. Global strategy, on the other hand, is applied by those business firms – large or small – that can do two things:

1 They can compete in all the markets that they choose to enter.
2 They can access and mobilise their worldwide resources – these resources are in the form of capital, products, technologies, know-how, labour, etc., – to the extent that is needed to develop new markets or maintain their existing markets.

To be global companies, these business firms must have the following characteristics in order to be considered truly global: first, they should have standardised products and apply the same marketing mix around the world – the more global a company is, the more homogeneous its core products and marketing mix tend to be. Second, they should be able and willing not only to outsource components, but capital, technologies, and know-how from around the world. The more global a company is, the less nationalistic it will be in terms of acquiring resources from its home country or selected countries. It will recognise opportunities for acquiring resources from anywhere in the world based on their availability, quality, and cost-efficiency. Third, they must internationalise their core competencies and functions. Fourth, global companies need to generate enough volume of sales to be able to cover the costs of their worldwide operations, mobilisation of resources, and their marketing mix strategies.

But we still have border bound countries!

The key issue with global strategies is that the world is still composed of independent countries with their own policies in trade and investments, and their own priorities of growth, labour protection, economic development, industrialisation,

▶

etc. All these policies mean that their governments intervene in the cross-border trade of goods and services. On the one hand, global companies enjoy their economies of scale in production, R&D, etc. These global firms also enjoy the advances in communications and transportation in the modern world. However, these firms still have to contend with border-bound trade policies enacted by the countries where these companies market their products. These issues force global companies to acknowledge the uniqueness of each market, not only in its cultural, social and economic differences, but also in terms of trade and investment regulations.

These government regulations can work as an advantage or as a disadvantage for global companies. One example in which they worked as an advantage is the semiconductor industry, where most domestic and foreign companies had located their operations in the Silicon Valley in the United States. They took advantage of the American government's strategic plan for developing this particular industry. To this end, various types of government incentives are granted to companies who establish their operations in this region.

Government regulations may also work as a disadvantage for the global firm. The experience of Kodak in Japan serves as a case in point. Kodak was trying to achieve a significant market share in Japan, only to see its efforts being limited by market barriers. Some of these market barriers were wholesale arrangements that favoured Fuji, the Japanese film-maker, allowing it in this way to secure the domestic market not only by restricting sales, but also by restricting strategies regarding price competition for Kodak.

And what about the subsidiaries?

Another issue that complicates the existence of these global strategies is the functions and roles of the subsidiaries. They are located in the line of fire. They know the market, its conditions and its characteristics. Should the subsidiaries be allowed to modify the products to meet the needs and wants of their market? Should the subsidiaries be allowed to access the local technologies and know-how to modify the products so as to promote new product development? Such decisions are made by some companies that allow their subsidiaries overseas to modify their products. In this manner, not only do they develop new products, but they simplify the entry into new markets. When the subsidiary is allowed to modify the product because of the sociocultural characteristics of the market, legal or regulatory limitations, or any other reason, the global strategies of the parent company then become less relevant as the local strategies become more important.

Subsidiaries can also circumvent some of the trade barriers in their own country because they can be viewed as domestic companies. Subsidiaries can also facilitate the entry into other markets where quotas, standards or other barriers are not so severe for the subsidiary's country as they would be for the parent company's country. Sometimes the entry into a new market by a subsidiary is not as threatening for the local competition as for the parent company who is the one coming in full force. When the threat of a multinational firm is seen as too big to deal with, local manufacturers will request their government to enact protectionist policies. Then, global strategies are again reduced to what a global firm can and cannot do.

In a global firm, where did you say the decision is made?

Global business firms find they have a number of global, regional or local decisions to make. There is a need for the integration of the organisational structure, a 'greater view' of the company's mission and goals. Functions such as finance and R&D need to be made at global level. At regional level, global firms found that functions such as marketing and sometimes manufacturing are better performed closer to the market. Finally, at local level, there are decisions regarding channels of distribution, local regulations and the sociocultural characteristics of the individual markets.

All these different levels of decisions produce a network of interrelated companies. Some of these companies are internal (subsidiaries) and others are external (suppliers and channels) to the global firms. This complex network of different players in many cases limits the influence and authority of the parent company, while at the same time increasing the need for co-ordination and for a coherent organisational culture, values, missions and goals.

Source: Adapted from Cateora and Graham (1999).

Questions

1 Discuss the different points made in the case in relation to the feasibility of 'true global strategy'.
2 How important are the four features that a global business firm must have in order to be called a global company?
3 Select a global company and evaluate how much of its strategy is global, regional or local. Discuss the reasons why you think that the business firm you selected is a global company.
4 Identify three or four countries where the company that you selected markets its products. Discuss the different trade barriers it contends with, and how the company has to change its strategies to be able to enter those countries.

Further reading

Baldwin, R.E. (1989) *Trade Policy in a Changing World Economy*, Chicago: University of Chicago Press. New issues in trade policies have emerged as the political response to trade deficits and to the belief of unfair trade by trade partners. This book contains a series of essays that are very relevant to the issues discussed during the GATT's Uruguay Round concerning the reduction of trade barriers.

O'Brien, R. (1997) *Subsidy Regulations and State Transformation in North America, the GATT, and the EU*, International Political Economy Series New York: St Martins Printing. The author focuses on the US and Canada and how difficult it has been to reach an agreement on the appropriate role of government in the economy. The author analyses the various subsidy arrangements agreed by the EU and during the GATT's Uruguay Round. Issues analysed are agriculture, aerospace, regional development and culture.

Sanderson, F.H. (1990) *Agricultural Protectionism in the Industrialized World*, New Brunswick, NJ: Resources for the Future. This book analyses the agricultural policies of the United States, the EU, Canada, Japan, Australia and New Zealand. It discusses the future trends of agricultural trade and the costs of protectionist policies in place today. The author projects the differences that would exist if the world had free trade in agricultural products.

References

Cateora P. and Graham, J. (1999) *International Marketing*, New York: Irwin/McGraw Hill.

Crossborders Monitor (1996) Chile, 4 September: 2.

Economist Intelligence Unit (1999) Communication trends in Asia: talk is cheap, 7 March.

Graham T. (1983) Global trade: war and peace, *Foreign Policy* 50 (Spring): 124–7.

Griffin, R.W., and Pustay, M.W. (1999) *International Business. A Managerial Perspective*. 2nd edn, New York. Addison-Wesley.

Hill, C. (1998) *International Business*, New York: Irwin/McGraw Hill.

Krugman, P., and Smith, A. (eds) (1994) *Empirical Studies of Strategic Trade Policy*, Chicago: The University of Chicago Press.

Lieberman, M., and Montgomery D. (1988) First mover advantages, *Strategic Management Journal* 9 (Special Issue, Summer): 41–58.

Magnier, M. (1989) Blockades to food exports hide behind invisible shields, *The Journal of Commerce*, 18 September.

Ohmae, K. (1990) *The Borderless World*, New York: Harper Collins.

Porter, M. (1990) *The Competitive Advantage of Nations*, New York: The Free Press.

Tayeb, M. (1997) *The Global Business Environment. An Introduction*, London: Sage Publications.

The New York Times (1999) Mystery of global spending: where the money went? 27 February.

The New York Times (1999) US raises tariffs for luxury goods, 4 March.

www.wto.org/about/org/, February. 1999

CHAPTER 12

National Institutions and Resources

Monir Tayeb

Learning objectives

By the end of this chapter you will:

■ know about major national institutions which constitute a society as a coherent and consistent entity

■ have an understanding of the significant role these institutions play in shaping the character of a society at any given time

■ know about the differences that exist among various countries around the world regarding their national institutions

■ be able to analyse the implications of these institutional differences for organisations in general and for international firms in particular.

Opening Case Study:
Singapore government's grip on society loosens slightly

Having once faced political threat from an opposition that voiced its dissatisfaction through Chinese travelling theatre, it clearly was not easy for Singapore to decide to permit street actors and musicians. But in the past year, as the authorities made a conscious effort to find new ways to make the city state more enticing to both foreigners and locals, Singapore announced that busking would be permitted – under certain conditions and in specific places.

To outsiders the decision seemed a small one. But to Singaporeans it was a prime example of how the authorities are trying, ever so carefully, to loosen their grip on society without losing their tight hold on political control. And for a growing number of Singaporeans who have travelled, been educated or lived abroad, and in those places experienced freedoms unheard of at home, it is most welcome.

▷

Many in their twenties, especially the women who do not undergo the intense two years of national military service that instill in men the importance of being part of a larger nation, complain that Singapore is stifling and believe incremental changes such as those instituted to date will never be enough. They loathe a system they complain quashes political dissent, bars satellite television, censors the internet, controls local media and constantly pressures them to buy into Singapore's material dream, content to live in a government-subsidised flat, get married and have children.

Singapore's most exploratory theatre, TheatreWorks, probed some of these feelings in a play called *Descendants of the Eunuch Admiral,* which paralleled the castration of ancient China's eunuchs with that endured by Singaporean yuppies as they climb the corporate ladder society lifts up to them. This, after all, is the home of the yuppie rallying cry, the four Cs: condoms, cash, cars and credit cards. 'It's a country that encourages that. You tend to lose sight of things that are intangible and things having to do with your soul,' says Tay Tong, TheatreWorks' general manager. 'The government saw that as becoming a predominant factor, so much so that they have come out with committees and sub-committees to deal with the betterment of society.' That in turn has led to the decision to turn Singapore into a regional arts hub.

Many may have difficulty picturing Singapore as a hotbed of bohemian abandon in a country where selling chewing gum is illegal because it sullies the sidewalks. George Yeo, minister for information and the arts, admits there is 'a constant tension' in Singapore between the desire to retain the youth and draw in foreigners from what he considers 'the ocean' while still maintaining the uniqueness of the city state's 'lagoon'. He puts it this way: 'The environment in the lagoon must always be different from the ocean. Then we have our own identity. Then we have our usefulness to the rest of the world ... It means everyday worrying about what's coming in and what's going out.'

The authorities do not believe they must entirely liberalise society to have the type of flourishing arts centre that will continue to entice people into the lagoon. They are focusing first on developing museums, building theatres, launching an arts radio station, hosting an annual arts festival.

Some of the results in the Singapore Art Museum already show a tolerance for questioning society. One piece that stands out attacks the oppression of women in patriarchal communities, comparing the pain of women who bound their feet in nineteenth century China with those today who bind their torsos to conform to society's image of feminine beauty.

But there are clearly areas that are out of bounds for Singaporean artists and it comes across most clearly on stage. The Boom Boom room, which is billed as satirical theatre, is overwhelmingly adolescent. Its shows touch on sexual taboos such as cross-dressing, and appear to snigger at national service in a dance of navy men in torn shirts, but stay quite clear of anything more controversial.

Artists say the authorities consider much to do with race, religion, politics and sex off-limits. Government censors recently provoked controversy by cutting a tame nude scene from the Hollywood film *Titanic* though, interestingly enough, let minutes of Demi Moore's breasts slip by in the film *Striptease.*

Source: *Financial Times* CD-ROM, 1 January–31 December 1998.

Introduction

Modern complex societies, unlike their relatively simple primitive ancestors, are divided into various institutions and organisations, as shown in Table 12.1, each of which contributes to the running of their affairs. Economic, political, educational, cultural and similar functions are performed either separately or in combination with others by various institutions. Some of these institutions are purely internal and some are supernational and external to the society, such as regional and global institutions discussed in Chapter 3. These take on board some of the functions of the member countries and influence the shape and running of some of their internal affairs.

Table 12.1 Major national institutions

Institutions	Examples
Education	Kindergartens, primary and secondary schools, colleges of further education, universities
Culture and the arts	Arts councils, museums, festivals, public libraries
Mass-communication media	Radio, television, press (conventional and on-line)
Political economy	Trade unions, political parties, pressure groups
Community and wildlife	Charities, community halls and clubs
Accounting practices	Financial accounting, management accounting
Communication infrastructure	Roads, railways, airports, ports, telecommunications
Financial infrastructure	Stock and capital markets, banks, insurance houses, building societies
Legal system	Employment and business laws and regulations
National and local security	Armed forces, police, intelligence services
Economy	Predominantly rural, predominantly industrial, capitalist, socialist, protectionist, liberal
Social structure	Class, caste
Taxation	Tax as source of revenue, tax as means of wealth redistribution

National institutions and their implications for business

Before discussing the most significant institutions among those listed in Table 12.1, it should be noted that these institutions strongly bear the hallmark of the national culture of the country in which they are situated. If they are home-grown, the goals they pursue and the way in which they go about performing their functions are ultimately rooted in that culture. If they are of foreign origins and have been imported by or imposed on the country, they usually tend to adapt to the host culture. This is so because people's values, attitudes, preferences and tastes filter through national institutions not only as citizens, founders, managers, employees and members, but also as their customers, clients and audiences.

Take political systems, for example. The American republican model, with an elected president and members of the Congress and the Senate, and elaborate checks and balances, remains largely true to its founders' ideals in the US. But the same model, imitated by many other countries of non-Western origins, has lost much of its character, to the extent that in some cases, the president is not elected any more and/or remains in office for life. The parliament, if it does exist, is either packed with the president's nominees and appointees or is an elected body with virtually no power to act as a checks-and-balances mechanism. If you examine each case carefully you will find the traces of the national culture, a much more stable and enduring factor, at the root of the character of the relatively younger imported political system.

In the UK, to give another example of another institution, a few daily tabloid newspapers print, usually on their page three, pictures of bare-bosomed young women. Can you imagine such pictures appearing in the Saudi Arabian press? This is not because the feminist and moralist groups and the general public in Britain approve of such pictures, but may be because they have a strong belief in the freedom of expression, and consider such pictures as a harmless price to pay for its safeguard. By contrast, in Saudi Arabia, where people's way of life and society as a whole are dominated by their religion, Islam, and the media are tightly controlled by the central government, the contents of their newspapers conform to the rules of Islam and the regulations set by the political elite.

However, some of the national institutions shown in Table 12.1 develop to some extent their own culture, preferences and priorities somewhat different from, but not incompatible with, that of the national culture as a whole. In other words, national culture should not be conceived of as a catch-all, all-encompassing envelope embracing everything and everybody within its reach.

Take France and its economic policies as an example. The country's economic system is a capitalist one, but under a Gaullist government, such as that headed by Alain Juppé, it became relatively more pro-market with less emphasis on government intervention, compared to a socialist administration, with a more active role for the government, such as the one formed by Lionel Jospin who succeeded him in the 1997 General Election – same country, same national culture, but two different economic policies based on two different philosophies and principles.

Similar contrasts of political and economic and indeed other social policies could be observed under Binyamin Netanyahu (Liqud) and Shimon Perez (Labour) in Israel, Ronald Reagan (Republican) and Jimmy Carter (Democrat) in the US, Margaret Thatcher (Conservative) and James Callaghan (Labour) in the UK.

These social institutions undergo many changes over time with respect to their policies, priorities and the ways in which they are organised. These changes could be caused by a change of government, through elections or through more drastic means such as *coups d'état* and revolutions. The changes also could come about because of wider regional and global events to which almost all modern societies are increasingly exposed. Technological breakthroughs, for instance, have introduced to greater or lesser extent new methods of teaching and learning using videos, personal computers and Internet facilities into many educational establishments around the world.

A review of the literature in different disciplines shows that nations are different from one another in the way in which they set priorities for their social institutions and run their affairs. The following pages discuss some of these differences and explore their implications for business organisations.

Education

The major aspects of educational systems in which we can observe variations across nations are macro- and micro-level priorities, teaching and learning practices, and management and ownership.

At the macro level, some nations emphasise the importance of free and universal schooling for their young in order to equip them with a firm foundation to start a vocation or go on to higher education, which may not necessarily be free. In many cases students are expected to find ways of financing their higher education, such as part-time jobs, deferred-payment loans, sponsorship, scholarship and parental assistance. Many South-East Asian countries, New Zealand and recently the UK are among the nations that have adopted policies along these lines. The top priority in these cases is to ensure the maximum possible literacy rate for the population as a whole. Policies of this kind mean that as far as business organisations are concerned, the workforce at all levels has a minimum standard of education, if not higher for some at least. This obviously enhances the company's overall skill levels and competencies.

There are some countries, like India, which are top heavy, so to speak: they have an excellent university-level educational system, but poorly maintained and resourced primary and secondary level education. Here the literacy rate is rather low and managers are handicapped by a shortage of skilled workers at shop-floor levels. Training these employees to become operators of sophisticated machinery and computerised equipment could be a tall order for many, especially small- and medium-sized firms.

At the micro level, that is the educational establishments, there could also be differences in priorities among nations. In some countries, like Germany's vocational education, apprenticeship and technical courses are highly valued, and employees with engineering degrees are well remunerated. Doing things by hand is as good as if not better than doing things by brains. By contrast, in the UK, traditionally the reverse has been the case. The top two universities, Oxford and Cambridge, dating back a few centuries, dominate major political and managerial positions, whose graduates have always prided themselves in being excellent at the arts, literature, philosophy and pure sciences. Courses in business and management for instance are relatively new in these establishment and their beginnings go back to the 1960s. For many years it was left to polytechnics (recently reorganised as universities) and the so-called red-brick universities with specialist courses in technological and engineering courses to train the bulk of the university educated workforce for the manufacturing sector. Most of these establishments were created in the second half of the mid-nineteenth and twentieth centuries.

Another aspect of education is learning and teaching practices. In some countries teaching is student-centred: that is students are actively involved in the learning and teaching process, through experimentation, trial and error, participation in class discussions and self-directed small group activities, and practical as well as theoretical learning. Students are generally encouraged to challenge, to explore, to criticise, to analyse, to make mistakes and to learn from mistakes in a constructive manner. In some countries, by contrast, teaching is a one-way activity, performed by the teacher, learning is a passive activity, and students are expected to accept facts as imparted in lectures and read in textbooks.

There are a whole range of forms on an imaginary continuum between these two extreme teaching styles, and in any given country a combination of them could exist. But what is important to note is that in some countries the overwhelming proportion of educational establishments may be closer to one end and in others closer to the other end of the continuum.

For instance, as Sayigh (1982) points out, education in Arab countries has little relevance to the needs and problems of society and the economy, and is not primarily of the problem-solving type. The system essentially prepares individuals for their successful upgrading in their attempt to climb the economic and social ladder, and is minimally oriented to the implanting of the notions of public service in Arab youth. As far as methodology is concerned, education still fails to provide sufficient scope for innovation and intellectual stimulation, and concentrates instead on cramming the students' memories with information. Also, there is insufficient practical work and experimentation in workshops, classrooms and laboratories. Only a small proportion of secondary education is actually in technical training.

Finally, although in many countries state- and privately-owned and managed educational establishments at all levels exist side by side, the degree to which the state determines and controls the content of the curricula varies from country to country. In some the central government sets minimum requirements to ensure that all students are taught certain courses necessary for their future careers; some leave it totally to the schools or local educational authorities to decide their curriculum; in some others, schools and other educational establishments are controlled by the political elite to ensure that the 'party line' is followed. In such cases certain courses that oppose the current political ideology may never be taught; other courses are monitored closely, censored and even deliberately distorted. Some of the ex-communist countries are examples of this sort of educational policies.

Both macro- and micro-level educational policies determine to a large extent the level of technological advancement as well as the quality of a country's workforce. A quick look at the composition of the world shows a wide range from highly advanced nations such as Japan, Germany, France, to middle-of-the-road countries, such as Brazil and Turkey, to certain destitute African nations whom most of the advances of the twentieth century have passed by. The discussion regarding the complex causes of these variations is beyond the scope of this chapter. But the implications of these variations for business organisations are obvious.

Political economic systems and the role of state

Nations are different from one another in the extent to which their citizens participate in the political process. Similarly, the extent to which governments intervene in the private and public life of citizens, from the economy and trade to artistic activities and individual rights and responsibilities, varies across the world. We could draw the following continuum along which various nations could be located.

Dictatorship	Democracy
Strong central government	Weak central government

The picture, however, is more complicated than this. For instance, China's political system is based on a strong central government and there is no provision for a multiparty parliamentary system or for the citizens' freedom of expression, of the kind prevalent in Western democracies. However, as far as the economy and certain business activities are concerned there are certain regions which are practically run on a capitalistic, market-oriented model. Moreover, Hong Kong, which was returned to China in 1997, has been more or less guaranteed for at least 50 years to enjoy a special status and to maintain its free-enterprise, *laissez-faire* economic structure.

In India, by contrast, the political regime is, in principle, a democracy, even though in practice there are many flaws in the system which compares it unfavourably with, say, Western European and North American democracies. The economy, on the other hand, is run largely on a protectionist principle, even though a change of direction in trade policies started in the early 1990s. Privatisation of state-owned enterprises, removal of trade restrictions, and exposure of domestic firms to competition from foreign firms are gradually taking place. However, the speed of the reform and its future are uncertain (*The Economist*, 7 March 1998).

Everywhere, with a few notable exceptions, the general trend of economic and trade policies in the last two decades of the twentieth century has been towards liberalisation, deregulation, privatisation and 'small government', a trend which is set to continue into the twenty-first century.

Infrastructure

A country's infrastructure, such as roads, water supply, railways, airports, ports, telecommunications and energy resources (renewable, nuclear and fossil fuels) are important factors that enhance or hinder the smooth and efficient running of organisations operating within its boundaries. There is nothing more frustrating for managers, and indeed other citizens, if they cannot communicate properly with their partners, suppliers and a host of other individuals and organisations. Fax machines, mobile phones, teleconferencing, and e-mail and Internet facilities are today essential tools to help people perform their tasks.

However, the spread and use of these facilities vary from country to country. Obviously the more technologically advanced a nation is the more it is likely that a vast majority of its citizens have some if not all of these facilities at their disposal. But in certain countries political considerations may limit the use of such facilities, regardless of their technological capabilities. Strict allocation and installation policies and procedures, interception and monitoring of telephone, Internet, e-mail and fax communications by some governments are not at all uncommon.

Similar points can be made about other mass-communication media, such as press, radio and television. There are countries where these media are either owned by the state or their editorial policies are heavily controlled by it. There are those in which people can broadcast and publish anything they like so long as they do not libel others or infringe people's privacy. In modern times, where satellites can beam any radio or television programmes into any home, the state's ability to control such media is being challenged but, as was mentioned earlier, it has not been eliminated. Recently, a media firm which provides satellite television services to, among other nations, an Asian country, cancelled its contract with a world-class broadcasting corporation. It was allegedly because the corporation's news programmes, which followed its tradition of impartiality and of telling the truth, were not welcomed by the officials of the host country.

Exhibit 12.1 Media: striking fear in political hearts

How, in any free society, do you determine whether the press is doing a decent job? Doubtless media pundits will come up with various criteria, all of them wise and valid.

The pundits may not give the Indian press a clean bill of health, but they will have to concede that after 50 years of independence it has one big achievement to its credit: it has managed to strike fear in the heart of politicians.

Recently, I met a middle-rank Congress politician with a legendary reputation for wheeler-dealing and financial corruption. He was not a happy man. 'These days, when I go to the toilet I look behind the flush to see if some journalist is waiting to trap me.' (This is expressed much more colourfully in Hindi.) There was, he said, no future in India for a professional politician engaged in making 'a little money on the side' while toiling for the masses.

For at least three decades after independence those who ruled India managed to manipulate the press. It was generally assumed that these gentlemen – and a few ladies – were of unimpeachable integrity and dedicated to serving the people. As a result, most of their shenanigans went unreported.

Mrs Indira Gandhi's brief flirtation with totalitarianism in 1975 opened a can of worms, and since then investigative journalism, concentrating largely on public men with itchy fingers, has developed and matured. It is now an essential component of the Indian press.

In spite of some egregious reporting errors, investigative journalism enjoys huge credibility with the reading public. 'When a paper tells me a politician is corrupt, and the politician tells me he is innocent, my first instinct is to believe the paper,' a retired army general said. He reflects the national mood.

Obviously, there are long-term dangers. Note has to be taken of the destructive mood that has taken hold of the republic: a conviction that all politicians in the country are corrupt and incompetent. This mood always existed, but was tempered by moderation and balance. Now – especially in the past two years – with many politicians having to answer charges ranging from subversion and criminal conspiracy to harbouring gangsters, and others in jail or on bail, cynicism has settled with certitude.

Two pillars of Indian democracy – the courts and the press – have played a decisive role in establishing the 'anti-politician' mood in the country. They have frequently worked in tandem and worked very effectively. Not surprisingly, opinion polls show that judges and journalists are held in high esteem, while politicians are at the bottom of the ladder, just above smugglers and pimps. Clearly, if this mood persisted the functioning of the democracy would be endangered. But, in the short term, it is not such a bad thing that politicians should look warily before they enter their bathrooms.

There was much celebration in the country when Mr I.K. Gujral was appointed Prime Minister. Although he had no grassroots support, his arrival was welcomed because he was seen to be 'clean'.

It would be wrong to believe that the press has purged the country of corrupt politicians, but it has instilled sufficient fear to make habitual offenders think twice. Not only have the offenders become more circumspect, but some have come to the conclusion that the increased possibility of exposure makes wrong-doing too risky.

The cleansing of Indian public life will, no doubt, be a long and drawn-out affair, but the process has started – and is irreversible. The new print press activism has meant that today the profession is much more self-assured. Government largesse – including newsprint quotas and official advertisements – no longer decide the destiny of publications. The consumer is king, and cut-throat competition – Delhi alone has more than a dozen English broadsheet dailies – keeps editors and managers on their toes.

Alas, savage price wars and the downgrading of journalists' status has crept in. Proprietors and managers frequently make senior editorial appointments and take editorial decisions without consulting editors.

In the past, the Indian print media produced a succession of strong editors who stood up to both governments and owners. Many of these have now either left the profession or succumbed to a new culture.

In spite of turbulence and tension, the media are generally healthy. Print and television have learned to co-exist: the latest figures show that 62 per cent of advertising expenditure is in print. Above all, the print media and particularly daily newspapers enjoy high credibility. One reason for this is the lack of any tabloid culture. The press may be solemn, over-politicised, ponderous and longwinded, but is relatively free from triviality, sleaze and celebrity muck-raking. It is an asset not to be squandered.

Source: *The Financial Times* website (1997).

Legal, financial and distribution infrastructure are also important business facilitators. Thomas (1994), comparing China and India as hosts to foreign direct investment, makes the following observations in this regard:

compared to India there are some serious limitations about China which should cause concern to discerning foreign investors. There is no legal system or independent judiciary, and it will take another generation to create them. The whole financial system including banks, financial institutions and stock market is yet to be organised. A commercial, privately operated wholesale and retail distribution system independent of the old party network has yet to evolve. As a result, working capital tied up in stocks under distribution is very high. India also has a very well-established and very efficient private trader-based distribution system. (p. 39)

Business laws, rules and regulations

Companies like individuals are subject to the laws of the country in which they operate, and all nations regulate work to some degree. Latin American and socialist countries have explicitly incorporated labour provisions in their national constitutions.

There are laws that govern general operational aspects of a company, such as where and how to register as a business concern, permission and license requirements for foreign firms to operate within their jurisdiction. Then there are rules pertaining to more specific aspects, such as off-shore investment, impact on the environment, preparation and disclosure of financial accounts, corporate taxation, employees rights and pension provisions. In the case of foreign companies, in addition to these, there could be further rules and regulations with regard to such matters as the amount of assets and shares they may own and the proportion of the profit they would be allowed to repatriate.

In some countries the government might set out the broad boundaries and limits beyond which firms are not allowed to operate, but within which they can do what their business and market imperatives require them to do. In some others these rules are quite tight and govern minute details of strategic and operational aspects of business firms, especially those of foreign origins.

Sometimes rules and regulations are used as tools to implement governments' trade and industrial policies. For instance, if a country wishes to encourage inward investment it will make it easier for foreign firms and individuals to bring in their capital and to start up a business either on their own or in partnership with local firms. By contrast, if the government wishes to curtail and deter foreign investment, without appearing overtly to do so, it could create a web of red-tape and bureaucratic procedures the unravelling of which might take months if not in some cases years before a permission to operate is granted to a foreign firm.

Business laws could also cover specific internal organisation activities such as human resource management (HRM) and health and safety. Maternity and paternity leave, statutory minimum wage, physical working conditions, protection of employees against dust and noise pollution, pension and medical provisions, and childcare facilities are examples of areas which in various countries are governed by laws and regulations.

Business laws and regulations can sometimes create confusion and difficulties, particularly for multinational firms. For instance, the Japanese practice of forcing older managers into 'voluntary' retirement by withholding their work assignments (Namiki and Sethi 1988) would violate the Age Discrimination in Employment Act if done in the US. Quality circles, a well-known vehicle for participatory decision making in Japan, would be illegal in the US in unionised settings if the bargaining agent objected to their implementation (Sockell 1984).

The laws regulating HRM practices are sometimes tied in with other government policies and programmes. In some developing countries HRM must be in line with the national development plans that have been prepared by planning authorities. The Ecuadorian Development Plan, for instance, endorses the idea of industry-wide collective bargaining. In Japan, HRM practices are scrutinised in terms of their ability to generate long-term comparative advantage. In France HRM practices reinforce protectionism or neo-mercantilism. In Sweden and The Netherlands, they enhance social welfare and in the US they comply with market regulation (Johnson 1985).

Accounting practices

Nations differ from one another in the way in which they regulate the financial affairs of the companies, both domestic and foreign, which operate within their territories. This difference in a way reflects not only the macro-level requirements but also the companies' needs and preferences. Rules governing accounting practices are one of the tools employed for this purpose.

At the macro level some countries are only interested to receive tax revenues and therefore set out rules and regulations as to how companies should prepare their accounts in order to make it clear to the tax authorities how much profit they made in any given financial period. What the companies might want to do with their financial reports thereafter is up to them. In some countries companies are required, in addition to information needed by tax authorities, to give detailed accounts about their financial performance to their shareholders.

At the micro level, companies themselves might want to use their financial reports as a management-information tool, and therefore might employ management accounting as well as financial accounting.

As was mentioned earlier, at both macro and micro levels the choice of one option or the other is largely dictated by the countries' and companies' needs and preferences. For instance, in many developing countries, especially those that are predominantly agricultural, the level of economic activities may not have reached a point where the use of sophisticated and elaborate accounting practices is warranted. In such cases, it is mostly financial accounting, usually geared to satisfy the taxman's requirements, that various companies employ. Another function of financial accounting in such countries is to help the government in overall national economic planning. However, this latter function is not confined to developing countries alone. In some advanced countries, like France and Sweden, national government plays an active part in the management of the country's resources, and business enterprises are expected to accomplish the government's policies and macroeconomic plans. Governments also ensure that companies have adequate capital and would loan or even invest in them if necessary. Financial accounting in those countries is therefore oriented toward decision making by government planners. Firms follow uniform accounting procedures and reporting practices, which are aimed to facilitate better government decisions.

In many industrialised countries companies prefer to have management accounting as well, which helps them in their strategic planning and top-level managerial decision making. As regards the content of financial reports, in some countries like Germany and Japan public share ownership is limited and major investors and creditors are also members of the Board of Directors. Consequently, in such cases, those interested in detailed information are also closely involved in the running and monitoring of the company's financial affairs and do not need financial reports to tell them what is happening. By contrast, in countries like the US and the UK, where there is a widespread public shareholding, financial reports have to be detailed enough to give the necessary information to big and small investors alike.

For the multinational companies that have interests and operations around the world, some of the differences in accounting practices would make their tasks more complicated compared with their single-nation counterparts. For instance, they might have to prepare multiple financial reports not only to satisfy their respective host and home-countries' requirements but also to satisfy their own internal needs. There is also an additional complication in terms of the level and type of knowledge and training of the staff that they employ in various countries. Because the requirements and practices vary from one country to another, local accountants may have appropriate knowledge and skills as far as their own country is concerned, but which may not be of much use for certain other requirements as far as the multinational company is concerned. This means that the company needs to train their local employees to learn new sets of skills as well as holding on to their existing ones.

Exhibit 12.2 NCB auditors fear shareholders may sue

Century Audit, the accountants to Nippon Credit Bank (NCB), are conducting an internal inquiry into why their recent audits failed to spot that the bank was under-reporting its bad loans.

The inquiry marks an attempt by Century Audit to stave off growing government and shareholder criticism of its role in NCB's recent demise. The government recently announced it would nationalise NCB, and revealed that its bad and potentially bad loans were over Y3700bn ($32bn), compared with the previously published total of Y3200bn.

Century Audit's move comes as some Japanese accountants fear they could soon be forced to take greater responsibility for the shortcomings of Japanese bank accounting. In particular, there is growing concern that some could soon face shareholder lawsuits as bank reform gathers pace.

Japanese accountants have played a relatively toothless role in the country's financial sector, and thus escaped public criticism for the banks' bad loan problems. But shareholders at Yamaichi Securities, which collapsed last year, have recently sued the broker's auditors, Chuo Audit, for failing to reveal that Yamaichi was conducting tobashi, the practice of shuffling losses between accounts to hide them.

Hiromi Uda, spokesman for Century Audit, said the company was uncertain if it would be sued by shareholders. But he acknowledged Century had certified NCB's accounts and 'had not found problems at the bank'.

Century Audit operates in partnership with KPMG, the UK accountancy group. KPMG has refused to comment on the case.

Source: *Financial Times* CD-ROM, 1 January–31 December 1998.

Taxation policies

Taxation is another area in which countries differ from one another. Tax can be used as a means to redistribute wealth, or just to finance certain public services unattractive to the private sector, or to reduce, limit, or even eliminate pollution and other damages to the environment. Different nations place different degrees of emphasis on these or any other macro-level concerns when devising their taxation policies, which are in any case dynamic and change over time. There is, for instance, currently an emphasis on 'small government' in certain Western countries, notably the US and the UK. Here, in the past two decades or so, there has been a tendency to reduce direct income tax and to increase the indirect or value-added tax. The small government trend is also noticeable to a lesser or greater extent in many ex-socialist countries and some developing nations where it is being incorporated in their nascent open-door economic policies.

Membership of regional trade agreements also tend to entail certain broad taxation policies in common with other fellow member states. The European Union is a good example of such a regional agreement.

As a result of these variations in taxation policies among regions and countries, multinational companies face a myriad of rules and regulations across their subsidiaries, to which they have to adapt both at operational and strategic levels.

Table 12.2 shows some of the major areas of difference in legal, accounting and taxation policies and practices among nations.

Table 12.2 National differences in accounting practices, legal systems and taxation policies

Legal system

	Areas of difference and variation		
Source	Code law	Common law	
Authority	State/länder	National/federal government	Super-national, regional, global

Accounting practices

	Areas of difference and variation		
Type	Financial accounting	Management accounting	Both
Purpose	To inform shareholders	To determine taxes	Both
Legal requirement	Legalistic approach	Non-legalistic approach	
	Laws stipulate the minimum standard requirements	Laws establish the limits beyond which it is illegal to venture	
Dealing with inflation	Historic cost principle	Inflation accounting	
Degree of sophistication	Very sophisticated and elaborate, requires skilled accountants	Simple, suitable for nations with unsophisticated economy, shortage of skilled accountants	

Taxation

	Areas of difference and variation
Direct (income and corporate)	Rates, exemptions, flat-rates, progressive rates
Indirect (value–added)	Variable versus flat rates, exemptions
Geographical scope	Local, state/länder, national/federal

Trade unions and other pressure groups

Trade unions and all other similar groupings of people are generally formed to influence decisions made by people in a position of authority, either by direct participation or by indirect means such as lobbying the authorities and influencing citizens' behaviours and preferences. These institutions are fundamentally the product of cultures in which dissent and opposition are not only tolerated but also considered as necessary for the smooth running of societal and other forms of group activities.

An examination of the world scene shows that there are differences in the extent to which such groupings are accepted as a legitimate constituent part of society. We could imagine a continuum, at one end of which is a total absence of pressure groups of any sort, and at the other end a total freedom of expression and action by all sorts of groups. Along the continuum we could locate countries with various degrees of tolerance and acceptance of dissent: some would allow social and economic challenge dissent but not a political one, some curb cultural activities of certain types, some might allow pressure groups to exist but keep a close eye on them.

In the past few decades pressure groups such as those concerned with environmental issues have instigated significant changes in consumers' attitudes to various products and services from fur coats to mass-produced factory chickens, to processed foods with chemical additives and preservatives, to polluting means of transport, to waste management. These changes of attitudes have been noted by companies and gradually translated into 'environmentally friendly' products and services. The production processes have also undergone changes and there has been a general tendency to move from polluting technologies to less-damaging ones. This has to a large extent been because of the successful lobbying of politicians by environmental groups and the general increase of awareness of environmental issues.

Multinational companies, when locating their operations in various countries, have to take note of environmental rules and regulations of their host countries as well as the expectations of their customers in general.

Trade unions are an example of pressure groups that are primarily concerned with the internal organisational aspects of companies and the way in which it might affect their members, such as human resource management and working conditions. But strategic activities of the firm would also be of concern if they directly or indirectly affect their members. For instance, a company might decide to relocate its operations from one country to another, or to start up a joint venture with a foreign partner in its country, or to set up a subsidiary in a customer country instead of exporting to it. All these could have serious implications for employees in the sites which are at the 'giving' end: some might lose their jobs, for example, or be expected to go and live in a foreign country for a while.

The amount of power that trade unions have varies across both space and time. There were times, for instance, when British trade unions wielded an enormous amount of power both within organisations and outside through politicians. Since 1979, after a series of reforms and acts of parliament, they have lost much of their power and influence. Economic downturns and recessions, resulting in mass redundancies, have also played their part. Another factor was a change in the industrial composition of the country, in that there was a shift from heavy industries, such as coal mining and ship building, traditionally a 'bastion' of trade unionism, to new electronics and other high-technology industries with little or no strong trade union traditions.

There are countries where trade unions do not exist at all and are not allowed to operate even if some people would think them desirable. And there are those nations where trade unions exist only on paper; in practice there is not much they can do to influence decisions affecting their members.

In most countries where trade unions are active the unions and management are considered to be two different sides of the enterprise, each defending the interests of their respective side. Japan is an interesting case, though, where trade unions are plant-based. A company has its own unions to which both management and workforce belong and negotiations take place within a framework where the two-sidedness of the enterprise is underplayed. However, although we could trace the absence of horizontal grouping of Japanese culture in such arrangements, it is important not to overemphasise their cultural roots. The harmonious character of Japanese trade unions is not inherently a Japanese cultural phenomenon. Rather it is a consequence of the government's deliberate post-war policies. The industrial relations were completely restructured, through various laws, with the express aim of avoiding destructive disputes and conflicts and of building the economy after the devastation and ravages of the war (see also Child and Tayeb 1983).

Chapter summary

This chapter has described the characteristics of major societal institutions which make up the character of a nation and on which a coherent society is based. These institutions individually and collectively perform certain functions, be it economic, educational, political and administrative, without which modern societies are unable to survive. Some, like education, play a significant role in the early formative years of individuals, and some, like political systems and trade unions, reflect this learning experience as well as reinforcing it.

Nations were shown to differ from one another in the character of their institutions and in the way in which they organise them. Companies with business involvement in countries other than their own will have to deal with these institutional differences and respond to them without being incompatible with them but at the same time further their own business interests.

Discussion questions

1 In what respects might the educational system of a country be important to its business companies?
2 What are the major areas in which accounting practices in various countries might differ from one another?
3 What roles can and do governments play in the economy of their respective countries?

Closing Case Study:
An American company in Scotland

Multinationals have to handle differences in national industrial relations one way or another. Sometimes they can and do override host-country's traditions, if they do not meet with serious local opposition. But sometimes they have to adapt to local conditions if there is a strong resistance by the workforce to the parent company's pressures.

NCR Dundee is a subsidiary of the American company NCR Inc. and is a good example of such an adaptation to local conditions.

Scotland in general, and Dundee in particular, have a long history of strong unionism. Employees have traditionally voiced their views through their unions. A few years ago an American car-manufacturing company changed its plans to set up a plant in Scotland because it could not get the local workforce to agree not to join unions. The would-be employees were prepared to let the opportunity slip through their fingers rather than lose their right to unionisation.

Moreover, industrial relations there, much like elsewhere in the United Kingdom, is characterised by a 'them and us' attitude. A few years ago a subsidiary of another multinational company located in Dundee provided a sad example of how things might go badly wrong in this respect.

Industrial relations apart, the Scots are a people with a distinctive cultural heritage, characterised by, among others, individualism, yet caring for the community, austerity, hard work, integrity and honesty. They are, moreover, very proud of their Scottishness and wish to emphasise it *vis-à-vis* other nations, especially their neighbours, south of the border.

NCR Dundee managers, themselves Scots, are well aware of all this. They have devised their HRM policies and practices in such a way as to avoid conflicts with the culture of the country and be compatible with it. To this end they have sometimes changed or even ignored some of the parent-company's strategies. It has paid off handsomely in terms of both employee satisfaction and commitment and the overall financial performance of the company.

Traditionally, the City of Dundee in central Scotland has had a heavily unionised workforce. This tradition exists in NCR Dundee as well. Around 1200 of the employees are currently unionised and are represented by three unions.

The current trend among many companies, especially NCR Dundee's competitors, is to have single union representation or even to derecognise trade unions in their organisations. Certain HRM tools are utilised as a substitute for traditional employee representation through trade unions. And the parent company wanted the Scottish subsidiary to follow this trend, which was also a policy pursued in other parts of the company. The Dundee plant has not gone along with this trend because of a strong local feeling for their union tradition and heritage. Instead, the company has worked with the tradition.

The leadership of the company since the early 1980s has placed great emphasis on building trust between unions and management, and judging by the attitudes of the employees and the culture of the company it has succeeded in doing so.

The personal style of the management, which is reflected in the 'walk about' and 'open door' company culture, has created an atmosphere in which people of all levels talk and listen to each other directly about the issues that concern them.

The management, in conjunction with the unions, has since the early 1980s made a conscious effort to break down traditional barriers between manual workers and staff, which had in part been a result of the differentiated treatments of the two groups, especially with regard to working conditions. For instance, in the past if a clerk was off sick for two or three days she or he would get full pay, but a manual worker in the same circumstances would receive social security payment. If there was a heavy snowfall and people arrived late at work, members of staff would still get fully paid, but manual employees would be penalised. This sort of differentiation, along with the traditional staff employees –manual employees structure, has now disappeared.

Management is very good at communicating information to the employees, through such means as meetings, conferences, and internal-circuit television monitors placed in various locations in the company premises. The information given to employees is wide-ranging, from setting up a new plant overseas to new models to be produced, to assembly workers' workload, and to the day's visitors to the company. For example, when the company had decided to set up a manufacturing subsidiary in China, they organised a meeting in a special venue and took all the employees there and put them in the picture. The meeting was also intended to allay fears that some employees might have had about the project. In mass meetings such as this employees are encouraged to question directors and other senior managers who introduce the new plans.

On their part, the workforce, both unionised and non-unionised sections, have contributed greatly to the good relationship between management and employees. They have learned to adapt to the changes management has had to introduce in their working patterns and other aspects of the company in response to the market and business environment. Through consultation processes and meetings, they have come to recognise the benefits such changes might bring.

As a result, the fortunes of the company are perceived as those of the employees. The infamous 'them and us' attitude which seems to characterise industrial relations in many British companies does not exist in NCR Dundee. Here the image of the company, both inside and outside in the wider community, is that of a caring company. Many employees have been with the company for a long time and labour turnover is low relative to similar companies in the region.

Source: Tayeb (1998).

Questions

1 What are the major characteristics of Scottish industrial relations?
2 To what extent could the company potentially benefit or suffer from these characteristics?
3 How did the managers of this American subsidiary manage industrial relations within the company?
4 How successful were they in their efforts?

Further reading

Alhashim, D.D. (1992) *International Dimensions of Accounting,* 3rd edn, Boston: PWS-Kent Publishing Company. This book covers a wide range of accounting issues of relevance to multinational companies and has also a chapter which discusses succinctly financial regulations in 12 major established and emerging economies.

Whitley, R. (1992) *European Business Systems: Firms and Markets in their National Contexts,* London: Sage Publications. This edited book is a collection of papers that discuss the implications of various national institutions for business organisations.

Wilkinson, B. (1994) *Labour and Industry in the Asia Pacific: Lessons from the Newly Industrialized Countries,* Berlin: De Gruyter. This book looks at labour relations in various countries in the region and also discusses issues such as national and company-level policies for employees' training and skills.

References

Child, J. and Tayeb, M.H. (1983) Theoretical perspectives in cross-national organizational research, *International Studies of Management and Organization* XII: 23–70.

Johnson, C. (1985) The institutional foundations of Japanese industrial policies, *California Management Review* 27: 59–69.

Namiki, N. and Sethi, S.P. (1988) Japan, in R. Nath (ed.) *Comparative Management: A Regional View,* Cambridge, Mass: Ballinger, pp. 1–22.

Sayigh, Y (1982) *The Arab Economy: Past Performance and Future Prospects,* New York: Oxford University Press.

Sockell, D. (1984) The legality of employee-participation programs in unionised firms, *Industrial and Labour Relations Review* 19: 357–94.

Tayeb, M.H. (1998) Transfer of HRM policies and practices across cultures: an American company in Scotland, *International Journal of Human Resource Management* 9 (2): 332–58.

The Economist (1998) Indecisive India, 7 March, pp. 16–17.

The Financial Times website (1997) Media: Striking fear in political hearts, 1 August, written by Vinod Mehta, http://www.ft.com.

Thomas, R. (1994) Change in climate for foreign investment in India, *Columbia Journal of World Business* 29 (1): 33–40.

CHAPTER 13

National Cultural Characteristics

Monir Tayeb

Learning objectives

By the end of this chapter you will:

■ know what is meant by national culture

■ be familiar with the main natural causes and primary social institutions which together give birth to national culture

■ have learned about major cultural characteristics on which nations are known to differ from one another and which also have implications for business organisations

■ know about the various cultural models and dimensions proposed by scholars and be aware of the strengths and weaknesses of the most widely used of these models.

Opening Case Study:
A Christian secular Moslem

The Moslem month of pilgrimage approaches. The Hajj, that set of arcane rituals performed in the Saudi desert by a multitude of white-robed Moslems, is due to begin on 6 April.

It's probably fair to say that so irreducibly have Islam and Moslems become associated in the 'Western' mind with a whole set of negative characteristics – everything from terrorism to general backwardness – that to a modern European the spectacle may be rather threatening, like some atavistic tribal gathering.

I think that is a very real mistake. But here's the rub: the very reasons which I believe make the pilgrimage non-threatening to non-Moslems are the very same reasons that, to put it bluntly, make it a cause of considerable terror to me.

Mine is a kind of mirror image experience to that described by Edward Said and G. N. Giladi, the former a Palestinian Christian and the latter an Israeli Jew of Arab (Iraqi) extraction. Both have asserted that they are 'Arab Islamic' in culture.

I suppose that makes me 'Christian secular' in terms of culture and Moslem by confessional status. Maybe as a result of the minority status of Islam in Europe and the endless crises of the Moslem world, I had developed a view of Islam that was determinedly rationalist and profoundly ecumenical in outlook, and sincerely inoffensive to non-Moslems.

When I consulted various analyses of the meaning and purpose of pilgrimage in Islam, my problems only deepened. It seemed to me I was just exactly the Moslem to whom so many commentators referred when they talked about the Islam of empty ritual:

> Islamic scholarship, worthy of its title, has been at best crippled and made anaemic. With very few exceptions, the naïve are being led by the semi-ignorant charlatans posing as Islamic leaders. Yesterday's loyal servants of the enemy have changed their garb, memorised some verses and, *ad nauseum*, talk of an Islamic renaissance. Their slogans are hollow, their hearts weak and their souls have been sold to many gods.
>
> The 'Moslem Nation', while it speaks of Panummatic goals, is entangled in a myriad of internal contradictions. It has no identity, no selfhood, no oneness. It has wrapped the Koran in silk and shelved it. It has consigned the Prophet to remote memory and forgotten its covenant with God. With its head comfortable in the lap of a godless enchantress, in a state of materialistic trance, it daydreams of the Prophet's Madinah, long gone, or a future 'Islamopolis' still uncharted. It is stranded in a sea of hypocrisy in the depths of self-deception. (From Ali Shariati, *Hajj Reflections on its Rituals*, 1981, Abjad).

I think it is obvious why any one recognising themselves in such a description, as I do myself, would be upset and feel a deep need for spiritual renewal. But why should non-Moslems feel encouraged by the awesome spectacle of the Hajj?

Well, to be honest – and here I hope you don't feel cheated – my reasons are not particularly logical and are certainly untestable. Moslems do not go on the pilgrimage in the spirit of separation from the rest of humanity. Far from it. They see themselves as responding to God's invitation on behalf of humanity as a whole. They see the Hajj as confirming God's love for everyone, regardless.

Source: *Financial Times* CD-ROM, 1 January–31 December 1998.

Introduction

This chapter defines national culture and discusses some of its origins such as family, religion and ecological conditions. Examples from various countries will be given to demonstrate how various nations are different from one another in this respect. The discussion then concentrates on major characteristics that modern societies share in common but, again, to different degrees. We then look at some work-related attitudes and values which have on the one hand one foot in national culture and on the other influence people's behaviours and actions within their workplace.

What is culture?

Culture as a concept is very difficult to define. Virtually every author who has written on a topic that in some way deals with culture has given a different definition from those offered by others. Culture has been conceived of as a 'woolly concept' (Tayeb 1992), as a 'recognisable whole' (Tayeb 1988), as 'collective mental programming' (Hofstede 1980) and as 'total patterns of values, ideas, beliefs, customs, practices, techniques, institutions, objects and artefacts' (Komin 1994). We can liken it to the air: it is everywhere, we cannot see it but we know it is there, we breathe it and we cannot exist without it. Culture is not a biological necessity and we will not die if we are deprived of it. But it is rather improbable, if not impossible, for a person to be devoid of the traces of his or her cultural upbringing and separated from his or her cultural context.

As human beings we are social animals and as such we engage in social intercourse with one another in various capacities throughout our life. From our social surroundings we pick up clues and hints as to correct and acceptable behaviours in different circumstances; we learn how to cope with events and situations; we model our behaviour, initially at least, on those around us; we find workable solutions to the various problems we face in our day-to-day life. All these and many more build up to a set of coherent, time-honoured preferences, tastes, beliefs, values, assumptions and meanings that make up our cultural upbringing.

As a social construct culture has certain features that help identify it from other constructs, such as opinion. It is enduring and changes very little over time; it persists across generations. Let's consider an example. The English are known to be an individualistic nation, in the sense that they value their autonomy and individuality as opposed to being group-oriented and collectivist. Macfarlane (1978), a scholar of English culture, was able to trace the origins of individualism in England as far back as 1000 years ago, through an examination of extant documents in English parish churches and town halls which reflected social norms and practices of their time.

This long-held tradition of individualism is qualitatively different from, say, what English people think about homosexuals now as opposed to what their forebears thought only a generation ago. To give another example, not so long ago some of the famous English writer D.H. Lawrence's books were deemed by the court of law as corrupting and were burnt publicly. It would be inconceivable for any of his books to be treated like this now. English people's opinions and with it the law of their land have changed within a space of a generation or two. But their individualism, as a cultural characteristic, has survived intact over hundreds of years.

A further feature of culture is that its constituents are shared by the community, even though there are variations, and indeed sometimes deviations, at both personal and geographical levels. We know, for instance, that in general the Japanese are group-oriented; 'face' is the most important element in Chinese social psychology; an overwhelming majority of marriages are arranged in India by the relatives of the couples involved; the British are pragmatic; the Germans are good at organisation; and the Iranians express their emotions, such as anger and joy, in public as well as in private. I shall come back again to the issue of cultural characteristics attributed to various peoples later in the chapter.

A cultural community does not necessarily correspond with clear-cut political or geographical boundaries. The Chinese people, spread across a large number of central and South-East Asian countries, not to mention the immigrant communities in Europe, America, Australia and New Zealand, are a good example of a cross-border cultural community. The Kurdish people, who live in the border areas of Turkey, Iraq and Iran, are another example.

Muna (1980) writes of Arab nations thus:

> Nationals of these countries have a common bond: a strong feeling of identity and commonality. They share the same language, religion, and history. While there are elements of diversity in these three bases of identity, the feelings of brotherhood and common destiny among nationals of Arab countries make it possible in the final analysis to refer to them as Arabs. (p. 5).

The flip side of this proposition is that within a political or geographical entity there could be more than one cultural community, quite distinctive from one another but living side by side as citizens of the same nation. The Chinese, Muslims and Hindus of Singapore, the Irish, Scots, Welsh and English in the UK, and a whole range of cultural communities in the US, such as those of African, Hispanic, Irish and Jewish origins, are relevant examples here.

A final point to make in this regard is that culture in the sense discussed here also applies to other levels of society: industry, corporation, department/function, a class of university student attending an international business course in their final year. In fact, any two or more people who engage in and sustain a relationship over a length of time would develop their own culture with its own unique recognisable features.

This chapter, however, deals with a wider cultural grouping – that of national culture – as the context within which various organisations, including business companies, operate.

Origins of culture

We first encounter culture in our own upbringing and socialisation process at home, with our parents and siblings. Our parents, having learned cultural characteristics from theirs and other circles of relatives, friends and fellow country men and women, pass them on to us. The family unit is a powerful influential factor in our early formative years and leaves a long-lasting impression on us. Research evidence shows that these early imprints stay with us almost intact for life and we carry them as part of our general cultural baggage along with other 'items' we pick up later in life.

Table manners, relationships with others such as politeness and respect for elders, attitudes to others' property, emotional and physical spatial distance from others, and the expression of emotions are but a few examples of what we learn at home.

Another factor, permeating and shaping our early upbringing, is religion. Our parents may or may not be religious people. Later in life, we may or may not hold on to our religious beliefs, and God or other supernatural beings may or may not exist as far as we are concerned, but we are still influenced by religion. An average, 'normal' person does not go around routinely stealing or damaging other people's property, or killing others, or harming people deliberately, etc. The underlying values and assumptions forbidding these and other antisocial behaviours are not in the law of nature but can be traced to primitive rituals in pagan societies and in later civilisations to established religions. And we carry them in our cultural baggage whether or not we believe in the religions that advocate them.

Sherif (1975) identified nobility, patience, self-discipline, good appearance, abstinence, resolve, sincerity, truthfulness, servitude and trust as major Islamic values. Similarly, Endot (1995), following his review of the literature, identified a number of major Islamic values that would lead to a 'respectable nation': trust-worthiness, responsibility, sincerity, discipline, dedication, diligence, cleanliness, co-operation, good conduct, gratefulness and moderation.

Latifi (1997), in a study of traditional and modern Islamic texts, identified the following work-related characteristics, which she later found present among the Iranians who participated in her studies: equality before God; individual respon-sibility within a framework of co-operation with others; a view that people in positions of power should treat subordinates kindly, as if their subordinates are their brothers or sisters; fatalism but also a recognition of personal choice; and encouragement of consultation at all levels of decision making, from family to the wider community, to the country as a whole.

Other religions have similarly been argued to create and influence people's values and attitudes. Individualism, a preference for personal choice and auton-omy, and pursuance of personal goals are said to be some of the hallmarks of Protestantism, a division of Christianity (Weber 1930). By contrast, Confucianism is characterised by family and group orientation, respect for age and hierarchy, a preference for harmony and an avoidance of conflict and competition (Lin 1939; Chan 1963; Hsu 1963)

Various religions, although they share a great deal in common with one another, usually assert their individuality by emphasising their distinctive features through certain rituals and functions that the followers are expected to observe.

Hindus, in greeting or in parting from one another, raise their hands, their palms held together and their fingers pointing upward. This gesture is most com-monly used in showing respect to a superior but it is also used by Hindus when approaching the image of a deity.

Muslims pray to God five times a day, make an annual pilgrimage to Mecca and fast for a whole month every year in Ramadan (one of the 12 months in the Islamic calendar) and the wealthy among them are expected to regularly pay a portion of their income to their poorer fellow Muslims.

Sikh men wear a turban, do not cut their hair and carry a dagger as a symbol of their religion.

Saturdays for the Jewish community are the Sabbath when the faithful are expected to abstain from carrying out certain normal week-day activities.

For many Christians the weekly worship on Sundays, the midnight mass on the eve of Christmas and the annual commemoration of the rise of Christ at Easter are some of the means by which the distinctiveness of their religion from others is highlighted.

Religions usually lay down rules for both public and private spheres of life. Here is an example of what Confucius says on the relationship between the ruler and the ruled:

> A ruler who governs his state by virtue is like the north polar star, which remains in its place while all the other stars revolve around it. . . . Lead the people with governmental measures and regulate them by law and punishment, and they will avoid wrong-doing but will have no sense of honor and shame. Lead them with virtue and regulate them by the rules of propriety (*li*) and they will have a sense of shame and, moreover, set themselves right. (Chan 1963: 22)

In Hinduism, a hierarchical and inherently unequal relationship between people is institutionalised in the caste system. The position of a person in society is determined at birth by the caste into which they are born. The hierarchical scale, with five distinct castes and numerous sub-castes, ranges from the untouchables at the lowest level to Brahmin priests at the apex. The system is not an abstract, hidden principle of social organisation; it is a visible dimension of everyday life in urban and rural India and dominates a Hindu's personal identity throughout his or her life, wherever he or she might be. The strict tradition of within-caste marriages does not allow movement between the castes, which are thus perpetuated and sustained over generations.

In modern societies the role of religion in overtly regulating people's public and private life varies greatly from one country to another. In secular societies this role is much more circumscribed officially and only imperceptibly underlies the organisation of society and the acceptable behaviours of its people. For example, in Turkey, which has a secular constitution, the officials, supported by the army, are wary of the rise of the Islamic movement in the county. They recently banned the Islamic Welfare (Refah) Party, which has a sizeable following in the country, on the ground that its policies jeopardise the secularism of the state. As a measure to further circumscribe the influence of religion, the government has recently banned entry to university premises by female students wearing Islamic dress and male students wearing beards (*BBC Radio News Bulletins*, 10 March 1998).

In countries that are expressly modelled after a religious ideal, the role of religion is far more extensive and inclusive than those that have secular constitutions. In the Islamic Republic of Iran, for instance, all social institutions, such as educational establishments and their priorities, the media, the arts, the political structure, the army, and private and public sector organisations, are all required to conform to Islamic values and instructions.

The *Taliban* regime in Afghanistan, especially in the urban and rural areas under its control, does not allow women to work outside their home or girls to attend schools and other educational institutions. The authorities have even ordered the windows of all houses to be painted over so that unveiled women cannot be seen from outside. A woman's face is considered to be a cause of men's corruption and therefore has to be covered. Men are told to grow beards.

In Pakistan in the early 1980s General Zia Islamised the country's law and introduced new codes of conduct. For instance, government employees had to give up their European-style clothing and adhere to strict Islamic dress. Education in state schools was segregated and girls had to wear head scarves. The economy was to be run on Islamic lines, including the reinstitution of an old Islamic wealth tax, *zakat*, and Islamic banking practices. Many of General Zia's Islamic laws are still in force in the country.

In Israel, which owes its origins as a nation to religion, prominent religious figures, especially when their political representatives hold influential positions in coalition governments, have a significant say in the way in which the society is organised and how people should behave. There was, for instance, recently a news item (*BBC Television Ceefax*, Tuesday 24 February 1998) according to which a panel of rabbis had declared that married women in Israel must return home by midnight. The ruling was made by a religious court in Haifa as it approved a divorce suit from a husband because his wife had stayed out all night. The wife protested that her husband has been 'sleeping with other women'. The court conceded that this was 'insufferable' but it ruled that nevertheless it was the wife who must be home by midnight.

Religion has been argued to have a significant bearing on nations' macro-level activities such as economic performance, as well as on individual behaviour as seen above.

Weber (1930), for instance, argued that the change of the economic structure in England from feudalism to capitalism and private ownership occurred in the sixteenth century. One of the contributory factors to this change was the peculiar 'ethic' which stressed untiring, never-ending acquisition which developed in certain parts of Protestant Europe. In Weber's view, Protestantism stood at the cradle of the modern economic person, and Calvinism in particular stressed the individual, one's own ability and initiative. Thus, although modern capitalism 'was derived from the peculiarities of the social structure of Occident, it was inconceivable without Calvinism' (p. 25), for it 'had the psychological effect of freeing the acquisition of goods from the inhibitions of traditionalistic ethics' (p. 171).

Confucianism, too, has been said to be, in part at least, responsible for the economic success of certain South-East Asian nations in the recent past (King and Bond 1985; Castaldi and Soerjanto 1988).

This does not mean that other religions hinder economic progress. In South-East Asia, Thailand is a Theravada Buddhist country. Indonesia and Malaysia are predominantly Muslim and, along with Turkey, as Seizaburo (1997) points out, will probably be the first Islamic countries to achieve true industrialisation without depending on oil and other underground resources.

India, where a vast majority of the population are adherents of Hinduism, and where the caste system remains deeply ingrained, is showing new signs of growth. It is true that this growth is largely as a result of its shift from a policy of protecting domestic industries by import substitution to a policy of economic development through liberalisation and export promotion. But it is also true that Hinduism and a rigid caste system do not pose a serious obstacle to the country's economic progress.

Climatic conditions and other ecological factors and historical events, whereby a people accumulates shared experiences over time, are among other 'creators' and perpetuators of culture. It is arguable, for instance, that harsh and 'unfriendly' climates and poor agricultural land would make it harder for their inhabitants to earn a living from the land. Such people tend to become, over time and across generations, hardworking, resilient, patient, tough and even aggressive.

Misumi (1994), a Japanese scholar, makes the following point regarding the Japanese, known to be a hard-working people:

historically the Japanese who made a living from farming in their small island country have always been condemned to work hard to survive. Moreover, until very recently, Japan was an agriculture-centred society. Socio-psychologically, the social character of the Japanese people and those various customs of Japanese society may be attributed, at least to some extent, to the farming life that has continued from time immemorial in this small and populous country with so few natural resources. ... Since Japan is a small country, people have to work hard to keep their farmlands well to achieve self-sufficiency. Thus it became a norm of life for farmers, both men and women, to work on the farm, brushing through the dewy grass and coming home late in the starlight. Their farmland, if neglected, would be overgrown with weeds and would be ruined. (p. 257)

Tayeb (1992) makes a similar point regarding Iranian and Indian peoples:

Thousands of years ago Arian tribes migrated from Central Asia to, among other places, India and Iran. In India, they found a fertile land with plenty of water and rivers and a relatively mild climate. In Iran, they faced harsh variable seasons, salt deserts and very few rivers. It was not perhaps an accident of history that Hinduism, a religion noted for its non-violence and passivity, found roots in India and the country was so frequently invaded and ruled by others. The same race, when they settled in Iran, became an aggressive nation, fought other nations, conquered their lands and built up the Persian Empire which ruled over a vast area for centuries. (p.122)

In this connection, Reader (1997) argues that much of Africa's history can be explained by its fragile soils and erratic weather. They make for conservative social and political systems. The communities that endured were those that directed their available energies primarily towards minimising the risk of failure, not maximising returns. This created societies designed for survival, not development; the qualities needed for survival are the opposite of those needed for developing, i.e. making experiments and taking risks. Some societies were wealthy, but accumulating wealth was next to impossible; most people bartered and there were few traders. Everybody had to keep moving. Africans were nomads or pastoralists or farmers constantly shifting as land became exhausted. This is why experience of the past was all-important and why gerontocracy became, one way or another, Africa's political system. Its societies were organised in age-sets in which the oldest ruled. They still do: few of Africa's leaders are under 60, well above the average life expectancy. In Kenya the 'young Turks' are all in their mid-fifties.

History could also have similar effects on a people's social psychology. The builders of empires might leave behind a sense of pride for their descendants even though the empires have long since vanished. Nations that have lived through wars might adopt a more co-operative and tolerant attitude towards their neighbours in order to avoid further destructive and hostile flare-ups. The European Union is a successful living example here.

Religion, family, history and ecological conditions all contribute in their own way to our cultural make-up. It is important to note, however, that the effects of these factors should be considered in conjunction with one another, and not in isolation. For instance, a people's religion might be fatalistic but this feature could well be offset by other factors. So that, for example, a country like India, where the predominant religion is Hinduism, a religion known for passivity and fatalism, gives birth to a strong movement headed by Gandhi which puts an end to 200 years of colonial rule by the British – a non-violent movement but certainly not a passive and fatalistic one.

Major cultural characteristics

So what does it all mean for business organisations? Managers, employees, customers, clients, suppliers and all other persons and institutions that deal with a business organisation are part of the culture of the society in which they live and work. They all share in common similar 'items' in their cultural baggage that they carry with them at all times. This baggage contributes to the way in which a company and its relationship with its surrounding environment are managed. The very survival of the company depends on how well this is all done.

It is therefore important to know what these baggage items, these cultural characteristics, are and how they might influence the management of a company as well as other spheres of life.

Numerous anthropologists and social anthropologists, social and organisational psychologists, and management researchers have written volumes on the kind of values and attitudes that various nations hold and the degree to which these might vary from nation to nation.

At the end of this chapter a list of useful references is recommended for further reading. It suffices to say here that some of these values and attitudes have more direct relevance for business organisations than others. A selection of these are discussed below to illustrate the connection between culture and the management of organisations.

But first two points need to be stressed. The cultural characteristics generally attributed to various peoples and discussed here are based on the findings of research studies and not on 'stereotypes' that we might have heard or read about other cultures.

Second, culture cannot really be simplified and reduced to a handful of neat boxes into which some nations are placed and from which others are excluded. To do this will give us only a myopic and not a realistic complete picture of a nation. Neither is it possible to attribute a certain degree of cultural characteristics to a nation and their opposites to others and then pigeon-hole them there forever. Many of these characteristics and their opposites are present in all of us and manifest themselves in one form or other in different situations. In other words, national culture is too vibrant and dynamic an entity to be confined to clear-cut boxes.

Given the above reservations, here are a selection of cultural characteristics that arguably have significant implications for organisations and the management of their affairs. In this chapter the implications of these as a wider context for firms are discussed. In Chapter 18 we see their effects on the internal organisation and management of firms.

Table 13.1 Major cultural characteristics observed in various nations

Level	Values, preferences, attitudes towards:
Individual	Honesty, truthfulness, trustworthiness
	Independence of mind
	Control of emotions
	Assertiveness, ambition, achievement-orientation
	Ability to cope with uncertainty, ambiguity, anxiety and stress
	Care for quality of life
	Competitiveness
	Resilience
	Hardworking, work ethic
	Easy going, laid-back
	Modesty, arrogance, self-confidence
Relationship with others	Interpersonal trust
	Co-operation, competition
	Respect for people in senior positions
	Fear of the powerful
	Expect equality, acceptance of inequality
	Kindness, generosity, politeness,
	Appreciation of favours
	Acceptance of responsibility
	Caring
	Group-orientation, collectivism
	Self-orientation, individualism
	Small in-group, large in-group
	Family ties, kinship
	Keeping promises
	Punctuality
	Respect for others' viewpoints
	Conflict, harmony
	High-context communication
	Low-context communication
Relationship with environment	Submission to nature, fatalism
	Mastery over the environment
	Living in harmony with the environment
	Nature is a resource for us to exploit
	Nature belongs to our children, we have it on loan
Relationship with the society and the state	Law abiding, law breaking
	Community orientation, family orientation
	Welfare state, social net
	Statism, individual responsibility (big government, small government)
	National health service
	Universal education
	Private insurance

Expectations from companies	Active role in the community (schools, hospitals)
	Active interest in employees' private life and well-being
	Separation of private and company life
	Care for the environment
	Contribution to charities
	Sponsorship of sporting and cultural events
Political views and activities	Republicanism, monarchism,
	Participation, indifference, revolution
	Attitudes to women's position in society, human rights, minority rights, animal rights, workers rights, homosexuality, etc.
Economic views and activities	Entrepreneurial spirit, spirit of capitalism, socialism, private enterprise, state capitalism, public ownership of means of production, mixed economy

Research evidence shows that national cultures are different from one another in the extent to which they subscribe to the above and similarly common characteristics. And that these differences manifest themselves in their institutions and the make-up of their sociopolitical systems. Chapter 11 discussed some of these institutions and their implications for organisations in detail. Here salient findings of some of the major empirical studies conducted by researchers working within management and other closely related disciplines will be examined.

Values and attitudes related to management and organisations

In this section various cultural characteristics relevant to work and organisation are discussed is some detail. Of these, the cultural dimensions proposed by Hofstede, which have received a great deal of attention by scholars and managers alike, will be examined closely, together with major criticisms that have been levelled against it. The section then goes on to discuss other dimensions and models proposed by various researchers.

Hofstede's proposed cultural dimensions

Hofstede's original four cultural dimensions are based on two attitude surveys conducted in a large American multinational corporation around 1968 and around 1972. The surveys covered over 116,000 completed questionnaires from employees in 50 different occupations and 66 different nationalities. Each questionnaire contained about 150 questions dealing with values, perceptions and satisfactions.

For technical reasons the analysis of the data, which led to Hofstede's main propositions, centred around the questionnaire responses from employees from

40 countries. Thirty-nine of the organisations were subsidiaries of the same large US-based multinational company. The fortieth was a Yugoslav worker-managed organisation which among other activities imported and serviced the American firm's products in the former Yugoslavia.

Of the 150 items included in the questionnaire, only 20 were used to construct the indices, which formed the basis of four cultural dimensions and which Hofstede labelled as: Power Distance, Uncertainty Avoidance, Individualism/Collectivism and Masculinity/Femininity.

'Power distance' indicates the extent to which a society accepts that power in institutions and organisations is distributed unequally. This is reflected just as much in the values of the less powerful members of the society as in the values of the more powerful ones. Some national and regional cultures are characterised by large inequality, concentration of power in the hands of a small and permanent elite, centralised organisations with tall hierarchical pyramids, and restricted upward communications. Some national and regional cultures are characterised by smaller inequality, more social mobility, less concentration of power in the hands of a small elite, decentralised organisations with flatter hierarchies, and relatively free upward communications.

'Uncertainty avoidance' indicates the lack of tolerance in a society for uncertainty and ambiguity, which expresses itself in higher levels of anxiety and energy releases, a greater need for formal rules and absolute truth, and less tolerance for people or groups with deviant ideas or behaviours. Some cultures represent higher levels of activity and personal energy. The more active cultures tend to apply more specialisation, formalisation and standardisation in their organisations. They put a higher value on uniformity and are less tolerant of, and interested in, deviant ideas. They tend to avoid risky decisions. The less active cultures attach less importance to formal rules and specialisation, they are not interested in uniformity and are able to tolerate a large variety of different ideas. They take risks more easily in personal decisions.

'Individualism' refers to a loosely knit social framework in society in which people are supposed to take care of themselves and of their immediate families only; and 'collectivism' to one in which they can expect their relatives, clan, or work organisation to look after them. More collectivist societies call for greater emotional dependence of members on their organisations. In a society in equilibrium the organisations in turn assume a broad responsibility for their members.

The predominant pattern of socialisation in almost all societies is for men to be more assertive and for women to be more nurturing. Various data on the importance of work goals show near consistency on men scoring advancement and earnings as more important; women quality of life and people. With respect to work goals, some societies are nearer the 'masculinity' end of the masculinity/femininity dimension, others nearer the 'femininity' end.

Table 13.2 shows scores for 40 countries for Hofstede's original proposed four cultural dimensions.

A few years later Hofstede and his colleague (Hofstede and Bond 1984, 1988), in two questionnaire surveys in which they measured the attitudes of a sample of students from 10 and 23 countries respectively, identified a fifth dimension, which they first termed Confucian Dynamism and then renamed as 'Time Orientation'. This dimension is argued to embrace two contrasting poles and distinguish 'short-term oriented' cultures from the 'long-term oriented' ones.

Table 13.2 Values of Hofstede's original four dimensions for 40 countries

Country	Power distance	Uncertainty avoidance	Individualism	Masculinity
Argentina	49	86	46	56
Australia	36	51	90	61
Austria	11	70	55	79
Belgium	65	94	75	54
Brazil	69	76	38	49
Canada	39	48	80	52
Chile	63	86	23	28
Colombia	67	80	13	64
Denmark	18	23	74	16
Finland	33	59	63	26
France	68	86	71	43
Germany (FR)	35	65	67	66
Great Britain	35	35	89	66
Greece	60	112	35	57
Hong Kong	68	29	25	57
India	77	40	48	56
Iran	58	59	41	43
Ireland	28	35	70	68
Israel	13	81	54	47
Italy	50	75	76	70
Japan	54	92	46	95
Mexico	81	82	30	69
Netherlands	38	53	80	14
New Zealand	22	49	79	58
Norway	31	50	69	8
Pakistan	55	70	14	50
Peru	64	87	16	42
Philippines	94	44	32	64
Portugal	63	104	27	31
Singapore	74	8	20	48
South Africa	49	49	65	63
Spain	57	86	51	42
Sweden	31	29	71	5
Switzerland	34	58	68	70
Taiwan	58	69	17	45
Thailand	64	64	20	34
Turkey	66	85	37	45
USA	40	46	91	62
Venezuela	81	76	12	73
Yugoslavia	76	88	27	21

Sample: Employees of multinational companies.
Source: Hofstede (1980: 315).

Long-term orientation involves persistence (perseverance), ordering relation-ships by status and observing this order, thrift, and having a sense of shame. Short-term orientation involves personal steadiness and stability, protecting your face, respect for tradition, and the reciprocation of greetings, favours and gifts.

Table 13.3 ranks 23 countries according to their scores on long-term orienta-tion (LTO).

Table 13. 3 **Long–term orientation**

Country/region	LTO score	LTO rank
Australia	31	15
Bangladesh	40	11
Brazil	65	6
Canada	23	20
China	118	1
Germany, FR	31	14
Great Britain	25	18
Hong Kong	96	2
India	61	7
Japan	80	4
Netherlands	44	10
New Zealand	30	16
Nigeria	16	22
Pakistan	00	23
Philippines	19	21
Poland	32	13
Singapore	48	9
South Korea	75	5
Sweden	33	12
Taiwan	87	3
Thailand	56	8
USA	29	17
Zimbabwe	25	19

Sample: Students
Source: Fang (1998): based on Hofstede (1991: 160).

Hofstede's colleagues, King and Bond (1985) argue that the long-term orientation found in certain South-East Asian countries, such as China, Hong Kong, Taiwan and South Korea, has something to do with the Confucian traditions prevalent there. These traditions, it is argued, emphasise thrift and perseverance, virtues associated with long-term orientation. However, these virtues, as Hofstede (1994) rightly points out, are not unique to countries with a Confucian heritage.

These dimensions are then argued to have implications for employees' behav-iour in work-related contexts (see also Chapter 18) and the economic performance of a nation as a whole. Some of these five dimensions were later refined (Schwartz and Bilsky 1987, 1990) and further elaborated (Triandis 1995).

Triandis and colleagues (Triandis 1987, 1995) developed a theory of individualism and collectivism that can be used both at the cultural and the individual or psychological level. Fiske (1990, 1992) identified four universal patterns of social behaviour, which were called Communal Sharing, Equality Matching, Market Pricing, and Authority Ranking, that can be used to explain the similarities and differences in cultures. Schwartz and colleagues (Schwartz 1992; Schwartz and Bilsky 1987, 1990) presented a theory of the universal structure of value that can be used to cluster cultures into different groups and explain their similarities and differences.

It is important to note that Hofstede's research findings, and the consequent emerging cultural dimensions, although they made a major contribution to cross-cultural comparative management, have not gone uncontested (Tayeb 1994a, 1996; Yeh and Lawrence 1995; Fang 1998).

Some criticisms are on methodological grounds (Tayeb 1996). For instance, the research is entirely based on an attitude-survey questionnaire, which is certainly the least appropriate and desirable way of studying culture. Moreover, the respondents, employees of a multinational corporation's subsidiaries, are an extremely narrow and specific sample of their countries' populations. They belong to the middle class of their society rather than to the upper, working or rural classes. The company is an American one, with a well-known strong organisational culture, which might well have 'ironed out' certain manifestations of local national cultures.

Besides, as was mentioned earlier, confining national culture to a handful of dimensions gives us only a simplistic and unidimensional picture of reality. It is too simple, for instance, to say that country A is lower on avoiding uncertainty compared to country B. Country A may in fact be higher on this characteristic when it comes to driving habits (an uncertainty- and anxiety-generating activity), but lower on sexual conduct expected of the young (another activity with an uncertain outcome), in comparison with country B (Chapman and Antoniou 1994). Attitude to power and authority, to give another example, is also highly situation-based: an Indian man might feel more powerful than his wife at home, but less so at work if he happens to be the director of a firm of which she is the owner-chairman. There may in fact be a whole host of complicated reasons why some people behave one way under one condition, and a different way under another (Tayeb 1996).

Given the complexity and dynamism of culture, it is arguable that Hofstede's findings reflect the values and attitudes of a large sample of employees in relation to their specific work environment at the time the study was conducted: nothing more, nothing less.

The connection between the first four dimensions identified in the US multinational company surveys and organisational structure and management styles suggested by Hofstede is speculative and not based on empirical evidence. There is no evidence that the author actually extended the study to include an investigation into the organisational and managerial features. For instance, there is no indication as to how each of the subsidiaries of the American company was organised and to what extent their employees' attitudes and values as measured in the two questionnaire surveys were reflected in their management styles.

The causal linkages that Hofstede argues exist between cultural dimensions on the one hand and employees' behaviour in work-related contexts, or national performance of various countries as a whole, on the other are also problematical. For instance, in one country uncertainty avoidance may be the cause of low labour turnover; in another the economic downturn and high unemployment may be the culprit. In some countries individualism and masculinity might be related to economic advancement, in others collectivism and patriotism might be behind their progress. If in a country organisations do not use many written rules and regulations, this may have nothing to do with their employees' low uncertainty avoidance; it may be because of a high rate of illiteracy among the employees, especially manual workers (Tayeb 1988).

In this connection, Yeh and Lawrence (1995) similarly question Hofstede's suggestion that cultural dimensions such as individualism and Confucianism are causally linked to national economic growth. The authors argue that 'while certain cultural orientations may be necessary conditions for economic growth, they do not appear to be sufficient. This suggests that this simple model of the relationship between culture and economic growth is inadequate' (p. 665). They then give examples of fluctuations of growth rates over a period of three decades in certain developing countries which could not be explained by their individualism and/or Confucianism. In the case of China, for instance, they point out that the country's 9.5 per cent growth rate during the 1980s has been largely attributed to Deng's market-oriented reforms rather than to changes in the culture of the Chinese people (Shirk 1993).

It should, however, be noted that Hofstede in a later publication (Hofstede 1991: 169) accepted that 'culture in the form of certain dominant values is a necessary but not a sufficient condition for economic growth'. But as Yeh and Lawrence (1995) point out, he and his associates explore the relationship between culture and economic growth without giving consideration to other factors that affect economic growth.

Fang (1998) strongly criticises the fifth dimension, Confucian dynamism, on the ground of its philosophical flaw and inconsistency with the cultural reality. He points out, for instance, that in a study (The Chinese Culture Connection 1987) of this dimension across a group of Western and Eastern countries, the Chinese scored far lower than respondents from the US, Britain and Canada. Given the constituent parts of the Confucian dimension mentioned above, this means that people from these Western countries are more face-conscious than the Chinese from China, Hong Kong, Taiwan and Singapore. Fang finds this result strange in view of the fact that face-saving is a prominent cultural characteristic of the Chinese.

Fang further argues that in the Chinese mind, Hofstede's fifth dimension, which divides specific Confucian values into a 'positive' pole on the one hand and a 'negative' pole on the other, suffers from a philosophical flaw. Perhaps the best-known symbol of East Asia is Yin Yang – the Chinese philosophical principle of dualism in the manifest world (Cooper 1990). The Chinese believe Yin and Yang exist in everything, or everything embraces Yin and Yang. Confucian values are no exception: each Confucian value has its bright side and dark side. Furthermore, these values on either pole of Hofstede's fifth dimension are essentially intertwined and do not contrast to one another (Fang 1998: 15).

Exhibit 13.1 America through the rose-tinted spectacles of a Briton

We British love and hate the US. We are mesmerised by its vibrancy, envious of its enterprise and captivated by its vastness. We are appalled by its inequalities, bewildered by its brutalities and condescending of its culture. Sometimes the sentiments co-habit in a half-objective assessment of the world's last superpower. More often we choose sides.

Jonathan Freedland makes no excuses for so doing. After three years in Washington as a correspondent for *The Guardian* newspaper he loves it all – the meritocracy, the individualism, the inventiveness, the libertarianism, the Baptist confessional culture.

All else is forgiven: the vast urban battlefields of the Bronx and south-central LA, the massive (mainly Black) underclass and even, it seems, the state-licensed murder of (mainly Black) violent criminals. What Britain needs, Freedland asserts, is not less of America's Big Macs, Nike trainers and Hollywood hullabaloo, but more of its political culture. If only the British would peer beyond their prejudices, they would discover a society at once more radical, more democratic and more egalitarian.

Freedland starts as he means to go on. Forget the tired clichés about a nation riven by race, riddled with crime and obsessed with money. Instead, breathe the freedom, the diversity and the zest for life. We meet South Carolina's legendary Senator Strom Thurmond, at 93 often incoherent but still running for office. Never mind he is sometimes confused enough to mistake Russians for Mexicans, or that he once championed the South's opposition to integration. Thurmond is an icon of the vibrant local democracy. By Freedland's account, even those African-Americans he had sought to deny basic civil rights know in their hearts that good Ol'Strom delivers to his constituents.

This the-people-are-the-masters democracy expresses itself in a different way in Northampton, Massachusetts. A small town of 30,000, west of Boston, it boasts the largest population of gay women in the world. It calls itself Lesbianville. More important, its gay women can pull the levers of American democracy to guarantee their rights. And if we need further testament to the rich diversity of American life it comes from Maricopa County, Arizona. Here the popular (elected) sheriff, Joe Arpaio, has found a novel way of fighting crime. Convicted felons bake in the sun in tents at the edge of the desert. They are shackled, badly fed and humiliated. We wishy-washy liberals might think that such barbarity has no place in a civilised society. But for Freedland it is a small price to pay for local freedom.

Here is Freedland's enduring theme. For all the abrasiveness of the US, it is free. Its constitution, separation of powers between federal and state government, freedom of information law, the election of officials at every level of society are vital guardians of the people's rights. Even the nation's barbaric propensity to execute people is held as evidence of the triumph of popular will.

Source: *Financial Times* CD-ROM, 1 January–31 December 1998.

Other proposed cultural dimensions and work–related values and attitudes

Trompenaars' seven dimensions of culture

Trompenaars' (1993) dimensions, although they are different from those of Hofstede's, have been argued (Gately *et al*. 1996) to be conceptually related to 'individualism' and 'power distance', and as such could be interpreted as supportive of Hofstede's model by emphasising some of the consequences of those two dimensions for organisational behaviour, attitudes and beliefs.

Trompenaars' cultural model consists of seven dimensions, five of which are grouped under 'relationships with people', the other two concerned with time and environment:

- 'relationships with people':
  - universalism versus particularism
  - individualism versus collectivism
  - affective versus neutral cultures
  - specific versus diffuse relationships
  - achieving versus ascribing status
- 'perceptions of time'
- 'relating to nature'

Universalism versus particularism
This concerns 'rules' in contrast to 'relationships' as the principal determinants of interpersonal behaviour. In a strongly universalist culture personal relationships should not interfere with business decisions. Nepotism is frowned on and contractual agreements are the referees of conduct. Logical, rational analytical thinking and impartial professionalism are ideal characteristics to cultivate and standards to maintain. In particularist cultures, institutionalised obligations to friendship and kinship are considered 'moral' requirements which are maintained through personalism, 'face', paternalism and other social network mechanisms.

Individualism versus collectivism
Trompenaars' second dimension is almost identical to Hofstede's dimension of the same name.

Affective versus neutral culture
This concerns the extent to which emotions or feelings may be expressed in interpersonal communication.

Specific versus diffuse relationships
This highlights the difference between 'specific' or low-context cultures where relationships are separated by the role of each party and 'diffuse' or high context cultures where relationships exist in multiple areas of our lives and at several levels of personality at the same time. This distinction means that in a diffuse society personal, leisure and family life is not rigidly distinct from life at work, and relationships transcend many or all aspects of life.

Achieving or ascribing status

In some societies status is accorded on the basis of achievement whereas others ascribe status on the basis of durable characteristics such as age. Achievement in ascriptive cultures is less an individual and more of a collective concern and organisations in these societies justify a high-power distance and the resulting hierarchy as requisite 'power-to-get-things-done'. Power in such cultures does not require legitimising in the same way as in achievement-oriented cultures and abuse of power is checked by the moral responsibilities inherent in patron–client type relationships.

Perceptions of time

Different attitudes towards time (past, present and future) are reflected by the contrast between notions of time as linear and 'sequential' and notions of time as circular and 'synchronic'. Such differences affect how we co-ordinate, plan and organise. A 'sequential' culture, where the focus is rational efficiency, is epitomised by maxims such as 'there is a time and a place for everything'. In contrast, a synchronic culture allows parallel activities and is less oriented towards punctuality. The focus in a synchronic culture is more likely to be on effectiveness than efficiency.

Relating to nature

The distinction here concerns different attitudes towards the natural environment and beliefs about nature's ability to be controlled. 'Inner-directed' cultures wish to subdue nature and tend to identify with mechanical models for institutions whereas outer-directed cultures feel more dependent on the environment and see themselves more as a part or product of the environment.

In a later study (Hampden-Turner and Trompenaars 1994) the 'affective versus neutral' dimension was replaced with another one which the authors called 'equality versus hierarchy'.

High-context and low-context cultures

Hall (1977) introduced the concept of low- and high-context cultures which he argued reflect the way in which people in any given culture communicate with one another. 'Context' is the information that surrounds an event. In a low-context culture, information is explicit and vested in words of precise and unambiguous meaning; in a high-context culture information is implicit, vested in shared experience and assumptions, and conveyed through verbal and non-verbal codes.

High-context cultures are those in which people are deeply involved with each other, and where simple messages with deep meaning flow freely; low-context cultures are those highly individualised, somewhat alienated, fragmented cultures in which there is relatively little involvement with people.

In low-context communication, the listener knows very little and must be told practically everything. In high-context communication the listener is already 'contexted' and so does not need to be given much background information.

Attitudes to achievement

In all societies the majority of people want to do well and have certain goals they strive to achieve. However, in some cultures, notably those characterised by individualism, people's objectives to do well do not go beyond themselves and their immediate nuclear family (spouse and children). Their success is theirs to enjoy, and their failures bring shame or sadness only to themselves.

In collectivist culture the scope of ambition and achievement encompasses the extended family as well; if your second cousin gets a first-class degree at university or is offered a prestigious job, the joy and pride are felt by all the members of the family, and if he or she fails the exams, or gets into trouble with the law, everybody shares in the shame and disgrace.

Exhibit 13.2 Why can't the present be just like the past?

Behind the Umma-yad mosque in Damascus' old city, the young Damascenes sit in a café drinking tea and listening to Abu Shadi, the hakawati. Perched on a chair placed over a table, he tells the epic story of a thirteenth-century Mamluk Sultan who fought the crusaders and accumulated victories in battle. Abu Shadi draws a sword and strikes it on the ground to portray the sultan's anger.

Story-telling spread during the Mamluk rule as a popular form of educational culture, and was promoted in Ottoman times to occupy a potentially hostile population. Weakened by the invasion of radio and television, it disappeared from Damascus in 1970. But the Damascenes have been eager to bring it back. So a few years ago, Abu Shadi abandoned his grocery business to take up the hobby full-time. It is fitting for the Damascenes to have gone back to listening to his stories. A city lost between the past and the future, Damascus is all too happy to hold on to tradition and hesitant to embrace anything that seems to upset its reclusive existence.

The weight of a rich civilisation and a proud past give the Damascenes a sense of security. Claiming to be the oldest city in the world, Damascus was the capital of the first Islamic empire. It is said that the prophet Mohammed, arriving at the gates of Damascus, refused to go in; he could not enter paradise twice, he said. With a once-cosmopolitan society and a rich trading culture, Damascus was known as a caravan city on the western edge of the great silk road. Yet today, Damascus is one of the few places in the Arab world to maintain an eerie isolation and to live as if unaffected by the ideas and events that occupy everyone else. The Syrian capital remains consumed by its conflict with Israel, which has occupied Syria's Golan Heights since 1967, and is unable to focus its energies on anything else. While neighbouring Beirut buzzes with excitement, Damascus has the feel of a small town, where a big night out means going to a café at the Sheraton hotel or in the old city to smoke a waterpipe.

While Egypt, Lebanon and Jordan become part of an 'emerging' market-oriented Middle East, Syria clings on to a mostly command economy which produces figures and rosy forecasts that seem out of touch with reality.

Damascus' location, at a crossroads between Asia, Africa and Europe, historically had made it the centre of caravan trade. But the city has piled up trade
barriers and a jungle of laws and regulations which stifle the most enthusiastic entrepreneur. The banks are so dysfunctional that obtaining a loan is an
unusual luxury, reserved for those who already have money.

Fiercely nationalistic, Damascus refuses to believe it might be missing out
on advances the rest of the world now takes for granted. There are only 150
mobile telephones in the city, serving the small coterie of regime officials
and favourites. Everyone else, it is said, will have to wait until the government can afford an efficient network. A similar number of privileged people
and government institutions are allowed to hook up to the local Internet
server. Others connect through Lebanon, turning the Internet into an
expensive luxury which can only be afforded by the elite.

Satellite dishes dot the roofs of many houses, but officially they remain
banned. Like many other laws in Damascus, they are there to be broken.
Many suspect, however, that the law can suddenly be invoked to demonstrate that an unfortunate has fallen out of favour. In a country where the
media is controlled by the government, and newspapers merely echo official
views, Damascus intellectuals survive in a 'word of mouth' culture and move
in small informal networks. They have no chance of constituting an organised opposition but can help to inform public opinion.

That Damascus remains in a state of war with Israel colours much of its
behaviour and, to many, justifies a cautious approach to the future. But
the stalemate in the peace process also seems to have frozen attempts at
even modest progress, as the regime focuses on building an Arab front to
counter Israel.

If the Damascenes cannot tell you where they are heading, it is mainly
because their future is so closely tied to the vision and the fate of one man.
For nearly 30 years, Damascus has been so overshadowed by the reign of
Hafez al Assad, its President, that no one dares plan for a post-Assad period.
'Any discussion of the future is dangerous,' explains a historian. 'The
Damascenes have not been able to build institutions that would transcend
the transition.'

There are, however, forces that even Damascus cannot resist. Salim
Nassan, whose family history spans that of modern Syria, can testify to this.
He lives in a palace in the Christian quarters of the old city and his family is
known to have been among the first to start making Syria's famed brocaded
silks. He loves to tell stories of his grandfather, whom he claims was the first
to make Syrian 'mosaics', the wooden objects such as backgammon tables
and furniture designed with different kinds and colours of wood and
mother-of-pearl.

Nassan would have liked nothing better than quietly to keep living off the
old family business. But as more tourists discovered Syria, the old city was
invaded with cheaper, lower-quality mosaics. Refusing to compromise his
standards and needing to maintain his status in the community and create
jobs for the neighbourhood, he decided to go into tourism and is turning
five houses near his palace into a hotel.

> The Zitona restaurant he leased a year ago is set in a traditional Damascene house with a fountain in the centre and arched painted doors. Its enchanting mood is only upset by the 1980s pop music sung by a Syrian with an Italian accent. But the pub in the upstairs balcony is closed because there are not enough customers, and a busy night means being able to fill just a few tables. But he is not discouraged. 'We didn't move forward for a long time, but now things are changing,' he says. 'We see what is happening elsewhere, and we ask why not us?'
>
> Source: *Financial Times* CD-ROM, 1 January–31 December 1998.

Attitudes to conflict and harmony

In every social grouping disagreement and conflicts are bound to occur from time to time, but it seems that cultures develop different ways of handling conflict, as indeed other social issues. In some cultures, especially in individualistic ones, conflict is seen as healthy: it reflects the belief that every individual has the right to express his or her views, even if this contradicts his or her superiors or other members of the group. People are generally encouraged to bring contentious issues into the open, discuss them, try to resolve them, and reach consensus if possible. In some cultures, social harmony takes precedence over an individual's right to express his or her views rigorously against the interests of the groups. Traditions such as Confucianism, Taoism and Buddhism, for instance, stress harmony in social relationships, and between people and their environment.

Interpersonal trust

Trust refers to the extent to which we are willing to ascribe good intentions to and have confidence in the words and actions of other people (Cook and Wall 1980). Some cultures are characterised by honesty and mutual trust and others by distrust.

The implications of some of the characteristics mentioned above will be discussed in Chapter 19.

Chapter summary

This chapter defined national culture and discussed how it is created within a society's primary institutions, such as family and religion. We also saw how natural conditions of a country, such as its geographical location and climate, might lead to some of the values and attitudes held by the people who inhabit it. The chapter then discussed major national cultural traits that are argued to be present in most modern nations in varying degrees. Certain models of national culture were discussed and their relationships with organisations were explored. The chapter also gave a critique of Hofstede's model which is widely used by researchers and managers as a means to explain the cultural origins of workplace behaviour.

Discussion questions

1 What makes a person's cultural characteristics different from their genetically inherited traits?
2 What are the origins of national culture?
3 What are the major culturally rooted work-related attitudes and values?

Closing Case Study:
Japanese and British cultures

Japanese society is characterised by a strong sense of group and community. A typical Japanese person's loyalty is to his or her own group or team, and he or she has no great willingness to accept influence from those outside it. One of the paradoxes that every Japanese person has to face is how to be a winner in a society that encourages group loyalty and discourages individual assertiveness. The Japanese in school, business and industry have long known the answer to this problem: compete as a member of a group, rather than as an individual.

In contrast, Britain's is an individualist culture, rooted in centuries-old religious heritage and kinship traditions, where individual responsibility, ability, initiative and competitiveness are encouraged.

British individualism and Japanese collectivism are reflected in their respective employee-organisation relationships. The concept of in-group is of relevance here. The in-group in Britain, like many other individualist nations, includes only the immediate nuclear family: spouse, children, and sometimes parents. In collectivist cultures the extent of the in-group is much wider. In Japan, the company for which a person works is a member of this wide in-group.

Another manifestation of collectivism and individualism in employee-organisation relationships is the extent to which these relationships are personal and emotional.

In Japan, employees expect their superiors to look after them and to help them with their personal difficulties. In individualist Britain, employees, unlike their collectivist counterparts, do not expect, and indeed do not want, their superiors to deal with their personal difficulties. This would be an invasion of their privacy. To them a manager who is concerned with the employees' well-being is one who, for instance, provides them with up-to-date equipment so they can perform their tasks better. In other words, managers and workers have an impersonal, task-oriented relationship with one another.

Individualism/collectivism can also be observed in the physical structures and the designs of buildings in which organisations are housed. If you visit any British university, for instance, you will see most lecturers have their own offices: little personal territories. The open-plan office is an imported phenomenon which has been adopted by a relatively small number of firms whose managers are keen to learn lessons from their Japanese counterparts.

Similarly, a love of privacy and individualism may be behind British managers' preference for formal and clearly defined job territories and regulations. In collectivist Japan, organisations are characterised, among other things, by job flexibility and job rotation.

▶

Employee training is another aspect of management that could be argued to be influenced, in part, by national culture. The large amount of time and money invested by Japanese companies in their employee training is well known. In Britain the situation is in most cases quite the opposite. The managers' reluctance to allocate a great deal of time and financial resources to employee training seems to have one foot in societal culture and another in the country's short-termist capital market.

British employees, like many other individualistic people, and unlike the Japanese 'company man', pursue occupational advancement through their career rather than within their workplace. Job-hopping and moving from company to company, rather than life-time employment and cradle-to-grave commitment to one company, are the rules of the game. As a result, British managers see the expenditure on training as a waste of their precious capital, and not as a long-term investment in human resources.

Class differentiation is another feature of the two societies that has a profound implication for their respective organisations.

Japanese society, unlike many other modern countries, is not horizontally stratified by class or caste. The overall picture of the society is that of vertical stratification by institution or group of institutions. For example, shop-floor technicians do not identify themselves with all the technicians in the country or with the working class in general. They identify themselves with their work organisation and all those people who work below and above them within it.

In contrast, Britain is horizontally stratified. Most Britons are conscious of class differentiation. Almost everybody one speaks with can place themselves in one class or other. Family background, education, and even accent, betray people's social class. The class hierarchy broadly consists of upper class (a very small proportion of the total population), middle class and working class, but there are subtle gradations within classes. However, there is no sharp and rigid division between these strata and the structure is a dynamic one in that there is movement between classes.

Class structures and their characteristics appear to have been reflected in employee–management relationships and industrial relations.

In most British companies managers and other white-collar employees have greater advantages over manual workers in many respects, such as power, status, pay, physical working conditions, eating places, rules for lunch and tea breaks, and holidays. Shopfloor workers are usually subject to a tighter control at work. They have to clock in and out at specific times, and in some of the companies that produce chemicals and drugs, they may even be subject to physical search every time they leave company premises.

Japanese companies operate a rigidly hierarchical system, but the barriers between blue- and white-collar workers are not synonymous with class, as in Britain. Class markers such as different dining rooms, segmented car parks, and others are absent. Open-plan offices accommodate directors and other senior managers together with the rank-and-file employees under the same roof. This illustrates the 'egalitarian' nature of the Japanese management system. However, the absence of these class markers is misleading, since status is so clearly signalled in other ways. For instance, the finely graded hierarchy that exists within the organisations is explicitly mirrored in the language, and is thus apparent to all.

Source: Tayeb (1994b).

Questions

1 Where would you place British and Japanese culture on a collectivism/individualism continuum?
2 How is the difference between these two cultures reflected in their management–employee relationship?
3 The Japanese are a very competitive nation. How is this reconciled with their group orientation?
4 To what extent is social stratification in Britain different from that in Japan? What does this mean for their peoples' respective workplace behaviour?

Further reading

Cray, D. and Mallory, G.R. (1998) *Making Sense of Managing Culture*, London: International Thompson Business Press. In this book the authors critically evaluate traditional approaches to cross-cultural comparison of management and organisations and propose a new approach to international management.

Gately, S., Leesem, R. and Altman, Y. (1996) *Comparative Management: A Transcultural Odyssey*, London: McGraw-Hill. In this book the issue of culture and organisations is discussed using innovative metaphors, imagery and analogies.

Hall, E.T. and Hall, M.R. (1990) *Understanding Cultural Differences*, Yarmouth, USA: Intercultural Press. The authors elaborate on the concepts of low and high context and their implications for understanding and communicating with people from different cultural backgrounds.

References

Castaldi, R.M. and Soerjanto, T. (1988) Post-Confucianism management practices and behaviors: a comparison of Japan versus China and South Korea, paper presented to the Western Academy of Management Meeting, Big Sky, MT, March.

Chan, W.-T. (1963) *A Source Book in Chinese Philosophy*, Princeton: Princeton University Press.

Chapman, M. and Antoniou, C. (1994) Uncertainty avoidance in Greece: an ethnographic illustration, paper presented to the annual Academy of International Business (UK) Conference, Bradford, April.

Cook, J. and Wall, T. (1980) New work attitude measures of trust, organizational commitment and personal need non-fulfilment, *Journal of Occupational Psychology* 53: 39–52.

Cooper, J.C. (1990) *Taoism; the Way of the Mystic*, revised edn, Wellingborough: The Aquarian Press.

Endot, S. (1995) *The Islamisation Process in Malaysia*, PhD thesis, University of Bradford.

Fang, T. (1998) Reflection on Hofstede's 5th dimension: a critique of Confucian Dynamism, paper presented to the Academy of Management Meetings, International Management Division, San Diego, California, 9–12 August.

Fiske, A.P. (1990) *Structures of Social Life: The Four Elementary Forms of Human Relations*, New York, NY: Free Press.

Fiske, A.P. (1992) The four elementary forms of sociality: framework for a unified theory of social relations, *Psychological Review* 99: 689–723.

Gately, S., Leesem, R. and **Altman, Y.** (eds) (1996) *Comparative Management: A Transcultural Odyssey*, London: McGraw-Hill.

Hall, E.T. (1977) *Beyond Culture*, New York: Doubleday.

Hampden-Turner, C. and **Trompenaars, F.** (1994) *The Seven Cultures of Capitalism*, London: Piatkus.

Hofstede, G. (1980) *Culture's Consequences*, California: Sage Publications.

Hofstede, G. (1991) *Cultures and Organizations: Software of the Mind*, London: McGraw-Hill.

Hofstede, G. (1994) The business of international business is culture, *International Business Review* 3: 1–14.

Hofstede, G. and **Bond, M.H.** (1984) Hofstede's culture dimensions: an independent validation using Rockeach's value survey, *Journal of Cross-Cultural Psychology* 15: 417–33.

Hofstede, G. and **Bond, M.H.** (1988) Confucius and economic growth: new trends in culture's consequences, *Organizational Dynamics* 16: 4–21.

Hsu, F.L.-K. (1963) *Caste, Clan and Club*, Princeton: Van Nostrand.

King, A.Y.C. and **Bond, M.H.** (1985) The Confucian paradigm of man: a sociological view, in W. Tseng, and D. Wu, (eds) *Chinese Culture and Mental Health*, New York: Columbia University Press.

Komin, S. (1994) Culture and work-related values in Thai organizations, in H.S.R. Kao, H.S.R.D. Sinha and S.-H. Ng, *Effective Organizations and Social Values*, New Delhi: Sage Publications, pp. 137–63.

Latifi, F. (1997) *Management Learning in National Context*, unpublished PhD thesis, Henley Management College.

Lin, Y. (1939) *My Country and My People*, revised edn, London: William Heinemann.

Macfarlane, A. (1978) *The Origins of English Individualism*, Oxford: Basil Blackwell.

Misumi, J. (1994) The Japanese meaning of work and small-group activities in Japanese industrial organizations, in H.S.R. Kao, D. Sinha and S.-H. Ng, *Effective Organizations and Social Values*, New Delhi: Sage Publications, pp. 256–68.

Muna, F.A. (1980) *The Arab Executive*, London: Macmillan.

Reader, J. (1997) *Africa: A Biography of a Continent*, London: Hamish Hamilton.

Schwartz, S.H. (1992) Universals in the content and structure of values: theoretical advances and empirical tests in 20 countries, in M Zanna (ed.) *Advances in Experimental Social Psychology*, New York, NY: Academic Press, Vol. 25, pp. 1–66.

Schwartz, S. and Bilsky, W. (1987) Toward a universal psychological structure of human values, *Journal of Personality and Social Psychology* 53: 550–62.

Schwartz, S. and Bilsky, W. (1990) Toward a theory of the universal content and structure of values: extensions and cross-cultural replications, *Journal of Personality and Social Psychology* 58: 878–91.

Seizaburo, S. (1997) Clash of civilisations or cross-fertilization of civilisations?, *JAPANECHO*, October: 44–9.

Sherif, M.A. (1975) *Ghazali's Theory of Virtue*, Albany: State University of New York Press.

Shirk, S. (1993) *The Political Logic of Economic Reform*, Berkeley, California: University of California Press.

Tayeb, M.H. (1988) *Organizations and National Culture: A Comparative Analysis*, London: Sage Publications.

Tayeb, M.H. (1992) *The Global Business Environment*, London: Sage Publications.

Tayeb, M.H. (1994a) National culture and organizations: methodology considered, *Organization Studies* 15(2): 429–46.

Tayeb, M.H. (1994b) Japanese managers and British culture: a comparative case study, *International Journal of Human Resource Management* 5(1): 145–66.

Tayeb, M.H (1996) Hofstede, in M. Warner (ed.) *International Encyclopaedia of Business and Management*, London: Thomson Business Press (Routledge Group), Vol. 2, pp. 1771–6.

The Chinese Culture Connection (1987) Chinese values and the search for culture-free dimensions of culture, *Journal of Cross-Cultural Psychology* 18(2): 143–64.

Triandis, H.C. (1990) Cross-cultural studies of individualism and collectivism, in J. Bremen (ed.) *Nebraska Symposium on Motivation 1989*, Lincoln: University of Nebraska Press.

Triandis, H.C. (1995) *Individualism and Collectivism*, Boulder, CO: Westview Press.

Trompenaars, F. (1993) *Riding the Wave of Culture*, London: Economist Books.

Weber, M. (1930) *The Protestant Ethic and the Spirit of Capitalism*, London: George Allen & Unwin.

Yeh, Ryh-song and Lawrence, J.J. (1995) Individualism and Confucian dynamism: a note on Hofstede's cultural root to economic growth, *Journal of International Business Studies* 26(3) 655–70.

Part V The Internal Challenges of International Firms

CHAPTER 14

Strategic Management in Emerging Markets

Sue Bridgewater

Learning objectives

By the end of the chapter you will:

■ understand the reasons behind the growing investment in emerging markets

■ be aware of the major challenges of operation in these turbulent markets

■ understand the strategic implications for firms.

Opening Case Study:
Engineers braced against the wind from the East

As the economies of South-East Asia have slid into turmoil in recent months, Britain's engineering companies have held their breath. Not only is the region an important export market, but much of the engineering and capital goods industry would suffer almost immediately from any broad fall in investment triggered in other countries by a general slowing in economic growth linked to the Asia crisis. With the strong pound, which is once again touching DM3 after signs of weakening two weeks ago, eroding export margins, it is no wonder the UK's engineering sector has been a stock-market weakling in recent months. But so far few engineering companies have followed the lead of Siebe, one of Britain's biggest in this sector, which this month announced 2000 job cuts worldwide to cope with economic shocks, including turbulence in East Asia.

Most are putting a brave face on events. They hold out few hopes of immediate increases in growth in the region but point to good longer-term prospects – or even refer to specific business opportunities linked to the crisis. GKN, which divides its business between vehicle components, helicopters and pallet distribution, has taken the chance to strengthen its long-term position in Thailand and South Korea by pushing from about 50 per cent to 100 per cent its ownership of two motor-parts manufacturing ventures. GKN's partners in the plants, both hit by the region's problems, were anxious to sell their stakes at a fairly low price, while the Thai and Korean governments relaxed their previous tough rules on foreign

▶

ownership because of the need to attract more overseas investment. 'You could say the crisis has had a silver lining for us,' said C.K. Chow, GKN's chief executive. While Mr Chow does not hide his concern about the possibilities of a further worsening of the Asian turmoil, particularly the possibility of it spreading to China and India, he points out that last year the worst-hit 'tiger' economies of South-East Asia accounted for only 0.3 per cent of GKN's £3.4bn revenues.

Also fairly sanguine is Gary Allen, chief executive of IMI, a maker of valves, pneumatic products and drinks dispensers for cafés and other soft-drinks outlets. About 5 per cent of the company's £1.5bn annual sales come from Asia, with China accounting for a large share of this. 'We are still bullish about China, particularly in drinks dispensers where we are seeing good interest from breweries,' said Mr Allen.

In valves, in 1997 IMI set up its first manufacturing venture in South Korea, only to see demand knocked back by the economic trouble. 'There are now signs of demand coming back again, with orders beginning to reappear from Korea and Thailand for projects such as power stations,' said Mr Allen. Other companies say the effect of Asia's problems has been offset by strong growth in other important markets, particularly the US and continental Europe.

Sir Ron Garrick, chief executive of Weir, one of the world's biggest pumpmakers, said that since 1995 Asia had been responsible for a diminishing share of his company's order book. The South Korean shipbuilding industry – a big buyer of pumps – has so far been little affected by the turbulence because it is heavily export-driven; if anything this business has been made more competitive by the devaluation of the currency. 'Demand from the region is not very good at the moment but I don't see any mammoth impact on us,' said Sir Ron.

At Rotork, the world's biggest maker of control systems for heavy-duty valves used in industries such as oil and gas, about a third of the company's £93m sales last year came from Asia-Pacific. Specific 'problem' countries including Thailand, Malaysia and Indonesia accounted for 9 per cent of total sales. 'We had been looking to expand our sales in these (problem) nations by 7–10 per cent this year – now we are expecting the business to be similar to last year,' said Bill Whiteley, Rotork's Chief Executive. 'I have some concerns about the prospects for next year but the impact of any weakness in the region is reduced by the good business we are seeing in other parts of the world such as North America.'

At Babcock, a big maker of materials-handling systems for Asian markets, John Parker, Chief Executive, said business in the region was 'difficult'. Last year, of Babcock's £200m of non-UK sales, about a third was in Asia – with the 'problem' countries such as Thailand and Malaysia which have devalued their currencies accounting for about a third of this. 'If we had more of our manufacturing in Asia, it would be more of a problem,' said Mr Parker. 'But because we design our equipment away from the end market and use local subcontractors for much of the production, we are in a better position to turn our attention to other parts of the world where prospects are better.'

Other companies in 'niche' markets say they are likely to suffer less than more broadly based competitors. Indeed, those with products that enhance productivity, such as Cookson, say they may step up investments in Asia as businesses there respond to the pressures by trying to become more competitive. Provided the Asian virus is contained, it seems British engineers may emerge relatively unscathed. The present worries may be overdone. But the fear remains that if Western economies begin to suffer from Asia's upsets, many engineers will prove vulnerable to any general economic slowdown.

Source: Financial Times CD-ROM, 1 January–31 December 1998.

Introduction

Although on a map of the world the stable, advanced economies might immediately appear the most attractive investment targets, a significant (and growing) proportion of international investment activity involves emerging markets. These emerging markets are characterised by rapid growth in GDP and include a number of 'mega-markets' with large populations. India has a population of 900 million, China 1.2 billion and Russia 300 million. However these emerging markets are fraught with difficulties for potential investors. In East and Central Europe the transition towards a market economy has brought short-term economic crisis. In countries such as China and India there are large gaps between rich and poor and the mass-market middle class is still at an early stage of development. Restrictive and emergent government policies may make emerging economies unpredictable host markets for investing firms. Nonetheless the high levels of uncertainty of mega-markets are justifiable to investors, given the potential longer-term rewards. This chapter identifies the challenges of emerging markets, such as Central and Eastern Europe, China and India. It identifies the strategic implications for firms of operation in emerging and less-developed markets.

Investment in emerging markets

Many international corporations have long been represented in the majority of advanced, industrialised Triad economies (Japan, North America and Europe). While these economies tend to be stable and incrementally changing, they are also subject to intense competition between global rivals, which makes it difficult for firms to make further significant advances in penetration. As a result, the focus of investment attention is increasingly drawn towards emerging and less-developed countries.

These economies may be politically unstable and potential profits may be long-term, but they are viewed by many firms as the last 'virgin territories' to be contested by global rivals. Furthermore, many of these countries are rich in raw materials, such as oil and gas, and have large amounts of relatively cheap labour. As a result, the question of how best to serve emerging mega-markets has risen to the top of the strategic agenda for managers and management theorists.

Macro–environmental challenges of emerging markets

Political issues

At times, the political situation in emerging markets has favoured foreign investment. Mexico's open-door policy of the early 1990s attracted significant inflows of foreign investment. China's market economy reforms under Deng Xiao Ping seemed to point forward to a promising future. However, an ongoing problem faced by entrants into emerging economies is their extreme political turbulence. Many of the political crises blow up suddenly but have a profound impact on international trade. Until March of this year, Russia, under Mr Chernomyrdin, appeared to be moving towards a market economy, but it is now in the grip of political turmoil which may ultimately see a reversion to central planning. The past few years have seen political uncertainty over the continuity of market reform in China after the death of Deng Xiao Ping, conflict between India and Pakistan over nuclear testing, and continued tensions in East and Central Europe. The unpredictability of the political climate for foreign investors in emerging markets poses a significant challenge.

Economic crisis

The extract from the *Financial Times* at the beginning of this chapter shows the impact of the South-East Asian crisis not only on foreign investors, but on investment in China and India. Similarly the political crisis in Russia, highlighted in Exhibit 14.1, has caused stock markets to fall around the world as many banks had financial investments in Russia.

Emerging markets, especially the transitional economies of East and Central Europe, have been subject to a series of economic crises. In 1993, after breaking away from the rouble zone, hyperinflation in Ukraine had reached 5800 per cent per annum (see Johnson Wax case study at the end of the chapter). Russia has defaulted on international loans and may be forced to print more currency, as did Bulgaria in 1996. This may further fuel inflation (*Financial Times*, 29 August 1998). Russia has called on advisors from Argentina, which restructured its economic debt in 1989. Such economic crises represent a major problem for firms operating in the local currency.

Level of technology

While many emerging markets lag behind more advanced nations technologically, they cannot necessarily be assumed to do so. As a result, firms may find themselves returning to basic products and technologies in one area, but requiring leading-edge technologies in others. One example of a basic technology which provides benefits is that of clockwork radio in South Africa. However, in many East and Central European countries, a market only exists for luxury, foreign cars. This apparent incongruity of demand in emerging markets stems from the dispersion of income. Most disposable income resides among a small minority of individuals who want luxury cars as status symbols. The poorest people often cannot afford cars at all or will buy cheaper domestic models. There is as yet no market for smaller, economy foreign cars as the middle class has yet to reach a sufficient level of disposable income.

Exhibit 14.1

In 1993, Warwick Business School was involved in a Technical Assistance to the Commonwealth of Independent States (TACIS) project in Ukraine. Correspondence with the host institution in Kiev proved problematic. The French co-ordinating firm advised that telex was the only means of overcoming the problems caused by the outmoded Ukrainian telephone system. Having finally located the last remaining telex machine in a corner of the University and sent a telex, at great expense, the author returned to her office to find an E-mail reply awaited her on the computer. To overcome the legacy of technological obsolescence from the Soviet state, foreign investors in Ukraine had set up electronic mail via the Internet.

Social issues

The extreme dispersion of wealth in emerging markets is a principal cause of social tension. Other social issues include ethnic tensions, such as those that have exploded disastrously in Central Europe. Economic crises in the transitional period have also brought worse living conditions for the majority, who question whether a return to central control might not be preferable. In Russia, China and India there is also a considerable difference in lifestyles between more cosmopolitan urban and remote rural areas. Especially in East and Central Europe and China there is a legacy of political repression.

Strategic challenges of emerging markets

Assessing attractiveness

Theorists refer to the rapid and unpredictable environmental change of emerging markets as 'discontinuous change'. Discontinuous change has been a feature of the international climate since the mid-1970s, and has been intense in emerging markets in the 1990s. Among the many consequences for international business and corporate strategy is the question of whether traditional models for assessing market attractiveness are applicable to these countries.

Methods proposed for the assessment of international risk range from observation to quantification via Delphi techniques and multivariate analyses. There are a variety of aims, such as understanding the cyclicality of economic and political development (Smith 1971), the composition of political and economic risk

(Rummel and Heenan 1978; Perlitz 1985) and ranking countries by assigning scores (Litvak and Banting 1968; Goodnow and Hansz 1972). Matrix approaches not only look at environmental risk, but also assess market attractiveness on the basis of organisational capabilities. Cushman (1979) and Perlitz (1985) both adapt the Boston Consultancy Group (BCG) matrix to international markets. However, as with the original BCG matrix, their models are open to criticism of the measures used on the axes.

However, all of these techniques were developed in advanced economies in the more stable 1960s and 1970s. Kami (1976) claims:

> Corporate planning during the 1960s was relatively easy. Businesses could concentrate on international operations, because external assumptions were 'givens' with long-range predictability and few fluctuations . . . planning techniques of extrapolation and mathematical computation of future trends based on past history worked quite well.

However, they may not be applicable to countries changing discontinuously. Matrices give a snapshot of the market attractiveness. The underlying assumption is that the country will change only gradually so data can be extrapolated forwards to give a reasonably accurate prediction of future attractiveness. However, the situation may change much more rapidly in emerging markets and assessments may soon be outdated.

Furthermore, the data may not be available, or may not be reliable in emerging markets. Models are only as accurate as the data on which they are calculated. In former Soviet countries, for example, figures for unemployment and economic data, such as inflation rates, were disguised under the previous system. Some market measures are still unavailable or cannot be verified. Models also rely on 'hard' quantitative measures of attractiveness, and cannot easily incorporate 'soft' social or cultural measures.

In situations of discontinuous change, Leemhuis (1985) supports the use of scenario planning, which considers a range of possible futures. Assessment of the worst and best case macro-environmental outcomes can incorporate both quantitative and qualitative data.

Deciding the best type of international operation

However market attractiveness is measured, emerging markets are likely to be assessed as high risk, although also with high long-term potential. The decision of which of the potential mega-markets to enter and how best to capitalise on the opportunities, at the lowest risk to the firm, is one that preoccupies many firms.

One Western investor in East and Central Europe comments on his firm's assessment that Ukraine, together with Russia, Bulgaria, Romania and Croatia, represented the highest level of risk:

> We haven't any plans to retreat from projects in any of those countries . . . but, ultimately, particularly investment in production follows the markets that are developing. (Roth 1994)

A better understanding of the choices firms make comes from distinguishing between 'uncertainty' and 'risk'. Uncertainty is caused by many factors, with unpredictable outcomes, and so is immeasurable (Knight 1921). Risk is the measurable (often-financial) effect of uncertainty (Miller 1992). High levels of uncertainty increase risk (Miles and Snow 1978; Miller 1992; Aharoni 1966). So investment in emerging markets poses significant risks.

Research suggests that the level of risk a firm is prepared to accept plays a key role in determining its choice of how to operate in a market. Cardozo (1985) suggests that high risk does not make an investment unattractive, but may require high levels of return in justification. Anderson and Gatignon (1986) suggest a trade-off between risk and control. However, literature from different roots suggests different ways to reduce risks in uncertain markets. While Johanson and Vahlne (1977) suggest entry using low levels of commitment in uncertain markets (see Chapter 6 for a fuller discussion), the internalisation school of economics literature suggests that firms take control of assets and capabilities which they wish to protect from inefficient markets (Buckley and Casson 1976; Rugman 1980). In contrast, corporate strategy literature suggests that joint venture agreements may enhance competitiveness where firms have complementary capabilities (Porter and Fuller 1986; Jarillo 1988; Hamel *et al.* 1989). These divergent views are reflected in data on how firms are actually entering East and Central Europe (McCarthy *et al.* 1993; Shama 1995, 1996) (see Table 14.1)

The predominant entry mode for East and Central Europe is a joint venture with a local partner, with the remainder split between low- and high-investment entry modes. A similar predominance of joint ventures can be seen in India and China. This phenomenon can be explained in a number of ways. First, it may be dictated by host-market legislation, as was the case in India prior to 1985 (*Fortune*, 16 November 1992) and was also the preference of Chinese and East and Central European governments (Schlegelmilch *et al.* 1991; Shama 1995). Second, the local partner may offer a quicker route through local bureaucracy, as in China (Johnston 1991) and in the Soviet Union (Johanson 1994):

Table 14.1 **How firms are entering East and Central Europe**

| Author | Host country | Number of ventures | | | | |
		Export/distributor	License	JV/SA	100% subsidary	100% manufacturing subsidary
McCarthy *et al.* 1993	Russia	8	20	10	–	–
Shama 1995, 1996	Ukraine	8	2	5	0	0
	Russia	28	4	46	8	0
	Other	2	3	4	3	0
	Total Russia/FSU	38	9	55	11	0
	Central Europe a)[1]	27	9	54	30	2
	Central Europe b)[2]	1	2	5	5	0
	Central Europe	28	11	59	35	2
	Total	66	20	114	46	2

1 Hungary, Poland, Czech Republic
2 Romania, Bulgaria, Slovakia

> Given the turbulent situation in the Soviet market and the difficulties for out-
> siders in perceiving how the Soviet economy works, knowledge about this area
> is a crucial factor for the firm in entering the Soviet market. (p. 151)

These findings seem nearest to strategy literature (Hamel *et al.* 1989) as local
knowledge is, in this case, the complementary skill that enhances the ability of
the market entrant to compete.

The case study of Johnson Wax at the end of this chapter shows a firm that
entered Ukraine via a joint venture but did not do so until it was possible to
take a majority equity stake. For many investing firms, the need to control the
operation seems to be motivated by the protection of the firm's brands in the
international market. This seems nearer to the expectations of internalisation
theory (Buckley and Casson 1976; Rugman 1980). This need to control seems
to explain the preference of some firms for wholly owned or high-stake co-
operative mode.

One key distinction is whether the firm aims to serve the local market, that it
has a *host market focus*, or is serving international customers or regulatory bodies
in its home or other international markets (Bridgewater 1995), that it has a *home
market focus*. Examples of investment with a *host market focus* are tobacco goods
firms, Philip Morris and R.J. Reynolds entering Russia to serve one of the few
growing cigarette markets in the world, or soft drinks firms PepsiCo and Coca-
Cola serving the growing middle market in India. Examples of *home market focus*
are accounting firms, who gain a substantial proportion of business from multinational corporations and regulatory bodies such as the EC and World Bank.
Other types of home market focus include firms entering emerging markets to
capitalise on raw materials. Examples of this are oil and gas firms, who will re-
export the raw material, and firms who establish production facilities in
countries with low labour costs, as with automotive companies in Mexico.

Firms with a home-market focus accept substantially lower levels of risk when
entering emerging markets than do those with a host-market focus, as they are
gaining returns from customers in more stable economies. Firms aiming to pene-
trate the host market face the full consequences of the uncertainty in these
countries. Whether they opt to establish manufacturing facilities or serve the
markets by export or through a distributor depends on their readiness to accept
high levels of risk. It is clear that export and the use of distributors can only
allow firms to skim the markets: that is, gain access to a small number of price-
insensitive customers, as they will be unable to compete on price with locally
produced products. While this may be attractive for high-margin products, such
as Rolls Royce cars, it might be less so for lower-margin competitors, such as Ford
or General Motors. An alternative motivation for using export and distributors is
that of overcoming uncertainty by gaining a better understanding of the country
before making a larger investment (Johanson and Vahlne 1977). Firms who enter
Eastern Europe using these entry strategies often describe this in financial terms
as 'taking an option' on a favourable development of the emerging market.
However, those exporting tended to be disappointed in the level of understanding they gained from operation on the periphery of the market. Firms with a
local partner or distributor gained better understanding of the way the market
worked (Bridgewater 1995).

Partners in progress

One issue which taxes multinational corporations who operate in emerging or less-developed countries is that of the 'duty of care' they have to the host market. As described in the previous section, firms may have invested to capitalise on raw materials or cheap production. They may also view these countries as offering the opportunity to sell products at the end of the product life-cycle. The use of basic products may be sensible and appropriate to the level of technology of the market (see earlier). However, selling products that are detrimental to, or fail to provide benefits in, the market is more problematic. There has been considerable debate over the impact of Nestlé selling baby formula in less-developed markets (Gilly and Graham 1988).

Critics believe that heavy promotion of formula encourages women to switch away from breastfeeding their children. If the formula is given at the wrong strength, to cut costs, or prepared in unhygienic conditions, this may have a detrimental effect on the health of babies. Nestlé argues that it is only switching people from competitors' brands, not to the product category from breastfeeding.

Shell has also faced controversy over its activities in Ogoni Land, Nigeria. Opponents suggest that Shell should have intervened more strongly in the trial and subsequent hanging of Ogoni rebel Ken Saro Wiwa, and that it is responsible for environmental damage to the region Shell protests that it is socially responsible, has taken appropriate environmental measures together with funding schools and hospitals in the region and cannot become involved in national politics.

The following example about the spread of Aids in less-developed countries highlights the complex demands on pharmaceutical companies. The essential question is whether multinational corporations should abide by laws stricter than those of the host market and, if so, whether at an acceptable international level or the most stringent level (Donaldson 1996). Moreover, it is questionable whether they have a responsibility to help their host countries behave in a morally acceptable way.

Exhibit 14.2 Tamed in the West by expensive drugs, Aids is exploding among the poor

Virtually no one in the developing world, where 90 per cent of the world's 30m HIV victims live, can possibly afford the drugs that are working miracles in the West. Since 1996, triple cocktails of anti-retroviral drugs have successfully suppressed HIV levels, allowing North American and European patients to lead comparatively normal lives. Without the drugs, HIV brings certain death from Aids.

Thus, while the epidemic is being tamed in the West, it is exploding in much of the developing world. In many southern African countries, one in four adults is HIV-positive. Life expectancy in Botswana, which recently touched 68, is likely to drop to the low 40s. India has 4m people with HIV, the highest total in the world. And although the disease has been slow to spread in China, it is now present in every province. That could lead to millions of new infections.

The contradiction between scientific progress in the West and the disease's acceleration in the Third World produces mixed emotions in Sam Kalibala, a Kenyan research associate of the Population Council in Nairobi. First, he is annoyed at his own government and those of many other developing countries whose economic mismanagement, he believes, has rendered them too poor to aspire to advanced treatment. Kenya, for example, can muster a health budget of just $10 a person a year. That is enough to pay for six hours of anti-retroviral treatment; to be effective it must be taken for life.

But Dr Kalibala is also angry with drug companies, which he believes are profiteering at the expense of the world's poor. 'There is a sadness that, knowing we are so poor, they're still trying to make money out of us.' Those drugs that do find their way to Africa – sometimes, though not always, at reduced prices – are used to treat high-ranking government and military officials, not the general public, he says.

Some countries, such as Brazil, have pledged to do all they can to make advanced anti-retroviral treatment widely available. Brazil plans to spend $600m next year on therapy, twice the amount the international donor community will come up with for the entire world.

'If they can afford it, that's great,' says Mead Over, a health economist at the World Bank and co-author of a Bank policy-research report entitled *Confronting Aids*. But, he cautions, such a treatment-for-all policy is unlikely to be sustainable even in relatively prosperous Brazil. In Africa and the poorer countries of Asia it is out of the question. This is not the counsel of despair, he insists. There are many practical policies leaders and donors can pursue.

Governments must concentrate on putting their prevention efforts where they are most effective, says Mr Over. This can often involve some very tough political choices, skewing scarce resources towards high-risk groups such as prostitutes or drug-users who are not always top of everyone's priority list. Thailand, for instance, pursues a policy of 100 per cent condom use in brothels. Since the policy began in 1991, the number of sexually transmitted diseases has fallen dramatically and the country appears to have the HIV epidemic in check.

Data collection is also vitally important, says Mr Over. If you do not know who is spreading the disease you cannot stop it. Many governments, for example, find it hard to accept that their militaries – full of sexually active, mobile young men – are an important conduit of infection. 'How many countries have realised that their own soldiers are their biggest internal security threat?' he asks. Governments should also spread information, both on how to avoid the disease and how to cope with it once infected. Mr Over supports big efforts on the treatment of infections such as malaria and tuberculosis which prey on people whose immune systems are weakened.

Callisto Madavo, the Bank's Vice-President for Africa, calls the epidemic the biggest single threat to the continent's development. 'By 2010, life expectancy in Zimbabwe will be virtually where it was in the late-1940s,' he says. 'If the epidemic is left unchecked, we will have wiped out all the development gains we have made in the last four decades.'

Source: *Financial Times* CD-ROM, 1 January–31 December 1998.

Chapter summary

Emerging markets offer considerable opportunities for international investors. However, firms must operate in highly uncertain environments in order to capitalise on them. Environmental problems include political stability, economic crises, technological obsolescence and cultural distance from many investing firms. Firms may find it difficult to accurately assess market attractiveness. If the decision is made to enter, firms must decide on the level of risk they are prepared to accept and whether they will accept long- rather than short-term returns on their investment. Moreover, firms may have to decide to what extent they have a 'duty of care' if they are operating in countries whose laws are more lax than their own.

Discussion questions

1 What macro-environmental challenges do multinational firms face when operating in emerging markets?
2 What issues should the firm consider in deciding the level of technology of its products or services?
3 What ethical stance do you believe multinational corporations should take when operating in countries with lax laws?

Closing Case Study:
Johnson Wax in Ukraine

In December 1991, in a popular referendum, the people of Ukraine voted to become an independent state. The period of Soviet central planning had officially ended. Amid the general euphoria, the people of Ukraine looked forward to a prosperous future as a nation state trading in the world market. Ukraine was widely heralded as the former Soviet Republic with the greatest potential for reform.

As a result, Ukraine became an attractive investment opportunity for multinational firms operating in highly competitive global industries. It had a population of 52 million people, who were 'short of absolutely everything' and its location between the more stable but relatively small Czech and Hungarian markets, and the even larger but highly unstable Russian market, made it a good gateway to Eastern Europe.

However, the transition to a free market economy brought severe difficulties for Ukraine. Premature severance of ties with Russia resulted in the loss of previous markets without gaining replacements. The temporary currency, the Karbovanet or coupon, failed to hold parity with the rouble. The financing of Ukraine's trade deficit by printing more money and the issue of massive compensatory credits to striking miners fuelled hyperinflation. *The Economist* quoted an inflation rate of 72 per cent per month, an aggregate 5800 per cent per annum (7 May 1994). This environmental turbulence has posed enormous challenges for international firms operating in Ukraine.

▶

The rate of transition in Ukraine is such that information is often outdated before it can be published. Legal decrees change with such frequency that it has become current practice to publish these in the local newspapers. Western businesses operating in the market report that they monitor this press to discover changes that are significant to them. The contradictory and often draconian measures the government imposes may have significant impact on Western investors.

Official data were controlled under the Soviet system. While they are, in many cases, the only data available, their reliability is doubtful. Variation between different sources is considerable. Even those sources, which should be reliable, such as banks and official government bodies, produce incomplete, misleading or erroneous data. Gross domestic product figures, produced by the Ukrainian National Bank, are not adjusted for inflation. Moreover, the inflation rates are not given anywhere on the report. Without these the data are useless.

The previously punitive culture in Ukraine has instilled an anxiety about revealing information, no matter how trivial. Consequently, sources are seldom revealed. Without the date and means of calculation, data cannot be validated. There is an unwillingness to speak on the telephone, as the KGB used to monitor calls. It is suggested that the major hotels, frequented by Westerners, are still monitored. Also culturally specific is the unwillingness of Ukrainians to admit to weakness. Work with Ukrainian students on projects with Ukrainian interpreters and colleagues has shown that the first response to a question 'Do you know anything about . . . ?' would invariably bring a claim of knowledge or expertise, which might later transpire not to be the case.

Manninen and Snelbecker's 1993 survey into criteria and barriers to foreign investment in Ukraine shows high profit potential (48 per cent) and local demand (37 per cent) as the primary motivations for investment, although the availability of cheap materials (30 per cent) and low labour costs (23 per cent) are also major attractions. However, contradictory and confusing legislation, lack of banking facilities and poor communications are seen as significant obstacles.

The current period of discontinuous change in Ukraine makes it difficult to extrapolate any clear picture of investment potential. Looking at the economic indicators alone gives a bleak picture of the attractiveness of the market for potential investors. However, this does not reflect the positive atmosphere that has arisen, at times, from favourable turns in legislation and political events, from the peaceful resolution of problems and the extreme good nature of the Ukrainian people.

Johnson Wax in Ukraine

Johnson Wax, Ukraine, is a subsidiary of S.C. Johnson and Son Ltd. It is a family-owned multinational, based in Racine, Wisconsin, in the USA. It is a large player, worldwide, in the household products and cleaners market. Founded in 1886, the company is in its fifth generation of family ownership and went public in 1987. The family retained its ownership interest and voting control. The firm had sales of $3400 million in 1991. Johnson Wax is traditionally a firm that adopts a pioneering approach to international expansion. In the 1930s, S.C. Johnson was the first US chemical company to invest in South America. In the early 1980s there were only three areas in which Johnson Wax was not yet present: India, Pakistan and the USSR. The firm began to look at ways of entering the Soviet Union, one of the possible targets. However, S.C. Johnson has a policy of investing in a controlling interest in its subsidiaries and Soviet law prevented it from owning more than 50 per cent of any joint venture.

In 1988, the law on joint ventures changed. The limit on the percentage of foreign investment was relaxed. Prior to the liberalisation of Eastern Europe, three years before the break-up of the Soviet Union, Johnson Wax began the process of finding a suitable joint venture partner. All negotiations had to be channelled via the Ministry for the Chemical Industry in Moscow. After meetings with a number of chemical plants throughout the European part of the Soviet Union, a suitable partner was identified in Kiev, Ukraine, in 1989. This was a state-owned producer of waxes and soaps, owned by the Ukrainian Chemical Association, a consortium of six chemical factories. The final agreement was signed in 1990.

Johnson Wax has an 80 per cent stake in a manufacturing joint venture. Its input consists of the investment necessary to update production facilities, marketing and managerial expertise and brands. The local partner brought local knowledge, premises and staff, as well as the base level of production facilities. Johnson Wax's strategy is simple: 'to be there before the others and develop a volume/cost competitive advantage in order to build up strong barriers to late entrants.'

A number of challenges face Johnson Wax. When first it entered Ukraine, it was still part of the Soviet Union. On liberalisation at the end of 1991, the environmental conditions altered dramatically. When it entered the market, Johnson Wax was hard pushed to keep up with local demand levels: 'Priced at roughly 30 per cent of their Western counterparts, [their products] were "gobbled up" by "a market screaming for new products."' *Business Central Europe*, February 1994.

It was then distributing through the old state-owned distribution system of 'baza' (wholesalers) and 'gastronom' (retail grocery stores). However, since April 1993, the factory has run at only 50 per cent of its capacity. This is not because of a decline in demand. Rather, the problems Johnson Wax is now facing result from the transition process.

The structure of the former state economic system has gradually disappeared and no stable private sector has appeared to take its place. Supply between wholesalers and retailers has now almost been severed. Little privatisation has taken place. In the absence of any proper distribution channels, a type of parasitic trader has developed. They take commission for arranging a deal by phone, but there is no added value in terms of distribution. As a result of this additional mark-up, the prices of Johnson Wax's products have soared. Furthermore, legislative measures change rapidly and can be draconian. The VAT levied on the firm's products has fluctuated from 0 per cent to 20 per cent then 28 per cent and now back to zero. Taxes can be up to 90 per cent of revenue, not profit. One foreign investor in the market says that the conditions are so hostile that 'it is like operating in the Wild West'. Bribery, corruption and organised crime are widespread.

In February 1994, the General Manager of C1 was uncertain what the future of the firm in Ukraine might be. He concluded:

There was a time when we thought Ukraine was the country with the best prospects in the Soviet Union. [Now] our arguments to the Board of Directors are much more subjective. I have no idea what will happen in Ukraine next year . . . We took a risk here, and it's one C1 can afford. The question is: can we survive until Ukraine goes back up, and are we building up a competitive advantage in the meantime?

Questions

1 What are the major opportunities and threats facing Johnson Wax in Ukraine?
2 What was Johnson Wax's market entry strategy?
3 What issues must the company resolve in order to be successful in Ukraine?

Further reading

Buckley, P.J. and **Ghauri, P.** (1994) *The Economics of Change in East and Central Europe*, London: Academic Press. This provides a good collection of articles relating to this region.

Paliwoda, S. (ed.) (1991) *New Perspectives on International Marketing*, London: Routledge. This gives good coverage to entry to the Chinese market.

References

Aharoni, Y. (1966) *The Foreign Direct Investment Process of the Firm*, Boston: Harvard University Press.

Anderson, E. and **Gatignon, H.** (1986) Modes of foreign entry: a transaction cost analysis and propositions, *Journal of International Business Studies* 17 (3): 1–26.

Bridgewater, S. (1995) The Entry mode choices of multinational corporations in turbulent markets: the case of Ukraine. Unpublished PhD dissertation, Warwick University.

Buckley, P.J. and **Casson, M.** (1976) *The Future of the Multinational Corporation*, London: Macmillan.

Cardozo, R.N. (1985) Risk return approach to product portfolio strategy, *Long Range Planning* 18 (2): 77–85.

Cushman, R. (1979) Norton's top-down, bottom-up planning process, *Planning Review* 7, November.

Donaldson, T. (1996) Values in tension: ethics away from home, *Harvard Business Review*, September–October: 307.

Freeland, C. Thornhill, J. and **Warn, K.** (1998) Yeltsin pledges to serve a full term as crisis deepens: Chernomyrdin hurries to create economic strategy for Russia, *Financial Times*, 29 August.

Gilly, M.C. and **Graham J.L.** (1988) A macroeconomic study of the effects of promotion on the consumption of infant formula, *Journal of Macromarketing*, Spring: 332.

Goodnow, J.D. and **Hansz, J.E.** (1972) Environmental determinants of overseas market entry strategies, *Journal of International Business Studies* 3: 33–55.

Hamel, G., Prahalad, C.K. and **Doz, Y.** (1989) Collaborate with your competitors and win, *Harvard Business Review* 67 (1): 133–40.

Jarillo, J.C. (1988) On strategic networks, *Strategic Management Review* 11: 479–99.

Johanson, M. (1994) Viking raps – a case study of joint venture negotiation in the former Soviet Union, in P. J. Buckley, and P. Ghauri, (eds) *The Economics of Change in Eastern and Central Europe*, London: Academic Press.

Johanson, J. and **Vahlne, J.E.** (1977) The internationalisation process of the firm: a model of knowledge development on increasing foreign commitments, *Journal of International Business Studies,* Spring/Summer: 23–32

Johnston, W. (1991) Alternative approaches to buyer-seller relations with the People's Republic of China, in S. Paliwoda, (ed.) *New perspectives on International Marketing,* London: Routledge.

Kami, M.J. (1976) Planning in times of unpredictability, *Columbia Journal of World Business,* Summer: 26–34.

Knight, F. (1921) *Risk, Uncertainty and Profit,* London: London University Press.

Leemhuis, J.P. (1985) Using scenarios to develop strategies, *Long Range Planning* 18 (2): 30–37.

Litvak, I.A. and **Banting, P.M.** (1968) A conceptual framework for international business arrangements, *Marketing and the New Science of Planning,* in R.L. King (ed.) AMA Fall Conference Proceedings.

Manninen, K. and **Snelbecker, D.** (1993) Obstacles to doing business in Ukraine, *Working Paper, Project for Economic Reform in Ukraine,* Harvard University, April.

McCarthy, D. Puffer, S.M. and **Simmonds, P.J.** (1993) Riding the rollercoaster: US firms' recent experience and future plans in the former USSR, *California Management Review* 36 (3): 106–9.

Miles, R.E. and **Snow, C.C.** (1978) *Organisational Strategy, Structure and Process,* New York: McGraw-Hill.

Miller, K. (1992) A framework for integrated risk management in international business, *Journal of International Business Studies* 2: 311–30.

Perlitz, M. (1985) Country-portfolio analysis – assessing country risk and opportunity, *Long Range Planning* 18 (4): 11–26.

Porter, M.E. and **Fuller, M.B.** (1986) Coalitions and global strategy, *Competition in Global Industries,* Boston, Mass: Harvard Business School Press.

Rahul J. (1992) India is opening for business, *Fortune,* 16 November: 129.

Roth, T. (1994) Gap widens between winners and losers: western domestic investors act as judges, *Central European Review,* Spring: 5.

Rugman, A. (1980) General theory of foreign direct investment (FDI): a re-appraisal of the literature, Weetwirtschaftliches Archiv, pp. 365–77.

Rummel R.J. and **Heenan, D.A.** (1978) How do multinationals analyse political risk? *Harvard Business Review,* 56: 67–76.

Schlegelmilch, B., Diamantopoulos, A. and **Petersen, M.** (1991) Conquering the Chinese market: a study of Danish firms' experiences in the People's Republic of China, in S. Paliwoda, (ed.) *New Perspectives in International Marketing,* London: Routledge.

Shama, A. (1995) Entry strategies of US firms to the newly independent states, Baltic states and Eastern European Countries, *California Management Review,* 37 (3): 90–109.

Shama, A. (1996) Cracking the former Soviet bloc markets: an empirical study, *International Journal of Management* 13 (2): 184–92

Smith, C.N. (1971) Predicting the political environment of international business, *Long Range Planning,* September: 7–14.

The Economist (1994) Surveys of Ukraine (2): How to wreck your economy, 7 March.

CHAPTER 15

Integrating Strategic Planning with Technology Management in the Global Firm[1]

Farok J. Contractor and V.K. Narayanan

Learning objectives

By the end of this chapter you will:

- understand a strategic planning framework that explicitly incorporates technology-management issues in global companies.

- know about the three stages of the planning process

- know about technology and knowledge management in multinational firms

- understand how the use of a strategic planning framework can serve to integrate managers from different parts of the company into a formalised technology-planning exercise.

Opening Case Study:
Doing the knowledge: a new species of corporate official

Do you have a chief knowledge officer in your company? No? It may be only a matter of time before this new corporate species, classified and categorised with its very own identifiable set of traits and characteristics, takes flight among the multinationals. That, at least, is one suggestion in a study from London Business School. The study by Professor Michael Earl and Ian Scott recognises that some companies may already possess executives of similar plumage without the word 'knowledge' in their job titles – an obvious alternative would be head of intellectual capital – but for the purposes of the LBS research, the study was confined to individuals who include the magic word somewhere in their title.

The main reason, explains Professor Earl, was to distinguish the job from that of the more widespread chief information officer, whom he perceives to have a more technical function. The knowledge officer, it seems, is a more exotic creature, often a creation of the chief executive. Professor Earl notes that the post is so reliant on the CEO's patronage that the position would most likely expire with the demise of its sponsor. The study estimates that some 25 knowledge officers are so named worldwide.

Given the job's precarious existence, it is not surprising that the research covers itself by acknowledging that in some companies it may be destined for an evolutionary dead end. Indeed, this appeared to be the hope of some of the officers themselves when they stepped into the role, looking at the job in some ways as an extended project of limited tenure. In practice, says the study, many found their task lasting longer than they had expected. So what does a chief knowledge officer do? One definition quoted in the report is that they 'co-ordinate and promote knowledge activities throughout the organisation' and 'drive forward the knowledge agenda'. What does this mean?

In practice, according to Elizabeth Lank, programme director (mobilising knowledge) at ICL, the computer company, it often means, initially at least, doing something of identifiable value in the dissemination of information such as setting up an intranet – an internal Internet – and demonstrating to fellow employees how it can be used to their advantage. But she sees the role quickly developing beyond that of an information specialist. 'The job title at first was programme director, knowledge management, but I changed that because I thought "knowledge management" had too much of a systems feel to it,' she says.

The job emerged from an internal knowledge management network, a kind of investigatory working party set up three years ago in recognition that ICL had turned from a manufacturing to a service company. Ms Lank, who had been head of management development, was appointed to the new job created by Keith Todd when he became Chief Executive in 1996. The job, she says, is still changing, but at present it concentrates on three main areas. The first involves running management workshops to get over the idea of knowledge as an asset and what it means in the company.

Managers are expected to draw up personal action plans at the workshops they use in their jobs. A second area is the identification and the plugging of gaps in corporate knowledge, and a third is to make knowledge accessible among employees and shared across functions. Ms Lank has a small support team which includes information technology expertise she did not have herself. The team does not belong to any specific department but works across functions. Measuring its worth, she accepts, is difficult. 'It's easier,' she says, 'to measure the cost of not doing it. We have 19,000 people across 80 countries. How can anyone find what projects we have done to re-use the learning? A manager in Stockholm may waste two months' work researching a project that has already been completed in the UK.'

The prevention of wasted work would seem to have much merit but there may be a limit to how far companies can go in attempting to harness the so-called 'tacit knowledge' we carry around in our heads.

A corporate focus on employee knowledge has proved threatening in the past. One of the aims of F. W. Taylor, the inventor of scientific management which broke down and measured the constituent parts of a job, was to ascertain the true capabilities of an individual. This met with resistance personified by Nels Alifas, a US trade union leader and one of Taylor's chief critics.

Alifas held that workers tried to keep knowledge to themselves in order to exercise control over their working lives. 'We haven't come into existence for the purpose of seeing how great a task we can perform through a lifetime,' said Alifas. 'We are trying to regulate our work so as to make it an auxiliary to our lives.' His observations are worth remembering among companies struggling to secure the knowledge of their employees. Those human assets are not like bricks and mortar and machinery designed as tools for profit. They have other lives outside the company.

Another source of resistance to knowledge sharing is the historical perspective of 'trade secrets', the idea of the guild that protected the workings of a craft among initiates. The approach of the knowledge officer is diametrically positioned to that of the worker who is unwilling to share his know-how. Personality testing of a sample of the officers in the LBS study found that openness was the predominating trait beyond that of extroversion. Most, according to Professor Earl, were confident, passionate and bubbly people. It may be significant that about a third of those covered by the study were women.

This open approach may prove the worth of such officers. As Ms Lank stresses, she sees her job as pointing out sources of knowledge in the company rather than that of extracting an individual's know-how. As knowledge management progresses, companies will need to create ways of recognising the expertise of certain employees. The sophistication of intranets has created the potential for systems to track the way individuals are being tapped for their know-how by colleagues. This is likely to throw up some surprises. We may soon be looking at a new group of worker heroes whose value to the company has been consistently underestimated by senior managers focused myopically on productivity. In the meantime, it is a good one for the CV. As one of those in the study remarked: 'I have the honour of having the most pretentious title in the company.'

Source: *Financial Times* CD-ROM, 1 January–31 December 1998.

Introduction

This chapter proposes a strategic planning framework that explicitly incorporates technology-management issues in global companies. It divides the planning process into three stages: scanning, strategy development (at the product level) and implementation (at the country level). The first stage treats the question, 'What technologies (as distinct from businesses) are we, or should we be in?' In the second stage, the aim is to develop a strategy for each of the products from the chosen technologies. In the third stage, details of implementation on a country-by-country basis are worked out.

Technology, for all its vital importance to a global company, cannot be treated as a profit centre. This is part of the difficulty in implementing the technology-management function, especially in multidivisional and global firms. The use of this framework will serve to integrate managers from different parts of the company into a formalised technology planning exercise.

Many multidivisional and multinational companies feel there is a poor coupling between technology development and strategic planning, possibly because of a lack of adequate planning frameworks for technology. The divisionalisation of companies tends to compartmentalise and fragment technology strategy. Some product divisions may not be aware of valuable technologies available from other divisions. The problem is often acute when units of a global firm are geographically and administratively scattered in distinct regional or national profit centres. The management of technology – that is, its development, transfer and optimal utilisation in the multinational firm – is a function that cuts across the product as well as the geographic dimensions of the company. Increasingly, technology needs to be developed and used by more than one product group or nation for maximum efficiency and exploitation. Moreover, a typical technology cycle from research to commercialisation takes much longer than a corporate planning cycle. Finally, the R&D function may be overly centralised, so that its planning is not well integrated with the needs of many country markets.

A global planning framework should address the following concerns. First, the R&D process can no longer be considered sequential, but rather synchronous with global manufacturing and global marketing decisions. This calls for an enlarged role for the R&D manager. But most firms are organised with regions or global product divisions as profit centres. How to harness the apparently different technology strategies and capabilities of various divisions into an overall global strategy direction for the firm is a key issue tackled by this chapter. Second, today technology acquisition from other firms may have as great a strategic importance as internal development, or the sale of technology beyond the firm's boundaries. Third, multiproduct and multinational companies have begun to focus on the critical issue of the interdivisional transfer of technology and co-ordination between different R&D facilities. Finally, the effective utilisation of the company's technical assets across the many country markets the firm operates in, is an issue growing in importance.

Managing technology in the multinational and multiproduct company

Managements used to product divisions or countries as profit centres may neglect the development of an overall technology strategy. It is difficult to think in terms of a technology as a profit centre or as a unit of measure since its boundaries are often fuzzy and spill over into several product areas. A company that has developed a technology has to know whether to use it exclusively in-house or also transfer it to other firms and industries in several nations for a full return on its investment. It must decide which end-applications it will exploit internally, by itself manufacturing and marketing products, and which end-applications or nations it will serve by co-operative alliances and contractual knowledge transfers. When the end-applications are very diverse, such as in information systems, no computer firm these days can claim to have fully exploited its commercial opportunities without allies and licensees internationally.

The second reason why it is difficult to think of technology as a profit centre is because the life-cycle of a technology may be longer or shorter than that of a product, depending on how narrowly we define each.

Third, ordinary capital budgeting and manager-evaluation methods break down when a technology is the unit of measurement (Leonard-Barton and Kraus 1985). Ordinary ROI criteria may not correctly measure the true strategic benefits and costs of a technology programme because its externalities are not well measured. For instance, investments in computer-aided manufacturing and robotics often appear to generate a poor ROI because their benefits (external to the manufacturing division) such as superior service and delivery to customers are not incorporated into the analysis. Using another example, the ROI from a transfer of technology under licensing or joint venture may appear to be superior to that from a fully-owned subsidiary – until, that is, the negative externality of subsequent competition from the licensee or partner is factored in (Contractor 1999).

On the input side, technology transcends the product and country dimensions since research, development and manufacturing involve numerous techniques, all of which may not be possessed by the firm. This requires a worldwide search followed by an internal development versus external acquisition decision. Globalisation presents the manager with two additional strategy decisions at the manufacturing level. First, the configuration of pieces of the manufacturing and distribution chain must be optimised geographically. The cost of internal technology transfer and co-ordination of foreign affiliates are two determining variables (Bartlett and Ghoshal 1987). Second, the costs of internal development and manufacture are weighed against the alternative of an intermediate product simply being bought in. There can be strikingly different strategy solutions in the same industry. 'Lean' automobile producers, for instance, may have less than 20 employees per thousand vehicles produced, compared to over 60 employees for others. The bulk of the difference is not productivity, but the vastly greater level of subcontracted parts and component purchases in the lean firms.

Such differences are not just technological, but cultural and organisational. A useful planning framework would link these issues and provide criteria for evaluating questions such as the optimal degree of integration with suppliers, the optimal level of global standardisation, and the degree to which the firm will utilise its technical assets by establishing fully owned foreign subsidiaries versus sharing its technologies with corporate allies.

This chapter proposes that such decisions need to be made at the same time as the R&D function and fed back into it. Technology development and international strategy can no longer be separate or sequential decisions. They have to be synchronous.

The analytical framework presented here is intended to initiate a common thinking process in a company, between the technologists, business managers, and country or marketing specialists who frequently have very different assumptions, approaches to risk, time values and 'rules of evidence'. This framework is an important first step in initiating a systematic analysis of technology policy by different personnel in a global company. However, there is an equally important set of process, behavioural and organisational learning issues, relating to the interaction of diverse personnel from various parts of the firm (Maidique and Zirger 1985).

A technology–planning framework

As was mentioned earlier, this chapter presents a three-stage planning process:

1 Technology scanning and audit (firm level)
2 Development strategy (technology/product level)
3 Implementation and utilisation (country level).

The first stage is a company-wide inventory, categorisation and selection of technologies and an assessment of the firm's overall competitive position. It asks questions such as 'What technologies are, or ought we to be in?'

The second stage occurs at the technology-specific or product level. For those technologies that are chosen for development, the second level treats questions such as the allocation of costs over various aspects of the development process, the optimal configuration of global suppliers and co-development partners, speed/cost tradeoffs, the optimal level of global standardisation and the degree of vertical integration. Here the focus is on formulating a development and commercialisation strategy for a particular product type.

The third stage, called implementation and utilisation, treats the optimum utilisation of a developed technology at the country level. It incorporates criteria such as the characteristics of the technology, its codifiability, transferability to other nations, the appropriability of profits from the fully owned subsidiary mode versus a joint venture or a licensing arrangement, and other external factors such as the diffusion of technology to potential competitors. Each stage is now described in some detail.

Stage 1: technology audit

During the first stage the firm strives to answer the question 'What technologies should we be in?' This means identifying actual and potential technologies inside and outside the firm; assessing the product applications that might emerge; categorising technologies that define the distinctive competence of the company; and deciding how to fill the gaps in the technology portfolio by either internal development, joint research with another firm or external acquisition. As part of planning Stage 1, two subordinate issues are also tackled: namely, technology progression and an intellectual property strategy in a global arena.

Technology inventory

Technology inventory refers to the process of identifying all technologies strewn throughout the global firm, as well as technical developments external to the firm that may affect its future. It may appear surprising, but many companies are unaware of the complete set of technologies in their technology portfolio. To be meaningful, identification should be specific, not general. For example, a general identification as 'biotechnology' is valueless since biotechnology is a cluster of widely differing technologies from genetic engineering to biogas.

Entirely new strategic directions are sometimes revealed by changing the unit of measurement or analysis from a product or nation to a technology. For

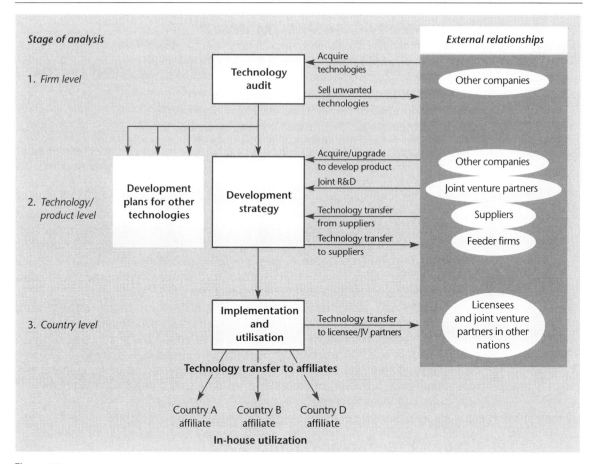

Figure 15.1 A technology-planning methodology for the multinational firm

instance, a defence company's portfolio of businesses or divisions included aero-space, as well as construction aggregates obtained from quarrying operations. Quarrying cost and efficiency depend on the proper placement of explosive charges so as to produce fragments of optimal size, detonated and placed opti-mally for easy collection. For defence applications the aerospace division had developed ultra-high-speed imaging techniques to track missiles and projectiles. By defining the technology rather than the business as the unit of analysis, the company spotted the applicability of this new technique to the construction aggregates division. The new technology – which can record images of a mil-lionth of a second or less in (literally) explosive environments – was put to use in improving rock-fragmentation efficiency through an optimum distribution and timing of charges in a quarry face, improving productivity in quarries by 15–30 per cent. Such a technology can also be sold or licensed externally.

The famous strategy question 'What business are we really in?' may thus be restated to read 'What technologies or knowledge areas are we really in?' Otherwise, opportunities are missed for want of asking the right question.

A technology-inventory process thus identifies and enables the application of a proprietary technology to other divisions of the firm. It also identifies external

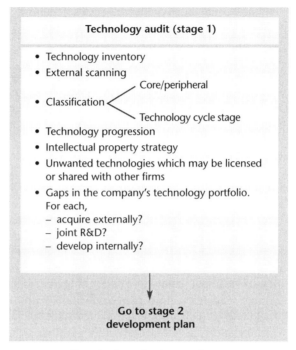

Technology audit (stage 1)

- Technology inventory
- External scanning
- Classification
  - Core/peripheral
  - Technology cycle stage
- Technology progression
- Intellectual property strategy
- Unwanted technologies which may be licensed or shared with other firms
- Gaps in the company's technology portfolio. For each,
  - acquire externally?
  - joint R&D?
  - develop internally?

Go to stage 2 development plan

Figure 15.2 Steps in the technology-audit process

technology-transfer opportunities whose competitive impact may first be assessed by members of the planning team called 'gatekeepers' (Goldstein 1987).

Technology scanning and knowledge-seeking foreign investments

This is the process of identifying evolving knowledge areas external to the firm that may affect its technology profile. Scanning complements the inventory process to determine the firm's desired technology portfolio and because critical 'make or buy' decisions hinge on an awareness of external developments.

Besides an investigative element, scanning requires maintaining interpersonal and organisational linkages with relevant actors. Foreign direct investment (FDI) may be made to exploit proprietary knowledge in foreign markets. Equally well, and increasingly, FDI is undertaken to serve as a window on developments in the foreign nation.

Classification of company knowledge

The next step would be to classify each technology as base, core or peripheral. Since base technologies are known to most competitors, transferring these to other firms outside the industry need not have competitive implications. An example would be ovens and furnaces which are basic to the steel industry but find applications in several others. Core technologies, on which competitive advantage is based, may not be easily shared outside the firm even in the mature stage. An example of a peripheral technology is the rather complex art of galvanising a car body which requires precise application of currents and control over bath chemistry. This kind of technology is peripheral to a large auto company, but it is a very desirable technology to other industries. Some firms have established 'technology marketing groups' to fully exploit the potential of peripheral but valuable technical assets.

Each technology may also be classified according to its stage in its technology cycle. This forces focus on the time element, on how the firm is doing *vis-à-vis* competitors, and on the technology-progression issue.

Technology progression

Technology progression refers to managing a 'technology portfolio' so that it contains products and technologies at various stages of development and maturity. This is important for balanced long-term growth and strategic direction, as well as to ensure that the 'cash cows' will finance new developments – and conversely that the company will in fact have new developments to be financed in the future. Technology progression is an especially crucial aspect for start-up firms to manage. New high technology firms exhibit a high dependence on technology transfer to and from external companies in the early years (Smith and Fleck 1988). Technology acquisitions are for rapid starts. Technology sales are to raise crucially needed cash. In a later stage there is a greater use of in-house development and commercialisation. The firm's business may make a corresponding progression. A biotechnology firm may move from contract research and testing for others, to the manufacture of diagnostic kits, and finally to the mass-marketing of drugs. In pharmaceuticals and computers the marketing function presents a formidable, capital-consuming obstacle to be tackled last. Technology progression is therefore a joint technology and financial-planning exercise. The entire technology-planning exercise has to be multidisciplinary, drawing personnel from several parts of the company.

Intellectual property strategy

For the majority of industries in the past, patents were seen as having symbolic value, applied for on defensive grounds, rather than as valuable cash-generating assets in their own right. A company's technology was judged to reside mainly in unpatented 'know-how' rather than in the patent, *per se*, in most industries. Worse, in the past, two-thirds of judgements in US courts were made against the patent holder (Kerr 1988). And a vastly greater number of patents were, and to a considerable extent continue to be, 'worked around' by competitors without legal challenge. Worst of all, the very act of filing in some nations could reveal proprietary secrets, while an underdeveloped legal system provided no effective protection there.

In the 1990s the environment has changed considerably for the computer, semiconductor, pharmaceutical, chemical and other industries that depend on intellectual property protection. For these industries, intellectual property protection has become a crucial strategy and marketing consideration. As the number of technologically proficient firms has increased globally, as competitors are better able to assimilate and reproduce technology, the importance of patent protection is more keenly felt. At the same time, all over the world, the rights of patent-holders are upheld more frequently than in the past. Enforcement and recourse are also beginning to be tighter in emerging markets.

Today intellectual property has a far more important competitive strategy implication than its cash value in accounting terms or in dispute settlements. It is used to stake out a market, to negotiate cross-licensing arrangements, and for technology and territorial swaps rather than for cash value.

Exhibit 15.1 **A new chip from diverse blocks**

The name of the game in designing semiconductors is to build as many functions as possible on to a single microprocessor, producing devices that amount to 'a system on a chip'. But with 20m transistors on the latest chip, the time needed to design one often exceeds the probable shelf life of the products in which it is to be used.

'This is a productivity gap that cannot be filled by today's designers on their own,' explains Jim Tully, a semiconductor analyst at Dataquest. 'The only way it can be filled is by slotting in predesigned blocks of intellectual property (IP) from other designers.' Trade in these blocks – often called virtual components or VCs – is 'taking off like a rocket', he says, growing by 65 per cent worldwide in 1997.

An important step has been taken recently to make this trade in virtual components (which may be just lines of code on a diskette or tape) as simple as buying and selling hardware. A Virtual Component Exchange (VCX) will begin some operations next year.

The VCX is based in Scotland, a country better known for producing electronic hardware than for designing it. But it has a powerful set of players among its ten founding members: semiconductor design companies such as Cadence Design Systems and Mentor Graphics of the US, Arm and Iss of the UK, and semiconductor producers such as Motorola, Toshiba and Siemens.

The VCX is part of the Alba Centre, a semiconductor-design campus at Livingston, near Edinburgh, set up by Scottish Enterprise, the development agency, to complement the establishment in the town of a system-on-a-chip design centre by Cadence which should eventually employ 1900 people.

'There are many hurdles to be overcome before you can use a block of somebody's else's intellectual property,' says Andy Travers, the VCX's interim director. First, he says, a semiconductor design company can spend a long time locating the VC it needs because VC providers, often small companies, are dispersed around the world and present their IP in different ways.

It can take 20 weeks to negotiate a contract between provider and user because there is no standard agreement under which a user can evaluate a VC to assess whether it suits him and then obtain the full use of it under licence. Even after a deal has been concluded the provider of the VC may find it difficult to audit the use the customer makes of it and collect royalties, leaving scope for disputes.

Because it is a new industry, says Mr Tully, 'VC providers don't know how much to charge and whether they are getting a good deal or not.' When the

VCX gets going, says Mr Travers, user companies will log on to it via the Internet and scroll through lists of tradeable ICs. The VCX will provide the electronic tools for an exchange of virtual signatures to allow the user to have an overview of the IC, followed by a full technical evaluation and a test of its compatibility.

Finally the parties would begin a contracting process, leading to agreement on price, delivery and product support. 'All this will be built into the contract in a form provided by the VCX,' says Mr Travers. The VCX will set a model for royalty agreements and protection of IP rights, and lay down rules to govern mediation and arbitration.

They can make deals under any legal jurisdiction but could find the Scottish legal system attractive. Jack Harding, President and Chief Executive of Cadence, says the fact that the Scottish system reaches decisions quickly and does not have a long list of precedents are two reasons his company is setting up in Scotland.

Mr Travers believes the VCX will cut the time it takes to conclude transactions by 50 per cent and achieve a similar reduction in dealing costs. It will not set prices, leaving this to the parties, nor charge a percentage on deals. Instead it will levy membership fees and charge for writing contracts and for the use of its tools and technical support. It is constituted as a not-for-profit organisation.

Mr Tully believes OEMs such as IBM and Nokia will become involved. 'They are realising they are sitting on a mountain of IP embedded in their products and would like to find a way of releasing and commercialising it.'

Source: *Financial Times* CD-ROM, 1 January–31 December 1998.

Outcome of the technology audit

The technology audit process results in the identification and categorisation of knowledge areas or technologies to be abandoned, developed further, and those which may be exchanged, licensed or shared with joint venture partners. The latter may be handed over to a 'technology marketing' department for external exploitation. The rest are intended for internal development, and a development plan drawn up for each (in Stage 2 of the technology-planning methodology). At the same time, gaps in the company's technology portfolio are identified, with a recommendation to fill the gap by either external acquisition, joint R&D, or by internal development.

Stage 2: the development strategy for each technology – the impact of international factors

Stage 2 of the planning process is concerned with the development of one technology at a time. This may lead to one, or a multiplicity of products, applications and manufacturing processes. Nevertheless, it is important, during the development stage, to keep the manufacturing and tooling aspects in mind from the very start for the most important expected products. Two teams may be

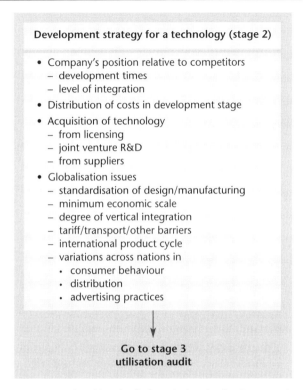

Development strategy for a technology (stage 2)

- Company's position relative to competitors
  - development times
  - level of integration
- Distribution of costs in development stage
- Acquisition of technology
  - from licensing
  - joint venture R&D
  - from suppliers
- Globalisation issues
  - standardisation of design/manufacturing
  - minimum economic scale
  - degree of vertical integration
  - tariff/transport/other barriers
  - international product cycle
  - variations across nations in
    - consumer behaviour
    - distribution
    - advertising practices

**Go to stage 3
utilisation audit**

Figure 15.3 Consideration in formulating the development plan

set up simultaneously. While the development venture team is working on the technical aspects, a manufacturing process team is already formulating design and manufacturing specifications. For many industries, we are no longer a comfortable, sequential world where production and manufacturing innovation became crucial only in the later stages of the technology cycle.

At the technology development stage itself, the firm has to plan for:

- development time versus cost tradeoffs
- the anticipated level of integration (or quasi-integration with joint venture partners, suppliers, etc.). This affects development costs and time, as well as later manufacturing decisions
- allocation of total development costs over various sub-activities such as tooling, pilot plant, startup and market studies
- anticipated speed of imitators and the expected dominant design standards in the industry
- optimal degree of globalisation.

Development costs and time

There has been a resurgence of ideas about the value of speed as a competitive tool, not only in production (Schmenner 1988) but also in development of new products (Takeuchi and Nonaka 1986). We discuss here the development cost versus time tradeoff. In general, development costs are spread over the subcategories of (a) product or process specifications; (b) pilot plant; (c) tooling and equipment; (d) startup including training of personnel; and (e) market studies.

Two planning decisions are needed:

1 Overall level of expenditure versus development time
2 Allocation of budgeted expenditures over the above subcategories.

In a world of accelerating product cycles the company that can develop an item faster has a survival edge. In a classic study, Mansfield's (1988) work compared 30 matched pairs of American and Japanese firms and showed that, in part, Japanese companies have a faster development and commercialisation time because of their greater expenditures to *consciously* shorten the development stage. For all industries Mansfield found the Japanese operating on the time–cost tradeoff function at a point where their costs would show a 9 percentage points increase in order to reduce time by 1 per cent; by comparison the US all-industry mean elasticity was about four. That is to say, Japanese firms appeared willing to expend on average twice the funds to achieve equivalent reductions in development and commercialisation time, as a strategic imperative.

Many Japanese firms on the other hand had lower development costs than comparable American firms in the same industry. There are two explanations. The first has to do with the allocation of development costs within the subcategories shown in Table 15.1. The Japanese allocated a far higher percentage of expenditures to tooling and equipment compared to US firms which spent more than double the Japanese level on market studies. Second, the Japanese placed a far greater reliance on external technical relationships with suppliers and subcontractors. The value added to sales ratio in Toyota or Nissan's factories was about 15 to 20 per cent compared to 48 per cent for GM in the 1980s (Eckard 1984). But the term subcontracting or outsourcing was a relationship that was not merely contractual. Interlocking equity ownership, intense transfers of technology both ways, and non-adversarial, co-operative behaviour make for what is really a co-development and co-manufacturing relationship. Mansfield's all-industry comparison from a sample of 30 matched pairs of Japanese and American companies concluded that the speed and lower cost of development in Japanese industry is partially explained by their external network or 'keiretsu' relationships.

Table 15.1 Percentage distribution of innovation costs, 100 firms, Japan and the United States, 1985

				Percent of innovation cost going for:			
	Applied research	Preparation of product specifications	Prototype or pilot plant	Tooling and manufacturing equipment and facilities	Manufacturing startup	Marketing startup	Total
All industries combined							
Japan	14	7	16	44	10	8	100
United States	18	8	17	23	17	17	100

Source: Mansfield (1988).

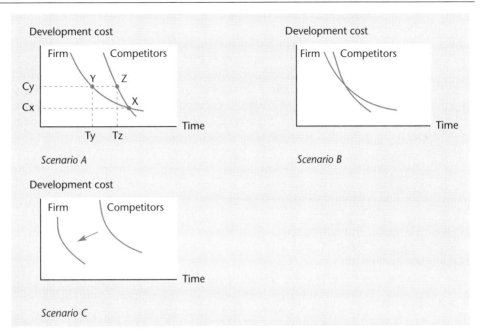

Figure 15.4 Alternative scenarios for development cost–time tradeoffs

Figure 15.4 depicts three alternative scenarios the planning group should consider. Scenario A shows our firm having a shallower slope than competitors on the development cost–time tradeoff. If so, it may consider moving from a point such as X to point Y. Even if competitors matched the higher level of expenditures to point Z, our firm would still enjoy time advantage Tz – Ty. The increase in expenditure Cy – Cx is justified only if the consequent lead time over competitors Ty – Tx enables the firm to descend the experience and scale curve first and capture a larger market share – or by having the company's standards adopted as the industry norm. In scenario B our firm and competitors have fairly similar time–cost tradeoff curves. Increased development expenditures are not justified as they may set off negative-sum, oligopolistic countermoves. In Scenario C our firm is able to move to an entirely new, and lower, curve by using external relationships such as co-development joint ventures and help from suppliers.

These diagrams are not entirely theoretical abstractions. Some firms calculate alternative budgets for the development expenditure on a particular technology and assess times for each. At the very least, the figures provide the basis for an informed discussion within the planning group. Companies worldwide, and not just the Japanese, today appear very conscious of the strategic value of such an exercise.

With global competition, it is becoming imperative for a firm to examine each technology in the development stage for:

- the time–cost tradeoff
- competitors' time/cost functions
- determining at what point on the function the firm chooses to be – that is, what it will spend
- relationships with suppliers and partners that may lower development times and cost.

Acquisition of technology

The alternative of acquiring the technology (or pieces of it) externally should form part of the planning process at this stage. There are various arrangements such as R&D partnerships, development joint ventures, licensing and contracted research. While we will not examine the benefits and costs of each, we can state some general criteria for evaluating them against each other and the in-house development alternative.

We begin with an overall valuation criterion, useful not only during negotiations, but also useful in identifying acquisition targets.

> A technology sale between companies may occur when the value of a technology is perceived to be considerably higher by the purchaser than by the company that developed it – so much so, that the incremental profitability to the acquiring firm less the transaction and adaptation cost to the acquirer must be greater than the technology's perceived profitability to the developer (seller), with the final purchase price lying somewhere in between.

Otherwise there would be no sale.

Why would the buyer and seller place unequal values on a technology? The reasons are both structural and perceptual.

Among structural reasons are: capital constraints in the developer firm; diversification advantages to the acquiring firm, not enjoyed by the present technology owner. These could be geographical, as well as product line diversification advantages; incremental costs of commercialisation and launch greater in the developer firm than in the acquiring company; pre-emption of a third competitor from acquiring a significant technology; and other complementarities or externalities eventually accruing to the purchaser, which the seller cannot enjoy.

In regard to the last point, it is still worth reiterating that the long-term strategy implications and complementarities are often far more important than the narrow calculations of capital budgeting and profit estimates can capture – especially if the time values and perceptions embedded in the calculation do not incorporate the viewpoints of the technology/R&D personnel, as well as executives in different parts of the global firm.

Among perceptual reasons (why a technology's value is rated differently across companies, as well as across departments in the same firm) are: variations in perceptions of the speed versus cost tradeoffs shown in Figure 15.4; sensitivity to the competitive ramifications of linking the firm to a technology developed by others; questions of whose designs will dominate the industry; the perceived maturity of the technology; and the possible atrophying of internal technical capability. Stopford and Baden-Fuller (1987) reported that it was not so much the economics of production, as perceptions of the 'strategic future' of the European appliance industry, that explained the variations in technology, scale and productivity between European companies. Italian firms were described as believing in a unified European market, and as having a longer-term orientation than their British counterparts who were said to pursue a policy of defending their 'national niche'.

Later in the chapter, we discuss the third alternative of co-developing a technology via contracted or co-operative relationships. There are benefits and costs. For instance, joint ventures and co-development alliances are often quicker and entail lower overall development costs; but the market has to be shared, and today's partners may become tomorrow's enemies.

Exhibit 15.2 Siemens and 3Com in joint venture deal

Siemens of Germany and 3Com, the US computer-networking company, are forming a $100m joint venture to target the rapidly growing market for converged voice and data networks.

The 50:50 owned enterprise will design equipment that allows companies to handle their telephone calls over their computer networks. This relatively new market, which is expected to grow to $4bn over the next three years, has a number of uses. In the management of call centres, for example, it would allow someone viewing a company's web site to connect instantly to a live salesman. It would also facilitate video conferencing through personal computers.

As well as designing the equipment at the core of such networks, the new company will provide software that allows phone calls to be made by computers and telephones that communicate over the Internet.

The new operation, which will be launched with about 200 engineers and assets of $100m including intellectual property from both companies, will work solely on research and development. The products will be manufactured and marketed by the two joint venture partners under their existing brand names.

The move comes during a radical restructuring at Siemens and reflects 3Com's need to find its way back into higher-margin product markets, especially in the US, where it has been losing ground to rivals such as Cisco Systems.

The deal also marks an increasingly close relationship between the two companies which already have an alliance to cross-market each other's products, and which are also working with Newbridge Networks of Canada to develop high-speed data-networking equipment for telecommunications groups.

Ron Sege, Senior Vice-President of large enterprise business at 3Com, defended his company's strategy of working through alliances as the best way to approach the market for converged voice and data equipment, which has been driving a number of mergers and acquisitions in the industry. 'We would contrast our approach with the go-it-alone route or the acquisition route, both of which have significant pitfalls,' he said.

Big mergers between data companies and telecoms groups, most notably the takeover of Bay Networks by Nortel, merely act as a management distraction, he said, while data-networking groups such as Cisco, which have decided to attack the market on their own, underestimate the challenge they face.

However, analysts are likely to view the alliance as a defensive move by two companies that are finding it hard to compete in an aggressive marketplace.

Source: *Financial Times* CD-ROM, 1 January–31 December 1998.

Globalisation and its link to technology planning

Globalisation involves, in part, international plant location and product-design decisions. These are determined by minimum economic scale, transport cost, protectionist barriers, aftersales service, flexible manufacturing and other design and production technology questions best considered at the development stage and not after manufacturing methods and specifications are finalised.

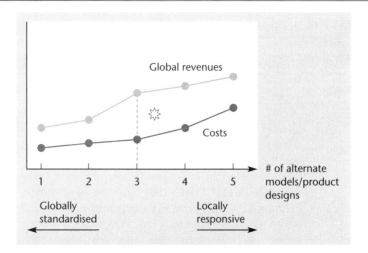

Figure 15.5 The optimum level of globalisation

Consider two alternative strategies depicted in Figure 15.5. A 'global' approach strives to cut costs and realise efficiencies by reducing the differences in models of a product sold in different nations. In the development and engineering stages, economies of scale and rationalisation are planned from a few large, low-cost plants to serve the world market.

A 'local responsiveness' strategy on the other hand tries to introduce variations, from one country to another, in product design, aftersales service and other technical parameters, in order to suit local customers and governments better. The scale of production is necessarily smaller and the number of plants worldwide is larger compared with a global strategy. The multinational firm can afford to be more decentralised, enabling local managers to be more responsive to local country conditions. Many designs of the product are needed, preferably with adaptability to different customer tastes or technical standards. (Also, the overall strategy of the firm can more easily include joint venture and licensing arrangements in certain nations, a theme we return to in Stage 3, the utilisation audit.)

Which of the two strategies is best? As Figure 15.5 suggests, 'neither' is the likely answer for the majority of industries. The optimum lies somewhere in between. A local responsiveness strategy is rewarded by worldwide total sales revenue increasing with a larger number of models adapted to conditions in each national market. But costs would then increase as well, with a larger number of smaller scale plants and a duplication of facilities and staff. Hence the optimum level of local responsiveness versus globalisation is likely to be found in an intermediate position.

At the development stage we need to consider technical as well as managerial variables which will affect the optimal degree of globalisation of a product. Some are shown in Figure 15.6, such as the minimum efficient scale (MES) of manufacture. Consider the evolution of the television receiver industry. MES has gone from 50,000 receivers per year in the early 1960s, to 500,000 sets in the late 1970s, to 2.5 million in the 1990s. This is more than one maker can hope to sell in many countries. Globalising firms have therefore to assess the ratio of MES over the mean size of the market in the countries they serve. By comparison,

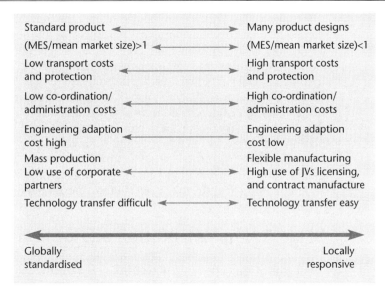

Figure 15.6 Variables affecting the optimal degree of globalisation

pharmaceutical manufacture is amenable to the very small scale of efficient manufacture, enabling formulations to be easily varied to suit local medical practice and regulations, without a large cost penalty.

Such strategy questions should be considered at the development stage and not after engineering and specifications are finalised. If considered early enough, it may be possible to develop manufacturing processes that are efficient at smaller scales of operation. This is especially true with computer-aided design and manufacturing, and with the flexible use of corporate partners overseas. An alternative approach is to design the product so as to build in easy, or relatively low-cost adaptability to local tastes and conditions.

Despite years of talk, the market for domestic appliances in Europe is not unified because of persistent cultural distinctions, brand loyalty and high national entry barriers in the distribution end of the business. Some companies, however, believe that globalisation is setting in and that there is a convergence in buyer preferences. In these companies, appliances are being redesigned with substantially fewer parts and flexible manufacturing systems which enable variations in output types despite production on a larger scale. In such a case the engineering adaptation costs for switching from one model to another are dramatically reduced. For the large appliance industry in general, entrenched national firms resist the further concentration of manufacture in fewer and larger plants.

Compared to one factory in each nation, a multinational firm that attempts to serve many markets from a few plants has significantly higher co-ordination and administrative costs, and risks arising from supply interruptions, currency and political fluctuations. These act counter to the tendency to entirely centralise global operations. These risks may also be perceived by customers, who do not wish to be so dependent on a foreign supplier. In the telecommunications and other 'strategic' industries, customers who are often governments, mandate local value-added activity and joint ventures with local firms to reduce such perceived risks.

Today, alert companies make the search for the globally optimum number of models part of their development planning. While some industries such as large appliances move towards fewer variations, others such as automobiles and consumer electronics may be moving towards more choice. For some firms, the incremental development and production costs of introducing an additional model may be more than recouped by the incremental global revenue resulting from offering customers a larger choice responsive to local tastes. It is the old story of 'incremental revenue versus incremental cost', but applied in this strategy-planning exercise to a product design (or model) as the unit of analysis.

Thus each firm hunts for its optimum between the extremes of complete global standardisation and producing a different model for each country market: an engineering and strategy exercise that should begin at the development stage.

Stage 3: implementation and utilisation audit

The focus at this level of the technology-planning exercise is on maximising the international utilisation of the developed product. One country at a time is examined to determine the optimal mode of business. In the broadest sense the firm needs to decide whether to extend its own organisation into the foreign nation by means of a fully-owned subsidiary (S), or whether to go in for a contractual mode such as contract manufacture (C), or licensing (L) the process and/or product design to an independent firm which learns the technology and manufactures the item in the country. In the middle of the spectrum are various quasi-contractual or quasi-integrated modes such as minority-owned joint ventures (JVM), and majority-owned joint ventures (JVS) which function like a subsidiary despite some shareholding by another firm.

Overall, the company ends up with a global pattern of business shown in Figure 15.8, a planning matrix of products versus countries. In the majority of product/country combinations the markets would simply be served by imports; or no business at all is feasible because of impediments to investment and trade such as protectionist barriers, transportation costs, restriction on foreign investment in certain sectors, and political risks.

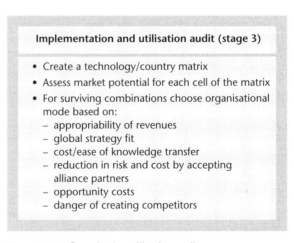

Figure 15.7 Steps in the utilisation audit

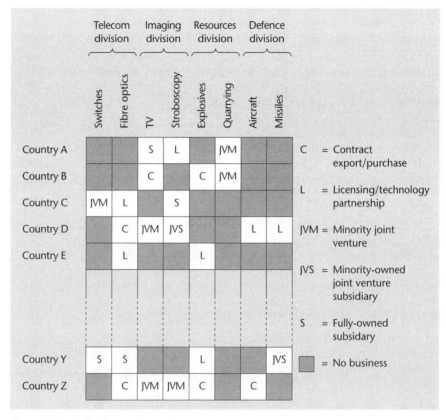

	Telecom division		Imaging division		Resources division		Defence division	
	Switches	Fibre optics	TV	Stroboscopy	Explosives	Quarrying	Aircraft	Missiles
Country A			S	L		JVM		
Country B			C		C	JVM		
Country C	JVM	L		S				
Country D		C	JVM	JVS			L	L
Country E		L			L			
Country Y	S	S			L			JVS
Country Z		C	JVM	JVM	C		C	

C = Contract export/purchase

L = Licensing/technology partnership

JVM = Minority joint venture

JVS = Minority-owned joint venture subsidiary

S = Fully-owned subsidary

= No business

Figure 15.8 Utilisation–audit matrix

For a newly developed product, how does a firm decide on which mode is best for a country? Choosing between a firm's own controlled and integrated subsidiary, or a contractual transfer of technology, or quasi-integration with another partner firm is a complex exercise. For each option not only do market revenues and production costs vary, but with joint venture partners and licensees the share of revenues and costs allocated to each firm is also subject to negotiation. Other strategic implications such as creating a potential competitor also need to be considered. Figures 15.9 and 15.10 provide some strategic guidance.

Figure 15.9 shows a decision tree of major options, and it plots them on an expected return versus degree of control map (Contractor 1999). In general, a fully owned subsidiary provides the highest potential return as well as control over strategy and operations. But as Figure 15.10 indicates it also carries the highest level of risk since the largest invested assets are at stake. Contracted modes carry the lowest degree of control in a long-run strategic sense, especially if a significant technology is transferred to an independent licensee who could eventually become a competitor. But such a risk can be contained by agreement provisions, a strong patent position or, most effectively, by remaining technologically one step ahead of licensees and joint venture partners. Moreover licensing bears the lowest level of commercial risk to the licensor who does not bear the capital investment, and typically earns a royalty-income stream linked to sales

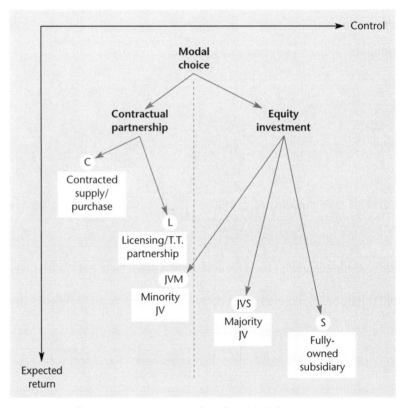

Figures 15.9 Control versus return mapping of model choices

rather than share of profits. Thus a royalty stream is *axiomatically* less volatile over the business cycle than profits, and sales are relatively steady, even if profits disappear in a severe downturn (Contractor 1985). Most of the capital investment and business-cycle risk is borne by the licensee company.

On the other hand, a fully owned foreign investment affords the firm the opportunity to appropriate the entire return on the investment and make its investment congruent with global strategy, unhindered by the possibly divergent

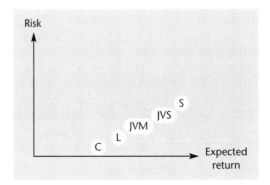

Figure 15.10 Risk versus return map of alternatives

and parochial objectives of partners. Fully owned investments are preferred by firms that dominate the designs of products and have a strong patent position.

Figures 15.9 and 15.10 depict joint ventures as occupying the middle ground on the (1) return (2) risk (3) control and (4) competitor risk dimensions. However, we should remember that in recent years companies have found that joint ventures in some cases offer the best overall mix on these four dimensions – to the extent that firms often prefer them over the fully owned subsidiary alternative. For instance a company that enters a foreign market alone bears all the investment risk, and its unfamiliarity with the local market may carry a heavy penalty in reduced sales. This penalty can be mitigated by taking a local partner who also shares in the investment risk of a joint venture. Moreover, the local partner can significantly reduce investment costs if it has an existing manufacturing and distribution establishment in the nation. In such cases joint ventures are preferred over fully owned investments.

In the case of a license, the risk is shifted ever further away; the licensee makes the investment and bears the investment risk, allocating the technology-supplying company a relatively safe, fixed percentage of revenues. Licensing is chosen when a company possesses a desirable technology but is unwilling to muster the managerial or financial investment, or face the perceived high risk in the nation, contenting itself with receiving a fixed royalty in return for very little or no incremental investment (over and above the sunk cost of development).

We should not make the mistake of assuming that licensing is undertaken mainly by small technology firms which lack the financial or management-personnel resources to make their own investments. Larger, multidivisional and multinational companies have a much larger potential for a profitable licensing and joint venture programme for their non-core technologies. The largest of companies such as a GM or a General Electric will typically have about 100 or fewer majority or fully controlled foreign investments for its core businesses. It is administratively and financially undesirable to have more. That still leaves hundreds or thousands of possible technology-country combinations unexploited on the matrix in Figure 15.8. Recall our earlier example of the auto company which had developed a new metal-galvanising technology with better rust protection of its cars in mind. Instead of neglecting the utilisation of this technology with applications in other industries in virtually every nation, it can be licensed, or joint ventures set up to greatly increase the return on the R&D investment. And this may be done without the fear that there will be an adverse competitive impact on its main business of selling automobiles.

Medium and large companies have dozens to hundreds of such valuable but under-utilised technologies strewn throughout the firm. It takes a technology inventory (Stage 1) plus a utilisation audit (such as the one recommended in Stage 3) to maximise the return on a company's R&D investment.

Chapter summary

This chapter has presented a methodology for strategic and technology planning in the global and multidivisional firm. Since corporate knowledge or a technology cannot be operationalised into profit centres, nor easily regarded as a unit of administrative measurement, the role of technology in formulating strategy is often *ad hoc*, or neglected in many larger, multidivisional companies. This is not because of lack of awareness. It is because corporate-planning procedures have not fully integrated the technology-management aspect.

This chapter presents a three-stage planning framework. The first stage, called technology audit, is a company and worldwide identification of technologies or knowledge competencies within and outside the firm. At this stage of the planning exercise, the planning group examines the technology-progression issue and intellectual property strategy, and makes a broad assessment of technologies that may be shared with other firms and those to be reserved for the company's exclusive development. At the same time, gaps in the company's strategy are identified, with a recommendation for how they may be filled by internal development, external purchase of the technology, or by means of a joint venture partnership.

The second stage of the planning exercise, called the development strategy, focuses on one technology at a time. It treats issues such as development cost and time *vis-à-vis* competitors, time–cost tradeoffs in the development budget, allocation of the budget over subcategories, acquisition of pieces of the technology from partners and suppliers, and the anticipated degree of globalisation versus local responsiveness which in turn feeds back into product design and manufacturing technology decisions.

The third stage of the planning exercise is called the implementation and utilisation audit. A technology/country matrix is created; each cell is then assessed for market potential. For large, and even medium-sized firms, the matrix can have hundreds of cells. Many of these will be eliminated as having little potential. For a new technology or product the analysis next recommends the mode of business, ranging from fully owned direct investments to arms-length licensing, with varieties of quasi-integrative or quasi-contractual options such as joint ventures, in between. While the methodology is presented in three steps, in practice it is iterative. In essence, the exercise integrates the national and functional diversity of the firm into a formalised consideration of the most critical component of its long-run strategic success technology.

Source: This chapter is a revised and adapted version drawn from an earlier article, Technology development in the multinational firm: a framework for planning and strategy. *R&D Management* 20 (4) October 1990.

Discussion questions

1 What are the main stages of a strategic planning process?
2 What is meant by 'technology progression' and why is it an especially crucial aspect for startup firms to manage?
3 What are the major differences between 'global' and 'local responsiveness' strategies?

Closing Case Study:
ABB aims to maximise payoffs and at the same time avoid stifling risk-taking

Monir Tayeb

Early next year a large pumping system will be placed on the bottom of the North Sea to separate oil from water and rocky debris and direct it to the surface.

The event hardly seems earth shattering. But it will be an important test for a technology-management system pioneered by ABB, the Swedish–Swiss company, one of the world's biggest engineering suppliers. Like many other large companies, ABB has been trying hard to maximise the chances of commercial payoffs from its R&D budget, without subjecting its technologists to so much pressure that they fail to take risks.

Where ABB differs from most other businesses is the scale of its spending on research, development and engineering: this amounts to some $2.6bn a year or about 8 per cent of sales.

Working on the projects are 20,000 engineers, the majority of whom are in ABB's six main business divisions, covering areas such as electricity generation and transmission, and process automation. At the less-applied end of the spectrum are 1300 scientists and technical people who work in ABB's nine research laboratories worldwide.

A team of technology experts, led by Markus Bayegan – a former Director of the company's Norwegian corporate laboratory who took over as ABB's head of technology in January – co-ordinates the efforts.

Mr Bayegan's main job is to steward a system of fast-track technology management that ABB has been introducing during the 1990s. The aim is, first, to bring together people from different parts of ABB's business to work in multidisciplinary teams, with research scientists often collaborating closely with engineers who spend most of their time dealing with customers.

The second aspect concerns the speed with which individual projects get off the ground, or are dropped if they do not show promise. 'When we decide on a new project we make the money available quickly and go for it,' says Mr Bayegan. 'We are trying to lead in a number of key technology areas, but with minimal bureaucracy.'

The subsea pumping system is an example of a so-called 'high-impact' project of a type introduced by ABB in 1994. The aim was to tackle important areas of technology that could have a big effect on ABB's business areas but involved a big risk.

High-impact projects are one of four broad types of technology programmes supported by ABB in this area. ABB has 10–15 specific high-impact programmes going on at any one time. Together they cost some $200m a year and invariably involve special groups of ABB people from different business and research divisions.

The pumping system was devised by one such team of 25. It will see service in so-called 'marginal' oilfields where the oil comes mixed with a large amount of water and debris. This mixture is normally pumped to the surface where it can be separated in large units mounted, for instance, on a platform. In the past, it has been a lot easier to put the separation unit on the surface – where maintenance, for instance, is relatively simple.

However, oil companies convinced ABB that a subsea system was preferable. Such a system would cut the cost of getting the material to the surface and reduce the weight of the equipment needed on the platform. The problem was to find the combination of mechanical engineering and control systems that would work with minimum supervision on the sea.

After a $25m development programme that started three years ago, the new subsea unit will be installed by ABB for the Norsk Hydro oil company in April 1999. It will be in the Troll C field 60km west of Bergen.

Similar systems could be used by oil and gas companies elsewhere. Mr Bayegan says the development time for the new unit was about a third to a half of what would have been needed using technology management techniques favoured during the 1980s. Even if development of such a system had found the necessary managerial support and finance, it would almost certainly have taken longer to bring together the development people and bring the programme to fruition.

A crucial element in the success of 'high impact' projects is an internal ABB computer network which links about 1500 of the company's scientists and engineers. Using this system, workers in different fields can swap ideas – for instance, about new control techniques or power semiconductors – that are applicable to a range of businesses. 'We use information technology to make research programmes more transparent,' says Mr Bayegan.

Source: *Financial Times* CD-ROM, 1 January–31 December 1998.

Questions

1 Why has ABB put in place a system of fast-track technology management?
2 Why is ABB convinced that a subsea pumping system is preferable to other technologies for its oil-exploration purposes?
3 How does ABB ensure the success of its 'high impact' projects?

References

Baden-Fuller, C. *and* **Stopford, J.M.** (1987) Why Global Manufacturing?, *Multinational Business*, Spring, pp. 15–25.

Bartlett, C. and **Ghoshal, S.** (1987) Managing across borders: new strategic requirements, *Sloan Management Review*: 7–17.

Contractor, F. (1985) *Licensing In International Strategy: A Guide for Planning and Negotiations,* Westport, CT: Quorum Books.

Contractor, F. (1999) Foreign market entry strategies, in *International Encyclopedia of Business Management,* London: Routledge.

Eckard, E. (1984) Alternative vertical structures: the case of the Japanese auto industry, *Business Economics*, October: 57–61.

Goldstein, M. (1987) Gatekeepers fit the key into new technology, *Industry Week*, 16 November: 75–7.

Kerr, J. (1988) Management's new cry: fight for your technology rights, *Electronic Business*, 15 August: 44–8.

Leonard-Barton, D. and Kraus, W. (1985) Implementing new technology, *Harvard Business Review*: 102–10.

Maidique, M. and Zirger, B. (1985) The new product learning cycle, *Research Policy*, December: 35–48.

Mansfield, E. (1988) The speed and cost of industrial innovation in Japan and the United States: external versus internal technology, *Management Science*: 1157–68.

Schmenner, R. (1988) The merit of making things fast, *Sloan Management Review*, Fall: 11–17.

Smith, J. and Fleck, V. (1988) Strategies of new biotechnology firms, *Long Range Planning* 21 (3): 51–8.

Stopford, J. and Baden-Fuller, C. (1987) Regional-level competition in a mature industry: the case of European domestic appliances, *Journal of Common Market Studies*, December: 173–92.

Takeuchi, H. and Nonaka, l. (1986) The new, new product development game, *Harvard Business Review*, Jan–Feb: 137–46.

CHAPTER 16

International Marketing Planning

Svend Hollensen

Learning objectives

By the end of this chapter you will be able to:

■ define and explain the five main decisions in international marketing planning

■ understand the importance of having a carefully designed information system as a starting point for the different phases of international marketing planning

■ understand the principles of standardisation and adaptation of international marketing strategies

■ discuss the influences that lead a firm to standardise or adapt its international marketing programme

■ explain the purpose of an international marketing budget.

Opening Case Study:
Cultural barriers as Europe dials M for middleman

In spite of success in Spain, Direct Line faces an uphill task elsewhere.

Nestling between the offices of longer established multinationals in an urban sprawl just north of Madrid, a small call centre is selling car insurance to Spanish, Catalan and English-speaking customers. Investing heavily in television advertising, it has doubled the number of policyholders on its books in the past 18 months and aims to be profitable by 2000.

Linea Directa is hoping that the removal of commission-seeking middlemen from the distribution chain will enable it to replicate the success of Direct Line, its parent, in the UK. The odds are not favourable. The telesales revolution in car insurance, pioneered by Direct Line in the 1980s, has been almost exclusively English.

Attempts to export such marketing techniques to the rest of Europe have shown only that the struggle for market share will be desperate in most countries.

In Germany and France, the continent's biggest insurance markets, telephone-based insurers account for just 0.9 per cent and 1.2 per cent of gross written premiums, says a report by Datamonitor.

Direct Line argues Spain is different from France and Germany. 'Commissions and costs in the established distribution channels were relatively high when we set up. Telephone banking had also enjoyed some success,' says Chris McKee, technical director. Spain's insurance market was deregulated quicker than elsewhere and car ownership is growing because of the rapidly improving transport system.

The difficulty elsewhere is partly cultural. Buying habits across much of continental Europe are conservative and relationships between policyholders and the local tied agents of big domestic insurers strong.

Competition has increased after EU directives four years ago freed policy terms and premium rates, and allowed insurance companies to operate across the EU on the basis of regulations in their home country. Premium income from business sold via the telephone should rise nearly 50 per cent to $12.4bn by 2002, according to Datamonitor. But telephone-based insurers will be most successful in Spain, The Netherlands and Scandinavia.

It is these markets' peculiarities that have helped the growth of direct insurers. In The Netherlands, the state health system has for some time encouraged consumers to use the telephone and most personal health insurance is sold direct. Much insurance in Scandinavia is distributed through company sales forces rather than via agents, so the telephone does not threaten relationships between insurers and intermediaries.

In France, mutually owned insurers have a tight grip on different customer segments through traditional links with professions. The initial investment in a call centre and the high costs of advertising mean profitability depends on the acquisition of sizeable market share, a process which could take between five and ten years. Linea Directa has 155,000 policies and earned Ptas8.8bn ($57.7m) of premiums last year. It made a loss of £1.6m ($2.61m).

Royal Bank of Scotland, which owns Direct Line, had invested in Spain through a link with Banco Santander and was represented on the board of Bank Inter, Direct Line's joint venture partner. Bank Inter was familiar with call-handling technology.

As a result, the red telephone that has bounced on to Britain's television screens for more than a decade is now recognised by nearly 90 per cent of Spanish television viewers. Linea Directa, which employs some 350 people, takes more advertising space than Mapfre, the country's biggest insurer.

Direct Line is cautiously considering expansion in other European countries. While it is already licensed to write business in Portugal, it has so far chosen not to do so. 'The ability to write insurance is not simply based on answering telephone calls. You have to have a physical presence for people to go and assess claims,' says Mr McKee.

Furthermore, underwriting business in a new country would require detailed knowledge of postcodes, car models and loss ratios, as well as the pricing and profit margins for existing operators. A 'pan-European' call centre marketing out of one country could offer efficient distribution, but would need to be supported by a local presence to manage claims and develop networks of repairers. All this could push up operating costs.

Bob Yates, insurance analyst at Fox-Pitt Kelton, suggests that other distribution methods, the Internet for example, could have overtaken the telephone by the time deregulation has had a noticeable effect on European markets. 'It may be that the idea of talking to someone on the telephone will be considered just as expensive as talking to an agent is now.'

Source: Financial Times CD-ROM, 1 January–31 December 1998.

Introduction

In the next decade companies will face markets that are globally competitive and globally integrated. International marketing is no longer only about domestic manufacture and exports.

Though the international marketing activities are in focus in this chapter they cannot be separated from the other value chain functions of the company: product development, production, and sales/service. All internationally oriented firms must consider an eventual internationalisation of these value chain functions.

The role of international marketing

The primary role of marketing management, in any organisation, is to design and execute effective marketing programmes that will pay off. Companies can do this in their home market or they can do it in one or more international markets. Going international is an enormously expensive exercise, in terms of both money and, especially, top management time and commitment. Because of the high cost, going international must generate added value for the company beyond extra sales. In other words: the company needs to gain a competitive advantage by going international. So, unless the company gains by going international, it should probably stay at home.

The task of international marketing management is complex enough when the company operates in one foreign national market. It is much more complex when the company starts operations in several countries. Marketing programmes must, in these situations, adapt to the needs and preferences of customers that have different levels of purchasing power as well as different climates, languages and cultures. Moreover, patterns of competition and methods of doing business differ between nations and sometimes also within regions of the same nation. In spite of the many differences, however, it is important to hold on to similarities across borders. Some co-ordination of international activities will be required, but at the same time the company will gain some synergy across borders, in the way that experience and learning acquired in one country can be transferred to another.

The major international marketing decision

Marketing practitioners face five main decisions in connection with the international marketing process. In Figure 16.1 the five phases of the decision process are linked to the information needed in each phase.

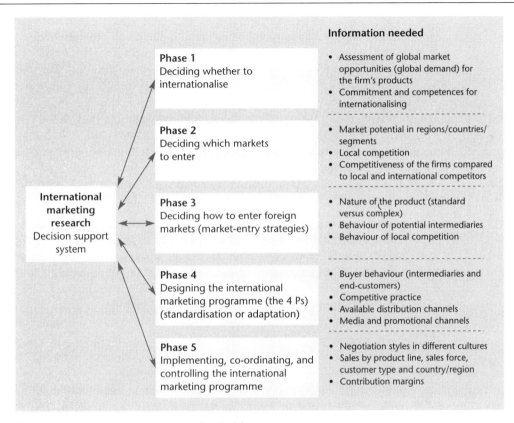

Figure 16.1 Major international marketing decisions

The role of international marketing research

The prime function of global marketing is to make and sell what international buyers want, rather than simply selling whatever can be most easily made. Therefore, what customers require must be assessed through marketing research and/or through establishing a decision support system (see Figure 16.1) so that the firm can direct its marketing activities more effectively by fulfilling the requirements of the customers.

Figure 16.2 summarises the principal tasks of international marketing research according to the major decision phases of the global marketing process. As can be seen, both internal (firm-specific) and external (market) data are needed. The role of a firm's internal information system in providing data for international marketing decisions is often forgotten.

How the different types of information affect the major decisions have been thoroughly discussed in the different parts and chapters of this book. Besides the split between internal and external data, the two major sources of information are primary data and secondary data:

- *Primary data* These can be defined as information that is collected first-hand, generated by original research tailormade to answer specific current research questions. The major advantage of primary data is that the information is specific ('fine grained'), relevant and up to date. The disadvantages of primary data are, however, the high costs and amount of time associated with the collection of this type of data.
- *Secondary data* These can be defined as information that has already been collected for other purposes and is thus readily available. The major disadvantage is that the data are often more general and 'coarse grained' in nature. The advantages of secondary data are the low costs and amount of time associated with its collection. For those who are unclear on the terminology, secondary research is frequently referred to as 'desk research'.

If we combine the split of internal/external data with primary/secondary data, it is possible to place data in four categories. On the basis of the data categorisation in Figure 16.2 four areas emerge, each having different demands as regards the collection of data. The generating of data in areas 1 and 2 can be done via desk research, and this is the point where the Internet comes into the picture. For many years, small companies especially have refrained from carrying out a systematic market selection because they have not had the resources to visit libraries, etc. with the purpose of gathering the necessary comprehensive data from 'thick' books. But this is where small companies can benefit from technological development. The Internet is available to all companies, not just the big ones.

The Internet is not the solution to all information needs, and by moving to the lower part of Figure 16.2 (areas 3 and 4) the secondary data gathering from the Internet should be followed by a primary data gathering before making the final decision on market selection and the setting up of a marketing plan. You can visit the market in question and carry out interviews with intermediaries and final customers (area 3). This can, through an estimation of the company's strengths and weaknesses compared to those of the competitors (area 4), form a basis for setting up a list of priorities for the penetration of new markets. It can also provide input for the subsequent elaboration of a marketing plan for this particular foreign market.

A very basic method of finding international business information is to begin with a public library or a university library. The Internet (World Wide Web, or www) can help in the search for data sources. The Internet has made available thousands of databases for intelligence research (i.e. research on competitors).

Figure 16.3 gives an example of how external data sources can be grouped geographically on a homepage on the Internet, where international marketing data are organised according to the presented structure. The international market researcher is recommended to start with the global sources and then move on to the particular region/country they are interested in.

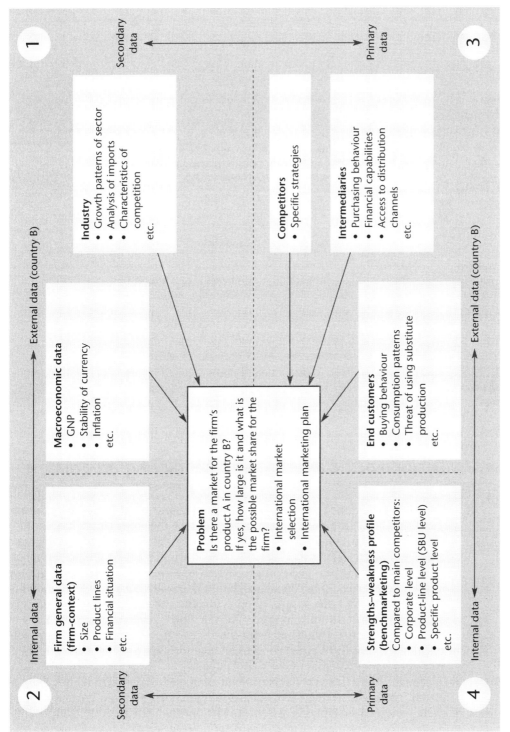

Figure 16.2   Categorisation of data for assessment of market potential in a country

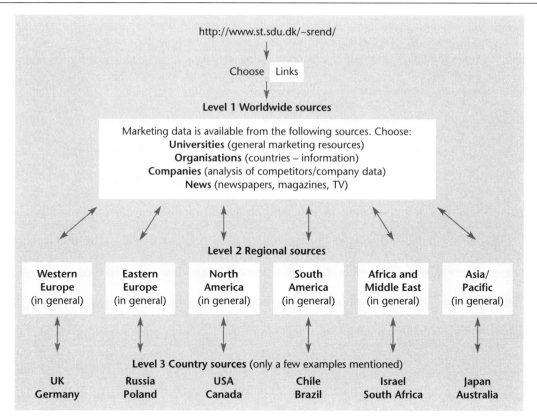

Figure 16.3 International marketing data sources

Designing the international marketing programme

After having decided which markets to enter and what penetration strategy to use (Figure 16.1) the next issue is how to design the global marketing mix.

Since the beginning of the 1980s, the term 'globalisation' has increasingly become a matter of debate. Levitt's contribution on 'The globalisation of markets' (Levitt 1983) provoked much controversy concerning the most appropriate way for companies to become international. Levitt's support of the globalisation strategy received both support and criticism. Essentially, the two sides of this debate represented local marketing versus global marketing and focused on the central question of whether a standardised, global marketing approach or a country-specific differentiated marketing approach has the most merits. Figure 16.4 shows the extremes of the two strategies.

Hence, a fundamental decision that managers have to make regarding their global marketing strategy is the degree to which they should standardise or adapt their international marketing mix. The following three factors provide vast opportunities for marketing standardisation (Meffert and Bolz 1993).

- *globalisation of markets* Customers are increasingly operating on a worldwide basis and are characterised by an intensively co-ordinated and centralised purchasing process. As a countermeasure, manufacturers estab-

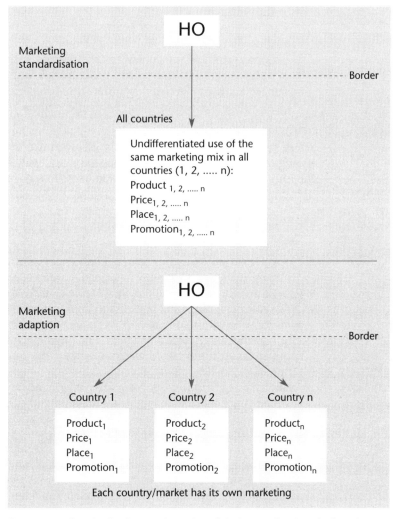

Figure 16.4 Standardisation or adaptation of the international marketing mix
Source: Hollensen (1998: 332).

lish a global key account management in order to avoid individual country subsidiaries being played off against each other in separate negotiations with, for example, global retailers.

- *globalisation of industries* Many firms can no longer depend on home markets for sufficient economies of scale and experience curve effects. Many industries, such as computers, pharmaceuticals and automobiles, are characterised by high R&D costs which can be recouped only via worldwide high-volume sales.
- *globalisation of competition* As a consequence of the worldwide homogenisation of demand, the different markets are interrelated. Therefore the firms can plan their activities on a worldwide scale and attempt to establish a superior profile *vis-à-vis* other global competitors. Hence, country subsidiaries no longer operate as profit centres but are viewed as parts of a global portfolio.

The standardised marketing concept can be characterised by two features:

- standardisation of marketing processes is mainly concerned with a standardised decision-making process for cross-country marketing planning. By standardisation of the launching of new products, controlling activities, etc, rationalisation of the general marketing process is sought.
- standardisation of marketing programmes and the marketing mix is concerned with the extent to which individual elements of the 4Ps (product, price, place, promotion) can be unified into a common approach for different national markets.

These two characteristics of standardisation are often interrelated. For many strategic business units, process-oriented standardisation is the precondition for the implementation of standardised marketing programmes.

Exhibit 16.1 Two cultural marketing mistakes in Japan

Proctor & Gamble's worst cultural experiences occurred in Japan as they introduced their Pampers brand. They had a commercial on the air in the US that showed an animated stork delivering Pampers diapers to homes.

The American managers in Japan thought that this would be a terrific piece of advertising to introduce Pampers to Japanese consumers. They dubbed the copy into Japanese, substituted the Japanese package for the American one and put the commercial on the air. To their great dismay, the advertising failed to build the business.

Finally, after showing the copy to several Japanese consumers, we discovered that they were confused about why this bird was delivering disposable diapers. According to Japanese folklore storks don't deliver babies. Babies arrive in giant peaches that float on the river to deserving parents.

By their marketing efforts in the Asia-Pacific region Procter & Gamble learned that the Asian consumer is extremely diverse. Unlike the consumers in North America, Europe and even Latin America, there are very few social or economic bonds that tie the consumers of the Asia-Pacific region together.

There are very savvy consumers in Japan who scrutinise every aspect of our products, compared with relatively naïve consumers in China, who are just getting used to having a choice of brands.

We have consumers with Western values in Australia and New Zealand, and very Confucian values in most of the region.

Source: *Advertising Age International*, January 1998: 8.

A US-based food processor, knowing that Pacific Rim household kitchens have little room for a full-sized oven, developed a cake mix that could be prepared in a rice cooker, an appliance found in virtually every household between Hong Kong and Kuala Lumpur.

The product was introduced to Japanese consumers – and failed miserably. Unfortunately, the food processor did not know that to the Japanese it is anathema to put anything but rice in a rice cooker, let alone a sticky cake mix.

Source: Crain's small business, *Chicago Edition*, Dec.1996/Jan.1997, vol. 4 Issue 10, p.12.

Many writers discuss standardisation and adaptation as two distinct options. The commercial reality, however, is that few international marketing mixes are totally standardised or adapted. Instead it is more relevant to discuss degrees of standardisation or adaptation. Exhibits 16.1, 16.2 and 16.3 show that in markets with high cultural distance, cultural adaptation of the marketing strategy is necessary.

Exhibit 16.2 **International in a local way**

Unilever describes itself as 'a truly multi-local multinational', and is dedicated to meeting the everyday needs of people everywhere. With 300 local operating units in some 90 countries and with sales in over 60 more, it caters for consumers around the world, in both new and established markets. Unilever has a portfolio of global, regional and local brands. Some, such as *Magnum* ice cream and *Dove* personal wash, have become world leaders; others are the top choice for consumers in specific countries.

Unilever's strength lies in its deep understanding of local culture and markets. Building on a presence that in places stretches back nearly a century, it is closely in tune with local consumers and invests in understanding and meeting their needs.

Since consumers vary from country to country in their preferences and habits, Unilever adjusts many of its brands to suit local tastes. For instance, among its many teas, Unilever produces 18 separate brands of black tea specifically tailored for consumption in 18 different countries and it is constantly sharpening the flavours to suit all its local markets. Likewise in detergents, Unilever's brands are also adapted. For example, in Brazil, *Omo* detergent has been modified to take into account differences in water conditions and laundry habits.

Source: *Introducing Unilever* (1999)

Exhibit 16.3 **McDonald's 'globalisation' strategy**

McDonald's may have taken its logo worldwide but still it makes a lot of adaptation of its product and advertising.

Product adaptations

In India they serve the 'Maharaja Mac'. This burger features two mutton patties, since most Indians consider cows sacred and don't eat beef.

In 'spicy' Singapore they serve a 'Pepper-burger', and in the fastidious green Germany they introduce a 'Vegetarian burger'.

In the depressed Indonesia they decided in 1998 to introduce a sort of 'crisis burger'. Concurrently with the 80 per cent decline of the Indonesian currency, the Rupiah, since last summer the price of the traditional Big Mac-burger, has risen from 4500 Rupiah to 10,400 Rupiah (approx. DKK 4.50). This has led to a drastic fall in turnover in McDonald's original 101 restaurants in Indonesia – and so far 21 restaurants have been closed down.

The new product has very little in common with a traditional hamburger. The name will be RiceEgg and will consist of a one-egg omelette mixed with strips of beef and vegetables, all served on a 'rice bun'. The price will be a modest 2000 Rupiah: less than twenty cents.

Advertising adaptation

Today they also produce the majority of their advertisements locally.

The advertising agency Leo Burnett and the competitor DDB share McDonald's advertising in more than 60 countries. Everywhere the aim is to promote the burger-chain as the near-by family restaurant with fast quality food. But the campaigns have been adapted to the family values of each nationality and also to the period in which the burger empire has existed in the country.

Australia is an 'old' market with the largest number of McDonald's restaurants per inhabitant in the world. Here they try to maintain the consumers' focus on the brand with the Australian song 'MacTime' and a series of trick movies with James Dean and Marilyn Monroe.

In China the burger chain is new in the market, so here they use children to introduce and explain McDonald's excellence to the older generation.

Hong Kong lies in between, both geographically, culturally, and as regards the life cycle of the burger chain. Here they also use children, but with a humour that is tailormade for the more Western-oriented customers.

Source: Across the Board, February 1997, 34(2): 5.

Table 16.1 summarises the main factors favouring international marketing standardisation versus adaptation.

The standardisation of physical product attributes (size, weight, colour, etc.) affords the greatest potential for cost benefits, since economies of scale are made principally at the manufacturing stage. On the other hand, the service attributes of a product (maintenance, aftersales service, spare parts availability, etc.) are fairly difficult to standardise, as circumstances for service delivery differ widely from one country to another. Most services are performed in direct relation to local customers. Service attributes are more dependent on culture.

Even though a part of the above factors points towards standardisation, the examples in Exhibits 16.2 (Unilever) and 16.3 (McDonald's) show that even the largest multinational companies are now moving towards the adaptation strategy.

After having determined the company's general international marketing strategy the next issue is the specific combination of the international marketing mix.

This chapter will not focus on every one of the 4Ps (product, price, place, and promotion). However, regarding the promotion mix, Exhibit 16.4 demonstrates the significance of translating slogans, etc into local languages without causing any misunderstandings. This also illustrates the importance of local advertising agencies being involved in the planning of local marketing campaigns.

Table 16.1 Main factors favouring standardisation versus adaptation

Factors favouring standardisation	Factors favouring adaptation
Rapid technology shifts in industry meaning shorter product life cycles (rapid worldwide penetration is necessary)	Slow technology shifts in industry meaning longer product life cycles
Economies of scale in R&D, production and marketing (experience curve effects)	Local environment-induced adaptation: government and regulatory influences (no experience of curve effects)
Global competition	Local competition
Short cultural 'distance' to the foreign market	Long cultural 'distance' to the foreign markets
Convergence of tastes and consumer needs (consumer preferences are homogeneous)	Variation in consumer needs (consumer needs are heterogeneous)
Centralised management of international operations	Fragmented and decentralised management with independent country subsidiaries
A standardised concept is used by competitors	An adapted concept is used by competitors
International product standards (e.g. ISO 9000 family)	Local product standards (e.g. industrial safety standards for electricity supply)
Favourable image of imported products, company, or brand	Unfavourable image of imported products, company, or brand

Exhibit 16.4 **Examples of slogans with 'problematic' translations**

- When General Motors introduced the Chevy Nova in South America it was apparently unaware that 'no va' means 'it won't go'. After the company figured out why it wasn't selling any cars it renamed the cars in its Spanish markets as the Caribe.
- Ford had a similar problem in Brazil when the Pinto flopped. The company found out that Pinto was Brazilian slang for 'tiny male genitals'. Ford prised all the nameplates off and substituted the name with Corcel, which means horse.
- In Taiwan, the translation of the Pepsi slogan 'Come alive with the Pepsi Generation' came out as 'Pepsi will bring your ancestors back from the dead'.
- Also in Chinese, the Kentucky Fried Chicken slogan 'finger-lickin' good' came out as 'eat your fingers off'.
- The American slogan for Salem cigarettes, 'Salem – Feeling Free', got translated in the Japanese market into 'When smoking Salem you feel so refreshed that your mind seems to be free and empty'.

▶

- When Parker Pen marketed a ballpoint pen in Mexico its ads were supposed to say 'It won't leak in your pocket and embarrass you'. However, the company mistakenly thought that the Spanish word 'embarazar' meant embarrass. Instead the ads said that 'It won't leak in your pocket and make you pregnant'.
- An American T-shirt maker in Miami printed shirts for the Spanish market which promoted the Pope's visit. Instead of the desired 'I saw the Pope' in Spanish, the shirts proclaimed 'I saw the Potato'.
- A Danish company made the following slogan for its cat litter on the British market: 'Sand for Cat Piss'. Unsurprisingly, sales of the firm's cat litter did not increase!
- Another Danish company translated 'Teats for baby's bottles' into 'Loose tits'.

Source: Hollensen (1998: 177/448).

Controlling the international marketing programme

The final, but often neglected, stage of international market planning (phase 5 in Figure 16.1) is the control process. Not only is control important to evaluate how we have performed, but it completes the circle of planning by providing the feedback necessary for the start of the next planning cycle. Unfortunately, however, 'control' is often viewed by the people of an organisation as being negative. If individuals fear that the control process will be used not only to judge their performance, but as a basis for punishing them, it will be feared and reviled.

There is no such thing as a 'standard' system of control for marketing. However, Figure 16.5 presents an example of annual control in the form of an international marketing budget for a manufacturer of consumer goods. Included in the budget are those marketing variables that can be controlled and changed by the sales and marketing functions (departments) in the home country and in the export market. In Figure 16.5 the only variable that cannot be controlled by the international sales and marketing departments is variable costs.

The global marketing budget system (as presented in Figure 16.5) is used for the following (main) purposes:

- allocation of marketing resources among countries/markets to maximise profits. In Figure 16.5 it is the responsibility of the global marketing director to maximise the total contribution 2 for the whole world
- evaluation of country/market performance. In Figure 16.5 it is the responsibility of export managers or country managers to maximise contribution 2 for each of their countries.

Co-operation is required between the country managers and the international marketing manager/director to co-ordinate and allocate the total marketing resources in an optimum way.

Please note that besides the marketing variables presented in Figure 16.5 the international marketing budget normally contains inventory costs for finished

International marketing budget	Europe			America	Asia/Pacific			Other markets	Total world Σ
	UK	Germany	France	USA	Japan	Korea		
Year = _____	B A	B A	B A	B A	B A	B A	B A	B A

Net sales (gross sales, less trade discounts, allowances, etc.

÷ **Variable costs**

= **Contribution 1**

÷ **Marketing costs:**

Sales costs (salaries, commissions for agents, incentives, travelling, training, conferences)

Consumer marketing costs (TV commercials, radio, print sales promotion)

Trade marketing costs (fairs, exhibitions, in-store promotions, contributions for retailer campaigns)

= Σ **Total contribution 2**

(marketing contribution)

B = budget figures; A = actual

Figure 16.5 An example of an international marketing budget for a manufacturer exporting consumer goods

goods. As the production sizes of these goods are normally based on input from the sales and marketing department, the inventory of unsold goods will also be the responsibility of the international marketing manager or director.

Furthermore, the international marketing budget may also contain customer-specific or country-specific product-development costs, if certain new products are preconditions for selling in certain markets.

In contrast to budgets, long-range plans extend over periods from two years up to ten years, and their content is more qualitative and judgemental in nature than that of budgets.

Chapter summary

Going international must generate added value for the company. So, unless the company gains by going international, it should probably stay at home.

International marketers face five main decisions in the international marketing process:

1 Deciding whether to internationalise
2 Deciding which market(s) to enter
3 Deciding how to enter foreign markets (market-entry strategies)
4 Designing the international marketing programmes (the 4Ps)
5 Implementing, co-ordinating and controlling the international marketing programmes.

In order to make good decisions and assess what international customers require, a marketing research/decision support system (DSS) is needed. In this chapter a systematic approach for gathering international marketing data has been presented.

Standardisation and adaptation of the international marketing strategy are presented as two distinct options. However, in reality only a few international marketing strategies are totally standardised or adapted. Instead it is more relevant to discuss the degrees of standardisation or adaptation. As a controlling tool it is also important to establish an international marketing budget.

Discussion questions

1 What problems can an international marketing manager expect to encounter when creating a centralised marketing research system (decision support system)?
2 An American manufacturer of shoes is interested in estimating the potential attractiveness of his products in China. Identify and discuss the sources and the types of data the company will need in order to obtain a preliminary estimate.
3 If you had a contract to do marketing research in Saudi Arabia, what problems would you expect in obtaining primary data?
4 Would Tokyo be a good test market for a new brand planned to be marketed worldwide? Why or why not?
5 Why don't more companies standardise advertising messages worldwide? Identify the environmental constraints that act as barriers to the development and implementation of standardised international advertising campaigns.

Closing Case Study:
Charlotte Sparre Ltd

The Danish designer Charlotte Sparre finished her fashion show in Copenhagen last week. Charlotte Sparre had convinced the Danish supermodel Helena Christensen to do one of her last cat walks and present the new Charlotte Sparre collection for Spring 1999. The following day Charlotte Sparre is on a plane to Stockholm in order to prepare the collections for a meeting there, and she is thinking about how sales on the Danish market are satisfactory but on the export markets the situation is not as good. She has sold some goods in Scandinavia and also in Germany, but the big break-through is yet to come.

The company Charlotte Sparre Ltd is a small Danish company situated in Hørsholm north of Copenhagen. The company was established in September 1993 with a production line consisting exclusively of silk scarves. Today new collections are produced four times a year, and many of the patterns in the collection are maintained through several seasons. Furthermore, in the near future the company plans to manufacture 'haute couture'.

Charlotte Sparre's basic aim is to supply the demand for exclusive silk garments combined with chiffon and jersey for women aged 25–45, and to supply the demand for exclusive silk scarves for women aged 15–75.

Today the company counts four employees: an accounts manager and two employees who, in co-operation with Charlotte Sparre, handle the other activities of the company. In 1997 sales amounted to DKK10m and the gross profit was in the millions.

The company uses outsourcing since almost all the production takes place in Denmark, Poland and South Korea. The primary reason is to minimise labour costs.

Charlotte Sparre's scarves are handmade, and the process takes two hours per scarf. The scarves are sewn in South Korea where they have the expertise in this particular field. All finished products are sent to Hørsholm for the final quality check.

Charlotte Sparre designs the collections herself and she makes her own prints on the basis of watercolour paintings that are printed on the scarves. This process also takes place in South Korea, and the minimum quantity to be bought for each new print is 1000 metres of silk. The inspiration for the colour combinations on the fabric is gathered at trend conferences and textile fairs in Paris. Ethnic vegetation and animal life are often repeated in the collections.

Charlotte Sparre's success in Denmark is, among other things, due to an extensive PR effort. Charlotte Sparre works systematically with person-oriented PR with the purpose of having a lot of press coverage in newspapers, weeklies and fashion magazines. The media can also borrow the current collection with the aim of having it depicted in weeklies and fashion magazines.

Export markets

Today the company sells the entire collection in Denmark and Sweden. Export to Norway, Germany, Switzerland, Spain, Portugal and Australia includes scarves, sarongs and dresses. The company is also working on an agreement on the sale of scarves with an English department store which also co-operates with other department stores in Europe.

The export is characterised as direct export and is handled by agents or importers in each particular country. In the countries in which the company uses an agent, he or she functions as a *reaching-out* salesman. When the orders are placed, the goods are delivered directly from Charlotte Sparre's warehouse in Hørsholm to the client abroad. Agents working for Charlotte Sparre receive a commission of 10 per cent of the turnover on that particular market. The importers have a higher profit percentage.

In the countries in which the company uses agents Charlotte Sparre, as a rule, holds the fashion fairs herself. However, in some cases they may be held by the agent. In both cases the costs for the fairs are covered by Charlotte Sparre. The importers are in charge of the fairs themselves and they also cover all the costs.

The company's turnover in 1997 was generated as follows:

Denmark	80%
Sweden	2%
Norway	4%
Germany	10%
Switzerland	1%
Rest (Australia, Spain, Portugal)	3%
Total	100%

The sale of scarves constituted approximately 90 per cent of the turnover in 1997.

Questions

1 Charlotte Sparre Ltd uses a relatively high degree of standardisation in the international marketing strategy. Discuss the pros and cons of Charlotte Sparre's standardisation of each of the Ps in the marketing mix: product, price, place, and promotion. Conclude on that basis.
2 Charlotte Sparre Ltd is considering setting up a homepage on the Internet with the aim of achieving a higher degree of profiling on the export markets. Make a proposition about the main contents of that homepage.

Further reading

Hollensen, S. (1998) *Global Marketing – A Market-Responsive Approach*, Europe: Prentice Hall. A textbook with a decision-making approach to international marketing using the value chain as a starting point. Many case studies and illustrative examples. An appendix with links to international marketing databases.

References

Advertising Age International, Jan., 1988:8, The Ad Age Group.

Levitt, T. (1983) The globalisation of markets, *Harvard Business Review*, May – June: 92–102.

Meffert, H. and **Bolz, J.** (1993) Standardisation of marketing in Europe, in C. Halliburton and R. Hünerburg (eds) *European Marketing: Readings and cases*, Wokingham: Addison Wesley.

CHAPTER 17

International Logistics

Alan McKinnon

Learning objectives

By the end of this chapter you will:

■ understand what is meant by the term logistics and appreciate its contribution to the competitiveness of international businesses

■ be aware of the differing logistical requirements of international businesses and the factors that influence these requirements

■ be familiar with key concepts such as logistical cost tradeoffs, time compression and the postponement principle

■ recognise the implications for logistics management of major trends, such as the geographical extension of sourcing, production and distribution operations, the centralisation of inventory, the reduction in order lead times and the growth of local customisation.

Opening Case Study:
Ocean in drive to enter global logistics arena

Ocean Group, the international freight company, is to merge its freight-forwarding and road-haulage interests as part of its strategy to join the ranks of emerging global logistics businesses. Ocean's freight-forwarding division, MSAS, which moves cargo across international borders, is to be put together with the group's smaller road distribution companies, Intexo and McGregor Cory. The merged entity will operate under the name MSAS Global Logistics and have sales of about £1.1bn.

John Allan, Chief Executive, said the group had decided on the merger because the traditional distinction between freight-forwarding and distribution was eroding. 'Multinational customers increasingly want to deal with a single organisation with good geographical coverage handling the entire supply chain,' he said.

▶

US logistics businesses such as Ryder and Penske, the latter backed by GE Capital, have moved into the European market in recent years, seeking to offer a global distribution service to multinational companies. Mr Allan said the US entrants were still building up their European networks, so had yet to make significant inroads into the business handled by their indigenous competitors. But he said it was important Ocean met the long-term competitive threat head on.

MSAS, with sales of about £900m last year, is one of the world's largest freight-forwarding companies. Intexo and McGregor Cory, which have sales of approximately £200m, enjoy strong positions in the healthcare and packaged consumer goods markets. Their networks cover the UK and Europe. Ocean is also building a distribution presence in Asia.

Mr Allan said the biggest hole in the group's distribution coverage was in the US. Ocean is understood to be seeking to rectify this.

Source: *Financial Times* CD-ROM, 1 January–31 December 1998.

Introduction

Over the past 30 years, the term logistics, which traditionally had strong military connotations, has become widely used in industry and commerce. As it has come into more common usage, many people have wrongly assumed that it is simply another word for transport. In fact, freight transport accounts for only around a third of total logistics costs. Logistics also involves a range of other related activities, including storage, inventory management, materials handling and order processing. The key objective of logistics is to co-ordinate these activities in a way that meets customer requirements at minimum cost.

In many companies this co-ordination has only been achieved over the past 20 years with the development of integrated logistics management. Previously the various activities were managed separately, subordinated to the requirements and budgeting of other functions and typically regarded as 'necessary evils'. Today logistics is well established as an important management function in its own right, with Board-level representation in many businesses alongside production, marketing and finance. It is now widely acknowledged that logistics managers can make a vital contribution to the competitiveness and profitability of a business. They can do this both by cutting costs and improving service quality.

Importance of logistics and supply–chain management

It has been estimated that in 1996 roughly $3425 billion was spent worldwide on freight transport, warehousing and related IT and administration (University of Michigan, quoted in *Financial Times* 1998). Expenditure on these activities represented on average around 11.7 per cent of national GDP. The inclusion of inventory costs would be likely to add a further 5–6 per cent to this figure. Given this high level of expenditure on logistics, even quite small cost savings can yield large economic benefits.

In practice, there have been dramatic improvements in the efficiency of logistics operations over the past decade. Surveys undertaken by A.T. Kearney Ltd for the European Logistics Association show that, across large samples of European companies, logistics costs were reduced, on average, from 14.3 per cent of sales revenue in 1987 to 7.5 per cent in 1998 (*Financial Times*, 1 December 1998). Much of this saving has accrued from tighter inventory management and greater productivity in freight transport.

Logistics can also improve the revenue side of the balance sheet. By providing customers with faster and more reliable services, it is possible to win additional sales and secure greater customer loyalty. Market research studies have established that in the ranking of industrial purchasing criteria, the standard of logistical support usually runs a close second to product design and quality in influencing the choice of supplier (Farmer and Ploos van Amstel 1992). There is no evidence to show that in cutting the cost of logistics, companies have been prepared to sacrifice customer service. On the contrary, service standards appear to have been rising when measured in terms of product availability, speed and reliability of delivery, order accuracy and the condition of goods of arrival.

The efforts of individual firms to improve the quality and efficiency of their logistical systems are inevitably constrained by the activities of outside suppliers, distributors and customers. If firms at different levels in the supply chain try to optimise their logistics independently, the management of product flow across the whole chain, or 'pipeline', is likely to be suboptimal. For example, inventory tends to accumulate at points in the chain where the ownership of goods is transferred from one company to another, adding significantly to distribution costs. Only by co-ordinating their logistical operations and more freely exchanging information can firms improve the overall efficiency of the supply chain while responding more flexibly to variations in customer demand. As Schary and Skjott-Larsen (1995) explain, 'All members of the chain, including carriers, intermediaries and telecommunications agencies have stakes in the performance of the chain.' By more effectively managing their supply-chain links, this performance can be improved to the mutual benefit of the various stakeholders.

While all companies can benefit from effective logistics and supply-chain management, it is a paramount requirement for businesses with extensive international operations. As Christopher (1998) observes, 'For global companies . . . the management of the logistics process has become an issue of central concern. The difference between profit and loss on an individual product can hinge upon the extent to which the global pipeline can be optimised, because the flows of goods and materials are so great.' Such firms not only have to manage the movement of products over greater distances, but also have to contend with the additional restrictions imposed on cross-border traffic and international differences in the structure of distribution systems, the quality of transport infrastructure and the numerous regulations governing logistical operations.

This chapter examines the logistical challenges facing businesses which source and distribute products internationally. In particular it will concentrate on the logistical activities of three types of company:

1 Companies whose core operation (e.g. manufacturing or retailing) is confined to a single country, but which import and export a significant quantity of products

2 Multinational firms which carry out their core activity in several countries within a single trading bloc, such as the EU, but may source and distribute products further afield

3 Corporations that source, manufacture and distribute products around the world, managing their logistics at a truly global scale.

The following section examines the distribution options available to firms in the first category, which are primarily concerned with exporting from their home country.

International distribution systems

If it wished, a company could avoid all responsibility for logistics. A manufacturer, for instance, might export its entire output on an *ex-works* basis requiring the foreign customer to arrange the collection of the goods and bear all the freight and insurance costs. Conversely, all its imports could be purchased on a delivered price basis. Most international trade, however, is sold on terms that require the exporter to assume at least some responsibility for delivery. The official terms of trade (known as Incoterms) define the point at which responsibility transfers from exporter to customer. This can be at the customer's premises, as in the case of 'delivered duty paid' (DDP) or at some intermediate point, when the goods are sold on a free-on-board (FOB) or cost-insurance-freight (CIF) basis. Companies have been increasing their relative use of delivered pricing, particularly within trading blocs. This allows them to sell their exports in foreign markets on the same basis as most domestically produced goods and also to use logistics more effectively as a marketing tool (Davies *et al.* 1988).

Companies that assume responsibility for delivering their products to foreign customers can organise their distribution in several ways. Picard (1982) provided a simple four-fold classification of the distribution systems available to exporters, based on an earlier taxonomy of distribution channels proposed by Bowersox (1978):

1 *Direct system* Orders are despatched from a factory or warehouse in the home country directly to the foreign customer.

2 *Transit system* Exports are channelled through a transit (or 'satellite') depot in another country which acts as a 'break-bulk' point. This makes it possible to transport goods more economically over long distances in bulk loads, disaggregating them into smaller consignments for final delivery to the customer within the foreign market.

3 *Classical system* Exports are distributed via warehouses in each of the foreign markets. These warehouses have a stockholding as well as break-bulk function, supplying foreign customers more rapidly from locally held inventory than through the direct or transit systems.

4 *Multicountry system* This closely resembles the classical system, though instead of having a separate warehouse(s) in each foreign country, one warehouse can serve several adjoining countries. This has the advantage of economising on warehousing and inventory costs.

Table 17.1 summarises the main advantages and disadvantages of each of these systems. The choice of system is determined mainly by four factors:

1 *Nature of the foreign customer base* If, for example, it is composed of a small number of large customers capable of receiving goods in large consignments, the direct system can be the most appropriate.
2 *Volume of export traffic* To be economically viable, the establishment of a break-bulk or warehousing facility in other countries requires a certain minimum volume of export business.
3 *Value density of the product* Products with a high ratio of value to weight or volume (i.e. 'value density') can withstand the higher transport costs associated with direct delivery. It is, for example, profitable to distribute a single personal computer through an international express parcel network to an individual customer.
4 *Order lead time requirements* In sectors where customers demand fast and reliable delivery and where the value of the product does not justify international express delivery, a manufacturer may have little choice but to hold stock locally.

Table 17.1 International distribution systems

Type of system	Advantages	Disadvantages
1 Direct	• No need for foreign warehouse • Greater inventory centralisation/ lower inventory level	• Longer order lead time • Less load consolidation/higher transport costs • More packaging and administration
2 Transit	• Permits breaking of bulk • Greater load consolidation/ lower transport costs • Less packaging and administration	• Extra handling costs in foreign market
3 Classical	• Permits breaking of bulk • Greater load consolidation/lower transport costs • Less packaging and administration • Shorter order lead times • Local stock availability • Lower import dues	• Incurs full warehousing cost • Decentralisation of inventory increases total stockholding
4 Multi-country	• Higher degree of inventory centralisation and lower unit warehousing costs than 3	• Longer lead times to customers • Higher local delivery costs • Difficult to co-ordinate with nationally based sales organisation

Source: Picard (1982).

The direct, transit and multicountry systems appear to be expanding at the expense of the classical system. The growth of Internet retailing, for example, is increasing the demand for international personalised (or 'just-for-you' J4U) delivery via parcel networks. Meanwhile, companies continuing to hold inventory in foreign markets have been concentrating in fewer locations. This latter trend has been particularly pronounced among multinational companies within the European Union. Companies such as Philips, Rank Xerox, Nike, Kelloggs and IBM have closed most of their national warehouses and moved to a system of 'pan-European' distribution based on a small number of European distribution centres (EDCs). Some companies, such as Compaq, now serve the continent from a single EDC while others use several: Sony, for example, has five distribution locations.

Restructuring of European distribution systems

The centralisation of inventory has been one of the dominant trends in logistics over the past 30 years. By reducing the number of stockholding points in their logistical systems firms can exploit the so-called 'square root law', cutting the amount of safety stock required to provide a given level of customer service (Maister 1976). For example, according to this law, moving from a decentralised system of ten warehouses to a completely centralised system should, *ceteris paribus*, cut the amount of safety stock by two-thirds. The resulting stock reductions can yield large financial benefits. In addition to these inventory savings, firms can also take advantage of economies in scale in warehousing. These combined savings usually far exceed any transport-cost penalty associated with centralisation, as illustrated by the experience of one manufacturer which closed nine national warehouses to concentrate inventory at a single distribution centre in Rotterdam (Table 17.2). This illustrates a classic logistical cost tradeoff in which a company incurs higher cost in one activity (local delivery) to achieve an overall reduction in total distribution costs.

Many companies have been able to minimise the additional delivery costs by continuing to break-bulk locally at 'satellite' depots around the continent. The stockholding and break-bulk operations which have traditionally been performed in the same locations can be geographically separated, with the former becoming more centralised while the latter remains dispersed (McKinnon 1989). This represents a combination of the 'transit' and 'multicountry' systems in Picard's classification.

Having reached an advanced stage within individual countries, inventory centralisation is now occurring at a larger geographical scale within the Single European Market as companies take advantage of the removal of frontier controls, the deregulation of international road haulage and improvements to road and rail infrastructure. This trend, however, has not proceeded as far or as quickly as some studies predicted (e.g. Cooper *et al.* 1991; O'Laughlin *et al.* 1993). Four factors appear to have retarded it. First, in many sectors, there has been less standardisation of products for the European market than expected.

Table 17.2 Cost comparison: centralised versus decentralised distribution

| Cost element | Costs in Million US $ | | Difference |
	Decentralised system	Centralised system	
Inventory	7.65	4.65	–3.00
Inbound freight	4.76	4.10	–0.66
Outbound delivery	4.58	4.84	+0.26
Labour	0.55	0.25	–0.30
Warehouse rental	0.33	0.15	–0.18
Equipment	0.18	0.6	–0.12
Total	18.15	14.05	–4.00

Centralised system: single warehouse in Rotterdam.
Decentralised system: warehouses in the UK, Germany, The Netherlands, Denmark, France, Belgium, Switzerland, Italy and Spain.
Source: Buck (1992).

National and regional differences in tastes and preferences have remained quite wide. As a result, companies have still had to make much of their output country-specific and hold separate stocks for each country. This reduces the potential benefits of centralisation. Second, many companies have experienced difficulty in co-ordinating a centralised distribution operation with a sales function which, for good reason, remains nationally based (Abrahamsson 1993). Third, no pan-European logistics companies have yet emerged capable of providing a Europe-wide distribution service to companies wishing to out-source this function (Browne and Allen 1994; Pellew 1998). Finally, increasing traffic congestion on major international corridors has deterred some firms from trying to distribute by road over long distances from centralised facilities (European Centre for Infrastructure Studies 1996).

The process of centralisation has not only affected inventory. Manufacturers have also been concentrating production capacity in fewer locations, imposing greater demands on the logistical system. In some cases this has resulted in a net reduction in the total number of factories; in others it has involved greater plant specialisation. The traditional system of nationally based production, where a factory would manufacture a broad range of products for the local market has, in many sectors, been replaced by 'focused manufacturing' where the entire production of a particular product for a continent or, in some cases, the world market is based at a single location. This allows companies to max-imise economies of scale in the production operation, but at the expense of making their logistical systems more transport-intensive and lengthening lead-time to customers. Christopher (1998) suspects that some manufacturers may not have fully assessed the logistical implications of this strategy. He observes that, 'a number of crucial logistical tradeoffs may be overlooked in what might possibly be a too-hasty search for low-cost producer status through greater economies of scale'.

Changing logistical requirements of global corporations

As companies expand their operations at a global scale, their logistical requirements change. The nature of these requirements reflects the particular globalisation strategy they adopt. Cooper (1993) identifies five strategies that impose very different demands on the global transport system. Each strategy is associated with a particular type of company:

- *invader* A manufacturer sets up a branch plant in a foreign market where it assembles kits obtained from the 'parent' and from which it distributes the finished product to national or continental markets. Such a company organises inbound logistics at a global scale but distributes finished products across a more limited market area. For example, in 1982, Mitsubishi set up a video-recorder plant in Scotland to supply the European market. For its first few years, this was a basic 'screwdriver' operation relying on kits imported from Japan.
- *settler* A firm undertakes more fundamental processing at a branch plant and sources a much larger proportion of its supplies locally. Invaders typically evolve into settlers, especially where regulatory pressures force companies to increase the proportion of local content in the finished product. The substitution of locally sourced parts reduces the demand for transcontinental flows of supplies. Logistical requirements are then largely confined to a single country or trading bloc. Mitsubishi's Scottish video-recorder plant and the Sony television factory in South Wales are good examples of manufacturing operations that have gained 'settler' status.
- *cloner* A company expands by replicating similar branch operations around the world, often on a franchise basis, which draw heavily on local sources of supply from the start. The McDonald's fast-food chain and Coca-Cola well exemplify this type of company. They often require large inputs of local raw materials and, because of the nature of the finished product (e.g. soft drinks), serve only a limited area, probably a national or regional market.
- *baron* A manufacturer concentrates its production capacity in the home country and continues to rely heavily on local suppliers. Finished products, on the other hand, are delivered worldwide from this base. Scotch whisky producers are good examples of 'barons'.
- *outreacher* This type of manufacturer also centralises its production, often in a single country, but sources and distributes its products worldwide. The Boeing aircraft corporation falls into this category.

In recent decades, 'invaders' have been evolving into 'settlers' and 'barons' into 'outreachers', dramatically altering their logistical requirements. Underlying these shifts has been a steady geographical expansion of companies' sourcing and distribution operations. The term 'logistics reach' is often used to describe the length of companies' supply lines upstream and distribution channels downstream. The extension of this 'reach' at a continental and global scale has been one of the dominant trends in international logistics over the past 30 years.

Wider sourcing and distribution

The average consumer is unaware of the distance that many products are transported before they reach the shop. For example, some of the materials in training shoes sold in the UK travel 60,000km before they are bought. Oil originating in the Middle East is exported to Indonesia for processing in a petro-chemical plant. A by-product of this process is shipped to England for manufacture into plastic toe and heel puffs. These are returned to the Far East for assembly into training shoes in a factory in Vietnam, from which the finished products are exported back to the UK, sometimes via The Netherlands or Belgium. Only by mapping the global supply chain, do we get a feel for just how transport-intensive modern systems of production and distribution have become.

Such complex trading networks have evolved chiefly to exploit labour-cost differentials and the availability of raw materials in particular countries. Their development has also been facilitated by deregulation and technological change. Trade liberalisation, mainly within trading blocs such as the EU and NAFTA, has removed constraints on cross-border movement and reduced related 'barrier costs'. Advances in telecommunications and information technology have given companies the means to manage the physical movement of products over long, often circuitous, routes. Many carriers have invested heavily in 'track and trace' systems to be able to establish the location of any consignment at any time, improving the visibility of the global supply chain to shippers and their customers.

Exhibit 17.1 Moving vehicles made easier

Car exporters are being offered a new way to containerise vehicle shipments which, it is claimed, will allow vehicles to be moved from factory to showroom using standard land and sea intermodal freight-transport networks.

Car-Rac International, the UK-based developer, admits that the basic idea of carrying cars in containers is not new in many parts of the world, but claims such operations have to date suffered from a lack of purpose-designed equipment.

'People have been trying to stuff cars into standard freight containers for 20 years and it has not really worked,' says John Evans, international director of Car-Rac. 'The big difference with our system is that we have designed a container specifically for cars. Automotive industry manufacturers already use intermodal containers and swapbodies extensively for inbound logistics. Car-Rac offers the same intermodal solution for finished vehicle delivery. We consider automobiles to be the last great cargo to be containerised.'

The new equipment, called a Car-Rac, is basically a collapsible, 40-foot freight container with two decks and space for six vehicles. Although initially developed as a 40-foot container, the Car-Rac has specially designed endgates which allow vehicles to project beyond that length if necessary. Units can also be fitted with slip-on post extenders which will enable them to carry tall vehicles of up to 2.6 metres in height, such as 4x4 sports models. If required, Car-Racs will also be available as 45-foot, or even 48-foot, units.

Because it is effectively a standard container unit, the equipment will allow cars to be carried door-to-door – from factory to showroom – by established general land and sea intermodal transport networks. 'We consider automobiles to be the last great cargo to be containerised,' says John Evans.

'Basically, the Car-Rac is not unlike a road transporter in container form. However, in just 30 seconds it can be picked up, complete with six vehicles, and transferred from one mode of transport to another – truck, train, ship or barge – with no individual movement of the vehicles inside,' says Mr Evans.

Mr Evans says Car-Racs would cost in the region of $8,500 to $9,000. 'If you take one on an operating lease for five years, that would work out at about $1 per car per day.'

Source: *Financial Times* CD-ROM, 1 January–31 December 1998.

The emergence of a new generation of intermodal 'mega-carriers' has also made it easier for multinational companies to organise logistics on a global scale. Companies such as Nedlloyd, Sealand, NYK and P&O combine deep-sea container shipping with land-based distribution coverage. Express carriers, such as DHL, Fedex, UPS and TNT closely integrate air-freight services with road-based collection and delivery to provide a rapid, reliable service for time-sensitive consignments. In addition to operating these services, carriers often become heavily involved in the planning and design of logistics systems for their multinational clients.

The real cost of international freight movement has been declining as the carrying capacity of ships and aircraft has expanded and transport operators enjoyed greater economies of scale. Competitive conditions in the shipping industry have further depressed rates. In the bulk-carrier market, for instance, a tonne of grain can be shipped from the Mississippi to Rotterdam for as little as $8.60 per tonne, a tonne of iron ore from Brazil to Rotterdam for only $2.60 per tonne. It is astonishing to think that for the price of a hamburger, you can transport a tonne of product 12,000 kilometres. In the unitised market, some vessels are now capable of carrying over 7000 TEU (20-foot equivalent unit) containers, each weighing up to 25 tonnes. Table 17.3 shows the typical costs of transporting a range of manufactured goods from the Far East to the UK, expressed as a percentage of the retail price of the product. These transport costs generally represent a small fraction of the difference in production costs that exists between Western Europe and the Far East.

The total logistical costs incurred in moving products internationally, however, can be many times the basic transport cost. For example, it can cost as much per tonne to unload cargo from a ship as to transport it hundreds of kilometres. Allowance has also to be made for the cost of financing, storing and insuring the inventory while in transit. As transit times for containers travelling between the Far East and Western Europe can be 3–4 weeks, these time-related costs can be greater than the distance-related (transport) costs. This time dimension in inter-

Table 17.3 Deep–sea container shipping costs per item

Product	Country of origin	Shipping cost per item
20" colour TV	Singapore	$10.03
Video recorder	Japan	$2.78
Cassette recorder	Hong Kong	$1.34
Squash racket	Taiwan	$0.17
Training shoes	Malaysia	$0.36
Canned tuna	Philippines	$0.02

Source: European Commission (1995).

national logistics has become increasingly important as competitive pressures to cut inventory levels have intensified. This major logistical trend is explored in the next section.

Acceleration of material flow

The prime goal of logistics is to make products available to customers. The speed with which it achieves this is generally measured by the order-lead time, i.e. the time elapsing from the placing of the order to the delivery of the goods. Order-lead times have been steadily reducing. A.T. Kearney Ltd (see *Financial Times* 1998) estimates that within Europe they have declined from an average of 27 days in 1987 to 12 days in 1998. These average figures conceal wide variations between sectors and countries. Particular attention has been paid in recent years to the rate at which products flow through grocery supply chains. This has been expressed as the number of days it takes products to move from the end of the packing line in a factory to the retail checkout, thus including time spent in the shop. This ranged from approximately 75–80 days in the US to only 28 days in the UK (Figure 17.1) (Kurt Salmon 1993; GEA 1994). These wide international variations can be attributed to differences in trading practices, the degree of retail concentration, the level of co-operation between retailers and suppliers, the level of IT support and the size of the country. To be competitive in a foreign market, an exporter must meet the prevailing delivery standards and this can prove more difficult in some countries than in others.

By increasing the speed with which products flow through the production and distribution system, firms can obtain a range of benefits:

- *savings on inventory costs* Inventory can represent 30 per cent or more of a manufacturer's total assets and typically accounts for around a third of total logistics costs. Cutting inventory levels releases working capital either for investment in more productive activities or to improve gearing. It also enables companies to economise on warehousing and insurance costs.

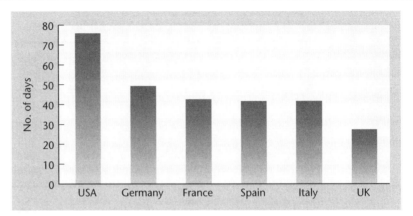

Figure 17.1 International variations in the average length of the grocery supply chain, 1993–4: Average number of days of inventory between the end of the packing line in the factory and the retail checkout

Source: Kurt Salmon (1993); GEA (1994).

- *reducing the risk of obsolescence* In many sectors, most notably in the electronics and consumer electrical sectors, the rate of new product development is accelerating while the 'product life cycle' is shortening. Having cut the time it takes to develop new products, firms naturally want to maximise their sales potential by minimising the 'time to market'. Once the products are flowing, the aim is to minimise the amount of inventory in the logistical channel to avoid being left with large amounts of obsolete stock when the new product is superseded.
- *responding more rapidly to variations in demand* Where order lead times are short, firms can adjust supplies more flexibly to variations in consumer demand and minimise their dependence on longer-term sales forecasts, which tend, on the whole, to be fairly inaccurate.

A series of new management principles and approaches, such as just-in-time (Hutchins 1988), quick response (Fernie 1994), lead-time management (Christopher and Braithwaite 1989), time compression (Warwick Manufacturing Group 1995), lean logistics (Jones *et al*. 1997) and efficient consumer response (Kurt Salmon 1993), have been developed over the past 20 years to help firms accelerate their logistical operations. Process-mapping techniques have been developed to analyse the expenditure of time in the supply chain and assess the opportunity for eliminating slack time and non-value adding activities (Scott and Westbrook 1991; Jones *et al*. 1997).

This mounting pressure to 'time-compress' logistical systems may seem at odds with the lengthening of supply chain links outlined earlier, particularly where these links cross international frontiers. Long transit times from distant factories can, after all, make the international supply chain unresponsive to short-term variations in demand.

One way in which firms can reconcile these apparently conflicting trends is by making greater use of air-freight services. Between 1985 and 1995, the world air-freight market grew at an annual average rate of 9.1 per cent (measured in revenue tonne-kilometres), much faster than world trade as a whole (Boeing 1996). Moreover, an increasing proportion of air-freight cargo is being handled by integrated air carriers which provide express services at premium rates. Their share of the global air-freight market is expected to grow from 5 per cent in 1995 to 37 per cent by 2015. The real cost of carriage by air has been steadily declining, broadening the range of commodities that can be carried economically by this mode.

Within trading blocs, new land-based services have developed offering international express delivery. Within Europe, these services are currently confined mainly to the road network. The movement of freight by rail across the continent is still relatively slow mainly because of delays at frontiers and a lack of co-ordination between national rail administrations. The European Commission has, nevertheless, estimated that the average speed at which rail-freight is moved could be increased by a factor of four from only 16km per hour to around 60km per hour (*European Freight Management*, 30 June 1998).

By switching from slower to faster modes and carriers, firms can substantially reduce transit times. Figure 17.2 shows how Scottish-based electronics companies have been able to reduce the time it takes to export their products to customers on the European mainland, a trend they expect to continue (SPEED Ltd 1998).

It is important to note, however, that transit time represents only a part, sometimes a very small part, of the total logistical cycle time. If, for example, we define this cycle time as the time elapsing from the arrival of the first components at the manufacturing assembly point to the delivery of the finished article at a retail outlet, the period spent in the transport system is usually a very small proportion of the total, even in the case of internationally traded goods. Relative to the total cycle time, the longer transit times experienced by these goods may have little net effect on their overall competitiveness. Several studies have suggested that in the typical manufacturing operation, only around 5 per cent of the total time that products spend on site is genuine value-adding time (Jones *et al.* 1997). The remainder is idle time, when products in the form of raw materials, components, subassemblies or finished items, lie around incurring stockholding

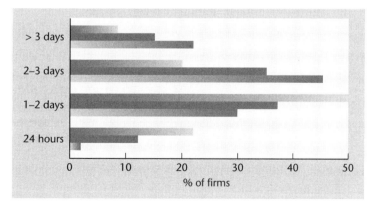

Figure 17.2 Dominant transit time requirement for exports of electronic equipment from Scotland to mainland Europe.
Source: SPEED Ltd (1998).

costs without having their value enhanced in any way. By rescheduling internal processes and managing lead times more effectively across the full spread of their activities, companies can offset longer transit times to foreign customers. Fynes and Ennis (1994) describe how Microsoft was able to time-compress processes at its plant in Ireland.

Exhibit 17.2 Supply chain logistics: In pole position in the race to innovate

Intense market competition, tightly managed production and increasing globalisation have combined to put the automotive manufacturing industry at the forefront of logistics sector innovation. Established trends in that context include reducing inventory, cutting supply lead times, consolidating overall logistics activities, rationalising the number of service providers employed and developing much closer business partnerships with those that are retained.

More recently, automotive sector logistics operations have also had to contend with a growing move among leading manufacturers towards build-to-order (BTO) rather than forecast-driven production. Much of the initial impetus for that development came from Japanese car manufacturers with their well-documented just-in-time and lean production concepts but BTO has now become a significant issue for the global automotive industry as a whole.

Some of the global implications of that trend are highlighted in a report, *Worldwide Logistics – The Future of Supply Chain Services*, published by the Holland International Distribution Council. 'Today, the key logistics indicator in the US, European and Japanese car manufacturing industry is the total cycle time. It used to be more than two months but industry goals are now set at around two weeks,' says the report. 'The improvement programmes include the well co-ordinated line-feed of parts and components into the assembly lines, on a just-in-time, just-in-sequence basis.' The HIDC report adds that such operations require 'particularly flexible and agile supply chains', forcing logistics service suppliers to 'proactively develop customised solutions rather than employ established, off-the-shelf systems'.

An example of that sort of development in the UK involves a new Rover Group Integrated Logistics Centre (ILC) at Oxford, southern England, opened earlier this year. Developed jointly with supply chain management specialist Exel Logistics, part of the NFC group, the £10m facility is designed to function as a 'supplier village'. In that context, Exel now receives, configures and despatches correctly sequenced inbound components to each of 140 build stations within Rover Oxford's recently constructed assembly building. Initially, the operation is servicing the production of the new Rover 75 car.

'The greater volume and complexity of build variations of the new Rover model meant that bringing components into a number of receiving points and then re-handling them in the conventional way was no longer good enough,' says Leigh Pomlett, managing director of Exel Logistics Automotive. Prior to development of the ILC, Rover's Oxford plant was served by five separate logistics buildings. However, in line with general automotive industry trends, Rover wanted to develop far shorter lead times between the placing of an order for a new car and its delivery to a dealer. That led to the manufacturer and Exel devising a system to assemble everything together under one roof.

'Within the assembly area, the lineside inventory of components has been minimised and Exel is able to supply configured components in the right sequence, at the right time and present them for despatch to the assembly personnel in the easiest way for fitting,' says Barrie Hunt, Logistics Director for Rover Oxford.

In keeping with trends on the inbound logistics side, automotive manufacturers are also outsourcing more of their outbound vehicle delivery activities. This year, for example, Vauxhall awarded a three-year contract to UK delivery company Walon, part of the AutoLogic group, for the management of its new purpose-built storage centre near Luton, Bedfordshire. The site, which includes a 10,000 square foot pre-delivery inspection workshop, is equipped with barcoding to track vehicles through the delivery process.

Another clearly established trend in automotive logistics is a move by manufacturers to reduce the number of service suppliers they employ. When it comes to inbound flows of parts and components for production lines, most leading companies in that sector are now looking to work with a handful of international companies: lead logistics suppliers (LLPs), as they call them.

The latter may, in turn, contract out part of that work to second- and third-tier service operators. Similar trends are also becoming apparent when it comes to the shipment and delivery of finished vehicles. As a result, the European automotive logistics sector, in particular, is experiencing considerable consolidation as leading service operators seek to develop pan-European coverage through company mergers and acquisitions.

UK-based logistics service company AutoLogic Holdings, for instance, recently acquired French operator Remorquage Automobile Depenage (RAD). The latter, which is based south-east of Paris, specialises in the transportation and delivery of fleet vehicles.

The acquisition of RAD came just weeks after AutoLogic bought the Mansped European automotive industry logistics service division of UK-based transport and distribution company United Carriers. More established operations in the AutoLogic group include Walon UK and Walon BNL.

On the logistics technology side, the automotive industry has also seen the launch of an interesting innovation which could open up new opportunities for shipping vehicles via standard intermodal road/rail/shipping container services (see also Exhibit 17.1).

Source: Financial Times CD-ROM, 1 January–31 December 1998.

Order lead times can vary for a particular product sourced from the same supplier. Research by Farmer and Ploos van Amstel (1992), for example, revealed that the delivery of a component from Japan to a factory in The Netherlands could take as little as seven days or as long 16 days, with an average order lead time of 12 days. By tracking the product and analysing the reasons for such variation, companies can try to reduce the average lead time to the minimum, cutting inventory and improving reliability. As mentioned earlier, customers generally attach more importance to the reliability of delivery than to the average or quoted delivery time. They are often prepared to trade longer transit times for greater reliability. By gaining a reputation for dependable delivery, therefore, firms exporting goods over long distances can compensate for any transit time penalty.

Local customisation

The desire to minimise inventory levels is also, theoretically, in conflict with the marketing objective of adding value to products by tailoring them more closely to consumer needs and tastes. For most companies, this involves broadening the product range and increasing the number of separate 'stock-keeping units' (SKUs). As a general rule, the greater the number of SKUs the larger the inventory holding, other things being equal. This can create a much greater inventory-management dilemma for a global manufacturer than for one serving only a national or regional market, partly because of the greater diversity of the global market but also because of the longer order lead times, especially where the production is focused in a few strategic locations.

An increasingly common way of resolving this dilemma is to centralise the core production of standard products, often in low labour cost countries, and decentralise their customisation to regional markets. This represents an application of the **postponement principle**, which suggests that companies should hold inventory in generic form as long as possible and defer their final configuration until they have a good idea of the likely demand for particular models or types (Zinn and Bowersox, 1988; van Hoek *et al.* 1998). This delays the 'explosion' in SKUs which occurs at the point of customisation, thus reducing the amount of inventory in the global supply chain and the risk of over- or under-supplying a particular market with a specialist product.

This strategy reduces inventory costs, but at the expense of adding an extra node to the international supply chain. This inflates facility costs, but often has only a minor effect on total transport costs. In most cases, after all, there would be a need for a break-bulk operation within regional markets anyway. Furthermore, as products are being moved in generic form on the longer trans-global link, loads can be more tightly consolidated, economising on transport costs. Packaging, manuals, attachments and ancillary products are then added close to the customer, minimising the distance they need to be transported.

Local customisation is increasingly being outsourced to logistics service providers, many of whom had their origins in transport or warehousing but have now extended their service portfolio to include activities that were traditionally the preserve of manufacturing. The Dutch logistics firm, Nedlloyd, for example, provides a European customisation service for IBM at a distribution centre in Amsterdam, which can involve any combination of 120 different tasks.

Chapter summary

The management of logistical operations has undergone a complete transformation over the past 30 years. This has enabled companies to improve standards of customer service while cutting operating costs and depressing inventory levels. Major challenges remain, however, particularly for logistics managers working in the international arena. Major business trends such as globalisation, mass customisation, time-compression and the move to focused production heavily impinge on the logistics function and, in some cases, exert conflicting pressures. The lengthening of supply lines and the expansion of product ranges, for example, run counter to the obsessive drive to reduce inventory. Those companies whose logistics strategies effectively reconcile these conflicts stand to gain a major competitive advantage.

Discussion questions

1 In what ways can international businesses derive competitive advantage from the management of logistics?
2 A manufacturer of CD racks is keen to export his products for the first time, but does not know how they should be distributed. What advice would you give him?
3 The current logistical trends of inventory centralisation, geographical extension and time compression are unlikely to continue indefinitely. What factors are likely to constrain them in the longer term?

Closing Case Study:
NIKE

The sports company NIKE is a good example of a global corporation with a highly complex logistical system. Its main strength is often considered to be its innovative and intensive marketing, based on the distinctive 'swoosh' logo. The success of the company, however, has relied just as much on its ability to distribute its products cheaply and reliably to customers throughout the world. As a report by Touche Ross (1995) explains, 'NIKE recognise that creating market demand is of little use unless it is also in a position to deliver its product, so they put logistics at the centre of their business strategy for the 1990s and beyond'.

Most NIKE products are designed in the US and manufactured, often on a subcontract basis, in the low labour-cost countries of the Far East, such as South Korea, Indonesia and Vietnam. The manufacturing process can involve the assembly of numerous components obtained from other countries. For example, training shoes are assembled in Indonesia from 52 separate parts sourced from suppliers in Japan, South Korea, Taiwan, the US and elsewhere in Indonesia (Christopher 1998). Upstream of the assembly operation, therefore, there is a dense network of supply lines, some of which require intercontinental freight movement.

▶

Downstream of the main production point, the dominant flows are from the Far East to Europe and North America. For these transglobal movements, NIKE can take advantage of the relatively low deep-sea container rates discussed in the chapter. Shipping costs per unit are very low relative to the differences in production costs between the Far East and the main markets of Western Europe and North America.

Managing NIKE's logistical operation is further complicated by its large product range, the high rate of product innovation, the seasonality of much of its sales, customer demand for matching sets of sportswear and the need for local customisation:

- *product range* Across its footwear, clothing and equipment divisions, there are many thousands of stock-keeping units (SKUs), with different product varieties available in different countries. In the early 1990s, for example, the company's European product range comprised 10,000 SKUs across Europe, but the number of SKUs available in any single country did not exceed 5000 (Ashford 1997a). The company requires a highly sophisticated IT system to process and track orders for such a diverse product range.
- *new product development* As sportswear has become increasingly fashion-sensitive, the number of new styles introduced each year has grown. In recent years, for instance, NIKE has been introducing around 300 new shoe designs per annum (Christopher 1998). This has major implications for logistics. Other things being equal, the proliferation of product lines exerts an upward pressure on inventory levels. As the product life cycle for fashion items is relatively short, it is essential to match replenishment closely to demand, thus minimising the amount of residual inventory left in the supply chain when fashions change. Such inventory can clog the distribution channel and inhibit the launch of new products. NIKE uses the term 'close-out' to describe inventory left at the end of a season or fashion cycle. According to Ashford and Naish (1995), who analysed NIKE's European logistics operation in 1992, the amount of discount that had to be offered to dispose of 'close-out' was 'one of the biggest logistics costs [they] identified at NIKE'. With the installation of more advanced IT systems, improved sales forecasting, the centralisation of inventory and reduction in order lead times, these costs have been sharply reduced during the 1990s.
- *seasonality* Demand for sportswear and equipment is highly seasonal, reflecting the times in the year when particular sports are played. For a global supplier, such as NIKE, seasonal differences between the northern and southern hemispheres helps to smooth these fluctuations, though as most demand is concentrated in North America and Europe this has only a minor effect. Variations in the nature and volume of product flow during the year make it difficult to maintain the utilisation of logistics assets at a high level.
- *matching sets* People often buy a collection of NIKE products at the same time, because they have a matching style or colour scheme or form a particular team strip. This means that an outlet has to stock several related items in the customer's size. As these items are often manufactured in different locations on different product cycles, a sophisticated order-replenishment system is required to bring them all together at the right place and time to meet customer requirements.
- *local customisation* It is common in the clothing and footwear sector for manufacturers to provide 'pre-retailing' services, such as ticketing, labelling, barcoding and repacking. These 'value-adding' services are usually performed

at the distribution centre rather than as part of the original production process and so become the responsibility of logistics managers. Sports equipment can also require modifications prior to final distribution: footballs, for example, are inflated close to the final point of sale to minimise transport costs across the supply chain.

Like many global businesses, NIKE has been trying to improve the quality of its distribution service, while at the same time increasing the efficiency of its logistical system. One way in which it has done this is by centralising inventory. In 1992, for example, the company operated approximately 20 main warehouses in 11 European countries (Ashford 1997a). Most countries had at least one warehouse and they each received direct deliveries, primarily from factories in the Far East. Following a strategic review of NIKE's European distribution operation in 1992–3, it was decided initially to centralise the inventory of clothing products at a single distribution centre in Meerhout in Belgium, close to the Dutch border. The 75,000 square metre warehouse was opened in 1994. Around this time a plan to concentrate the inventory of footwear products at two locations was abandoned in favour of an alternative proposal also to centralise these stocks at the Meerhout site (Ashford 1997b). A separate 30,000 square metre warehouse was built to accommodate the footwear. More recently, the company has established a central European distribution point for sports equipment at Eersel in The Netherlands.

The closure of national warehouses and the move to pan-European distribution based on major hubs has yielded numerous benefits. In accordance with the 'square root law', inventory levels have declined relative to sales, while the sharp reduction in the number of stock locations has cut warehousing costs. Meanwhile, the level of product availability has increased and order lead times shortened. The provision of value-adding, pre-retail services has also been improved. It has been estimated that the payback period for the Meerhout distribution centre, which cost 'well over $100,000', was under two years (Ashford 1997b).

NIKE has also been part of the worldwide trend to outsource logistics. For example, in 1997 its Equipment Division formed a logistics partnership with Menlo Logistics, an American logistics service provider. Menlo manages NIKE's distribution centre in Atlanta from which sports equipment is delivered across the United States. It worked closely with NIKE in developing a new distribution strategy for its range of sports equipment and uses its proprietary warehouse and order-management software to control the order-replenishment process. In 1998, Menlo and its sister company, Emery Global Logistics, were awarded the contract for the Equipment Division's European logistics operation based at the new distribution in Eersel (Menlo Logistics 1998). The director of operations at NIKE Equipment explains this move as follows:

> We have undertaken a fundamental paradigm shift and started to contract out distribution services. This enables us to focus more on our core competency, which is to strengthen the NIKE brand by creating, developing and marketing innovative products.

While NIKE, like many other international businesses, is prepared to entrust much of the responsibility for its distribution operation to outside contractors, logistics will remain a fundamental part of the company's competitive strategy.

Questions

1 Why is Nike's logistical system crucial to its successful operation?
2 What factors have contributed to the complexity of Nike's logistical operation?
3 How did Nike benefit from centralising its inventory system?

Further reading

Walter, D. (ed.) (1999) *Global Distribution and Logistics Planning*, London: Kogan Page. This book contains chapters on all the main aspects of logistics written by 15 specialists in the field.

Taylor, D. (1997) *Global Cases in Logistics and Supply Chain Management*, London: International Thomson Business Press. Taylor has assembled 34 case studies focusing on a broad range of logistics and supply chain issues. Many of these cases concern the management of international logistics operations.

References

Abrahamsson, M. (1993) Time-based distribution, *International Journal of Logistics Management*, 4: 75–83.

Ashford, M. (1997a) NIKE Europe, in D. Taylor (ed.) *Global Cases in Logistics and Supply Chain Management*, London: International Thomson Business Press.

Ashford, M. (1997b) NIKE Europe, in D. Taylor (ed.) *Global Cases in Logistics and Supply Chain Management: Teachers' Notes*, London: International Thomson Business Press.

Ashford, M. and **Naish, S.** (1995) NIKE's dream, *Logistics Europe* 3(1): 26–32.

A.T. Kearney Ltd. (1999) *Survey of European Logistics 1998*, Brussels: European Logistics Association.

Boeing (1996) *World Air Cargo Forecast 1996/1997*, Seattle.

Bowersox, D. (1978) *Logistical Management*, 2nd edn, New York: Macmillan.

Browne, M. and **Allen, J.** (1994) Logistics Strategies for Europe, in J. C. Cooper (ed.) *Logistics and Distribution Planning: Strategies for Management*, London: Kogan Page.

Buck, R. (1992) Choosing a distribution strategy, *Site Selection Europe* 9: 60–63.

Christopher, M. (1998) *Logistics and Supply Chain Management*, London: Financial Times/Pitman Publishing.

Christopher, M. and **Braithwaite, A.** (1989) Managing strategic lead times, *Logistics Information Management* 2(4)

Cooper, J.C. (1993) Logistics strategies for global businesses, *International Journal of Physical Distribution and Logistics Management* 23(4): 12–23.

Cooper, J.C., Browne, M. and Peters, M. (1991) *European Logistics: Markets Management and Strategy*, Oxford: Blackwells.

Davies, G., Fitchett, J. and Gumbrell, K. (1988) The benefits of delivered pricing, *European Journal of Marketing* 21(1): 47–56.

European Centre for Infrastructure Studies (1996) *The State of European Infrastructure 1996*, Rotterdam.

Farmer, D. and Ploos van Amstel, R. (1992) *Effective Pipeline Management*, London: Gower.

Fernie, J. (1994) Quick response: an international perspective, *International Journal of Physical Distribution and Logistics Management* 24(6): 38–46.

Financial Times (1998) A survey on supply chain logistics, 1 December.

Fynes, B. and Ennis, S. (1994) From lean production to lean logistics: the case of Microsoft Ireland, *European Management Journal* 12(3): 32–40

GEA (1994) *Supplier Retailer Collaboration in Supply Chain Management*, London: Coca-Cola Retailing Research Group-Europe.

Hutchins, D. (1988) *Just in Time*, Aldershot: Gower.

Jones, D., Hines, P. and Rich, N. (1997) Lean logistics, *International Journal of Physical Distribution and Logistics Management* 23: 153–73.

Kurt Salmon (1993) *Efficient Consumer Response: Enhancing Consumer Value in the Supply Chain*, Washington, DC: Kurt Salmon.

Maister, D.H. (1976) Centralisation of inventories and the 'square root law' *International Journal of Physical Distribution* 6(3): 124–35.

McKinnon, A.C. (1989) *Physical Distribution Systems*, London: Routledge.

Menlo Logistics (1998) *NIKE Equipment Signs Up Menlo Logistics to Manage Distribution Centers in North America and Europe*, web page: http://www.menlolog.com/news/

O'Laughlin, K.A., Cooper, J. and Cabocel, E. (1993) *Reconfiguring European Logistics Systems*, Oak Brook, Ill.: Council of Logistics Management.

Pellew, M. (ed.) (1998) *Pan-European Logistics*, London: Financial Times Management Report, 1998.

Picard, J. (1982) Typology of physical distribution systems in multinational corporations, *International Journal of Physical Distribution and Materials Management* 12(6): 26–39.

Schary, P.B. and Skjott-Larsen, T. (1995) *Managing the Global Supply Chain*, Copenhagen: Munksgaard International Publishers.

Scott, C. and Westbrook, R. (1991) New strategic tools for supply chain management, *International Journal of Physical Distribution and Logistics Management* 21(1): 23–33.

SPEED Ltd (1998) *1998 Survey of Distribution and Logistics in Scottish Manufacturing Industry*, Edinburgh.

Touche Ross (1995) Touche Ross and NIKE team-up to reengineer NIKE's European logistics, *Logistics News* 16.

van Hoek, R., Commandeur, H.R. and **Vos, B.** (1998) Reconfiguring logistics systems through postponement strategies, *Journal of Business Logistics* 19(1): 33–54.

Warwick Manufacturing Group (1995) *Time Compression Self-Help Guide*, Warwick: University of Warwick.

Zinn, W. and **Bowersox, D.** (1988) Planning physical distribution and the principle of postponement, *Journal of Business Logistics* 9(2): 117–36.

CHAPTER 18

Structuring International Organisations

Anne-Wil Harzing

Learning objectives

By the end of this chapter you will be able to:

- describe and explain the major types of organisational structures used in managing international operations

- analyse the advantages and disadvantages of each of these structures and the factors that impact the choice for a certain structure

- understand why the focus on structural characteristics is giving way to a more integrated view to managing international organisations

- understand the logic of the different typologies of multinational companies.

Opening Case Study:
Percy Barnevik eliminates hierarchy

Following the merger between Asea and Brown Boveri under Percy Barnevik's leadership, the period 1987–91 was marked by radical restructuring, lay-offs, plant closures, product exchanges, and disposals.

Barnevik described in 1993 how he was operating a matrix organisation with fewer than 100 headquarters staff running 1200 companies worldwide. He claimed he could cut the headquarters staff in any traditionally centralised corporation by 90 per cent in one year: 30 per cent into free-standing service centres that deliver value; 30 per cent decentralised into the line businesses; and 30 per cent eliminated as unnecessary.

Staff levels in the headquarters of ABB's subsidiaries were also cut drastically: from 600 to 100 for one in the US, from 1600 to 100 for ABB Germany and from 880 to 25 for Stromberg. By 1993 around 250 senior line managers operated in a matrix of 50 business areas and geographical operations, co-ordinated directly through the centre with comprehensive information management.

ABB's approach has now evolved further in response to the personal stresses and co-ordination problems caused by the new approach.

▶

The manager as transferor of knowledge at BP

Between 1987 and 1997, BP changed from an unfocused, mediocre performer back to a high performer with 90 business units and $70bn turnover. Employee numbers have fallen from 129,000 to 53,000. A new management approach started with Project 1990 under Bob Horton. It involved substantial delayering and attempts to create new roles for middle managers but there were serious short-term problems.

David Simon took over in 1992 with a focus on 'performance and teamwork'. Restructuring proceeded with outsourcing of non-core activities such as IT and accounting. John Browne, who succeeded Simon in 1995, has focused on BP's ability to leverage its organisational assets and technological know-how world-wide in critical areas such as drilling.

Browne has focused on an organisational structure that will promote learning, with nothing between the nine-member executive group and the business unit managers. A massive investment in getting over 1000 managers on to a network of 'virtual teams' is underway with a new emphasis on behaviour that shares knowledge across the company. This should enable best practice to be trans-ferred anywhere in the world.

Source: *Financial Times* CD-ROM, 1 January–31 December 1998.

Introduction

As companies internationalise, their structures have to be adapted to reflect their international involvement. This chapter discusses the structuring of interna-tional organisations. We start with a discussion of the different organisational structures and the factors that influence the choice for a particular structure. In doing so, we pay particular attention to the so-called strategy–structure argu-ment. However, in the current turbulent international arena organisational structure 'proved to be unequal to the task of capturing the complexity of the strategic task facing most organisations' (Bartlett and Ghoshal 1992: 516). It is therefore not very useful to look at organisational structure in isolation. The second part of the chapter therefore presents a more integrated approach and looks at configurations of strategy–structure and control mechanisms in multina-tional companies (MNCs).

Organisational structures for multinational firms: traditional approaches

Early studies on the structure of MNCs were usually based on the work of Chandler (1962) who proclaimed a deterministic relationship between strategy and structure. Chandler distinguished four growth strategies: expansion of volume, geographic dispersion, vertical integration, and product diversification. These strategies called for different structures, hence his adage 'structure follows strategy'. Stopford and

Wells's (1972) classic study investigated this relationship in an international context. In an empirical investigation of 187 large American multinational companies, they identified two strategic variables that were able to 'predict' organisational structure: foreign product diversity and percentage of foreign sales. A model was constructed (see Figure 18.1) that showed how MNCs adopt different organisational structures at different stages of international expansion.

When firms start to internationalise and both their foreign sales and foreign product diversity are limited, the preferred organisational structure is usually an international division. The domestic organisational structure is left untouched and all international activities are simply concentrated in one international division. This might be an advantage if international presence is still very limited. It does not require a complete overhaul of the organisation and the structure is simple and understandable. It also creates a central pool of international experience and expertise.

The international division structure does create a number of problems, however. First, it tends to underplay the importance of international activities, since the international division is only one of the many divisions of the company. It also underestimates the diversity that might be inherent in international operations: the head of the international division is assumed to represent the interest of all countries in which the company operates. The isolation of domestic and international activities may also create duplication of efforts and limits the transfer of knowledge in the company. Because of the structural separation, there is a complete lack of co-ordination between domestic and foreign operations, which might hinder both the company's effectiveness and efficiency.

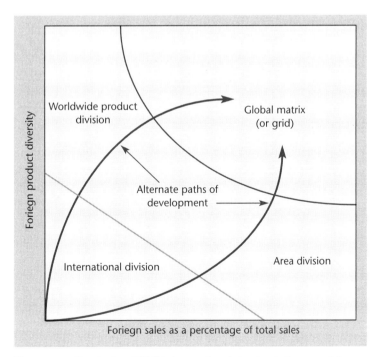

Figure 18.1 Stopford and Wells's international structural stages model
Source: Adapted from Stopford and Wells (1972).

Therefore, once companies expand their international operations, they usually choose one of two worldwide structures: the area division structure or the product division structure. The choice is again dependent on the two variables identified by Stopford and Wells (1972). For companies that increase their foreign sales without significantly increasing product diversity, the most likely choice is a worldwide area division. In this type of structure, the world is divided into separate areas, which might be either a country or a group of countries, depending on the size of the market. In this case, the country in which the headquarters is located is simply one of the areas. Each area division usually operates in a rather autonomous way and oversees its own production, R&D, marketing, etc. This approach might work well if the company has a narrow product line (low level of foreign product diversity), which needs to be adapted to different local tastes and values. Local responsiveness is usually a key competitive advantage of these structures. Even more so than for the international division structure, however, this type of structure suffers from a lack of co-ordination. Activities will be duplicated and because each unit functions independently, essential information and experience may not be transferred from one unit to another. Area structures are therefore usually complemented with staff specialists for specific product categories. These staff specialists facilitate information transfer and strive to limit duplication.

Companies that are reasonably diversified (high level of foreign product diversity) usually adopt a worldwide product structure. In this type of structure, divisions are created for each major product or product group. Again divisions are relatively independent and autonomous and are responsible for their own value-creating activities (production, R&D, marketing, etc). A major advantage of this approach is that it improves efficiency, because activities can be easily co-ordinated and rationalised within the product group. Transfer of core competences and knowledge is also much easier than in the area division structure. This structure works well for industries in which cost-efficiency and co-ordination are of paramount importance. In contrast to the area structure, however, this structure makes attention to local differences far more difficult, sometimes resulting in a lack of local responsiveness.

According to Stopford and Wells (1972), yet another structure may be necessary if the company enters a subsequent stage, one in which both foreign sales and product diversity are high. They see the global matrix as the ideal structure for this stage of international development. This structure should combine the advantages of the area and product structure: local responsiveness and global efficiency. In the matrix structure, responsibility for a particular product is shared by both product and area managers. Many managers will have to report to two bosses: one in the product division and one in the area division. The advantage of the matrix is that it should enable a company to balance product and area requirements and achieve both efficiency and responsiveness. The reality is often different. Many matrix structures are associated with conflict, bureaucracy and slowness of decision making. Because of shared decision making, it is difficult to assign individual responsibility and the result may be chaos, lack of direction and inflexibility. Both in academic literature and in practice, attention has therefore shifted from matrix structures to matrix cultures and in general to the 'softer' aspects of the organisation, such as people, processes and control mechanisms. This signals the limits of organisational structure, something we come back to in detail later in this chapter. First, however, we take a closer look at some of the variables that determine organisational structure in MNCs.

In this chapter, we concentrate on theories and developments related to multinational organisations. In general management literature, however, we also see a move away from the focus on structural variables and a tendency to bring 'the soft side of the organisation' into the picture, combined with an emphasis on flexibility. Mintzberg, for instance, sees the **adhocracy** (one of his organisational configurations, the others being the simple structure, the divisionalised form, the machine bureaucracy and the professional bureaucracy) as the organisation of the future (Mintzberg 1983: 275). The adhocracy is a highly organic organisation, flexible and decentralised to cope with dynamic and complex environments, with mutual adjustment as a rather informal co-ordination mechanism. Mintzberg himself states that diversified markets formerly led multinationals to using the divisionalised form, grouping their major divisions either by area or by product line. However, 'those multinational firms with interdependencies among their different product lines, and facing increasing complexity as well as dynamism in their environment, will feel drawn toward the divisionalised adhocracy hybrid' (Mintzberg 1983: 269). More than 30 years ago Burns and Stalker (1961) already identified the organic organisation – with characteristics such as continual adjustment, lateral communication and commitment – as opposed to the mechanic organisation. And finally, in Peters and Waterman's bestseller *In Search of Excellence* (1982) the 'soft' aspects of organising – skills, shared values, style (of management) and staff – are at least as important as the formal aspects of structure, strategy and systems.

What determines organisational structures?

In the previous section, we discussed one of the most important determinants of an MNC's structure: its strategy. Although strategy was defined in a rather specific way, using the variables foreign product diversity and foreign sales, in a more general sense strategy will be an important determinant of an organisation's structure. A well-accepted typology of strategy is Porter's (1985) dichotomy of cost-efficiency and differentiation. For companies focusing on cost-efficiency the worldwide product structure would be an ideal type of structure, while the area-divisions structure might be more suitable for companies that focus on the differentiation of products to local tastes and preferences.

A number of other external and company-related factors can influence the type of structure a company chooses. Two important factors, industry and the home country of the MNC, will be discussed in detail later in this chapter. The host government and the availability of local managers can be influential as well. Host governments will usually be keen on local ownership and local content and will promote the delegation of authority to local subsidiaries. Whether a more autonomous structure is possible also depends, however, on the human resource capability of the country in question. If there is a lack of qualified local managers, MNCs will tend to centralise their structures and take major decisions at headquarters.

Since early work by Woodward (1958/1987), technology has been recognised as a factor that may have an important impact on the type of structure used in organisations. More recently, however, developments in information technology and telecommunications are giving rise to no less than a revolution in the structuring of (multinational) companies. Computer networks can be used to link subsidiaries all over the world to create a very integrated type of company. Many types of work, such as telemarketing, hotel and airline reservations and computer programming need not necessarily be performed close to the customers. Activities can be performed where wages are lowest or where the necessary skills are most easily available. And although these types of companies may seem to run the risk of getting 'out of control', controlling employees' output and behaviour is actually much easier if they are linked through computer networks or telephone lines.

From strategy–structure to process: modern approaches to structuring MNCs

On pages 420–23 we discussed the early approaches to the structuring of MNCs, based on Stopford and Wells's seminal work. We also indicated that today more sophisticated approaches have developed. These approaches take a more integrated approach by looking at the interaction between environment, strategy, structure and processes. Table 18.1 summarises these ideas. It is based on the environment-strategy-structure paradigm, which suggests that superior company performance comes from a good fit between strategy and environmental demands, and between organisational structure (and processes) and strategy.

In contrast to earlier work on MNC strategy and structure (Stopford and Wells 1972; Franko 1976; Daniels *et al.* 1984, 1985; Galbraith and Kazanjian 1986; Egelhoff 1988), we do not presuppose a one-way deterministic relationship between any of these five variables. Especially the link between strategy and structure has been discussed extensively since Chandler's (1962) seminal work and various authors (see, for instance, Hall and Saias 1980) have argued that strategy might be just as dependent on structure as structure is on strategy. Most of the authors discussed in this section belong to the process school of international management (Doz and Prahalad 1991), that had its origins in the

Table 18.1 Environment, strategy, structure, systems and processes in MNCs

Environment: historical	Environment: industry	Strategy	Structure	Systems and processes
Changes in international environment	Pattern of international competition	Company's strategic response	Company's organisational structure	Company's control mechanisms

dissertations of Prahalad (1975) and Doz (1976) and adhere to a more flexible and less deterministic relationship between environment, strategy, structure and process. The overall balance, fit or match is what counts.

Control mechanisms

In view of the topic of this chapter, we mainly focus on structure and control mechanisms, although we pay some attention to the other elements as well. Control mechanisms can be defined as the instruments that are used to make sure that all units of the organisation strive towards common organisational goals. Numerous control mechanisms have been identified, with some authors seeing organisational structure as one of the control mechanisms. Still other authors use the term co-ordination mechanism to describe the same process. However, an extensive literature review (Harzing 1999) resulted in a synthesis of four major types of control mechanisms, as summarised in Table 18.2.

Table 18.2 Classification of control mechanisms on two dimensions

	Personal/cultural (founded on social interaction)	Impersonal/bureaucratic/technocratic (founded on instrumental artefacts)
Direct/explicit	Category 1: Personal centralised control	Category 2: Bureaucratic formalised control
Indirect/implicit	Category 4: Control by socialisation and networks	Category 3: Output control

Source: Adapted from Harzing (1999).

- *personal centralised control* This control mechanism denotes the idea of some kind of hierarchy, of decisions being taken at the top level of the organisation and personal surveillance of their execution. The terms used by various authors to describe this control mechanism are: centralisation, hierarchy and direct personal kind of control.
- *bureaucratic formalised control* The control mechanisms in this category are impersonal (also called bureaucratic) and indirect. They aim at pre-specifying, mostly in a written form, the behaviour that is expected from employees. In this way, control can be impersonal because employees can and should refer to the 'manual' instead of directly being told what to do. The terms used by various authors to describe this type of control are: bureaucratic control, formalisation, rules, regulations, paper system and programmes.
- *output control* The main characteristic of this category is that it focuses on the outputs realised instead of on behaviour (as the other three control mechanisms do). These outputs are usually generated by the use of reporting or monitoring systems and can take any form from rather general aggregated

financial data to detailed figures regarding sales, production levels, productivity, investments, etc. The key element that distinguishes this control mechanism from the two previous ones is thus that instead of particular courses of action certain goals/results/outputs are specified and monitored by reporting systems. The terms used by various authors to describe this type of control are: result control, plans, output control, goal setting.

- *control by socialisation and networks* The fourth type of control mechanism is mainly defined by what it is not: it is not hierarchical, it is not bureaucratic, there are no fixed targets, it is usually not very formal. Compared to the other categories this control mechanism is rather informal, subtle and sophisticated. We can distinguish three main subcategories in this broad category:

  - *socialisation* This can be defined as ensuring that employees share organisational values and goals; that is, they are socialised into a common organisation culture. Another frequently used term is cultural control.
  - *informal, lateral or horizontal exchange of information* This is the use of non-hierarchical communication as a control mechanism. Terms used are: mutual adjustment, direct (managerial) contract, informal communication and co-ordination by feedback.
  - *formalised lateral or cross-departmental relations* This category has the same objectives as the second one, increasing the amount of (non-hierarchical) information processing, with the difference that in this case the relationships are (temporarily) formalised within the organisational structure. Examples are task forces, cross-functional teams, integrative departments.

As a common denominator for this category, we propose the term *control by socialisation and networks*. Networks comprise both the second and third subcategory, as the aim of both mechanisms is to create a network of communication channels that supplements the formal hierarchy. The term network is chosen because in organisation theory it is frequently used to denote non-hierarchical relations.

Typologies of MNCs

A prime example of the more integrated type of approach described above is Bartlett and Ghoshal's (1989) typology of international firms that includes a discussion of the changing international and industry environment as well as the company's strategy, structure and processes. Bartlett and Ghoshal distinguish four types of MNCs: multidomestic,[1] international, global and transnational.

Multidomestic organisational model

The period between the two world wars was characterised by a rise in nationalistic feelings. Countries became more and more protectionistic and erected high tariff barriers. There were large national differences in consumer preferences and communication and logistical barriers remained high. These circumstances favoured national companies. For *multinational* companies, the strategy of centralised production in order to capture economies of scale, combined with exports to various countries, was made impossible by high tariff and logistical barriers. In order to be able to compete with national companies, multinational firms had to set up a larger number of foreign manufacturing subsidiaries. Differences in consumer preferences and high communication barriers led to a decentralisation of decision making, so that the foreign subsidiaries were relatively independent of their headquarters. Even now, however, many industries have multidomestic characteristics. A prime example of a multidomestic industry is the branded packaged products industry (e.g. food, and laundry detergents). Companies in these industries preferably follow a multidomestic strategy, which gives primary importance to national responsiveness. Products or services are differentiated to meet differing local demands.

Responsiveness to the differences that distinguished national markets led multidomestic companies to decentralise organisational assets and decision making. This resulted in a configuration that can be described as a decentralised federation. The decentralised federation is organised by area: that is, by geographical region. This kind of structure – which is comparable to the area division structure of Stopford and Wells – was particularly compatible with the management norms of the mainly European companies that sought international presence in that particular era. Family ownership had been the dominant tradition and therefore organisational processes were built on personal relationships and informal contacts rather than formal structures and systems. Operational decisions were simply delegated to trusted parent-company nationals who were assigned abroad. The main approach to controlling and co-ordinating foreign subsidiaries was a rather informal one: direct personal contact between headquarters and subsidiary managers. Some simple financial control systems often supplemented this informal co-ordination.

International organisational model

The postwar years were characterised by a worldwide boom in demand. Consumers were catching up for the years of scarcity and soberness. The US was in a predominant economic position during this period and led the way. Most European companies were preoccupied with the reconstruction of their domestic operations, while American companies were almost untouched by the war. US companies developed new technologies and products. They were almost forced into the international market by spontaneous export orders and opportunities for licensing. Later they started making their products in manufacturing facilities in Western Europe and in developing countries. The adjective 'international' refers to the international product life cycle, which describes the internationalisation process in this type of industry. The critical success factor in these industries is the ability to transfer knowledge (particularly technology) to units abroad. It involves sequential diffusion of innovations that were originally developed in the home market.

A classic example of an international industry is telecommunications switching. In the international organisational structure, transfer of knowledge and expertise to countries that were less advanced in technology or market development is the essential task. Local subsidiaries do still have some freedom to adopt new products or strategies, but co-ordination and control by headquarters is more important than in the multidomestic type. Subsidiaries are dependent on the parent company for new products, processes or ideas. A co-ordinated federation, often structured by function, is the name for the structural configuration of this organisational model. The managerial culture of these companies provided a good fit with this structure. This culture was based on professional management, which implied a certain willingness to delegate responsibility. At the same time, however, these companies used sophisticated management systems and specialist corporate staffs to retain overall control.

Global organisational model

In the 1960s and 1970s, the successive reductions in tariff barriers began to have their full impact. They were accompanied by declining international transport costs and communication barriers. Furthermore, new electronic technologies increased the minimum efficient scale in many industries. Finally, consumer preferences became more homogeneous because of increased international travel and communication. All these developments made centralised and relatively standardised production with exports to various countries profitable again. In a global industry, standardised consumer needs and scale efficiencies make centralisation and integration profitable. In this kind of industry, a firm's competitive position in one country is significantly influenced by its position in other countries, and rivals compete against each other on a truly worldwide basis.

A classic example of a global industry is consumer electronics. The preferred strategy in these industries is one strategy that gives primary importance to efficiency. Global companies integrate and rationalise their production to produce standardised products in a very cost-efficient manner. This is the strategy traditionally followed by Japanese multinationals. In a global organisational configuration, assets, resources and responsibilities are centralised. The role of subsidiaries is often limited to sales and service. Compared with subsidiaries in multidomestic or international organisations, they have much less freedom of action. The structural configuration of this organisation is called a centralised hub – comparable to Stopford and Wells's product-division structure. This configuration was particularly compatible with the managerial norms and processes in Japanese companies. Centralised decision making and control allowed these companies to retain their complex management system requiring intensive communication and personal commitment.

Transnational organisational model

By the late 1970s, there was rising concern on the part of host countries about the impact of MNCs on their balance of trade, national employment levels, and on the international competitiveness of their economies. Consequently, they gradually started to exercise their sovereign powers. Trade barriers were erected again to limit exports and foreign direct investments were regulated by industrial policies. Other forces also counteracted the previous globalisation process.

Flexible manufacturing reduced the minimum efficient scale by employing robotics and CAD/CAM technologies. The use of software became important in a growing number of industries (from telecommunications to computers and consumer electronics). This development facilitated conformity to consumers, who were again asking for products tailored to their local needs.

The problem is that we do not see a complete reversal to the multidomestic era again. The worldwide innovation of the international era and the global efficiency of the global era remain important competitive factors and companies should pay attention to global efficiency, national responsiveness and worldwide learning at the same time. In order to do this their strategy must be very flexible. The strategy (literally) is to have no set strategy, but to let each strategic decision depend on specific developments. Strategy becomes unclear and it may become dissolved into a set of incremental decisions with a pattern that may only make sense after the fact. Issues are shaped, defined, attended to, and resolved one at a time in a 'muddling through' process. A transnational strategy would be a deliberately planned strategy to have an 'adaptive' (Mintzberg 1988a), 'incremental' (Quinn 1988), 'muddling through' (Lindblom 1987) or 'emergent' (Mintzberg 1988b) strategy.

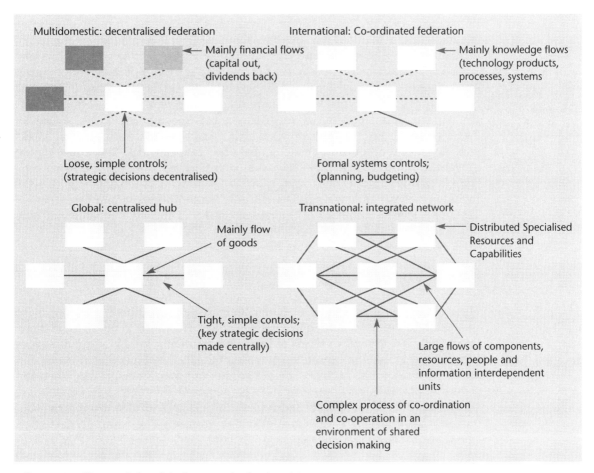

Figure 18.2 Characteristics of the four organisational models
Source: Adapted from Bartlett and Ghoshal (1992).

The type of organisation structure that fits a transnational strategy is very flexible. Bartlett and Ghoshal refer to an integrated network structure that links major subunits of the company together. Assets, resources and capabilities are neither centralised nor completely decentralised. Expertise is spread throughout the organisation and subsidiaries can serve as a strategic centre for a particular product –market combination. To use a popular term, companies are creating 'centres of excellence' for each activity. It is important to realise that this concept upsets the traditional notion of having one headquarters and many dependent subsidiaries. The company becomes a kind of network with different centres for different activities. Each centre can have a strategic role for a particular area. The main characteristics of these four organisational models are summarised in Figure 18.2.

An empirical test of the configurational approach

Bartlett and Ghoshal's typology as described in the previous section, is one of the most popular typologies of MNCs in both academic and professional circles. Their typology, however, was based on an in-depth study of just nine multinational companies in three different industries. Although the typology gives some general ideas, it includes few specifics about structural elements and the use of different control mechanisms. This section therefore describes the results of a large-scale test of their typology in over 100 MNCs from nine different countries (USA, Japan, Germany, France, UK, Sweden, Switzerland, Finland, and The Netherlands). Subsidiaries in 22 different countries were included in the study (for a more detailed description of the results see Harzing 1999). Based on Bartlett and Ghoshal's typology, ideal profiles of three different types of MNCs were constructed: multidomestic, global and transnational. The international model was not included since previous studies had shown that this differed little from the other models. A large number of subsidiary characteristics were included, so that the original Bartlett and Ghoshal model could be extended. Table 18.3 gives a summary of the characteristics of the three models that were found to be significantly different between the different models.

Global companies

These operate in industries with rather standardised consumer needs that make the realisation of economies of scale very important. These companies are therefore usually rather large in terms of their number of employees. Many industries have turned global during the last decades, but the consumer electronics, computer and automobile industry remain prime examples. Since price competition is very important, the dominant strategic requirement is efficiency, and these companies therefore integrate and rationalise their production to produce standardised products in a very cost-efficient manner. The result is that their subsidiaries are also relatively large.

Table 18.3 **Configurations of multinational companies**

Organisational model	Multidomestic	Global	Transnational
Headquarters characteristics			
Size of the company	Relatively small	Relatively large	Average size
Subsidiary characteristics			
Average size of subsidiaries	Relatively small	Relatively large	Average size
Total level of interdependence	Low	High	High
Level of HQ dependence	Low	High	Medium
Level of subsidiary dependence	Low	Medium	High
Local responsiveness	High	Low	High
% autonomous subsidiaries	High	Low	Medium
% receptive subsidiaries	Low	High	Low
% active subsidiaries	Low	Low	High
% production subsidiaries	High	Low	High
% R&D subsidiaries	Low	Low	High
% acquired subsidiaries	High	Low	Medium
Level and type of control			
Total level of control	Low	High	High
Level of personal centralised control	Low	High	Medium
Level of bureaucratic formalised control	Low	High	Medium
Level of output control	Medium	Medium	Medium
Level of control by socialisation and networks	Low/Medium	Medium	High
Level and type of expatriation			
Extent of expatriate presence	Low	High	High
Type of expatriate control	More indirect	More direct	More indirect

Subsidiaries in global companies are usually very dependent on headquarters for their sales and purchases, and are not supposed to respond actively to the local market demands in terms of, for instance, product adaptation. Their role is receptive rather than active or autonomous, and they are typically greenfields rather than acquisitions. A relatively low percentage of subsidiaries have 'strategic' functions such as production or R&D. The total level of control exercised by headquarters towards these subsidiaries is rather high. A high level of the two direct control mechanisms – personal centralised control and bureaucratic formalised control – mainly causes this. The indirect control mechanisms, output control and control by socialisation and networks, are not used to a higher than average extent. Expatriate presence in subsidiaries of this type of company is high, and the main role of these expatriates is to exercise direct control through the supervision of decisions taken at headquarters. The global configuration is most typical of German and Japanese MNCs.

Multidomestic companies

These are the complete reverse of global companies. Products or services are differentiated to meet differing local demands, and policies are differentiated to conform to differing governmental and market demands. Local demand is determined by cultural, social and political differences between countries. The food and beverages industry is a classical example of a multidomestic type of industry, but many firms in the paper industry also score high on multidomestic characteristics.

Since economies of scale are unimportant in these types of companies, both the company as a whole and the different subsidiaries are rather small in terms of employees. Subsidiaries operate relatively independent from headquarters, in a sense that they buy and sell a very low proportion of their input/output from headquarters. They are responsive to the local market, and adapt both products and marketing to local circumstances. This is made easier by the fact that products are often produced locally, which is reflected in a relatively high percentage of subsidiaries that have a production function. The role of subsidiaries can therefore be characterised as autonomous. A relatively large number of these subsidiaries are acquisitions and, partly because of that, subsidiaries in multidomestic companies are usually older than in other companies. Not surprisingly, the total level of control exercised by headquarters towards these subsidiaries is rather low. Especially the two direct control mechanisms, personal centralised control and bureaucratic formalised control, are used to a very low extent, while the use of output control and control by socialisation and networks lies around average. Expatriate presence is low. If expatriates are present their role is providing informal, rather than formal, control. The multidomestic configuration is most typical of French and British and to a lesser extent Finnish and Swedish MNCs.

Transnational companies

In a sense, these combine characteristics of both global and multidomestic companies, in that they try to respond simultaneously to the sometimes conflicting strategic needs of global efficiency and national responsiveness. The transfer of knowledge is also very important for these companies. Expertise is spread throughout the organisation, and subsidiaries can serve as a strategic centre for a particular product–market combination. Although we cannot yet identify 'typical' transnational industries, the pharmaceutical industry comes close and many MNCs in the food industry are moving towards a more transnational type of company.

In terms of size, transnational firms and their subsidiaries can also be located between global and multidomestic companies. Subsidiaries in this type of company are more dependent on other subsidiaries for their input and outputs than on headquarters, which confirms the network type of organisational structure, that is said to be typical for transnational companies. Subsidiaries are usually also very responsive to the local market, and many of them play an autonomous role. The level of active subsidiaries, that is subsidiaries that are both highly integrated and responsive to the local market, is highest in these types of firms. Subsidiaries are also more likely to have a strategic role such as production or R&D. The level of control exercised towards subsidiaries in transnational companies is nearly as high as for global companies. This is mainly due, however, to a high level of control by socialisation and networks. Relatedly, although expatriate presence in subsidiaries is also rather high, the main role of expatriates in this type of companies is to facilitate an informal and indirect, rather than a direct type of control. The transnational configuration is most typical of American, Dutch and Swiss MNCs.

Chapter summary

This chapter has discussed the structuring of international organisations. Four traditional structural arrangements and their advantages and disadvantages were discussed. Several factors were shown to influence the choice of organisational structure. It was argued that more recently academics and practitioners have moved away from a focus on structure alone to look at more integrated models of companies including strategy, structure and control mechanisms. Four major types of control mechanisms were discussed and the most popular typology of organisational models, constructed by Bartlett and Ghoshal, was outlined. A final section described a large-scale empirical test and extension of this popular theory.

Discussion questions

1 Describe the major types of multinational organisational structures according to the Stopford and Wells stages model and mention their respective advantages and disadvantages.
2 Mention at least three factors that influence the choice of organisational structure and explain their impact.
3 Describe the key characteristics of multidomestic, international, global and transnational companies. Would you agree that it would be best for most companies to follow the transnational model?
4 Take a multinational company of your own choice and describe its organisational model. Do you feel this model is effective, given the company's product–market?

Closing Case Study:
The Organising Logic of ABB

Headquartered in Zurich, ABB was formed through a merger of two European companies: the Swedish Asea, founded in 1890 and the Swiss Brown Boveri, which came into existence a year later. In August 1987, Percy Barnevik (President and CEO of ABB Asea Brown Boveri from 1987 to 1996) announced that Asea, where he was Managing Director, would merge with Brown Boveri to combine forces in the competitive market for electrical systems and equipment. In 1997

▶

ABB generated annual revenues of more than \$31 billion, employed 213,000 people and operated in 140 countries around the world.

ABB Asea Brown Boveri is a global organisation of staggering business diversity. Yet its organising principles are stark in their simplicity. Along one dimension, the company is a distributed global network. Executives around the world make decisions on product strategy and performance without regard for national borders. Along a second dimension, it is a collection of traditionally organised national companies, each serving its home market as effectively as possible. ABB's global matrix holds the two dimensions together.

At the top of the company sit CEO Percy Barnevik and 12 colleagues on the executive committee. The group, which meets every three weeks, is responsible for ABB's global strategy and performance. The executive committee consists of Swedes, Swiss, Germans and Americans. Several members of the executive committee are based outside Zürich, and their meetings are held around the world.

Reporting to the executive committee are leaders of the 50 or so business areas (BAs), located worldwide, into which the company's products and services are divided. The BAs are grouped into eight business segments, for which members of the executive committee are responsible. For example, the 'industry' segment, which sells components, systems and software to automate industrial processes, has five BAs, including metallurgy, drives and process engineering. The BA leaders report to Gerhard Schulmeyer, a German member of the executive committee, who works out of Stamford, Connecticut.

Each BA has a leader responsible for optimising the business on a global basis. The BA leader devises and champions a global strategy, holds factories around the world to cost and quality standards, allocates export markets to each factory, and shares expertise by rotating people across borders, creating mixed-nationality teams to solve problems, and building a culture of trust and communication. The BA leader for power transformers, who is responsible for 25 factories in 16 countries, is a Swede who works out of Mannheim, Germany. The BA leader for instrumentation is British. The BA leader for electric metering is an American based in North Carolina.

Alongside the BA structure sits a country structure. ABB's operations in the developed world are organised as national enterprises with Presidents, balance sheets, income statements and career ladders. In Germany, for example, Asea Brown Boveri Aktiengesellschaft, ABB's national company, employs 36,000 people and generates annual revenues of more than \$4bn. The managing director of ABB Germany, Eberhard von Koerber, plays a role comparable with that of a traditional German CEO. He reports to a supervisory board whose members include German bank representatives and trade-union officials. His company produces financial statements comparable with those from any other German company and participates fully in the German apprenticeship programme.

The BA structure meets the national structure at the level of ABB's member companies. Percy Barnevik advocates strict decentralisation. Wherever possible, ABB creates separate companies to do the work of the 50 business areas in different countries. For example, ABB does not merely sell industrial robots in Norway. Norway has an ABB robotics company charged with manufacturing robots, selling to and servicing domestic customers, and exporting to markets allocated by the BA leader.

There are 1100 of such local companies around the world. Their presidents report to two bosses: the BA leader, who is usually located outside the country, and the President of the national company of which the local company is a subsidiary. (Taylor 1991: 93)

In 1997 Göran Lindahl became ABB's new President and CEO, while Percy Barnevik retained his role as Chairman. In August 1998 ABB realigned its business segments to form eight divisions, having previously consolidated the eight business segments mentioned in the case into four larger ones. It also dissolved its regional matrix management (consisting of three regional organisations: Europe, America and Asia) that had been introduced to co-ordinate ABB's expansion in these areas. The country organisation structure as described continues to form the key force behind building ABB's multidomestic presence in markets around the world.

In managing the matrix, informal control mechanisms are very important. ABB relies on control by socialisation and networks and output control rather than personal centralised control and bureaucratic formalised control to manage its complex organisation (Harzing 1999).

Source: *Harvard Business Review*, March–April 1991 and ABB Homepage.

Note

1 Because we prefer to use the term multinational as a general term describing companies operating in more than one country, we have consistently substituted Bartlett and Ghoshal's term multinational with the comparable term multidomestic.

Questions

1 Analyse how ABB's organisational structure helps it to realise its dual goal of local responsiveness and global efficiency.
2 Why do you think ABB has managed to implement the matrix structure, which has a danger of becoming bureaucratic and cumbersome, successfully?

Further reading

Nohria, N. and **Ghoshal, S.** (1997) *The Differentiated Network: Organizing Multinational Corporations for Value Creation*, San Francisco: Jossey-Bass Publishers. This book gives an excellent summary and integration of Nohria and Ghoshal's stream of work on MNC structure since the mid-1980s.

References

Bartlett, C.A. and Ghoshal, S. (1989) *Managing Across Borders: The Transnational Solution*, Boston, Mass: Harvard Business School Press.

Bartlett, C.A. and Ghoshal, S. (1992) *Transnational Management: Text, Cases and Readings in Cross-Border Management*, New York: Irwin.

Burns, T. and Stalker, G.M. (1961) *The Management of Innovation*, London: Tavistock Publications.

Chandler, A.D. (1962) *Strategy and Structure: Chapters in the History of the Industrial Enterprise*, Cambridge, Mass: M.I.T. Press.

Daniels, J.D., Pitts, R.A. and Tretter, M.J. (1984) Strategy and structure of US multinationals, *Academy of Management Journal* 27(2): 292–307.

Daniels, J.D., Pitts, R.A. and Tretter, M.J. (1985) Organizing for dual strategies of product diversity and international expansion, *Strategic Management Journal* 6(3): 223–37.

Doz, Y.L. (1976) *National Policies and Multinational Management*, unpublished doctoral dissertation, Harvard Business School.

Doz, Y. and Prahalad, C.K. (1991) Managing DMNCs: a search for a new paradigm, *Strategic Management Journal* 12: 145–64.

Egelhoff, W.G. (1988) Strategy and structure in multinational corporations: a revision of the Stopford and Wells model, *Strategic Management Journal* 9: 1–14.

Franko, L.G. (1976) *The European Multinationals*, London: Harper & Row.

Galbraith, J.R. and Kazanjian, R.K. (1986) Organizing to implement strategies of diversity and globalisation: the role of matrix designs, *Human Resource Management* 25(1): 37–54.

Hall, D. and Saias, M. (1980) Strategy follows structure, *Strategic Management Journal* 1(2): 149–63.

Harzing, A.W.K. (1999) *Managing the Multinationals: an International Study of Control Mechanisms*, Cheltenham: Edward Elgar.

Lindblom, C.E. (1987) The science of muddling through, in D.S. Pugh, *Organization Theory: Selected Readings*, Harmondsworth: Penguin Books, pp. 238–55.

Mintzberg, H. (1983) *Structures in Fives: Designing Effective Organizations*, Englewood Cliffs, N.J.: Prentice Hall.

Mintzberg, H. (1988a) Strategy-making in three modes, in J.B. Quinn, H. Mintzberg, and R.M. James, *The Strategy Process*, Englewood Cliffs, N.J.: Prentice-Hall, pp. 82–8.

Mintzberg, H. (1988b) Opening up the definition of strategy, in J.B. Quinn, H. Mintzberg, and R.M. James, *The Strategy Process*, Englewood Cliffs, N.J.: Prentice-Hall, pp. 13–20.

Peters, T.J. and Waterman, R.H. (1982) In Search of Excellence: *Lessons from America's Best-Run Companies*, New York: Harper & Row.

Porter, M.E. (1985) *Competitive Advantage: Creating and Sustaining Superior Performance*, New York: The Free Press.

Prahalad, C.K. (1975): *The Strategic Process in a Multinational Corporation*, Unpublished doctoral dissertation, School of Business Adminstration, Harvard University.

Quinn, J.B. (1988) Strategic change: 'logical incrementalism', in J.B. Quinn, H. Mintzberg and R.M. James, *The Strategy Process*, Englewood Cliffs, N.J.: Prentice-Hall, pp. 94–103.

Stopford, J.M. and **Wells, L.T.** (1972) *Managing the Multinational Enterprise*, New York: Basic Books.

Taylor, W. (1991) The logic of global business: an interview with ABB's Percy Barnevik, *Harvard Business Review*, March–April 1993.

Woodward, J. (1958-1987) Management and technology, in D.S. Pugh, *Organization Theory: Selected Readings*, Harmondsworth: Penguin Books, pp. 52–66.

CHAPTER 19

Understanding and Managing a Multicultural Workforce

Monir Tayeb

Learning objectives

By the end of this chapter you will:

■ be familiar with the debate regarding the influence of culture on organisations

■ be able to relate certain cultural characteristics to certain aspects of organisational behaviours and relationships

■ be aware of the extent to which host-country national cultures might have a bearing for organisations with international business interests

■ have an understanding of the role of the host culture for a company's relationships with its environment and for its internal management style.

Opening Case Study:
France and the United States: two countries divided by more than an ocean

A young and talented American with an international reputation was offered a transfer to a senior position in another division of Rhone Poulenc, the French pharmaceuticals group. Her excitement turned to shock when she saw the risible salary offer. Following its usual procedures, the personnel office had calculated her new pay by considering just two factors: her age and her university qualifications. Its method was akin to that used in the French public sector.

The story, one of a number of anecdotes in a new book,* highlights just how great the cultural divide can be between French companies and their foreign counterparts. In a country proud of its traditions, and with a vocal elite probably more opposed than anywhere else in the world to the 'Americanisation' of its values, the experience of French companies acquiring US ones is particularly interesting.

Guillaume Franck, professor of management at HEC, one of France's top business schools, analyses eight acquisitions of US groups. They include the agro-chemicals division of Union Carbide, bought by Rhone Poulenc in 1987 after the Bhopal disaster in India; and Motel 6, the budget hotel chain bought by Accor.

Such deals were all the more striking because they had been so rare. Rhone Poulenc's purchase was the first time chemists had flown the French flag on American soil since the Dupont brothers 200 years earlier.

Mr Franck highlights mutual incomprehensions from the moment negotiations about takeovers start. The French complain about American lawyers' hair-splitting and an obsession with budgets; the Americans think the French put the cart before the horse by discussing 'typically French big, general ideas'.

The Americans were often struck by the far greater importance in French companies of spending time in the corporate headquarters to build up a personal network. They had difficulty understanding the vaguely described but extremely important hierarchical responsibilities, status and power of French managers. They sought in vain for clearly laid-out contracts that defined their roles.

'I learned to not publicly contest a French manager who starts criticising individuals rather than just their actions,' says one American expatriate quoted in the book. Perplexed by the conduct of meetings, he says: 'We need to rank our actions; the French are content to simply rank ideas. We have difficulty knowing where to concentrate our energy and our efforts.'

When the insurer Axa acquired Equitable, the US managers were frustrated by the obsession of top executives at their new French owner with asking questions on every detail of the business.

A la conquête du marché américain. By Guillaume Franck.
Editions Odile Jacob, Paris.

Source: *Financial Times* CD-ROM, 1 January–31 December 1998.

Introduction

This chapter introduces the issue of national culture and organisations. It first concentrates on the debate that has been taking place within the academic world and the business community since the early 1960s, and then brings the debate to the present time. The chapter then spells out the relationship between work-related values and attitudes and organisations and illustrates the discussion with appropriate examples. The discussion moves on to examine the implications of national culture for international firms. Here we explore contextual issues such as host-country expectations and business ethics, and internal matters, such as human resource management, expatriation and inpatriation.

Background debates

The study of management and organisation as a discipline in its own right is essentially a twentieth-century phenomenon, even though the management of people and organisations goes back into the mist of history. Within the discipline, different strands of thought, such as Fordism, human relations, systems theory and contingency theory have been debated and backed up from time to time by empirical evidence. The question of national culture and management came to the fore in the 1960s, and gained momentum two decades or so later following Japan's spectacular economic performance, which catapulted it from a feudal society into one of the most modern industrialised nations.

Among the early studies some only identified distinctive characteristics of organisations and managers across nations (Haire *et al.* 1966), while others tried to relate these to the cultural traits of the peoples involved. For instance, Crozier (1964), in his seminal study of the French bureaucracy, attributed certain dysfunctions of French organisations to certain cultural characteristics of French people, which he argued were created and reinforced by various French social institutions, especially the educational system.

Kakar (1971) reported that paternal type of superior-subordinate relationships, especially in the form of assertive superior behaviour, dominated the authority relations in Indian organisations. He argued that this pattern was related to sociocultural factors in Indian traditions as well as to the hierarchical development of modern work organisations in India.

In the same vein, De Bettignies (1973) reported that the cultural characteristics of Japanese people, rooted in their history and family structure, are manifested in their organisational behaviour. He argued that these deeply rooted values influence organisational relationships in the forms of (1) a strong sense of group or community; (2) a strong sense of obligation and gratitude; (3) a strong sense of 'we' versus' they; (4) an underlying emotionality and excitability which is controlled by a somewhat compulsive attention to details, plans and rules; (5) a willingness to work hard and to persevere toward long-range goals; (6) a total devotion to the boss; (7) an emphasis on self-effacement and a tendency to attribute responsibilities to others rather than taking responsibility for one's own actions; and (8) a strong belief that competence comes automatically with seniority.

Later still, researchers engaged in studies that involved comparing management and organisations in two or more countries, such as Pascale (1978) and Ouchi (1981) who compared Japanese and US companies; Maurice *et al.* (1980) who studied closely matched factories in France, the then West Germany, and Great Britain; Jamieson (1980) who investigated the structural characteristics and attitudes of managers of five British companies closely matched with six American subsidiaries; and Tayeb (1988) who compared national cultures, employee attitudes and values, and organisational structures of seven English companies with their near-exact counterparts in India.

As we saw in Chapter 13, a research project that involved two questionnaire surveys of a large number of countries was conducted by Hofstede (1980) in the late 1960s and early 1970s. Using organisational structural dimensions identified and proposed by the Aston Research Group (Pugh *et al.* 1968), Hofstede argued that two of his four cultural dimensions lay behind these structural parameters: 'power distance' is conceptually related to 'concentration of authority' (centralisation), and 'uncertainty avoidance' is related to 'structuring of activities' (formalisation, specialisation, standardisation). Further, he argued that these two, together with individualism/collectivism and masculinity/femininity dimensions greatly influence people's attitudes, values and behaviours within their workplace and their company's management style.

Hofstede, by demonstrating the differences among nations on these four dimensions, made a strong case to invalidate Anglo–American-based theories of management and leadership in other countries. He further argued that for those theories, and indeed technologies developed in West, to work in countries other than their birthplace certain cultural adjustments should be made. He then cited two countries, Iran and Japan, to illustrate his point:

> Attempts at the transfer of leadership skills which do not take the values of subordinates into account have little chance of success . . . Technologies are not neutral with regard to values: in order to work, they assume that certain values are respected. Making these technologies work means that people in the receiving countries must learn new leadership and subordinateship skills, change old institutions and shift their values . . . Cultural transposition, in the ideal case, means finding a new cultural synthesis which retains from the old local values those elements deemed essential but which allows the new technologies to function. Probably the country which has most successfully done this so far is Japan; a country where it has clearly failed is Iran. (Hofstede 1980: 300)

Another development was the so-called convergence (universalism) versus divergence (particularism) debate. Some authors have emphasised the universality of organisations and the similarities between them (for example, Kerr *et al.* 1952; Cole 1973; Hickson *et al.* 1974; Form 1979; Negandhi 1979, 1985), and others the cultural uniqueness of organisations (for example, Crozier 1964; Meyer and Rowan 1977; Hofstede 1980; Lincoln *et al.* 1981; Laurent 1983). There are those who argue that technology carries its own imperatives: for an assembly-line automobile technology to be utilised properly a certain organisational design and management style must be adopted. An electronics company, on the other hand, would find a different design more appropriate; and so on.

Tayeb (1988) argued, however, that the various sides of this debate are not mutually exclusive. Rather, they complement one another. That is, certain aspects of organisations are more likely to be universal, such as shop-floor layout (influenced in part by technological requirements), hierarchical structure and division of functions, whereas some areas are more culture-specific, such as human resource management. Moreover, the fact is that organisations and their employees do not live in a vacuum, separated from their societal surroundings. National culture, as a set of values, attitudes and behaviours, includes elements that are relevant to work and organisation. These are carried into the workplace as part of the employees' cultural baggage. Work-related values and attitudes, such as power distance, tolerance for ambiguity, honesty, pursuance of group or individual goals, work ethic, and entrepreneurial spirit, form part of the cultural identity of a nation (Hofstede 1980; Tayeb 1988), and although employees may be required to perform certain *practices* at work, they cannot be deprived of their *values* (Hofstede *et al.* 1990).

National culture apart, as we saw in Chapter 12, there are other societal factors, such as government policies, industrial relations' rules and regulations, the power of pressure groups, and membership of regional and global agreements and institutions, all of which have a direct or indirect bearing on an organisation's management practices (see also Tayeb 1996, 1998).

Organisations and cultures

The work-related values and attitudes discussed above influence organisational structure and its management style in different ways. Moreover, the influence of individual values and attitudes is in some cases reinforced by others, and in some cases cancelled out by them. The reason, as was mentioned in Chapter 13, is that culture is too complex and dynamic to be confined to clear-cut dimensions expected to result in clear-cut cause-and-effect relationships. For instance, Indians are believed to be a collectivist people, just like the Japanese. However, when it comes to workplace behaviour, the Indians are far less group-oriented and committed to their organisation's goals than are their Japanese counterparts (Tayeb 1995).

In addition, because of the effects of non-cultural factors on organisations, even within the same country we encounter a range of organisational structural configurations and management styles: democratic, decentralised companies operating side by side highly centralised and authoritarian ones, may even be in the same industrial estate a few yards from one another.

Research evidence shows that non-cultural factors such as size (number of employees), technology, ownership, status, industry and competition, could have similar effects on organisations in terms of their organisational structure and management style, irrespective of the cultural setting within which they operate.

For instance, in all countries large organisations tend to be more decentralised than smaller ones. Publicly owned companies are likely to have more written rules and regulations and standard procedures than their private-sector counterparts. Companies that operate in competitive markets usually spend more on R&D and their 'front-line' staff have more authority to react to market conditions than those that operate in low-competition environments. In a hospital or a university, doctors and lecturers tend to have more control over how they organise and perform their task than, say, non-specialist manual workers on a car-factory shop-floor. Managers of a subsidiary of a multinational company, or a bank branch, or a shop in a retail chain would probably have much less decision-making power than their counterparts in an independent company.

Moreover, there is evidence that some aspects of organisations are less prone to cultural influences than others. For instance, the use of computers and robots in offices and shopfloors does not presuppose certain cultural characteristics. By contrast, human resource management and leadership styles are more likely to reflect employees' and their managers' cultural background and upbringing. We come back to this issue again in Chapter 21.

Given the above qualifications and caveats, some of the consequences of cultural characteristics are discussed below, on the basis of the research evidence available to date.

In high-power distance countries, organisations tend in general to be more centralised, in that power resides in the hands of a few at the apex of the hierarchy, and only the authority to make minor non-strategic decisions may be delegated down the line. In small-power distance nations, organisations tend to be run on a participative model and decision-making processes may spread downwards and across.

In high-uncertainty avoidance nations, people tend to shield themselves against uncertainty and ambiguity by making decisions collectively. The Japanese organisations' *ringi* style of decision making is a good example of this process. Well-structured organisations with clear-cut procedures and rules, such as those we observe in Germany, can also be argued to be an effect of the German people's low tolerance for ambiguity and uncertainty. In a country like the UK, where people have a relatively higher degree of tolerance for uncertainty, organisations tend to be less structured, and use less written and formal rules and regulations.

In individualistic countries, such as the US, where achievement and ambitions are self-oriented, motivational policies such as pay, benefits and promotion are based on individual employees' achievement. By contrast, in certain collectivist cultures such as Japan, group performance forms the basis for rewards allocation. Interestingly, in a vast majority of Japanese companies, employees' wage level and promotion is also based in part on seniority. This fits in well with the high regard and respect the Japanese are said to hold for their aged compatriots.

In feminine societies, at national, organisational and individual levels, the emphasis is on quality of life rather than material achievement *per se*; achievement in the professional sphere would not be at the expense of family life; the 'rat race' is frowned on, losers are not shunned, the weak are provided for through a social safety net and environmental considerations are not overlooked by the profit-maximisation drive. In masculine societies the opposite of these is generally the case.

In cultures that are characterised by short-term orientation, the share-holders' horizon is usually the next financial year's dividends; they buy and sell shares to maximise their earnings, and loyalties do not reside with any single company. The managers in turn pursue short-term policies and strategies to remain competitive not only as providers of goods and services but also as satisfiers of their shareholders' goals. In long-term oriented cultures, medium- to long-term growth and market share take precedence over short-term profits; companies tend to be owned by a handful of shareholders and institutions whose financial well-being does not depend on short-term cash and dividends.

In high-context countries, the flow of communication among people is helped along with understated but perfectly understood clues; a hint, a nudge or a wink, might go unnoticed by outsiders or puzzle them, but they speak volumes to insiders. To a person from a low-context culture visiting a high-context country, words, statements, promises and expressions may not necessarily mean what they appear to be. In some countries, if at the end of an uncomfortable meeting, a manager says to a client 'I'll see what I can do, phone me later,' both sides know that he is saying no, and that there is no point in making that phone call. To a person unfamiliar with the nuances and context of the conversation, this statement is seen as a promise, and the inevitably disappointing phone call would later leave him bitter and angry.

High interpersonal trust could in principle mean decentralised organisational structure and management style, where managers tend to have sufficient confidence in their subordinates to let them make certain decisions without referring back to higher levels.

International companies and national culture

For companies that have business interests and activities in countries other than their own, the above and similar characteristics would form the cultural contexts within which they have to operate. They manifest themselves in various forms and have to be taken into consideration by international companies if they wish to succeed in those contexts, at both macro and micro levels.

Before going further in the discussion it is worth noting that the extent to which an international company is affected by other countries' national culture depends on the extent of the company's internationalisation. For example, a company that exports its products abroad needs above all to take into account the customers' tastes and preferences and the host-country's rules and regulations; deeper cultural characteristics, such as group-orientation, achievement motivation and the like, are not directly relevant to the exporting company. But if a company is involved in a joint venture or has a subsidiary abroad, the situation is quite different. Here it not only has to take into account foreign customers, governments and other social institutions. Because it employs people from the host country, it has also to take into consideration their different work experiences and preferences for workplace relationships, such as management style and authority structure.

Relationships with the 'environment'

Host-countries' codes of behaviour, cultural norms and general expectations from companies are usually understood and respected by foreign firms, unless they go against their fundamental beliefs and principles. In which case either they adapt or leave. What they cannot and should not do is to try to change the local culture.

For instance, in a country where people expect business organisations to play an active role in the community, it may not go down well with the local population if the foreign company remains indifferent to and aloof from local cultural, educational and other social events.

Muna's (1980: 30–32) description of the pressures from the business and social community on Arab executives is quite instructive. According to him, there is a fusion of business, social and personal life and the executives are unable, for sociocultural reasons, to separate business affairs from social or personal life. They are often one and the same. Business meetings may have to take place out of office hours and at home. On the other hand they also have to receive social visits at the office, and find it difficult to discourage such customs since they stem from the strong societal norm of hospitality. In fact, their and their family's reputation is at stake if they do not conform to the community's norms and expectations. The executives have to live up to their standing in the community. What matters above all is the opinion of family members, close friends and/or employees and the larger community.

The sociocultural context also exerts pressures on various other activities of a foreign company, and sometimes the very existence of the company in a country could be at stake.

In India, for example, one of the major political parties, the Bharatiya Janata Party (BJP) advocates certain policies that have serious implications for foreign investors. The party has a fringe wanting to throw out all foreign multinationals. The party mainstream, although more moderate, still expresses 'fear' that Indian culture may be eroded by foreign investment in food and drinks, and so would be likely to curtail future investment in alcoholic and soft drinks, potato crisps, pizza parlours and the like.

The BJP might also curb foreign portfolio investment, which it regards as volatile hot money. However, the party is aware of the need to maintain foreign confidence, and wants to champion Indian business without scaring away foreigners. It welcomes foreign investment in the infrastructure, which alone could cost $10bn a year (*The Economist*, 7 March 1998).

In Colombia, Occidental Petroleum (also known as Oxy), a US company, has experienced a direct clash with local traditions. Five thousand U'Wa Indians have been threatening for years to commit mass suicide over Oxy's plans to explore their tribal lands. Oxy got a permit to explore the Samore field, 20 per cent of it lying beneath the U'wa reservation, in early 1995. The U'wa promptly fired off their suicide threat. They say their ancestors carried out such a threat in the conquistadors' days. They believe that their lands are the heart of Mother Earth, and oil is her blood. Its extraction would kill their culture, they said; they would sooner kill themselves. After a great deal of argument, mediation and court actions, the oil company is discussing a new contract with the government, the result of which may exclude all U'wa land from exploration (*The Economist*, 6 June 1998).

Business ethics

Business ethics is a tricky issue in the context of international business. There are many obvious clear-cut cases, such as Mafia-driven operations and social and criminal offences that characterise business environments in certain countries. Sometimes, there may not be any corruption involved in conducting business with partners across borders but the business itself may be considered by some as unethical, such as selling arms to undemocratic countries with less than clean human rights records.

However, there are also grey areas with which companies have to deal: one person's bribe is another's gift to build trust; someone's nepotism is the other's networking; who can tell for sure which is which?

It is also worth noting that what might appear as an unethical behaviour or custom to an outsider, is the result of years, decades, even centuries of the shared experience of people who develop specific solutions to their specific problems, not shared by others outside that experience.

What do you do if your child is very ill and the doctor's page boy will not let you see him unless you discreetly put a few coins in his hand? If you don't, others will, and your child may not be alive by the time your turn eventually comes. It is not for outsiders to question the system; the insiders have worked out a practical way of coping with the situation, and if it works for them, so be it.

In this connection Taylor *et al.* (1997) explain the corrupt practices prevalent in post-communist Russia in historical and political terms. They argue that conditions in Russia today are the result of a long history of authoritarianism, a tradition and heritage that have left deep scars and deformed perceptions that present awesome difficulties for developing a substantial civil society. More recent history, the authors further argue, encompassing the communist period from 1917 until the beginning of democratic and market reforms in the late 1980s, has been characterised by the head of the Russian Orthodox Church (*Moscow News*, 22–28 April 1994: 6) as a 'seventy-year spiritual vacuum'.

According to Taylor *et al.* (1997: 11) recent literature is replete with depictions of the devastating effects on Russian society emanating from this long period. The communist frame of reference served to 'blur the line between the permitted and the forbidden, the acceptable and the unacceptable . . . stripping, cheating, theft and dishonesty of their moral repulsiveness' (Dimitov 1992). The centrality and power of the state went so far in depoliticising the people 'that cynicism, hopelessness and passivity developed as a shield against the authorities' (Bialer 1991–2: 168).

What stance do multinational companies take when faced with corruption and other 'unethical' practices? Some companies argue that if they do not go along with the tide and, say, bribe their way into a permission or a contract, their competitors will, and a lucrative business is lost. However, research has not always supported such arguments (Graham 1983).

Many companies develop their own ways of handling corruption and other unethical situations. Some may devise their own code of ethics with detailed guidelines, in addition to their own country's legal requirements, with which they are compatible. Naturally, like other organisational policies and practices, codes of ethics to some extent reflect each company's own culture and specific preferences and priorities. France's Renault, for example, stopped negotiations with Italy's Fiat a few years ago after discovering that a number of the Italian company's top executives had been implicated in bribes (Stajkovic and Luthans 1997).

Exhibit 19.1 Coping with corruption

'Hindustan Lever, the Anglo-Dutch maker of products from Lux to Lipton tea, was the first multinational to Indianise, combining the best of both worlds,' says Mr Amit Sharma, managing director of Motorola India. 'It's a role model for companies that want to succeed in India.' Hindustan Lever earned a reputation for probity in a country where political interference and red tape prompted companies to bribe their way round bureaucrats. The group adopted a different method to persuade the mandarins to ease up on import or production limits: it made the case for job creation, export earnings and rural development.

Such lessons stuck with Mr Muktesh Pant, with Hindustan Lever for 16 years and now Managing Director of Reebok, the sportswear maker firm. When he wanted to start making shoes locally, he faced a problem. Importing samples, even a single pair, was banned to protect local industry.

'Everyone in the shoe trade imported the left shoe into Bombay and the right shoe into Madras,' he says. Determined to find a legal alternative, Mr Pant met officials time and again until he convinced them that foreign prototypes would help upgrade India's industry. Eventually, the government granted Reebok a special licence to import 10,000 pairs.

Source: *Financial Times* CD-ROM, 1 January–31 December 1998.

Some Japanese companies have business codes specifically for their international operations which generally recommend 'enlightened self-interest' (Taka and Foglia 1994) and are in accordance with the host-country's ethical concerns, values and expectations.

Most countries obviously have laws that govern broad, and sometimes specific, areas of business ethics. These laws usually cover both domestic situations and those arising out of dealings with foreign nationals within or outside their national boundaries. The US for instance has a Foreign Corrupt Practices Act that explicitly prohibits the bribery of foreign nationals by US businesses. Whether or not legislation prevents unethical practices, however, is another question. China, for example, has legislation prohibiting the pirating of intellectual property, but, as Stajkovic and Luthans (1997) point out, enforcement has been less than satisfactory:

> Not only is it estimated that 90 per cent of computer software in China has been pirated from US firms, but today there are highly visible fake cans of Coca-Cola, fake MacDonald's hamburger restaurants, and even fake versions of the Jeeps that Chrysler manufactures with a joint-venture partner in Beijing. (p. 24)

Relationships with the employees

Human resource management

A multinational company with operating subsidiaries abroad in which local people work as employees is by definition a multicultural company. Managing human resources, reconciling employees' interests and expectations with the company's other resources and priorities, is a complex enough task in a single-nation, single-culture firm. The complexities could increase astronomically as a company adds more and more country-specific operations to its business and its workforce becomes more and more culturally diverse.

Culture, as was discussed in Chapter 13, is a social construct. This means that within an organisation the level at which culture manifests itself is where the employees interact with one another formally and informally on innumerable occasions: over a cup of coffee, around a table in a committee room; as team members; in a manager-subordinate situation, and so forth. We saw how complicated and different national cultures are with regard to their values, attitudes and beliefs, etc. We know how differently people might behave around the world even if they are in similar situations. These differences are also reflected within organisations with a culturally diverse workforce.

In a company with a homogeneous workforce, everybody knows the rules of the game, thanks largely to the cultural baggage everybody brings in and whose contents they mostly share. But in a culturally heterogeneous multinational company there is more than one set of rules of the game; each subsidiary has its own set and may like to play the game by it.

For instance, in sharply stratified cultures, be it on the basis of class or caste systems, people roughly know their place. A manager is a manager and a worker is a worker; never one indulges in doing the other's job. The manager leads and manages, the worker obeys and does the actual production work. In a more egalitarian society, the division between people may be less sharp, and therefore you might have workers who might sit on the Board of Directors and managers who would not mind putting on an overall and getting their hands dirty on the shop floor. Management style here allows people to participate in both managerial and manual work.

What do you do if some of your subsidiaries are located within a culture of the first kind and others in the second? Do you let each subsidiary go its own way and do as the locals do and before you know it you lose control over your operations as a whole? Or do you keep a tight rein and make all subsidiaries sing to the same tune regardless what their fellow locals do, and before you know it ambitious locals with a desire to take initiative leave you for greener pastures elsewhere?

Multinational firms have three broad subsidiary-management options at their disposal: they can choose to implement similar HRM policies and practices to those customary in the home country and ignore local conditions entirely (an ethnocentric policy); they can largely follow the practices prevalent in individual host countries (a polycentric policy); they can devise and implement a universal company-wide policy, fostered through organisational culture and philosophy (a global policy) (Perlmutter 1969).

Specific characteristics in the countries in which subsidiaries are located, however, might interfere with a straightforward choice of options and force multinationals to opt for a 'hybrid' strategy. In a study of manufacturing and service subsidiaries of Japanese multinational companies, for example, differences were found in the degree and nature of home-grown practices that these companies introduced into their US subsidiaries (Beechler and Yang 1994).

Another factor that might complicate HRM policy choices is the manner in which subsidiaries are set up. It is easier to impose home-grown policies on a green field subsidiary than on one that has joined the parent company through acquisition or merger (Tayeb 1994). Old companies with established cultures and 'mannerisms' are more likely to resist the imposition of policies than brand new companies. In the latter case employees are still finding their way around and are more open to experimentation with new ideas; the organisational culture has not yet taken definite shape.

The above discussion shows that relationships between a parent company and its subsidiaries are inherently prone to tension and conflicts, which arise mainly from a need to maintain the integrity of the company as a coherent, co-ordinated entity, while allowing for subsidiaries to respond to their differentiated environments (Laurent 1986; Bartlett and Ghoshal 1989, 1992; Schuler et al. 1993).

The concepts of differentiation and integration, originally a focus of debate among sociologists, were first discussed within the context of management and organisation studies by Lawrence and Lorsch (1967). They argued that for an organisation to perform effectively in diverse environments, it must be both appropriately differentiated and adequately integrated in order that the separate units and departments are co-ordinated and work towards a common goal. In the context of international business, their model has been used to explain the dynamics of managing organisations operating across borders.

Doz (1976) described the need for differentiation in political terms, emphasising the tension that exists between the 'economic imperative' (large-scale efficient facilities) and the 'political imperative' (local content laws, local production requirements). Prahalad (1976) developed a typology of multinational companies that stressed 'the need for managerial interdependence' (integration) versus the 'need for managerial diversity' (local responsiveness), so highlighting the need for differentiation on a geographical basis. To maintain an equilibrium between these two conflicting forces, Prahalad and Doz (1987) suggested a multifocal solution where the focus of decision making shifts between the international and the local depending on the problem under consideration. They argue that the mindset of managers should have a global framework, balancing the needs between local responsiveness and a global vision of the firm. However, the appropriate mix of differentiation and integration may vary from company to company depending on the form and extent of their internationalisation, their industry and the markets they serve, and the kind of employees they have (Tayeb 1996).

A relevant point to make here is that there is a qualitative distinction between HRM *policies* and HRM *practices* (Schuler *et al.* 1993). Whereas multinational firms might find it feasible to have company-wide philosophies and policies of a global or ethnocentric nature, they might find it necessary to be responsive to local conditions when it comes to HRM practices and adopt polycentric practices. The guiding principle in such cases is to keep the company as a whole intact and integrated, while at the same time allowing for a measure of differentiation when needed or desirable (Prahalad and Doz 1987; Welch 1994).

A recent study by Tayeb (1998) shows that the power and influence of subsidiaries could play a significant role in the parent–subsidiary relationship, especially with regard to HRM. In the subsidiary investigated the managers interpreted their parent company's HRM policies into practices that were compatible not only with their specific business priorities and market conditions, but also with their local traditions and their own organisational ways of doing things. The subsidiary was able to exert such an influence mainly because it was half a century old and had established a strong rapport with its employees and local environment. It was also able to demonstrate to the parent company that its spectacular success in the international market was due to its own brand of management style and HRM practices.

Exhibit 19.2 **A language to unite our multicultural team: Geoff Unwin's secret weapon**

Geoff Unwin is the Chief Executive of Cap Gemini, the European information technology consultancy, which employs more than 30,000 people worldwide. He began his career in 1963 as a chocolate-taster for Cadbury Schweppes. Five years later, he joined Hoskyns Group, a UK computer services company. In 1984, he became Managing Director of Hoskyns, which was acquired by Cap Gemini in 1990.

'People ask why this very French company put a Brit in charge. My answer is that it was because I was different. I thought differently. Not better, just differently. When people think differently, it puts a different perspective on problems. We exploit that.

'It is a very, very multicultural organisation. This diversity brings a lot to the company. In the early days, I spent a fair amount of time travelling, getting to understand people and getting some feeling for what is different about the cultures. If one can factor that in, one can get more out of the team. The French involve themselves in much more analysis than the Brits. I remember a French manager making the classic comment: "It will work in practice but what about the theory?"'

'The very analytical approach does have some dangers. The danger is that you will believe what you write down. The best indicators are your eyes and ears.

'A German manufacturing company once asked me for our five-year plan. I just giggled. It is positively dangerous to talk about five-year plans in this industry, which is changing all the time.

'You have to be very flexible. I have always found that the most powerful way of doing that is to operate in a team. Very often it will take braver decisions. Things can be executed faster, provided tasks are allocated across the team.

'The analogy is with a professional football team. A lot of organisations operate like children playing football, with people lurching off to the right and left. But people have to stay in position. You have to be able to trust them to do what they are meant to be doing.

'People need to be aware that you change the team regularly. In the first two years after I started, we changed 40 per cent of the top 150 people. It was done quietly. There was no blood on the floor. A 20 per cent change every 18 months is healthy. The organisation is growing very strongly. It is like climbing Everest. Some people won't make it to the next stage. Some have got tired in the climb. It is best to move them to another part of the field to rejuvenate them. Some will leave.

'Long before I joined, Cap Gemini decided that English was going to be the language of the company. It was a remarkable decision for a French company to make. Even so, when I came into this job I realised that a great deal of transactions would be in French. I had rusty schoolboy French and I realised it would be important to speak it and understand it. For two and a half years, a French lady studying at the London School of Economics would come to my house at 8.30am and try to teach me.

'I had a very highly educated French minder as my operational assistant. He would sit in a meeting and tell me what it was really about. When you are in a business meeting in a foreign language, you recognise just how difficult it is. English speakers have a huge advantage, as international companies increasingly adopt English as their business language. We take it for granted but it is a national asset. My secret weapon is English.'

Source: Financial Times CD-ROM, 1 January–31 December 1998.

Expatriation

Many multinational companies send their staff, usually from headquarters and usually rather senior people, to their foreign subsidiaries from time to time and for varying periods of time. The objectives are manifold. First, expatriation is a means to transfer technical and managerial skills over a sustained period to the subsidiaries until they are mastered by the company's local employees. Second, it helps integrate the subsidiaries into the company and form a coherent whole, all aiming at achieving the same goals. Third, it broadens the horizon of especially the senior staff and creates an international, indeed global mindset, which is vital for companies operating in competitive global markets. Finally, until recently most multinationals used to allocate senior positions in their subsidiaries only to their home nationals. This practice is being increasingly met with disenchantment and dissatisfaction of many talented local employees, who at times would see a glass ceiling in their way to the top. As a result, and because of the danger of losing such employees, most multinationals are now allowing their top local positions to be filled by suitably qualified local people.

But how do you prepare employees for foreign assignments? Candidates for expatriate assignments are normally selected not only for their technical and managerial expertise but also for their cross-cultural adaptability. Training beforehand and mentoring the expatriate while abroad would be of great help here.

In the past three decades or so, with the proliferation of international trade and business, both researchers and practitioners have realised the importance of cross-cultural training as a useful, if not necessary, means of preparing people who have to work in a country other than their own.

Cultural training could take various forms, from the use of videos prepared by professional agencies, to in-house or external short courses and seminars, to fully developed extensive intercultural training programmes, such as culture assimilators, and a spell of working experience abroad.

Companies might use any combination of these approaches as they see fit to enable their employees to perform their jobs well while on foreign assignment. Expatriate training and performance records at both company and national levels are mixed.

Tung's (1984) survey of a sample of American and Japanese multinationals and their human resource management practices regarding their employees abroad found that, on the whole, Japanese companies had a better record compared to their American counterparts in terms of their employees' performance, among other things.

She found that such characteristics as employees' high level of commitment, managers' familiarity with and understanding of their subordinates' personal and family circumstances, extensive training programmes, including a spell of time spent abroad, a long-term perspective regarding employee performance and attitudes, all helped to create a better record of employee performance abroad compared to the American firms studied. These had adopted expatriates' policies which were almost all opposite to those of their Japanese counterparts.

In a subsequent survey (1988) Tung compared the management strategies and practices of Japanese and American multinationals' expatriates with those of a sample of European ones. Here she found that American multinationals fared worse compared to both their Japanese and European counterparts. The Americans had a much higher failure rate, which was found to have roots in its shorter time perspective and less positive attitudes to and understanding of foreign cultures.

In the study mentioned above Tayeb (1998) found the headquarters of the company concerned had no formal training programmes for its staff before they were sent on foreign assignments. However, once they arrived in the UK subsidiary they would get help and support from the locals.

There was, for instance, a half-day programme put together not to train the newcomers, but to familiarise them with the living conditions there, such as cultural and social issues, and what they needed to be aware of. The company would also put together an information pack, a little handbook, informing people how to drive in their new 'country', where they could go to have fun, what the theatres were like, and so forth.

One of the expatriate managers, on the basis of his own experience, has taken additional initiatives in this respect:

> I was trying to find the best way to provide support both for the families and for the expatriates. So what I actually did was, I hired an expatriate wife, so she works for me. She has already been through the experience and the problems of getting used to living here, transitioning from US life to here. It's her job and her responsibility to help other expatriates settle into life and usually it's the spouse. The spouse is usually at home, etc., so she, for example, when they first come here, she actually gets them in a car and gives them an orientation of the area, drives them round, shows them the area. She finds houses for them rather than throwing them to the estate agents, she finds the houses, she contacts the estate agents. She finds out what kind of housing they are looking for and then I tell her the limits and she goes out and finds the houses. She takes them round and shows them the houses, they decide, she helps them through the transition to local lifestyles. Plus a social network has been created of all the expatriates. The wives get together from time to time, they used to get together on a weekly basis, and so when a new ex-pat comes over they join the circle. It's a support circle and they get together, have lunch once a week, they had a sewing circle at one point, everyone would try sewing and embroidery. I think we were pretty creative, we created something called 'gourmet dinners'. We would pick a different country of the world and then we would take recipes and pass the recipes out and each family member would bring one and we'd have a pot-luck. So those are the kind of things we did and that was a real support network. (Tayeb 1998: 350–51)

In addition to these informal arrangements, this UK subsidiary encourages exchange of expatriates to and from the UK in order to develop a global mindset in the workforce, and to enable them to communicate easily with people from other parts of the world. Managers in particular are encouraged to participate in various international conferences and multicultural events.

Inpatriation

This is a process whereby staff, usually in senior positions, from the subsidiaries are invited to join the headquarters, sometimes on a short-term basis, to be trained and acculturated, sometimes for a much longer period in order to create a multicultural team at the home base. As Harvey and Buckley (1997) argue, as global competition becomes more intense, a logical step for global companies would be to evolve into multicultural multinational organisations. The authors go on to demonstrate that major world competitors are embarking on the retooling of their management to reflect a diversity of cultural perspectives (p. 36):

Asea Brown Boveri (ABB), a Swedish-Swiss electrical engineering MNC, has a board of directors consisting of eight individuals from four different nationalities; an executive committee of eight with five managers from countries other than Sweden or Switzerland; its official corporate language is English; and all financial results are reported in US dollars. The European energy company, Royal Dutch/Shell, has over 38 nationalities represented in its London headquarters and nearly as diverse a workforce in its operating units throughout the world. (Pechter 1993; Thronhill 1993; Copeland 1995)

The Japanese are reducing their unicultural orientation in their global businesses. Yoichi Morishita, president of Matsushita, has ordered that top management must reflect the cultural diversity of the countries where Matsushita does business. Sony sells 80 per cent of its products overseas and recently recognized the need to become multicultural. It has appointed two foreigners to its Board of Directors and has plans to hire host-country nationals who are to be integrated into the top management of the parent organization. At the same time, the Chairman of Sony has stated that in five years the Board of Directors of Sony will reflect the diversity of countries that are important to the future of the company. Similarly, Toshiba plans to have a more representative top management and Board of Directors to facilitate long-run global strategies. (Harvey and Buckley 1997: 36)

Chapter summary

This chapter has focused on the debate about the influence of national culture on organisations. Following a brief history of the debate within the academic and business communities, specific relationships between certain work-related values and attitudes on the one hand and specific areas of organisational behaviours on the other were spelt out. The discussion was then brought down to the implications of host-country culture for international companies. It was argued that the degree to which organisations are affected by other countries' culture depends on the extent of their internationalisation. This issue was examined with respect to a company's relationship with its external environment and its employees, with special emphasis on human resource management, expatriation and inpatriation.

Discussion questions

1 What aspects of organisations are more likely to be influenced by national culture?
2 What aspects of organisations are said to be culture-free?
3 To what extent are international organisations influenced by the culture of those with whom they do business?

Closing Case Study:
Business protocols? What do you mean?

Angelica Cortes

John Dunning goes to Chile

As the day to depart for Santiago, Chile, approaches, John Dunning is optimistic and enthusiastic about the prospect of travelling to South America. John is a 27-year-old electronic engineer who has been working with Alpha Corp. for the past three years as sales manager. His company manufactures time-precision equipment that is used to programme and control industrial machinery involved in assembly lines or other lines of equipment that need to function in precise time spans. As Alpha Corp. is contemplating expanding its market to Latin America, Chile offers good possibilities: the product is not produced in Chile, and there is a good market because of the emphasis in the industrialisation of their economy.

To do this, Alpha Corp. is contemplating the idea of entering into a joint venture with a Chilean company. They feel that partnering with a local business will facilitate their entrance to the market because of their local partner's knowledge and familiarity of the business customs and also their connection with suppliers, buyers and financial institutions. To this end Alpha had identified Astac S.A. as a good candidate for this alliance.

Astac S.A. manufactures numerical control equipment that complements Alpha's products and through previous contacts they feel comfortable with the idea of forming this strategic alliance. This opportunity to visit Chile and possibly to negotiate this business agreement was a signal of confidence on the part of management. John was competent in his field and even when he was fairly new in sales, he had been doing well with their American customers. Alpha Corp. selected him for this negotiation, thinking it will give him experience and international exposure that will be valuable for their future market expansion. He had never been in Chile – or outside the United States – but he had heard that the country is a promising emerging market in South America. The country has a very stable democratic system which is pro-business, and it has a strong market economy that provides a positive environment for international business.

As John carefully prepared for the business negotiation regarding the terms of the joint venture, he decided to ask for advice from his colleague Marianne McCallaghan who has been in Brazil and Argentina for vacations. Marianne indicated that Latin Americans tend not to be so punctual with respect to their business appointments, and they also tend to extend the first meeting into personal conversations rather than concentrating on business discussions. John made mental notes of these two observations.

A flying start

Finally the day for departure arrived and John left for Chile. His company had already made hotel reservations and his first meeting was at three o'clock that afternoon, giving him some time to rest and review his notes. On his arrival at the Chilean company he was greeted by the Marketing Vice-President's secretary and immediately guided into the meeting room where he met the management of the firm: Luis Jose Sandoval, President; Sergio Albornoz, Comptroller; Alberto

Agustinas, Marketing Vice-President; and Patricia Vargas, Director of Engineering, all of them ranging in age from mid-thirties to late fifties. After a few questions about his trip and first impressions, the meeting concentrated on the business discussion. John felt very comfortable, feeling that it was not different from the manner in which business meetings are conducted in the US. All the managers spoke fairly good English, so there was no need for an interpreter, eliminating time-consuming translations and allowing a more direct interaction among the managers. John immediately moved into addressing them by their first name, and felt that any difference in age and organisational rank was ignored because of his professional competence. At the end of the meeting, it was agreed to have another meeting at 9:00 the next morning.

Dark clouds are gathering

John arrived promptly at 9:00 am at the meeting and was greeted by Alberto Agustinas who explained that Patricia Vargas was joining them, but Mr Sandoval and Mr Albornoz would not come because they had previous appointments. The meeting concentrated on business and technical descriptions of the complementarity of the products. John felt that the meeting, even when it was cordial, was more polite than friendly. Close to lunch time he was invited by Alberto and Patricia to a restaurant and the conversation centred on John's experience, his organisational rank, and his long-term goals with Alpha Corp. Again John got the impression that the tone of the interactions was more polite than friendly and began to ask himself if yesterday had been the same or was it that he had concentrated so much on the details that he did not notice a certain degree of coldness in the interaction. Maybe it was just his imagination.

Disaster looms

The last meeting was held the following morning and he again met with Alberto and Patricia. Thirty minutes into that meeting, the President came in unexpectedly and announced that, after reviewing the information, he had decided that Astac would not go ahead with the joint venture. The President was polite but nevertheless lacked the cordiality he had showed at the beginning of the first meeting.

On his flight back to the US, John reviewed his mental notes about what happened in the first meeting. He had a feeling that something went wrong, but he couldn't pinpoint exactly what it was. One thing he was certain of: he had lost the opportunity to close any business agreement with that company, but how would he explain that to his management if he did not even know what the problem was and what went wrong? He was sure that it was not the products themselves or the terms of the agreement: it was something else.

Questions

1 What did go wrong in John Dunning's encounter with Astac SA. executives during the first meeting?
2 What kind of information should Alpha Corp have collected before sending a manager to Chile for a negotiation of a joint venture? Why was that information important?
3 Why is understanding the issues of power distance so important in negotiating with different cultures?
4 How does power distance influence the degrees of formality found in business protocols?

Further reading

Joynt, P. and **Warner, M.** (1996) *Managing Across Cultures: Issues and Perspectives*, London: International Thomson Business Press. This book is a collection of 22 papers that discuss various aspects of the culture and management issue. Some papers are concerned with theoretical models and arguments while others also present findings of empirical studies conducted in various countries.

Jackson, T. (1995) *Cross-Cultural Management*, London: Butterworth-Heinemann. There are ten chapters in this book, each of which includes a number of papers written by various authors from around the world. The papers cover a wide range of comparative management topics and national geographical areas.

Hickson, D. J. and **Pugh, D. S.** (1995) *Managing Worldwide*, Harmondsworth: Penguin Books. This book covers the management styles and practices of a wide range of countries around the world.

References

Bartlett, C. A. and **Ghoshal, S.** (1989) *Managing across Borders: The Transnational Solution*, London: Century Business.

Bartlett, C. A. and **Ghoshal, S.** (1992) What is a global manager?, *Harvard Business Review* 92: 124–32.

Beechler, S. and **Yang, J. Z.** (1994) The transfer of Japanese-style management to American subsidiaries: contingencies, constraints, and competencies, *Journal of International Business Studies* 25: 467–91.

Bialer, S. (1991–2) The death of Soviet communism, *Foreign Affairs* 70(5) 166–181.

Cole, R. E. (1973) Functional alternatives and economic development: an empirical example of permanent employment in Japan, *American Sociology Review* 38: 424–38.

Copeland, A. (1995) Helping foreign nationals adapt to the US, *Personnel Journal*, February: 83–7.

Crozier, M. (1964) *The Bureaucratic Phenomenon*, London: Tavistock Publications.

De Bettignies, H. C. (1973) Japanese organizational behaviour: a psychological approach, in D. Graves (ed.) *Management Research: A Cross Cultural Perspective*, Amsterdam: Elsevier Scientific Publishing.

Dimitov, P. (1992) Freeing the soul from communism, *Wall Street Journal*, 23 March: A10.

Doz, Y. (1976) *National Policies and Multinational Management*, DBA dissertation. Cited in J. Roure, J. A. Alvarez, C. Garcia-Pont and J. Nueno (1993) Managing international dimensions of the managerial task, *European Management Journal* 11: 485–92.

Form, W. (1979) Comparative industrial sociology and the convergence hypothesis, *Annual Review of Sociology* 5: 1–25.

Graham, J. L. (1983), Foreign corrupt practices: a manager's guide, *Columbia Journal of World Business*, Fall: 89–94.

Haire, M., Ghiselli, E. E. and Porter, R. W. (1966), *Managerial Thinking: An International Study*, New York: John Wiley.

Harvey, M. G. and Buckley, M. R. (1997) Managing inpatriates: building a global core competency, *Journal of World Business* 32(1): 35–52.

Hickson, D. J., Hinnings, C. R., McMillan, C. J. M. and Schwitter, J. P. (1974) The culture-free context of organization structure: a tri-national comparison, *Sociology* 8: 59–80.

Hofstede, G. (1980) *Culture's Consequences*, California: Sage Publications.

Hofstede, G., Neuijen, B., and Ohavy, D. (1990) Measuring organizational cultures: a qualitative and quantitative study across twenty cases, *Administrative Science Quarterly* 35: 286–316.

Jamieson, I. (1980) *Capitalism and Culture: A Comparative Analysis of British and American Manufacturing Organizations*, Farnborough: Gower.

Kakar, S. (1971) The theme of authority in social relations in India, *Journal of Social Psychology* 84: 93–101.

Kerr, C. J., Dunlop, J. T., Harbison, F. H. and Myers, C. A. (1952) *Industrialism and Industrial Man*, Cambridge, Mass.: Harvard University Press.

Laurent, A. (1983) The cultural diversity of Western management conceptions, *International Studies of Management and Organizations* 8: 75–96.

Laurent, A. (1986) The cross-cultural puzzle of international human resource management, *Human Resource Management* 25: 91–102.

Lawrence, P. R. and Lorsch, J. W. (1967) *Organization and Environment: Managing Differentiation and Integration*, Boston: Harvard University Press.

Lincoln, J., Hanada, M. and Olson, J. (1981) Cultural orientations and individual reactions to organizations: a study of employees of Japanese-owned firms, *Administrative Science Quarterly*, 26: 93–115.

Maurice, M., Sorge, A. and Warner, M. (1980) Societal differences in organizing manufacturing units: a comparison of France, West Germany and Great Britain, *Organization Studies* 1(1): 59–86.

Meyer, J. W. and Rowan, B. (1977) Institutionalized organizations: formal structure as myth and ceremony, *American Journal of Sociology* 83: 340–63.

Muna, F. A. (1980) *The Arab Executive*, London: Macmillan.

Negandhi, A. R. (1979) Convergence in organizational practices: an empirical study of industrial enterprise in developing countries, in C. J. Lammers and D. J. Hickson, *Organizations Alike and Unlike*, London: Routledge & Kegan Paul, pp. 323–45.

Negandhi, A. R. (1985) Management in the Third World, in Pat Joynt and Malcolm Warner, *Managing in Different Cultures*, Oslo: Universitetsforlaget, pp. 69–97.

Ouchi, W. (1981) *Theory Z: How American Business Can Meet the Japanese Challenge*, Reading, Mass.: Addison-Wesley.

Pascale, R. T. (1978) Zen and the art of management, *Harvard Business Review* 56: 153–62.

Pechter, K. (1993) The foreigners are coming, *International Business*, September: 55–60.

Perlmutter, H. V. (1969) The tortuous evolution of the multinational corporation, *Columbia Journal of World Business* 4: 9–18.

Prahalad, C. K. (1976) Strategic choices in diversified MNCs, *Harvard Business Review*, July–August: 67–78.

Pralahad, C. K. and Doz, Y. L. (1987) *The Multinational Mission: Balancing Global Demands and Global Vision*, New York: Free Press.

Pugh, D. S., Hickson, D. J., Hinings, C. R. and Turner, C. (1968) Dimensions of organization structure, *Administrative Science Quarterly* 13: 65–105.

Schuler, R. S., Dowling, P. J., and De Cieri, H. (1993) An integrative framework of strategic international human resource management, *Journal of Management* 19: 419–59.

Stajkovic, A. D. and Luthans, F. (1997) Business ethics across cultures: a social cognitive model, *Journal of World Business* 32(1): 17–34.

Taka, I. and Foglia, W. D. (1994) Ethical aspects of Japanese leadership style, *Business Ethics* 13: 135–48.

Tayeb, M. H. (1988) *Organizations and National Culture*, London: Sage Publications.

Tayeb, M. H. (1994) Japanese managers and British culture: a comparative case study, *International Journal of Human Resource Management* 5: 145–66.

Tayeb, M. H. (1995) The competitive advantage of nations: the role of HRM and its sociocultural context, *International Journal of Human Resource Management* 6(3): 588–605.

Tayeb, M. H. (1996) *The Management of a Multicultural Workforce*, Chichester: John Wiley.

Tayeb, M. H. (1998) Transfer of HRM policies and practices across cultures: an American company in Scotland, *International Journal of Human Resource Management* 9(2): 332–58.

Taylor, T. C., Kazakov, A. Y. and Thompson, C. M. (1997) Business ethics and civil society in Russia, *International Studies of Management and Organisation* 27(1): 5–18.

Thronhill, A. (1993) Management training across cultures: the challenge for trainers, *Journal of European Industrial Training* 17(10): 43–51.

Tung, R. L. (1984) *Key to Japan's Economic Strength: Human Power*, Lexington, MA: D. C. Heath.

Tung, R. L. (1988) *The New Expatriates*, Cambridge, Mass.: Ballinger.

Welch, D. (1994) Determinants of international human resource management approaches and activities: a suggested framework, *Journal of Management Studies* 32: 139–64.

Part VI National Models of Management Styles and their Transferability

CHAPTER 20

Major Management Styles and Practices in a Selected Group of Countries

Monir Tayeb

Learning objectives

By the end of this chapter you will:

■ be familiar with a variety of management styles and workplace behaviours in a number of major countries

■ be aware of some of the opportunities that multinationals could seize on while operating there

■ understand some of the problems these companies might experience working away from home in unfamiliar settings

■ understand the challenges these unfamiliar settings might pose and how difficult or easy it might be for foreign companies to rise to these challenges.

Opening Case Study:
In Egypt red tape has been turned into high art

Cairo ministry's foreign investor unit employs 1400 to do the work of 50–60

During the 1980s, Abdel-Rahman Ahdel-Meguid, the late Deputy Prime Minister, was fond of telling his many Western friends: 'We did not invent bureaucracy, but we've had 5000 years to perfect it – to the point where we consider it an insult for anything to be completed.'

He would say that a new file, on being handed to a ministry official, might need processing by say, ten departments, from point A to point J, before being completed and returned to its owner.

However, no self-respecting civil servant present at the creation of such a file would deign to open it without first placing it at a safe distance, whence it could

▶

be observed for several weeks in case it showed dangerous tendencies, such as moving without permission. It would then be allocated a resting place on his desk. From that vantage point, it could be safely used in the construction of a pyramid of similar tiles, or as a repository for dust, feet or cigarette ash. It could also be picked up and shown to any passing colleague before being replaced to gather dust and, if damp enough, act as a 'wet nurse' for spores of mushrooms.

After years of fruitless struggle, during which no file in any of his ministries got beyond point C, Mr Abdel-Rahman resigned and emigrated to Boston, where he died, reconciled to the fact that, in Egypt at least, some things never change.

Ibrahim Fawzi will confirm this. Mr Fawzi, a former minister of industry and mineral wealth, is now the respected president of the General Authority for Investment and Free Zones (GAFI), part of the economy ministry.

The sole aim of Mr Fawzi's official life is to entice foreign investors and ease their way into the mainstream of Egypt's economy by helping them set up plants or offices in one of the country's numerous free zones. 'Little is being done to reform Egypt's bureaucracy,' he says.

'Free zones or not,' groaned one prospective investor emerging into the bumper-to-bumper chaos of Adly Street in downtown Cairo after a meeting with Mr Fawzi, 'I still have to deal with the *Mugamma.*' The *Mugamma* is special.

The mere mention of the word gets the same kind of reaction from an Egyptian as the words KGB or Lubyanka prison can from a Russian.

Dominating Tahrir Square in central Cairo, the *Mugamma* is the 'headquarters' of Egypt's bureaucracy: a gaunt and massive monument of Nasserite socialism and the glories of Soviet 1950s architecture.

The prospective free zone investor was right: he can have his plant in a free zone but, if he wants to live in Egypt, send his children to school, get a driving licence or permit for a power or water connection, he cannot avoid the *Mugamma.*

In the two years since the *Mugamma* last opened its doors to public scrutiny, two conspicuous changes have taken place. Not improvements, changes. The shoeshine boy, who used to do a brisk trade on the ninth floor, has had to move his stand to outside the building. 'I could not get a permit,' he said, grinning sheepishly. Does he have one now? He rolls his head and grins from ear to ear. His shoeshines are still brilliant.

On the ground floor, a large crowd gathers in front of four elevators. By the resigned look on the faces, some could have been waiting two years. No change there. But above the elevator doors have appeared great white chalk marks informing the visitor that the two lifts on the right go to the floors with even numbers and the two on the left to the floors with odd numbers.

Innovation indeed. So why is everyone concentrated at the door of the lift on the far right? Because after two years, it is still the only one working.

As Mr Fawzi says, in Egypt they like to do things gradually.

Source: *Financial Times* CD-ROM, 1 January–31 December 1998.

Introduction

National culture, as we saw in some of the earlier chapters in this book, plays a significant role in shaping organisations and their management styles. With the ever-increasing internationalisation and indeed globalisation of business, multi-national firms tend to take a keen interest in how other nations organise their business affairs and how this in turn might impact on their own business activities and work organisation.

This chapter focuses on the major organisational and managerial characteristics of a number of countries around the world, from the US in north America, to the current economic powers and emerging economies of Europe, to some of the tigers and would-be tigers of Asia. The countries covered in the chapter are intended to provide a broad representation of established and emerging economies with significant potential and actual contributions to the global economy in general and international business in particular.

The chapter ends with a case study on South Africa, a newcomer and respected member of the international community. The case study highlights the implications of the post-apartheid regime for domestic and foreign companies with business interests in South Africa.

The chapter is divided into three sections: section one deals with a selection of countries in Europe. The second is devoted to the US to represent the Americas. The final section concentrates on major Asian countries.

Section One: Europe

Management in Western Europe with Special Emphasis on the UK, Germany and France

Chris Brewster

Western Europe: similarities and differences

This section examines the business environment in Western Europe, paying particular attention to the UK, France and Germany. This is a challenging task. These are not homogeneous countries and Western Europe (however defined) is not a homogeneous region. However, there are sufficient similarities within each country and sufficient differences between them to make such comparisons a valuable learning opportunity: and there are sufficient similarities within Western Europe and between it and the other regions of the world to make that a valuable level of analysis too. Elsewhere (Brewster 1994) I have used the image of the scenes disclosed by turning the focus screw on a telescope to make the point that each level of magnification inevitably blurs some things, but reveals others. That is the purpose of this section.

Hofstede (1993: 5) has argued that 'culturally, "Europe" does not exist', but Brunstein (1995: 2) points out that 'Europe is clearly marked by statistical characteristics which are unique' and she sums up the point in a memorable phrase: 'Europe is a distinct area that can be studied as one entity. On one condition! It must not be forgotten that what marks Europe is that within a certain homogeneity, a lot of room is assigned to and taken up by the differences.' That approach is adopted here.

Rather than examine each of these three major countries in turn, the section examines first some of the factors they share in common in the areas of society, politics, working population, business and, then, because it is a fascinating microcosm of the different ways that business operates, human resource management. The section then examines each of these headings again to explore some of the differences between these countries. The final part of the section briefly draws some conclusions.

Almost by definition, writing this section is going to involve an uncomfortable amount of generalisation about very complex, different countries, each of which has their own internal complexities and differentiation. I have, for example, written about the UK, but accept the point made by Tayeb (1993) that England is not the same as the UK: there are Scotland and Wales, not to mention the disputed status of Northern Ireland, to consider. I have (almost) ignored the disputed boundaries of what is now Germany and the fact that the country was divided for nearly half a century. I have written as if each *Länd* is the same. I have had to ignore the cultural differences within France. And so on.

Furthermore, the factors that I have chosen to highlight are a matter of my personal choice and emphasis – others may well have chosen other issues. The reader must bear the level of generality and choice of material in mind throughout the section: the task is worthwhile because deeper understanding of our circumstances, in business as elsewhere, can only come about through comparison – of each country with others and each region with others.

Identifying similarities

The societies of Western Europe, and the UK, France and Germany in particular, share some important similarities which, taken together, make the region unique. There is no other geographical area of such a limited size in the world which has even close to the number of long-established countries, cultures and languages within it. No other region has had such a turbulent and bloody history over so many centuries. No other region in the world has taken such dramatic steps in choosing to subordinate its national governments to the authority of a supranational Union. This part of the chapter examines the similarities between these countries in, successively, overall societal terms, in politics, in relation to the working population, business and human resource management.

Societal similarities

These countries are the Old World. They have existed in some form or other for centuries. They were themselves part of the Holy Roman Empire. These are societies in which, despite the diversity within and between them, and despite increasing secularity, most people share an approach to their lives which is informed by the Christian religion. Largely because of the early development of language and recording in these countries, much of known history, of the discoveries and artefacts that we use in everyday life, of our philosophies and civilisation, stems from this part of the world. It is not that the region was in any way superior in these respects to, for example, the even longer established civilisations of China, but the influence of recording and writing, the first industrial revolution and the worldwide spread of these countries' power meant that they had a disproportionate and still largely dominant influence.

The UK, France and Germany share, with other Western European countries, an extensive and influential history. They each had traditions of exploration and of empires (enormous in the case of the UK). They have sent significant numbers of their populations out to these foreign lands and been the recipients of immigration over many generations. International business has been part of their experience for longer than the US has been in existence. They are the earliest countries to have industrialised. This has made them rich and given them many advantages. But it has also become a problem as their deeply embedded cultures, structures and institutions struggle to adapt to the latest industrial revolution based on the microchip.

These are countries too which have over many centuries learnt from each other. A historical record of the last thousand years reveals the extent to which habits and manners spread from one country to another (Elias 1936,1969,1980) and any European with teenage children, even those who do not holiday in other European countries, will tell you that this process continues! And significantly here this continues to be the case in business. There are many companies who have adopted (and often adapted) ways of working that they have seen to be successful in other European countries: a particularly pertinent factor in the ever more common cross-border mergers.

And despite Hofstede's strictures there are clearly ways in which the values and cultures of these nations have much in common. The UK, France and Germany share an individualistic culture, based on a fundamentally mixed (public and private sector) economy. They show a respect for legislation, in business as elsewhere, and for learning. They have strong state systems for dealing with the sick, the old and the otherwise disadvantaged.

Political similarities

Europe is the home of one of the boldest experiments ever made in terms of international co-operation. Most of the Western European countries have voluntarily agreed to become part of the European Union (others are applying, or have agreed to follow many of the EU's laws). For the first time in history a group of major and minor nation states have subordinated their own legislative processes to a common one. And, by and large, it is working. The effects on business within Europe are considerable; the implications, for international co-operation everywhere in the world, are immense.

The UK, France and Germany are, like most other states in Europe, unequivocally social democratic in form and government. The differences between the parties in government and opposition in these countries become less obvious each decade. Politicians are nowhere regarded with much respect, but there seems little prospect of any major challenge to the established system or even the political parties involved.

A key to the political system in each of these countries is that they have a well-established, generally respected and honest civil service, applying the laws fairly and without bias. This is such a feature of these countries that it is rarely remarked on: but it is fundamental to the way they work.

Similarities in working population

These three countries are also representative of much of Europe in the trends in their workforces, although they are clearly much larger than most. In all three the birth rate has dropped drastically in recent years and continues to fall. At the same time the population in general is ageing. People are staying on longer in education, retiring earlier (half the workforce in these countries has already ceased employment by the normal retiring age), and living longer. The result is an increasingly problematic 'dependency ratio' (the number of people economically active as a proportion of the whole population). Already, these three countries have no more than between three and four out of every ten people economically active. There is severe and increasing pressure on the various governments as they attempt to handle the consequent imbalances.

The European countries are also unusual in the proportion of women at work: almost half of the working population is female. And the proportion is growing. It is a proportion that is concentrated at the lower end of the wage market – the 'glass ceiling' is still firmly in place.

And the meaning of work is also changing. There are, partly associated with the growth in the numbers of women in the workforce, increasing amounts of flexibility in employment patterns (Brewster *et al.* 1997). There are more and more part-timers (more than a quarter of all jobs in the UK, for example), temporary employees, employees on fixed term contracts, weekend workers and a host of other options. Long-term, full-time employment now applies to an ever-shrinking minority of the workforce in Europe.

Similarities in the business environment

In the business world in particular, these are countries where the state is still strong. Public sector ownership is still extensive: and governments have a crucial impact on business. These are countries with a tradition of legal intervention in business and comparatively high tax rates. On the other hand they are countries with well-educated, skilled and, in certain circumstances, adaptable workforces. They are also countries with good modern communications, where business is conducted according to clear rules and where contracts are honoured. They are, in broad terms, favourable places to do business.

Compared to other significant economic competitors such as the USA and Japan, there is an argument that Western Europe has been hampered economically by three things: a diversity of currencies; a diversity of languages; and a willingness to spend additional riches on leisure and leisure activities rather than consumer goods. The first is being addressed: the creation of a single European currency is the latest, and perhaps one of the boldest, steps in the unique experiment that is the European Union. The diversity of languages (there are 23 within the 15 countries of the EU) is being fostered by programmes aimed at helping to preserve the minor tongues, but in business terms English is slowly coming to dominate the way Europe works together. The European fascination with leisure has meant that the region enjoys the longest holidays in the world: most French people, for example, expect to get four or five weeks off work in blocks, plus another 20 or so in separate single or double days. With weekends, they will be working the equivalent of less than four days out of every week. To workers in the US or Japan, these seem almost incredible figures. One result is that the leisure industries, tourism and the arts are much stronger in Western Europe; another is that the multiplier effects of consumerism apply less strongly and our economies have grown less fast.

The vast majority of the business dealings of the European countries are conducted within Europe. Even when the focus is restricted to trade external to the individual countries, it remains the case that the vast majority of the trade of Western European countries is with other Western European countries.

Similarities in human resource management

The ways in which people are managed may be seen as a touchstone of different approaches to business. It is where cultural assumptions are most apparent.

Human resource management (HRM) is notably different in Western Europe, both theoretically and practically, from the approaches in, say Japan or the US (Brewster 1994, 1999). The European approach sees compliance with legislation as of equal importance with profitability; expects governmental involvement in employment relationships; accepts a social role for the organisation; sees the trade unions as social partners (more than seven out of every ten major organisations negotiates with trade unions – and often for senior employees as well as manual workers); and expects to debate all key issues with employees. The EU supports the national systems in encouraging legally backed 'works councils' or equivalents at which key managerial decisions have to be explained to employee representatives.

Identifying differences

This depiction of the European similarities, however, conceals a wide range of differences in history, values and approaches to business issues. The second main part of this section uses the same headings to identify some of the critical differences.

Societal differences

Linguistically and culturally the UK, France and Germany are distinct. Hofstede (1980, 1984) contrasts the importance of hierarchy and the acceptance of power distance in France with the British comfort with a comparative absence of rules and preparedness to adapt pragmatically. Others (Lawrence 1991; Warner and Campbell 1993) have pointed to the German desire for clear and unambiguous principles and a preference for consensus and a joint professional approach to problems, linking it to the corporatist social partnership that has characterised both politics and business.

Historically, these countries have pursued different paths. France and the UK have existed, in some identifiable form, for centuries and they and the German states or Germany itself, have spent much of the time since at odds – even at war. In these terms, Germany is a relatively recent creation. The borders of Germany have been much more fluid, covering, even relatively recently, both a much larger and a smaller area than its current boundaries. Neither the UK nor Germany, unlike France, spent most of the First and Second World War under occupation; but Germany, unlike France and the UK, lost those wars. Even in its current form Germany has only existed as it is now since the collapse of communism in Europe was heralded by the fall of the wall dividing the six Eastern *Länder* from the rest of Germany at the end of the 1980s. The effects of the two world wars and their aftermath have been profound, for Germany in particular. The challenge of communism on its borders and the fears of inflation have dominated political thinking and had a significant effect on business.

The three countries are Christian, but whereas France has remained within the Roman Catholic tradition, the UK developed its own and increasingly different form of Protestantism centuries ago. Germany, the original home of Protestantism, has both traditions of Christianity firmly established, with Catholicism still strong in the south.

Though each country had its empire, Germany is essentially landlocked and has seen its sphere of influence as Europe itself. Historically it has tried to dominate the region by force: ironically, it is now probably more influential in its role as the largest country and dominant power within the EU, with the new European currency based on the deutschmark, as it tries its best to be a good EU citizen and not to be too dominant. At present, the country, or at least its political and business leaders, assume it has a special role and responsibility for central Europe and anticipate a key role in economic development there. The British, by contrast, are an island race, and their focus, both politically and in business, has tended to be outside Europe. Like the French they still have linguistic and cultural (and economic) ties to their former colonies.

Both the UK and France are relatively centralised countries. France is a particularly centralised one. All major organisations in France are headquartered in Paris and the link between leading government officials and business is strong; all major road and rail connections go to and from Paris. The limited steps that have been taken to reduce the dominance of London in the UK, with the establishments of representative assemblies (though with very limited powers) in Scotland and Wales, are hardly being contemplated in France. Germany, by contrast is a Federal Republic. It is an essentially decentralised country. Its various local state (*Länder*) governments have considerable powers. There is no single leading city: Berlin, Munich, Frankfurt, Hamburg are all important. Unlike the UK or France where major companies, financial institutions and government can all be found in the same city, in Germany elements of these can be found in all the major cities.

There are discernible differences in the backgrounds of business leaders in the three countries. The UK system is still class influenced with many business leaders coming from the separate education system set up for the wealthier section of the population. To some degree business ('trade') is still seen in the UK as a less respectable option than the arts or classics. The French system is rigorously and nationally egalitarian and elitist. Egalitarian in that applications to university or, better, the *grandes écoles* is by open national competition. Elitist in that these systems then dominate the closely interwoven networks of senior civil servants and business leaders. It is hard for a French person from outside this elite to get established in politics or business. The German system is based on the importance of *technik*: knowledge and skills about work and particularly about manufacture. The country's education system is focused on it: and the country's economy is now under pressure, partly as a result.

These differences are reflected in the approaches to working with each other: essentially hierarchical in France, with offices representing status; hierarchies in the UK being moderated by networks of contacts and a more informal mode of address; open-plan offices and less hierarchy in Germany, but with more formal modes of address.

Political differences

Although there is much on which the governments of these countries can agree, they have different political parties in power with different objectives. In both Germany and France there are right-wing nationalist parties, polling significant proportions of the total votes. There are important differences in the role of the government and in their powers versus, for example, the almost unchallengeable written constitution of Germany with its nationality clauses still based on genetics rather than residence and its key role for local state governments. The Conservative governments that controlled the UK in the 1980s and much of the 1990s, 'privatised' many of the industries and utilities that remain under public control in France and Germany, and deliberately made it more difficult for the government to play a role in business.

Differences in working population

Unemployment is disproportionately high in Germany: a key problem given that the Germans have experienced lesser levels of unemployment than many other European countries in the last 50 years. The reunification of Germany, despite the actions of the German government and EU support, has combined with a failure to respond quickly enough to the changing nature of the economy, to leave a problem that currently seems to be intractable. One early critic argued that the famous 'dual system' of training, which gave the country such high levels of competence in manufacturing, actually created 'the best trained dole queue in the world' (Spiers 1985: 24)

Germany tends to have a wider skill base and to be more functionally flexible, but has less working time or contractual flexibility than the UK, for example.

Differences in the business environment

A critical difference in the business environment concerns ownership. The public sector is a major owner in all three countries certainly, but is much less so in the UK. The stock market is a key influence in the UK, even on unquoted companies, and the short-termism and aggressive takeover battles that result have been seen as a source of the UK's comparatively poor economic performance since the Second World War (Hutton 1995). By contrast, a larger proportion of the French economy is still family owned and run, including some of the famous-name giants of the French economy. At the same time, the French government has traditionally taken a much more interventionist, directing and supporting role in French business, often driving through major projects such as the Channel Tunnel. The German system is different again: here most major businesses are owned by a combination of interlocking bank holdings. The banks own the businesses, and their competitors, and the businesses own the banks. The effect is that German companies are, in Randlesome's (1990) instructive phrase, 'in business to be in business'. In other words, their focus is on survival and continuity rather than growth or domination – or even profit. A longer-term view is widespread. Kristensen (1997: 21), drawing on Lane (1992), makes the point strongly about the importance in Germany of the 'bureaucratic way in which business associations, banks and cartels created a very regulated system of co-operation and competition among the larger firms'. And Streeck (1992) has pointed out the virtual impossibility in the German system of discerning where state bureaucracy ends and the private sector begins.

Differences in human resource management

A European approach to HRM is identifiable, but the differences between countries are considerable. In some respects these differences are reducing: the most obvious example is as a result of the decision by the Labour Government in the UK to accept the EU's Social Chapter. The UK has joined the other countries now in having a minimum wage, and employee representative structures have been promised.

However, in other respects there are still crucial differences in employment legislation, in trade unionism and representation, and in managerial attitudes. Thus, the legislation on employment contracts differs between France and Germany but in both countries is generally much more restrictive than that in the UK. Established German civil servants have clearly determined rights under their constitution, as do the senior managerial grades (the *cadre*) in France. Trade union membership covers approximately a third of the UK and German workforces, but less than half that in France. On the other hand, almost all the workforce in Germany and France have their terms and conditions set by collective bargaining, a lesser proportion in the UK. In major German organisations there is a Supervisory Board, with considerable powers, on which between a third and a half of the seats will be held by employee representatives. And they have the right to establish a Works Council to oversee HR issues. In France employees in all organisations with more than 50 people working there can insist on the establishment of a *comité d'entreprise* which has significant consultation rights. In the UK, such committees are established only where there is agreement between employers and employees. Finally, the effects of these various factors on managerial attitudes is that the committees in France moderate the hierarchical nature of the French enterprise – and the managers are aware that there will often be a political appeal outside the organisation. In Germany managers expect to work more closely with their subordinates, to consult with them and to have to explain their decisions. The result is often more record keeping and bureaucracy, but also there is easier implementation of resulting decisions. The UK is moving from an antagonistic management/union relationship. There are some interesting examples of partnership arrangements (Allen 1998), but it is still arguably managements that are reluctant to open the books and invest the trust required to make these work on a widespread scale.

Conclusions

In practice, in these as in all societies, there is a continual interplay and reinforcement of the relationship between managerial styles and approaches, their manifestation in HR practices of recruitment, task allocation and work, the institutional framework, products and markets (Lane 1989; Sorge 1991, 1996).

The overriding conclusion from this brief charge through the business environment of these three major European countries must be that there are both important similarities within Europe, that make it valuable to consider the region as distinct to other regions; but also important differences between the countries within the region. There are critical developments, changing the nature of business in these countries and in many cases making them more similar. The growth of stock-market influence, even in Germany; the great EU experiment and its impact through, for example, restrictions on the role of the state in French business, and the imposition of employee consultation on the UK's European businesses is creating further similarities. The ever-growing influence of the European market is playing a key role in forcing businesses in all the European countries to compete with each other. This does not, though, amount to convergence. The head-to-head competition, and even the co-operative arrangements that are increasingly common between businesses as others learn from the typically Germanic system of long-term relationships with suppliers and customers, give opportunities to pick up ideas from each other, and force companies to offer increasingly common goods and services. But at the same time, business leaders in each country still tend to believe in their own national ways of doing business and even argue that it gives them an 'edge'.

This variety may be one of the central advantages of European business. Unlike major competitor economies Europe has no monolithic belief in a one-best-way of doing business; it is language aware; it has opportunities to learn from different approaches and attitudes to business from within its own resources. The example of the European Union is not that business becomes more alike, but that it is possible to do business effectively despite the obvious differences – if the will is there. This is partly why European businesses are more accepted internationally than say the US or Japanese businesses and why Europeans are more successful as expatriates (Brewster and Harris 1998). Rather than its differences being a problem for European businesses, the ability to exploit its differences may be a key to future success.

Further reading

Marx, E. (1996) *International Human Resource Management Practices in Britain and Germany: London and Berlin Compared*, UK: Anglo-German Foundation.

References

Allen, M. (1998) All-inclusive, *People Management*, 11 June 1998.

Brewster, C. (1994) HRM: the European dimension, in J. Storey (ed.) *Human Resource Management: A Critical Text*, London: Routledge.

Brewster, C., Mayne, L. and Tregaskis, O. (1997) Flexible working in Europe: a review of the evidence, *Management International Review*, Special Issue 1/97, 37: 1–19

Brewster, C.J. (1999) Different paradigms in strategic HRM: questions raised by comparative research, in P. Wright, L. Dyer, J. Boudreau, and G. Milkovich, (eds), *Research in Personnel and HRM*, Connecticut: JAI Press.

Brewster, C. and Harris, H. (eds) (1998) *International HRM: Contemporary Issues in Europe*, London: Routledge.

Brunstein, I. (1995) *Human Resource Management in Western Europe*, Berlin/New York: Walter de Gruyter.

Elias, N. (1936,1969,1980) *Über den Prozess der Zivilisation: soziogenetische und psychogenetische Untersuchungen*, Vols 1 and 2, Frankfurt/Main: Suhrkamp.

Hofstede, G. (1980) *Culture's Consequences*, Berkeley CA: Sage.

Hofstede, G. (1984) *Culture's Consequences: International Differences In Work-Related Values*, abridged edn, London: Sage Publications.

Hofstede G. (1993) Intercultural conflict and synergy in Europe, in D.J. Hickson (ed.) *Management in Western Europe*, New York: Walter de Gruyter.

Hutton, W. (1995) *The State We're In*, London: Jonathan Cape.

Kristensen, P. H. (1997) National systems of governance, in R. Whitley and P.H. Kristensen (eds) *Governance at Work: the Social Replication of Economic Relations*, Oxford: Oxford University Press.

Lane, C. (1989) *Management and Labour in Europe*, Aldershot: Edward Elgar.

Lane, C. (1992) European business systems: Britain and Germany compared, in R. Whitley (ed.) *European Business Systems*, London: Sage.

Lawrence, P. (1991) The personnel function: an Anglo-German comparison in C. Brewster and S. Tyson (eds) *International Comparisons in Human Resource Management*, London: Pitman.

Randlesome, C. (1990) *Business Cultures in Europe*, Oxford: Heinemann.

Sorge, A. (1991) Strategic fit and societal effects: interpreting cross-national comparisons of technology, organisations and human resources, *Organisation Studies* 12: 161–90.

Sorge, A. (1996) Societal effects in cross-national organisation studies, in R. Whitley and P.H. Kristensen (eds) *The Changing European Firm*, London: Routledge.

Spiers, B. (1985) Does myth blur the facts of West German training?, *BACIE Journal*, September: 22–4.

Streeck, W. (1992) *Social Institutions and Economic Performance: Studies of Industrial Relations in Advanced Capitalist Economies*, London: Sage.

Tayeb, M. (1993) English culture and business organisations, in D.J. Hickson (ed.) *Management in Western Europe*, New York: Walter de Gruyter.

Warner, M. and Campbell, A. (1993) Germany, in D.J. Hickson (ed.) *Management in Western Europe*, New York: Walter de Gruyter.

Changing Management Style in Central and Eastern Europe: the Case of Hungary

Katalin Illes

Introduction

The transformation of Central and Eastern European countries has now been in progress for ten years. During this period a wealth of knowledge has been accumulated based on theoretical models, empirical research and personal experience.

The countries of Central and Eastern Europe represent an enormous geographical, demographic and cultural diversity. They provide new markets, cheap, often well-trained work forces and untapped resources for Western investors. They also have the potential for making a great impact on the global economy in the future.

Though the 40 years of communism left its mark in the form of some similarities on these countries (such as central planning, hidden unemployment, state subsidies, shortage-based excess demand, etc.) each country has to be looked at and appreciated individually because of historic, cultural, economic and political differences. Rather than skimming over the surface and giving only snapshots of all the countries in the region, we decided to select one country, Hungary, and attempt a more detailed analysis. However, as and when it is appropriate, we support our argument with examples from other countries.

The Czech Republic, Hungary and Poland will join the European Union in the next few years and are described as countries that 'present the characteristics of democracy, with stable institutions guaranteeing the rule of law, human rights, and respect for and protection of minorities. [They] can be regarded as functioning market economies, and should be able to cope with competitive pressure and market forces within the European Union in the medium term' (European Union, 1997). These are economically the most advanced countries of Central and Eastern Europe. They started the transformation process with certain advantages. For example, under Polish communism most farms remained private; while the economic reforms that started in Hungary in the 1970s gave a considerable headstart to economic transformation at the beginning of the 1990s.

All these countries experienced and continue to experience dramatic political, economic and social changes.

Transition or transformation?

Transition

The dominant way of considering transition among economists and political scientists in the late 1980s and early 1990s was that the change of the formerly socialist countries of Central and Eastern Europe was from one type of socioeconomic regime to another type. Internal institutional continuity was over-looked and ignored. Transition was interpreted as a once and for all shift from a political-economic regime based on the logic of the central planning to another political-economic regime based on the logic of the market (Makó 1997). It means a total break with the social and economic institutions of the ex-socialist system and the creation of brand new institutions, patterns of behaviour of social and economic agents. It considers the legacy of the socialist past to be institutionally deficient, overestimating the level of homogeneity of institutions in the former social-economic regime and neglecting the diversity of regulations. This view underestimates the importance of time for the social learning process in creating market economy of consistent institutions in the post-socialist countries of the Central and Eastern European countries (Makó and Simonyi 1992).

Transformation

Transformation is a more balanced view that stresses the importance of the whole process. It is an evolutionary approach that recognises the 'path dependence' in the emergence of the new institutions of the market economy. According to Stark, with this approach we can get a better understanding of the variety of forms of development in the post-socialist countries (Stark 1992).

Some key events before 1989

In fact transition began much before the late 1980s. The slow erosion of the Soviet-type model of organising economic activity started in the late 1960s. In Hungary, for example, the following main events happened before the collapse of communism:

The new economic reform

The new economic reform in 1968 increased the autonomy of social actors in organising economic activities (Kornai 1980). Managers got more freedom to use financial incentives instead of administrative ones.

The firms were, however, still characterised by excess physical resources, and limited financial and managerial resources (Peng and Heath 1996). Empirical research shows that during this period several organisational and managerial innovations were introduced into the labour process (Bossányi and Nyikos 1987). For example, tasks were divided between groups rather than between individuals; in certain places job evaluation was also introduced; and there was a tendency to improve employee participation in decision making.

Inside contracting group

The liberalisation process continued in the 1980s with a 'policy package' to allow the development of 'inside contracting groups'. The aim of this central economic policy initiative was to overcome the macro-rigidity of the socialist economic system. The inside contracting groups operated at the company's premises after regular working hours and fully replaced the company's need for overtime. Their members were selected on a voluntary basis and these groups of workers were bargaining with the management on the price of work-contract without involving the trade union (Makó 1997). This movement gave an opportunity for organisational innovation and stimulated an entrepreneurial spirit within the companies. In 1981–2 the liberalisation package also gave entrepreneurs an opportunity to set up their business independently from any state-owned company. These entities were mainly small, limited-liability companies and co-operatives. The initiative was so popular that over a hundred thousand people started different kinds of enterprises and became managers but also kept their full-time employee status. Some of these companies started a steady growth and still exist today. Other companies which are successful today started their activities as independent working groups. The members of these working groups organised their activities within the organisational network and integrated both horizontally and vertically. The experiences of these working groups became an integral part of the development of organisational and management culture in Hungary. Many of the internal groups used the state company almost as an incubator and when they became strong enough in this safe environment they moved out of the company's premises and started an independent life. The co-operation within and between these entrepreneurial groups developed a network-type of social relation. There was a growing contrast between the rigidity of the over-centralised management structure of the state company and the flexible, team-oriented, lean managerial set-up of these inside working groups.

Enterprise councils

Enterprise councils were established as the highest collective body of management of the state-owned companies between 1985 and 1990. The aim was to make these councils into the body of 'self-management' in the company. However, this aim has never been achieved. The majority of firms were underfinanced and, in spite of the innovations, the managerial resources were very unequally developed.

The supervisory role of the state and the various ministries became so loose, both legally and in practice, that sometimes even the leaders were confused about the ownership of the company. On the one hand it meant greater independence for the companies; on the other no one felt really responsible.

The shortage economy forced managers to run their business as 'a just-in-case' system to hoard physical resources, which is in contrast to the 'just-in-time' system pioneered by the Japanese. As a result, excess physical resources could often be found in the socialist firms (Peng and Heath 1996). The inefficiency in manufacturing processes in the former socialist countries is well illustrated by the Kornai ratio, which is the indicator of input inventories versus output inventories. The high ratio signals the resource hoarding of socialist managers in Table 20.1.

Table 20.1 Kornai ratio for manufacturing enterprises 1981–5

Countries	Kornai ratio
Planned economies	
Bulgaria	5.07
Czechoslovakia	3.07
Hungary	6.10
Poland	4.49
Soviet Union	3.16
Market economies	
Canada	0.92
Japan	1.09
Sweden	0.89
United Kingdom	1.02
United States	1.02
West Germany	0.71

Source: Adapted from Kornai (1992a).

The growing liberalisation of the economy and the positive changes at company level eased slightly the tension. However, it could not change the unfavourable macro-economic performance of the planned economies which were characterised by:

- slow reaction time in macro-economic decision making
- economic shortage created regular bottlenecks in the production process and led to the tendency of using a huge size of buffer stocks
- resource hoarding instead of resource saving, combined with the 'wait and see' attitude of the socialist managers.

Some key events after 1989

The Czech Republic, Hungary, Poland, East Germany and Slovak, started the transitional process from a command to a market economy in 1989. If we examine the similarities and differences, we can see the effects of the previous institutional factors. There were similarities and also differences in the legal and regulatory environment of these countries.

The main similarities are:

- increasing corporate autonomy by privatisation
- globalisation of economic activities
- key role of foreign direct investment in the modernisation process.

The main differences are:

- uneven development in the forms of privatisation
- industrial relations system: from patterns of co-operation to confrontation
- variety in forms of foreign direct investments. (Makó 1997)

Table 20.2 shows the difference in private sector employment and the share of private sector contribution in the national GDP in the four so called Visegrad Countries.

Table 20.2 A comparison of Visegrad countries

Countries	Private sector share in employment		Private sector share in GDP	
	1989%	1994%	1989%	1994%
Czech Republic	16	65	0–10	56
Hungary	20	65	20	55–56
Poland	47	61	25–28	58
Slovak Republic	<10	55	10	58

Source: Borish and Noel (1996).

The change of management style

The effects of privatisation

The role of privatisation has been overestimated in all the transitional economies. Sometimes it was considered as the answer to all the economic problems. Now it is obvious that in itself privatisation is not and cannot be a remedy to all the problems.

> While market-oriented operation had public support at least at the beginning of the transition, the attitude towards privatisation was ambivalent from the very beginning. Small property holding was accepted, but there was a strong negative feeling against the private ownership of large companies. (In Global Competition Research Programme 1998)

These negative feelings were mainly against the following two groups:

- those multinational companies that bought the Hungarian companies purely for the sake of increasing their market share and started to shut down production and made employees redundant as soon as they took over the company
- those Hungarians in high positions who used their position and contacts to privatise prospering companies for themselves.

Privatisation is an ongoing process and 'contrary to the optimistic scenarios of domestic politicians and Western economists who foresaw a rapid transfer of assets from state-owned enterprises to private ownership, the overwhelming bulk of the Hungarian economy remains state property' (Stark 1996: 998). In 1999 there are state-owned companies such as the Post Office Bank still to be privatised. The government appoints the members of the Board of Directors and the supervisory committee of the state-owned companies. It is up to the discretion of the government when and how to change these members. It means that the management of the company needs to learn to work under such conditions. When there is a change in government it could mean the change of priorities and a change of strategies. It leads to an increased level of uncertainty because companies can lose or gain economic importance almost overnight. This is just one illustration of the extremes of unpredictability that companies need to learn to cope with.

Contrary to the hopes of the evolutionary economists, considerable evidence suggests that the second economy has not become a dynamic, legitimate private sector. Though the number of registered companies increased sharply, many are 'dormant' or 'dummy' firms. Tax evasion is pervasive, and many entrepreneurs still engage in private ventures only as a second job (Laky 1992; Gábor 1994, 1996). And although employment is increasing in the sector, most researchers agree that the proportion of unregistered work is increasing faster (Kornai 1992b: 13).

These tendencies, together with new forms of corruption, extortion and exploitation made Endre Sik call this transition one 'from second economy to informal economy'. He argues that the current conditions in Hungary are similar to those in Latin America (Sik 1994).

> When private entrepreneurs look at government policy, they see only burdensome taxation, lack of credits, virtually no programs to encourage regional or local development, and inordinate delays in payments for orders delivered to public sector firms. Through violations of tax codes, off-the-books payments to workers, and reluctance to engage in capital investment, much of the private sector is responding in kind. Such government policies and private sector responses are clearly not a recipe for the development of a legitimate private sector as a dynamic engine of economic growth. (Stark 1996: 999)

Privatisation and management style

In Hungary the composition of company size moves between two extremes. On the one hand there are large national and multinational organisations; on the other there are almost one million so-called micro firms employing between one to ten people. There are only relatively few small- and medium-size enterprises in the country.

There is often only a fine line between public and private ownership and using David Stark's (1996) term the properties are recombinant in Eastern Europe.

> Recombinant property is a form of organisational hedging in which actors respond to uncertainty by diversifying assets, redefining and recombining resources. It is an attempt to hold resources that can be justified by more than one legitimating principle.
>
> Property transformation in post-socialist Hungary involves the decentralised reorganisation of assets and the centralised management of liabilities.

Together they blur the boundaries of public and private, the boundaries of enterprises, and the boundedness of justificatory principles. Enterprise-level field research, data on the ownership structure of Hungary's 2200 largest enterprises and banks, and an examination of the government's recent debt consolidation programmes suggest the emergence of a distinctively East European capitalism that will differ as much from West European capitalisms as do contemporary East Asian variants. (Stark 1996: 993)

The change in ownership brought radical change into the management system of the companies. The Soviet-type organisational structure which had been adopted in all former communist countries is essentially based on the early stages of Western business organisation and management. According to Chandler (1962) the dominant management organisation was the functional-unitary bureaucratic form of organisation, which served to realise traditional and vertical expansion strategies.

The Hungarian development of organisational forms between 1945 and 1980 has achieved the first stage of the US and Western European companies which was completed by the fifties and sixties. (Dobák and Tari 1996)

The first structural change came in the form of the matrix organisations, followed by the divisionalisation of companies. Though the managers of the centralised economies had some useful managerial skills, they were often ignored and managers were exposed to the so-called knowledge deficiency model, which assumes that managers in the post-socialist countries are deprived from the fundamental elements of the competence necessary under new circumstances of the market economy (Thompson 1994). The supporters of this view thought that with the help of Western consultants the ex-socialist managers could just simply be retrained and then they would act and behave like their Western partners. Surveys, observations and empirical studies challenged the validity of the knowledge-deficiency model and revealed not only the complex nature of the transformation process but also the necessity of the mutual learning process, i.e. both foreign and local managers have to learn from each other (Adorján *et al.* 1996).

Diversity of management styles

Through the privatisation process many multinational companies entered Central and Eastern Europe bringing not only capital and new technology but also new organisational structure and management style.

The amount of change that is introduced into the acquired Central and Eastern European company depends mainly on the national and organisational culture of the parent company. To date the only empirical research on management in Hungary has been gathered through Hofstede's valued research.

The data for Hofstede's classical culture study in IBM was collected around 1970. This survey did not include the countries of this region. The first replication of this research was carried out in Hungary (Varga 1986) and put Hungary in the group of the German-speaking countries of Austria, Switzerland, Germany and Finland with small power distance and with stronger uncertainty avoidance.

According to Hofstede, uncertainty avoidance describes a society's fear of the unknown; it indicates 'to what extent a culture programs its members to feel either uncomfortable or comfortable with difference (Hofstede 1992).

Power distance is the extent to which the less powerful members of the organisation and institutions accept and expect that power is distributed unequally. Hofstede relates this to notions of inequality. Thus according to Hofstede, nations with this mixture 'show little social inequality, but more need for structure' (Hofstede 1993).

A more recent study (Dobák 1998) that used a similar concept to Hofstede's study found a slightly lower level of uncertainty avoidance and a definitely higher power distance. This study also revealed a strong demand for value change both at national and organisational level. The biggest demand at national level is for the reduction of power distance and at organisational level for the increase of achievement orientation and the decrease of power distance. The implication of this in terms of management style suggests a need for less hierarchically structured organisations so that the pressure is reduced.

Little has been written about the style itself, however, and to what degree they reflect Western managerial styles can be seen from the type of innovations that have been introduced.

According to a recent survey (Makó *et al.* 1997) Hungarian-owned firms use considerably less innovation than foreign owned ones (see Table 20.3).

Table 20.3 Percentage of firms reporting organisational innovation

Has the company introduced the following:	Hungarian-owned firms	Foreign-owned firms
TQM	18.4	37.5
Group work	55.1	66.7
Profit of cost centres	44.9	62.5
Interorganisational networking	34.7	37.5
Benchmarking	4.1	37.5
Flat hierarchies	22.4	50.0
Interdisciplinary design teams	18.4	33.3
Just-in-time delivery	10.2	41.7
Outsourcing	8.2	29.2
System suppliers	10.2	20.8
ISO9000	34.7	62.5
Information technology	28.6	70.8

Source: Makó *et al.* (1997).

This example clearly illustrates that larger, multinational companies are able to achieve more advantageous economies of scale in research and development than smaller, domestic companies. Makó and Ellingstad (1997) report that foreign-owned firms are more proactive, particularly in the areas of quality improvement, product development and cutting the cost of personnel. Outsourcing happens mainly because of flexibility and not because of cost saving. They also observed that there is little employee loyalty and sometimes companies find it difficult to maintain a stable workforce.

The transformation of management style and organisations is very uneven in all countries of the transitional economies. However, reports show that at one end of the scale there are the young managers who acquired their MBAs either in the US or Britain and follow a totally Westernised managerial approach. This new generation of managers typically work for multinational companies and use English as the common language of the global business. These managers use participative rather than autocrative managerial techniques, enjoy working in multinational teams and are open to new, creative problem-solving techniques. At the other end of the scale we can find those who have worked for 30–40 years in the centralised system and are very reluctant to change. They prefer the clear hierarchical system where the boundaries and responsibilities are clearly defined and easy to follow. They see change as a threat and try to prolong the *status quo* as long as possible. The main objective for them is to muddle through the jungle of changes until retirement. We must not forget those who fall between these two extremes. These are the top and middle managers who started their careers in the old system. Most of these people work hard to find their niche of survival in the new system through language and management courses. It is seen to be a considerable problem.

Hungarian managers are also criticised for their inability to use management decision techniques, and for being years behind Western counterparts, and that the role of the personality of the decision-maker is too large. There are many assumptions in these statements. They have been built on practices based in a different culture with a different trajectory, and set of dynamics of change. While many Western companies are moving away from this centralised and distant form of controlling, this may well be an appropriate or effective way in Hungary. The fact that the role of personality of the decision-maker is too large also reflects the lack of democracy and the centralising tendency under the Soviets.

Conclusions

In the last ten years all the Central and Eastern European countries have made some progress towards the market economy and three of them are already considered to have a market economy. The political and economic change, however, are much more tangible and certainly quicker to achieve than the change of values and attitudes of people. It is also easier to follow the change process through different numerical indicators than through interviews, questionnaires and observation. When it is the question of survival then organisations and people adjust to the new requirements relatively quickly. In many well-documented cases for a foreign owner manager it takes two to three years to change the management style and organisational culture of a state owned company. However, when there is no direct pressure for change the process is much slower, more evolutionary. It will take time for all the countries of Central and Eastern Europe to fully develop their market economies and integrate into Europe and into the global economy as equal political and economic partners without losing their own unique national characteristics.

A more in-depth study of organisational life, a historic analysis of the change process over the centuries and an understanding of the unique evolution process of national culture and character could advise both researchers and practitioners in the West how to best assist these countries in their development.

References

Adorján, M., Balaton, K., Galgóczi, B., Makó, C and **Ternovsyky, F.** (1996) Gazdasági szervezetek az átalakulás idöszakában -szereplök és stratégiák, *Vezetéstudomány* 7–8: 5–25.

Borish, M.S. and **Noel, M.** (1996) *Private sector development during transition*, Washington: World Bank Discussion Papers 318: 87.

Bossányi, K. and **Nyikos, L.** (1987) Vjitások a vállalati vezetésben, *Nepszabadság*, 30 November, Budapest, Hungary.

Chandler, A.D. Jr. (1962) *Strategy and Structure: Chapters in the History of the American Enterprise*, Cambridge: Cambridge University Press.

Dobák, M. (1998) Menedzsment és versenyképesség, *Mühelytanulmányok*, PZ6, Budapest: Közgazdaságtudományi Egyetem.

Dobák, M. and **Tari, E.** (1996) Evolution of organisational forms in transition period of Hungary, *Journal for East European Management Studies* 1 (2): 7–35.

European Union (1997) *Agenda 2000*, European Union.

Gábor, I. (1994) Modernity or a new type of duality? The second economy of today, in J.M. Kovács (ed.) *Legacy of Communism in Eastern Europe*, New Brunswick, N.J.: Transaction Books, pp. 3–21.

Gábor, I. (1996) Too much, too small: small businesses in post-socialist Hungary, *Restructuring Networks: Legacies, Linkages, and Localities in Post-socialist Eastern Europe*, in G. Grabher and D. Stark (eds) New York: Oxford University Press.

Hofstede, G. (1980) *Culture's Consequences: International Differences in Work-Related Values*, Beverly Hills CA: Sage Publications.

Hofstede, G. (1992) The reintegration of Eastern Europe in the family of nations, Research Working Paper 92–3, Institute for Research on Intercultural Cooporation, University of Limburg, Maastricht.

Hofstede, G. (1993) The nation-state as a source of common mental programming: similarities and differences across Eastern and Western Europe, in S. Gustavsson and L. Lewin (eds) *The Future of the Nation State*, London: Routledge.

In Global Competition Research Programme (1998) *Report on Competitiveness of the Hungarian Enterprise Sphere*, Budapest: University of Economic Science.

Kornai, J. (1980) *Economics of Shortage*, Amsterdam: North Holland.

Kornai, J. (1992a) *The Political Economy of Communication*, Princeton: Princeton University Press, p. 250.

Kornai, J. (1992b) The post-socialist transition and the state: reflections in the light of Hungarian fiscal problems, *American Economic Review* 82 (2): 1–21.

Laky, T. (1992) Small and medium-size enterprises in Hungary, *Report for the European Commission*, Budapest: Institute for Labour Studies.

Makó, C. (1997) Transferring managerial competence and organization from Western to Eastern Europe, *Research Output, Final Report*, Budapest: Centre for Social Conflict Research.

Makó, C. and **Ellingstad, M.** (1997) A forgotten dimension of the 'transformation economies' : the case of the managerial labour process, paper presented at the 13th EGOS Colloquium: Organisational Responses to Radical Environment Changes, Budapest: Budapest University of Economic Sciences, 3–5 July.

Makó, C., Ellingstad, M. and **Kuczi, T.** (1997) *REGIS: Székesfehérvár Region Survey Results and Interpretations*, Budapest: Centre for Social Conflict Research, Hungarian Academy of Science, January.

Makó, C. and **Simonyi, Á** (1992) Labour Relations in Transition in Eastern Europe, in G. Széll (ed.) *Spaces and Acting Society*, Berlin: Walter de Gruyter & Co.

Peng, M.W. and **Heath, P.S.** (1996) The growth of the firm in planned economies in transition: institutions, organisations, and strategic choice, *Academy of Management Review* 21 (2): 492–528.

Sik, E. (1994) From the multicoloured to the black and white economy, *International Journal of Urban and Regional Research* 18 (1): 46–70.

Stark, D. (1992) Path-dependence and privatisation strategies in East-Central Europe, *East European Politics and Societies* 6: 17–51.

Stark, D. (1996) Recombinant property in East European capitalism, *American Journal of Sociology* 101 (4) January: 993–1027.

Thompson, P. (1994) Corporate culture: myths and realities, West and East, in C. Makó and P. Novoszáth (eds) *Convergence versus Divergence: the Case of the Corporate Culture*, Budapest: Centre for Social Conflict Research, Hungarian Academy of Science, Communication and Consultation Co: 179–200

Varga, K. (1986) *Az emberi és szervezeti eröforrás fejlesztése*, Budapest: Akadémiai Kiadó.

Section Two: USA

What You See Is What You Get: Thoughts on American Management

Peter Lawrence

Introduction

There are some societies that are quite good at internally partitioning them-selves, so that knowing about one bit does not tell you anything about 'the other bits'. Take France, for example. It would be possible for a foreigner (a non-French person) to visit France often, and get to know it well in tourist terms. Such a person might well learn French and thereby achieve some access to French intel-lectual life, and become a devotee of French culture. But none of this, no matter how intrinsically rewarding, would give this interested foreigner any idea of what it would be like to work in a French company, of how work relations and corporate culture might differ from those of, say, Britain. And this is because France is in many ways closed to outsiders, it is partitioned, the French them-selves keep work and non-work apart, distinguish between the professional and the personal, practice role segregation as a fine art.

But America is not like this. America is a what you see is what you get society. The values of American business are the values of American society. The strengths of American management are the virtues of American society. American management style is an occupationally focused version of national style. We could indeed imagine rather accurately what working in an American organisation would be like on the basis of our tourist travel and encounters. This is an up-front, nothing to hide, strongly communicating society.

Business, management and history

In the US, business has been shaped by history and society. European accounts of the history of the US tend to focus on the colonial period, and thus emphasise the thousands of people who went there from the sixteenth and the eighteenth centuries seeking a religious and political freedom not afforded them in 'old Europe'. This is fine but we would rather choose to emphasise the millions of immigrants to the US in the nineteenth and twentieth centuries who went there in the expectation that they would have a higher standard of living, would earn more, own more, make more, be able to spend more than in the countries of their birth. These millions, and their legitimate expectations, have made the US more openly materialistic than most societies, where striving for wealth, success and possessions needs no excuse, is basic to the human condition.

In discussing management it may be helpful to distinguish between management as an activity (something that people do), management as an idea (a consciousness of management as a discrete task having its own dynamics, and susceptible to analysis and discussion), and management as a subject (something that is taught). The first of these, management as an activity, has always been with us since mankind embarked on collective endeavour – the building of the pyramids, to take an example from the ancient world. But management as an idea and management as a subject were pretty much invented in the US (Lawrence 1986).

It would seem that the word management came into common use in America in the nineteenth century, and this betokens a consciousness of the phenomenon – what we have called management as an idea. The formula goes something like this:

Opportunity + Resources – People = Management

That is to say, the US in the nineteenth century offered the unique combination of a superabundance of land, space, natural resources and opportunities for enrichment together with a relative shortage of people to exploit these advantages. The result is an emphasis on individual resourcefulness and versatility, and on the effective organisation of (scarce) human resources. The same scarcity of people in the formative period of the nineteenth century is a spur to mechanisation and to the development of labour-saving devices.

It is the same with management as a subject. The US has some of the earliest business schools, beginning in the 1880s. By the 1950s more undergraduates in America were studying business administration than any other subject (a state of affairs not achieved in Britain until the 1990s). Or again the US pioneered the MBA, and produced large numbers of them. Some management subjects, most obviously marketing and corporate strategy, are heavily dominated by the Americans; indeed, over 80 per cent of all the books that have ever been written about management have been written by American citizens.

The size of America also affected the development of business. Because it was a big country, everything it did was on a big scale. So, to take the classical example, its railroads were bigger than anyone else's, needed more substantial capitalisation and this fostered the early growth of joint stock companies. America was not just a large geographical area: it also came to have a large population (the US is population-wise the world's third biggest country after China and India) and a very different one. It is disposed of a huge domestic market, its manufacturing companies became correspondingly large, benefiting by economies of scale to a high degree. Reaching this large but dispersed market was a challenge that stimulated the development of marketing; reaching customers physically also posed a logistical challenge that made Americans leaders in the organisation of distribution. These large companies, with their economies of scale, their marketing and distribution capability were also among the first to internationalise, both by establishing overseas subsidiaries and by means of cross-border acquisition.

Individualism and management

In Hofstede's (1980) famous study of the work-related values of IBM employees, individualism versus collectivism is one of the four key dimensions, and the country that 'came top' with the highest score for individualism was the US. But American individualism is not expressive, it is not about being different or being high on interiority. American individualism focuses on achievement and, above all, on economic achievement. As the slogan on a popular T-shirt has it:

Failure is not an option

This individualism informs and inspires American management. There is a heavy and undisguised investment in career success. There is high mobility between companies in the pursuit of success. High management incomes reward success, and the salary hierarchy tends to be steep: that is to say, every promotion means a significant pay raise. An ethic of personal achievement runs through US management: it justifies demonstrably hard work and long hours when necessary, it fuels personal initiative and underpins the strong presentation of personal image. It is also part of the readiness to take decisions: in America, as opposed to Japan, individuals not groups take decisions, and they are discrete rather than consensus (Athos and Pascale 1982). The individualism X success syndrome serves in American eyes to legitimise the means to the end, and there is often more than a touch of amorality here. While gathering material for a book on American management (Lawrence 1996), I interviewed a lot of managers working at companies in the US and among other things asked them to give an outline of their careers to date. Their answers were often surprisingly frank, including episodes where they had faked, bluffed and deceived; taken morally dubious short cuts; figured everything would be forgiven if they succeeded in the end. They would round off their accounts with remarks like:

I'm the second highest paid executive in the company.
I make my own luck!
I've got the office next to the CEO.

Communication

Individualism and communication go together. For individuals to connect, contrive and impact, they must communicate. Communication is a strength of American management. First of all American managers engage proactively in communication.

First it is recognised as a necessary part of the management role, not to be slighted or ignored. Second in the American scheme of things language is a means not an end; that is to say you can do anything you like with the language so long as you convey meaning (communicate) effectively to others. Third, Americans will not leave unsaid anything that needs to be said for reasons of delicacy. American communication is direct, meanings are not packaged. They actually ask questions like:

What kind of dollars are we talking about (= how much?)
What is her motive?
What does he want?
What do I need to know?

Fourth, Americans check for understanding in the course of a verbal exchange. They will ask:

Do you understand what I am saying?
Does this make sense to you?

Again in the American scheme it is OK if you do not understand first time round, but you are not allowed to 'walk away' without having understood. You will be given the option of an 'action replay' and if you need it, you had better use it!

Knowledge and information

It is not so easy to distinguish between knowledge and information – but we will try! Knowledge has a context, it is embedded, implies a wider understanding. But information is no more than an aggregation of bits, it is 'hard', i.e. separate from a larger entity that will effect our understanding of it, it is often expressed in a numeric form.

Americans like information. Its appeal is that it is uncomplicated. It is also acceptable – everyone can get hold of it, you do not need a PhD from MIT to master information. Therefore it is rather egalitarian, all Americans can partake in it, it is not exclusive or dependent on class or educational status. Americans exchange information in the 'social space' that in England is filled by discussing the weather.

But information is also the essence of management. Information fuels decisions. Information enables control. Gathering information – about markets, costs, prices, competitors, options – makes management rational and gives it the capability to be effective. Information is inseparable from the great American management strength – systems.

Systems

Systems are the essence of American efficiency. Whenever possible managerial acts and administrative procedures have been *systematised*, reduced to a number of simple stages in a rational order, programmed and transmitted. Systems abound in such areas as costing, budgetary control, financial planning, production control, purchasing, gathering and analysing marketing information, and of course in personnel administration. We are not positing here a black and white contrast between American companies and comparisons in other countries. It is rather that:

- American systems are more numerous and cover a wider range of operations
- American managers are temperamentally inclined to put more reliance in the systems
- these systems tend to compensate for low levels of vocational training and employee education, to compensate for what Lester Thurow has called the 'dumbing down' of the American workforce. (Thurow 1996)

Furthermore, the systems are fuelled by information, and enable decisions to be rationalised and standardised. An American bank, for example, will have a system for evaluating the performance of individual branches. Such a system will be in the form of gathering transaction, turnover, and profitability data under prespecified headings. Built into the design of the system will be some trigger points that tell you when, for example, a particular branch is so unprofitable that it should be closed: number of accounts, loan value over customer base, profitability per head of staff, and so on. So the decision to close a branch is depersonalised, built into the system, and in consequence is more likely to be accepted. One intangible aspect of American organisations is that there is a more diffuse acceptance of decisions and outcomes; this probably derives from the way they have been 'objectified' by systems and data.

Strategy

It is not an accident that the corporate strategy literature is primarily American, and there is clearly a parallel between American interest in strategy and the importance attached to wealth: what, after all, is corporate strategy but a set of precepts and proposals to keep a company profitable in the future?

Again the American emphasis on strategy does not represent a black and white contrast between American managers and managers in other countries, but a difference of degree. It is, however, noticeable that American managers seem to attach more importance to strategy. Senior managers in the US, if asked open-ended questions about the nature of their jobs, their priorities or tasks, will inevitably put strategy high on the list. This executive concern with strategy is also more open: there is more discussion, more accumulation of relevant data, and more emphasis on communicating this strategy, 'on cascading it down', so that it may inform the actions of organisational members. It is also noticeable that American executives tend to be very well informed about their industries and about developments in these industries.

Proactivity

The energy and dynamism that is popularly attributed to American society finds its parallel in American management, which is striking in its proactivity.

Europeans who go to work in American companies, whether in the US or elsewhere, often make the critical comment that these companies seem to change direction more than do their European counterparts and also that they 'screw up' more frequently. Whether or not these charges are fair, they are probably indicative. That is to say American companies change course more often because they are resolved to keep trying until they find something that gives the desired result; and they sometimes get things wrong because they are typically resolved to DO SOMETHING.

To restate this last point a little, when an issue is genuinely complicated, such that we are really unsure what to do for the best, Europeans may be inclined to do nothing for fear of making it worse, but Americans will be inclined to do something; if it doesn't work they do something else!

To put it another way, American managerial behaviour is 'solution driven'. The focus on analysis is limited, and is merely a preliminary to deciding what action to take. The emphasis is on a plausible solution, rather than on a perfect solution.

The over-riding proactivity is very much in evidence at meetings in American companies. At the end of the meeting you always know:

- what is going to be done
- who is going to be responsible for which actions
- how long it is going to take
- when we are going to meet to review progress.

This is claiming a good deal.

Balance sheet

The combination of systems, strategy and proactivity outlined in the last few pages gives Americans a strong claim to be the exemplars of professional management (and they pretty much invented it). The case becomes stronger when we add the natural advantages of a large, resource rich country, becoming the world's largest affluent market, and doing everything on a larger and more challenging scale than anyone else and therefore speeding down the learning curve.

We are conscious of having given a positive picture of American management, which in turn prompts the question: What are its weaknesses?

First I would have to say that the American business establishment is probably hamstrung by its short-termism, its need to produce escalating short-term profits for the benefit of shareholders. This disadvantage has been critical in the duel the US has fought, and largely lost, with Japan – a battle for both domestic and world markets. Second, the mindset of American management is more suited to playing a strong hand than a weak one: it worked fine when the US was the dominant economic power and could play its strengths, but seems now a little dated and sometimes inappropriate. Third, and it is a related point, Americans have difficulty relating to the cultural differences of other societies unless it is from a position of leadership and dominance – they can show other people how to do it (the American way) but not adapt *to* them.

But probably the most serious charge is that in a certain sense American management is too good. So good, in fact, with its systems and organisation and proactivity, that it has served to mask the 'dumbed down' limitations of an American workforce.

References

Athos, A.G. and **Pascale, R.T.** (1982) *The Art of Japanese Management*, London: Allen Lane.

Hofstede, G. (1980) *Culture's Consequences*, Beverley Hills, Los Angeles: Sage Publications.

Lawrence, P. (1986) *Invitation to Management*, Oxford: Basil Blackwell.

Lawrence, P. (1996) *Management in the USA*, London: Sage Publications.

Thurow, L. (1996) *The Future of Capitalism*, London: Nicholas Brealey.

Section Three: Asia

Management in Japan

D.H. Whittaker

Introduction

Japanese management has a number of interrelated features which together constitute a distinctive style of management, although there are variations according to sector and product focus, size, ownership and organisation culture. I first outline the key features and how they fit together, then look at variations and limitations. Japanese management should not be understood as a static set of practices; it is the product of evolution in a specific – and changing – political, economic and sociocultural environment. After looking briefly at this process of evolution, I discuss current challenges and the directions in which Japanese management is continuing to evolve.

Human resources

Human resource management is at the core of most conceptions of 'Japanese-style management'. Indeed, 'Japanese-style management' is frequently used synonymously with the 'three pillars' of lifetime (or long-term) employment, *nenko* (seniority plus merit) wages and promotion, and enterprise unions.

'Lifetime employment' refers to the preference for hiring fresh school or college graduates, and employing them until a mandatory retirement age, currently around 60 for many companies. Graduates are hired on the basis of potential rather than readily applicable skills, with school or college taken as an indicator of potential. Since employment is long term, recruiting is a careful process, for both parties, and is followed by an induction period in which new recruits are socialised into their new corporate 'community' before their initial workplace training. Subsequent assignments reflect long-term human resource development objectives, strategic development and current production considerations. In return for an implicit, not contractual, promise of long-term employment, employees are expected to accept job assignments flexibly.

Long-term employment applies to 'regular' employees. Other categories, such as part-time, temporary or contract workers, who may be employed on the basis of existing skills, for specific jobs and specific periods, add flexibility to the system. 'Lifetime employment' is most fully realised in large, prestigious companies, and even here there is a certain amount of turnover, particularly on the part of young workers (hence the preference by some for the term 'long-term employment').

Long-term employment is reinforced by the wage and promotion system, which rewards loyalty with seniority increments. *Nenko*, however, has a merit element as well, which is evaluation-based, and hence discourages the coasting or complacency that might creep in with job security. Differences based on evaluation are kept small for the first few years of a given cohort, but widen later on, encouraging employees to work hard for higher pay and promotion later in their careers. Twice-yearly bonuses totalling four to five months' wages are also designed to encourage identification with the company, and welfare benefits are extensive for regular employees. Non-regular workers, on the other hand, tend to be employed for a fixed rate, without many of the fringe benefits and bonuses offered to regular workers.

Internalised career structures and wage systems weaken the rationale for occupation or class-based worker organisation, and encourage an enterprise focus, although enterprise unions are the product of a chequered industrial relations history, and not just a functional fit with the first two 'pillars'. Although industrial federations are important for wage-bargaining co-ordination, the basic unit of union organisation corresponds with the employing organisation, and all regular employees below a certain junior management level belong, irrespective of their 'collar' status or current job. One result is harmonised conditions between blue-collar and white-collar employees. Enterprise unions, moreover, tend to adopt co-operative relations with management, passive in some cases, active in others. In this sense they enhance stability, and are often referred to as the 'third pillar' of 'Japanese-style management'. One in four workers belongs to a union, mainly in larger enterprises where the other 'pillars' are most strongly established.

Companies benefit from an education system that produces highly literate and numerate recruits. They then expend considerable effort developing their human resources over a long time period. HRM is a key corporate function.

Corporate governance and strategic management

Three-quarters of the directors of listed companies have spent most or all of their working life in the same company. They are promoted employees. One in six has served as an executive of the enterprise union. They are divided from those they manage by belonging to an earlier cohort rather than an 'us–them' divide, predisposing them to take employee interests seriously. Corporate finance and share ownership features also reduce pressure on managers to prioritise shareholder returns. 'Main banks' have played an important role in providing both indirect and direct finance. Majority shares are owned by companies with business relationships, or companies in the same industrial group, often on a reciprocal basis. Their interests are served by the long-term growth and viability of the company, and not simply high dividends. Dividends are basically fixed and low.

A high proportion of profits is retained within companies, leading to high rates of investment, and contributing to a growth and market-share orientation. Many industries are dominated by a 'big five' or 'big six', which engage in 'referential competition' by carefully monitoring their competitors in all aspects of their business. Competition has been marked more by internal mobilisation, innovation and investment than strategic differentiation or mergers and acquisition activity. Competitors, however, co-operate in industry associations to advance common interests, especially in their dealings with the government.

Key decisions are made by senior directors rather than the Board of Directors, although normally after extensive consultation which extends well down into the organisation. These decisions are then often relayed in a general and even vague form, with lower levels of the organisation giving them concrete shape. Some researchers have pointed to ambiguity in structure and job descriptions as well as strategy as a spur to mobilisation, knowledge creation and innovative activity (e.g. Nonaka and Takeuchi 1995; see also Itami 1987).

In sum, capital markets, like labour markets, feature long-term commitments – rather than spot allocative efficiency, and corporate governance exhibits a 'stakeholder' rather than (shareholder) agency orientation. Senior management seeks to mobilise employees through 'referential competition'.

Shop-floor-based innovation

Consistent with this style of corporate governance and mobilisation is a strong emphasis on shop-floor-based process and product innovation, in the context of daily work activities, small group activities and matrix teams. This has been a prominent factor in dramatic productivity increases in Japanese manufacturing in the postwar period. New methods were pioneered for inventory reduction, tooling and changeover time reduction, and continuous improvements enhancing quality and price competitiveness, often simultaneously. Manual workers as well as engineers have been agents of change and organisational learning.

Human resource management – the 'three pillars' – is an important precondition for such innovation, but organisational characteristics should also be noted. Many manufacturing companies have multifunctional and multiproduct factories, and have been somewhat ambivalent about divisionalisation. Fruin (1992, 1997) attributes the emergence of such factories to historical conditions: limited resources, rapid growth, technology transfer and absorption – and their persistence to the favourable environment they provide for learning and innovation.

Interfirm relations and subcontracting

For historical and functional reasons, such as the desire for a relatively homogeneous and stable workforce, corporate activities are relatively focused, either by sector or by stage of production or sales. This focus is complemented by interfirm linkages, such as in corporate groupings, through subcontracting, and sales' distribution networks. Japanese management and industrial structure are therefore interrelated, and the management of interfirm relations is an important corporate task.

So extensive is subcontracting that large 'manufacturers' may be more accurately described as 'assemblers' (and new product developers and marketers). Subcontractors are frequently organised in tiers, in which large numbers of small firms doing basic or machining processes supply a smaller number of larger firms producing subassemblies, which are then supplied to the assembler. In volume assembly industries, subcontracting relations complement internal processes in just-in-time management. They are typically long term, and managed by carrots and sticks, encouraging continuous improvement rather than simply spot-price efficiency. Once seen as a vehicle for large firms to exploit smaller firms, in recent years observers have stressed mutuality and the competitive advantages offered by division of labour specialisation and market-sensitive flexibility. This is another aspect of Japanese management that foreign competitors have sought to emulate.

Small firms

Although more than half of manufacturing SMEs (small and medium-sized enterprises; up to 300 employees) subcontract for at least part of their income, it would be a mistake to see them simply as appendages of large firms. Many are not subcontractors, while others may start out by subcontracting before developing their own product or service. Thus they must be seen in terms of their own management dynamics, and not just those of large firms. 'Wanting to be one's own boss' is a key reason for starting a small business in many countries, and Japan is no exception. (This aspect of Japan's culture has received much less attention than large firm-based 'groupism'. In fact, Japan ranks alongside Italy as having the highest proportion of small firms, and employees in them, of any OECD country.) Once they have 'raised their flag', owners will go to great lengths to keep it raised. Such motivations are an important reason for the large number of small firms in Japan – and an important source of innovativeness.

The 'three pillars' are less evident in small firms than in the large firms described above, although many small firms have a core of long-serving employees. Ownership and corporate governance are obviously different; many small firms are family owned and run. There is great diversity in terms of objectives and management style, from livelihood businesses to growth-oriented large firms, aspirants that emulate the practices of large firms. This diversity makes it difficult to construct an alternative management model to that based on large firms.

Women and Japanese management

'Japanese-style management' is premised on and reinforces a male breadwinner, female homemaker social division of labour. The proportion of working women is by no means low by international standards, but it is not easy to combine family on the one hand, and the career commitments that 'Japanese-style management' requires on the other. Typically women graduates are hired as regular employees, much the same as male employees, but job rotation and training are less extensive. The majority will leave to have children. This helps companies to maintain lower seniority wage costs. After initial childrearing, many women find work again, but in a part-time capacity, which again lowers company wage costs and enhances flexibility. While not unique to Japan, these practices are highly institutionalised.

Long working hours of male regular employees, too, are premised on women managing the 'home front'. There is some resistance to this social division of labour; women are marrying later, if at all, and having fewer children. Rather than pursuing equality under unreformed Japanese management, however, career-oriented women and feminists advocate greater compatibility between work and home for both men and women.

Evolution and change

Japanese management is not a static set of practices. It is the product of evolution through response to challenges in a specific – and changing – political, economic and sociocultural environment. The interwar years, the Second World War and the postwar, high-growth years each saw significant developments. Following the First World War companies began to introduce long-term employment and incremental wage increases for core workers in order to reduce chronic labour turnover, to retain the workers they had trained, and to ward off the burgeoning labour movement. The slump following the First World War, too, taught them the dangers of building up excessive production capacity, and they began to use subcontracting as a management tool. These practices were made more systematic in the 1930s and during the Second World War, when labour turnover was suppressed, and subcontracting practices institutionalised to enhance the war effort. Reforms to capital markets curtailed the role of the stock market, and restrictions were placed on dividend returns.

Against a background of poverty and turbulence following the Second World War, newly recognised labour unions pressed for employment security and an end to blue-collar white-collar wage and status differentials. When managers regained the upper hand, they modified rather than negated the concessions. They sought to encourage 'moderate' unionism, and employee identification with the company through wage and promotion reform. These in turn paved the way for the spread of small group activities such as zero defect and quality control circles. The key elements of Japanese management were largely in place by the late 1960s, and they were fine-tuned in the 1970s.

Challenges

Given that Japanese management has evolved in response to environmental and strategic challenges, it is reasonable to believe that it will continue to evolve, unless it becomes a victim of its past success and ossifies. There is by no means a shortage of challenges, both endogenous and exogenous.

An obvious challenge is that of internationalisation and globalisation, both in terms of corporate development and changing competition. Given the sociocultural context in which it developed, it is not easy to transfer the 'soft' aspects of

Japanese management. Localisation has been problematic, as has the development of sophisticated global management. Companies are also faced with the challenge of reorienting domestic operations as more and more production is moved offshore.

Other challenges include structural changes in the economy, rapidly changing technology, deregulation, prolonged domestic recession, and turmoil in overseas markets, particularly Asia. Unlike some of their nimble foreign competitors, who for instance might rapidly shed jobs in response to a downturn, or hive off parts of the business and buy into new areas to adapt to structural or technological change, long-term commitments, not least to regular employees, force Japanese companies to take a more gradualist approach. Financial deregulation is increasing participation by foreign institutions and, through corporate finance, prompting companies to take shareholder interests more seriously.

Endogenous challenges include ageing workforces, which increase direct and indirect wage costs and exacerbate promotion bottlenecks. Increasing numbers of 'knowledge workers' engaged in R&D and corporate planning require modifications to personnel and HRM systems.

Companies have responded to these challenges by modifying long-term employment (by 'loaning' or transferring older workers, extending the sphere of long-term employment), hiring contract workers and increasing differentiation among regular employees, (re)emphasising results-based pay and reducing the seniority weighting. Removal of the legal ban on holding companies is likely to accelerate restructuring, and corporate governance is being modified to make accountability more transparent. For some, these changes mark the beginning of the end of Japan's distinctive form of management, a convergence towards 'global standards'. More probably, they mark a significant new chapter in its evolution.

Further reading

Imai, **K.** and **Komiya, R.** (eds) (1994) *Business Enterprise in Japan*, Cambridge MA: MIT Press. Views of leading Japanese economists before the 1990s recession really began to bite.

Japan Commission on Industrial Performance (1997) *Made in Japan*, Cambridge MA: MIT Press. Researched and written as a response to *Made in America*, MIT Commission on Industrial Performance (1989), Cambridge MA: MIT Press when the recession was beginning to bite.

Sako, M. and **Sato, H.** (eds) (1997) *Japanese Labour and Management in Transition*, London: Routledge. A good overview of developments in HRM and labour relations in the 1990s.

References

Fruin, **M.** (1992) *The Japanese Enterprise System*, New York: Oxford University Press.

Fruin, **M.** (1997) *Knowledge Works*, New York: Oxford University Press.

Itami, H. with Roehl, T. (1987) *Mobilizing Invisible Assets*, Cambridge MA: Harvard University Press.

Nonaka, I. and Takeuchi, H. (1995) *The Knowledge-Creating Company*, New York: Oxford University Press.

Management in the Arab Middle East

David Weir

Introduction

Classical organisation theories and principles of management do not have universal acceptability and validity regardless of cultural and environmental diversity. Studies of management in the Middle East have demonstrated the existence of a coherent though varied style of management related at least as much to the indigenous culture and the environmental and historical features of those societies as to the influence of any external paradigms deriving from North America or the Far East. It is now possible to talk of a 'Fourth Paradigm' (Weir 1998) which characterises management experience in the region. Much of the uniqueness of this paradigm derives from the Islamic culture which is the dominant pattern of belief and social organisation, much from the specifically Arabic influence of the population and demography. Some, it is argued, derives from the specific physical environment, the influence of the desert and the cultural practices deriving from the Bedouin way of life, counterpointed with the experience of the culture of cities, trade and travel over several centuries. Some specific distinguishing factors mark the management styles found in Maghreb, Tunisia, Algeria and Morocco, but they may also be considered under this heading. That is not to say there is uniformity of practice or any lack of development, change and reaction to the global economy, in the Middle East.

Al-Rasheed (1994a) has argued that the influences of globalisation, industrialisation and changing technology are as significant as those of the Islamic and Arabic legacy. Al Buraey (1985) has characterised Islamic administrative practices in a comprehensive account.

Management styles in the Arab Middle East

An early attempt to characterise the management styles found in the region is in Muna's (1980) study *The Arab Executive*. Muna's sample included Lebanese, Syrian and Egyptian managers but was in any event relatively small. Badawy (1980) finds that organisational characteristics and management practices are strongly influenced by the indigenous culture. Attiyah (1993) in a series of significant contributions, examined the influence of culture on managerial organisation. He concludes that most studies in Arab society and culture are impressionistic and speculative while there has been until recently a significant absence of field surveys and rigorous research. Moreover, ideological and political considerations have influenced the direction of some studies. This situation is now much improved and it is possible to base contemporary characterisation on a significant number of empirical researches in each of the main arenas in which managers operate in the Middle East.

Attiyah indicates that the superficial expectation that managers in Middle East environments would necessarily tend towards autocratic and hierarchical modes while managing is not borne out by the evidence. He finds that while managers in an Arab context use more than one style, there is a strong tendency towards participative and consultative styles. Experiences, management training and development are a significant mediating factor.

Studies of the macro organisation of society in the region indicate that Islamic and religious-based models of social organisation are both significant constraints on managers in societies such as Iran, Libya and Syria which for different combinations of political and social events have passed through or are continuing to experience periods of strong authoritarian control and the imposition of a dominant ideology, whether based on religious fundamentalism or militaristic nationalism.

The region is experiencing a particular form of economic development in which the values, norms, customs and patterns of behaviour that characterise a regionally based and religiously justified culture are being challenged in a wide variety of societal contexts. The Middle East represents a political and cultural mosaic of enormous diversity and simple characterisations such as 'Islamic fundamentalism' tend to be at best misleading. Nonetheless, 90 per cent of Arabs are Muslim and all Arabs speak Arabic although there are differences in dialect and accent.

Islam comprises a common matrix of cultural practices and religious belief among the Semitic tribes (originally nomadic within the Arabian peninsula) who over 2000 years colonised and conquered the neighbouring regions of Syria, Egypt, Mesopotamia, Persia and North Africa. This tradition permits us to seek a unifying structure of management behaviour within these regions.

A major attempt to characterise management direction and identity across the Arab world is found in Dadfar (1993), who demonstrates the significance of sociocultural influences on the behaviour of Arab managers in their own sociocultural context. He identified tribalism, Islam, Westernisation and government intervention as significant factors influencing Arab management practices. Ali (1990) similarly characterises Arab management in three groups: Westernised, Arabised and Islamised.

Dadfar's characterisation is based on a study of historical and literary sources and on empirical studies of project management. As with many scholars who have worked in this field, Dadfar's theoretical and empirical understanding is reinforced by the experience of consulting in an Arab context and the attempt to mediate classical Western values of management to a Middle Eastern environment.

Dadfar's typology is based on the triangulation of the three master influences, Islam, Westernisation and Tribalism. However, he further differentiates along these three dimensions to create a ninefold typology.

This contains such complex characterisations as the 'tribo-Westernised' managers who do not like Western democracy and do not apply Western management principles but nonetheless desire to adopt Western lifestyles, technology and techniques. Among these managers the importance of authority and the respect allocated to other tribes results in deliberate choices, to specialise in areas of business that are not perceived as within the sphere of influence of other tribes.

This approach to management is contrasted with the 'Western tribalised' form found in modern organisations with significant numbers of ex-patriate professional managers. In these organisations 'the last word is always the Arab manager's word. Functional structure and systematised management at the end of the day are subordinate to family and tribal interests.'

Dadfar concludes that there is in principle an ideal type of management available to organisations in the region, which he characterises as 'the ideal man'. This characterisation recognises loyalty as a key feature and argues that loyalty to tribe and individual should be replaced by loyalty to the organisation. Similarly, pride in tradition, dynasty and tribe could provide the basis for pride in work. Rivalry 'should be shifted from tribe to organisation' and the core Islamic pillar of dedication to work, supported by the practices of Islamic worship, can provide a powerful basis for new management practices emphasising productivity, motivation and effective working values.

A similar basis in Islamic principle concerning respect for knowledge should justify the continuing need to study and master up-to-date technology. Dadfar is ambivalent about whether these changes in working practice, rooted in Islamic and Arabic belief patterns, still nonetheless require the introduction of democratic Western values. Rather, he argues that participative decision making involving consultation with those charged with the implementation of decisions is more consistent with underlying Islamic and Arabic values. Education is another pillar of Islamic belief and practice but the theoretical, and what Dadfar describes as the 'poetic', approach needs to be replaced by 'practical knowledge that complies with real life'. Dadfar argues that in several key respects the fundamentals of Islamic belief and Arabic social organisation are consistent with contemporary trends in Western management.

This argument is taken further by Weir (1998) who argues that these same tendencies in fact permit organisations in an Arab context to be both focused on key organisational imperatives because of the inward and family-driven nature of ownership, but to provide successful models of organisational decision making because of the emphasis on participation and consultation rooted in such social structures as the Majlis (of Persian rather than Arabic origin) but nonetheless widespread throughout the Arab world.

Various scholars have pointed to the neglect and even hostility towards Arabic managerial organisation encountered in the West especially in North America. This feature not merely implies ignorance of contemporary Arabic management organisation but also of the historical and philosophical origins of management thought. Mubarak (1998) has recently examined the core concepts underlying Western theories of motivation in the sacred writings of Islam and found surprising similarities between Western and Islamic conceptualisations related to the world of work. Indeed, it is arguable that the fundamental concepts, which in the West are believed to arise autonomously as a result of the agricultural and industrial revolutions, in Western societies are in fact borrowed from Islamic writing before the renaissance period and that scholars such as Ibn Khaldun and Ghazzali were familiar with many of these ideas.

Several authors have used Hofstede's (1980) work on cultural variations in 50 countries and three regions as the basis for examining the specific influence of culture on organisation structure and managerial organisation. The four dimensions of power, distance and certainty avoidance, individualism/collectivism and masculinity/femininity have proved an illuminating basis for characterising and comparing the impact of national culture. Sabri (1995) examines the roots of organisational culture in four Jordanian organisations to investigate if this culture is indeed congruent with the Jordanian Arab national culture. She shows that significant differences exist between Jordanian managers and other groups in their preferred cultures, Jordanians having a stronger preference for power and role cultures and less for achievement and support. She compares the organisational management culture with that of employees to show that Jordanian organisations are higher on power than role achievement or support. Employees emphasised achievement rather than power. A small sample and the different technological basis of the organisations do not rule out the possibility that technology operates as a mediating variable, but Sabri does not find that Jordanian organisations uniformly show higher scores on power and role culture than organisations in national cultures that are relatively low on power distance and weak on uncertainty avoidance. These findings indicate that technology and the rate of national industrial development are significant variables. Specific industry differences are significant in Middle Eastern as in a Western context. Industrial, regional and organisational factors may vary within a specific regional context. It is not possible to adopt a simplistic characterisation of the way in which Middle Eastern managerial culture operates in a specific context. Many scholars demonstrate the variability of managerial practice within a recognisably core central set of structures, practices and belief patterns.

The Gulf region contains some of the richest and the fastest growing economies in the world. Many are small city-state economies with strong possibilities for critical control, direction and comprehension of major societal resources. A number of studies attempt to characterise the behaviour and attitude of managers in these societies. A number of multinational companies operate in this region with success. They have been concerned to identify the appropriate organisational modes of response to their host societies and cultures and to obtain good levels of productivity and performance from multicultural workforces with a large proportion of ex-patriates in a context in which there are political pressures towards reducing the number of ex-patriates and progressively nationalising the professional, technical and managerial labour forces. There are profound implications for national and organisational labour markets.

In the development of the Gulf economies, education has been a major emphasis. Over the past 30 years, and specifically since the oil-price rise, the growing relative affluence of these economies has permitted the systematic exposure to European and North American modes of management and technical education.

The emerging managerial elite in Bahrain is increasingly well educated even by North American norms. It is developing a realistic self-image, setting strict performance standards, taking advantage of opportunities for professional self-renewal and, within the context of the authoritarian and autocratic power structures of Bahraini organisations, demands inclusion in the decision-making process.

Al Hashemi and Najjaz's (1990) study identifies a number of key tasks for managers and the organisational leadership in Bahrain before a balance can be found between the development needs of the economy and the aspirations for 'managerialism' of the emerging cadres of world-qualified, world-trained Bahrainian managers. The study clearly indicates, however, the existence of pressures towards professionalisation and increasing consciousness of management as a class within Bahrain society.

Mezal (1988) compared the managerial background patterns and attitudes of Arab managers in Kuwait and Egypt. Egyptian and Kuwaiti managers are well educated, the majority of them holding college degrees. This and the Bahrain studies emphasise a finding of growing significance. Managers in the Middle East have tended to be older than their Western counterparts and respect for seniority has been a feature of organisation structure. In the Gulf economies, however, this is changing and Mezal finds that the Kuwaiti managers in this sample are younger, better qualified and in many respects more Westernised than their Egyptian counterparts.

Younger managers in Egypt are less mobile and tend to be more embedded in specific industrial and commercial situations, thus making them more dependent for their career success on the decisions of older, less qualified managers in the organisation.

Both samples emphasise job security as both a desirable organisational characteristic and as a preferred outcome, even of more significance than promotion opportunities.

Participation and consultation are preferred values in both samples. Mezal's study emphasises the findings of many others, including Attiyah, that autocratic and authoritarian management structures are not perceived as desirable *per se* in the Arab world of organisations.

These findings are reinforced in the most authoritative source of data about Gulf managers, the MEIRC (1985) report on the making of Gulf managers under the direction of Farid Muna. This provides a benchmark for many subsequent studies conducted since.

More Gulf managers hold university degrees than their counterparts in the US, UK, France, Germany and Japan. Gulf managers receive more management training per year than American and British managers.

The most important characteristics for managerial success are family upbringing, quality of education and early experience. Therefore, recruitment and selection have been highly emphasised processes within Gulf organisations. Training and development, however, are also important. The MEIRC findings emphasise gaps in education and training facilities and the proposed ways of dealing with them. But they draw attention to the increase of good and even 'outstanding' practice in the large Gulf employers. For many small and medium enterprises and for developing organisations it is from local sources and examples rather than from Western or Far Eastern models that illumination will be drawn.

A finding of great significance is that there is a higher degree of homogeneity among managers from the six GCC countries, supervening nationality as a statistically significant factor. Though there are differences they are overshadowed by similarities.

Gulf managers prefer the consultative style of decision making while believing that their own bosses' style was still largely autocratic. The study points to an emerging and evolving Gulf managerial style which is neither Western nor Eastern and is greatly influenced 'by the distinctive and particular culture of the Gulf'. Consultation is the natural and preferred decision style. Subordinates in the Gulf 'do not expect to participate' in decision making on an equal footing with their managers but do expect to be consulted. The Japanese style of bottom–up consensus decision making is unlikely to be effective, nor is Western-style organisational democracy.

Gulf managers prefer organisations that provide relatively stable, 'even fixed' structures and known loci of decision making. They prefer their superior's decision making to be decisive and responsible. They do not expect to have major decisions delegated to them. They do expect to be incorporated in the thinking and explanation that lies behind the need for specific senior management decisions.

The cultural and philosophical underpinnings of belief patterns and behavioural practices are demonstrated by the explanations for particular beliefs being rooted in traditional and religious examples. This culture of management has its own mythology. Thus the practice, which has come to be known in the West since the well-known work by Peters and Waterman (1982), *In Search of Excellence*, as 'management by walking about' is supported and justified among Gulf managers by reference to the practice of the Caliph Omar, Ibn Al Khattab, who visited his people to see and hear at first hand their problems and grievances. The need for the highest level of management in an organisation to be personally above reproach is also demonstrated in the role modelling of Caliph Omar who was known for 'his piety, justice and patriarchal simplicity ... his irreproachable character became an example for all conscientious successors to follow'. Muna (1980) comments that this interpersonal style 'practised in the early days of Islam was found to be still effective by some Gulf managers even in today's complex organisations'.

Likewise the traditions of the Majlis or Diwaniah in which senior managers get together on a regular basis with employees and supervisors from various levels reduces the problems of bypassing that results from 'open door' policies, favoured in some Western organisations.

Other practices are seen as significant: one which resonates with good management and practice in the West is to encourage subordinates to formulate solutions to problems before coming to senior management with a statement of the difficulty. This avoids upward delegation. Systems in relation to time keeping and organisational performance requirements are seen by successful Gulf managers as reducing the necessity for personal intervention. The Gulf management culture is based on talking, not writing, so memos are not usually successful. This relates to the widely understood basis of communication throughout the Middle East and the Arab world. Letters are less significant than personal visits. Important matters are better dealt with face to face. The use of personal networks, connections and coalitions to support face-to-face interaction is also widespread. It is difficult within the culture of the Middle East to say 'no' face to face, however, so successful managers are seen as those who have developed a capability to give negative messages while maintaining strong interpersonal rapport.

Finally, successful organisations in the Gulf are seen as embodying family or tribal virtues. Some senior managers spoke explicitly about being 'the head of the family'. The head of a family or tribe provides both the necessary capabilities for decision making and decisive intervention but also the ability to offer social support, sustenance and development. Powerful people are seen as having *Wasta*, roughly translateable as network power and influence.

Organisations in the Gulf context are brought up, therefore, on an explicit decision-making culture based on interpersonal connections, hierarchical in essence, but offering both rights and responsibilities upwards and downwards.

This study has created a benchmark for comparison. Its findings are not necessarily universal but they embody themes that are undoubtedly widespread throughout the Arab world.

A key focus of research on management styles and behavioural practice in the Arab world has been motivation. An initial stream of studies attempted to apply characteristically Western and North American models of motivation to the inappropriate context of Middle Eastern organisations. Not surprisingly this approach produced mixed results. However, more recently, attempts have been made to map, describe and explain the patterns of motivation that are in fact found in this context. An important review is provided by Al-Rasheed (1994b), who reviews a number of empirical studies of the contemporary field of Arab management. He engages with a number of typological approaches, in particular Attiyah's (1991) attribution of the Arab organisation problems to organisational, bureaucratic, economic and political factors. He also engages with the argument that the cultural discontinuity experienced in the Middle East deals with seven processes of industrialisation that have deracinated the Arab management cadre from their own legitimate historical, cultural and traditional experiences. Al-Rasheed also dialogues with Weir's conceptualisation of the 'fourth paradigm', pointing out that in its initial exposition this typology is based on theoretical as much as on empirical grounds. He is similarly critical of Dadfar's more complex typology leading to the 'ideal man scenario'. Al-Rasheed's approach represents a decisive step forward in the efforts to identify a distinctively appropriate pattern of beliefs and behaviours, based on original research.

Al-Rasheed identifies a 'limited focus on future organisation' leading to a lack of relevant human resource management policies and management development and planning, a lack of delegation of authority, highly personalised superiors and subordinate relationships deriving from loyalty to individuals and paternalistic hierarchical organisational relationships. These lead to a number of barriers to effective organisational practice, short-sighted training policies, primitive human resource management policies, uncohesive and unelaborated organisational structures, little scope for advancement and promotion and, in particular, little opportunity for women in management.

These features derive from dimensions of society prevalent throughout the Arab world, family ownership and management, under qualified middle management and a limited job market. All these features are exacerbated by the relative youth of Arab business organisations and their relatively small size and scale compared to Western organisations in similar markets.

In many ways they are the obverse of the paradigmatic features noted in the Fourth Paradigm and the MEIRC study. 'Traditional religious values' are not necessarily taken-for-granted but are the focus of criticism and development. 'Traditional Islam' is not a taken-for-granted concept with the same meaning in all parts of the Islamic world. Al-Rasheed refers to the conflicting nature of Arab values in which tradition and modernity are present in an as yet unresolved admixture. Among the cultural tensions present therefore are the dilemmas of fatalism and freewill, shame and guilt, conformity and creativity, past and future, heart and mind, form and content, correctivity and individuality, closed and open mind, obedience and rebellion, charity and justice and vertical against horizontal values.

Al-Rasheed also points out that there is a fundamental difference between Western and Arab nation states. In the former, democracy is a key major premise underlying most forms of social organisation. In the Arab world this kind of political democracy is almost entirely absent. Al-Rasheed is also critical of what he identifies as a traditional educational system and non-innovative management scholarship. In this he reinforces the critique by Ali (1990) of the lack of impact of scholarship and the supporting infrastructures of science in changing organisational practices in the Arab world.

This critique is still to a large extent justified and the field of Arab management has not so far become a mature field of enquiry. There are no major centres of research dedicated to this topic. For five years from 1993 the annual Arab management conference at Bradford Management Centre provided a focus for this research.

The situation, however, is developing and improving in many diverse ways. Many writers have built on the earlier generation of benchmark studies in reinforcing the characterisation of management practice described above.

A major contemporary focus of research is on management training and development. Here a number of writers including Abudoleh and Weir (1997) have added to the empirical literature.

Despite the widespread lack of use of Western-style management practices such as assessment centres, as documented by Abudoleh and others, nonetheless sophisticated companies which accord to traditional Arab practices but compete in global markets, such as Emirates Airlines, have produced a meld of the best practices of global management, suitably tailored to Middle Eastern conditions.

A key dimension of the success of many of these organisations has been the appropriate use of expatriate managers. The expatriate manager has become another research focus. But still the benchmark analysis comes from the MEIRC report. Expatriate managers are not only Western in origin and orientation. Within most of the Middle East there are a very significant number of mangers from an Asian background usually from the Indian sub-continent. Within one particular Middle Eastern country, expatriates can come from other countries in the region and bring different expectations and behavioural practices that may not always be in tune with local behaviours.

In the MEIRC sample, Western ex-patriate managers are valued for their know-how and expertise, hard work, professionalism, discipline, organisational attention to detail and ability to work within and tolerate the hardships of foreign culture. But they may be disliked for their arrogance, lack of respect for local cultures, materialism, opposition to the training and development of nationals and their capacity for stereotyping nationals based on one bad experience. Other Arab expatriates may be valued for their hard-driving behaviours, for being essentially from the same culture and background, for being loyal and trustworthy and decisive but disliked when they are cliquish, stand in the way of the development of local managers, put a low value on time and behave autocratically. Indian and Asian expatriates are valued for their hard work, technical competence, discipline and obedience and capabilities as good desk people. They are disliked when they stand in the way of the development of nationals, behave as yes men, lack creativity and behave in a cliquish way.

There is now a growing literature on the expatriate experience. The replacement of expatriate senior managers by nationals is now official policy throughout most if not all of the Middle Eastern world. So the questions of Al-Rasheed and others will have to be resolved if Arab organisations are to continue to compete in the global economy in a way in which their natural resources of the region and high educational level of managers ought to facilitate.

A number of other specific themes have also engaged recent and contemporary researchers. The position of women managers varies dramatically throughout the nations in the region. It is perhaps most highly developed in Jordan and the Palestinian communities. Salman (1993) and Abuznaid (1993) have documented the emergence of a cadre of women managers vital to the economic development of these communities. Others have studied the growth of women managers in the Gulf countries. Salman and others have studied small business and its impact on the Palestinian economy, but studies of small enterprises are relatively lacking throughout the region. The world economy is now paying more attention to environmental and resource-friendly management. This management philosophy, still unusual and marginal in a Western context, is arguably more central in terms of Islamic and Bedouin values and thus can expect greater prominence in decision making in the Arab world.

Another strongly emphasised theme in many Western organisations in the past decades has been total quality management. In a path-breaking study Medhat Ali (1997), himself a senior quality manager in one of the largest Saudi organisations, has demonstrated that a total quality management programme of impressive dimensions can produce similar or even improved results to those reported in Western literature when introduced into a traditionally directed but competitive Arab organisation. These findings are consistent with the experience of such companies as Emirates Airlines.

Special attention in many studies has been paid to management in the public sector, building on the landmark studies of Badawy (1980) and others. A critical note has been represented by others. The heavy bureaucracy, a legacy of the Ottoman era, and colonial managerial organisation is associated not merely with delay and over-complication of decision making but explicitly with the problems associated with corruption and venality. For obvious reasons this is not a popular theme for organisations to fund research on. But it is undoubtedly a factor that should not be ignored.

Finally, new generations of researchers have returned to some of the master themes, in particular the role of Islam. Many studies have documented and attempted to sympathise with the importance of traditional Islamic values in such areas as Islamic banking. Some others have shown that the key tenets of Islam are compatible with modern business organisation. Mubarak (1998) has attempted a new synthesis of traditional themes by arguing that concepts regarded since Tawney and Weber as endemic to the Protestant ethic and the rise of capitalist work organisation may be prefigured in the work of medieval Islamic scholars.

But this, like all aspects of management in the Middle East, is a developing theme awaiting the empirical study and a more comprehensive theoretical rationalisation. This is a live dynamic field and the path of knowledge is continuing to unfold. The Fourth Paradigm is an emergent reality. 'The dogs bark, but the caravan moves on.'

References

Abudoleh, J. and **Weir D.T.H.** (1997) Management training and development needs analysis: practices in Jordanian private companies, *Middle East Business Review* 2 (1).

Abuznaid, S. (1993) *Palestinian Women From Followers to Leaders*, Bradford,* pp. 38–54.

Al-Buraey, M.A. (1985) *Administrative Development: An Islamic Perspective*, London: Kegan Paul.

Al Hashemi, I. and **Najjaz**, G. (1990) *Gulf 2000: The Making of Bahraini Managers*, Bahrain: University of Bahrain Press.

Ali, A. J. (1990) Management theory in a transitional society: the Arabs' experience, *International Studies of Management and Organisation* 20: 7–35.

Al-Rasheed, A. (1994a) Traditional Arab management: evidence from empirical comparative research, in *Proceedings of Arab Management Conference*, Bradford: 89–114.

Al-Rasheed, A. (1994b) *Factors Affecting Managers Motivation and Job Satisfaction: The Case of Jordanian Bank Managers*, Bradford, pp. 163–88.

Attiyah, H. S. (1993) *Management Development in Arab Countries of the Middle East*, Bradford, pp. 183–202.

Attiyah, H.S. (1991) Research in Arab Countries, *Arabic Organisation Studies* 13: 105–112.

Badawy, M.K. (1980) Styles of Mid Eastern Managers, *California Management Review* 22: 51–8.

Dadfar, H. (1993) *In Search of Arab Management Direction and Identity*, Bradford, pp. 260–75.

Hofstede, G. (1980) *Culture's Consequences*, London: Sage Publications.

Medhat, Ali (1997) *TQM in a Major Saudi Organisation*, PhD thesis, Bradford University.

MEIRC (1985) *The Making of the Gulf Manager*, Dubai: MEIRC Consulting Company.

Mezal, F. (1988) *An Empirical Assessment of Managerial Characteristics in Development Countries. The Case of Arabic Managers in Kuwait and Egypt*, Baghdad: Institute of Administration.

Mubarak, A. (1998) *Motivation in Islamic and Western Management Philosophy*, PhD Thesis, Bradford University.

Muna, F. (1980) *The Arab Executive*, London: Macmillan.

Peters, T. and **Waterman, R.** (1982) *In Search of Excellence: Lessons from America's Best-Run Companies*, New York: Harper & Row.

Sabri, H. (1995) *Cultures and Structures: The Structure of Work Organisations Across Different Cultures*, Bradford.

Salman, H. (1993) *Palestinian Women and Business Education*, Bradford.

Salman, H. (1995) *The Contribution of Palestinian Women to Business Development*, Bradford, pp. 471–88.

Weir, D.T.H. (1998) The Fourth Paradigm, in Ali A Shamali and J. Denton *Management in the Middle East*, Gulf Management Centre.

* 'Bradford' identifies the Annual Proceedings of the Arab Management Conference held at Bradford Management Centre 1992–7.

Indian Management Style and HRM[1]

Pawan S. Budhwar

Introduction

This section is divided into two parts. In the first, an attempt has been made to present a general picture of the Indian management style. It attempts to answer the question: Do environmental and economic pressures significantly affect the traditional personnel function in India? The second part analyses the impact of recent liberalisation of economic policies on Indian HRM.

Indian management

India is one of the world's most ancient nations and has a continuous and documented history which dates back to about 2000 BC. Over the centuries, large numbers of invaders and immigrants bringing with them different cultures and religions have settled down in India. As a result, Indian society has turned out to be a mixture of various ethnic, religious, linguistic, caste and regional collectivities which further differ because of historical and sociocultural specificities. These diversities are reflected in patterns of life, styles of living, land-tenure systems, occupational pursuits, inheritance and succession rules (Sharma 1984). The current Indian population (which is 900 million, the second largest in the world) consists of people with thousands of distinct ethnic identities, a stratified caste system, enormous income gaps between the rich and the poor, a middle class of 120 million people (the largest middle-class market in the world) and distinctive Marxist, Muslim, Sikh and other religious minorities (Thomas and Philip 1994). Of all these, the Hindu religion is the most dominant. Because of such diversities it is difficult to pin down a coherent Indian management system (Jain 1991).

However, research evidence shows the strong impact of the East India Company (which established British rule in India) on Indian industry and government. Current public servants reflect similar 'mistrust' towards the general public as shown by the Company towards the Indian natives. The Company also bequeathed India with the legacy of a red-tape-ridden bureaucratic system, which they themselves inherited from the Moghuls. Some researchers (see Silveria 1988: 8–9) blame the British rule for leaving India without an industrial culture, as a result of which after independence Indian businessmen thought and behaved like traders and commission agents rather than entrepreneurs and industrialists.

To a great extent, the current Indian management system is a product of a mixture of social, economic, religious and political factors, which have now prevailed in India for a long time. Indians are socialised in an environment that values strong family ties and extended family relationships; they are more likely to develop stronger affiliative tendencies or greater dependence on others. So in the work context interpersonal relations are more salient to them and, as a result, their job-related decisions might be influenced more by interpersonal considerations than by task demands (Kanungo and Mendonca 1994). Further, factors such as the long British rule, a strong caste system, religion and an agrarian-based society, an extended family system, a high rate of illiteracy and poverty, and weak and unimportant ties between state and individual (because the presence of intermediate groups like family, caste and village have catered for individual needs) have created a management system that is based on social and family relationships.

Indian organisations both in the past and present have made attempts to emulate Western or Eastern (Japanese) patterns of management. This is because Indian managers are often trained in the West and most of the Indian management institutes have adopted the Western education system. However, because of the strong family, social and religious influence on the one hand and Western education on the other, Indian managers internalise two separate sets of values. The first is acquired from their family and community and is related to affiliation, security, dependency and social obligation. The second is drawn from their education and professional training and relates to personal growth, efficiency and collaborative work (Sahay and Walsham 1997). In practice, the first set of values is very dominating.

Several researchers have compared Indian management practices with that of other regions such as the US, the UK and Japan. For example, in cultural terms compared to an English person, an Indian person is more fearful of people in power, obedient to superiors, dependent on others, fatalistic, submissive, undisciplined, friendly, modest, unreserved, collectivist, caste conscious and clan orientated, law abiding but less self-controlled, tenacious and less willing to take account of other people's views (Tayeb 1988). Similarly, Sharma (1984) in his study contrasted the high efficiency and achievement-orientated US management style with a more fatalistic style in India. Given their daily exposure to a scarce economy and an indifferent society in the face of poverty, Indian managers are more inclined to believe events are predetermined by a 'hidden hand' that shapes their destiny. They also demonstrate tough resilience in the face of hazards, reinforced by an infinite capacity to bear sufferings. Similar findings were reported recently by Sparrow and Budhwar (1997). Such attitudes have led to risk aversion on the part of managers and a tendency to dither when decisions have to be made.

Hofstede (1991) found that India is a low to moderate uncertainty-avoidance culture. However, in contrast, some analysis by Indian academics characterises the management style as one that demonstrates an unwillingness to accept organisational change or take risks, a reluctance to make important decisions in work-related matters or lack of initiative in problem solving, a disinclination to accept responsibility for job tasks and an indifference to job feedback (Singh 1990; Kanungo and Mendonca 1994).

Hierarchy and inequality are deeply rooted in India's tradition and are also found in practice in the form of unequally placed caste and class groups. Indian organisational structures and social relations are therefore hierarchical and people are status conscious. They find it comfortable to work in superior–subordinate relationships, which are personalised. India's positioning in Hofstede's (1991) research as a high power distance culture then reflects the hierarchical nature of Hinduism (evidenced by the caste system), the early socialisation process that highlights the importance of the family structure and the remnants of British colonial influence. Age also matters greatly in India, and seniority can be expected to play a significant role in decisions about promotion and pay. Apart from these, one's caste, religion and social contacts also matter significantly. Intergroup relationships are characterised by suspicion of other groups, a search for small group identity and a strong inclination to affiliate with people in power (Sharma 1984; Sahay and Walsham 1997). Such inequalities have persisted and remained in equilibrium because of organic linkages between them and the ingrained interdependence of the different socioeconomic groups.

India is also a low masculinity culture in Hofstede's terms. This is reflected in a paternalistic management style and preference for personalised relationships rather than a more divorced performance orientation (Kanungo and Jaeger 1990). This generates a 'tendermindedness' and 'soft work culture' that is associated with a reluctance to take bold decisions and see them through to the end (Sinha 1990). Success is judged on a 'moral consideration of the text' and strict observance of ritual, not on actual behaviour, absolute principles or rules. Indian work culture dictates a distinctive style of transformational leadership, which has been called the 'nurturant-task leadership' style (Mathur et al. 1996; Sinha and Sinha 1990). This draws on the use of familial and cultural values (such as affection, dependence and the need for personalised relationships) to temper the firm and structured task direction expected in situations of high-power distance. In such conditions the motivational tools have to have a social, interpersonal and even spiritual orientation (Sinha and Sinha 1990).

Low individualism (as per Hofstede's results for India) implies that family and group attainments take precedence over work outcomes. The primary purpose of work is not to express or fulfil one's self, but as a means to fulfil one's family and social obligations. Indeed, family and social networking is an important method for obtaining work, securing promotion and advancing pay (Sparrow and Budhwar 1997). A self-reinforcing circle exists, whereby culture dictates that political connections and ascribed status, not achievement status, underpins the selection, promotion and transfer systems, such that loyalty of appointees is more towards the appointing authorities than the goals of the organisation, and job-related decisions are influenced more by interpersonal relations than by task demands (Kanungo and Mendonca 1994). Moreover, low social and intellectual mobility forces owners to recruit managers from their own families, castes and communities, reinforcing old customs, values and beliefs. The top Indian industrial houses (such as Tatas, Birlas) are very good examples of this. The high prevalence of owner–managers within the business structure fits well with this cultural tendency.

Based on a detailed analysis of Indian national culture and its impact of Indian management, Sharma (1984: 76) summarises that:

> it presents a plausible picture of the average Indian's resistance to change, his willingness to delegate but unwillingness to accept authority, his fear of taking an independent decision, his possessive attitude towards his inferiors and his abject surrender to his superiors, his strict observance of rituals and his disregard of them in practice, his preaching of high morals against personal immorality, and his near-desperate efforts at maintaining the *status quo* while talking of change.

In the light of this characterisation of Indian management we are tempted to ask the question: Do Indian managers currently behave in the same way as discussed above? Have they changed? Or are they trying to change their practices to cope with the pressures thrown up by the recent liberalisation of Indian economic policies? A number of institutions are changing their pre-liberalisation stance, such as trade unions, labour laws, the educational and vocational training set-up, and government policies. What are the effects of such changes on the Indian personnel function?

HRM in the newly liberalised Indian economy

Formalised personnel functions have been common in Indian organisations for decades. The origins of the personnel function can be traced back to the 1920s with the concern for labour welfare in factories. The Trade Union Act 1926 gave formal recognition to workers' unions. Similarly, the recommendations of the Royal Commission on Labour gave rise to the appointment of labour officers in 1932 and the Factories Act 1948 laid down the duties and qualifications of labour welfare officers. These developments all formed the foundations for the personnel function in India (Sparrow and Budhwar 1996).

In the early 1950s two professional bodies were set up: the Indian Institute of Personnel Management (IIPM), formed at Calcutta, and the National Institute of Labour Management (NILM) at Bombay. During the 1960s the personnel function began to expand beyond its welfare origins with the three areas of labour welfare, industrial relations and personnel administration developing as the constituent roles for the emerging profession. In the 1970s the thrust of the personnel function shifted towards the need for greater organisational 'efficiency' and by the 1980s personnel professionals began to talk about new concepts such HRM and HRD. The two professional bodies of IIPM and NILM were merged in 1980 to form the National Institute of Personnel Management (NIPM) at Bombay. The status of the personnel function in India has therefore changed over the years. However, it is currently changing at a much more rapid pace then ever. Why?

On independence in 1947, India was among the two most industrialised nations of Asia. There were no 'tigers' or 'dragons' at that time and even Japanese goods were of poor quality. Things deteriorated at a rapid pace since then. Possible reasons in this regard include poor planning, increasing population and poverty, and a state-regulated economy. India claims to have the third largest pool of technically qualified persons in the world. However, over 40 per cent of its educated people (mainly graduates) remain unemployed. Year after year the world competitiveness report declares India to be the least competitive among the ten newly industrialised countries (Ratnam 1992). By the beginning of the 1990s the Indian economy experienced decelerating industrial production, double-digit inflation, increasing external and government debt with a high ratio of borrowing to GNP, and foreign exchange reserves sufficient to cover only three weeks of imports (Ahluwalia 1994; Sparrow and Budhwar 1996).

It was against this background that funds were secured from the World Bank and the International Monetary Fund to restructure the Indian Economy from a state-regulated regime to a free market system. In line with the development the currency was devalued and most of the economic policies such as the fiscal, trade, industrial, financial, agricultural and HR policies were reformed (Krishna and Monappa 1994; Ratnam 1995). These liberalised policies have had wide-ranging implications for Indian economy in general and Indian HRM in particular.

Liberalisation heralded sudden competition for indigenous firms as international firms were allowed to operate in India. This has created a pressure on Indian firms to switch from labour-intensive to more capital-intensive methods of production, and hence the emergence of a new requirement for organisations to remove surplus labour and generate new sustainable employment (Budhwar and Sparrow 1997). Indian organisations are now attempting to improve quality and match world standards such as ISO 9000. The aim is to increase productivity, reduce costs and over-manning, while generating employment, improving quality and reducing voluntary and involuntary absenteeism (Krishna and Monappa 1994).

Organisations are also having to cope with the subsequent de-skilling, re-skilling and multi-skilling problems, workforce reduction policies and retention and career development issues. These require the training and development of a new work culture (Ratnam 1995). As a result of such pressures, there is a high emphasis on human resource development (HRD) in Indian organisations. In fact HRD is the more often-used term to denote personnel function than HRM in India (Budhwar 1998).

The faster the speed at which Indian organisations can modernise and mechanise plants, introduce new technology, revamp plant layout for easier and efficient material handling and eliminate waste, the more successful they will be. In such conditions, the significance of personnel function in tackling these pressures is being realised in Indian managements. Although the recent reforms have created tremendous pressures on the traditional Indian management system it is too early to judge whether there is any noticeable change in the way organisations are managed in India. Since the traditional Indian management system developed over a very long time, understandably it will take some time to change.

However, some early symptoms of change are appearing. HRM is playing a noticeable role in bringing about changes in Indian organisations. More and more Indian organisations are creating a separate HRM/HRD department. There has been a significant increase in the level of training and development of employees (Budhwar and Sparrow 1997). The constitutional pressures are forcing organisations to employ people from backward and reserved categories (Ratnam and Chandra 1996). There are also indications of a movement towards performance-related pay and promotions. However, these are more evident in the private sector (Bordia and Blau 1998). Similarly, in comparison to the public sector, the internal work culture of private enterprises now places greater emphasis on the internal locus of control, future orientation in planning, participation in decision making, effective motivation techniques and an obligation towards others in the work context (Mathur *et al.* 1996). There is also an attempt to select new recruits on the basis of merit in the private sectors (at least at the lower and middle levels).

The antagonist role of trade unions is also on the verge of change. However, because of the strong political support the pace of this change is very slow. There is still a strong need to amend the provisions of many labour legislations (which are strongly pro-labour). The giant public sector organisations need to downsize to reduce their surplus labour so as to improve their efficiency. There are some attempts in this regard in the form of the introduction of 'voluntary redundancy schemes'. There is a small shift towards flexible and part-time work. The nature of HRM function is reported to be becoming proactive (for more details on HRM in India see Budhwar 1998). The required movement for change in the Indian management has been started (primarily because of the economic reforms). It needs to pick up the momentum and sustain it in the long run.

Note

1 I wish to thank Yaw Debrah and Paul Sparrow for their useful comments on an earlier version of this section.

References

Ahluwalia, M.S. (1994) India's quiet economic revolution, *The Columbia Journal of World Business*, Spring: 6–12.

Bordia, P. and Blau, G. (1998) Pay referent comparison and pay level satisfaction in private versus public sector organizations in India, *The International Journal of Human Resource Management* 9 (1): 155–67.

Budhwar, P. (1998) *Comparative Human Resource Management: A Cross-National Study of India and Britain*, unpublished PhD thesis, Manchester: Manchester Business School.

Budhwar, P. and Sparrow, P.R. (1997) Evaluating levels of strategic integration and devolvement of human resource management in India, *The International Journal of Human Resource Management* 8 (4): 476–94.

Hofstede, G. (1991) *Culture's Consequences: Software of the Mind*, London: McGraw-Hill.

Jain, H. C. (1991) Is there a coherent human resource management system in India?, *International Journal of Manpower*, 12 (1): 10–17.

Kanungo, R.N. and Jaeger, A.M. (1990) Introduction; the need for indogenous management in developing countries, in A.M Jaeger and R.N. Kanungo (eds) *Management in Developing Countries*, London: Routledge.

Kanungo, R.N. and Mendonca, M. (1994) Culture and performance improvement, *Productivity* 35 (3): 447–53.

Krishna, A. and Monappa, A. (1994) Economic restructuring and human resource management, *Indian Journal of Industrial Relations* 29: 490–501.

Mathur, P., Aycan, Z. and Kanungo, R.N. (1996) Work cultures in Indian organisations: a comparison between public and private sector, *Psychology and Developing Society* 8 (2): 199–222.

Ratnam, C.S.V. (1992) *Managing People: Strategies for Success*, New Delhi: Global Business.

Ratnam, C.S.V. (1995) Economic liberalization and the transformation of industrial relations policies in India, in. A. Verma, T. A. Kochan and R. D. Lansbury (eds) *Employment Relations in the Growing Asian Economies*, London: Routledge.

Ratnam, C.S.V. and Chandra, V. (1996) Sources of diversity and the challenge before human resource management in India, *International Journal of Manpower* 17 (4/5): 76–108.

Sahay, S. and Walsham, G. (1997) Social structure and managerial agency in India, *Organization Studies* 18 (3): 415–44.

Sharma, I.J. (1984) The culture context of Indian managers, *Management and Labour Studies* 9 (2): 72–80.

Silveria, D.M. (1988) *Human Resource Development: The Indian Experience*, New Delhi: New India Publications.

Singh, J.P. (1990) Managerial culture and work-related values in India, *Organisation Studies* 11 (1): 75–101.

Sinha, J.B.P. (1990) *Work Culture in Indian Context*, New Delhi: Sage Publications.

Sinha, J.B.P. and Sinha, D. (1990) Role of social values in Indian organisations, *International Journal of Psychology* 25: 705–14.

Sparrow, P. and Budhwar, P. (1996) Human resource management in India in the new economic environment, in A. Saxena and H. Devedi (eds) *HRM in the New Economic Environment*, Jaipur: National Publishing House, pp. 28–73.

Sparrow, P.R. and Budhwar, P. (1997) Competition and change: mapping the Indian HRM recipe against world wide patterns, *Journal of World Business* 32 (3): 224–42.

Tayeb, M. (1988) *Organisations and National Culture*, London: Sage Publications.

Thomas, A.S. and Philip, A. (1994) India: management in an ancient and modern civilisation, *International Studies of Management and Organisation* 24 (1–2): 91–115.

Chinese Style of Business: *Ji* and Others

Tony Fang

Travelling in China, international business students can hardly fail to notice that Sun Tzu (Sunzi) is the best-known Chinese in the local Chinese business literature; Chinese businesspeople are taught to apply his *Art of War* in doing business. Moreover, military terminology is extensively used in Chinese business and economic life. Zhu Rongji, 'China's economic czar', provided an example recently. At his first press conference as China's fifth premier in the Great Hall of the People on 19 March, 1998, Zhu declared:

> No matter what is ahead of me, whether landmines or an abyss, I will brace myself for it. I have no hesitation and no misgivings, and I will do my very best and devote myself to the people and country until the last day of my life.[1]

Zhu's firm commitment to reform left a strong impression on the public. In the light of the obstacles, challenges and dangers incumbent in transforming China into a market-oriented economy, and of the pressures of current Asian financial turmoil, Zhu was certainly making a serious declaration rather than a symbolic statement. Equally impressive, however, was the military terminology Zhu used to express his ambition; Zhu sounded like a general commander in a battlefield rather than a chief economic architect in a marketplace.

Sun Tzu's strategic teaching has significant impact on Chinese style of business. Sun Tzu was a famous ancient Chinese military strategist who lived 2300 years ago. He once served as a general commander for the King of Wu and demonstrated his superb talents in military strategy. Sun Tzu's *The Art of War*, a 13-chapter military treatise, is heralded as 'the earliest of known treatises on the subject, but has never been surpassed in comprehensiveness and depth of understanding' (Hart 1982: v). *The Art of War* has been regarded as the most influential classical strategic thinking in East Asia which has significant influence not only on Chinese, but also Korean and Japanese styles of business (Chen 1995).

The key to understanding Sun Tzu's strategic thinking lies in an indigenous Chinese word that is largely unknown to the West: *ji*. *The Art of War* opens with the 'Chapter of *Ji*' in which the art of war is described as manipulation of various kinds of *jis*. Sun Tzu (1982: 66) said:

> If a general who heeds my strategy [*ji*] is employed, he is certain to win. Retain him! When one who refuses to listen to my strategy [*ji*] is employed, he is certain to be defeated. Dismiss him![2]

In Chinese, *ji* means idea, plan, ruse, stratagem, tactics (as a noun); meter, gauge (as a noun); and to count, compute, calculate, number (as a verb). *Ji* can be understood as a carefully devised scheme with which to cope with difficult situations and gain psychological and material advantages over opponents. Chinese culture offers many *ji*-related sayings. One, for example, goes like this: 'The *ji* for the whole year lies in the spring; the *ji* for the whole day lies in the morning; the ji for the whole family lies in harmony; and the *ji* for the whole life lies in diligence.' *Ji* is a neutral word that can convey both positive and negative meanings depending on how it is used. *Ji* is neither strategy, nor tactics, but rather a combination of both. I prefer to translate *ji* into English as *Chinese stratagem*.

A variety of Chinese stratagems are taught in *The Art of War*: e.g. comparison, leadership, shared vision, delegation of power, conquer by stratagems, create a situation, prudence, initiative, quick fighting, deception, extraordinary troops, flanking, flexibility, focus and espionage (Mun 1990). If asked to telescope them into one sentence, I point to Sun Tzu's (1982: 77) famous aphorism: 'To win one hundred victories in one hundred battles is not the acme of skill. To subdue the enemy without fighting is the acme of skill.' Sun Tzu's strategic thinking strikes chords in harmony with Taoist Wu Wei ('to do nothing') principle, the true meaning of which, however, is not 'to do nothing' but 'to do without doing', 'to fight without fighting', or 'to manage without managing'. Hence, *The Art of War* is virtually about the 'art of non-war': a skilful strategist conquers the enemy without fighting it and takes the enemy's cities without bloodying swords.

Exhibit 20.1 The 36 Chinese Stratagems (*Ji's*)

Ji 1   Cross the sea without Heaven's knowledge.
Ji 2   Besiege Wei to rescue Zhao.
Ji 3   Kill with a borrowed knife.
Ji 4   Await leisurely the exhausted enemy.
Ji 5   Loot a burning house.
Ji 6   Clamour in the east but attack in the west.
Ji 7   Create something out of nothing.
Ji 8   Openly repair the walkway but secretly march to Chen Cang.
Ji 9   Watch the fire burning from across the river.
Ji 10   Hide a knife in a smile.
Ji 11   Let the plum tree wither in place of the peach tree.
Ji 12   Lead away a goat in passing.
Ji 13   Beat the grass to startle the snake.
Ji 14   Borrow a corpse to return the soul.
Ji 15   Lure the tiger to leave the mountains.
Ji 16   In order to capture, first let it go.
Ji 17   Toss out a brick to attract a piece of jade.
Ji 18   To capture bandits, first capture the ringleader.
Ji 19   Remove the firewood from under the cooking pot.
Ji 20   Muddle the water to catch the fish.
Ji 21   The golden cicada sheds its shell.
Ji 22   Shut the door to catch the thief.
Ji 23   Befriend the distant states while attacking the nearby ones.
Ji 24   Borrow the road to conquer Guo.
Ji 25   Steal the beams and change the pillars.
Ji 26   Point at the mulberry tree but curse the locust tree.
Ji 27   Play a sober-minded fool.
Ji 28   Lure the enemy on to the roof, then take away the ladder.
Ji 29   Flowers bloom in the tree.
Ji 30   The guest becomes the host.

Ji 31   The beautiful woman stratagem.
Ji 32   The empty city stratagem.
Ji 33   The counterespionage stratagem.
Ji 34   The self-torture stratagem.
Ji 35   The stratagem of interrelated stratagems.
Ji 36   Running away is the best stratagem.

Source: Fang (1999: 166).

China's 5000-year-long history, with its wars, misery, famine, trickery, large population and intensified interpersonal interactions, has enabled the Chinese people to summarise their wisdom of surviving disasters, overcoming hardships, and handling subtleties of interpersonal relationships into a short compendium: *The 36 Stratagems* (see Exhibit 20.1).[3] The work, known as *Sanshiliu Ji* in Chinese, was compiled by an anonymous Chinese writer in the late Ming (1368–1644) and/or early Qing (1644–1911) dynasties. These 36 Chinese stratagems are a mirror image of Sun Tzu's philosophy of victory without fighting: deal with the opponent by using deception, a 'borrowed knife', or an external force instead of engaging in head-on fighting. *The 36 Stratagems* provides a key to much of Chinese thinking (von Senger 1991) and a means for comprehending Chinese behaviour, including both deliberate and inadvertent actions (Gao 1991).

China has had a rich '*ji* culture' (*jimou wenhua*) since ancient times. The Chinese learn the concept of *ji* early in their childhood from folklore, theatre, radio and TV plays, or even grandfather's bedtime stories of *The Art of War*, *The 36 Stratagems*, *Romance of the Three Kingdoms*, *Water Margin*, *Journey to the West*, etc. Chinese stratagems are expressed in the form of idioms, most of which contain no more than four Chinese characters arranged so that when recited they produce a rhythmic effect, making it easy even for children to remember them. Chiao (1981: 429) maintains that Chinese stratagems 'form a highly sophisticated, extensive and enduring tradition in Chinese culture; what are manifested by the contemporary Chinese, communist or non-communist alike in this regard are basically the continuation of this everlasting tradition.'

The following is a Chinese proverb: 'The marketplace is like a battlefield.' Behind the proverb lies the Chinese belief that the wisdom that guides the general commander in the battlefield is the same one that guides all of us in our daily life, including business life (Chu 1991). Therefore, military strategies, tactics and terminology can be utilised logically in business and economic settings, according to the Chinese. Chinese organisations place high value on morale, discipline, flexibility and information collection, an orientation reminiscent of many insights from military operations.

My research into Chinese business negotiating style shows that when a highly trusting relationship is absent, *ji* is most likely to be employed, deliberately or inadvertently, by the Chinese as influence tactics to gain advantage over the other party (Fang 1999). Look at Chinese negotiating tactics. A Chinese negotiator typically does not force you to cut your price but rather subtly hints that your competitors are offering better offers next door. This is a typical 'Kill with a borrowed knife' (*Ji* 3, Exhibit 20.1) trick. Penetrating beneath various Chinese negotiating tactics that are often talked about in business management literature, we find the Chinese tend to use deception, a 'borrowed knife', an external force, or a created situation to induce you into doing business the Chinese way. The distinctiveness of Chinese negotiating tactics lies in the Chinese capacity to play *ji* – like playing Tai Chi – borrowing the opponent's force to knock the opponent off balance. Some of these tactics are listed as follows:

- playing competitors off against one another ('Kill with a borrowed knife'; *Ji* 3, Exhibit 20.1)
- attacking the opponent's weaknesses ('Besiege Wei to rescue Zhao'; *Ji* 2, Exhibit 20.1)
- utilise one's own weaknesses ('The self-torture stratagem'; *Ji* 34, Exhibit 20.1)
- playing home court ('Await leisurely the exhausted enemy'; *Ji* 4, Exhibit 20.1)
- making 'ridiculous' demands ('Clamour in the east but attack in the west'; *Ji* 6, Exhibit 20.1)
- stalling ('Watch the fire burning from across the river'; *Ji* 9, Exhibit 20.1)
- making surprising actions ('Openly repair the walkway but secretly march to Chen Cang'; *Ji* 8, Exhibit 20.1)
- teaming up with a strong partner ('Borrow a corpse to return the soul'; *Ji* 14, Exhibit 20.1)
- flattering ('Hide a knife in a smile'; *Ji* 10, Exhibit 20.1)
- shaming ('Beat the grass to startle the snake'; *Ji* 13, Exhibit 20.1)
- feigning anger ('Point at the mulberry tree but curse the locust tree'; *Ji* 26, Exhibit 20.1)
- playing the white face/red face ('Let the plum tree wither in place of the peach tree'; *Ji* 11, Exhibit 20.1)

Although Chinese business style can be explained from the *ji* perspective, we must not forget the influence of other sociocultural factors. Chinese culture has been moulded fundamentally by Confucianism, a philosophical doctrine founded by Confucius (551–479 BC). Confucianism influences Chinese behaviour through the Confucian values, such as moral cultivation, the importance of interpersonal relationships, family orientation, respect for age and hierarchy, the need for harmony, and the concept of face (Tu 1984; Lockett 1990; Tan 1990; Child and Markoczy 1993; Fang 1999). From the Confucian perspective, we see that the Chinese view business transactions essentially as an ongoing problem-solving relationship (*guanxi*) instead of a one-off legal package. The Chinese attach great importance to mutual trust and benefit in doing business, a direct manifestation of the reciprocal Confucian attitude toward interpersonal relationships, known in Chinese as *li shang wang lai* ('Courtesy demands reciprocity' or 'Deal with a person as he or she deals with you'). Chinese lawyers seldom formally show up at the international business negotiation table; the Confucian aversion to law can be discerned from behaviour. The Chinese like to do business with large international famous firms and *face* is an important cultural and psychological factor. In Chinese organisations, management is centralised, authoritarian, charismatic, personalised, hierarchical, and consensus seeking, a style that owes much to the legacy of Confucianism.

We also need to refer to China's basic national conditions, especially its political-economic system, to understand Chinese business mentality. China's ideological linkage to communism, centralised economic planning and control structure, unsophisticated legal regime, lack of technology and capital, underdeveloped infrastructure, large population, low average education level, low per capita living standard, ongoing reforms, and fast changes all have their imprints on Chinese business style. The Chinese Communist Party (CCP) and Chinese government play a decisive role in the management of Chinese economy. The central government has never loosened its political control despite reforms and economic decentralisation (Huang 1996). Chinese politics has an all-pervasive influence on Chinese decision making that can be either 'crazily quick' or 'tremendously slow' (Huang, Leonard, and Chen 1997). Understanding China's political and economic situations and providing the right technologies and products to satisfy China's priority needs and wants are the key to success. China is one of the world's largest countries in both geographic (9,600,000 sq km) and demographic (1.2112bn in 1995) terms. The Chinese seem to know the monetary value of their market as well as that of advanced foreign technologies. To exchange the large China market for advanced foreign technologies is China's state policy guiding Chinese firms' attitude toward foreign technology transfer to China. The Chinese are technology and price sensitive in Sino-Western business negotiations, a style considerably influenced by China's basic conditions. The Chinese are tough business negotiators because bargaining is a Chinese way of life within Chinese bureaucratic institutions.

For a long time in the past, Chinese economy, a copy of the former Soviet Union's economic model, were extremely centralised. Chinese enterprises were simply the government's appendages rather than independent economic entities and they lacked decision-making power in business management. Market, competition, customer, quality, service and innovation were unknown concepts in Mao's China. Pre-reform HRM, for example, was characterised by Maoist *tiefanwan* ('[Everyone has an] iron rice bowl') and *daguofan* ('[Eating from the same] big rice pot'): everyone was offered guaranteed lifetime employment and more or less the same 'from cradle to grave' welfare package regardless of whether they were doing a good job or not. As a result, as Wall (1990: 22) observes: 'Many do not choose to work hard; they are indifferent to quality standards; they avoid responsibility; and they consider customers a nuisance.'

China is in the process of dramatic change. Market-oriented reforms since 1978 have gradually decentralised Chinese economy. Now, local governments are enjoying more economic decision-making power and enterprises greater operational autonomy. By the end of 1995, China had approved a total of 258,000 foreign-invested enterprises with contractual foreign investment of $395.7bn and actual invested capital of $135.4bn (Xu 1996). Competition has been introduced into the economy. State-owned enterprises (SOEs), private businesses, joint ventures (JVs), wholly foreign owned enterprises (WFOEs), etc. are now operating side by side in China. Foreign trade is now handled not only by foreign trade corporations (FTCs) under MOFTEC (Ministry of Foreign Trade and Economic Cooperation) as it previously was, but also by a large number of FTCs under various ministries and even by individual plants. *Tiefanwan* and *daguofan* are being broken down to allow a more market-oriented mechanism to regulate the HRM. A large-scale survey of Chinese cities shows that despite complaints, 85 per cent of interviewees agree that reforms have provided unprecedented opportunities for people to demonstrate individual talents (Tan 1993).

Contrary to the past, market, competition, customer, quality, service, innovation, technology and R&D have entered into the new China business lexicon. As this is being written, millions of Chinese workers are being or will be laid off in China's ambitious process of privatising the debt-ridden firms from among China's 300,000 SOEs. The reform-minded Zhu Rongji government will certainly bring many new changes to Chinese economy in the years to come, which in turn will impact on Chinese business style. We have reason to believe that, in the future, Chinese managers will be more open-minded and internationally adapted; more Chinese will be able to use English and other foreign languages to communicate efficiently with their foreign counterparts; legalism will be more respected in China and Chinese lawyers will increasingly show up at the international business negotiation table. China's continuing market-oriented reform and acquisition of foreign investments will speed up this process.

Notes

1 *China Daily*, (1998) Zhu promises no delay over reforms, 20 March: 1.
2 *Ji* is translated by Samuel B. Griffith as 'strategy' in Sun Tzu 1982.
3 For a detailed historical and legendary account of *The 36 Stratagems*, interested readers are referred to Chu (1991), Gao (1991), and von Senger (1991).

Further reading

Burstein, D. and **de Keijzer, A.** (1998) *Big Dragon: China's Future: What it Means for Business, the Economy, and the Global Order*, New York: Simon & Schuster. This book is about the impact China will have on the global balance of wealth and power in the twenty-first century. A valuable debate on China's politics, economy, and other basic national characteristics as well as their implications for the economy, business, and global order.

Child, J. (1994) *Management in China during the Age of Reform*, Cambridge: Cambridge University Press. This book analyses management issues in current China in both Chinese state-owned enterprises and Sino-foreign joint-venture contexts. It covers areas such as enterprise leadership, decision making, the management of marketing and purchasing transactions, the work roles of senior managers, personnel practices and reward systems.

References

Chen, M. (1995) *Asian Management Systems: Chinese, Japanese and Korean Styles of Business*, London: Routledge.

Chiao, C. (1981) Chinese strategic behaviours: a preliminary list, in *Proceedings of the International Conference on Sinology*, Taipei, 15–17 August 1980, Academia Sinica, Taipei, pp. 429–40.

Child, J. and **Markoczy L.** (1993) Host-country management behaviour and learning in Chinese and Hungarian joint ventures, *Journal of Management Studies*, 30 (4): 611–31.

Chu, C.-N. (1991) *The Asian Mind Game*, New York: Rawson Associates.

Fang, T. (1999) *Chinese Business Negotiating Style*, Thousand Oaks: Sage Publications.

Gao, Y. (1991) *Lure the Tiger out of the Mountains: The Thirty-Six Stratagems of Ancient China*, New York: Simon & Schuster.

Hart, B.H.L. (1982) Foreword to *Sun Tzu: The Art of War*, trans. by Samuel B. Griffith, London: Oxford University Press, pp. v–vii.

Huang, Q., Joseph, L. and **Tong, C.** (1997) *Business Decision Making in China*, New York; International Business Press.

Huang, Y. (1996) *Inflation and Investment Controls in China: the Political Economy of Central–Local Relations during the Reform Era*, Cambridge: Cambridge University Press.

Lockett, M. (1990) The nature of Chinese culture, in J. Child and M. Lockett (eds) *Advances in Chinese Industrial Studies*, vol. 1, Part A, Greenwich: JAI Press, pp. 269–76.

Mun, K.-C. (1990) The competition model of Sun Tzu's art of war, in Hong Kuang (ed.) *Encyclopedia of Modern Marketing*, Beijing: Economics and Management Press, pp. 930–5 (in Chinese).

Sun, T. (1982) *Sun Tzu: The Art of War*, (trans. Samuel B. Griffith), London: Oxford University Press.

Tan, C.-H. (1990) Management concepts and Chinese culture, in J. Child and M. Lockett (eds) *Advances in Chinese Industrial Studies*, vol. 1, Part A, Greenwich: JAI Press, pp. 277–88.

Tan, H.-K. (1993) Urban dwellers try to keep pace with reforms, *China Daily*, 21 January, Beijing.

Tu, W.-M. (1984) *Confucian Ethics Today: The Singapore Challenge*, Singapore: Federal Publications.

von Senger, H. (1991) *The Book of Stratagems*, New York: Viking Penguin.

Wall, J.A. Jr. (1990) Managers in the People's Republic of China, *Acadamy of Management Executive* 4 (2): 19–32.

Xu, Y.-C. (1996) Good prospects for further expansion of Sino-Swedish trade and economic co-operation, in *China: Marketplace* (May), Stockholm: Grossistförbundet Svensk Handel.

Chapter summary

This chapter discussed various HRM and other managerial practices in the US, Western and Eastern Europe, China, India, Japan and the Middle East Arab countries. According to these discussions, a wide variety of management styles and ways of doing business exists in the world. They offer both opportunities and pose a challenge to multinational firms. It is therefore crucial for these firms to understand these opportunities and challenges, their sociocultural and political-economic roots, and prepare their workforce and managers for their tasks.

Closing Case Study:
Changes on the shop floors in South Africa
Monir Tayeb

A welter of legislation has defined a new constitution for the workplace. Few places in South Africa have felt the impact of majority rule more keenly than the shop floors of its factories.

Since the African National Congress assumed power in 1994 its allies in the trade union movement have probably benefited more than any other group. A welter of legislation, beginning with the Labour Relations Act of 1996, has defined a new constitution for the workplace. It has yet to win investors' confidence.

The dismantling of apartheid legislation has brought immediate benefits by removing many arcane labour practices. Industrial unrest has declined and productivity is rising faster than other indicators. Stoppages because of strikes have fallen from 3.1m working days in 1992 to 650,000 in 1997, the lowest since 1987.

The progress has been largely discounted in the capital markets for three reasons. First, the improvements come off a very low base and are based on comparisons with an era when political protests routinely distorted the labour market.

Second, they are firmly based on the co-operation of trade unions, whose influence has been enshrined in statute. Third, there are more battles ahead as the government prepares to implement its most controversial labour legislation yet, an Employment Equity Bill.

The increased influence of the Congress of South African Trade Unions, the largest labour federation, has not resulted in higher wage settlements. Average wage increases have outpaced inflation and are forecast to continue this year at the 1997 level of 9–10 per cent while inflation falls towards 5 per cent. But settlements in unionised sectors have been consistently lower than in those that fall outside the new negotiating framework.

Stripped of its political role, organised labour is learning a new pragmatism. Rising competition in most sectors, and an overall reduction in jobs as companies adjust to a less protected environment, have provided an incentive to avert industrial action. This trend has been encouraged by new statutory structures, which require industry-wide collective bargaining to be mandatory in most sectors.

New mechanisms for conciliation and arbitration have reduced the proportion of strikes triggered by non-wage related issues. Pay disputes triggered 71 per cent of strikes in 1997 compared with 57.4 per cent in 1996.

Settlements have also been handled more swiftly as centralised bargaining chambers have removed many of the most contentious issues from the factory floor. Despite this record, the relatively sophisticated structures inherent in the new legislation have been widely criticised by business as ill-suited to a developing country. Correcting the worst inefficiencies of apartheid labour practices has proved an easier task than creating a simple structure to please investors.

A recent report by BOE Securities, a Johannesburg stockbroker, rates the labour market as 'an unqualified negative' in investors' perceptions. 'The external environment is not only reshaping economic policy but causing a fatalism among policy-makers,' says Ebrahim Patel, secretary-general of the South African Clothing and Textile Workers' Union. 'Whatever one's view, the labour movement is the most articulate exponent of an alternative strategy.'

These differences came to a head last year during an emotive and largely rhetorical debate between trade unions and organised business over the Basic Conditions of Employment Act.

The law will impose a 45-hour working week, increase rates of overtime pay, entrench the role of trade unions in sectoral bargaining and introduce statutory conditions of employment in even the lowest-paid, and previously unregulated, industries.

Its sequel, this year's Employment Equity Bill, will trigger similar antagonism at the National Economic Development and Labour Council, a tripartite body set up to represent the interests of labour and business in policy making.

The law will compel companies with more than 50 staff to draw up plans to develop a workforce whose racial composition reflects that of the country. A government watchdog will monitor progress.

The Bill recognises mitigating factors that could frustrate efforts to achieve these targets. Employers are not compelled to fire existing staff to make room for Blacks. The unavailability of skills, a shrinking labour force or lower-than-expected labour turnover will also count as valid excuses. But, after five years, companies deemed not to have tried hard enough will face fines.

Source: *Financial Times* CD-ROM, 1 January–31 December 1998.

Questions

1 South Africa now has in place a new labour relations legislation. What triggered it off?
2 What have been the major impacts of various Labour Relations Acts?
3 What are the main criticisms of the new labour legislation?

CHAPTER 21

Transferring Management Policies and Practices across Borders

Monir Tayeb

Learning objectives

By the end of this chapter you will:

- be familiar with the general debate surrounding the issue of transferability of management policies and practices across nations

- have an understanding of the cultural prerequisites of certain Japanese management practices that in the past two decades or so especially have attracted Western companies' attention

- be aware of the need for the compatibility of imported management practices with local cultures and the need to train home employees to master such practices

- be aware of the similar compatibility between imported management teaching practices and courses with local cultural and non-cultural environments within which managers attending such courses have to operate.

Opening Case Study:
East meets West: Western classical music in China

The British Council in China is about to bring off a coup: it plans to import the Royal Opera to christen an opera house in Shanghai. Covent Garden's *Tosca* will be backed by a Chinese chorus and Chinese technicians. One more sign, if any were needed, of the renaissance that Western classical music is enjoying in a city where it flourished before Mao snuffed it out.

That renaissance seems nationwide. Other signs include mezzo Jiang Guan being voted Cardiff Singer of the World; Beijing stampeding for tickets when Pavarotti comes to sing; and a piano being the status symbol for the pampered Chinese child.

▶

For a land where Western music was not long ago calibrated in purely negative terms – Debussy being 'useless', Schumann 'unhealthily introspective' and Beethoven at best 'harmless' – this change is dramatic. But is it real, or just skin-deep?

The music students playing non-stop in my hotel foyer are impressively accomplished, as are the teenage instrumentalists of the Hua Yin Youth Orchestra. None of the middle-class children in this sparky band intend to make music a career, but many will clearly be first-rate amateurs. Dropping in on them practising at the Conservatory with the ebullient Jiang Guan, I find blowers, bangers and scrapers every bit as good as their coevals in London.

I get an upbeat view from conductor Chen Zuohuang, artistic director of the China National Symphony Orchestra (and in his spare time, Music Director of its counterpart in the Kansas city of Wichita). The middle-class urge to buy pianos betokens a big new audience in the future, he says; sales of his orchestra's first two CDs – 600,000 in one year – indicate the already existing audience. 'What strikes me, when we tour the Chinese provinces, is how hungry people are for classical music. Our recent concert in Nanjing was the first in that city's history, and they turned it into a festival. By the time we arrived, every pump-attendant knew about us. It didn't feel like a normal concert – it was from the heart, to the heart. That is what Chinese people love about Western classical music, and it goes for my young players too. They're not jaded, as so many are in the West.'

But he concedes that Western classical music in China has a hard row to hoe. The country has just 20 symphony orchestras – for a population comprising 22 per cent of the entire human race – and many of those only perform sporadically. Funding is the problem: the sudden emergence of a market economy has left state-funded orchestras – and above all opera companies – high and dry, with enough cash for salaries, but not enough to finance productions. Chen balances his books with the aid of money from Exxon, Boeing, General Motors and sundry firms in Hong Kong.

Some musicians gloomily predict that Western classical music will never be truly enshrined in the Chinese consciousness. The flautist Liu Ning, who teaches at Tsinghua University, thinks it can never cross the divide between town and country. 'In China it will always be the music of the educated classes. Poor peasants will never understand it. Their music will always be home-grown Chinese.'

But what strikes me is the tenacity with which Liu and his friends are fighting for the music they love. Liu's secondary schooling was dominated by Red Guard thugs; and his real education continued at home where his parents secretly taught him to play the 'corrupt' music of the West. Chen, too, recalls clandestine studies: 'I had to learn music in a totally silent world.'

Professor Yang Hongnian is an intense little man with Lisztean locks who receives me flanked by his piano-professor wife and 30-year-old conductor son, Li. Yang the elder had a glittering career as a composer and chorus-master, but then came the Cultural Revolution, during which he and his wife were forced to work in the fields. When I ask if this brought his musical activities to a halt, he proudly hands me a thick book, *The Art of Choral Training*, which he penned during the long nights of exile. 'Because my father lost all that time,' explains Li, 'he now feels he must work twice as hard to regain it.'

They play me some recordings of the Children and Young Women's Choir that Yang has created: exhilarating stuff, Kodaly with a Chinese tinge. Meanwhile Li, who has just finished his conducting studies in Stuttgart, stresses the fact that, along with other musician friends, he has decided to come home. 'We believe in the future of classical music in China.'

Source: *Financial Times* CD-ROM, 1 January–31 December 1998.

Introduction

In this chapter the discussion of culture and organisations is extended to encompass the transferability of management policies and practices across borders, with special emphasis on issues related to human resource and people management. In order to examine the effectiveness of cross-national transfers, certain fashionable Japanese HRM practices are analysed with a view to examining their cultural roots, and the policies importing companies might adopt to make such transferred practices workable for them. This issue is then discussed within the context of Central and Eastern European nations which are moving away from a centrally planned system to a more decentralised and non-socialist one. The case of developing countries will also be considered here. The chapter then focuses on the issue of imported management-teaching models that certain developing countries try to emulate in order to equip their managers for the challenges ahead.

Transfer of management practices across cultures

Many managers understandably attempt to learn from their more successful counterparts elsewhere. As *The Economist* (1996) puts it, today's ambitious managers spend their holidays not on the beach, but on pilgrimages to the world's best-run companies. They visit Florida's Disney World to study Uncle Walt's 'pixi dust' formula for managing people, or small American firms such as Springfield Re-Manufacturing and Johnsonville Sausage, which have pioneered new fads, or visit Toyota City to learn about lean production.

Managers pay such visits abroad with the primary intention of improving their own companies' performance (Womack *et al.* 1990; Osterman 1994; Macduffie 1995). But sometimes, in the name of modernisation and learning from foreigners, they force through changes in their organisational structure and management practices which might otherwise provoke a great deal of resentment and resistance from their employees (Arthur 1987).

If we look back and examine the development of management thinking and models, we notice that initially it was the US companies and, perhaps to a lesser extent, Western European firms that provided 'best' models. Many countries, especially the developing ones, looked to these models for inspiration on their way to industrialisation (see, for instance, Amante 1995; Latifi 1997). Some, notably Japan, succeeded and others failed miserably, quite possibly on national cultural grounds (Hofstede 1980). Currently, the transitional economies of Central and Eastern Europe look to capitalist countries to learn new 'ways of doing things', with varying degrees of success.

Job flexibility, teamwork, quality circles, no-strike agreements, local as opposed to national pay bargaining, and de-unionisation, in short Japanisation, are very fashionable in some Western countries, notably the US and Britain. Other foreign practices such as Sweden's Volvo and Saab approach have also had their followers.

But are management practices originated in a country with its own specific sociocultural characteristics transferable to another country with different traits?

The answer seems to be a qualified yes. Human beings, throughout their history have always tried, sometimes quite successfully, to learn from others. Management techniques, including human resource management practices, are no exception.

Academic researchers have debated the issue for a long time. The arguments range from the 'universality' of such ideas to their 'strictly culture-bound and non-transferable' nature. In practice, however, a position somewhere between these two extremities is more likely to be the case.

There are certain practices that can easily be imported from abroad with few difficulties, such as assembly-line production techniques. There are some more complex practices which need to be modified and adapted to local conditions in order to be properly operational, such as quality circles. Some practices such as participative management require extensive management and employees training and reorientation. In these latter cases it is important that these ideas be implemented with due regard to local conditions. Let us discuss these points in detail.

In Chapter 19 it was argued that there are certain aspects of organisations that are more prone to cultural influences than others. We could apply the same argument to the question of cross-national transfer of management practices. Those practices that affect the universal, hard aspects of organisations, such as technology, it is argued, could more easily be transferred from one country to another compared with the soft, culture specific aspects, such as human relations.

Take operating computers and robots in offices and shopfloors, for example. There is nothing inherently cultural in being able to work these machines. It is sometimes simply a matter of willingness on the part of the operators and their supervisors to arrange for suitable on-the-job training. Educational establishments from school to universities can also be funded and encouraged to teach these skills to the pupils and students and equip them for their future employment.

Culture in its narrow sense, in terms of values and attitudes such as, for instance, individualism and collectivism, has no significant role to play here. It is rather the socioeconomic and political institutions of society that prepare people for using the technology. True, technologies and their application may require applying specific subordinate–superior relationships and people-management styles, which might be rooted in culture. But these can be learned and mastered in due course through training and shared experiences.

At a more strategic level, such as fighting off competition, the acquisition of new plants, merging, exporting, importing and setting up subsidiaries abroad, business imperatives, rather than culture, may dictate the way in which companies have to function. For instance, if an emerging economy of Eastern Europe allows only joint ventures with local firms as the only foreign investment mode within its territory, for a company wishing to enter that market a joint venture is the only option, regardless of its managers' cultural values and attitudes.

We could argue that these national level policies are in turn influenced by culture. This might be true, but not slavishly so. The wind of trade liberalisation, privatisation, deregulation and the like, which is currently sweeping through many countries, covers in its course a wide range of cultures, from the individualistic France to the collectivist India, from the high-power distance Brazil to the low-power distance Britain, from the masculine Japan to the feminine Thailand.

Then there is the soft, people-management aspect of the organisation: human resources management, leadership style, authority relationships and the like.

These were argued in the previous chapter to be strongly influenced by culture. In this chapter it is argued that management practices that involve these aspects of organisations may be more difficult, sometimes even undesirable, to transfer across cultural divides.

Exhibit 21.1 The 'fisherman mentality' of Icelanders and foreign management techniques

Probably the best way to understand certain aspects of Icelandic society and the working of its organisations is to define the 'fisherman mentality'. The fishing industry is and has been the most important sector of Iceland's economy and has had to contend with a very unstable economic environment, which complicates the running of companies. Nevertheless, a short-term orientation and slowness in adopting new approaches to management cannot be explained by history and the unfavourable business environment alone. There is something more far-reaching to it, and this is the fisherman mentality.

A fisherman is dependent on luck and therefore sees no need to plan how long he will fish. He goes fishing and hopes for fast results. If he does not catch any fish soon, he may give up fishing for the day or try to find a better location. A fisherman may fish in the company of colleagues but is not necessarily concerned about what they have on their hooks or how much they catch. All that matters is how much he personally catches. A fisherman is not constrained by punctuality or by much organisation. He is flexible and will work hard when the fishing season is good. Finally, the fisherman tends to think he knows his job and is thus not very eager to adopt new or different fishing techniques.

These characteristics are reflected in the organisation and management of Icelandic companies. In fact, many Icelanders still have a very pragmatic approach to management. 'A fisherman society does not have the same need for management as industrial societies,' says Sigurlaugsson (1995), in order to explain why Icelanders have been slow to introduce new management techniques. Management in Iceland tends, therefore, to be marked by a lack of long-term goals and the required tenacity to hold on to them, as well as relatively low productivity, despite long working hours (Idntaeknistofnun Islands and Idnadarraduneyti 1987).

Because of the unorganised and individualistic nature of Icelandic society, a common orientation and perspective toward future achievement within companies and in the governing of the country is seriously lacking (Aflvaki 1994). Managers tend to be preoccupied with running their own departments and often ignore what is happening in other parts of the company.

Furthermore, Icelanders, through their short experience of business, have not developed any distinctive approach to organisational structures. As a consequence, there are mostly flat hierarchies within companies, owing to the egalitarian nature of the society, but there are also some steeper hierarchies, adopted some years back, in response to North American theories of task specialisation and accountability. Management with steep hierarchies

▶

and division of tasks is likely to undermine the success of some Icelandic companies because it does not fit well with local social mores and thus is not very likely to derive benefits from the existing Icelandic culture. Integrity, organisational commitment, and co-operative ability are what managers in Iceland can best harness for the purpose of running companies.

Source: Eyjolfsdottir and Smith (1997).

Let us illustrate the point about the problematic nature of the cross-culture of transfer of management techniques and styles at both national and organisational levels.

Take democracy and dictatorship as models of national management style. The political system of a society, like its other social institutions, creates and is created by the culture of that society. A democratic political system is developed and flourishes in cultures where people believe in sharing power and responsibility, where consultation and respect for other people's opinions are considered as strengths rather than weaknesses and where people demand to be consulted and regard themselves as equal to those in positions of power. These values and attitudes are, in turn, reinforced and perpetuated by the political climate they have helped to create. A non-democratic regime is usually seen in countries where the opposite values are held by people in general.

In countries where a certain type of political regime is imposed on people by foreign powers or through military coups, and that might be incompatible with the local culture, the regime will either collapse after a few years, or will lose much of its initial characteristics and will be modified to allow for local preferences.

Recent history gives us examples of the rejection of authoritarian regimes in fundamentally democratic countries: the short-lived Greek military government which was replaced after a few years by a democratic parliamentary regime in the 1970s; the return of constitutional monarchy to Spain after the death of General Franco; the rejection in 1989 of over 40 years of communism, which was imposed by the Soviet Union on the peoples of Central and Eastern European countries, are examples of this kind.

India is a case of democracy having been adapted over time to a culture that does not share all the prerequisite values to sustain it in its original form. Parliamentary democracy was imposed on India by outgoing British colonial rulers, and has changed in fundamental ways since it was first installed. The new features are much more in line with other sociocultural characteristics of the country as a whole (see, for instance, Segal 1971; Tayeb 1988).

At the organisational level, we can consider Japanese quality circles, teamwork, total quality management (TQM) and job flexibility, which many companies in both West and East have in the past two decades tried to emulate.

Quality circles

A quality circle, which is a vehicle for employee participation, is a small-group activity in which ordinary blue- and white-collar workers, usually employed on broadly similar work and led by their supervisor, volunteer to participate. Such volunteers are trained in problem-identification and problem-solving techniques. Quality-circle members may identify problems to solve themselves, or these may be suggested by others. Either way it is generally the members who select which specific problem to work on. Applying the training they have been given, they analyse the problem and try to arrive at solutions to it. The circle formally presents its analysis and findings to management who may accept or reject their recommendations. If its proposals are accepted and implemented, the circle will monitor progress for a period of time, making adjustments where appropriate, before moving on to another project (Hill 1987).

Cultural prerequisites for quality circles are, among others, employee commitment to organisational goals and objectives, a strong work ethic, group orientation, a willingness to participate in decision-making processes on the part of employees, a willingness to delegate authority and take other people's views into consideration on the part of their managers. It seems a culture that possesses all or some of these characteristics stands a better chance of instituting, importing and implementing quality circles successfully than other cultures.

Teamwork

Teamwork too is congruent with a collectivist culture, and may not necessarily find fertile grounds in individualistic countries. Moreover, it presupposes a willingness on the part of both employees and their managers to engage in collective decision making, to participate in decisions that may or may not affect their job directly, to hear other people out and value their views and contributions. This cultural argument aside, teamwork, as in the Japanese model in any case, goes hand in hand with team-based appraisal and reward policies.

Total quality management

TQM is an integrated approach to management that represents a holistic management philosophy rather than a series of techniques. In traditional British quality management, for example, usually after a batch of products or components are made by shopfloor workers, a quality inspector examines them for defects. If they do not like the finished product it will be thrown into the waste bin and may or may not be recycled at a later stage. TQM, by contrast, emphasises a built-in quality control at every stage of production and as a continuous process. More importantly, the inspector and the operator is one and the same. As a consequence, defects are noticed in the process of production and not after it is finished. This procedure in turn results in low wastage and even zero defects. The system does not preclude a final overall inspection of the finished product before leaving the shopfloor.

Here again the unstated assumption is that the operator is sufficiently committed to the organisation to pay careful attention to what they are doing and to prevent damages and defects. Furthermore, it is assumed that the manager has enough confidence and trust in the operator to let them make the product and check its quality as well.

This style of quality inspection works perfectly in companies and countries where there is a co-operative relationship between management and employees. It will be rather problematic in companies and countries where the management–worker relationship is characterised by a 'them and us' attitude.

Job flexibility

One of the features of many Japanese companies is that employees on recruitment work in various departments and learn how to perform various tasks, before eventually settling down in their 'own' job. This experience gives the new recruits a holistic view of the company and will make them a generalist rather than a specialist. The holistic view helps them have all other parts of the company in mind when making various decisions. The generalism gives them more technical and managerial flexibility and enables them to perform different tasks as and when required. Certain managerial styles and organisational and national cultural characteristics make such working arrangements obviously easier.

To be transferable to non-Japanese cultures, therefore, quality circles, teamwork, TQM, job flexibility and other practices, require the same cultural and organisational contexts as there are in Japan. However, this is a fatalistic view and is not entirely supported by evidence. What is important to note here is that these and other foreign models can be successfully implemented, given modifications to allow for local cultural and other contextual characteristics and also appropriate employee training.

This is what a British shopfloor employee told me recently in an interview:

> We had the traditional assembler who was just asked to sit down and put two things together, you know, for example. They are now being asked to assemble, to verify, to inspect, to test, now the situation is: 'There's the product, get on and build it.' How you do that, right, and if it means you instead of just doing assembly, and then somebody else inspecting it, now you just get it done, which creates more skills you know. It takes a long time in certain jobs to build up that skill and the same in what we call our main lines, where a person has different jobs, these people build the machines from A to Z, and some of them it takes up maybe one machine or two machines a day just because of the enormous bulk, different skills, and they acquired these skills on the job.

Moreover, the importation of foreign policies and practices calls for sensitivity to both national and organisational cultures and other characteristics inside and outside the organisation. It is ultimately this sensitivity to local sociocultural characteristics, rather than a crude imitation of foreign practices, that should be learned and mastered by managers when they consider adopting foreign practices.

Sensitivity to local conditions applies to foreign companies operating in a host country as well as the home-based firms that wish to learn from their foreign counterparts. Research evidence shows that a vast majority of multinational companies adopt a selective approach to taking their home-grown practices to their foreign subsidiaries. And even then they might in some cases introduce only variants of the originals (see, for instance, Oliver and Davies 1990; Oliver and Wilkinson 1992; Yang 1992; Tayeb 1994; Shadur *et al.* 1995).

Central and Eastern Europe and capitalist management models

Many companies in the ex-socialist countries of Central and Eastern Europe are tempted to import some of the capitalist countries' management practices. Multinationals with wholly owned subsidiaries or joint ventures located there are also keen to take their home-grown practices with them. However, the process of transfer from capitalist countries to ex-socialist ones is a great deal more complicated than when the transfer takes place between two capitalist countries.

This is because in capitalist countries companies generally perform *similar functions* but maybe in *different ways*. But in ex-socialist countries, when they were under communism, companies did not perform certain functions at all. In other words, the difference between capitalist and socialist countries is not only that of *style* but also of *substance*. For instance, an average manufacturing company in any capitalist country will have functions such as marketing, R&D, accounting, personnel/HRM, as a matter of course. In ex-socialist countries many of these functions were either out of the company's control or were not performed at all.

A company based in a capitalist country has also already developed these functions in accordance with its existing socioeconomic structure. When importing new ways of doing things from abroad, it may need to make certain adjustments to make them workable and to train its employees to work in new ways.

In ex-socialist countries, by contrast, companies have to start by adapting their existing functions to their new domestic economic conditions, then learn to perform new sets of functions that would be necessary to survive in the market. Then at a later stage they have to decide whether, for instance, to go for the Japanese or the German or the American style of doing things, or none at all.

From a Western multinational company's perspective, when deciding to transfer its home-grown practices to Central and Eastern European countries, there is yet another added complication: the cultural heterogeneity of these countries. It is true that the Soviet Union imposed on these countries similar political economic structures and institutions, but national character, which lies behind people's behaviour, is more than just the sum of a nation's social institutions. Culture, in term of values, attitudes and beliefs, is a deeply-rooted construct which may not necessarily be eradicated by an imposed regime. The stories of invasions, occupations and colonisation of various countries throughout history tell us as much.

As Kovach (1994) rightly points out, 'What may work in Warsaw may not work in Budapest. For example, the pervasiveness of the state security system in Romania (Securitate), compared with that in Hungary, has led to a relatively greater lack of trust between management and employees in Romanian organizations' (p.95).

Developing countries and advanced nations' management models

The question of the transfer of management practices is of crucial importance especially for less-developed nations. Many of these countries, in an attempt to upgrade their organisational systems and improve their performance, import various management techniques from the more advanced industrialised nations, especially the US. It is, however, important for managers from less-developed countries to be aware of the sociocultural and technological characteristics that are unique to their own societies, and to recognise the implications of these characteristics for their work organisations.

Let us consider the cultural characteristics of Arab Middle East nations and the US. Tables 21.1 and 21.2, extracted from an article by Bakhtari (1995), show major similarities and differences between the two cultures.

Table 21.1 **Major characteristics of American culture**

- Americans are very informal. They tend not to treat people differently even when there are great differences in age or social standing
- Americans are direct. They do not talk around things. They tend to say exactly what they mean. To some foreigners, this appears abrupt or even inappropriate behaviour
- Americans are competitive. They are self-focused and goal-oriented. Some foreigners find Americans assertive or overbearing
- Americans are achievers. They like to keep scores, whether at work or at play. They emphasise accomplishments
- Americans are independent and individualistic. They place a high value on freedom and believe that individuals can shape and control their own destinies
- Americans are questioners. They ask a lot of questions, even of someone they have just met. A significant part of an American student's education is learning to think, question and analyse
- Americans dislike silence. They would rather talk about the weather than deal with silence in a conversation
- Americans value punctuality. They keep appointments, calendars, and live according to schedules and clocks
- Americans are used to stability. They do not like uncertainty
- Americans value cleanliness. They often seem obsessed with bathing, eliminating body odours and wearing clean clothes
- Americans hold ethnocentric views. They believe that their culture and values are superior to all others

Source: Adapted from Bakhtari (1995).

Now imagine a company operating in the Middle East decides to import certain US-grown practices such as participative management style. The Americans themselves have, in general, the cultural prerequisites to function under this style, both as managers and as subordinates. The Middle Eastern employees and their managers' traditional upbringing has not, in general, prepared them for a participative management style. But there is nothing inherent in the participative management style that is beyond the ability of an average human being to learn; it might take time, determination and political will at both national and organisational levels, but it can be done.

Table 21.2 Major characteristics of Middle Eastern culture

- Middle Easterners are traditional. They appear to be religious. Islam has a tremendous effect on their lives. They strictly adhere to the rules and orders of Islam
- Middle Easterners are family-oriented. Family is the nucleus of Middle Eastern societies. They put special emphasis on family unity and coherence. Mothers in the family enjoy a divine respect
- Middle Easterners value friendship. They share all aspects of their lives with friends. Often, friends and neighbours are named in their wills
- Middle Easterners like consultation. Originating from Islam, consulting with others, particularly elders, is a common behaviour of Middle Easterners
- Middle Easterners are individualistic. Although their form of individualism is different from that of Americans, they are individualistic in the context of their own culture
- Middle Easterners are less participative, particularly in decision making. Important decisions are made only by high-level authorities
- Middle Easterners are very conservative in risk taking. They rely on intuition and instincts rather than data and procedures
- Middle Eastern societies and organisations are male-dominated. The level of female participation in management and social affairs is lower than that of most other societies.

Source: Adapted from Bakhtari (1995).

This point brings our discussion to teaching management practices.

Teaching management practices

The societal context of management practices plays a significant role in the character of such practices. It is argued here that the content and style of teaching of such practices should also reflect their wider context.

Nations differ from one another, among other things, in their needs, aspirations and objectives. Educational establishments reflect these and can respond effectively to them only if they tailor their practices accordingly. What, however, we observe in many business schools around the world is a separation of these schools from their wider context. Teaching style and content, exemplified in MBA and similar courses, seem to impart universal management-technique packages, while the learning needs of managers and students of management are far from being universal.

This point is particularly relevant to developing countries, many of which, in an attempt to upgrade their organisational systems and to improve their performance in the international market, import various management practices and educational techniques from the more advanced industrialised nations, without due regard to their own sociocultural and technological characteristics.

Take a developing country like India and a developed one like the UK, for example. India is a country that is trying to catch up with the industrialisation process and become a major player on the international scene. But it has to over-come certain obstacles and problems that are more or less unique to it: a colonial legacy, that slowed down its industrialisation; massive poverty; a high illiteracy rate; communal tension; poor infrastructure; and culturally rooted resistance to change (Tayeb 1996). As a consequence, the government has adopted a protec-tionist economic policy, among others, to encourage a restructuring of the economy and to protect disadvantaged sections of the population. Although there has been a measure of liberalisation of trade in recent years the economy is still far from being an open-door one. In a climate such as this, where market forces take a back seat to social priorities in determining strategies and actions, managers grapple with different needs and challenges than those in an advanced economy like the UK. The latter pursues a liberal open-door economic policy, and enjoys a modern infrastructure, an educated and skilled workforce and a fully developed industrial base. Here the internal market is competitive and keeps managers constantly on their toes. R&D, marketing, advanced technology and, in short, business priorities, are their main preoccupation, for which they need a different set of tools than do their Indian counterparts.

If Indian and British business schools and other institutions of higher educa-tion are to cater for the real needs of their respective managers and would-be managers, their curriculum should be vastly different from one another. Comparative empirical studies in these two and many other countries are needed to tell us to what extent such differences of approach actually exist in educa-tional establishments around the world.

In this connection Latifi (1997) reports that Iranian managers work in an econ-omy where government plays an active role in business and commercial activities and many major industries and companies are actually publicly owned. In an environment such as this, she argues, competition and similar market con-siderations are less prominent as an issue than in countries where private sector and open competition dominate the economy. As a result Iranian managers do not need to learn such skills as marketing and fighting off competitors as much as their counterparts do in a country such as the US. Moreover, because of the limited resources at their disposal Iranian managers tend to be generalists and need therefore many skills to be able to perform their multifaceted tasks. This is in sharp contrasts with the specialist nature of the tasks that many American managers perform. Management teaching practices should, again, reflect such differing needs.

Exhibit 21.2 MBA goes to Poland

At first glance the small, industrial town of Nowy Sacz in South-Eastern Poland, close to the snow-capped Tatra mountains and the border with Slovakia, is an unlikely place to find the cutting edge of transition in Poland. But it is here, in buildings that were once the headquarters and workshops of a building materials company that went bankrupt at the beginning of the 1990s, that one of the country's leading private business schools is taking shape.

From the outside the main office building and the nearby factory shells betray their industrial origins, despite their tidiness and the fresh paint. But inside they have been transformed into classrooms, lecture halls and a 230-seat lecture theatre. There is a library, both traditional and electronic, the school's own television studio and computer laboratories.

The Wyzsza Szkola Biznesu (Higher Business School) National-Louis University is part of the mushrooming non-state higher education sector in Poland, which now boasts 137 institutions, of which around 70 per cent are offering courses in business, finance and economics. 'We think about 15 per cent of students in the country are attending non-state colleges and this could increase to as much as 25 per cent in the next few years,' says Krzysztof Pawlowski, rector of the Nowy Sacz school.

Mr Pawlowski, a Solidarity and, later, Christian Democrat senator in the upper house of the Polish parliament from 1989 to 1993, has been the driving force behind the school. On one of his earliest visits to West Europe as a member of Poland's first freely elected parliament after the collapse of communism, he was taken to visit a private business school in Germany. 'I was trying to get a better understanding of the conditions of democracy.' He came away convinced, that such institutions would be vital in speeding up the transition from the command economy to the free market and private enterprise. 'The training of future managers is one of the most important tasks of our transformation. Poland's best resource in the global market is its people but they must be well trained. My idea was to multiply Poland's opportunities to compete through its people. It was a political idea. In the early 1990s the main problem was with the qualifications of the people in our economy. Now, for our integration into the European Union, our people can be our main advantage.'

Starting with the setting up of a foundation in 1991, the college took shape with the help of the business community locally and nationally. It received the support of aid organisations in the US, Germany and Sweden and, crucially, the co-operation and backing of the National-Louis University in Evanston, Chicago. NLU provided the first syllabus and essential expertise in the teaching of English as a foreign language. The high level of language tuition, in particular in English and German, has helped establish the school's reputation.

Beginning in 1992 the number of students has doubled each year to reach more than 2000 in the current academic year. Of these, 1550 are in full-time study – paying more than $1600 a year in tuition fees – 690 in part-time courses and 200 in postgraduate programmes. The school offers a three-year BA degree in business studies and the opportunity of one more year of study in the US to gain a US degree. There is a postgraduate MBA course in co-operation with the Maastricht School of Management in The Netherlands. From the next academic year it will also offer its own Masters degree.

The business school became financially stable in 1995 and is now able to develop on the basis of tuition and registration fees. The target number of BA students is 3000 and the strategic goal is 'to be recognised among the best business schools in Central and Eastern Europe'.

Source: *Financial Times* CD-ROM, 1 January–31 December 1998.

It is also important for developing nations, in parallel with learning from abroad, to build on their own resources and develop compatible indigenous management teaching practices. In other words, the transfer of such practices should not replace but complement local practices that are a culmination of the specific context of the particular society. As Marsden (1992) points out, current development efforts focus on building institutional capacity through the encouragement of local self-reliance. For these nations, the West, or Japan for that matter, is not the only source of valuable innovation and creativity. 'Local', 'traditional' or 'folk' knowledge is no longer the irrelevant vestige of 'backward' people who have not yet made the transition to modernity. Rather, they are the vital wellspring and resource bank from which alternative futures might be built.

Chapter summary

This chapter discussed the issue of the cross-cultural transfer of management policies and practices with special emphasis on human resource management. It was argued that management practices reflect not only the cultural attitudes and values of the people involved but also the wider national context within which they are developed. In order for imported practices to work they need to be modified and at the same time employees need to be trained to master these practices.

Examples were given of certain Japanese management practices and their cultural prerequisites to highlight the complications involved. The chapter also discussed the question of the transferability of management practices within the context of ex-socialist countries of Europe and developing nations in general. The discussion was then brought to a conclusion by discussing the transferability of management teaching across nations.

Discussion questions

1 What types of management techniques and practices are easily transferable across cultures?
2 What steps can be taken to make cross-cultural transfer of management policies and practices possible and successful?
3 What particular problems might the ex-socialist countries of Europe experience when importing foreign 'capitalist' practices?

Closing Case Study:
IMI Yorkshire Fittings and foreign management practices

IMI is one of Europe's leading manufacturers of brass compression fittings, stop cocks and radiator valves for the plumbing and heating industry. These products are made in two manufacturing plans in Dundee and Leeds and distributed via a network of four sales offices and depots in Glasgow, Belfast, Leeds and Wallingford, plus several in Europe and the Far East. The Dundee company dates from 1920 when the only materials used for domestic plumbing were lead and iron. Renowned as one of Scotland's finest fitting manufacturers, the company has become a highly efficient producer of quality Kuterlite compression fittings.

However, in the 1990s the company was in serious trouble and was stagnating: 'our work was market driven not price–cost driven. If demand dropped you dropped production. The market capacity was eight and a half million fittings, and was stable, we were not going any where.' The management team identified the manufacturing system as the root cause of their problems.

For many years the company had operated somewhat complacently traditional methods of production – assembly line, supervisors, foremen, skilled men. They had to run the machine all the time otherwise it was considered as waste. The production area was divided into process sections operating a batch-production system. High volumes of products were transported all over the factory through various processes in what was a labour intensive operation. The managing of each section was rigidly organised into groups of skilled and semi-skilled personnel, which made for compartmentalised attitudes and a non-flexible approach to work.

Pre- and post-machining sections were similarly organised. The supervision of each section or department was under the control of foremen and leader hands. The company had operated on a payment-by-results basis since its inception in 1920. In effect, it was an old-fashioned, brown field site organisation making an unchanging product with an ageing workforce who were very resistant to change.

During 1993, it became obvious to the senior management team that the company could not continue with the manufacturing methods that had sustained the factory for many years. There had to be a quantum change if the factory was to survive into the next decade. In 1994, in the face of fierce competition, the company embarked on a long-term strategic plan, to greatly improve the quality of products and customer service and to become a world-class operation.

The management team decided to replace their 'old-fashioned' production design by cell manufacturing and a self-directed work-group model. Cellular manufacture was seen as the most appropriate manufacturing system for their type of work. While there are other systems through which it could have been possible to achieve production targets the company felt that cellular manufacture was more conducive to a planned culture change throughout the factory. The cells were intended to have the following characteristics:

- every cell to be 'U' shaped
- raw material in, finished product out
- all products inspected from within cell
- zero WIP
- total floor space to be no more than twice the floor area of the process machinery
- skilled resource will be no more than 25 per cent of total cell resource
- only one generic group of product

▶

- availability through planned maintenance
- in-house manufacturing lead time to be less than one day, with no set-up time greater than one hour
- every cell to be capable of self-management

The next major undertaking was to convince the employees that the proposed plan was the best option and that it was needed if they were to survive. There was a great deal of suspicion and scepticism as to the reasons for change, which was perceived to mean redundancy. 'We told them if we go on as it is we all lose our jobs, we cannot guarantee a job for everybody but we can guarantee a continuous process of production, but in the end there was a reluctant acceptance of the principle.'

In order to prepare the workforce for the change its implementation was planned in the following stages over a period of two years:

- issues were discussed, people were persuaded and convinced
- decisions were communicated to the entire workforce
- working parties (staff and trade unions) were set up to develop different aspects of the cell/team
- team leaders were appointed, training team leaders started, machine moves started
- first three cells were created, team training started
- final machine move
- staff team training started. For each group of employees there was a 15-day training with the help of consultants and specialists brought in from outside
- support department training started
- managers were trained how to interview for the selection of new employees

The manufacturing cells were created in tandem with extensive teamwork training for all employees, which has been the key to making a success of this transition to cell working. Each individual cell is manned by self-directed work teams, who hold regular review meetings with both management and themselves. There are few restrictions as to how each cell achieve targets; many performance decisions are made by the teams themselves while keeping to basic guidelines.

In the past there were rows of machines and operations, with people being attached to each row. It would take on average four and a half people to produce one item. Now cells manufacture, inspect and pack finished products and, moreover, they have zero work in progress (WIP), whereas before there used to be a huge amount of raw material and WIP tied up at any given point in time.

Before the introduction of cell manufacturing, various sections did not know what others were doing, but now there are daily, weekly and monthly meetings between manufacturing managers and team leaders to make work teams involved in managerial level decisions and to pass on information to them. In general, employees are given more information compared to the past, even though sensitive issues, such as cost, productivity and redundancy are discussed among the managers only.

The organisational structure has also changed from a top heavy, tall pyramid with layers of managers, to a flat, three-level structure consisting of factory manager, manufacturing manager and team leader. The main problem was to convince the managers to buy this new process because they did not want to let go of the control they had over the rank and file.

The pay and bonus system too has undergone a dramatic change. Whereas in the past the same type of people with the same level of pay worked together, now there is an individual bonus scheme and people with a different pay base work together.

The productivity-based bonus has been replaced by a flat-rate one, because in the old style 'managers and employees used to make up the records to beat the system, we produced large quantities only to go to boxes because of our bonus system'. The bonus payment is not linked to productivity any more.

The company has dispensed with quality inspection and maintenance functions as specialist jobs.

> The quality inspector and maintenance men have gone, everybody now controls the quality and services the machines. They have service and maintenance plans, each group does its own maintenance. In the past if there was a breakdown, work would stop until the maintenance people came and sorted it out. Now it gets done by team members.

Management believes the success of this new work pattern is a result of the change in attitudes. They argue that no extra training for this process was needed because 'they had all been here for so long that they knew how to check quality and service the machines, they just didn't want to do it because it wasn't their job. This attitude has gone now.'

The cell-manufacturing system has given more control to the rank and file. They communicate and talk to others more now, and are not afraid of expressing their views, and discussing and trying out their own ideas. The 'them and us' attitude has gone and been replaced by mutual trust and sharing the interest of the company. The cells are given their jobs and targets, it is then up to cell members to organise the work and get on with it.

The new work organisation has not met with the approval of all employees, however. There was a group of employees who were not happy with the cell-manufacturing arrangement and preferred the old ways. The company has treated these with understanding and sensitivity. A special area has been allocated to them and they are organised on the traditional model, but they are welcome to join the cells if they wish. The company decided, following its long-held beliefs and traditions, which consider employees as its biggest assets, to accommodate rather than fire them. (The company has been granted the 'Investor in People' award, in recognition of its HRM policies and practices).

Since the introduction of team working productivity levels have progressively increased.

> We are engaged in a high volume product, producing 13–14 million items a year. It is important to know how best to produce it. With 180 people we make three times as much we would do before the change. We make a typical fitting in three seconds, a nut in two seconds, the longest from start to finish in four seconds.

The company's customer relations are also improving steadily. More insight for all employees into the business is encouraging greater attention to detail, higher quality and reliable documentation. Many people are keen to learn more and improve their skills: in short, take greater interest in their company.

Source: Tayeb (1999).

Questions

1 Why did IMI's managers feel it was necessary to restructure their company's management and operating structures and what models did they import from abroad to help them with their task?
2 How did they prepare their employees to accept these new practices?
3 What modifications did these imported practices have to undergo in order to be workable in their new home?
4 What else in the company, apart from structure and work organisation, had to change in the process?

Further reading

Kanungo, R.N. and Mendonca, M. (1994) *Work Motivation: Models for Developing Countries*, London: Sage Publications. In this book the authors discuss cross-cultural dimensions of work and ask whether management models from the industrialised world are applicable in Third World countries.

Tayeb, M.H. (1995) The competitive advantage of nations: the role of HRM and its sociocultural context, *International Journal of Human Resource Management* 6(3): 588–605. The author argues that some nations appear to have certain cultural traits which enable them better to adapt imported management practices to their particular needs, compared to other nations.

Roney, J. (1997) Cultural implications of implementing TQM in Poland, *Journal of World Business* 32(2): 152–68. The author demonstrates that thanks to decades-old management traditions under communism the adoption of total quality management by a Polish company has met with practical difficulties and impediments.

References

Aflvaki (Reykjavik Development Agency) (1994) *Report on the Scale of Competitiveness of Iceland*, Reykjavik: Aflvaki Rreykjavikur. Cited in H. M. Eyjolfsdottir and P. B. Smith (1997) Icelandic business and management culture, *International Studies of Management and Organization* 26(3): 61–72.

Amante, M.S.V. (1995) Employment and wage practices of Japanese firms in the Philippines: convergence with Filipino-Chinese and Western-owned firms, *International Journal of Human Resource Management* 6: 642–55.

Arthur, A. (1987) Japanisation and the harmonisation of employment conditions, paper presented to the Japanisation of British Industry Conference, Cardiff, September.

Bakhtari, H. (1995) Cultural effects on management style, *International Studies of Management and Organization* 25(3): 97–118.

Eyjolfsdottir, H.M. and Smith, P.B. (1997) Icelandic business and management culture, *International Studies of Management and Organization* 26(3): 61–72.

Hill, F.M. (1987) What British management can reasonably expect from a quality circle programme, paper presented to the Japanisation of British Industry Conference, Cardiff, September.

Hofstede, G. (1980) *Culture's Consequences*, California: Sage Publications.

Idntæknistofnun Islands and Idnadarraduneyti (State Publications) (1987) *Indicators of Productivity for Improved Quality of Life*, Reykjavik; Rikisprentsmidjan Guttenberg. Cited in H. M. Eyjolfsdottir and P. B. Smith (1997) Icelandic business and management culture, *International Studies of Management and Organization* 26(3): 61–72.

Kovach, R.C. Jr (1994) Matching assumptions in the transfer of management practices: performance appraisal in Hungary, *International Studies of Management and Organization* 24(4): 839–99.

Latifi, F. (1997) Management learning in national context, unpublished PhD thesis, Henley Management College.

Macduffie, J.P. (1995) Human resource bundles and manufacturing performance: organizational logic and flexible production systems in the world auto industry, *Industrial Labor Relations Review* 48: 197–221.

Marsden, D. (1992) Incomes policy for Europe? or, will pay bargaining destroy the European single market?, *British Industrial Relations* 30: 587–604.

Oliver, N. and Davies, A. (1990) Adopting Japanese-style manufacturing methods: a tale of two (UK) factories, *Journal of Management Studies* 27: 555–70.

Oliver, N. and Wilkinson, B. (1992) *Japanization of British Industry*, Oxford: Blackwell.

Osterman, P. (1994) How common is workplace transformation and who adopts it?, *Industrial and Labor Relations Review* 42: 173–88.

Segal, R. (1971) *The Crisis of India*, Bombay: Jaico Publishing House.

Shadur, M.A., Rodwell, J. J., Bamber, G. J. and Simmons, D. E. (1995) The adoption of international best practices in a Western culture: East meets West, *International Journal of Human Resource Management* 6: 735–57.

Sigurlaugsson, B. (1995) *From Manual Skills to Mental Skills*, Reykjavik: Framtikars'n. Cited in H. M. Eyjolfsdottir and P. B. Smith (1997) Icelandic business and management culture, *International Studies of Management and Organization* 26(3): 61–72.

Tayeb, M.H (1988) *Organizations and National Culture: A Comparative Analysis*, London: Sage Publications.

Tayeb, M.H. (1994) Japanese managers and British culture: a comparative case study, *International Journal of Human Resource Management* 5: 145–66.

Tayeb, M.H. (1996) Indian management behaviour, in M. Warner (ed.) *International Encyclopaedia of Business and Management*, London: International Thomson Business Press, Vol.3, pp. 2875–80.

Tayeb, M.H. (1999) Foreign remedies for local difficulties: the case of Scottish manufacturing firms, *International Journal of Human Resource Management* 10(5): 842–57.

The Economist (1996) Lean and its limits, 14 September, p. 85.

Womack, J.P., Jones, D.T. and Roos, D. (1990) *The Machine that Changed the World*, New York: Rawson Associates.

Yang, J.Z. (1992) A summary report of human resource management policies and practices of Japanese-owned firms in the US, paper presented to the Conference on the Human Resource Management in the New Europe of the 1990s, Ashridge Management College, July.

Microsoft, IBM and Intel
Juggernauts of the high-tech world

Monir Tayeb

This book has taken you through the world of international business from the theories that may explain the bases on which nations trade with one another and the ways in which the free flow of international trade might be interfered with by these very same nations, to the manner in which these theories are translated into policies and practices by international companies and their managers and employees.

The book has highlighted the role of international companies in our world not only as innovators, initiators, makers, traders and movers of goods and services but also as culture-builders, trend-setters and life-style changers. The major internal and external challenges, opportunities and threats that these companies face and deal with were also discussed.

It would be fitting to end the book with a case study about three of the most successful world-class companies which have made a huge difference in the way we communicate with one another and do business with our fellow human beings around the world.

Closing Case Study:
Microsoft, IBM and Intel

Microsoft, International Business Machines and Intel – three juggernauts of the high-technology world – rank second, fourth and ninth, respectively, among the world's most respected companies. Together, often in collaboration but at times competing aggressively, these three US companies have played a central role in creating today's information technology industry.

Microsoft's software and Intel's chips are core components of the personal computers that IBM initially launched in the early 1980s, radically changing the working lives of millions of people.

All three dominate their core markets and all three have global operations. Yet the most notable characteristic that these companies have in common is their demonstrated ability to adapt rapidly to shifting market and technology trends.

Microsoft changed course when it recognised the significance of the internet. Over the past year, Intel has restructured its business to address an increasingly segmented market for microprocessor chips used in different types of computers.

IBM, which has undergone far more drastic change, has rejuvenated itself by reinventing the mainframe computer, using the latest semiconductor technol-

▶

ogy, to make it cost-competitive with alternative 'distributed' computing systems. As well as keeping pace with change, Microsoft, Intel and IBM are now expanding into new markets.

Microsoft is moving beyond the desktop into 'enterprise computing' with software for powerful computer systems and networks. IBM is building a big new services business, while Intel is developing ever more powerful microprocessor chips for use in large-scale computers as well as in high-volume office, consumer and mobile PCs.

In size, each is the world's largest company in its segment of the information technology industry. Yet Microsoft's high ranking, in particular, may come as a surprise to some. Far from commanding respect, the software industry leader is facing charges, filed by the US Justice Department and the attorneys-general of 20 US states, that it has used anti-competitive business practices to maintain its monopoly in the market for personal computer operating systems software.

Microsoft is a company that people either admire greatly or despise. It is notable that Microsoft received greater support outside the US, where it has few direct competitors. Latin American Chief Executives gave the company more votes than top-ranking General Electric. In Europe, Microsoft almost tied with GE. Yet in North America, Microsoft trailed in fourth place behind not only GE but also Coca-Cola and Toyota.

However, Microsoft, with Bill Gates, its multibillionaire Chairman and Chief Executive, is also one of the most written about companies in the world. It features regularly in newspaper headlines and on the covers of business magazines. Microsoft has 'changed the way we live and communicate with each other,' said one survey participant. 'Among all the companies in the world it is the most competitive,' commented another.

Mr Gates came second only to Jack Welch of GE among the most respected business leaders. He was hailed as a 'genius' by several survey participants and admired for his 'brilliant strategic planning'. He is 'completely unintimidated by anything', said one Chief Executive, in a comment that would surely ring true among Microsoft's competitors.

International Business Machines, in fourth place, clearly won its votes as a 'comeback' company. 'They managed a spectacular turning point,' said one supporter. Another Chief Executive summed up the situation, describing IBM as a 'technology leader that proved itself capable of responding to dramatic changes in the past ten years'.

Lou Gerstner, IBM chairman and chief executive, gets all the credit. Ranked fourth among the most respected business leaders, he is admired for his 'single-mindedness' and 'customer focus'. He also wins plaudits for his 'ability to revive the company (by) creating a worldwide focused strategy'.

IBM was ranked even more highly by Chief Executives from its own industry sector. However, North American chief executives are not great fans of 'Big Blue', as the world's largest computer company is commonly known.

Their votes did not even rank IBM among the top ten companies. In contrast, Intel was ranked higher by its home crowd than in the worldwide rankings. The chipmaker came joint ninth among the world's most respected companies, but number five in North America.

Surprisingly, the most advanced semiconductor manufacturer in the world did not make the top ten in its own industry segment. Perhaps, as a components supplier, Intel did not get the recognition it deserves. Ironically, the products of most of the top ten companies in the industry, as ranked by survey participants, benefit greatly from Intel's rapid technology advances.

Andy Grove, Intel Chairman, was placed fifth among world business leaders. Mr Grove, who handed over the role of Chief Executive to Craig Barrett earlier this year, is held in even higher esteem within the US technology industry. He guided Intel from revenues of $2.9bn in 1988, to $25bn in 1997, a 27 per cent compound annual growth rate.

Known for his direct and sometimes abrasive comments, Mr Grove last year upbraided European executives for failing to adapt more quickly to e-mail. Yet Mr Grove is also widely admired for his disarming honesty. A refugee from Hungary who arrived in the US with nothing but great ambitions, Mr Grove has recently spoken out against those who would limit immigration in the US.

Although survey participants did not rank any of these companies number one, information technology was the only industry to have three companies placed among the top ten in the world. In North American rankings, these three were joined by Lucent, the communications equipment spin-off from AT&T, and America Online, the leading internet access service, with more than 14 million subscribers.

Source: *Financial Times* CD-ROM, 1 January–31 December 1998.

Index